D1715273

AMERICAN
SPEECHES

AMERICAN
SPEECHES

Wayland Maxfield Parrish

and

Marie Hochmuth

DEPARTMENT OF SPEECH
UNIVERSITY OF ILLINOIS

GREENWOOD PRESS, PUBLISHERS
NEW YORK

Copyright © 1954 by Longmans Green and Co.

Reprinted by permission of Longmans Green and Co.

First Greenwood Reprinting 1969

Library of Congress Catalogue Card Number 69-14028

SBN 8371-1962-6

PRINTED IN UNITED STATES OF AMERICA

815
P261a

Preface

The remarkable development of interest in the study of public speaking during recent years has been directed chiefly to the theory and practice of speech-making, rather than to an examination of the masterpieces of eloquence from which our precepts and theories should in large measure be derived. Many of the numerous textbooks in current use fail to direct the student's attention with sufficient emphasis to the great models of earlier times, and one frequently finds members of the modern generation of students and teachers of public speaking who have little acquaintance with these oratorical masterpieces. Collections of speeches have been published from time to time, but few of these volumes are at present readily available. It is to fill this gap, so far as American oratory is concerned, that the present volume has been prepared.

In preparing this collection we have had in mind various purposes that such a book may serve. It may be used to acquaint beginning students of public speaking with some of the great speeches of America's best speakers, and to supply students of argumentation and persuasion with models for imitation and materials on which to try their powers of analysis. Students of American oratory may find here some of the speeches that have been most influential in shaping our ideals, our culture, and our history. And the advanced student of rhetoric may use the texts of the speeches as material on which to test his principles of rhetorical criticism.

Amid such a wealth of material as American history affords the decision on what to choose and what to leave out has been a difficult one. In general, our aim has been to make available those addresses which most teachers will want their students to be familiar with, those which deserve, and repay, careful study. We have included speeches that make some notable contribution to the solution of an urgent problem, speeches representative of those men whose influ-

115141

ence was exerted chiefly through public address, speeches which voice American ideals and aspirations, speeches notable for their skillful adaptation to a particular situation, and we have not forgotten those whose worth seems apparent quite apart from the situation which called them forth, those which, like poetry, are enduring literature because of their apt or beautiful expression of universal truths or sentiments.

Knowing that many wish to study a speech in detail and in its entirety as a speaker's method of meeting a specific situation, we have presented all addresses except Webster's "Reply to Hayne" in a form as complete and accurate as existing evidence will permit. It follows that some parts of these addresses may be regarded today as feeble, pointless, and dull. But if a rhetorician is interested in an orator's total performance he will want to examine his worst as well as his best passages.

And in general what the critic wishes to study is the speech as actually spoken, not an advance copy prepared for the press, or an amended copy which represents what the speaker writing after the event wishes he had said. But such accurate texts are not always obtainable. Until modern times faithful reports of speeches as delivered have been hard to come by, and many texts of older speeches are quite unreliable. This lack of verbatim reporting does not, however, invalidate or defeat the purposes of rhetorical analysis. The critic may be interested in what the speaker *meant* to say, as well as in what he *did* say. If he is interested primarily in assessing the immediate effect of the speech he will want to have the words as spoken. But if he is concerned with the speaker's theory of speechmaking, or with his ideas, he will prefer to deal with his intention as revealed in his revised manuscript. And, of course, the intrinsic excellence of a speech does not depend upon its having been spoken. Shakespeare wrote fictitious speeches for his characters, and many of them deserve careful study as models of speech composition. The much-declaimed "Liberty or Death" of Patrick Henry and the "Supposed Speech of John Adams" by Webster were certainly never uttered by their imputed authors in the form in which we know them. But who would deny that they are specimens of excellent speech composition, worthy of study and imitation? We need not, then, be disturbed by the fact that some of the speeches in this book may not have been spoken by their authors exactly as we have represented them.

We have thought it best to present the speeches without editing or analysis since many teachers will wish to assign those tasks to their students, believing that the young rhetorician may profit more from making his own investigation and analysis than from having that work done for him. We have, however, supplied with each address some slight historical and biographical data. We have supplied also an introductory essay on rhetorical criticism and a complete analysis of Lincoln's First Inaugural Address in which students and teachers may find useful suggestions of method and procedure.

We acknowledge gratefully the advice and criticism of our colleagues, Richard Murphy and Karl Wallace.

W. M. PARRISH
MARIE HOCHMUTH

Urbana, Illinois
October 24, 1953

Contents

The Study of Speeches

WHY DO WE study the speeches of the past? What values do we seek in exhuming the long-silent utterances of dead orators on issues that are equally dead? Questions of burning interest in the time of Webster or of Lincoln have long since lost their heat, and an attempt to rekindle their embers may seem impertinent now when the whole world trembles before the problems of controlling atomic energy and containing communist Russia. And in any age what can be learned from orators that could not be better learned from the study of state papers, government reports, editorials, and scholarly essays in politics, enonomics, and philosophy?

When Socrates once referred to himself as "a pining man who was frantic to hear speeches," he defined a human trait which, in greater or lesser degree, is present in all of us. If, as Emerson said, "every man is an orator, how long soever he may have been a mute," perhaps we study speeches to find vicarious expression of our own unuttered eloquence. And both the lover of speeches for their own sake and the frustrated orator may find in their study something of "practical" value, for it is true of our age as it was of Aristotle's that "all men attempt to discuss statements and to maintain them, to defend themselves and to attack others," [1] and whether we do this in formal addresses or in informal discussions we may expect to learn from a study of the notable addresses of the past some lessons that we can apply to the preparation of our own speeches, for though the subjects of controversy that concern us may be quite different from those that exercised the talents of earlier speakers, yet the *methods* of discussion and argument remain very much the same from age to age.

[1] *Rhetoric*, I, i.

1

If we have progressed far enough in our study of rhetoric to have developed a coherent theory of speech construction we may wish to test it by applying it to the recorded speeches of the past. And if we do not have a method of our own and wish to develop one, it is surely the part of wisdom to observe carefully and analytically the practices of earlier speakers instead of depending entirely upon our own fumbling trials and errors. Any sound theory of speech-making must be derived from observation of the practices of the best speakers. In this book are recorded some of the best efforts of some of the best speakers in American history. They can be studied with profit by any aspiring rhetorician.

This suggests another reason for the study of public addresses that applies especially to more mature students of rhetoric. It is not always wise to accept uncritically the precepts of some standard textbook, whether by Aristotle, Cicero, or a modern writer, and assume its soundness and validity. The careful student will wish to compare these theories with the actual practice of masters of public address. If our textbook says, for instance, that a speaker should begin by conciliating his audience, let us examine the beginnings of a dozen or two representative addresses to see whether the theorist is supported by practice. And when Aristotle says we may argue that what is rare is a greater good than what is plentiful we may well examine a number of speeches to discover whether such an argument has actually been used.

The student who is interested in history will not lack a motive for the study of public address. He cannot be indifferent to the utterances of important men on important questions of the period he is studying. He will study speeches for the light they throw on contemporary events, and he will study events for the light they throw upon speeches. And he may discover that speeches have often been instrumental in shaping the course of history, in defining and strengthening a people's ideals, and in determining its culture.

Taking a deeper and more philosophical view, we may say that the study of speeches is worth while because all of man's activities are of interest to us and we assume that "in some sense human experience is worth while." [2] The Greeks believed that one of man's greatest pleasures lay in learning new things. Such a doctrine can hardly be questioned when we contemplate the insatiable modern drive for learning and discovery. In the physical sciences it has led to the quest for the innermost secrets of the atom, and in the philological sciences to the attempt to relearn all that was once known. To recover the great speeches of the past, to reconstruct the circumstances under which they were given, to discover the motives that prompted the orator to speak and the motives that prompted the audience to respond — these may surely be counted among interesting and worthy studies.

In recovering or in exploring the great thought currents of earlier times the speech may or may not be a more useful instrument than other writings, in prose or verse, but it is from its very nature likely to be more interesting and more vital. And this leads us to a consideration of the nature of public address.

What Is a Speech?

Typically, a speech is an utterance meant to be heard and intended to exert an influence of some kind on those who hear it. Typically, also the kind of influence intended may be described as persuasion. The hearer is to be moved to action or argued into the acceptance of some belief. The aim of the speaker is, in the words of William Caxton "to cause another man ... to believe or to do that thing which thou wouldst have him for to do." [3]

Such a purpose is plainly enough discerned in Webster's Reply to Hayne or in Patrick Henry's plea for war against England. But in some presidential addresses, public lectures, and eulogies it is not so clear. In such addresses the speaker's aim may incline toward pure exposition or pure self-expression, and certainly these are legitimate aims in public address. But even so, a persuasive purpose is pretty sure to be present, for the expositor wishes to have his ideas approved and accepted, and even the plowboy who declaims his

[2] David Daiches, *A Study of Literature* (Ithaca, N.Y.: Cornell University Press, 1948), p. 228.
[3] *Myrrour & Dyscrypcyon of the Worlde,* 1481.

own sentiments or another's while following the furrows may have an imaginary audience in his eye. A very popular and successful modern preacher once confessed that the chief appeal of the ministry for him was in its opportunity for self-expression, but it is not on record that he ever delivered his sermons in an empty church. The orator may say, and may believe, that he is merely giving vent to his inmost convictions, and this would seem to be true of some orations and parts of orations. "I know not what course others may take, but as for me—" cried Patrick Henry. Just so, many artists assert that their work is purely personal and deny that they have any intention to communicate with others. But Professor I. A. Richards contends that the artist's "conscious neglect of communication does not in the least diminish the importance of the communicative aspect. . . . Denial that he is at all influenced in his work by a desire to affect other people, is no evidence that communication is not actually his principal object." [4] Just so, a speech may have a persuasive efficacy even though the speaker denies any intention to persuade.

It should be noted, however, that lectures or addresses that are designed solely to give the hearer information or instruction,[5] to furnish him with facts, must, from their very lack of urgency, fall short of the highest eloquence. It is the essential nature of oratory that it be moving, that it be persuasive. All of the notable speeches in American history have, directly or indirectly, this persuasive purpose. All of those included in this volume have it.

It should be noted also that typically, but not always, a speech is designed to meet a specific situation, to affect a given audience, as when a United States Senator argues for the passage of a bill, or a prosecutor pleads before a jury for the conviction of a culprit. It follows, as we shall find later, that there can be no adequate judgment of the effectiveness of an address unless we understand fully the situation which it was designed to meet.

[4] See his chapter on Communication and the Artist in *Principles of Literary Criticism* (New York: Harcourt Brace & Co., 1952).

[5] W. M. Parrish, *Speaking in Public* (New York: Charles Scribner's Sons, 1947), pp. 308-16.

Many speeches, however, do not have such an immediate specific purpose or a sharply defined audience. A public lecture may be intended for repeated delivery to many audiences, and a president's address, though delivered before an immediate audience, may be intended for the whole nation or for the whole world. And such speeches may not be directed to any specific occasion but may aim generally at winning good will, creating confidence, allaying fears, strengthening loyalties and beliefs, warning of impending dangers, preparing the public mind for measures to come, or building a more tolerant or favorable attitude toward some person or proposal or institution. But whether the audience is specific or general, present or remote, a speech is likely to have more urgency, more directness of address, and more simplicity in vocabulary, style, and structure than compositions intended to be read in private.

Keeping in mind the exceptions and reservations and modifications discussed above, we may say, then, that a speech is a spoken discourse intended to work some kind of persuasive effect upon a given audience.

The Nature of Criticism

"Let us say that the task of literary criticism is to put the reader in possession of the work of art," says Cleanth Brooks.[6] He continues, "Is this a mere reading of the work or is it a judgment of it? Frankly, I do not see how the two activities can be separated. . . . The attempt to drive a wedge between close reading of the text and evaluation of the work seems to me confused and confusing." Let us say the same of rhetorical criticism. We are concerned with the interpretation of speeches, with analysis of their content, structure, and method; and we are concerned at the same time with judgment or evaluation of their excellences and defects.

It will be apparent from the definition above that putting a reader in possession of a speech involves more than analysis of its content and form. Since the purpose of a speech is to work persuasion upon an audience, we cannot properly explain or evaluate it until we have

[6] Foreword to R. W. Stallman, *Critiques and Essays in Criticism*, 1920-1948 (New York: The Ronald Press Co., 1949), p. xx.

learned a great deal about the occasion which called it forth, the speaker's relation to the occasion, the resources available to him, and the climate of opinion and current of events amidst which he operated. Particularly do we need to know the nature of the audience for whom the speech was intended so that we may understand why certain things were said and certain others omitted, and so that we may judge whether the speaker has wisely and skillfully adapted his ideas and methods to those for whom they are intended. It will help also to know something of the speaker's character, education, and experience, for these are important conditioners of what he says. And when we have formed an impression of the speech we may wish to test its validity by examining whatever evidence is available concerning its actual effect upon those who heard or read it.

If we study, for example, the First Inaugural Address of Franklin D. Roosevelt, how are we to understand and evaluate such phrases as "the only thing we have to fear is fear itself," "the money changers have fled from their high seats in the temple of our civilization," "a stricken nation in the midst of a stricken world"? We will have to make a careful examination of contemporary events and conditions as we find them recorded in newspapers, magazines, surveys, and histories of the period. Through similar sources we will need to examine the life and character of the speaker to discover why this kind of man was likely to say the kind of thing he did say. We will wish to know what advisers he consulted while preparing the address and how their advice influenced him. The composition of the immediate audience scattered over the Capitol Plaza is not of great importance, for the speech was addressed not to them primarily but to the nation at large, indeed to the whole world. Analysis of such an audience is a formidable task, but the critic must learn what he can of the fears and hopes of the people of the world at that time.

It is obvious that an attempt to discover and to analyze *all* the factors in the historical situation, in the consciousness of the audience, and in the baffling personality of the speaker on this occasion would require a lifetime of study and could never be complete. The critic must be selective. He must distinguish what is relevant to his purpose from what is merely interesting, and he must be limited by the prescribed scope of his study.

It is all the more important that he should not get lost in such studies, since they are, strictly speaking, extraneous to rhetoric. They are useful only insofar as they help in the rhetorical analysis of the speech itself. Properly speaking, they are excursions into the fields of history, sociology, or biography which furnish a background against which the speech itself may be studied.

It is even more important that the critic should not be diverted into an attempt to assess the *result* of a speech except as its effect may help us to judge the quality of the speech itself. Rhetoric, strictly speaking, is not concerned with the *effect* of a speech, but with its *quality*, and its quality can be determined quite apart from its effect. This is apparent when we consider that a properly qualified rhetorician should be able to analyze and to judge a written speech before it is delievered, and so before it can have had any effect. So also he should be able to criticize it after it is delivered without paying any attention to its effect.

It cannot be too often repeated that the effect of a speech *may* bear little relation to its intrinsic worth. A speaker's success in achieving a desired response from his audience is not necessarily proof that he has spoken well, or his failure, that he has spoken ill. His objective may have been too easy, or his audience may have responded as he wished despite the fact that they were actually repelled by his plea. Or, on the other hand, their votes may have been bought up in advance, or they may have had a stubborn prejudice against him or his proposal that nothing could dispel. Many of the great speeches of history have been made in lost causes. Some have been called forth by the speaker's very consciousness that his case was hopeless. Under such circumstances an orator may speak merely to put his views on record, or he may speak in defiant challenge to an opposition which he knows is invincible. Witness John Brown's moving defense when about to receive a sentence of death. One may say in such cases that the orator is speaking to posterity, or to the larger audience who will read his plea, and often that is true. But who can assess the effect of a speech on posterity? Who can determine today the effect of Woodrow Wilson's pleas for the League of Nations? How can one determine the actual influence of Lincoln's plea for malice toward none and charity for all? Indeed how can we be sure that a speech that "gets the votes" or "wins a verdict" is really the cause of the alleged results? The real reasons for a man's vote may lie hidden in his own mind. In most cases, all we know is that a plea was made, and the vote was so and so. The relation between the two is seldom discoverable.

Let us not be too confident, then, that we are measuring the effect of a speech. And in any case the totting up of such responses as are discernible is a task for a historian, a clerk, or a comptometer, not for a rhetorician. If the results of a speech are measurable, it is the job of the rhetorician to analyze the *causes* of its alleged success or failure as these are discoverable in the speech itself.

The Critic's Qualifications

It is true that anyone can pronounce judgment on speeches, and most everyone does, but only a judgment that comes from a qualified critic is worthy of respect. One of the first qualifications we look for in seeking a competent critic is a judicious temperament. Many of us are prone to make decisions before we have examined all the factors involved in a situation and weighed each in its relation to others. In judging speeches we must not hastily jump to conclusions merely because we have found something that pleases or displeases us. We must school ourselves to examine patiently all the factors relevant to a sound judgment and not to depend upon whim, prejudice, or individual preference. It is not opinion we seek, but truth.

But how can one speak of truth in a field so incapable of scientific certitude as rhetoric? We have no calipers or test tubes or mathematical formulas to help us. How can one be sure of the quality of a speech, or of its value? Sir William Osler's advice to young doctors is pertinent here. "At the outset," he said, "do not be worried about this big question — Truth. It is a very simple matter if each one of you starts with the desire to get as much as possible. No human being is constituted to know the truth, and nothing but the truth;

and even the best of men must be content with fragments, with partial glimpses, never the full fruition. In this unsatisfied quest the attitude of mind, the desire, the thirst . . . the fervent longing, are the be-all and the end-all. . . . The truth is the best you can get with your best endeavor, *the best that the best men accept* — with this you must learn to be satisfied, retaining at the same time with due humility an earnest desire for an ever larger portion." [7]

Besides a thirst for truth and a judicious temperament in dealing with it, the critic of rhetoric must have special education for his task. He must have, first, a wide general education in history, politics, literature, and all the liberal studies. The speeches he studies may range through all the fields of human knowledge, they may be rich in allusions to persons and events, and the critic must be able to follow all the workings of the orator's mind. If he comes across such phrases as "a house divided against itself," "a consummation devoutly to be wished," or "be in earnest, don't equivocate, don't excuse, don't retreat a single inch," he should be able to identify and explain them. In one paragraph of a speech by George William Curtis there are references to James Otis, Wendell Phillips, Quincy, John Quincy Adams, Whittier, Longfellow, Lowell, Emerson, Parker, Beecher, Jonathan Mayhew, Roger Williams, and William Ellery Channing, and an understanding of the paragraph requires some familiarity with their lives and achievements. In such cases one must, of course, consult encyclopedias, biographical dictionaries, histories, and so on, but with the understanding that they do not take the place of a well-furnished mind.

Second, the critic must know speeches. He must have read and heard and studied many of them if he is to know the nature of the genus, speech. Only from familiarity with a large number of representative specimens will he know what he should look for in a given speech and what its distinctive qualities and merits are. To understand or to evaluate a particular thing — a horse, a motor car, a drama, a painting — one must be familiar with many specimens of that thing. It is only thus that standards of judgment are formed.

---

[7] *Aequanimitas* (3rd ed.; Philadelphia: The Blakiston Co., 1932), pp. 397-98.

Until the student acquires such a background in public address, he is not qualified to interpret or judge speeches. One of the purposes of this book is to make available some materials for that background.

Men have been studying speeches for as long as speeches have been made, and through the ages many treatises have been written to define the principles of speech-making and to reduce them to a system. The third qualification of the modern critic is familiarity with these treatises on rhetoric. Where so many competent guides have mapped out the ground, it is folly for anyone to stumble alone over such difficult and treacherous terrain, especially so since among these writers on rhetoric are some of the most eminent minds in the history of the race. With the best of these works the modern critic of public address should become thoroughly familiar. The fact that some of them were written centuries ago does not measurably diminish their value for the criticism of speeches in the middle of the nineteenth century. Rhetoric deals in the main with man's motives and desires and, whether we like it or not, basic human nature has not changed essentially in two thousand years. The way to a man's heart in ancient Athens is still the way to a man's heart today. Styles and modes of speaking may change in different ages, but wherever the fundamental purpose of speaking is to influence human conduct its essence will remain the same.

So much has been written on rhetoric that its study might absorb a whole lifetime, but for most purposes such thorough study is not needed. It is enough if one knows the best of the treatises on the subject. It is not by swallowing whole libraries, but by repeatedly and intently contemplating a few very great works, that the mind is best disciplined. And as Lane Cooper has said, "The best-read man is the one who has oftenest read the best things." [8]

There is little disagreement among modern scholars on which are the best works on rhetoric, at least until we come to modern writings. The following list contains most, if not all, of the older works that modern scholars consider most worthy of study. They should be available in any good college library.

[8] *Two Views of Education* (New Haven: Yale University Press, 1922), p. 118.

Standard Works on Rhetoric

Plato: *Phaedrus and Gorgias*
Aristotle: *Rhetoric*
Cicero: *De Oratore*
Quintilian: *Institutio Oratoria*
Longinus(?): *On the Sublime*
Francis Bacon: *The Advancement of Learning,* Chapter III
George Campbell: *The Philosophy of Rhetoric*
Hugh Blair: *Lectures on Rhetoric and Belles Lettres*
Richard Whately: *Elements of Rhetoric*

These will serve as a base from which to examine the flood of modern studies, criticisms, and textbooks on public speaking which issue yearly from the press. A very useful summation of rhetorical theories with many suggestions of lines of study will be found in *Speech Criticism: The Development of Standards for Rhetorical Appraisal* by Lester Thonssen and A. Craig Baird.[9] Many model studies of orators may be found in *A History and Criticism of American Public Address,* sponsored by The National Association of Teachers of Speech and edited by W. N. Brigance.[10]

A word of caution may be needed against using any one of the works listed above as a sole guide in the criticism of an address. To derive all one's criteria from Whately, for instance, or even from so comprehensive a treatise as Aristotle's, is pretty sure to result in a criticism that is only partial, with neglect of some important matters and too much attention to others. So far as is possible one should be guided by all of "the best" theories of appraisal, difficult as this makes the task. Jacques Barzun has well said, "The critic's role is ... to see, hear, and talk about everything in the light of *some imaginary standard set by the books with the toughest lives.*" [11] Some suggestions for forming this imaginary standard will be found in the section that follows.

[9] New York: The Ronald Press Co., 1948.
[10] New York: McGraw-Hill Book Co., 1943.
[11] *Harper's Magazine* (July, 1949), p. 105. (Italics ours.)

The Basis of Criticism

There is general agreement among scholars that of all the books that have been written on rhetoric the one with the toughest life is Aristotle's *Rhetoric*. It has profoundly influenced nearly all subsequent writers, and its present liveliness is attested by the fact that it is available today in more English translations than probably any other ancient work. We shall lean heavily upon it in forming our "imaginary standard" of criticism.

Aristotle defined rhetoric as "the faculty of observing in any given case the available means of persuasion." Note first in this definition that rhetoric is a *faculty*. That is, it is not a definite technique with fixed rules of procedure, but merely the ability to find the elements of persuasion in a given speech. Note also that the rhetorician is not to limit his attention to the means of persuasion actually used, but is to consider all the means *available* to the speaker whether he used them or not. He should discover what the speaker *might* have said, what the situation called for, what resources were accessible to him. This, of course, points toward a careful analysis of the situation that called forth the address, the environment in which it was made, the problem that it was intended to solve. It suggests also that the critic's concern is not with the literal result of the speech, but with the speaker's use of a correct method; not with the speech's effect, but with its effectiveness. Persuasive always means persuasive to someone — a judge in a case at law, a prospective voter in an election, a listener in a popular audience. But the judge or listener as Aristotle conceives him is always a *qualified* judge — a person of good education, sound sense, and judicious temper. This is the kind of audience we must assume in assessing the effectiveness of a speech, for it is the kind of audience aimed at in the best efforts of all our orators. We admire Burke's great addresses, not because they were well adapted to the boozy country squires who sometimes sat in Parliament, but because they were designed for a better audience. In speech-making, as in life, not failure, but low aim, is crime. And so in criticism we interpret and evaluate a speech in terms of its effect upon an audience of qualified listeners.

The Means of Persuasion

With rhetorical criticism thus defined we proceed to consider some of the most important means by which a speech works persuasion in those who hear and judge it.

One of the most important elements in persuasiveness is the impression made by the speaker's character and personality. Much of this impression is made, of course, by his appearance, voice, manner, and delivery, and cannot be recovered from study of the printed speech. Many indications of his trustworthiness *can*, however, be found in the printed text. We can learn whether he possesses those personal qualities that Aristotle thought most persuasive — virtue, intelligence, and good will. When Theodore Roosevelt said, "There should be relentless exposure of and attack upon every evil man, whether politician or business man," and when Franklin D. Roosevelt said, "Happiness lies not in the mere possession of money; it lies in the joy of achievement, in the thrill of creative effort," they were revealing a moral bent that should have stimulated their hearers to greater confidence in their integrity. Most speeches are full of such indicators of the speaker's trustworthiness, and the critic must note them and assess their value. He may note such things as whether the speaker establishes his own authority with the audience, whether he has a sympathetic understanding of their way of life, their thoughts, and their problems, whether he impresses them as being well informed on his subject, whether he is given to dogmatism, exaggeration, and overstatement, whether he has a sense of humor, whether he seems sincere, friendly, fair-minded, modest, self-respecting, respectful, courteous, and tactful.[12] The presence or absence of one or more of these qualities may dispose the hearers so favorably or so unfavorably toward the speaker that they pay little attention to what he says.

This, however, is not always true, and the second element of effectiveness we must consider is the *content* of the speech. The essential question to ask here is: Did the speaker choose the right

[12] See the chapter, "The Speaker Himself," in James A. Winans, *Speech-Making* (New York: D. Appleton-Century Co., 1938).

things to say? It is desirable to separate *what* was said from *how* it was said — often a difficult task — and this may best be done by making a summary or précis of the speaker's thought which avoids the wording of the original. We must consider whether he seems to be acquainted with all the pertinent facts bearing on his subject and whether he uses those that are most significant or persuasive. We must determine also whether they really are facts, or only guesses, opinions, or hearsay, whether he has drawn valid inferences from them, and whether he has combined them into a coherent logical structure that will satisfy the understanding and win conviction.

It is helpful to separate the structure of the speech from the structure of the reasoning that supports it, and to outline both. Rarely will they coincide, for rarely do experienced speakers put their thoughts into the mechanical form favored by schoolboy debaters: "I will prove so and so, and my reasons are, first, second, third, etc." A chronological outline will reveal the order of the speaker's thoughts; a logical outline will reveal the structure and validity of his thinking. The main proposition (or propositions) may nowhere be specifically stated, but it should be ferreted out by the critic and clearly formulated, and the supporting arguments should be marshaled under it to form a logical brief. He should ask: Just what is this speaker trying to prove, and what does he adduce to support his thesis? By this means he will best discover the essential substance of the speech — or its lack of substance.

The critic should assess also the depth and weight of the ideas presented. A great speech cannot consist of mere eloquent nothings. It must deal with great issues, not with trivial ephemera. And the critic must consider whether the orator is actuated by lofty ideals of justice, honor, liberty, and the like, or whether he is concerned with such local and temporary matters as balancing this year's budget or getting a subsidy for farmers. It is true that persuasion may be as skillful in small matters as in great, but we cannot divorce the value of a speech from the value of the ideas with which it deals.

When the plan and structure of a speech are clearly perceived, the critic may note whether there is any persuasive effect in the *order* in which ideas are presented. In the given situation is there any advantage in presenting this idea first and that one second? The notion is as old as Plato that a speech should have a beginning, a middle, and an end, and the disposition of materials, *dispositio*, was a main consideration of Roman rhetoricians. In most speeches the threefold division — introduction, discussion, conclusion — is easily discernible. And in general it will be found that the introduction is designed to win an intelligent, sympathetic, and attentive hearing, and the conclusion to sum up what has been said and to make a final appeal. These are their time-honored functions. But what the critic should note is not merely whether the speech follows this classical pattern, but whether it proceeds step by step in conformity with the need, the mood, and the expectation of the audience. The hearers may require an analysis of a problem before they will attend to its solution. They may want certain objections answered before they will listen to a proposal. Or they may entertain certain doubts or suspicions that the speaker will have to remove before he can get a fair hearing. The situation may be such that he will need to establish a common ground of interest, of feeling, or of belief with his audience before he presents his proposal. And it may be that the presentation of an unpopular theme calls for a strategy whereby the hearers are led to agree with the speaker on several non-controversial matters so that they will continue to agree when a less acceptable matter is presented. That is, the critic must look not only to the *chronological* order of materials and their logical structure, but also to the *psychological* order of presentation if one exists.

Another means of persuasion, and perhaps the most important of all, is by appeal to certain *motives* to which an audience can be expected to respond. The most persuasive speaker is he who most effectively directs his appeal to the basic interests, desires, wants, instincts, and emotions of his hearers. A complete catalogue of such motives has never been made, but the critic may get most help in this matter from Aristotle's discussion of the "Constituents of Happiness" and "Goods," and his analysis of the emotions.[13] He will be

[13] *Rhetoric*, I, v, vi, vii; II, ii-xii.

helped also, by the analyses of audiences by the Reverend George Campbell [14] and James A. Winans.[15]

Sometimes the "motivation" of a speech will be immediately clear. Patrick Henry's "Liberty or Death," for instance, is obviously an appeal to our love of liberty, though it contains many other appeals also. Curtis's "Public Duty of Educated Men" appeals, of course, to the sense of duty of the young graduates to whom it was addressed. But often the motive to which the orator appeals is hidden or obscure. It may nowhere be mentioned, and the emotions he seeks to arouse may not be named. One of the most rewarding tasks of the critic is to search them out and to determine from a study of them what kind of audience the orator presumes himself to be addressing. Does he assume that his hearers will respond to such motives as group loyalty, honor, courage, fair play, altruism, or does he appeal only to self-interest and personal security? Does he assume that they are progressive and forward-looking, or that they are timid, conservative, and fearful of anything new? Does he rely more on challenges to reason than on appeals to emotion? Does he attempt to arouse fear, anger, hatred, jealousy, or confidence, temperance, and love? And so on.

When the nature of the appeal is understood one must consider the manner in which it is presented. A speaker may scold an audience for its failure in duty, or he may ridicule its negligence, or try to shame it into action. He may present an unpopular proposal with challenging bluntness, or skillfully identify it with accepted beliefs and habitual conduct. He may rely upon effective repetition to drum in an idea and get it accepted. He may arouse emotion by effective play upon the imagination. By moving examples and illustrations he may fix responsibility upon his hearers and compel them to face the truth. And he may win them to a favorable response, as Franklin D. Roosevelt so often did, by a serene and cheerful confidence that they *will* respond favorably. All such methods of presenting a proposal the critic will note and assess.

[14] *Philosophy of Rhetoric* (New York: Funk and Wagnalls Co., 1911), Book I, Chap. VII.
[15] *Op. cit.,* Chap. XV.

Style

Another important means of persuasion lies in the speaker's *style*. It is style, the choice and arrangement of words, that determines in the main the value of a speech as enduring literature. And it is style that more than any other factor gives a speaker the uniqueness by which he is distinguished from other speakers. Here the authenticity of the text of the speech becomes especially important, though the critic may be more interested in what the speaker *meant* to say than in what he *did* say. But he will want to know whether the words he is studying are the speaker's own or contributed by some adviser or ghost writer.

It has been a truism since Aristotle that the first virtue of style is to be clear. But clarity is a relative matter, and the critic must ask always: Clear to whom? The brilliant academic addresses of Curtis and Phillips with their wealth of allusions to literature and history make difficult reading today. Were they clear to the erudite audiences before whom they were spoken? In its effect on its audience a speech must, of course, be *immediately* clear since, once uttered, it cannot be called back for a rehearing (unless it was recorded). In its vocabulary, its allusions, its illustrations, and its sentence structure it must be suited to the intelligence of those for whom it is intended. These are the principal considerations in criticising the clarity of a speech.

Because audiences may be dull, indifferent, and subject to many distractions, we expect a speech to have a vividness and vivacity that will win and hold attention. This is the quality that Aristotle well described as "setting a thing before the eyes." Such an effect may be obtained by concrete wording, effective descriptions, flights of imagination and fancy, the use of metaphors, examples, illustrations, analogies, by vivid narratives and dramatic dialogues and rhetorical questions. Such devices may be used in connection with parallelism of phrase and antithesis. Vivacity is obtained also by conciseness of statement, economy of style, brevity of uttterance, though in this respect audiences and periods vary in their taste. Apparently the audiences of Webster's day tolerated an elaborateness of amplification that may impress us as mere flatulence and bombast. In this, as in other matters, the critic must consider the peculiar nature of the audience addressed. Finally, the vividness of a speech will depend largely upon whether the various oratorical elements are presented with appropriate variety, for any device if endlessly repeated loses its power to hold attention.

A third characteristic of a good style is its appropriateness. It should be suited to the speaker, to the audience, and to the occasion. Factors to be considered are vocabulary, the nature of the materials — facts, arguments, illustrations, and the like — the mood and temper of the speaker and of the audience, the gravity of the subject, the nature of the occasion, and so on. Here again, the validity of the criticism will depend upon how effectively the occasion has been analyzed.

Another quality to be considered is the orality or "speak-ability" of the style. There should be indications that it was meant to be spoken to an audience rather than read silently and privately by an individual reader. The factors that distinguish an oral from a written style have never been definitely set forth, but the critic will look for such things as directness of address, as revealed by personal pronouns and questions; simplicity of sentence structure; heat and vitality of expression demanded by the need for holding the attention of an audience; and a choice of words and phrases that allow for ease, smoothness, and force of utterance.[16]

In studying style one should look also for those occasional passages of sustained nobility and beauty which sometimes lift oratory into the realm of poetry. The ideas and sentiments that inspired them may no longer be meaningful, but still they live and move us by their intrinsic aptness and beauty. Sometimes, as occasionally with Ingersoll, they seem to be merely "purple patches" sewed onto the fabric of the discourse to attract attention, but often they are developed authentically from the orator's feeling and imagination. A thorough study of oratory cannot fail to take account of them.

[16] J. M. Clapp, "Oratorical Style and Structure," in S. B. Harding, *Select Orations Illustrating American Political History* (New York: The Macmillan Co., 1909).

There are other aspects of style, but those we have just discussed are perhaps the most important. For additional criteria and suggestions we recommend especially the works cited above by Aristotle, Campbell, and Blair.

Conclusion

These, then, are the principal means of persuasion that the critic of speeches will consider — character, content, logic, arrangement, motivation, and style. He will be interested also in the speaker's delivery and will learn what he can about it from available reports of the speech, but the text itself will seldom offer any suggestions about how the address was spoken. Students of classical rhetoric will note that this classification cuts across the Aristotelian three-fold division into ethical, pathetic, and logical proofs, and the five-fold Roman division of speech preparation into invention, disposition, style, delivery, and memorization. However, it will be found that all of these are accounted for, except the last.

We have been concerned chiefly with the analysis of single speeches, but it should be obvious that such analyses will prepare the student for other critical adventures. He may wish to attempt a comparative study of two or more orators, noting whether they appeal to the same or different motives, whether they arrange their materials in similar ways, how obtrusively each speaker's ego appears, how they compare in the use of illustrations and examples, how they differ or resemble each other in imagery, in vitality, in sentence form, in vocabulary, or in style. From such studies the critic will prepare himself for a sound judgment of what is unique and distinctive about a given orator. He may concern himself with the varying styles and methods that seemed to prevail in different periods of history. Or he may become interested in discovering certain recurring themes in oratory and changes in attitude toward them — such themes as liberty, democracy, human welfare, the function of government, the concept of honor, the hope of peace, the function of leadership.

These and many other lines of study may prove to be interesting and rewarding. The avenues of research are so various, and the possibility of getting lost in a blind alley is so great, that we feel impelled to warn that a rhetorical criticism is likely to be the less valuable the farther it strays from the central core of our discipline, which is the determination of whether the speaker has discovered and employed in the given case the available means of persuasion.

W. M. P.

Lincoln's First Inaugural

Part I

SPRING COMES GENTLY to Washington always," observed the poet-historian, Carl Sandburg. "In early March the green of the grass brightens, the magnolia softens. Elms and chestnuts burgeon. Redbud and lilac carry on preparations soon to bloom. The lovemaking and birthing in many sunny corners go on no matter what or who the blue-prints and personages behind the discreet bureau and departmental walls." [1] Spring of 1861 was little different from other springs in physical aspect. March 4th dawned as other March 4th's, no doubt, wavering between clearness and cloudiness. At daylight clouds hung dark and heavy in the sky. Early in the morning a few drops of rain fell, but scarcely enough to lay the dust. A northwest wind swept down the cross streets to Pennsylvania Avenue. The weather was cool ·and bracing, and on the whole, "favorable to the ceremonies of the day." [2] The sun had come out.

But if, on the whole, spring had come "gently" as usual, there was little else that bespoke the same rhythm. Out of the deep of winter had come the somewhat bewildered voice of President Buchanan asking, "Why is it ... that discontent now so extensively prevails, and the union of the States, which is the source of all these blessings is threatened with destruction?" [3] Spiritually and morally, the city, indeed the nation, were out of tune, cacophonous, discordant.

Would there be a harmonizing voice today from the gaunt "orator

---

[1] Carl Sandburg, *Abraham Lincoln: The War Years* (Harcourt, Brace and Co., 1939), I, 120.

[2] *New York Times*, March 5, 1861, p. 1, col. 1.

[3] James Buchanan, "Fourth Annual Message, December 3, 1860," *The Works of James Buchanan,* collected and edited by John Bassett Moore (Philadelphia: J. B. Lippincott Co., 1910), XI, 7.

of the West," about to take the helm of the nation? "Behind the cloud the sun is shining still," Abraham Lincoln had said three weeks before, as his train meandered across the Illinois prairies taking him on an "errand of national importance, attended ... with considerable difficulties." [4] Trouble had not come suddenly to the nation, of course. Only a year previously the country had been "eminently prosperous in all its material interests." [5] Harvests had been abundant, and plenty smiled throughout the land. But for forty years there had been an undercurrent of restlessness. As early as 1820, an occasional voice had urged the necessity for secession. Again in 1850, with somewhat greater vehemence, voices were raised as the distribution of newly acquired Mexican territory took place. Then came the repeal of the Missouri Compromise in 1854, the civil war in Kansas and the Sumner-Brooks combat in the Senate in 1856, the Dred Scott decision in 1857, and the spectacular John Brown's raid at Harper's Ferry in 1859, all giving rise to disorder, unrest, and threats of secession as abolition sentiment mounted. Finally, came the election of 1860, and the North appeared to have "capped the mighty pyramid of unfraternal enormities by electing Abraham Lincoln to the Chief Magistracy, on a platform and by a system which indicates nothing but the subjugation of the South and the complete ruin of her social, political and industrial institutions." [6] It was not merely that Lincoln had been elected president, but the "majorities" by which he was elected were "more significant and suggestive than anything else — more so than the election itself — for they unmistakably indicate the hatred to the South which animates and controls the masses of the numerically strongest section of the Confederacy." [7] Senator Clingman of North Carolina found the election a "great, remarkable and dangerous fact that has filled my

[4] Speech at Tolono, Illinois, February 11, 1861, as reported in *New York Daily Tribune*, February 12, 1861, p. 5, col. 3.

[5] Buchanan, *loc. cit.*

[6] *New Orleans Daily Crescent*, November 13, 1860, as quoted in *Southern Editorials on Secession*, edited by Dwight Lowell Dumond (New York and London: The Century Co., 1931), p. 237.

[7] *New Orleans Daily Crescent*, November 12, 1860, as quoted in *Southern Editorials on Secession*, p. 228.

section with alarm and dread for the future," since Lincoln was elected *"because he was known to be a dangerous man,"* avowing the principle of the "irrepressible conflict." [8] Richmond observers commented that a party "founded on the single sentiment, the exclusive feeling of hatred of African slavery," was "now the controlling power in this Confederacy," and noted that the question "What is to be done ... presses on every man." [9] In Charleston, South Carolina, the news of Lincoln's election was met with great rejoicing and "long continued cheering for a Southern Confederacy." [10]

Scarcely more than a month had passed when South Carolina led off in the secession movement. Her two senators resigned their seats in the United States Senate on November 10, 1860, and on December 20 an Ordinance of Secession was adopted,[11] bringing in its wake secessionist demonstrations throughout the South.[12] By the first of February of the new year, Mississippi, Florida, Alabama, Louisiana, Texas, and Georgia had "repealed, rescinded, and abrogated" their membership in the Union by adopting secession ordinances, standing "prepared to resist by force any attempt to maintain the supremacy of the Constitution of the United States." [13] The other slaveholding states held a position of *"quasi* neutrality,"* declaring that their adhesion to the Union could be secured only by affording guarantees against wrongs of which they complained, and dangers which they apprehended.[14] Already by the end of 1860, secessionists at Charleston were in possession of the post office, the federal courts, the customhouses, and forts Castle Pinckney and Moultrie.[15]

[8] Speech of Senator Thomas L. Clingman of North Carolina in the Senate, December 3, 1860, *The Congressional Globe,* Second Session, 36th Congress, Vol. 30, p. 3.

[9] *Richmond Semi-Weekly Examiner,* November 9, 1860, as quoted in *Southern Editorials on Secession,* p. 223.

[10] *The Daily Herald,* Wilmington, N. C., November 9, 1860, as quoted in *Southern Editorials on Secession,* p. 226.

[11] Daniel Wait Howe, *Political History of Secession* (New York: G. P. Putnam's Sons, 1914), p. 449.

[12] J. G. Randall, *Lincoln the President* (New York: Dodd, Mead and Co., 1945), I, 215.

[13] *New York Times,* February 11, 1861, p. 4, col. 2.

[14] *Ibid.*

[15] Randall, *loc. cit.*

It was not without clamor and fanfare that senators took their leave from familiar places. When, on December 31, Senator Judah Benjamin of Louisiana reported that he would make a parting secession speech, "every corner was crowded" [16] in the Senate galleries. His closing declaration that "you can never subjugate us; you never can convert the free sons of the soil into vassals . . . never, never can degrade them to the level of an inferior and servile race. Never! Never!"[17] was greeted by the galleries with "disgraceful applause, screams and uproar." [18] As the galleries were cleared because of misbehavior, people murmured in departing, "Now we will have war," "D—n the Abolitionists," "Abe Lincoln will never come here." [19] Critics observing the national scene remarked, "The President . . . enters upon one of the most momentous and difficult duties ever devolved upon any man, in this country or any other. No one of his predecessors was ever called upon to confront dangers half as great, or to render a public service half as difficult, as those which will challenge his attention at the very outset of his Administration." [20]

January of 1861 came without hope, and with little possibility of the cessation of unrest. Occasionally the newspapers scoffed at the recommendation of the *Richmond Inquirer* that an armed force proceeding from Virginia or Maryland should invade the District of Columbia and prevent the peaceful inauguration of Abraham Lincoln, dismissing it as the "exaggeration of political rhetoric." [21] The capital of the nation was beset by rumor, clamor, occasional attempts at compromise, and general misbehavior. "I passed a part of last week in Washington," observed a Baltimore reporter, "and never, since the days of Jerico [sic], has there been such a blowing of rams' horns as may now be heard in that distracted city. If sound and clamor could overthrow the Constitution, one might well expect to see it go down before the windy suspirations of forced breath that shock and vibrate on all sides." Almost everywhere he met "intem-

---

[16] *New York Times,* January 1, 1861, p. 1, col. 1.
[17] *Congressional Globe,* Second Session, 36th Congress, Vol. 30, p. 217.
[18] *New York Times,* January 1, 1861, p. 1, col. 1.
[19] *Ibid.*
[20] *New York Times,* February 11, 1861, p. 4, col. 2.
[21] *The National Intelligencer* (Washington), January 3, 1861, p. 3, col. 2.

perate and alarming disciples of discord and confusion." "War, secession, and disunion are on every lip; and no hope of compromise or
adjustment is held out by any one. The prevailing sentiment in
Washington is with the South." [22]

As secession went on apace in the South, Wendell Phillips declared in Boston's Music Hall that he hoped that all the slave states
would leave the Union.[23] Horace Greeley, impatient after forty
years of Southern threat, disclaimed a "union of force,—a union
held together by bayonets," and would interpose "no obstacle to
their peaceful withdrawal." [24] Meanwhile, however, a few held out
for compromise. On December 18, Senator Crittenden of Kentucky
introduced a series of compromises in the Senate,[25] but action
seemed unlikely. And when, on January 7, Senator Toombs of
Georgia made a "noisy and ranting secession speech, and at the
close was greeted with a storm of hisses and applause, which was
continued some time," Crittenden's "appeal to save the country,"
presented in "good taste," created "little or no additional favor for
his compromise measure." [26] While Crittenden appealed in the
Senate, a peace conference met in Washington at the invitation of
Virginia, with its announced purpose "to afford to the people of the
slaveholding States adequate guarantees for the security of their
rights." [27] Although delegates assembled and conducted business,
ultimately submitting to the Senate a series of resolutions, it appeared from the beginning that "no substantial results would be
gained." [28] It was clear that the sympathies of the border states
which had not yet seceded "were with those which had already done

[22] New York Times, January 15, 1861, p. 1, col. 5.
[23] New York Times, January 21, 1861, p. 1, col. 4; see also, complete text of
speech in Ibid., p. 8, cols. 5, 6 and p. 5, cols. 1, 2.
[24] Horace Greeley, Recollections of a Busy Life (New York: J. B. Ford and
Co., 1868), p. 398.
[25] Congressional Globe, Second Session, 36th Congress, Part I, Vol. 30, pp.
112-14.
[26] New York Times, January 8, 1861, p. 1, col. 1; see also, Congressional
Globe, Second Session, 36th Congress, Part I, Vol. 30, pp. 264-71.
[27] Howe, op. cit., p. 465.
[28] Ibid., p. 467.

so." [29] Ultimately, the propositions were rejected by the Senate, just as were the Crittenden resolutions, in the closing days of the Congress. In all, it appeared to be an era of "much talk and small performance," a dreary season of debate, with "clouds of dusty and sheety showers of rhetoric," a nation trying to live by "prattle alone," a "miserably betalked nation." [30]

When Lincoln left Springfield, February 11, to wend his way toward Washington, another president, Jefferson Davis, elected on February 9 to head the newly organized Southern Confederacy, was traveling from Mississippi to the Montgomery Convention of slaveholding states to help complete the act of secession, his trip being "one continuous ovation." [31] "The time for compromise is past," observed Davis, as he paused at the depot at Montgomery to address the crowd, "and we are now determined to maintain our position, and make all who oppose us smell Southern powder, feel Southern steel." [32] Clearly, people could agree that Lincoln was to inherit "a thorny wilderness of perplexities." [33] Would he "coerce" the seceded states and ask for the restoration of federal properties in possession of the secessionists? Would he respond to pressure "from all sides" and from a "fraction of his own party" to consent to "extension" of slavery, particularly below the line 36° 30'? Would he listen to "compromise" Republicans in Congress and only "*seem*" to compromise, "so as not to appear obstinate or insensible to the complaints of the Slaveholders"? [34] Would he stand by the Chicago Republican platform, severe in its strictures on the incumbent Democratic administration's acceptance of the principle that the personal relation between master and slave involved "an unqualified property in persons"? [35] Would he stand by the part of the platform which pledged "the maintenance inviolate of the rights of

[29] *Ibid.,* p. 467.
[30] *New York Daily Tribune,* March 13, 1861, p. 4, col. 4.
[31] *New York Daily Tribune,* February 18, 1861, p. 5, col. 6.
[32] *Ibid.,* p. 5, col. 6.
[33] *Ibid.,* March 4, 1861, p. 4, col. 2.
[34] *New York Daily Tribune,* February 18, 1861, p. 6, col. 1.
[35] M. Halstead, *A History of the National Political Conventions of the Current Presidential Campaign* (Columbus, Ohio: Follett, Foster and Co., 1860); p. 138.

the States, and especially the right of each State to order and control its own domestic institutions according to its own judgment exclusively"? [36] Was the belief that he had so often uttered representative of the true Lincoln: "A house divided against itself cannot stand"? [37]

On March 4 as the newspapers gave advance notice of what was to transpire during the day, there was a note of fear and uncertainty in regard to the safety of the President-elect, along with the general eagerness about the outlines of Lincoln's course of action to be announced in the Inaugural. "The great event to which so many have been looking forward with anxiety — which has excited the hopes and fears of the country to an extent unparalleled in its comparatively brief history — will take place to-day," observed the *New York Times*. "The occasion has drawn to the Federal Capital a greater crowd, probably, than has ever been assembled there on any similar occasion. . . . Whether the ceremonies will be marred by any untoward event is, of course, a matter of conjecture, though grave fears are expressed on the subject." [38] While visitors to Washington were seeking to get a glimpse of the tumultuous Senate in all-night session, General Scott and his advisers were together planning to take the "greatest precaution" for preventing "any attack upon the procession or demonstration against Mr. Lincoln's person." [39] Rumors of the presence of a "large gang of 'Plug Uglies' who are here from Baltimore," [40] circulated freely. Whether they were in Washington to make an attack on the person of the president or to "create a disturbance, and plunder private persons" [41] was a matter for general speculation. Whatever the purpose, General Scott and his advisers had decided to leave nothing undone to secure the safety of

[36] *Ibid.*

[37] "A House Divided: Speech Delivered at Springfield, Illinois, at the Close of the Republican State Convention, June 16, 1858," in *Abraham Lincoln: His Speeches and Writings,* edited with critical and analytical notes by Roy P. Basler (Cleveland, Ohio: The World Publishing Co., 1946), p. 372.

[38] *New York Times,* March 4, 1861, p. 4, col. 1.

[39] *New York Times,* March 4, 1861, p. 1, col. 2.

[40] *Ibid.*

[41] *Ibid.*

the president-elect. Riflemen in squads were to be placed in hiding on the roofs commanding buildings along Pennsylvania Avenue. Orders were given to fire in the event of a threat to the presidential carriages. There were cavalry regulars to guard the side-street crossings, moving from one to another as the procession passed. From the windows of the Capitol wings riflemen were to watch the inauguration platform. General Scott would oversee the ceremonies from the top of a slope commanding the north entrance to the Capitol, ready to take personal charge of a battery of flying artillery stationed there. District militia in three ranks were to surround the platform to keep back the crowd. Armed detectives in citizen's clothing were to be scattered through the great audience.[42]

The occasion must have seemed strange to the man who had been accustomed to being carried on the shoulders of admirers on speaking occasions in his years as a stump orator in the West, and to being the idol of many a torchlight procession during the combats with the "Little Giant" in the tumultuous debates of 1858. Even the Capitol grounds where the crowds had begun to assemble had a strangely unfamiliar look in contrast to its fixity during his years as congressman in 1847 and 1848. "The old dome familiar to Congressman Lincoln in 1848 had been knocked loose and hauled down," noted Sandburg. "The iron-wrought material on the Capitol grounds, the hammers, jacks, screws, scaffolds, derricks, ladders, props, ropes, told that they were rebuilding, extending, embellishing the structure on March 4, 1861." "On the slope of lawn fronting the Capitol building stood a bronze statute of Liberty shaped as a massive, fertile woman holding a sword in one hand for power and a wreath of flowers in the other hand for glory. Not yet raised to her pedestal, she looked out of place. She was to be lifted and set on top of the Capitol dome, overlooking the Potomac Valley, when the dome itself

[42] *Ibid.;* see also, Sandburg, *The War Years,* I, 120-21; Randall, *Lincoln the President,* I, 293, 294; William E. Baringer, *A House Dividing* (Springfield, Ill.: Abraham Lincoln Association, 1945), pp. 331-34; *The Diary of a Public Man,* Prefatory notes by F. Lauriston Bullard, Foreword by Carl Sandburg (Chicago: Privately printed for Abraham Lincoln Book Shop, 1945), pp. 73, 74; Clark E. Carr, *Stephen A. Douglas, His Life and Public Services, Speeches and Patriotism* (Chicago: A. C. McClurg and Co., 1909), p. 123.

should be prepared for her." [43] The carpenters had set up a temporary platform fronting the Senate wing for the occasion, with a small wooden canopy covering the speaker's table. [44] "The crowd swarmed about all the approaches leading to the capitol grounds," observed a witness, "while the spacious level extending from the east front of the capitol was one vast black sea of heads." [45] There were between 25,000 and 50,000 people there, waiting with expectancy. [46] "Every window in the north front of the Capitol was filled with ladies. Every tree top bore its burden of eager eyes. Every fence and staging, and pile of building material, for the Capitol extension was made a 'coyn of vantage' for its full complement of spectators." [47] It was noticeable that "scarce a Southern face is to be seen" [48] in the crowd, "judging from the lack of long-haired men." [49] While the crowd waited for the administration of the oath of the Vice-President, which took place in the Senate chambers, it was entertained with martial music, and "by the antics of a lunatic, who had climbed a tall tree in front of the capitol and made a long political speech, claiming to be the rightful President of the United States." Policemen were detached to bring him down, but he merely climbed higher and "stood rocking in the wind, and made another speech." [50] The ceremonies over indoors, the major figures of the occasion were seen emerging, Abraham Lincoln with James Buchanan by his side.

As Lincoln and Buchanan took places on the right side of the speaker's stand, Chief Justice Taney, who soon would administer the oath of office, took a seat upon the left. Many in the audience were seeing Lincoln for the first time. "Honest Abe Lincoln," the folks back home called him, or just "Old Abe" was the affectionate

[43] Sandburg, *The War Years*, I, 120.

[44] Baringer, *op. cit.*, p. 333.

[45] Correspondence of the *Cincinnati Commercial*, as quoted in *The Chicago Daily Tribune*, March 8, 1861, p. 2, col. 4.

[46] *New York Daily Tribune*, March 5, 1861, p. 5, col. 4.

[47] *Chicago Daily Tribune*, March 9, 1861, p. 3, col. 2.

[48] *New York Times*, March 4, 1861, p. 1, col. 2.

[49] *Chicago Daily Tribune*, March 5, 1861, p. 1, col. 2.

[50] Correspondence of the *Cincinnati Commercial*, as quoted in *The Chicago Daily Tribune*, March 8, 1861, p. 2, col. 4.

cry at the Chicago "Wigwam" as thousands cheered and shook the rafters "like the rush of a great wind, in the van of a storm," [51] when he was nominated. Walt Whitman thought "four sorts of genius, four mighty and primal hands, will be needed to the complete limning of this man's future portrait—the eyes and brains and finger-touch of Plutarch and Eschylus and Michel Angelo, assisted by Rabelais." [52] "If any personal description of me is thought desirable," Lincoln had written two years before, "it may be said I am, in height, six feet four inches, nearly; lean in flesh, weighing on an average one hundred and eighty pounds; dark complexion, with coarse black hair and gray eyes. No other marks or brands recollected." [53] He was "not a pretty man," his law partner, Herndon, thought, "nor was he an ugly one: he was a homely man, careless of his looks, plain looking and plain acting." But he had that "inner quality which distinguishes one person from another." [54] "I never saw a more thoughtful face," observed David Locke, "I never saw a more dignified face, I never saw so sad a face." [55] Emerson had found in him the "grandeur and strength of absolute simplicity," when, on occasion, he had heard him speak, seen his small gray eyes kindle, heard his voice ring, and observed his face shine and seem "to light up a whole assembly." [56] "Abraham Lincoln: one of nature's noblemen," he was sometimes toasted.[57]

"It was unfortunate," says the noted Lincoln scholar, J. G. Randall, "that Lincoln was not better known, North and South, in March of

[51] Halstead, *op. cit.*, pp. 149-51.

[52] *The Complete Writings of Walt Whitman* (New York: G. P. Putnam's Sons, 1902), II, 244.

[53] Lincoln to J. W. Fell, Springfield, Illinois, December 20, 1859, *Complete Works of Abraham Lincoln*, edited by John G. Nicolay and John Hay (New York: The Tandy-Thomas Co., 1905), V, 288, 289.

[54] Herndon MS fragment, quoted in Randall, *op. cit.*, p. 28.

[55] *Remembrances of Abraham Lincoln by Distinguished Men of His Time*, collected and edited by Allen Thorndike Rice (8th ed.; New York: Published by the *North American Review*, 1889), p. 442.

[56] John Wesley Hill, *Abraham Lincoln, Man of God* (4th ed.; New York: G. P. Putnam's Sons, 1930), p. 306.

[57] Carl Sandburg, *Abraham Lincoln, The Prairie Years* (New York: Harcourt, Brace and Co., 1926), I, 199, 200.

1861. Had people more fully understood his pondering on government, reverence for law, peaceful intent and complete lack of sectional bitterness, much tragedy might have been avoided." [58] "Gentle, and merciful and just!" [59] William Cullen Bryant was eventually to write. But now, in 1861, there was something unknown about Lincoln to many. It is true that after the Lincoln-Douglas debates he had gained recognition beyond the limits of his state. The Chicago *Democrat* called attention to the fact that "Mr. Lincoln's name has been used by newspapers and public meetings outside the State in connection with the Presidency and Vice Presidency, so that it is not only in his own State that Honest Old Abe is respected." "Even his opponents profess to love the man, though they hate his principles," it observed. [60] Again the *Illinois State Journal* took pride in reporting his growing fame. In "other states," it said, he had been found "not only . . . an unrivalled orator, strong in debate, keen in his logic and wit, with admirable powers of statement, and a fertility of resources which are equal to every occasion; but his truthfulness, his candor, his honesty of purpose, his magnanimity . . . have stamped him as a statesman whom the Republicans throughout the Union may be proud of." [61] In 1860, in New York, the "announcement that Hon. Abraham Lincoln, of Illinois would deliver an address in Cooper Institute . . . drew thither a large and enthusiastic assemblage," and William Cullen Bryant thought that he had only "to pronounce the name of Abraham Lincoln" who had previously been known "only by fame" in order to secure the "profoundest attention." [62] Lincoln had faced thousands of people along the way to Washington, at Indianapolis, Cleveland, Philadelphia, Albany, Harrisburg, and elsewhere, being greeted enthusiastically. Still, "in general," observes Randall, "it cannot be said that he had a 'good press' at the threshold of office. Showmanship failed to make capital of his rugged origin, and there faced the country a strange man

[58] *New York Times Magazine*, February 6, 1949, p. 11.

[59] "Abraham Lincoln," in *The Poetical Works of William Cullen Bryant*, edited by Parke Godwin (New York: D. Appleton and Co., 1883), II, 151.

[60] Quoted in *Daily Illinois State Journal*, November 15, 1858, p. 1, col. 1.

[61] *Ibid.*, November 12, 1858, p. 2, col. 1.

[62] *New York Times*, February 28, 1860, p. 1, col. 1.

from Illinois who was dubbed a 'Simple Susan,' a 'baboon,' or a 'gorilla.' " [63] "Our Presidential Merryman," *Harper's Weekly* had labeled him,[64] later carrying a caricature recounting the fabricated story of his incognito entry into Washington. "He wore a Scotch plaid Cap and a very long Military Cloak, so that he was entirely unrecognizable," the caption read.[65] Men like Stanton thought of him as a "low, cunning clown." [66] And the Associated Press reporter, Henry Villard, remembered his "fondness for low talk," and could not have persuaded himself "that the man might possibly possess true greatness of mind and nobility of heart," admitting to a feeling of "disgust and humiliation that such a person should have been called upon to direct the destinies of a great nation." [67]

In the South, there had been little willingness to know the Lincoln they "should have known," the Lincoln who "intended to be fair to the Southern people, and, as he had said at the Cooper Union in February of 1860, 'do nothing through passion and ill-temper,' 'calmly consider their demands, and yield to them where possible." [68] The South had made up its mind that whatever the North did to ingratiate Lincoln with them was done in deceit. "Since the election of Lincoln most of the leading Northern Abolition papers have essayed the herculean task of reconciling the Southern People to his Presidential rule," observed the *New Orleans Daily Crescent*. "Having succeeded to their heart's content in electing him — having vilified and maligned the South through a long canvass, without measure or excuse — they now tell us that Mr. Lincoln is a very good man, a very amiable man; that he is not at all violent in his prejudices or partialities; that, on the contrary, he is a moderate, kindly-tempered, conservative man, and if we will only submit to his administration for a time, we will ascertain that he will make one of

[63] Randall, *op. cit.*, I, 292.
[64] Vol. V (March 2, 1861), p. 144.
[65] *Ibid.* (March 9, 1861), p. 160.
[66] *The Diary of a Public Man*, pp. 48, 49.
[67] *Memoirs of Henry Villard* (Boston: Houghton, Mifflin Co., 1904), I, 144.
[68] J. G. Randall, "Lincoln's Greatest Declaration of Faith," *New York Times Magazine*, February 6, 1949, p. 11.

the best Presidents the South or the country ever had! 'Will you walk into my parlor said the spider to the fly.' " "Mr. Lincoln may be all that these Abolition journals say he is. But, we do not believe a word they say," the *Crescent* continued. "We are clearly convinced that they are telling falsehoods to deceive the people of the South, in order to carry out their own selfish and unpatriotic purposes the more easily. They know that, although Lincoln is elected to the Presidency, he is not yet President of the United States, and they are shrewd enough to know that grave doubts exist whether he ever will be. The chances are that he will not, unless the South is quieted. . . ." [69]

The South found it easier to view Lincoln as a stereotype, a "radical Abolitionist," and "Illinois ape," a "traitor to his country." Then, too, the escape through Baltimore by night could "not fail to excite a most mischievous feeling of contempt for the personal character of Mr. Lincoln throughout the country, especially at the South." [70]

Thus appeared Lincoln, who "without mock modesty" had described himself en route to Washington as "the humblest of all individuals that have ever been elevated to the presidency." [71]

Senator Baker of Oregon advanced to the platform and announced, "Fellow-Citizens: I introduce to you Abraham Lincoln, the President elect of the United States of America." [72]

Mr. Lincoln had the crowd "matched" [73] in sartorial perfection. He was wearing a new tall hat, new black suit of clothes and black boots, expansive white shirt bosom. He carried an ebony cane with a gold head the size of a hen's egg. He arose, "walked deliberately and composedly to the table, and bent low in honor of the repeated and enthusiastic cheering of the countless host before him. Having put on his spectacles, he arranged his manuscript on the small table,

[69] *Southern Editorials on Secession*, p. 229.

[70] *The Diary of a Public Man*, p. 46.

[71] "Address to the Legislature of New York, at Albany, February 18, 1861," in *Complete Works of Abraham Lincoln*, VI, 140.

[72] *New York Times*, March 5, 1861, p. 1, col. 3.

[73] Sandburg, *The War Years*, I, 122.

115141

keeping the paper thereon by the aid of his cane." [74] In a clear voice he began: [75]

Fellow-citizens of the United States:

In compliance with a custom as old as the government itself, I appear before you to address you briefly, and to take, in your presence, the oath prescribed by the Constitution of the United States, to be taken by the President "before he enters on the execution of his office."

I do not consider it necessary at present for me to discuss those matters of administration about which there is no special anxiety or excitement.

Apprehension seems to exist among the people of the Southern States, that by the accession of a Republican Administration, their property, and their peace, and personal security, are to be endangered. There has never been any reasonable cause for such apprehension. Indeed, the most ample evidence to the contrary has all the while existed, and been open to their inspection. It is found in nearly all the published speeches of him who now addresses you. I do but quote from one of those speeches when I declare that "I have no purpose, directly or indirectly, to interfere with the institution of slavery in the States where it exists. I believe I have no lawful right to do so, and I have no inclination to do so." Those who nominated and elected me did so with full knowledge that I had made this, and many similar declarations, and had never recanted them. And more than this, they placed in the platform, for my acceptance, and as a law to themselves, and to me, the clear and emphatic resolution which I now read:

"Resolved, That the maintenance inviolate of the rights of the States, and especially the right of each State to order and control its own domestic institutions according to its own judgment exclusively, is essential to that balance of power on which the perfection and endurance of our political fabric depend; and we denounce the

[74] New York Times, March 5, 1861, p. 1, col. 3.
[75] The text of the Inaugural being used is that contained in Abraham Lincoln: His Speeches and Writings, edited by Roy P. Basler, pp. 579-90.

lawless invasion by armed force of the soil of any State or Territory, no matter under what pretext, as among the gravest of crimes."

I now reiterate these sentiments: and in doing so, I only press upon the public attention the most conclusive evidence of which the case is susceptible, that the property, peace and security of no section are to be in any wise endangered by the now incoming Administration. I add too, that all the protection which, consistently with the Constitution and the laws, can be given, will be cheerfully given to all the States when lawfully demanded, for whatever cause — as cheerfully to one section as to another.

There is much controversy about the delivering up of fugitives from service or labor. The clause I now read is as plainly written in the Constitution as any other of its provisions:

"No person held to service or labor in one State, under the laws thereof, escaping into another, shall, in consequence of any law or regulation therein, be discharged from such service or labor, but shall be delivered up on claim of the party to whom such service or labor may be due."

It is scarcely questioned that this provision was intended by those who made it, for the reclaiming of what we call fugitive slaves; and the intention of the law-giver is the law. All members of Congress swear their support to the whole Constitution — to this provision as much as to any other. To the proposition, then, that slaves whose cases come within the terms of this clause, "shall be delivered up," their oaths are unanimous. Now, if they would make the effort in good temper, could they not, with nearly equal unanimity, frame and pass a law, by means of which to keep good that unanimous oath?

There is some difference of opinion whether this clause should be enforced by national or by state authority; but surely that difference is not a very material one. If the slave is to be surrendered, it can be of but little consequence to him, or to others, by which authority it is done. And should any one, in any case, be content that his oath shall go unkept, on a merely unsubstantial controversy as to *how* it shall be kept?

Again, in any law upon this subject, ought not all the safeguards

of liberty known in civilized and humane jurisprudence to be introduced, so that a free man be not, in any case, surrendered as a slave?
And might it not be well, at the same time to provide by law for the
enforcements of that clause in the Constitution which guarantees
that "the citizens of each State shall be entitled to all privileges and
immunities of citizens in the several States"?

I take the official oath to-day, with no mental reservations, and
with no purpose to construe the Constitution or laws, by any hypercritical rules. And while I do not choose now to specify particular
acts of Congress as proper to be enforced, I do suggest that it will be
much safer for all, both in official and private stations, to conform
to, and abide by, all those acts which stand unrepealed, than to
violate any of them, trusting to find impunity in having them held
to be unconstitutional.

It is seventy-two years since the first inauguration of a President
under our national Constitution. During that period fifteen different
and greatly distinguished citizens, have, in succession, administered
the executive branch of the government. They have conducted it
through many perils; and, generally, with great success. Yet, with all
this scope for [of] precedent, I now enter upon the same task for the
brief constitutional term of four years, under great and peculiar
difficulty. A disruption of the Federal Union, heretofore only menaced, is now formidably attempted.

I hold, that in contemplation of universal law, and of the Constitution, the Union of these States is perpetual. Perpetuity is implied,
if not expressed, in the fundamental law of all national governments.
It is safe to assert that no government proper, ever had a provision
in its organic law for its own termination. Continue to execute all
the express provisions of our national Constitution, and the Union
will endure forever—it being impossible to destroy it, except by
some action not provided for in the instrument itself.

Again, if the United States be not a government proper, but an
association of States in the nature of contract merely, can it, as a
contract, be peaceably unmade, by less than all the parties who
made it? One party to a contract may violate it — break it, so to
speak; but does it not require all to lawfully rescind it?

Descending from these general principles, we find the proposition that, in legal contemplation, the Union is perpetual, confirmed by the history of the Union itself. The Union is much older than the Constitution. It was formed in fact, by the Articles of Association in 1774. It was matured and continued by the Declaration of Independence in 1776. It was further matured and the faith of all the then thirteen States expressly plighted and engaged that it should be perpetual, by the Articles of Confederation in 1778. And finally, in 1787, one of the declared objects for ordaining and establishing the Constitution, was *"to form a more perfect Union."*

But if [the] destruction of the Union, by one, or by a part only, of the States, be lawfully possible, the Union is *less* perfect than before the Constitution, having lost the vital element of perpetuity.

It follows from these views that no State, upon its own mere motion, can lawfully get out of the Union, — that *resolves* and *ordinances* to that effect are legally void, and that acts of violence, within any State or States, against the authority of the United States, are insurrectionary or revolutionary, according to the circumstances.

I therefore consider that in view of the Constitution and the laws, the Union is unbroken; and to the extent of my ability I shall take care, as the Constitution itself expressly enjoins upon me, that the laws of the Union be faithfully executed in all the States. Doing this I deem to be only a simple duty on my part; and I shall perform it, so far as practicable, unless my rightful masters, the American people, shall withhold the requisite means, or, in some authoritative manner, direct the contrary. I trust this will not be regarded as a menace, but only as the declared purpose of the Union that it will constitutionally defend and maintain itself.

In doing this there needs to be no bloodshed or violence; and there shall be none, unless it be forced upon the national authority. The power confided to me will be used to hold, occupy, and possess the property and places belonging to the government, and to collect the duties and imposts; but beyond what may be necessary for these objects, there will be no invasion—no using of force against or among the people anywhere. Where hostility to the United States, in any interior locality, shall be so great and so universal, as to prevent competent resident citizens from holding the Federal offices, there will be no attempt to force obnoxious strangers among the people for that object. While the strict legal right may exist in the government to enforce the exercise of these offices, the attempt to do so would be so irritating, and so nearly impracticable with all, that I deem it better to forego, for the time, the uses of such offices.

The mails, unless repelled, will continue to be furnished in all parts of the Union. So far as possible, the people everywhere shall have that sense of perfect security which is most favorable to calm thought and reflection. The course here indicated will be followed, unless current events and experience shall show a modification or change to be proper; and in every case and exigency my best discretion will be exercised according to circumstances actually existing, and with a view and a hope of a peaceful solution of the national troubles, and the restoration of fraternal sympathies and affections.

That there are persons in one section or another who seek to destroy the Union at all events, and are glad of any pretext to do it, I will neither affirm or deny; but if there be such, I need address no word to them. To those, however, who really love the Union, may I not speak?

Before entering upon so grave a matter as the destruction of our national fabric, with all its benefits, its memories and its hopes, would it not be wise to ascertain precisely why we do it? Will you hazard so desperate a step, while there is any possibility that any portion of the ills you fly from have no real existence? Will you, while the certain ills you fly to, are greater than all the real ones you fly from? Will you risk the commission of so fearful a mistake?

All profess to be content in the Union, if all constitutional rights can be maintained. Is it true, then, that any right, plainly written in the Constitution, has been denied? I think not. Happily the human mind is so constituted, that no party can reach to the audacity of doing this. Think, if you can, of a single instance in which a plainly written provision of the Constitution has ever been denied. If, by the mere force of numbers, a majority should deprive a minority of any clearly written constitutional right, it might, in a moral point of view, justify revolution—certainly would, if such a right were a vital one. But such is not our case. All the vital rights of minorities, and of individuals, are so plainly assured to them, by affirmations and negations, guarantees and prohibitions, in the Constitution, that controversies never arise concerning them. But no organic law can ever be framed with a provision specifically applicable to every question which may occur in practical administration. No foresight can anticipate, nor any document of reasonable length contain express provisions for all possible questions. Shall fugitives from labor be surrendered by national or by State authority? The Constitution does not expressly say. *May* Congress prohibit slavery in the territories? The Constitution does not expressly say. *Must* Congress protect slavery in the territories? The Constitution does not expressly say.

From questions of this class spring all our constitutional controversies, and we divide upon them into majorities and minorities. If the minority will not acquiesce, the majority must, or the government must cease. There is no other alternative; for continuing the government, is acquiescence on one side or the other. If a minority, in such case, will secede rather than acquiesce, they make a precedent which, in turn, will divide and ruin them; for a minority of their own will secede from them whenever a majority refuses to be controlled by such minority. For instance, why may not any portion of a new confederacy, a year or two hence, arbitrarily secede again, precisely as portions of the present Union now claim to secede from it? All who cherish disunion sentiments, are now being educated to the exact temper of doing this.

Is there such perfect identity of interests among the States to compose a new Union, as to produce harmony only, and prevent renewed secession?

Plainly, the central idea of secession, is the essence of anarchy. A majority, held in restraint by constitutional checks and limitations, and always changing easily with deliberate changes of popular opinions and sentiments is the only true sovereign of a free people. Whoever rejects it, does, of necessity, fly to anarchy or to despotism. Unanimity is impossible; the rule of a minority, as a permanent arrangement, is wholly inadmissible; so that, rejecting the majority principle, anarchy or despotism in some form is all that is left.

I do not forget the position assumed by some, that constitutional questions are to be decided by the Supreme Court; nor do I deny that such decisions must be binding in any case, upon the parties to a suit, as to the object of that suit, while they are also entitled to very high respect and consideration in all parallel cases by all other departments of the government. And while it is obviously possible that such decision may be erroneous in any given case, still the evil effect following it, being limited to that particular case, with the chance that it may be over-ruled, and never become a precedent for other cases, can better be borne than could the evils of a different practice. At the same time, the candid citizen must confess that if the policy of the government upon vital questions, affecting the whole people, is to be irrevocably fixed by decisions of the Supreme Court, the instant they are made, in ordinary litigation between parties, in personal actions, the people will have ceased to be their own rulers, having to that extent practically resigned their government into the hands of that eminent tribunal. Nor is there in this view any assault upon the court or the judges. It is a duty from which they may not shrink, to decide cases properly brought before them; and it is no fault of theirs if others seek to turn their decisions to political purposes.

One section of our country believes slavery is *right*, and ought to be extended, while the other believes it is *wrong*, and ought not to be extended. This is the only substantial dispute. The fugitive slave clause of the Constitution, and the law for the suppression of the foreign slave trade, are each as well enforced, perhaps, as any law can ever be in a community where the moral sense of the people imperfectly supports the law itself. The great body of the people abide by the dry legal obligation in both cases, and a few break over in each. This, I think, cannot be perfectly cured; and it would be worse in both cases *after* the separation of the sections, than before. The foreign slave trade, now imperfectly suppressed, would be ultimately revived without restriction, in one section; while fugitive slaves, now only partially surrendered, would not be surrendered at all, by the other.

Physically speaking, we cannot separate. We cannot remove our respective sections from each other, nor build an impassable wall between them. A husband and wife may be divorced, and go out of the presence, and beyond the reach of each other; but the different parts of our country cannot do this. They cannot but remain face to face; and intercourse, either amicable or hostile, must continue between them. Is it possible, then, to make that intercourse more advantageous or more satisfacory, *after* separation than *before?* Can aliens make treaties easier than friends can make laws? Can treaties be more faithfully enforced between aliens than laws can among friends? Suppose you go to war, you cannot fight always; and when, after much loss on both sides, and no gain on either, you cease fighting, the identical old questions, as to terms of intercourse, are again upon you.

This country, with its institutions, belongs to the people who inhabit it. Whenever they shall grow weary of the existing government, they can exercise their *constitutional* right of amending it, or their *revolutionary* right to dismember or overthrow it. I cannot be ignorant of the fact that many worthy and patriotic citizens are desirous of having the national Constitution amended. While I make no recommendation of amendments, I fully recognize the rightful authority of the people over the whole subject to be exercised in either of the modes prescribed in the instrument itself; and I should under existing circumstances favor rather than oppose a fair opportunity being afforded the people to act upon it.

I will venture to add that to me the Convention mode seems preferable, in that it allows amendments to originate with the people themselves, instead of only permitting them to take or reject propositions, originated by others, not especially chosen for the purpose, and which might not be precisely such as they would wish to either accept or refuse. I understand a proposed amendment to the Constitution, which amendment, however, I have not seen, has passed Congress, to the effect that the federal government shall never interfere with the domestic institutions of the States, including that of persons held to service. To avoid misconstruction of what I have said, I depart from my purpose not to speak of particular amendments, so far as to say that holding such a provision to now be implied constitutional law, I have no objection to its being made express and irrevocable.

The Chief Magistrate derives all his authority from the people, and they have conferred none upon him to fix terms for the separation of the States. The people themselves can do this also if they choose; but the executive, as such, has nothing to do with it. His duty is to administer the present government, as it came to his hands, and to transmit it, unimpaired by him, to his successor.

Why should there not be a patient confidence in the ultimate justice of the people? Is there any better or equal hope, in the world? In our present differences, is either party without faith of being in the right? If the Almighty Ruler of nations, with his eternal truth and justice, be on your side of the North or on yours of the South, that truth, and that justice, will surely prevail, by the judgment of this great tribunal, the American people.

By the frame of the government under which we live, this same people have wisely given their public servants but little power for mischief; and have, with equal wisdom, provided for the return of that little to their own hands at very short intervals.

While the people retain their virtue and vigilance, no administration, by any extreme of wickedness or folly, can very seriously injure the government in the short space of four years.

My countrymen, one and all, think calmly and *well*, upon this whole subject. Nothing valuable can be lost by taking time. If there be an object to *hurry* any of you, in hot haste, to a step which you would never take *deliberately*, that object will be frustrated by taking time; but no good object can be frustrated by it. Such of you as are now dissatisfied, still have the old Constitution unimpaired, and, on the sensitive point, the laws of your own framing under it; while the new administration will have no immediate power, if it would, to change either. If it were admitted that you who are dissatisfied, hold the right side in the dispute, there still is no single good reason for precipitate action. Intelligence, patriotism, Christianity, and a firm reliance on Him, who has never yet forsaken this favored land, are still competent to adjust, in the best way, all our present difficulty.

In *your* hands, my dissatisfied fellow countrymen, and not in *mine*, is the momentous issue of civil war. The government will not assail *you*. You can have no conflict, without being yourselves the aggressors. *You* have no oath registered in Heaven to destroy the government, while *I* shall have the most solemn one to "preserve, protect and defend" it.

I am loth to close. We are not enemies, but friends. We must not be enemies. Though passion may have strained, it must not break our bonds of affection. The mystic chords of memory, stretching from every battle-field, and patriot grave, to every living heart and hearth-stone, all over this broad land, will yet swell the chorus of the Union, when again touched, as surely they will be, by the better angels of our nature.

With "more of Euclid than of Demosthenes" [76] in him, his delivery was not that of the spellbinder, agitator, or demagogue. His voice was a tenor that "carried song-tunes poorly but had clear and appealing modulations." [77] Habitually a little "scared" [78] when he spoke, he was "pale and very nervous" [79] on this occasion, but his "cheerfulness was marked." [80] "Compelled by nature, to speak slowly," [81] his manner was "deliberate and impressive" [82] and his voice "remarkably clear and penetrating." [83] There was little evidence in his voice of the fear that might have come as the result of knowing that

[76] Randall, *op. cit.*, I, 49.

[77] Sandburg, *The Prairie Years*, I, 305.

[78] [W. H. Herndon and J. W. Weik], *Herndon's Life of Lincoln*, with an introduction and notes by Paul M. Angle (Cleveland: The World Publishing Co., 1949), p. 220.

[79] *The Diary of a Public Man*, p. 74.

[80] Correspondence of the *Cincinnati Commercial*, as quoted in *Chicago Daily Tribune*, March 8, 1861, p. 2, col. 4.

[81] Herndon and Weik, *op. cit.*, p. 273.

[82] *New York Tribune*, March 5, 1861, p. 5, col. 4.

[83] *Ibid.*

there were "heavy bets" about his safety.[84] Some of the spectators noted a "loud, and distinct voice, quite intelligible by at least ten thousand persons below him"; [85] others found it a "clear, ringing voice, that was easily heard by those on the outer limits of the crowd"; [86] still others noted his "firm tones of voice," his "great deliberation and precision of emphasis." [87] Sandburg might have remarked that it gave out "echoes and values." [88]

As Lincoln read on, the audience listened respectfully, with "intense interest, amid a stillness almost oppressive." [89] In the crowd behind the speaker sat Horace Greeley, momentarily expecting the crack of rifle fire.[90] At one point he thought it had come. The speaker stopped. But it was only a spectator crashing down through a tree.[91] Otherwise, the crowd in the grounds "behaved very well." [92] Buchanan sat listening, and "looking as straight as he could at the toe of his right boot." [93] Douglas, close by on Lincoln's right, listened "attentively," showing that he was "apparently satisfied" as he "exclaimed, *sotto voce*, 'Good,' 'That's so,' 'No coercion,' and 'Good again.' " [94] Chief Justice Taney "did not remove his eyes from Mr. Lincoln during the entire delivery." [95] Mr. Cameron stood with his back to the President, on the opposite side to Mr. Douglas, "peering off into the crowd." [96] Senator Seward and the other Cabinet officers-elect "kept themselves in the background." [97] Senator Wigfall of

[84] *New York Times,* March 4, 1861, p. 1, col. 2.

[85] *National Intelligencer,* March 5, 1861, p. 3, col. 3.

[86] *New York Times,* March 5, 1861, p. 1, col. 3.

[87] Correspondence of the *Cincinnati Commercial,* quoted in *Chicago Daily Tribune,* March 8, 1861, p. 2, col. 4.

[88] Sandburg, *The Prairie Years,* I, 306.

[89] Frederick W. Seward, *Seward at Washington, as Senator and Secretary of State* (New York: Derby and Miller, 1891), I, 516.

[90] Greeley, *op. cit.,* p. 404.

[91] *Diary of a Public Man,* p. 74.

[92] *Ibid.*

[93] *New York Times,* March 5, 1861, p. 1, col. 3.

[94] *Ibid.*

[95] *Ibid.*

[96] Correspondence of the *Cincinnati Commercial,* as quoted in *Chicago Daily Tribune,* March 8, 1861, p. 2, col. 4.

[97] *Ibid.*

Texas, with folded arms "leaned conspicuously in a Capitol door-way," listening to the Inaugural, plainly wearing "contempt, defiance, derision, on his face, his pantomimic posture saying what he had said in the Senate, that the old Union was a corpse and the question was how to embalm it and conduct the funeral decently." [98] Thurlow Weed moved away from the crowd, reporting to General Scott at the top of the slope "The Inaugural is a success," as the old general exclaimed, "God be praised! God in his goodness be praised." [99] To a newspaper reporter surveying the scene, there was a "propriety and becoming interest which pervaded the vast assembly" and "impressed every spectator who had the opportunity of overlooking it." [100] The crowd "applauded repeatedly" and "at times, rapturously," [101] particularly at points where he "announced his inflexible purpose to execute the laws and discharge his whole constitutional duty." [102] When Lincoln declared, "I hold that in the contemplation of international law, and of the Constitution, the Union of these States is perpetual," the "cheers were hearty and prolonged." [103] When he said, "I shall take care that the laws of the Union be faithfully executed in all the States," he was met with a "tremendous shout of approval." [104] But the "greatest impression of all was produced by the final appeal," [105] noted one of the reporters. "With great solemnity of emphasis, using his gestures to add significance to his words," Lincoln remarked "You have no oath registered in Heaven to destroy this Government, while I shall have the most solemn one to preserve, protect and defend it," and the crowd responded with "round after round of cheering." [106] Finally, after

[98] Sandburg, *The War Years*, I, 123.

[99] Seward, *op. cit.*, pp. 516, 517.

[100] *New York Daily Tribune*, March 5, 1861, p. 5, col. 4.

[101] *Chicago Daily Tribune*, March 8, 1861, p. 2, col. 4, quoted from *Cincinnati Commercial*.

[102] *New York Daily Tribune*, March 5, 1861, p. 5, col. 4.

[103] *Chicago Daily Tribune*, March 8, 1861, p. 2, col. 4, quoted from *Cincinnati Commercial*.

[104] *Chicago Daily Tribune*, March 8, 1861, p. 2, col. 4, quoted from *Cincinnati Commercial*.

[105] *Ibid.*

[106] *Ibid.*

Lincoln had addressed his "words of affection" to the audience, ending his address, "men waved their hats, and broke forth in the heartiest manifestations of delight. The extraordinary clearnes [*sic*], straight-forwardness and lofty spirit of patriotism which pervaded the whole address, impressed every listener, while the evident earnestness, sincerity and manliness of Mr. Lincoln extorted the praise even of his enemies." [107] "The effect of the Inaugural on the country at large remains to be awaited and to be gathered from many sources," observed a reporter, "but it is conceded on all hands that its effect, already noticeable on the vast gathering here, upon the city, and the tone of feeling here is eminently happy, and the source of great gratulation on every side." [108]

Chief Justice Taney stepped forward, shrunken, old, his hands trembling with emotion, and held out an open Bible. Lincoln laid his left hand upon it, raised his right hand, and repeated with a "firm but modest voice" [109] the oath: "I do solemnly swear that I will faithfully execute the office of President of the United States, and will, to the best of my ability, preserve, protect, and defend the Constitution of the United States." Lincoln was now president. Below, the crowd "tossed their hats, wiped their eyes, cheered at the tops of their voices, hurrahed themselves hoarse," and "had the crowd not been so very dense, they would have demonstrated in more lively ways, their joy, satisfaction and delight." [110] Over on the slope the artillery boomed a salute to the sixteenth president of the United States.[111] The crowd ebbed away, and Lincoln rode down Pennsylvania Avenue with Buchanan, bidding him good-bye at the Presidential mansion.[112]

The address had taken thirty-five minutes in delivery, and now it was all over, at least until the nation in general turned in its response.

[107] *Chicago Daily Tribune*, March 8, 1861, p. 2, col. 4, quoted from *Cincinnati Commercial*.
[108] *Chicago Daily Tribune*, March 9, 1861, p. 3, col. 2.
[109] *New York Times*, March 5, 1861, p. 1, col. 3.
[110] *Ibid.*
[111] Sandburg, *The War Years*, I, 122.
[112] Baringer, *op. cit.*, p. 334.

Lincoln had spent six weeks in preparing it—six weeks and many years of lonely thought, along with his active experience on the circuit and the stump. Like the "House Divided Speech" and the "Cooper Union Address" it was deliberately and cautiously prepared, undergoing revision up to the moment of delivery. "Late in January," he told his law partner, Herndon, that he was "ready to begin" [113] the preparation of the Inaugural. In a room over a store, across the street from the State House, cut off from all intrusion and outside communication, he began the preparation. He had told Herndon what works he wanted to consult and asked to be furnished "Henry Clay's great speech delivered in 1850; Andrew Jackson's proclamation against Nullification; and a copy of the Constitution." He "afterwards" called for a copy of Webster's reply to Hayne, a speech which he regarded as "the grandest specimen of American oratory." [114] "With these few 'volumes,' and no further sources of reference," [115] he began his work on the address.

On February 2, 1861, he wrote a friend, George D. Prentice,[116] editor of the *Louisville Journal*, "I have the document blocked out; but in the now rapidly shifting scenes I shall have to hold it subject to revision up to the time of delivery." [117] He had an original draft printed by one of the proprietors of the *Illinois State Journal* to whom he entrusted the manuscript.[118] "No one else seems to have been taken into the confidence of Mr. Lincoln as to its contents until after he started for Washington on February 11." [119] Upon reaching Indianapolis, he presented a copy to O. H. Browning who had accompanied him from Springfield. According to Browning, "before parting with Mr. Lincoln at Indianapolis, Tuesday, he gave me a copy of his inaugural address, and requested me to read it, and

[113] Herndon and Weik, *op. cit.*, p. 386.
[114] *Ibid.*
[115] *Ibid.*
[116] *Lincoln Lore*, No. 308 (March 4, 1935).
[117] Louis A. Warren, "Original Draft of the First Inaugural," *Lincoln Lore*, No. 358 (February 17, 1936).
[118] *Ibid.*
[119] *Ibid.*

give him my opinion, which I did. I thought it able, well considered, and appropriate, and so informed him. It is, in my judgment, a very admirable document. He permitted me to retain a copy, under promise not to show it except to Mrs. Browning." [120]

Upon arriving in Washington, Lincoln submitted a copy to Secretary Seward with the same invitation to criticize it.[121] According to Louis A. Warren, "As far as we know these two men are the only ones who made any suggestions about certain revisions in the original copy," [122] even though a few others may have seen it.[123]

Reporters showed an avid interest in the preparation of the Inaugural, sometimes reporting inaccurately on the various stages of its preparation. Recording the activities of the President on Saturday night, March 2, one reporter erroneously observed: "Mr. Lincoln sent for Senator Seward, and at 11½ o'clock that gentleman reached the hotel. Mr. Lincoln read to him the Inaugural for the first time, and then asked his advice. Senator Seward took it up section after section and concurred heartily in a great part of it. He suggested a few modifications, an occasional emendation and a few additional paragraphs, all of which were adopted by Mr. Lincoln, and the Inaugural was declared complete and perfect by Senator Seward, who then retired." [124] On Sunday, the reporter remarked, "Mr. Lincoln stated this evening that the Inaugural could not be printed, as some points might require modifying or extending, according to the action of the Senate to-night. His son is now writing copies of what is finished, one of which will be given to the Associated Press when he commences reading it.[125] On the same day there were "reports of efforts in high quarters to induce the presi-

[120] *The Diary of Orville Hickman Browning,* edited with an introduction and notes by Theodore Calvin Pease and James G. Randall (Springfield, Ill.: Illinois State Historical Library, 1925), I, 1850-1864, 455, 456.

[121] Seward, *op. cit.,* p. 512.

[122] *Lincoln Lore,* No. 358.

[123] John G. Nicolay and John Hay, *Abraham Lincoln, A History* (New York: The Century Co., 1914), III, 319. Nicolay and Hay observe that "Judge David Davis read it while in Springfield," and "Francis P. Blair, Sr., read it in Washington, and highly commended it, suggesting no changes."

[124] *New York Times,* March 4, 1861, p. 1, col. 1.

[125] *New York Times,* March 4, 1861, p. 1, col. 2.

dent to tone down his inaugural, but it is not affirmed that they were successful." [126]

A final report on the preparation of the Inaugural records the activities on the morning of March 4th: "Mr. Lincoln rose at 5 o'clock. After an early breakfast, the Inaugural was read aloud to him by his son Robert, and the completing touches were added, including the beautiful and impassioned closing paragraph." [127]

As J. G. Randall has observed, "if one would justly appraise Lincoln's first presidential state paper, this inaugural of 1861 deserves to be read as delivered and to be set over against the alternative statements that Lincoln avoided or struck out in revision. Statements pledging maintenance of Federal authority were toned down and shorn of truculence, while promises of conciliation were emotionally underlined." [128] Mr. Browning advised "but one change," supposed by some authorities to be "the most important one in the entire document." [129] "Mr. Seward made thirty-three suggestions for improving the document and nineteen of them were adopted, eight were used after Mr. Lincoln had modified them, and six were discarded *in toto*." [130] Finally, Lincoln, "without suggestion from any one made sixteen changes in the original draft." [131]

And so, however much the country might criticize as it scanned the Inaugural, Lincoln could respond, as he did to the Douglas taunt in 1858 that the "House Divided Speech" had been "evidently well prepared and carefully written," [132] "I admit that it was. I am not master of language; I have not a fine education; . . . I know what I meant, and I will not leave this crowd in doubt. . . ." [133]

[126] *New York Daily Tribune,* March 4, 1861, p. 5, col. 1.
[127] *New York Times,* March 5, 1861, p. 1, col. 1.
[128] Randall, *op. cit.,* I, 309.
[129] Warren, *loc. cit.*
[130] *Ibid.*
[131] *Ibid.*
[132] Speech of Senator Douglas, delivered in Chicago, July 9, 1858, in *The Political Debates between Abraham Lincoln and Stephen A. Douglas,* with an introduction by George Haven Putnam (New York: G. P. Putnam's Sons, 1913), p. 24.
[133] Speech in reply to Douglas at Chicago, Illinois, July 10, 1858, in *Abraham Lincoln, His Speeches and Writings,* edited by Roy P. Basler, p. 392.

Lincoln did not have to wait long for a response from the country at large. As he delivered the address, little audiences unseen by the speaker dotted the land, clustering around newspaper offices and waiting for telegraphic reports of what was in the Inaugural. Between Washington and New York, the American Telegraph Company had placed at the disposal of the Associated Press three wires for the communication of the address.[134] Similar arrangements had been made with other key cities. The delivery of the Inaugural commenced at 1:30 P.M., Washington time, and the "telegraphers promptly to the minute" began its transmission. "The first words of the Message were received by the agents of the Press at 1:45, and the last about 3:30," observed the *New York Times*.[135] "Such rapidity in telegraphic communication has never before been reached in this country."[136] By four o'clock, "the entire document was furnished to the different newspapers,"[137] and special editions of the press were in the hands of readers within an hour. "People of all parties in this city, as elsewhere, were on tip-toe all day to know what was going on at Washington, and especially to hear what President Lincoln would say in his Inaugural," observed the *New York Times*.[138] "At length it was announced that the procession had reached the Capitol, and then, while the President was delivering his speech and the reporters were transmitting it by telegraph, there was a long period of unalloyed expectancy. Meantime, men given to talking, in the many crowds, discussed all sorts of topics, connected with the questions of the day, before little groups of gaping listeners. There was many a prophet among them, not without honor, before the Message was received, who knew exactly what it was going to contain, and foretold with marvelous preciseness the points which Mr. Lincoln would dwell on.

"It was nearly 5 o'clock when the eloquence of these worthies was suddenly quenched as by a wet blanket, and the wet sheets of the latest edition, with the President's Inaugural in black and white,

[134] *New York Times*, March 5, 1861, p. 8, col. 5.
[135] *Ibid.*
[136] *Ibid.*
[137] *Ibid.*
[138] *New York Times*, March 5, 1861, p. 8, cols. 4, 5.

leaped forth from the presses into the hands of all who could get copies. Then there was wild scrambling around the counters in publication offices, a laying down of pennies and a rape of newspapers, and the crowds began to disperse, each man hastening to some place remote from public haunt, where he might peruse the document in peace. The newsboys rushed through the city crying with stentorian lungs 'The President's Message!' 'Lincoln's Speech!' 'Ex-tray Times!' 'get Lincoln's Inau-gu-ra-a-a-il!' And an hour later everybody had read the Message and everybody was talking about it." [139]

Out in Mattoon, Illinois, a similar scene was being enacted. A roving reporter, heading south from Chicago to observe the reactions of the crowds, made a "tour of the town" and stopped at hotel lobbies, where the speech, fresh from the press, was being "read and re-read, silently and aloud, to groups of ardent listeners . . . As the reading in a crowd progresses, when the reader comes to the place where Mr. Lincoln 'puts his foot down,' down goes likewise every foot in the circle." [140]

The home folks whom Lincoln had bade an affectionate farewell three weeks before were among the most anxious of the unseen audiences. Whereas they spoke only for themselves at the time of the tearful departure, they were now ready to speak for the nation. "The Inaugural Address of our noble Chief Magistrate has electrified the whole country," they said. "It has satisfied people of all parties who love the Union and desire its preservation. In this city it gives almost universal satisfaction." [141] In Quincy, the scene of one of the debates of 1858, the address was received with "much enthusiasm," and the Republican Gun Squad fired thirty-four guns; [142] in Peoria, "so great was the anxiety felt to see what Mr. Lincoln said, that people came forty miles to get copies of the message," [143] reading it with "much enthusiasm." [144]

[139] *Ibid.*
[140] *Chicago Daily Tribune,* March 8, 1861, p. 2, col. 3.
[141] *Illinois State Journal,* March 6, 1861, p. 2.
[142] *Chicago Daily Tribune,* March 6, 1861, p. 1, col. 3.
[143] *Ibid.*
[144] *Ibid.*

But occasionally there was a dissenting voice back home, particularly in the Democratic press, as there was generally throughout the North. While the *Chicago Daily Tribune* was "quite sure that no document can be found among American state papers embodying sounder wisdom and higher patriotism,—breathing kindlier feelings to all sections of the country," [145] the Chicago *Times* denounced the Inaugural as "a loose, disjointed, rambling affair," concluding that the Union was now "lost beyond hope." [146] While the *New York Times* observed that "conservative people are in raptures over the Inaugural," and that "Its conciliatory tone, and frank, outspoken declaration of loyalty to the whole country, captured the hearts of many heretofore opposed to Mr. Lincoln," [147] the New York *Herald* found that "the inaugural is not a crude performance—it abounds in traits of craft and cunning. It bears marks of indecision, and yet of strong coercion proclivities . . . It is neither candid nor statesmanlike; nor does it possess any essential dignity or patriotism. It would have caused a Washington to mourn, and would have inspired a Jefferson, Madison, or Jackson with contempt." [148] There were those in Maine who found it a "poor, weak, trashy affair, a standing disgrace to the country, and a fit commentary on the fanaticism and unreasonableness which made him President." [149] Some in Pennsylvania found it "one of the most awkwardly constructed official documents we have ever inspected," and "pitiably apologetical for the uprising of the Republican party, and his own election to the Presidency, by it." [150] And there were those in Ohio "who never expected to see a Black Republican peaceably inaugurated in this White Republican country . . . but now the Rubicon is passed," and the Inaugural, "like its distinguished author," is "flat-footed. It is more *magazinish* in *sound*

[145] *Chicago Daily Tribune*, March 5, 1861, p. 1, col. 1.

[146] Quoted in Randall, *op. cit.*, p. 306.

[147] *New York Times*, March 5, 1861, p. 1, col. 4.

[148] Quoted in the *New York Daily Tribune*, March 7, 1861, p. 6, col. 6.

[149] *The Bangor Union*, as quoted in *New York Daily Tribune*, March 8, 1861, p. 6, col. 5.

[150] *The Philadelphia Evening Journal*, as quoted in *New York Daily Tribune*, March 7, 1861, p. 7, col. 3.

than in *style*, smelling strongly of gunpowder, and is *'coercion'* all *over*, as the South understands that word." [151]

"It is an interesting study" said a Douglas journal, the Peoria *Daily Democratic Union*, on March 7th, "to look over the various journals that have come to our table since the delivery of President Lincoln's Inaugural Address, and notice the different manner in which they speak of it." "All of these criticisms of the Address cannot be correct, for they clash materially; and that fact demonstrates very plainly that some of them were either the offspring of prejudice, or were written by men incapable of judging of the merits of this first state paper of President Lincoln." [152]

Whereas there was difference of opinion in the North, much of it stopped short of vehement denunciation. However, the South saw little hope from Lincoln, and expressed itself accordingly. "Mr. Lincoln's Inaugural Address is before our readers," observed the *Richmond Enquirer*, "couched in the cool, unimpassioned, deliberate language of the fanatic, with the purpose of pursuing the promptings of fanaticism even to the dismemberment of the Government with the horrors of civil war . . . Civil war must now come. Sectional war, declared by Mr. Lincoln, awaits only the signal gun from the insulted Southern Confederacy, to light its horrid fires all along the borders of Virginia." [153] The *Richmond Dispatch* was equally strong: "The Inaugural Address of Abraham Lincoln inaugurates civil war, as we have predicted it would from the beginning . . . The sword is drawn and the scabbard thrown away . . . ere long Virginia may be engaged in a life and death struggle. . . ." [154] The *Baltimore Sun* observed, "The Inaugural, as a whole, breathes the spirit of mischief," and found "no Union spirit in the address." [155] "We presume nobody is astonished to hear that Secessionists regard the Inaugural

[151] *Cleveland Plaindealer*, as quoted in *Chicago Daily Tribune*, March 9, 1861, p. 1, col. 3.

[152] Quoted in *Northern Editorials on Secession*, edited by Howard Cecil Perkins (New York: D. Appleton-Century Co., 1942), II, 643.

[153] Quoted in *New York Daily Tribune*, March 7, 1861, p. 7, col. 2. See also, *Southern Editorials on Secession*, pp. 474, 475.

[154] *Southern Editorials on Secession*, p. 475.

[155] Quoted in *New York Daily Tribune*, March 7, 1861, p. 7, col. 1.

as a 'declaration of war,' " noted one observer. "Before the Inaugural has been read in a single Southern State, it is denounced, through the telegraph, from every Southern point, as a declaration of war." [156] "I have heard but one construction of Mr. Lincoln's declaration of his intention to 'hold, occupy, and possess the property and places belonging to the Government, and to collect the duties and imposts,' " observed a special correspondent in Richmond. The Inaugural "is received with much disfavor," and "is regarded, if not as a declaration of war, as at least the expression of a determination to coerce the seceding States into compliance with the demands of the Federal Government." [157] Reporting from Charleston, South Carolina, another correspondent observed, "The part which, of course, attracted most attention and was read and re-read with deep interest, was that wherein Mr. Lincoln declares that to the best of his ability, he will take care, according to his oath and the Constitution, that 'the laws of the Union are faithfully executed in all the States,' and that he will use the power confided to him to 'hold, occupy and possess the property and places belonging to the Government, and to collect the duties and imposts.' " The verdict was, according to this correspondent, "that rebellion would not be treated tenderly by Mr. Lincoln, and that he was quite another sort of man from James Buchanan." [158]

At least a minority of the people of the South responded less vehemently. Occasionally a roving reporter, mingling among the crowds in southern cities, reported less fury. From Montgomery came word that Alexander Stevens had found the Inaugural "the most *adroit* State paper ever published on the Continent," and "a great moral impression has been produced" [159] in both Charleston and Montgomery. In Savannah, Georgia, "Not a word have we yet heard uttered against its tone," observed a reporter, predicting "a powerful and sweeping effect at the South." [160] Now and then a reporter noticed "a pretty general disappointment that the document con-

[156] *New York Times,* March 7, 1861, p. 4, col. 2.
[157] *New York Daily Tribune,* March 9, 1861, p. 6, col. 2.
[158] *New York Daily Tribune,* March 9, 1861, p. 6, col. 1.
[159] *New York Daily Tribune,* March 12, 1861, p. 6, col. 1.
[160] *New York Daily Tribune,* March 11, 1861, p. 6, col. 2.

tained so little 'blood and thunder.' " [161] "That the document should be calm and dignified in tone and style, logical in its conclusions, and plain and kind in its treatment of the great topic of the day, was annoying to the Rebels, who hoped to find in the address a provocation for extreme action." [162]

While the country at large read the speech and responded both favorably and unfavorably, Senator Clingman of North Carolina and Stephen A. Douglas engaged in debate over its meaning in the United States Senate. "If I understand it aright, all that is direct in it, I mean, at least, that purpose which seems to stand out clearly and directly, is one which I think must lead to war—war against the confederate or seceding State" [163] remarked Clingman. Douglas, on the other hand, who had "read it carefully" could not "assent to the construction" of the senator from North Carolina, believing he could "demonstrate that there is no foundation for the apprehension which has been spread throughout the country, that this message is equivalent to a declaration of war." [164]

Just as the country searched the Inaugural for the sentiments it contained, it also examined and appraised the language and style in which it was couched. The Toronto *Leader* could not admire the "tawdry and corrupt schoolboy style," even as it gave "credit" for its "good sense." [165] An Albany, New York, observer found it "useless to criticize the style of the President's Inaugural when the policy it declares is fraught with consequences so momentous." Nevertheless, he paused to describe it as a "rambling, discursive, questioning, loose-jointed stump speech." It consisted of "feeble rhetorical stuff." [166] While papers unfriendly to Lincoln were finding it "inferior in point of elegance, perspicuity, vigor, talent, and all the graces of composition to any other paper of a like character which

[161] *New York Daily Tribune,* March 9, 1861, p. 6, col. 1.

[162] *Ibid.*

[163] *Congressional Globe,* Second Session, 36th Congress, Vol. 30, Part II, p. 1436.

[164] *Ibid.*

[165] Quoted in *New York Daily Tribune,* March 7, 1861, p. 7, col. 3.

[166] *Albany Atlas and Argus,* as quoted in *Northern Editorials on Secession,* II, 628.

has ever emanated from a President of the Republic," [167] papers that were friendly found the contrary to be the case. "It is clear as a mountain brook," commented a Detroit reporter. "The depth and flow of it are apparent at a glance." [168] In Boston, the *Transcript* reporter commented at length: "The style of the Address is as characteristic as its temper. 'Right words in their right places'; this is the requirement of good rhetoric. Right words at the right times, should be the test by which we try the speech of statesmen; and this test Mr. Lincoln's address will bear. It has not one flaming expression in the whole course of its firm and explicit statements. The language is level to the popular mind, the plain homespun language of a man accustomed to talk with 'the folks' and 'the neighbors,' the language of a man of vital common sense, whose words exactly fit his facts and thoughts." [169] Occasionally, the concluding paragraph was singled out for praise. In Indianapolis, the reporter of the *Daily Journal* remarked: "The closing sentence, the only attempt at rhetorical display in the whole address, is singularly and almost poetically beautiful." [170]

Part II

Given the circumstances that brought forth the Inaugural Address, and removed in time from the passions which agitated the country, what may one say of Lincoln's address on March 4, 1861? The historian has often examined it for its effects, and has concluded that "Though not fully appreciated then, this was one of the great American inaugurals." [171] And the literary critic has sometimes observed its final passage, finding in it poetic beauty and enduring

[167] *Jersey City American Standard,* as quoted in *Northern Editorials on Secession,* II, 625.

[168] *Detroit Daily Tribune,* as quoted in *Northern Editorials on Secession,* II, 623.

[169] Quoted in *New York Daily Tribune,* March 7, 1861, p. 7, col. 1.

[170] Quoted in *Northern Editorials on Secession,* II, 619.

[171] J. G. Randall, "Lincoln's Great Declarations of Faith," *New York Times Magazine,* February 6, 1949, p. 23.

worth. Unlike the historian, we are not concerned merely with the Inaugural as a force in the shaping of American culture; nor are we concerned with its enduring worth as literature. The Inaugural was a speech, "meant to be heard and intended to exert an influence of some kind on those who heard it," [172] or those who read it. We must, therefore, be concerned with evaluating the Inaugural as a speech, a medium distinct from other media, and with methods peculiarly its own. We must be concerned with discovering in this particular case "the available means of persuasion" and with evaluating their worth.

Let us view the Inaugural as a communication, with a purpose, and a content presumably designed to aid in the accomplishment of that purpose, further supported by skillful composition in words, and ultimately unified by the character and manner of the person who presented it.

We must not casually assume that Lincoln's purpose is easily discernible in the occasion itself. It is true, of course, that this was an inaugural ceremony, with a ritual fairly well established by fifteen predecessors, "Yet, with all this scope for [of] precedent," Lincoln was keenly aware that he entered upon the same task "under great and peculiar difficulty. A disruption of the Federal Union, heretofore only menaced, is now formidably attempted." If we are to discern the purpose that Lincoln had when he addressed the American people on March 4, 1861, we must recall the experiences of the nation between his election as president and the day of his inauguration. During that time, he had been made keenly aware of Southern resentment to a "sectional" president. The rapid movement of the Secessionists followed closely on the announcement of his election, and of the ascendancy of the Republican party to a position of power. The South viewed the Republican platform as an instrument for its "subjugation" and the "complete ruin of her social, political and industrial institutions." [173] By its acts of secession, and its establishment of a provisional government of its own, the lower

[172] *Supra*, p. 3.
[173] *New Orleans Daily Crescent*, November 13, 1860, as quoted in *Southern Editorials on Secession*, p. 237.

South raised the very practical question: What is the authority of the federal government in regard to maintaining itself and in regard to reclaiming those federal properties possessed by retiring members?

Lincoln had also been made keenly aware of the doubts and skepticism that prevailed regarding his ability to lead his party and the nation. "I cannot but know what you all know," he had observed on his way to Washington, "that without a name, perhaps without a reason why I should have a name, there has fallen upon me a task such as did not rest even upon the Father of his Country ..." [174] In addition, he was keenly aware of both Northern and Southern distrust of his moral character and integrity. Even to members of his party, he was a "funny man," given to stories in bad taste, and an Illinois wag. And to the South, he was at best thought to be as radical as the most rabid of the left-wing Republicans, hence a "dangerous man." [175] That he was aware of the prevailing sentiments regarding him as a man is reflected in his casual remark en route to Washington when, for a moment, his address was misplaced. In a worried search, he described the Inaugural as "my certificate of moral character, written by myself." [176]

Although from the time of his election he was urged to state his views on the passing events, Lincoln had remained silent. That his silence was not due to a lack of anxiety is easily apparent. "Allusion has been made," he noted on his way to Washington, "to the interest felt in relation to the policy of the new administration. In this I have received from some a degree of credit for having kept silence, and from others some deprecation. I still think that I was right ...

"In the varying and repeatedly shifting scenes of the present, and without a precedent which could enable me to judge by the past, it has seemed fitting that before speaking upon the difficulties of the country I should have gained a view of the whole field, being at

[174] "Address to the Legislature of Ohio at Columbus, February 13, 1861," *Complete Works*, VI, 121.

[175] Speech of Senator Clingman of North Carolina in the Senate, December 3, 1860, *The Congressional Globe*, Second Session, 36th Congress, Vol. 30, p. 3.

[176] Ward Hill Lamon, *Recollections of Abraham Lincoln, 1847-1865*, edited by Dorothy Lamon Teillard (Washington, D. C.: Published by the editor, 1911), p. 36.

liberty to modify and change the course of policy as future events may make a change necessary.

"I have not maintained silence from any want of real anxiety." [177]

What, then, was Lincoln's purpose? Clearly, he intended to take the occasion of the inauguration to declare the position of the Republican party in regard to the South, to announce his considered judgment in regard to the practical questions raised by the movement of secession, and, in all, to give what assurance he could of his personal integrity.

In evaluating the Inaugural, we must keep in mind its purpose, for the purpose of the speech controlled Lincoln's selection of materials, his arrangement, his style, and his manner.

Let us turn to the speech itself in order to note the materials and methods he employed to sustain his purpose. Considering the general predisposition of the South to view the incoming administration with suspicion, and considering the fact that Lincoln had not spoken for his own party since his nomination, he found it necessary to take a moment to "press upon the public attention the most conclusive evidence of which the case is susceptible," the idea of the integrity of the Republican party and his own integrity as its helmsman. Wise judgment could scarcely have dictated otherwise, for the lower South had gone out of the Union partly on the grounds that it expected no fair consideration from the newly born party, and the border states were contemplating similar measures. Lincoln attempted to conciliate his audience by assuring the country that "the property, peace and security of no section are to be in any wise endangered by the now incoming Administration." In order to do this he called attention to the fact that he was taking a solemn oath in "your presence"; he committed himself again to previously spoken words [178] that have "all the while existed, and been open to their inspection"; to the Republican platform pertaining to the "maintenance inviolate of the rights of the States, and especially the right of each State to

[177] "Address to the Legislature of Ohio at Columbus, February 13, 1861," *Complete Works*, VI, 121, 122.

[178] "Mr. Lincoln's Reply," First Joint Debate, at Ottawa, August 21, 1858, *The Political Debates between Abraham Lincoln and Stephen A. Douglas*, p. 209.

order and control its own domestic institutions according to its own judgment exclusively"; [179] and to the clause "plainly written in the Constitution," pertaining to delivering up "on claim of the party to whom such service or labor may be due" [180] the escaping fugitive. He concluded his opening remarks with a reiteration of the avowal that he took the "official oath to-day, with no mental reservations, and with no purpose to construe the Constitution or laws, by any hypercritical rules." This was neither the material nor the method of a "deceitful" or "dangerous" man. By it, Lincoln was attempting to touch off those favorable responses that accrue to the appearance of honesty, straightforwardness, and obedience to the Constitution. One must remember that Lincoln's pledge of faith could not have given satisfaction to the Abolitionist group within his own party with whom he was constantly identified by the South; it did, however, serve to differentiate him from the radical element and hence to reassure the states yet within the Union. From the standpoint of persuasiveness Lincoln was undoubtedly wise in taking the advice of Seward to omit the two paragraphs immediately following his opening statement in the original draft of the Inaugural:

The more modern custom of electing a Chief Magistrate upon a previously declared platform of principles, supercedes, in a great measure, the necessity of restating those principles in an address of this sort. Upon the plainest grounds of good faith, one so elected is not at liberty to shift his position. It is necessarily implied, if not expressed, that, in his judgment, the platform which he thus accepts, binds him to nothing either unconstitutional or inexpedient.

Having been so elected upon the Chicago Platform, and while I would repeat nothing in it, of aspersion or epithet or question of motive against any man or party, I hold myself bound by duty, as well as impelled by inclination to follow, within the executive sphere, the principles therein declared. By no other course could I meet the reasonable expectations of the country.[181]

[179] Halstead, *op. cit.*, p. 138.

[180] Article IV, Sec. 2.

[181] For changes in the Inaugural, see MS of early printed version with secretarial reproductions of the changes, and accompanying letter of John Hay to Charles Eliot Norton, dated March 25, 1899, explaining the nature of the revisions, in Widener Library of Harvard University. See also, John G. Nicolay and

To have used the paragraphs would undoubtedly have incited anew the suspicion that he was merely a "sectional" president and an "abolitionist" or "party man."

Having spent time in an attempt to gain a fair hearing for the rest of his address, Lincoln next took up the question for which the whole country awaited an answer, namely, What is the duty and the policy of the Republican administration in regard to Secession? Without delay, he laid down the proposition, "I hold, that in contemplation of universal law, and of the Constitution, the Union of these States is perpetual. Perpetuity is implied, if not expressed, in the fundamental law of all national governments"; hence "no State, upon its own mere motion, can lawfully get out of the Union,—that *resolves* and *ordinances* to that effect are legally void, and that acts of violence, within any State or States, against the authority of the United States, are insurrectionary or revolutionary, according to circumstances." Furthermore, "if the United States be not a government proper, but an association of States in the nature of contract merely, can it, as a contract, be peaceably unmade, by less than all the parties who made it?"

To the North, the mere assertion of the principle of perpetuity would have been sufficient; no further proof would have been necessary. But to the lower South, already out of the Union, and to the border states and upper South contemplating similar action, clearly assertion was not sufficient. Therefore, Lincoln found his proposition "confirmed by the history of the Union itself." The Union, he pointed out, was "much older than the Constitution"; it was "formed in fact, by the Articles of Association in 1774"; it was "matured and continued by the Declaration of Independence in 1776"; it was "further matured and the faith of all the then thirteen States expressly plighted and engaged that it should be perpetual, by the

---

John Hay, *Abraham Lincoln*, III, 327 344; Louis A. Warren, "Original Draft of the First Inaugural," *Lincoln Lore*, No. 358 (February 17, 1936) and No. 359 (February 24, 1936). See, *The Robert Todd Lincoln Collection of the Papers of Abraham Lincoln*, Library of Congress. Microfilm in University of Illinois Library. This collection contains the most important source for the various working sheets of the Inaugural.

Articles of Confederation in 1778"; finally "in 1787, one of the declared objects for ordaining and establishing the Constitution, was '*to form a more perfect Union*'." Although Lincoln's support of his proposition was factual, the facts themselves carried with them the respect and loyalty that had always attached to the founding fathers who were held in esteem for their vision and their wisdom.

Having stated the principle that guided him, Lincoln continued logically with its application, holding that "to the extent of my ability I shall take care, as the Constitution itself expressly enjoins upon me, that the laws of the Union be faithfully executed in all the States." In discussing the policy of the government in enforcing the laws of the Union, Lincoln does not speak as the master or the mere advocate handing down a bloodless decision, but as a servant performing a "simple duty," the "American people" being "my rightful masters." As a skilled persuader, he was undoubtedly aware that lines of argument will often meet with varied responses according to whether they are put forward by those toward whom one feels sympathetic or antagonistic.[182] Nowhere in the Inaugural does Lincoln seek more earnestly to be conciliating and mild. He was aware that legalism alone would not sustain his purpose. He could have used the bold and confident assertion that appeared in the original draft of the Inaugural:

All the power at my disposal will be used to reclaim the public property and places which have fallen; to hold, occupy and possess these, and all other property and places belonging to the government and to collect the duties and imposts; but beyond what may be necessary for these objects, there will be no invasion of any State.

Even in the original draft, Lincoln had avoided the use of the names of specific forts to which he had reference. Pickens and Sumter were in a precarious position and were peculiarly explosive topics of discussion. However, Lincoln yielded even further in tempering his remarks, accepting the suggestion of O. H. Browning, and finally choosing only to say:

[182] Robert K. Merton, *Mass Persuasion* (New York: Harper and Brothers, 1946), p. 109.

The power confided to me will be used to hold, occupy, and possess the property and places belonging to the Government, and to collect the duties and imposts; but, beyond what may be necessary for these objects, there will be no invasion, no using of force against or among the people any- where.

Furthermore, "Where hostility to the United States, in any interior locality, shall be so great and so universal, as to prevent competent resident citizens from holding the Federal offices," he would make "no attempt to force obnoxious strangers among the people for that object," even though the "strict legal right may exist." And, the mails "unless repelled" would continue to be furnished. In doing this, "there needs to be no bloodshed or violence," he assured the country, and promised that "there shall be none, unless it be forced upon the national authority." Nowhere did Lincoln assert a power or a practice that he believed impossible of enforcement, or that he believed could be interpreted as "coercion" in its baldest and most belligerent form.

Having announced his specific policy, Lincoln turned to those "who really love the Union," neither affirming nor denying that there were those "who seek to destroy the Union at all events," being "glad of any pretext to do it." In his original draft, he had intended point- edly to observe "Before entering upon so grave a matter as the destruction of our national Union, would it not be wise to ascertain precisely why we do it?" In his final draft, however, he blotted out the word "Union" and substituted for it the unifying and figurative word "fabric," further inserting the words "with all its benefits, its memories and its hopes," thereby seeking to heighten feeling by suggesting appropriate attitudes.

Having passed the climax of his remarks, Lincoln moved, in the last half of the Inaugural, to a reasoned discussion of related topics. He denied that any right plainly written in the Constitution had been violated, observing that majorities and minorities arise as a result of that class of questions for which no specific constitutional answer has been provided. The alternative to accepting the "major- ity principle" was always either "anarchy or depotism." Not even the Supreme Court could serve as the final arbiter on questions "affecting the whole people," for unless it limited its activity to making decisions on specific "cases properly brought before them," the "people will have ceased to be their own rulers." He argued the impracticability of secession, contrasting it with the simple act of divorce between husband and wife who may remain "beyond the reach of each other," and concluded that "Physically speaking, we cannot separate." Not even war was a satisfactory solution to difficulties, for "you cannot fight always," and after much "loss on both sides, and no gain on either," the "identical old questions" are again to be settled. "This country, with its institutions, belongs to the people who inhabit it," he insisted, urging that when the whole people "shall grow weary of the existing government, they can exercise their *constitutional* right of amending it, or their *revolutionary* right to dismember or overthrow it."

Lincoln's appeal throughout was to the "patient confidence in the ultimate justice of the people." "Is there any better or equal hope, in the world?" he asked, even as he noted the human tendency of parties in dispute to insist with equal confidence on being in the "right." Rising to the position of impartial leader, he sought faith in a higher law, and in a disinterested Ruler: "If the Almighty Ruler of nations, with his eternal truth and justice, be on your side of the North or on yours of the South, that truth, and that justice, will surely prevail, by the judgment of this great tribunal, the American people."

Lincoln ended his address with both a challenge and a declaration of faith. "In *your* hands, my dissatisfied fellow countrymen, and not in *mine*, is the momentous issue of civil war. The government will not assail *you*." He was just about to take an oath, and to him an oath was a solemn pledge, not only in word, but in truth. It was an avowal of morality, binding him not only to duty to the people but to God, "the Almighty Ruler of nations." "*You* have no oath registered in Heaven to destroy the government," he pleaded in an attempt to secure the cooperation of all those who could help him in fulfilling the pledge he was to take, "while *I* shall have the most solemn one to 'preserve, protect and defend' it." His final appeal was to feeling rather than to reason. He undoubtedly realized that when men cannot achieve common ground through reason, they may achieve it through the medium of feeling. "I am loth to close," he observed. "We are not enemies, but friends. We must not be enemies. Though passion may have strained, it must not break our bonds of affection." No longer the advocate, or even the president performing official duties, Lincoln, taking the advice of Seward, became the affectionate father, the benevolent and hopeful counselor, trusting not only in reason, but calling on "memory," the "patriot grave," the "heart and hearth-stone," "the better angels of our nature" to "swell the chorus of the Union."

Whereas the disgruntled may have "found too much argumentative discussion of the question at issue, as was to have been expected from a man whose whole career has been that of an advocate," [183] obviously others could not have failed to notice that Lincoln sought valiantly to employ all the "available means of persuasion." He had sought to reach his audience not only through reason, but through feeling and through the force of his own ethical ideals.

Any fair-minded critic, removed from the passions of the times, must find himself much more in agreement with those observers of the day who believed the Inaugural met the "requirements of good rhetoric" by having "right words in their right places" and "right words at the right times," [184] than with those who labeled it "feeble rhetorical stuff," and found it "inferior in point of elegance, perspicuity, vigor, talent, and all the graces of composition to any other paper of a like character from a President of the Republic." [185] One who studies the revisions in phrase and word in the various drafts of the Inaugural must become aware that Lincoln was concerned not only with using the right argument, but with using words cautiously, and purposefully, to obtain a desired effect from his listeners and from his potential readers. To the rhetorician, style is not an aspect of language which can be viewed in isolation or judged merely by the well-attuned ear. Nor is it sufficient to apply

[183] *The Diary of a Public Man,* p. 75.

[184] *The Boston Transcript,* as quoted in *New York Daily Tribune,* March 7, 1861, p. 7, col. 1.

[185] *Jersey City Standard,* as quoted in *Northern Editorials on Secession,* II, 625.

such rubrics as clarity, vividness, elegance as absolute values, or as an adequate description of style. Words are an "available means of persuasion," and the only legitimate question is: Did Lincoln use words effectively to achieve his specific purpose?

Although Lincoln may have lamented that he did not have a "fine education" or that he was not a "master of language," [186] he had a keen sensitiveness for language. He "studied to see the subject matter clearly," said an early teacher, "and to express it truly and strongly. I have known him to study for hours the best way of three to express an idea." [187] And when his partner, Herndon, attempted the grandiose in expression, Lincoln sometimes remarked, "Billy, don't shoot too high—aim lower and the common people will understand you. They are the ones you want to reach—at least they are the ones you ought to reach. The educated and refined people will understand you any way. If you aim too high your ideas will go over the heads of the masses, and only hit those who need no hitting." [188] Lincoln had become adept at stump speaking, and knew how to use language to make himself clear and to make a point. That he knew the power of language to fire passions and to cloud understanding is amply demonstrated in his remarks at Indianapolis when he was en route to Washington. "Solomon says there is 'a time to keep silence,'" he observed, "and when men wrangle by the month with no certainty that they mean the same thing, while using the same word, it perhaps were as well if they would keep silence. The words 'coercion' and 'invasion' are much used in these days, and often with some temper and hot blood. Let us make sure, if we can, that we do not misunderstand the meaning of those who use them. Let us get exact definitions of these words, not from dictionaries, but from the men themselves, who certainly deprecate the things they would represent by the use of words." [189] Lincoln was keenly aware that words themselves were often grounds

[186] Speech in reply to Douglas at Chicago, Illinois, July 10, 1858, in *Abraham Lincoln: His Speeches and Writings,* edited by Roy P. Basler, p. 393.

[187] Herndon and Weik, *op. cit.,* p. 99.

[188] *Ibid.,* p. 262.

[189] "Address to the Legislature of Indiana at Indianapolis, February 12, 1861," *Complete Works,* VI, 112, 113.

for argument, systems of attitudes suggesting courses of action.[190]
Then, too, Lincoln knew that his "friends feared" and "those who
were not his friends hoped, that, forgetting the dignity of his position, and the occasion, he would descend to the practices of the
story-teller, and fail to rise to the level of a statesman." [191]

The desire for clearness, the desire to subdue passion, the desire
to manifest the integrity and dignity befitting a statesman in a
responsible position—these are the factors that influenced Lincoln
in his composition of the Inaugural, and to appraise his style without
constant awareness of them is likely to lead the critic far afield. Let
us consider Lincoln's style, then, as a system of symbols designed to
evoke certain images favorable to the accomplishment of his purpose and, in so far as he could, to prevent certain other images from
arising.

One of the most marked characteristics of Lincoln's style is its
directness. By it he attempts to achieve the appearance of candor
and honesty, traits that were eminently significant to the success of
the Inaugural, considering the doubts and suspicions that were
prevalent regarding his integrity. From the opening sentence to the
conclusion one notes the unmistakable honesty and straightforwardness that reside in direct address. "I appear before you," he remarks,
"to address you briefly, and to take, in your presence, the oath
prescribed by the Constitution of the United States . . ." Again, he
observes, "I have no purpose, directly or indirectly, to interfere
with the institution of slavery in the States where it exists"; "I now
reiterate these sentiments"; "I take the official oath to-day, with no
mental reservations"; "*You* have no oath registered in Heaven to
destroy the government, while *I* shall have the most solemn one to
'preserve, protect and defend' it." Direct and forthright throughout,
he could scarcely have used words to better advantage in emphasizing his honesty and integrity.

What doubts there were pertaining to inadequacies traceable to

[190] Kenneth Burke, "Two Functions of Speech," *The Language of Wisdom
and Folly,* edited and with an introduction by Irving J. Lee (New York: Harper
and Brothers, 1949), p. 40.
[191] L. E. Chittenden, *Recollections of President Lincoln and His Administration* (New York: Harper and Brothers, 1904), p. 88.

his humble origins and his lack of formal education must in some wise have been dispelled by his clearness, his accuracy, and his freedom from the awkward expression or the simple idiom of the Western stump speaker. Lincoln had felt his inadequacies when he addressed an Eastern audience of educated men at Cooper Union and was uncomfortable. In his Inaugural, prepared for an audience representative of the whole country, he had been cautious and careful to use language that was sustained in its dignity. Seward, sometimes known for his polished expression, had given him some aid in the choice of the proper word. Lincoln accepted advice in such word changes as "acquiesce" instead of "submit, "constituted" instead of "constructed," "void" instead of "nothing," "repelled" instead of "refused," and he also accepted such a change of phrase as "imperfectly supports the law itself" for "is against the law itself." Although the changes are minor, they reflect Lincoln's desire for correctness and conciseness. On his own better judgment, he deleted the one extended metaphor that appeared in the original draft. "I am, rather for the old ship, and the chart of the old pilots," he had originally written, with some of the tang and flavor of his speech in addressing popular Western audiences. "If, however, the people desire a new, or an altered vessel, the matter is exclusively their own, and they can move in the premises, as well without as with an executive recommendation." The figure was not equal in elevation to the rest of his remarks. His final draft read simply, "I cannot be ignorant of the fact that many worthy and patriotic citizens are desirous of having the national Constitution amended. While I make no recommendation of amendments, I fully recognize the rightful authority of the people over the whole subject..." Such phrasing, simple in its dignity, undoubtedly was more appropiate and suited to his needs.

That Lincoln sought to control the behavior of his audience and the reader through the appropriately affective word is apparent throughout his address. There are times when even the level of specificity and concreteness, usually thought to be virtues of style, is altered in favor of the more general word or allusion. For instance, Lincoln had originally intended to say, "why may not South Carolina, a year or two hence, arbitrarily, secede from a new Southern Confederacy . . . ?" Finally, however, he avoided being specific, altering his remarks to read "why may not any portion of a new confederacy, a year or two hence, arbitrarily secede again . . . ?" Again, the ridicule in his assertion, "The Union is less perfect than before, which contradicts the Constitution, and therefore is absurd," is eliminated and reason is substituted: "The Union is *less perfect* than before the Constitution, having lost the vital element of its perpetuity." Lincoln sometimes chose the longer statement in preference to the sharp, pointed word or phrase, if by a longer expression he could avoid truculence or the pointing of an accusing finger. Such a phrase as "be on your side of the North or on yours of the South," aided considerably in creating an image of impartiality, and was to be preferred for the shorter, but divisive phrase, "be on our side or yours." The changes that Lincoln made in the direction of fullness rather than compression were designed to aid in clearness, exactness, and completeness, for the country expected him to express himself fully on the disturbing problems of the time.

The close of Lincoln's address, often cited for its poetic beauty, reflects not only his aesthetic sense, but perhaps more importantly, his power of using words to evoke images conducive to controlling response. As is very well known, Lincoln was not merely trying to be eloquent when he closed the address. He achieved eloquence and cadenced beauty through his direct attempt to be "affectionate," Seward having reminded him that perhaps feeling should supplement reason, and having suggested a possible conclusion:

"I close. We are not we must not be aliens or enemies but ~~countrym~~ fellow countrymen and brethren. Although passion has strained our bonds of affection too hardly they must not ~~be broken they will not~~ I am sure they will not be broken. The mystic chords of memory which proceeding from ~~every ba~~ so many battle fields and ~~patriot~~ so many patriot graves ~~br~~ pass through all the hearts and ~~hearths~~ all the hearths in this broad continent of ours will yet ~~harmo~~ again harmonize in their ancient music when ~~touched as they surely~~ breathed upon ~~again~~ by the ~~better angel~~ guardian angel of the nation." [192]

[192] Facsimile of the original suggestion of Seward as reprinted in *Abraham Lincoln: His Speeches and Writings*, edited by Roy P. Basler, pp. 589, 590.

An image of great-heartedness, great humility, and great faith re-
sulted when Lincoln rephrased Seward's suggestion in his own style.
It was his final declaration of faith and had in it the emotional
intensity that often accompanies the hoped-for but unknown. It was
his final plea for a course of action befitting "friends."

Let us conclude our remarks on Lincoln's style by emphasizing
that it reflected the same purposefulness that was characteristic of
the arguments contained in the address. Through directness, clearness, dignity, and appropriately affective words, he sought to aid
himself in achieving his ends.

One further means of persuasion may be noted, namely, that of
his manner in oral presentation. Lincoln's delivery, of course, was
significant chiefly to those who composed his immediate audience,
and not to any great extent to the much larger audience throughout
the country, except in so far as eyewitnesses and newspaper reports
conveyed impressions pertaining to the character and personality
of the speaker. It is undoubtedly true that Lincoln's manner contributed heavily to his effectiveness on this particular occasion. It
may even be true that, had the whole country been immediately
present, it would have found further grounds for trust. Ethical
stature often shows itself not only in the selection of argument or
the composition of words, but in those "echoes and values" that
emanate from physical presence alone. "If I were to make the
shortest list of the qualifications of the orator," Emerson once
remarked, "I should begin with *manliness;* and perhaps it means
here presence of mind."[193] It must be remembered that when
Lincoln advanced to the platform to deliver his Inaugural, he did
so in face of threats on his life. That he manifested little fear is
apparent from practically all of the newspaper accounts of the day.
The most usual observation indicated that "the great heart and
kindly nature of the man were apparent in his opening sentence,
in the tone of his voice, the expression of his face, in his whole
manner and bearing."[194] In the judgment of many, he "gained the

[193] "Eloquence," *The Complete Works of Ralph Waldo Emerson* (New York:
Sully and Kleinteich, 1875), VIII, 123.
[194] Chittenden, *loc. cit.*

confidence of his hearers and secured their respect and affection." [195] Lincoln appears to have had a sense of communication, a complete awareness of what he was saying when he was saying it. His thought emerged clearly and appeared to be in no way obstructed by affectation or peculiarities of manner. With dignity and firmness coupled with mildness and humility he sought to enforce his plea by those powers that reside in personality. That they have stimulus value one can scarcely question.

Thirty-nine days after Lincoln delivered his Inaugural Address, Fort Sumter was fired upon. Civil war had begun. Lincoln had sought to save the Union by carefully reasoned argument, by regard for the feelings and rights of all the people, and by a solemn avowal of justice and integrity. That the Inaugural alone could not prevent the war is surely insufficient ground to condemn it for ineptness. "In speechmaking, as in life, not failure, but low aim, is crime." [196] There were many divisive forces, and these had gained great momentum by the time Lincoln addressed the American people. The South accepted the burden of his challenge, "In *your* hands, my dissatisfied fellow countrymen, and not in *mine*, is the momentous issue of civil war."

M. H.

[195] *Ibid.*, p. 90.
[196] *Supra*, p. 12.

Jonathan Edwards

SINNERS IN THE HANDS

OF AN ANGRY GOD

¶ JONATHAN EDWARDS, eighteenth-century champion of Calvinism, was born at East Windsor, Connecticut, on October 5, 1703. He entered Yale College at the age of twelve, graduating in 1720. After studying theology in New Haven and serving briefly as a tutor at Yale, he became assistant to his grandfather, Solomon Stoddard, pastor at Northampton, Massachusetts. In 1729 he succeeded his grandfather as pastor of the Congregational Church at Northampton, serving until 1750, at which time he was dismissed by the congregation over a dispute concerning admission requirements to the church. From 1750 to 1757 he preached at Stockbridge, Massachusetts, and served as a missionary to the Indians. On February 16, 1758, he was inducted into the presidency of Princeton College, but died a month later of smallpox.

The sermon, "Sinners in the Hands of an Angry God," was preached to a rural congregation at Enfield, Massachusetts, on July 8, 1741, at the peak of a period of religious revivalism known as The Great Awakening. Its powerful effect in generating religious enthusiasm is recorded in many contemporary accounts.

Their foot shall slide in due time. Deut. xxxii, 35.

IN THIS VERSE is threatened the vengeance of God on the wicked unbelieving Israelites, who were God's visible people, and who lived under the means of grace; but who, notwithstanding all God's wonderful works towards them, remained (as ver. 28.) void of counsel, having no understanding in them. Under all the cultivations of heaven, they brought forth bitter and poisonous fruit; as in the two verses next preceding the text.—The expression I have chosen for my text, *Their foot shall slide in due time,* seems to imply the following things, relating to the punishment and destruction to which these wicked Israelites were exposed.

1. That they were always exposed to *destruction;* as one that stands or walks in slippery places is always exposed to fall. This is implied in the manner of their destruction coming upon them, being represented by their foot sliding. The same is expressed, Psalm lxxiii. 18. "Surely thou didst set them in slippery places; thou castedst them down into destruction."

2. It implies, that they were always exposed to sudden unexpected destruction. As he that walks in slippery places is every moment liable to fall, he cannot foresee one moment whether he shall stand or fall the next; and when he does fall, he falls at once without warning: Which is also expressed in Psalm lxxiii. 18, 19. "Surely thou didst set them in slippery places; thou castedst them down into destruction: How are they brought into desolation as in a moment!"

3. Another thing implied is, that they are liable to fall *of themselves,* without being thrown down by the hand of another; as he that stands or walks on slippery ground needs nothing but his own weight to throw him down.

4. That the reason why they are not fallen already, and do not fall now, is only that God's appointed time is not come. For it is said, that when that due time, or appointed time comes, *their foot shall slide.* Then they shall be left to fall, as they are inclined by their own weight. God will not hold them up in these slippery places any longer, but will let them go; and then, at that very instant, they shall fall into destruction; as he that stands on such slippery declining ground, on the edge of a pit, he cannot stand alone, when he is let go he immediately falls and is lost.

The observation from the words that I would now insist upon is this.—"There is nothing that keeps wicked men at any one moment out of hell, but the mere pleasure of God"—By the *mere* pleasure of God, I mean his *sovereign* pleasure, his arbitrary will, restrained by no obligation, hindered by no manner of difficulty, any more than if nothing else but God's mere will had in the least degree, or in any respect whatsoever, any hand in the preservation of wicked men one moment.—The truth of this observation may appear by the following considerations.

1. There is no want of *power* in God to cast wicked men into hell at any moment. Men's hands cannot be strong when God rises up. The strongest have no power to resist him, nor can any deliver out of his hands.—He is not only able to cast wicked men into hell, but he can most easily do it. Sometimes an earthly prince meets with a great deal of difficulty to subdue a rebel, who has found means to fortify himself, and has made himself strong by the numbers of his followers. But it is not so with God. There is no fortress that is any defence from the power of God. Though hand join in hand, and vast multitudes of God's enemies combine and associate themselves, they are easily broken in pieces. They are as great heaps of light chaff before the whirlwind; or large quantities of dry stubble before devouring flames. We find it easy to tread on and crush a worm that we see crawling on the earth; so it is easy for us to cut or singe a slender thread that any thing hangs by: thus easy is it for God, when he pleases, to cast his enemies down to hell. What are we, that we should think to stand before him, at whose rebuke the earth trembles, and before whom the rocks are thrown down?

2. They *deserve* to be cast into hell; so that divine justice never stands in the way, it makes no objection against God's using his power at any moment to destroy them. Yea, on the contrary, justice calls aloud for an infinite punishment of their sins. Divine justice says of the tree that brings forth such grapes of Sodom, "Cut it down, why cumbereth it the ground?" Luke xiii. 7. The sword of divine justice is every moment brandished over their heads, and it is nothing but the hand of arbitrary mercy, and God's mere will, that holds it back.

3. They are already under a sentence of *condemnation* to hell. They do not only justly deserve to be cast down thither, but the sentence of the law of God, that eternal and immutable rule of

righteousness that God has fixed between him and mankind, is gone out against them, and stands against them; so that they are bound over already to hell. John iii. 18. "He that believeth not is condemned already." So that every unconverted man properly belongs to hell; that is his place; from thence he is, John viii. 23. "Ye are from beneath:" And thither he is bound; it is the place that justice, and God's word, and the sentence of his unchangeable law assign to him.

4. They are now the objects of that very same *anger* and wrath of God, that is expressed in the torments of hell. And the reason why they do not go down to hell at each moment, is not because God, in whose power they are, is not then very angry with them; as he is with many miserable creatures now tormented in hell, who there feel and bear the fierceness of his wrath. Yea, God is a great deal more angry with great numbers that are now on earth: yea, doubtless, with many that are now in this congregation, who it may be are at ease, than he is with many of those who are now in the flames of hell.

So that it is not because God is unmindful of their wickedness, and does not resent it, that he does not let loose his hand and cut them off. God is not altogether such an one as themselves, though they may imagine him to be so. The wrath of God burns against them, their damnation does not slumber; the pit is prepared, the fire is made ready, the furnace is now hot, ready to receive them; the flames do now rage and glow. The glittering sword is whet, and held over them, and the pit hath opened its mouth under them.

5. The *devil* stands ready to fall upon them, and seize them as his own, at what moment God shall permit him. They belong to him; he has their souls in his possession, and under his dominion. The scripture represents them as his goods, Luke xi. 12. The devils watch them; they are ever by them at their right hand; they stand waiting for them, like greedy hungry lions that see their prey, and expect to have it, but are for the present kept back. If God should withdraw his hand, by which they are restrained, they would in one moment fly upon their poor souls. The old serpent is gaping for them; hell opens its mouth wide to receive them; and if God should permit it, they would be hastily swallowed up and lost.

6. There are in the souls of wicked men those hellish *principles* reigning, that would presently kindle and flame out into hell fire, if it were not for God's restraints. There is laid in the very nature of carnal men, a foundation for the torments of hell. There are those corrupt principles, in reigning power in them, and in full possession of them, that are seeds of hell fire. These principles are active and powerful, exceeding violent in their nature, and if it were not for the restraining hand of God upon them, they would soon break out, they would flame out after the same manner as the same corruptions, the same enmity does in the hearts of damned souls, and would beget the same torments as they do in them. The souls of the wicked are in scripture compared to the troubled sea, Isa. lvii. 20. For the present, God restrains their wickedness by his mighty power, as he does the raging waves of the troubled sea, saying, "Hitherto shalt thou come, but no further," but if God should withdraw that restraining power, it would soon carry all before it. Sin is the ruin and misery of the soul; it is destructive in its nature; and if God should leave it without restraint, there would need nothing else to make the soul perfectly miserable. The corruption of the heart of man is immoderate and boundless in its fury; and while wicked men live here, it is like fire pent up by God's restraints, whereas if it were let loose, it would set on fire the course of nature; and as the heart is now a sink of sin, so if sin was not restrained, it would immediately turn the soul into a fiery oven, or a furnace of fire and brimstone.

7. It is no security to wicked men for one moment, that there are no visible means of death at hand. It is no security to a natural man, that he is now in health, and that he does not see which way he should now immediately go out of the world by an accident, and that there is no visible danger in any respect in his circumstances. The manifold and continual experience of the world in all ages, shows this is no evidence, that a man is not on the very brink of eternity, and that the next step will not be into another world. The unseen, unthought-of ways and means of persons going suddenly out of the world are innumerable and inconceivable. Unconverted men walk over the pit of hell on a rotten covering, and there are innumerable places in this covering so weak that they will not bear

their weight, and these places are not seen. The arrows of death fly unseen at noon-day; the sharpest sight cannot discern them. God has so many different unsearchable ways of taking wicked men out of the world and sending them to hell, that there is nothing to make it appear, that God has need to be at the expense of a miracle, or go out of the ordinary course of his providence, to destroy any wicked man, at any moment. All the means that there are of sinners going out of the world, are so in God's hands, and so universally and absolutely subject to his power and determination, that it does not depend at all the less on the mere will of God, whether sinners shall at any moment go to hell, than if means were never made use of, or at all concerned in the case.

8. Natural men's prudence and care to preserve their own lives, or the care of others to preserve them, do not secure them a moment. To this, divine providence and universal experience do also bear testimony. There is this clear evidence that men's own wisdom is no security to them from death; that if it were otherwise we should see some difference between the wise and politic men of the world, and others, with regard to their liableness to early and unexpected death: but how is it in fact? Eccles. ii. 16. "How dieth the wise man? even as the fool."

9. All wicked men's pains and *contrivance* which they use to escape hell, while they continue to reject Christ, and so remain wicked men, do not secure them from hell one moment. Almost every natural man that hears of hell, flatters himself that he shall escape it; he depends upon himself for his own security; he flatters himself in what he has done, in what he is now doing, or what he intends to do. Every one lays out matters in his own mind how he shall avoid damnation, and flatters himself that he contrives well for himself, and that his schemes will not fail. They hear indeed that there are but few saved, and that the greater part of men that have died heretofore are gone to hell; but each one imagines that he lays out matters better for his own escape than others have done. He does not intend to come to that place of torment; he says within himself, that he intends to take effectual care, and to order matters so for himself as not to fail.

But the foolish children of men miserably delude themselves in their own schemes, and in confidence in their own strength and wisdom; they trust to nothing but a shadow. The greater part of those who heretofore have lived under the same means of grace, and are now dead, are undoubtedly gone to hell; and it was not because they were not as wise as those who are now alive: it was not because they did not lay out matters as well for themselves to secure their own escape. If we could speak with them, and inquire of them, one by one, whether they expected, when alive, and when they used to hear about hell, ever to be the subjects of that misery: we doubtless, should hear one and another reply, "No, I never intended to come here: I had laid out matters otherwise in my mind; I thought I should contrive well for myself: I thought my scheme good. I intended to take effectual care; but it came upon me unexpected; I did not look for it at that time, and in that manner; it came as a thief: Death outwitted me: God's wrath was too quick for me. Oh, my cursed foolishness! I was flattering myself, and pleasing myself with vain dreams of what I would do hereafter; and when I was saying, Peace and safety, then suddenly destruction came upon me."

10. God has laid himself under *no obligation,* by any promise to keep any natural man out of hell one moment. God certainly has made no promises either of eternal life, or of any deliverance or preservation from eternal death, but what are contained in the covenant of grace, the promises that are given in Christ, in whom all the promises are yea and amen. But surely they have no interest in the promises of the covenant of grace who are not the children of the covenant, who do not believe in any of the promises, and have no interest in the Mediator of the covenant.

So that, whatever some have imagined and pretended about promises made to natural men's earnest seeking and knocking, it is plain and manifest, that whatever pains a natural man takes in religion, whatever prayers he makes, till he believes in Christ, God is under no manner of obligation to keep him a moment from eternal destruction.

So that, thus it is that natural men are held in the hand of God, over the pit of hell; they have deserved the fiery pit, and are already sentenced to it; and God is dreadfully provoked, his anger is as great towards them as to those that are actually suffering the executions of the fierceness of his wrath in hell, and they have done nothing in the least to appease or abate that anger, neither is God in the least bound by any promise to hold them up one moment; the devil is waiting for them, hell is gaping for them, the flames gather and flash about them, and would fain lay hold on them, and swallow them up; the fire pent up in their own hearts is struggling to break out: and they have no interest in any Mediator, there are no means within reach that can be any security to them. In short, they have no refuge, nothing to take hold of; all that preserves them every moment is the mere arbitrary will, and uncovenanted, unobliged forbearance of an incensed God.

Application

The use of this awful subject may be for awakening unconverted persons in this congregation. This that you have heard is the case of every one of you that are out of Christ.—That world of misery, that lake of burning brimstone, is extended abroad under you. There is the dreadful pit of the glowing flames of the wrath of God; there is hell's wide gaping mouth open; and you have nothing to stand upon, nor any thing to take hold of; there is nothing between you and hell but the air; it is only the power and mere pleasure of God that holds you up.

You probably are not sensible of this; you find you are kept out of hell, but do not see the hand of God in it; but look at other things, as the good state of your bodily constitution, your care of your own life, and the means you use for your own preservation. But indeed these things are nothing; if God should withdraw his hand, they would avail no more to keep you from falling, than the thin air to hold up a person that is suspended in it.

Your wickedness makes you as it were heavy as lead, and to tend downwards with great weight and pressure towards hell; and if God should let you go, you would immediately sink and swiftly descend and plunge into the bottomless gulf, and your healthy constitution, and your own care and prudence, and best contrivance, and all your righteousness, would have no more influence to uphold you and keep you out of hell, than a spider's web would have to stop a fallen rock. Were it not for the sovereign pleasure of God, the earth would not bear you one moment; for you are a burden to it; the creation groans with you; the creature is made subject to the bondage of your corruption, not willingly; the sun does not willingly shine upon you to give you light to serve sin and Satan; the earth does not willingly yield her increase to satisfy your lusts; nor is it willingly a stage for your wickedness to be acted upon; the air does not willingly serve you for breath to maintain the flame of life in your vitals, while you spend your life in the service of God's enemies. God's creatures are good, and were made for men to serve God with, and do not willingly subserve to any other purpose, and groan when they are abused to purposes so directly contrary to their nature and end. And the world would spew you out, were it not for the sovereign hand of him who hath subjected it in hope. There are black clouds of God's wrath now hanging directly over your heads, full of the dreadful storm, and big with thunder, and were it not for the restraining hand of God, it would immediately burst forth upon you. The sovereign pleasure of God, for the present, stays his rough wind; otherwise it would come with fury, and your destruction would come like a whirlwind, and you would be like the chaff of the summer threshing floor.

The wrath of God is like great waters that are dammed for the present; they increase more and more, and rise higher and higher, till an outlet is given; and the longer the stream is stopped, the more rapid and mighty is its course, when once it is let loose. It is true, that judgment against your evil works has not been executed hitherto; the floods of God's vengeance have been withheld; but your guilt in the mean time is constantly increasing, and you are every day treasuring up more wrath; the waters are constantly rising, and waxing more and more mighty; and there is nothing but the mere pleasure of God, that holds the waters back, that are unwilling to be stopped, and press hard to go forward. If God should only withdraw his hand from the flood-gate, it would immediately fly open, and the fiery floods of the fierceness and wrath of God, would rush forth with inconceivable fury, and would come upon you with omnipotent power; and if your strength were ten thousand times greater than it is, yea, ten thousand times greater than the strength of the stoutest, sturdiest devil in hell, it would be nothing to withstand or endure it.

The bow of God's wrath is bent, and the arrow made ready on the string, and justice bends the arrow at your heart, and strains the bow, and it is nothing but the mere pleasure of God, and that of an angry God, without any promise or obligation at all, that keeps the arrow one moment from being made drunk with your blood. Thus all you that never passed under a great change of heart, by the mighty power of the Spirit of God upon your souls; all you that were never born again, and made new creatures, and raised from being dead in sin, to a state of new, and before altogether unexperienced light and life, are in the hands of an angry God. However you may have re-formed your life in many things, and may have had religious affec-tions, and may keep up a form of religion in your families and closets, and in the house of God, it is nothing but his mere pleasure that keeps you from being this moment swallowed up in everlasting destruction. However unconvinced you may now be of the truth of what you hear, by and by you will be fully convinced of it. Those that are gone from being in the like circumstances with you, see that it was so with them; for destruction came suddenly upon most of them; when they expected nothing of it, and while they were saying, Peace and safety: now they see, that those things on which they depended for peace and safety, were nothing but thin air and empty shadows.

The God that holds you over the pit of hell, much as one holds a spider, or some loathsome insect over the fire, abhors you, and is dreadfully provoked: his wrath towards you burns like fire; he looks upon you as worthy of nothing else, but to be cast into the fire; he is of purer eyes than to bear to have you in his sight; you are ten thousand times more abominable in his eyes, than the most hateful venomous serpent is in ours. You have offended him infinitely more than ever a stubborn rebel did his prince; and yet it is nothing but his hand that holds you from falling into the fire every moment. It is to

be ascribed to nothing else, that you did not go to hell the last night;
that you was suffered to awake again in this world, after you closed
your eyes to sleep. And there is no other reason to be given, why you
have not dropped into hell since you arose in the morning, but that
God's hand has held you up. There is no other reason to be given
why you have not gone to hell, since you have sat here in the house
of God, provoking his pure eyes by your sinful wicked manner of
attending his solemn worship. Yea, there is nothing else that is to be
given as a reason why you do not this very moment drop down into
hell.

O sinner! Consider the fearful danger you are in: it is a great furnace of wrath, a wide and bottomless pit, full of the fire of wrath,
that you are held over in the hand of that God, whose wrath is provoked and incensed as much against you, as against many of the
damned in hell. You hang by a slender thread, with the flames of
divine wrath flashing about it, and ready every moment to singe it,
and burn it asunder; and you have no interest in any Mediator, and
nothing to lay hold of to save yourself, nothing to keep off the flames
of wrath, nothing of your own, nothing that you ever have done,
nothing that you can do, to induce God to spare you one moment.—
And consider here more particularly,

1. *Whose* wrath it is: it is the wrath of the infinite God. If it were
only the wrath of man, though it were of the most potent prince, it
would be comparatively little to be regarded. The wrath of kings is
very much dreaded, especially of absolute monarchs, who have the
possessions and lives of their subjects wholly in their power, to be
disposed of at their mere will. Prov. xx. 2. "The fear of a king is as the
roaring of a lion: Whoso provoketh him to anger, sinneth against his
own soul." The subject that very much enrages an arbitrary prince,
is liable to suffer the most extreme torments that human art can
invent, or human power can inflict. But the greatest earthly potentates in their greatest majesty and strength, and when clothed in their
greatest terrors, are but feeble, despicable worms of the dust, in
comparison of the great and almighty Creator and King of heaven
and earth. It is but little that they can do, when most enraged, and
when they have exerted the utmost of their fury. All the kings of the

earth, before God, are as grasshoppers; they are nothing, and less than nothing: both their love and their hatred is to be despised. The wrath of the great King of kings, is as much more terrible than theirs, as his majesty is greater. Luke xii. 4, 5. "And I say unto you, my friends, Be not afraid of them that kill the body, and after that, have no more that they can do. But I will forewarn you whom you shall fear: fear him, which after he hath killed, hath power to cast into hell: yea, I say unto you, Fear him."

2. It is the *fierceness* of his wrath that you are exposed to. We often read of the fury of God; as in Isaiah lix. 18. "According to their deeds, accordingly he will repay fury to his adversaries." So Isaiah lxvi. 15. "For behold, the Lord will come with fire, and with his chariots like a whirlwind, to render his anger with fury, and his rebuke with flames of fire." And in many other places. So, Rev. xix. 15. we read of "the wine press of the fierceness and wrath of Almighty God." The words are exceeding terrible. If it had only been said, "the wrath of God," the words would have implied that which is infinitely dreadful: but it is "the fierceness and wrath of God." The fury of God! the fierceness of Jehovah! Oh, how dreadful must that be! Who can utter or conceive what such expressions carry in them! But it is also "the fierceness and wrath of *Almighty* God." As though there would be a very great manifestation of his almighty power in what the fierceness of his wrath should inflict, as though omnipotence should be as it were enraged, and exerted, as men are wont to exert their strength in the fierceness of their wrath. Oh! then, what will be the consequence! What will become of the poor worms that shall suffer it! Whose hands can be strong? And whose heart can endure? To what a dreadful, inexpressible, inconceivable depth of misery must the poor creature be sunk who shall be the subject of this!

Consider this, you that are here present, that yet remain in an unregenerate state. That God will execute the fierceness of his anger, implies, that he will inflict wrath without any pity. When God beholds the ineffable extremity of your case, and sees your torment to be so vastly disproportioned to your strength, and sees how your poor soul is crushed, and sinks down, as it were, into an infinite gloom; he will have no compassion upon you, he will not forbear the executions of his wrath, or in the least lighten his hand; there shall be no moderation or mercy, nor will God then at all stay his rough wind; he will have no regard to your welfare, nor be at all careful lest you should suffer too much in any other sense, than only that you shall *not suffer beyond what strict justice requires.* Nothing shall be withheld, because it is so hard for you to bear. Ezek. viii. 18. "Therefore will I also deal in fury: mine eye shall not spare, neither will I have pity; and though they cry in mine ears with a loud voice, yet I will not hear them." Now God stands ready to pity you; this is a day of mercy; you may cry now with some encouragement of obtaining mercy. But when once the day of mercy is past, your most lamentable and dolorous cries and shrieks will be in vain; you will be wholly lost and thrown away of God, as to any regard to your welfare. God will have no other use to put you to, but to suffer misery; you shall be continued in being to no other end; for you will be a vessel of wrath fitted to destruction; and there will be no other use of this vessel, but to be filled full of wrath. God will be so far from pitying you when you cry to him, that it is said he will only "laugh and mock," Prov. i. 25, 26, etc.

How awful are those words, Isa. lxiii. 3, which are the words of the great God. "I will tread them in mine anger, and will trample them in my fury, and their blood shall be sprinkled upon my garments, and I will stain all my raiment." It is perhaps impossible to conceive of words that carry in them greater manifestations of these three things, *viz.* contempt, and hatred, and fierceness of indignation. If you cry to God to pity you, he will be so far from pitying you in your doleful case, or showing you the least regard or favour, that instead of that, he will only tread you under foot. And though he will know that you cannot bear the weight of omnipotence treading upon you, yet he will not regard that, but he will crush you under his feet without mercy; he will crush out your blood, and make it fly, and it shall be sprinkled on his garments, so as to stain all his raiment. He will not only hate you, but he will have you in the utmost contempt: no place shall be thought fit for you, but under his feet to be trodden down as the mire of the streets.

3. The *misery* you are exposed to is that which God will inflict to

that end, that he might show what that wrath of Jehovah is. God hath had it on his heart to show to angels and men, both how excellent his love is, and also how terrible his wrath is. Sometimes earthly kings have a mind to show how terrible their wrath is, by the extreme punishments they would excute on those that would provoke them. Nebuchadnezzar, that mighty and haughty monarch of the Chaldean empire, was willing to show his wrath when enraged with Shadrach, Meshech, and Abednego; and accordingly gave orders that the burning fiery furnace should be heated seven times hotter than it was before; doubtless, it was raised to the utmost degree of fierceness that human art could raise it. But the great God is also willing to show his wrath, and magnify his awful majesty and mighty power in the extreme sufferings of his enemies. Rom. ix. 22. "What if God, willing to show his wrath, and to make his power known, endure with much long-suffering the vessels of wrath fitted to destruction?" And seeing this is his design, and what he has determined, even to show how terrible the unrestrained wrath, the fury and fierceness of Jehovah is, he will do it to effect. There will be something accomplished and brought to pass that will be dreadful with a witness. When the great and angry God hath risen up and executed his awful vengeance on the poor sinner, and the wretch is actually suffering the infinite weight and power of his indignation, then will God call upon the whole universe to behold that awful majesty and mighty power that is to be seen in it. Isa. xxxiii. 12-14. "And the people shall be as the burnings of lime, as thorns cut up shall they be burnt in the fire. Hear ye that are far off, what I have done; and ye that are near, acknowledge my might. The sinners in Zion are afraid; fearfulness hath surprised the hypocrites," etc.

Thus it will be with you that are in an unconverted state, if you continue in it; the infinite might, and majesty, and terribleness of the omnipotent God shall be magnified upon you, in the ineffable strength of your torments. You shall be tormented in the presence of the holy angels, and in the presence of the Lamb; and when you shall be in this state of suffering, the glorious inhabitants of heaven shall go forth and look on the awful spectacle, that they may see what the wrath and fierceness of the Almighty is; and when they have seen it, they will fall down and adore that great power and majesty. Isa. lxvi. 23, 24. "And it shall come to pass, that from one new moon to another, and from one sabbath to another, shall all flesh come to worship before me, saith the Lord. And they shall go forth and look upon the carcasses of the men that have transgressed against me; for their worm shall not die, neither shall their fire be quenched, and they shall be an abhorring unto all flesh."

4. It is *everlasting* wrath. It would be dreadful to suffer this fierceness and wrath of Almighty God one moment; but you must suffer it to all eternity. There will be no end to this exquisite horrible misery. When you look forward, you shall see a long for ever, a boundless duration before you, which will swallow up your thoughts, and amaze your soul; and you will absolutely despair of ever having any deliverance, any end, any mitigation, any rest at all. You will know certainly that you must wear out long ages, millions of millions of ages, in wrestling and conflicting with this almighty merciless vengeance; and then when you have so done, when so many ages have actually been spent by you in this manner, you will know that all is but a point to what remains. So that your punishment will indeed be infinite. Oh, who can express what the state of a soul in such circumstances is! All that we can possibly say about it, gives but a very feeble, faint representation of it; it is inexpressible and inconceivable: For "who knows the power of God's anger?"

How dreadful is the state of those that are daily and hourly in the danger of this great wrath and infinite misery! But this is the dismal case of every soul in this congregation that has not been born again, however moral and strict, sober and religious, they may otherwise be. Oh that you would consider it, whether you be young or old! There is reason to think, that there are many in this congregation now hearing this discourse, that will actually be the subjects of this very misery to all eternity. We know not who they are, or in what seats they sit, or what thoughts they now have. It may be they are now at ease, and hear all these things without much disturbance, and are now flattering themselves that they are not the persons, promising themselves that they shall escape. If we knew that there was one person, and but one, in the whole congregation, that was to be the subject of this misery, what an awful thing would it be to think of! If we knew who it was, what an awful sight would it be to see such a person! How might all the rest of the congregation lift up a lamentable and bitter cry over him! But, alas! instead of one, how many is it likely will remember this discourse in hell? And it would be a wonder, if some that are now present should not be in hell in a very short time, even before this year is out. And it would be no wonder if some persons, that now sit here, in some seats of this meeting-house, in health, quiet and secure, should be there before to-morrow morning. Those of you that finally continue in a natural condition, that shall keep out of hell longest will be there in a little time! your damnation does not slumber; it will come swiftly, and, in all probability, very suddenly upon many of you. You have reason to wonder that you are not already in hell. It is doubtless the case of some whom you have seen and known, that never deserved hell more than you, and that heretofore appeared as likely to have been now alive as you. Their case is past all hope; they are crying in extreme misery and perfect despair; but here you are in the land of the living and in the house of God, and have an opportunity to obtain salvation. What would not those poor damned hopeless souls give for one day's opportunity such as you now enjoy!

And now you have an extraordinary opportunity, a day wherein Christ has thrown the door of mercy wide open, and stands in calling and crying with a loud voice to poor sinners; a day wherein many are flocking to him, and pressing into the kingdom of God. Many are daily coming from the east, west, north and south; many that were very lately in the same miserable condition that you are in, are now in a happy state, with their hearts filled with love to him who has loved them, and washed them from their sins in his own blood, and rejoicing in hope of the glory of God. How awful is it to be left behind at such a day! To see so many others feasting, while you are pining and perishing! To see so many rejoicing and singing for joy of heart, while you have cause to mourn for sorrow of heart, and howl for vexation of spirit! How can you rest one moment in such a condition? Are not your souls as precious as the souls of the people at Suffield,[1] where they are flocking from day to day to Christ?

Are there not many here who have lived long in the world, and are not to this day born again? and so are aliens from the commonwealth of Israel, and have done nothing ever since they have lived, but treasure up wrath against the day of wrath? Oh, sirs, your case, in an especial manner, is extremely dangerous. Your guilt and hardness of heart is extremely great. Do you not see how generally persons of your years are passed over and left, in the present remarkable and wonderful dispensation of God's mercy? You had need to consider yourselves, and awake thoroughly out of sleep. You cannot bear the fierceness and wrath of the infinite God.—And you, young men, and young women, will you neglect this precious season which you now enjoy, when so many others of your age are renouncing all youthful vanities, and flocking to Christ? You especially have now an extraordinary opportunity; but if you neglect it, it will soon be with you as with those persons who spent all the precious days of youth in sin, and are now come to such a dreadful pass in blindness and hardness.—And you, children, who are unconverted, do not you know that you are going down to hell, to bear the dreadful wrath of that God, who is now angry with you every day and every night? Will you be content to be the children of the devil, when so many other children in the land are converted, and are become the holy and happy children of the King of kings?

And let every one that is yet of Christ, and hanging over the pit of hell, whether they be old men and women, or middle aged, or young people, or little children, now hearken to the loud calls of God's word and providence. This acceptable year of the Lord, a day of such great favours to some, will doubtless be a day of as remarkable vengeance to others. Men's hearts harden, and their guilt increases apace at such a day as this, if they neglect their souls; and never was there so great danger of such persons being given up to hardness of heart and blindness of mind. God seems now to be hastily gathering in his elect in all parts of the land; and probably

[1] A town in the neighbourhood.

the greater part of adult persons that ever shall be saved, will be brought in now in a little time, and it will be as it was on the great out-pouring of the Spirit upon the Jews in the apostles' days; the election will obtain, and the rest will be blinded. If this should be the case with you, you will eternally curse this day, and will curse the day that ever you was born, to see such a season of the pouring out of God's Spirit, and will wish that you had died and gone to hell before you had seen it. Now undoubtedly it is, as it was in the days of John the Baptist, the axe is in an extraordinary manner laid at the root of the trees, that every tree which brings not forth good fruit, may be hewn down and cast into the fire.

Therefore, let every one that is out of Christ, now awake and fly from the wrath to come. The wrath of Almighty God is now undoubtedly hanging over a great part of this congregation: Let every one fly out of Sodom: "Haste and escape for your lives, look not behind you, escape to the mountain, lest you be consumed."

Patrick Henry

LIBERTY OR DEATH

¶ PATRICK HENRY (1736-1799) was born in Virginia and was all his life a resident of that state. He was not of the Virginia aristocracy but came from a middle-class family of considerable culture and attainments. After leaving the country school at the age of ten he was tutored for some years by his father. He experimented with business and farming, then studied law for a few months and in 1760 was admitted to the bar. He first achieved wide notice by his speech in the Parsons' Cause, defending the people against heavy taxation for the support of the clergy, and soon became one of Virginia's leading lawyers, orators, and statesmen, and a vigorous agitator for revolution. He was elected to the House of Burgesses in 1765, was Virginia's first elected governor, 1775, and served four subsequent terms in that office, attended two sessions of the Continental Congress, and declined various other offices. His championship of political liberty was always sectional and local, and when the Federal Constitution was presented for ratification he opposed it.

The speech commonly called "Liberty or Death" was delivered March 23, 1775, before the Virginia Convention in St. John's Church, Richmond. It had to do with a resolution Henry had introduced to put Virginia "in a state of defence" by raising and equipping an army. Washington and Jefferson, among others, supported the resolution, and it was carried by a narrow margin. No accurate report of the speech was made at the time, and the text here given is derived from the account in William Wirt's biography, *The Life and Character of Patrick Henry*, published in 1817, forty-two years after the speech was delivered. Wirt says that his text was derived from the accounts of witnesses. It is probable that its sustained brilliance of style is more Wirt's than Henry's.

91

M R. PRESIDENT: No man thinks more highly than I do of the patriotism, as well as abilities, of the very worthy gentlemen who have just addressed the house. But different men often see the same subject in different lights; and, therefore, I hope it will not be thought disrespectful to those gentlemen, if, entertaining as I do opinions of a character very opposite to theirs, I shall speak forth my sentiments freely and without reserve. This is no time for ceremony. The question before the house is one of awful moment to this country. For my own part, I consider it as nothing less than a question of freedom or slavery; and in proportion to the magnitude of the subject ought to be the freedom of the debate. It is only in this way that we can hope to arrive at truth, and fulfil the great responsibility which we hold to God and our country. Should I keep back my opinions at such a time, through fear of giving offense, I should consider myself as guilty of treason towards my country, and of an act of disloyalty toward the Majesty of Heaven, which I revere above all earthly kings.

Mr. President, it is natural to man to indulge in the illusions of hope. We are apt to shut our eyes against a painful truth, and listen to the song of that siren, till she transforms us into beasts. Is this the part of wise men, engaged in a great and arduous struggle for liberty? Are we disposed to be of the number of those, who, having eyes, see not, and having ears, hear not, the things which so nearly concern their temporal salvation? For my part, whatever anguish of spirit it may cost, I am willing to know the whole truth; to know the worst, and to provide for it.

I have but one lamp by which my feet are guided, and that is the lamp of experience. I know of no way of judging of the future but by the past. And judging by the past, I wish to know what there has been in the conduct of the British ministry for the last ten years to justify those hopes with which gentlemen have been pleased to solace themselves and the house. Is it that insidious smile with which our petition has been lately received? Trust it not, sir; it will prove a snare to your feet. Suffer not yourselves to be betrayed with a kiss. Ask yourselves how this gracious reception of our petition comports with those war-like preparations which cover our waters and darken our land. Are fleets and armies necessary to a work of love and reconciliation? Have we shown ourselves so unwilling to be reconciled, that force must be called in to win back our love? Let us not deceive ourselves, sir. These are the implements of war and subjugation; the last arguments to which kings resort. I ask gentlemen, sir, What means this martial array, if its purpose be not to force us to submission? Can gentlemen assign any other possible motive for it? Has Great Britain any enemy, in this quarter of the world, to call for all this accumulation of navies and armies? No, sir, she has none. They are meant for us: they can be meant for no other. They are sent over to bind and rivet upon us those chains which the British ministry have been so long forging. And what have we to oppose to them? Shall we try argument? Sir, we have been trying that for the last ten years. Have we anything new to offer upon the subject? Nothing. We have held the subject up in every light of which it is capable; but it has been all in vain. Shall we resort to entreaty and humble supplication? What terms shall we find, which have not been already exhausted? Let us not, I beseech you, sir, deceive ourselves longer. Sir, we have done everything that could be done, to avert the storm which is now coming on. We have petitioned; we have remonstrated; we have supplicated; we have prostrated ourselves before the throne, and have implored its interposition to arrest the tyrannical hands of the ministry and Parliament. Our petitions have been slighted; our remonstrances have produced additional violence and insult; our supplications have been disregarded; and we have been spurned, with contempt, from the foot of the throne! In vain, after these things, may we indulge the fond hope of peace and reconciliation. There is no longer any room for hope. If we wish to be free—if we mean to preserve inviolate those inestimable privileges for which we have been so long contending—if we mean not basely to abandon the noble struggle in which we have been so long engaged, and which we have pledged ourselves never to abandon, until the glorious object of our contest shall be obtained —we must fight! I repeat it, sir, we must fight! An appeal to arms and to the God of Hosts is all that is left us!

They tell us, sir, that we are weak; unable to cope with so formidable an adversary. But when shall we be stronger? Will it be the next week, or the next year? Will it be when we are totally disarmed, and when a British guard shall be stationed in every house? Shall we gather strength by irresolution and inaction? Shall we acquire the means of effectual resistance by lying supinely on our backs and hugging the delusive phantom of hope, until our enemies shall have bound us hand and foot? Sir, we are not weak, if we make a proper use of those means which the God of nature hath placed in our power. Three millions of people, armed in the holy cause of liberty, and in such a country as that which we possess, are invincible by any force which our enemy can send against us. Besides, sir, we shall not fight our battles alone. There is a just God who presides over the destinies of nations, and who will raise up friends to fight our battles for us. The battle, sir, is not to the strong alone; it is to the vigilant, the active, the brave. Besides, sir, we have no election. If we were base enough to desire it, it is now too late to retire from the contest. There is no retreat, but in submission and slavery! Our chains are forged! Their clanking may be heard on the plains of Boston! The war is inevitable—and let it come! I repeat it, sir, let it come.

It is in vain, sir, to extenuate the matter. Gentlemen may cry, Peace, Peace—but there is no peace. The war is actually begun! The next gale that sweeps from the north will bring to our ears the clash of resounding arms! Our breathren are already in the field! Why stand we here idle? What is it that gentlemen wish? What would they have? Is life so dear, or peace so sweet, as to be purchased at the price of chains and slavery? Forbid it, Almighty God! I know not what course others may take; but as for me, give me liberty or give me death!

Thomas Jefferson

FIRST INAUGURATION ADDRESS

¶ THOMAS JEFFERSON (1743-1826), although in no way a distinguished orator in his time, was noteworthy for the rhetorical effectiveness of his addresses. Born in 1743 in Virginia, the son of a planter, Jefferson attended William and Mary College, and studied law under George Wythe. Admitted to the bar in 1767, he rose quickly to an eminent position. In 1775 he was appointed to the Second Continental Congress, later being called upon to draft the Declaration of Independence. Jefferson served as a member of the Virginia Legislature from 1776-79; was governor of Virginia from 1779-81; minister to France, 1784-89; Secretary of State under Washington, 1789-94, and Vice-President, 1797-1801. Elected to the presidency in 1801, he served until 1809.

Jefferson's First Inaugural Address was delivered in Washington, March 4, 1801, the seat of government having been moved from Philadelphia in the previous year. The presidential campaign of 1800 which culminated in unseating the Federalists had been an exceedingly bitter one. In addition, the two Republican candidates, Jefferson and Aaron Burr, captured the same number of votes, thus throwing the election into the House of Representatives for final decision. The deadlock was not broken until February 17th, scarcely a fortnight before the day of Inauguration.

FRIENDS and Fellow Citizens:—

Called upon to undertake the duties of the first executive office of our country, I avail myself of the presence of that portion of my fellow citizens which is here assembled, to express my grateful thanks for the favor with which they have been pleased to look toward me, to declare a sincere consciousness that the task is above my talents, and that I approach it with those anxious and awful presentiments which the greatness of the charge and the weakness of my powers so justly inspire. A rising nation, spread over a wide and fruitful land, traversing all the seas with the rich productions of their industry, engaged in commerce with nations who feel power and forget right, advancing rapidly to destinies beyond the reach of mortal eye—when I contemplate these transcendent objects, and see the honor, the happiness, and the hopes of this beloved country committed to the issue and the auspices of this day, I shrink from the contemplation, and humble myself before the magnitude of the undertaking. Utterly indeed, should I despair, did not the presence of many whom I here see remind me, that in the other high authorities provided by our constitution, I shall find resources of wisdom, of virtue, and of zeal, on which to rely under all difficulties. To you, then, gentlemen, who are charged with the sovereign functions of legislation, and to those associated with you, I look with encouragement for that guidance and support which may enable us to steer with safety the vessel in which we are all embarked amid the conflicting elements of a troubled world.

During the contest of opinion through which we have passed, the animation of discussion and of exertions has sometimes worn an aspect which might impose on strangers unused to think freely and to speak and to write what they think; but this being now decided by the voice of the nation, announced according to the rules of the constitution, all will, of course, arrange themselves under the will of the law, and unite in common efforts for the common good. All, too, will bear in mind this sacred principle, that though the will of the majority is in all cases to prevail, that will, to be rightful, must be reasonable; that the minority possess their equal rights, which equal laws must protect, and to violate which would be oppression. Let us, then, fellow citizens, unite with one heart and one mind. Let us restore to social intercourse that harmony and affection without which liberty and even life itself are but dreary things. And let us reflect that having banished from our land that religious intolerance under which mankind so long bled and suffered, we have yet gained little if we countenance a political intolerance as despotic, as wicked, and capable of as bitter and bloody persecutions. During the throes and convulsions of the ancient world, during the agonizing spasms of infuriated man, seeking through blood and slaughter his long-lost liberty, it was not wonderful that the agitation of the billows should reach even this distant and peaceful shore; that this should be more felt and feared by some and less by others; that this should divide opinions as to measures of safety. But every difference of opinion is not a difference of principle. We have called by different names brethren of the same principle. We are all republicans—we are all federalists. If there be any among us who would wish to dissolve this Union or to change its republican form, let them stand undisturbed as monuments of the safety with which error of opinion may be tolerated where reason is left free to combat it. I know, indeed, that some honest men fear that a republican government cannot be strong; that this government is not strong enough. But would the honest patriot, in the full tide of successful experiment, abandon a government which so far kept us free and firm, on the theoretic and visionary fear that this government, the world's best hope, may by possibility want energy to preserve itself? I trust not. I believe this, on the contrary, the strongest government on earth. I believe it is the only one where every man, at the call of the laws, would fly to the standard of the law, and would meet invasions of the public order as his own personal concern. Sometimes it is said that man cannot be trusted with the government of himself. Can he, then, be trusted with the government of others? Or have we found angels in the forms of kings to govern him? Let history answer this question.

Let us, then, with courage and confidence pursue our own federal and republican principles, our attachment to our union and representative government. Kindly separated by nature and a wide ocean from the exterminating havoc of one quarter of the globe; too high-minded to endure the degradations of the others; possessing a chosen country, with room enough for our descendants to the hundredth and thousandth generation; entertaining a due sense of our equal right to the use of our own faculties, to the acquisitions of our industry, to honor and confidence from our fellow citizens, resulting not from birth but from our actions and their sense of them; enlightened by a benign religion, professed, indeed, and practiced in various forms, yet all of them including honesty, truth, temperance, gratitude, and the love of man; acknowledging and adoring an overruling Providence, which by all its dispensations proves that it delights in the happiness of man here and his greater happiness hereafter; with all these blessings, what more is necessary to make us a happy and prosperous people? Still one thing more, fellow citizens—a wise and frugal government, which shall restrain men from injuring one another, which shall leave them otherwise free to regulate their own pursuits of industry and improvement, and shall not take from the mouth of labor the bread it has earned. This is the sum of good government, and this is necessary to close the circle of our felicities.

About to enter, fellow citizens, on the exercise of duties which comprehend everything dear and valuable to you, it is proper that you should understand what I deem the essential principles of our government, and consequently those which ought to shape its administration. I will compress them within the narrowest compass they will bear, stating the general principle, but not all its limitations. Equal and exact justice to all men, of whatever state or persuasion, religious or political; peace, commerce, and honest friendship, with all nations—entangling alliances with none; the support of the state governments in all their rights, as the most competent administrations for our domestic concerns and the surest bulwarks against anti-republican tendencies; the preservation of the general government in its whole constitutional vigor, as the sheet anchor of our peace at home and safety abroad; a jealous care of the right of election by the people—a mild and safe corrective of abuses which are lopped by the sword of the revolution where peaceable remedies are unprovided; absolute acquiescence in the decisions of the majority —the vital principle of republics, from which there is no appeal but to force, the vital principle and immediate parent of despotism; a well-disciplined militia—our best reliance in peace and for the first moments of war, till regulars may relieve them; the supremacy of the civil over the military authority; economy in the public expense, that labor may be lightly burdened; the honest payment of our debts and sacred preservation of the public faith; encouragement of agriculture, and of commerce as its handmaid; the diffusion of information and the arraignment of all abuses at the bar of public reason; freedom of religion; freedom of the press; freedom of person under the protection of the *habeas corpus;* and trial by juries impartially selected—these principles form the bright constellation which has gone before us, and guided our steps through an age of revolution and reformation. The wisdom of our sages and the blood of our heroes have been devoted to their attainment. They should be the creed of our political faith—the text of civil instruction—the touchstone by which to try the services of those we trust; and should we wander from them in moments of error or alarm, let us hasten to retrace our steps and to regain the road which alone leads to peace, liberty, and safety.

I repair, then, fellow citizens, to the post you have assigned me. With experience enough in subordinate offices to have seen the difficulties of this, the greatest of all, I have learned to expect that it will rarely fall to the lot of imperfect man to retire from this station with the reputation and the favor which bring him into it. Without pretensions to that high confidence reposed in our first and great revolutionary character, whose preeminent services had entitled him to the first place in his country's love, and destined for him the fairest page in the volume of faithful history, I ask so much confidence only as may give firmness and effect to the legal administration of your affairs. I shall often go wrong through defect of judgment. When right, I shall often be thought wrong by those whose positions will not command a view of the whole ground. I ask your indulgence for my own errors, which will never be intentional; and your support against the errors of others, who may condemn what they would not if seen in all its parts. The approbation implied by your suffrage is a consolation to me for the past; and my future solicitude will be to retain the good opinion of those who have bestowed it in advance, to conciliate that of others by doing them all the good in my power, and to be instrumental to the happiness and freedom of all.

Relying, then, on the patronage of your good will, I advance with obedience to the work, ready to retire from it whenever you become sensible how much better choice it is in your power to make. And may that Infinite Power which rules the destinies of the universe, lead our councils to what is best, and give them a favorable issue for your peace and prosperity.

Daniel Webster

THE BUNKER HILL MONUMENT

❡ DANIEL WEBSTER (1782-1852) was born at Salisbury, New Hampshire. After graduating from Dartmouth College in 1801 he took up the practice of law, first in New Hampshire and after 1816 in Boston. He was twice elected to Congress from New Hampshire and once from Massachusetts. From 1827 till 1841 he was United States senator from Massachusetts. From 1845 to 1850 he was again in the Senate. He served as Secretary of State in the cabinets of Presidents Harrison, Tyler, and Fillmore. From 1832 on he was hopeful of receiving the Whig nomination for the presidency, but was always disappointed.

Webster won national fame as an orator by his address at Plymouth, 1820, on "The First Settlement of New England." Thereafter through his various occasional addresses, pleas at the bar, and debates in Congress he became, by common agreement, America's greatest orator.

The address that follows "was delivered in the open air at noon of a cool sunshiny day, June 17, 1825, the fiftieth anniversary of the Battle of Bunker Hill. It followed upon a procession from Boston Common, with two hundred veterans of the Revolution (including forty who had fought at Bunker Hill), riding in barouches; and upon the laying, by General Lafayette, of the cornerstone of the monument. The audience that gathered on the north declivity of the hill and at its base, may have numbered a hundred thousand. How many of these could hear Webster's voice and follow his words no one can say." (*A History and Criticism of American Public Address,* edited by W. N. Brigance, New York, 1943, p. 681.) The text of Webster's speeches that follow is from the *National Edition* of *The Writings and Speeches of Daniel Webster,* Boston, 1903. It is well to note that Webster made it a practice to revise his speeches for publication after they were delivered.

THIS UNCOUNTED MULTITUDE before me and around me proves the feeling which the occasion has excited. These thousands of human faces, glowing with sympathy and joy, and from the impulses of a common gratitude turned reverently to heaven in this spacious temple of the firmament, proclaim that the day, the place, and the purpose of our assembling have made a deep impression on our hearts.

If, indeed, there be anything in local association fit to affect the mind of man, we need not strive to repress the emotions which agitate us here. We are among the sepulchres of our fathers. We are on ground, distinguished by their valor, their constancy, and the shedding of their blood. We are here, not to fix an uncertain date in our annals, nor to draw into notice an obscure and unknown spot. If our humble purpose had never been conceived, if we ourselves had never been born, the 17th of June, 1775, would have been a day on which all subsequent history would have poured its light, and the eminence where we stand a point of attraction to the eyes of successive generations. But we are Americans. We live in what may be called the early age of this great continent; and we know that our posterity, through all time, are here to enjoy and suffer the allotments of humanity. We see before us a probable train of great events; we know that our own fortunes have been happily cast; and it is natural, therefore, that we should be moved by the contemplation of occurrences which have guided our destiny before many of us were born, and settled the condition in which we should pass that portion of our existence which God allows to men on earth.

We do not read even of the discovery of this continent, without feeling something of a personal interest in the event; without being reminded how much it has affected our own fortunes and our own existence. It would be still more unnatural for us, therefore, than for others, to contemplate with unaffected minds that interesting, I may say that most touching and pathetic scene, when the great discoverer of America stood on the deck of his shattered bark, the shades of night falling on the sea, yet no man sleeping; tossed on the billows of an unknown ocean, yet the stronger billows of alternate hope and despair tossing his own troubled thoughts; extending forward his harassed frame, straining westward his anxious and eager eyes, till Heaven at last granted him a moment of rapture and ecstasy, in blessing his vision with the sight of the unknown world.

Nearer to our times, more closely connected with our fates, and therefore still more interesting to our feelings and affections, is the settlement of our own country by colonists from England. We cherish every memorial of these worthy ancestors; we celebrate their patience and fortitude; we admire their daring enterprise; we teach our children to venerate their piety; and we are justly proud of being descended from men who have set the world an example of founding civil institutions on the great and united principles of human freedom and human knowledge. To us, their children, the story of their labors and sufferings can never be without its interest. We shall not stand unmoved on the shore of Plymouth, while the sea continues to wash it; nor will our brethren in another early and ancient Colony forget the place of its first establishment, till their river shall cease to flow by it. No vigor of youth, no maturity of manhood, will lead the nation to forget the spots where its infancy was cradled and defended.

But the great event in the history of the continent, which we are now met here to commemorate, that prodigy of modern times, at once the wonder and the blessing of the world, is the American Revolution. In a day of extraordinary prosperity and happiness, of high national honor, distinction, and power, we are brought together, in this place, by our love of country, by our admiration of exalted character, by our gratitude for signal services and patriotic devotion.

The Society whose organ I am [1] was formed for the purpose of rearing some honorable and durable monument to the memory of the early friends of American Independence. They have thought,

---

[1] Mr. Webster was at this time President of the Bunker Hill Monument Association.

that for this object no time could be more propitious than the present prosperous and peaceful period; that no place could claim preference over this memorable spot; and that no day could be more auspicious to the undertaking, than the anniversary of the battle which was here fought. The foundation of that monument we have now laid. With solemnities suited to the occasion, with prayers to Almighty God for his blessing and in the midst of this cloud of witnesses, we have begun the work. We trust it will be prosecuted, and that, springing from a broad foundation, rising high in massive solidity and unadorned grandeur, it may remain as long as Heaven permits the works of man to last, a fit emblem, both of the events in memory of which it is raised, and of the gratitude of those who have reared it.

We know, indeed, that the record of illustrious actions is most safely deposited in the universal remembrance of mankind. We know, that if we could cause this structure to ascend, not only till it reached the skies, but till it pierced them, its broad surfaces could still contain but part of that which, in an age of knowledge, hath already been spread over the earth, and which history charges itself with making known to all future times. We know that no inscription on entablatures less broad than the earth itself can carry information of the events we commemorate where it has not already gone; and that no structure, which shall not outlive the duration of letters and knowledge among men, can prolong the memorial. But our object is, by this edifice, to show our own deep sense of the value and importance of the achievements of our ancestors; and, by presenting this work of gratitude to the eye, to keep alive similar sentiments, and to foster a constant regard for the principles of the Revolution. Human beings are composed, not of reason only, but of imagination also, and sentiment; and that is neither wasted nor misapplied which is appropriated to the purpose of giving right direction to sentiments, and opening proper springs of feeling in the heart. Let it not be supposed that our object is to perpetuate national hostility, or even to cherish a mere military spirit. It is higher, purer, nobler. We consecrate our work to the spirit of national independence, and we wish that the light of peace may rest upon it forever. We rear a memorial of our conviction of that unmeasured benefit which has been conferred on our own land, and of the happy influences which have been produced, by the same events, on the general interests of mankind. We come, as Americans, to mark a spot which must forever be dear to us and our posterity. We wish that whosoever, in all coming time, shall turn his eye hither, may behold that the place is not undistinguished where the first great battle of the Revolution was fought. We wish that this structure may proclaim the magnitude and importance of that event to every class and every age. We wish that infancy may learn the purpose of its erection from maternal lips, and that weary and withered age may behold it, and be solaced by the recollections which it suggests. We wish that labor may look up here, and be proud, in the midst of its toil. We wish that, in those days of disaster, which, as they come upon all nations, must be expected to come upon us also, desponding patriotism may turn its eyes hitherward, and be assured that the foundations of our national power are still strong. We wish that this column, rising towards heaven among the pointed spires of so many temples dedicated to God, may contribute also to produce, in all minds, a pious feeling of dependence and gratitude. We wish, finally, that the last object to the sight of him who leaves his native shore, and the first to gladden his who revisits it, may be something which shall remind him of the liberty and the glory of his country. Let it rise! let it rise, till it meet the sun in his coming; let the earliest light of the morning gild it, and parting day linger and play on its summit.

We live in a most extraordinary age. Events so various and so important that they might crowd and distinguish centuries are, in our times, compressed within the compass of a single life. When has it happened that history has had so much to record, in the same term of years, as since the 17th of June, 1775? Our own Revolution, which, under other circumstances, might itself have been expected to occasion a war of half a century, has been achieved; twenty-four sovereign and independent States erected; and a general government established over them, so safe, so wise, so free, so practical, that we might well wonder its establishment should have been accomplished so soon, were it not far the greater wonder that it should have been established at all. Two or three millions of people have been augmented to twelve, the great forests of the West prostrated beneath the arm of successful industry, and the dwellers on the banks of the Ohio and the Mississippi become the fellow-citizens and neighbors of those who cultivate the hills of New England. We have a commerce, that leaves no sea unexplored; navies, which take no law from superior force; revenues, adequate to all the exigencies of government, almost without taxation; and peace with all nations, founded on equal rights and mutual respect.

Europe, within the same period, has been agitated by a mighty revolution, which, while it has been felt in the individual condition and happiness of almost every man, has shaken to the centre her political fabric, and dashed against one another thrones which had stood tranquil for ages. On this, our continent, our own example has been followed, and colonies have sprung up to be nations. Unaccustomed sounds of liberty and free government have reached us from beyond the track of the sun; and at this moment the dominion of European power in this continent, from the place where we stand to the south pole, is annihilated forever.

In the meantime, both in Europe and America, such has been the general progress of knowledge, such the improvement in legislation, in commerce, in the arts, in letters, and, above all, in liberal ideas and the general spirit of the age, that the whole world seems changed.

Yet, notwithstanding that this is but a faint abstract of the things which have happened since the day of the battle of Bunker Hill, we are but fifty years removed from it; and we now stand here to enjoy all the blessings of our own condition, and to look abroad on the brightened prospects of the world, while we still have among us some of those who were active agents in the scenes of 1775, and who are now here, from every quarter of New England, to visit once more, and under circumstances so affecting, I had almost said so overwhelming, this renowned theatre of their courage and patriotism.

Venerable Men! You have come down to us from a former generation. Heaven has bounteously lengthened out your lives that you might behold this joyous day. You are now where you stood fifty years ago, this very hour, with your brothers and your neighbors, shoulder to shoulder, in the strife for your country. Behold, how altered! The same heavens are indeed over your heads; the same ocean rolls at your feet; but all else how changed! You hear now no roar of hostile cannon, you see no mixed volumes of smoke and flame rising from burning Charlestown. The ground strewed with the dead and dying; the impetuous charge; the steady and success-ful repulse; the loud call to repeated assault; the summoning of all that is manly to repeated resistance; a thousand bosoms freely and fearlessly bared in an instant to whatever of terror there may be in war and death;—all these you have witnessed, but you witness them no more. All is peace. The heights of yonder metropolis, its towers and roofs, which you then saw filled with wives and children and countrymen in distress and terror, and looking with unutterable emotions for the issue of the combat, have presented you today with the sight of its whole happy population, come out to welcome and greet you with a universal jubilee. Yonder proud ships, by a felicity of position appropriately lying at the foot of this mount, and seem-ing fondly to cling around it, are not means of annoyance to you, but your country's own means of distinction and defence. All is peace; and God has granted you this sight of your country's happi-ness, ere you slumber in the grave. He has allowed you to behold and to partake the reward of your patriotic toils; and he has allowed us, your sons and countrymen, to meet you here, and in the name of the present generation, in the name of your country, in the name of liberty, to thank you!

But, alas! you are not all here! Time and the sword have thinned your ranks. Prescott, Putnam, Stark, Brooks, Read, Pomeroy, Bridge! our eyes seek for you in vain amid this broken band. You are gathered to your fathers, and live only to your country in her grateful remem-brance and your own bright example. But let us not too much grieve, that you have met the common fate of men. You lived at least long enough to know that your work had been nobly and successfully accomplished. You lived to see your country's independence established, and to sheathe your swords from war. On the light of Liberty you saw arise the light of Peace, like

> "another morn,
> Risen on mid-noon";

and the sky on which you closed your eyes was cloudless.

But ah! Him! the first great martyr in this great cause! Him! the premature victim of his own self-devoting heart! Him! the head of our civil councils, and the destined leader of our military bands, whom nothing brought hither but the unquenchable fire of his own spirit! Him! cut off by Providence in the hour of overwhelming anxiety and thick gloom; falling ere he saw the star of this country rise; pouring out his generous blood like water, before he knew whether it would fertilize a land of freedom or of bondage!—how shall I struggle with the emotions that stifle the utterance of thy name! Our poor work may perish; but thine shall endure! This monument may moulder away; the solid ground it rests upon may sink down to a level with the sea; but thy memory shall not fail! Wheresoever among men a heart shall be found that beats to the transports of patriotism and liberty, its aspirations shall be to claim kindred with thy spirit!

But the scene amidst which we stand does not permit us to confine our thoughts or our sympathies to those fearless spirits who hazarded or lost their lives on this consecrated spot. We have the happiness to rejoice here in the presence of a most worthy representation of the survivors of the whole Revolutionary army.

Veterans! you are the remnant of many a well-fought field. You bring with you marks of honor from Trenton and Monmouth, from Yorktown, Camden, Bennington, and Saratoga. *Veterans of half a century!* when in your youthful days you put everything at hazard in your country's cause, good as that cause was, and sanguine as youth is, still your fondest hopes did not stretch onward to an hour like this! At a period to which you could not reasonably have expected to arrive, at a moment of national prosperity such as you could never have foreseen, you are now met here to enjoy the fellowship of old soldiers, and to receive the overflowings of a universal gratitude.

But your agitated countenances and your heaving breasts inform me that even this is not an unmixed joy. I perceive that a tumult of contending feelings rushes upon you. The images of the dead, as well as the persons of the living, present themselves to you. The scene overwhelms you, and I turn from it. May the Father of all mercies smile upon your declining years, and bless them! And when you shall here have exchanged your embraces, when you shall once more have pressed the hands which have been so often extended to give succor in adversity, or grasped in the exultation of victory, then look abroad upon this lovely land which your young valor defended, and mark the happiness with which it is filled; yea, look abroad upon the whole earth, and see what a name you have contributed to give to your country, and what a praise you have added to freedom, and then rejoice in the sympathy and gratitude which beam upon your last days from the improved condition of mankind!

The occasion does not require of me any particular account of the battle of the 17th of June, 1775, nor any detailed narrative of the events which immediately preceded it. These are familiarly known to all. In the progress of the great and interesting controversy, Massachusetts and the town of Boston had become early and marked objects of the displeasure of the British Parliament. This had been manifested in the act for altering the government of the Province, and in that for shutting up the port of Boston. Nothing sheds more honor on our early history, and nothing better shows how little the feelings and sentiments of the Colonies were known or regarded in England, than the impression which these measures everywhere produced in America. It had been anticipated, that while the Colonies in general would be terrified by the severity of the punishment inflicted on Massachusetts, the other seaports would be governed by a mere spirit of gain; and that, as Boston was now cut off from all commerce, the unexpected advantage which this blow on her was calculated to confer on other towns would be greedily enjoyed. How miserably such reasoners deceived themselves! How little they knew of the depth, and the strength, and the intenseness of that feeling of resistance to illegal acts of power, which possessed the whole American people! Everywhere the unworthy boon was rejected with scorn. The fortunate occasion was seized, everywhere, to show to the whole world that the Colonies were swayed by no local interest, no partial interest, no selfish interest. The temptation to profit by the punishment of Boston was strongest to our neighbors of Salem. Yet Salem was precisely the place where this miserable proffer was spurned, in a tone of the most lofty self-respect and the most indignant patriotism. "We are deeply affected," said its inhabitants, "with the sense of our public calamities; but the miseries that are now rapidly hastening on our brethren in the capital of the Province greatly excite our commiseration. By shutting up the port of Boston, some imagine that the course of trade might be turned hither and to our benefit; but we must be dead to every idea of justice, lost to all feelings of humanity, could we indulge a thought to seize on wealth and raise our fortunes on the ruin of our suffering neighbors." These noble sentiments were not confined to our immediate vicinity. In that day of general affection and brotherhood, the blow given to Boston smote on every patriotic heart from one end of the country to the other. Virginia and the Carolinas, as well as Connecticut and New Hampshire, felt and proclaimed the cause to be their own. The Continental Congress, then holding its first session in Philadelphia, expressed its sympathy for the suffering inhabitants of Boston, and addresses were received from all quarters, assuring them that the cause was a common one, and should be met by common efforts and common sacrifices. The Congress of Massachusetts responded to these assurances; and in an address to the Congress at Philadelphia, bearing the official signature, perhaps among the last, of the immortal Warren, notwithstanding the severity of its suffering and the magnitude of the dangers which threatened it, it was declared, that this Colony "is ready, at all times, to spend and to be spent in the cause of America."

But the hour drew nigh which was to put professions to the proof, and to determine whether the authors of these mutual pledges were ready to seal them in blood. The tidings of Lexington and Concord had no sooner spread, than it was universally felt that the time was at last come for action. A spirit pervaded all ranks, not transient, not boisterous, but deep, solemn, determined,

> *"totamque infusa per artus*
> *Mens agitat molem, et magno se corpore miscet."*

War, on their own soil and at their own doors, was, indeed, a strange work to the yeomanry of New England; but their consciences were convinced of its necessity, their country called them to it, and they did not withhold themselves from the perilous trial. The ordinary occupations of life were abandoned; the plough was staid in the unfinished furrow; wives gave up their husbands, and mothers gave up their sons, to the battles of a civil war. Death might come, in honor, on the field; it might come, in disgrace, on the scaffold. For either and for both they were prepared. The sentiment of Quincy was full in their hearts. "Blandishments," said that distinguished son of genius and patriotism, "will not fascinate us, nor will threats of a halter intimidate; for, under God, we are determined that, wheresoever, whensoever, or howsoever we shall be called to make our exit, we will die free men."

The 17th of June saw the four New England Colonies standing here, side by side, to triumph or to fall together; and there was with them from that moment to the end of the war, what I hope will remain with them forever, one cause, one country, one heart.

The battle of Bunker Hill was attended with the most important effects beyond its immediate results as a military engagement. It created at once a state of open, public war. There could now be no longer a question of proceedings against individuals, as guilty of treason or rebellion. That fearful crisis was past. The appeal lay to the sword, and the only question was, whether the spirit and the resources of the people would hold out, till the object should be accomplished. Nor were its general consequences confined to our own country. The previous proceedings of the Colonies, their appeals, resolutions, and addresses, had made their cause known to Europe. Without boasting, we may say, that in no age or country has the public cause been maintained with more force of argument, more power of illustration, or more of that persuasion which excited feeling and elevated principle can alone bestow, than the Revolutionary state papers exhibit. These papers will forever deserve to be studied, not only for the spirit which they breathe, but for the ability with which they were written.

To this able vindication of their cause, the Colonies had now added a practical and severe proof of their own true devotion to it, and given evidence also of the power which they could bring to its support. All now saw, that if America fell, she would not fall without a struggle. Men felt sympathy and regard, as well as surprise, when they beheld these infant states, remote, unknown, unaided, encounter the power of England, and, in the first considerable battle, leave more of their enemies dead on the field, in proportion to the number of combatants, than had been recently known to fall in the wars of Europe.

Information of these events, circulating throughout the world, at length reached the ears of one who now hears me. He has not forgotten the emotion which the fame of Bunker Hill, and the name of Warren, excited in his youthful breast.

Sir, we are assembled to commemorate the establishment of great public principles of liberty, and to do honor to the distinguished dead. The occasion is too severe for eulogy of the living. But, Sir, your interesting relation to this country, the peculiar circumstances which surround you and surround us, call on me to express the happiness which we derive from your presence and aid in this solemn commemoration.

Fortunate, fortunate man! with what measure of devotion will you not thank God for the circumstances of your extraordinary life! You are connected with both hemispheres and with two generations. Heaven saw fit to ordain, that the electric spark of liberty should be conducted, through you, from the New World to the Old; and we, who are now here to perform this duty of patriotism, have all of us long ago received it in charge from our fathers to cherish your name and your virtues. You will account it an instance of your good fortune, Sir, that you crossed the seas to visit us at a time which enables you to be present at this solemnity. You now behold the field, the renown of which reached you in the heart of France, and caused a thrill in your ardent bosom. You see the lines of the little redoubt thrown up by the incredible diligence of Prescott; defended, to the last extremity, by his lion-hearted valor; and within which the corner-stone of our monument has now taken its position. You see where Warren fell, and where Parker, Gardner, McCleary, Moore, and other early patriots, fell with him. Those who survived that day, and whose lives have been prolonged to the present hour, are now around you. Some of them you have known in the trying scenes of the war. Behold! they now stretch forth their feeble arms to embrace you. Behold! they raise their trembling voices to invoke the blessing of God on you and yours for ever.

Sir, you have assisted us in laying the foundation of this structure. You have heard us rehearse, with our feeble commendation, the names of departed patriots. Monuments and eulogy belong to the dead. We give them this day to Warren and his associates. On other occasions they have been given to your more immediate companions in arms, to Washington, to Greene, to Gates, to Sullivan, and to Lincoln. We have become reluctant to grant these, our highest and last honors, further. We would gladly hold them yet back from the little remnant of that immortal band. *Serus in cœlum redeas.* Illustrious as are your merits, yet far, O, very far distant be the day, when any inscription shall bear your name, or any tongue pronounce its eulogy!

The leading reflection to which this occasion seems to invite us, respects the great changes which have happened in the fifty years since the battle of Bunker Hill was fought. And it peculiarly marks the character of the present age, that, in looking at these changes, and in estimating their effect on our condition, we are obliged to consider, not what has been done in our own country only, but in others also. In these interesting times, while nations are making separate and individual advances in improvement, they make, too, a common progress; like vessels on a common tide, propelled by the gales at different rates, according to their several structure and management, but all moved forward by one mighty current, strong enough to bear onward whatever does not sink beneath it.

A chief distinction of the present day is a community of opinions and knowledge amongst men in different nations, existing in a degree heretofore unknown. Knowledge has, in our time, triumphed, and is triumphing, over distance, over difference of languages, over diversity of habits, over prejudice, and over bigotry. The civilized and Christian world is fast learning the great lesson, that difference of nation does not imply necessary hostility, and that all contact need not be war. The whole world is becoming a common field for intellect to act in. Energy of mind, genius, power, wheresoever it exists, may speak out in any tongue, and the *world* will hear it. A great chord of sentiment and feeling runs through two continents, and vibrates over both. Every breeze wafts intelligence from country to country; every wave rolls it; all give it forth, and all in turn receive it. There is a vast commerce of ideas; there are marts and exchanges for intellectual discoveries, and a wonderful fellowship of those individual intelligences which make up the mind and opinion of the age. Mind is the great lever of all things; human thought is the process by which human ends are ultimately answered; and the diffusion of knowledge, so astonishing in the last half-century, has rendered innumerable minds, variously gifted by nature, competent to be competitors or fellow-workers on the theatre of intellectual operation.

From these causes important improvements have taken place in the personal condition of individuals. Generally speaking, mankind are not only better fed and better clothed, but they are able also to enjoy more leisure; they possess more refinement and more self-respect. A superior tone of education, manners, and habits prevails. This remark, most true in its application to our own country, is also partly true when applied elsewhere. It is proved by the vastly augmented consumption of those articles of manufacture and of commerce which contribute to the comforts and the decencies of life; an augmentation which has far outrun the progress of population. And while the unexampled and almost incredible use of machinery would seem to supply the place of labor, labor still finds its occupation and its reward; so wisely has Providence adjusted men's wants and desires to their condition and their capacity.

Any adequate survey, however, of the progress made during the last half-century in the polite and mechanic arts, in machinery and manufactures, in commerce and agriculture, in letters and in science, would require volumes. I must abstain wholly from these subjects, and turn for a moment to the contemplation of what has been done on the great question of politics and government. This is the master topic of the age; and during the whole fifty years it has intensely occupied the thoughts of men. The nature of civil government, its ends and uses, have been canvassed and investigated; ancient opinions attacked and defended; new ideas recommended and resisted, by whatever power the mind of man could bring to the controversy. From the closet and the public halls the debate has been transferred to the field; and the world has been shaken by wars of unexampled magnitude and the greatest variety of fortune. A day of peace has at length succeeded; and now that the strife has subsided, and the smoke cleared away, we may begin to see what has actually been done, permanently changing the state and condition of human society. And without dwelling on particular circumstances, it is most apparent, that, from the before-mentioned causes of augmented knowledge and improved individual condition, a real, substantial, and important change has taken place, and is taking place, highly favorable, on the whole, to human liberty and human happiness.

The great wheel of political revolution began to move in America. Here its rotation was guarded, regular, and safe. Transferred to the other continent, from unfortunate but natural causes, it received an irregular and violent impulse; it whirled along with a fearful celerity; till at length, like the chariot-wheels in the races of antiquity, it took fire from the rapidity of its own motion, and blazed onward, spreading conflagration and terror around.

We learn from the result of this experiment, how fortunate was our own condition, and how admirably the character of our people was calculated for setting the great example of popular governments. The possession of power did not turn the heads of the American people, for they had long been in the habit of exercising a great deal of self-control. Although the paramount authority of the parent state existed over them, yet a large field of legislation had always been open to our Colonial assemblies. They were accustomed to representative bodies and the forms of free government; they understood the doctrine of the division of power among different branches, and the necessity of checks on each. The character of our countrymen, moreover, was sober, moral, and religious; and there was little in the change to shock their feelings of justice and humanity, or even to disturb an honest prejudice. We had no domestic throne to overturn, no privileged orders to cast down, no violent changes of property to encounter. In the American Revolution, no man sought or wished for more than to defend and enjoy his own. None hoped for plunder or for spoil. Rapacity was unknown to it; the axe was not among the instruments of its accomplishment; and we all know that it could not have lived a single day under any well-founded imputation of possessing a tendency adverse to the Christian religion.

It need not surprise us, that, under circumstances less auspicious, political revolutions elsewhere, even when well intended, have terminated differently. It is, indeed, a great achievement, it is the master-work of the world, to establish governments entirely popular on lasting foundations; nor is it easy, indeed, to introduce the popular principle at all into governments to which it has been altogether a stranger. It cannot be doubted, however, that Europe has come out of the contest, in which she has been so long engaged, with greatly superior knowledge, and, in many respects, in a highly improved condition. Whatever benefit has been acquired is likely to be retained, for it consists mainly in the acquisition of more enlightened ideas. And although kingdoms and provinces may be wrested from the hands that hold them, in the same manner they were obtained; although ordinary and vulgar power may, in human affairs, be lost as it has been won; yet it is the glorious prerogative of the empire of knowledge, that what it gains it never loses. On the contrary, it increases by the multiple of its own power; all its ends become means; all its attainments, helps to new conquests. Its whole abundant harvest is but so much seed wheat, and nothing has limited, and nothing can limit, the amount of ultimate product.

Under the influence of this rapidly increasing knowledge, the people have begun, in all forms of government, to think, and to reason, on affairs of state. Regarding government as an institution for the public good, they demand a knowledge of its operations, and a participation in its exercise. A call for the representative system, wherever it is not enjoyed, and where there is already intelligence enough to estimate its value, is perseveringly made. Where men may speak out, they demand it; where the bayonet is at their throats, they pray for it.

When Louis the Fourteenth said, "I am the state," he expressed the essence of the doctrine of unlimited power. By the rules of that system, the people are disconnected from the state; they are its subjects; it is their lord. These ideas, founded in the love of power, and long supported by the excess and the abuse of it, are yielding, in our age, to other opinions; and the civilized world seems at last to be proceeding to the conviction of that fundamental and manifest truth, that the powers of government are but a trust, and that they cannot be lawfully exercised but for the good of the community. As knowledge is more and more extended, this conviction becomes more and more general. Knowledge, in truth, is the great sun in the firmament. Life and power are scattered with all its beams. The prayer of the Grecian champion, when enveloped in unnatural clouds and darkness, is the appropriate political supplication for the people of every country not yet blessed with free institutions:—

> "Dispel this cloud, the light of heaven restore,
> Give me to see,—and Ajax asks no more."

We may hope that the growing influence of enlightened sentiment will promote the permanent peace of the world. Wars to maintain family alliances, to uphold or to cast down dynasties, and to regulate successions to thrones, which have occupied so much room in the history of modern times, if not less likely to happen at all, will be less likely to become general and involve many nations, as the great principle shall be more and more established, that the interest of the world is peace, and its first great statute, that every nation possesses the power of establishing a government for itself. But public opinion has attained also an influence over governments

which do not admit the popular principle into their organization. A
necessary respect for the judgment of the world operates, in some
measure, as a control over the most unlimited forms of authority. It
is owing, perhaps, to this truth, that the interesting struggle of the
Greeks has been suffered to go on so long, without a direct interference, either to wrest that country from its present masters, or to
execute the system of pacification by force, and, with united strength,
lay the neck of Christian and civilized Greek at the foot of the
barbarian Turk. Let us thank God that we live in an age when
something has influence besides the bayonet, and when the sternest
authority does not venture to encounter the scorching power of
public reproach. Any attempt of the kind I have mentioned should
be met by one universal burst of indignation; the air of the civilized
world ought to be made too warm to be comfortably breathed by
any one who would hazard it.

It is, indeed, a touching reflection, that, while in the fulness of
our country's happiness, we rear this monument to her honor, we
look for instruction in our undertaking to a country which is now
in fearful contest, not for works of art or memorials of glory, but
for her own existence. Let her be assured, that she is not forgotten
in the world; that her efforts are applauded, and that constant
prayers ascend for her success. And let us cherish a confident hope
for her final triumph. If the true spark of religious and civil liberty
be kindled, it will burn. Human agency cannot extinguish it. Like
the earth's central fire, it may be smothered for a time; the ocean
may overwhelm it; mountains may press it down; but its inherent
and unconquerable force will heave both the ocean and the land,
and at some time or other, in some place or other, the volcano will
break out and flame up to heaven.

Among the great events of the half-century, we must reckon,
certainly, the revolution of South America; and we are not likely to
overrate the importance of that revolution, either to the people of
the country itself or to the rest of the world. The late Spanish
colonies, now independent states, under circumstances less favorable,
doubtless, than attended our own revolution, have yet successfully
commenced their national existence. They have accomplished the

great object of establishing their independence; they are known and acknowledged in the world; and although in regard to their systems of government, their sentiments on religious toleration, and their provisions for public instruction, they may have yet much to learn, it must be admitted that they have risen to the condition of settled and established states more rapidly than could have been reasonably anticipated. They already furnish an exhilarating example of the difference between free governments and despotic misrule. Their commerce, at this moment, creates a new activity in all the great marts of the world. They show themselves able, by an exchange of commodities, to bear a useful part in the intercourse of nations.

A new spirit of enterprise and industry begins to prevail; all the great interests of society receive a salutary impulse; and the progress of information not only testifies to an improved condition, but itself constitutes the highest and most essential improvement.

When the battle of Bunker Hill was fought, the existence of South America was scarcely felt in the civilized world. The thirteen little Colonies of North America habitually called themselves the "Continent." Borne down by colonial subjugation, monopoly, and bigotry, these vast regions of the South were hardly visible above the horizon. But in our day there has been, as it were, a new creation. The southern hemisphere emerges from the sea. Its lofty mountains begin to lift themselves into the light of heaven; its broad and fertile plains stretch out, in beauty, to the eye of civilized man, and at the mighty bidding of the voice of political liberty the waters of darkness retire.

And, now, let us indulge an honest exultation in the conviction of the benefit which the example of our country has produced, and is likely to produce, on human freedom and human happiness. Let us endeavor to comprehend in all its magnitude, and to feel in all its importance, the part assigned to us in the great drama of human affairs. We are placed at the head of the system of representative and popular governments. Thus far our example shows that such governments are compatible, not only with respectability and power, but with repose, with peace, with security of personal rights, with good laws, and a just administration.

We are not propagandists. Wherever other systems are preferred, either as being thought better in themselves, or as better suited to existing condition, we leave the preference to be enjoyed. Our history hitherto proves, however, that the popular form is practicable, and that with wisdom and knowledge men may govern themselves; and the duty incumbent on us is, to preserve the consistency of this cheering example, and take care that nothing may weaken its authority with the world. If, in our case, the representative system ultimately fail, popular governments must be pronounced impossible. No combination of circumstances more favorable to the experiment can ever be expected to occur. The last hopes of mankind, therefore, rest with us; and if it should be proclaimed, that our example had become an argument against the experiment, the knell of popular liberty would be sounded throughout the earth.

These are excitements to duty; but they are not suggestions of doubt. Our history and our condition, all that is gone before us, and all that surrounds us, authorize the belief, that popular governments, though subject to occasional variations, in form perhaps not always for the better, may yet, in their general character, be as durable and permanent as other systems. We know, indeed, that in our country any other is impossible. The *principle* of free governments adheres to the American soil. It is bedded in it, immovable as its mountains.

And let the sacred obligations which have devolved on this generation, and on us, sink deep into our hearts. Those who established our liberty and our government are daily dropping from among us. The great trust now descends to new hands. Let us apply ourselves to that which is presented to us, as our appropriate object. We can win no laurels in a war for independence. Earlier and worthier hands have gathered them all. Nor are there places for us by the side of Solon, and Alfred, and other founders of states. Our fathers have filled them. But there remains to us a great duty of defence and preservation, and there is opened to us, also, a noble pursuit, to which the spirit of the times strongly invites us. Our proper business is improvement. Let our age be the age of improvement. In a day of peace, let us advance the arts of peace and the works of peace. Let us develop the resources of our land, call forth its powers, build up its institutions, promote all its great interests, and see whether we also, in our day and generation, may not perform something worthy to be remembered. Let us cultivate a true spirit of union and harmony. In pursuing the great objects which our condition points out to us, let us act under a settled conviction, and an habitual feeling, that these twenty-four States are one country. Let our conceptions be enlarged to the circle of our duties. Let us extend our ideas over the whole of the vast field in which we are called to act. Let our object be, *Our Country, Our Whole Country, and Nothing but Our Country*. And, by the blessing of God, may that country itself become a vast and splendid monument, not of oppression and terror, but of Wisdom, of Peace, and of Liberty, upon which the world may gaze with admiration for ever!

Daniel Webster

———————

THE MURDER OF

CAPTAIN JOSEPH WHITE

¶ WEBSTER maintained, throughout his long career of public service, an extensive legal practice. In the summer of 1830, only a few months after his "Reply to Hayne" in the Senate, he was called to Salem, Massachusetts, to assist in the prosecution of the murderers of Captain Joseph White, a wealthy and aged merchant. Joseph Knapp, a distant relative of Mr. White, hoped through his death and the destruction of his will to fall heir to a large part of his fortune. He stole and destroyed the will and conspired with his brother Frank and with George and Richard Crowninshield to commit the murder. They were detected largely through interception of a blackmail letter from a young ex-convict named Palmer, who had been told of their plot. While the four were in prison Joseph Knapp agreed to confess the whole plot on promise of immunity, an agreement he failed to keep at the trial. Richard Crowninshield, who had alone accomplished the murder, committed suicide. Frank Knapp was first brought to trial as a principal in the crime. As the law then stood, an accessory in a murder could not be tried until a principal had been convicted. Webster's speech was delivered in summing up the government's case against Frank Knapp as a principal in the crime.

I AM little accustomed, Gentlemen, to the part which I am now attempting to perform. Hardly more than once or twice has it happened to me to be concerned on the side of the government in any criminal prosecution whatever; and never, until the present occasion, in any case affecting life.

122

But I very much regret that it should have been thought necessary to suggest to you that I am brought here to "hurry you against
the law and beyond the evidence." I hope I have too much regard
for justice, and too much respect for my own character, to attempt
either; and were I to make such attempt, I am sure that in this
court nothing can be carried against the law, and that gentlemen,
intelligent and just as you are, are not, by any power, to be hurried
beyond the evidence. Though I could well have wished to shun
this occasion. I have not felt at liberty to withhold my professional
assistance, when it is supposed that I may be in some degree useful
in investigating and discovering the truth respecting this most
extraordinary murder. It has seemed to be a duty incumbent on me,
as on every other citizen, to do my best and my utmost to bring
to light the perpetrators of this crime. Against the prisoner at the
bar, as an individual, I cannot have the slightest prejudice. I would
not do him the smallest injury or injustice. But I do not affect to be
indifferent to the discovery and the punishment of this deep guilt.
I cheerfully share in the opprobrium, how great soever it may be,
which is cast on those who feel and manifest an anxious concern
that all who had a part in planning, or a hand in executing, this
deed of midnight assassination, may be brought to answer for their
enormous crime at the bar of public justice.

Gentlemen, it is a most extraordinary case. In some respects, it
has hardly a precedent anywhere; certainly none in our New England history. This bloody drama exhibited no suddenly excited,
ungovernable rage. The actors in it were not surprised by any lion-
like temptation springing upon their virtue, and overcoming it,
before resistance could begin. Nor did they do the deed to glut
savage vengeance, or satiate long-settled and deadly hate. It was a
cool, calculating, money-making murder. It was all "hire and salary,
not revenge." It was the weighing of money against life; the counting out of so many pieces of silver against so many ounces of blood.

An aged man, without an enemy in the world, in his own house,
and in his own bed, is made the victim of a butcherly murder, for
mere pay. Truly, here is a new lesson for painters and poets. Whoever shall hereafter draw the portrait of murder, if he will show it as

it has been exhibited, where such example was last to have been looked for, in the very bosom of our New England society, let him not give it the grim visage of Moloch, the brow knitted by revenge, the face black with settled hate, and the blood-shot eye emitting livid fires of malice. Let him draw, rather, a decorous, smooth-faced, bloodless demon; a picture in repose, rather than in action; not so much an example of human nature in its depravity, and in its paroxysms of crime, as an infernal being, a fiend, in the ordinary display and development of his character.

The deed was executed with a degree of self-possession and steadiness equal to the wickedness with which it was planned. The circumstances now clearly in evidence spread out the whole scene before us. Deep sleep had fallen on the destined victim, and on all beneath his roof. A healthful old man, to whom sleep was sweet, the first sound slumbers of the night held him in their soft but strong embrace. The assassin enters, through the window already prepared, into an unoccupied apartment. With noiseless foot he paces the lonely hall, half lighted by the moon; he winds up the ascent of the stairs, and reaches the door of the chamber. Of this, he moves the lock, by soft and continued pressure, till it turns on its hinges without noise; and he enters, and beholds his victim before him. The room is uncommonly open to the admission of light. The face of the innocent sleeper is turned from the murderer, and the beams of the moon, resting on the gray locks of his aged temple, show him where to strike. The fatal blow is given! and the victim passes, without a struggle or a motion, from the repose of sleep to the repose of death! It is the assassin's purpose to make sure work; and he plies the dagger, through it is obvious that life has been destroyed by the blow of the bludgeon. He even raises the aged arm, that he may not fail in his aim at the heart, and replaces it again over the wounds of the poniard! To finish the picture, he explores the wrist for the pulse! He feels for it, and ascertains that it beats no longer! It is accomplished. The deed is done. He retreats, retraces his steps to the window, passes out through it as he came in, and escapes. He has done the murder. No eye has seen him, no ear has heard him. The secret is his own, and it is safe!

Ah! Gentlemen, that was a dreadful mistake. Such a secret can be safe nowhere. The whole creation of God has neither nook nor corner where the guilty can bestow it, and say it is safe. Not to speak of that eye which pierces through all disguises, and beholds every thing as in the splendor of noon, such secrets of guilt are never safe from detection, even by men. True it is, generally speaking, that "murder will out." True it is, that Providence has so ordained, and doth so govern things, that those who break the great law of Heaven by shedding man's blood seldom succeed in avoiding discovery. Especially, in a case exciting so much attention as this, discovery must come, and will come, sooner or later. A thousand eyes turn at once to explore every man, every thing, every circumstance, connected with the time and place; a thousand ears catch every whisper; a thousand excited minds intensely dwell on the scene, shedding all their light, and ready to kindle the slightest circumstance into a blaze of discovery. Meantime the guilty soul cannot keep its own secret. It is false to itself; or rather it feels an irresistible impulse of conscience to be true to itself. It labors under its guilty possession, and knows not what to do with it. The human heart was not made for the residence of such an inhabitant. It finds itself preyed on by a torment, which it dares not acknowledge to God or man. A vulture is devouring it, and it can ask no sympathy or assistance, either from heaven or earth. The secret which the murderer possesses soon comes to possess him; and, like the evil spirits of which we read, it overcomes him, and leads him whithersoever it will. He feels it beating at his heart, rising to his throat, and demanding disclosure. He thinks the whole world sees it in his face, reads it in his eyes, and almost hears its workings in the very silence of his thoughts. It has become his master. It betrays his discretion, it breaks down his courage, it conquers his prudence. When suspicions from without begin to embarrass him, and the net of circumstance to entangle him, the fatal secret struggles with still greater violence to burst forth. It must be confessed, it will be confessed; there is no refuge from confession but suicide, and suicide is confession.

Much has been said, on this occasion, of the excitement which has existed, and still exists, and of the extraordinary measures taken to discover and punish the guilty. No doubt there has been, and is, much excitement, and strange indeed it would be had it been otherwise. Should not all the peaceable and well-disposed naturally feel concerned, and naturally exert themselves to bring to punishment the authors of this secret assassination? Was it a thing to be slept upon or forgotten? Did you, Gentlemen, sleep quite as quietly in your beds after this murder as before? Was it not a case for rewards, for meetings, for committees, for the united efforts of all the good, to find out a band of murderous conspirators, of midnight ruffians, and to bring them to the bar of justice and law? If this be excitement, is it an unnatural or an improper excitement?

It seems to me, Gentlemen, that there are appearances of another feeling, of a very different nature and character; not very extensive, I would hope, but still there is too much evidence of its existence. Such is human nature, that some persons lose their abhorrence of crime in their admiration of its magnificent exhibitions. Ordinary vice is reprobated by them, but extraordinary guilt, exquisite wickedness, the high flights and poetry of crime, seize on the imagination, and lead them to forget the depths of the guilt, in admiration of the excellence of the performance, or the unequalled atrocity of the purpose. There are those in our day who have made great use of this infirmity of our nature, and by means of it done infinite injury to the cause of good morals. They have affected not only the taste, but I fear also the principles, of the young, the heedless, and the imaginative, by the exhibition of interesting and beautiful monsters. They render depravity attractive, sometimes by the polish of its manners, and sometimes by its very extravagance; and study to show off crime under all the advantages of cleverness and dexterity. Gentlemen, this is an extraordinary murder, but it is still a murder. We are not to lose ourselves in wonder at its origin, or in gazing on its cool and skilful execution. We are to detect and to punish it; and while we proceed with caution against the prisoner, and are to be sure that we do not visit on his head the offences of others, we are yet to consider that we are dealing with a case of most atrocious crime, which has not the slightest circumstance about it to soften its enormity. It is murder; deliberate, concerted, malicious murder.

Although the interest of this case may have diminished by the repeated investigation of the facts; still, the additional labor which it imposes upon all concerned is not to be regretted, if it should result in removing all doubts of the guilt of the prisoner.

The learned counsel for the prisoner has said truly, that it is your individual duty to judge the prisoner; that it is your individual duty to determine his guilt or innocence; and that you are to weigh the testimony with candor and fairness. But much at the same time has been said, which, although it would seem to have no distinct bearing on the trial, cannot be passed over without some notice.

A tone of complaint so peculiar has been indulged, as would almost lead us to doubt whether the prisoner at the bar, or the managers of this prosecution, are now on trial. Great pains have been taken to complain of the manner of the prosecution. We hear of getting up a case; of setting in motion trains of machinery; of foul testimony; of combinations to overwhelm the prisoner; of private prosecutors; that the prisoner is hunted, persecuted, driven to his trial; that every body is against him; and various other complaints, as if those who would bring to punishment the authors of this murder were almost as bad as they who committed it.

In the course of my whole life, I have never heard before so much said about the particular counsel who happen to be employed; as if it were extraordinary that other counsel than the usual officers of the government should assist in the management of a case on the part of the government. In one of the last criminal trials in this county, that of Jackman for the "Goodridge robbery" (so called), I remember that the learned head of the Suffolk Bar, Mr. Prescott, came down in aid of the officers of the government. This was regarded as neither strange nor improper. The counsel for the prisoner, in that case, contented themselves with answering his arguments, as far as they were able, instead of carping at his presence.

Complaint is made that rewards were offered, in this case, and temptations held out to obtain testimony. Are not rewards always offered, when great and secret offences are committed? Rewards were offered in the case to which I have alluded; and every other means taken to discover the offenders, that ingenuity or the most persevering vigilance could suggest. The learned counsel have suffered their zeal to lead them into a strain of complaint at the manner in which the perpetrators of this crime were detected, almost indicating that they regard it as a positive injury to them to have found out their guilt. Since no man witnessed it, since they do not now confess it, attempts to discover it are half esteemed as officious intermeddling and impertinent inquiry.

It is said, that here even a Committee of Vigilance was appointed. This is a subject of reiterated remark. This committee are pointed at, as though they had been officiously intermeddling with the administration of justice. They are said to have been "laboring for months" against the prisoner. Gentlemen, what must we do in such a case? Are people to be dumb and still, through fear of over-doing? Is it come to this, that an effort cannot be made, a hand cannot be lifted, to discover the guilty, without its being said there is a combination to overwhelm innocence? Has the community lost all moral sense? Certainly, a community that would not be roused to action upon an occasion such as this was, a community which should not deny sleep to their eyes, and slumber to their eyelids, till they had exhausted all the means of discovery and detection, must indeed be lost to all moral sense, and would scarcely deserve protection from the laws. The learned counsel have endeavored to persuade you, that there exists a prejudice against the persons accused of this murder. They would have you understand that it is not confined to this vicinity alone; but that even the legislature have caught this spirit. That through the procurement of the gentleman here styled private prosecutor, who is a member of the Senate, a special session of this court was appointed for the trial of these offenders. That the ordinary movements of the wheels of justice were too slow for the purposes devised. But does not every body see and know, that it was matter of absolute necessity to have a special session of the court? When or how could the prisoners have been tried without a special session? In the ordinary arrangement of the courts, but one week in a year is allotted for the whole court to sit in this county. In the trial of all capital offences a majority of the court, at least, is required to be present. In the trial of the present case alone, three weeks have already been taken up. Without such special session, then, three years would not have been sufficient for the purpose. It is answer sufficient to all complaints on this subject to say, that the law was drawn by the late Chief Justice himself, to enable the court to accomplish its duties, and to afford the persons accused an opportunity for trial without delay.

Again, it is said that it was not thought of making Francis Knapp, the prisoner at the bar, a principal till after the death of Richard Crowninshield, Jr.; that the present indictment is an afterthought; that "testimony was got up" for the occasion. It is not so. There is no authority for this suggestion. The case of the Knapps had not then been before the grand jury. The officers of the government did not know what the testimony would be against them. They could not, therefore, have determined what course they should pursue. They intended to arraign all as principals who should appear to have been principals, and all as accessories who should appear to have been accessories. All this could be known only when the evidence should be produced.

But the learned counsel for the defendant take a somewhat loftier flight still. They are more concerned, they assure us, for the law itself, than even for their client. Your decision in this case, they say, will stand as a precedent. Gentlemen, we hope it will. We hope it will be a precedent both of candor and intelligence, of fairness and of firmness; a precedent of good sense and honest purpose pursuing their investigation discreetly, rejecting loose generalities, exploring all the circumstances, weighing each, in search of truth, and embracing and declaring the truth when found.

It is said, that "laws are made, not for the punishment of the guilty, but for the protection of the innocent." This is not quite accurate, perhaps, but if so, we hope they will be so administered as to give that protection. But who are the innocent whom the law would protect? Gentlemen, Joseph White was innocent. They are innocent who, having lived in the fear of God through the day, wish to sleep in His peace through the night, in their own beds. The law is established that those who live quietly may sleep quietly; that they who do no harm may feel none. The gentleman can think of none that are innocent except the prisoner at the bar, not yet convicted. Is a proved conspirator to murder innocent? Are the Crowninshields and the Knapps innocent? What is innocence? How deep stained with blood, how reckless in crime, how deep in depravity may it be, and yet retain innocence? The law is made, if we would speak with entire accuracy, to protect the innocent by punishing the guilty. But there are those innocent out of a court, as well as in; innocent citizens not suspected of crime, as well as innocent prisoners at the bar.

The criminal law is not founded in a principle of vengeance. It does not punish that it may inflict suffering. The humanity of the law feels and regrets every pain it causes, every hour of restraint it imposes, and more deeply still every life it forfeits. But it uses evil as the means of preventing greater evil. It seeks to deter from crime by the example of punishment. This is its true, and only true main object. It restrains the liberty of the few offenders, that the many who do not offend may enjoy their liberty. It takes the life of the murderer, that other murders may not be committed. The law might open the jails, and at once set free all persons accused of offences, and it ought to do so if it could be made certain that no other offences would hereafter be committed; because it punishes, not to satisfy any desire to inflict pain, but simply to prevent the repetition of crimes. When the guilty, therefore, are not punished, the law has so far failed of its purpose; the safety of the innocent is so far endangered. Every unpunished murder takes away something from the security of every man's life. Whenever a jury, through whimsical and ill-founded scruples, suffer the guilty to escape, they make themselves answerable for the augmented danger of the innocent.

We wish nothing to be strained against this defendant. Why, then, all this alarm? Why all this complaint against the manner in which the crime is discovered? The prisoner's counsel catch at supposed flaws of evidence, or bad character of witnesses, without meeting the case. Do they mean to deny the conspiracy? Do they mean to deny that the two Crowninshields and the two Knapps were conspirators? Why do they rail against Palmer, while they do not disprove, and hardly dispute, the truth of any one fact sworn to by him? Instead of this, it is made matter of sentimentality that Palmer has been prevailed upon to betray his bosom companions and to violate the sanctity of friendship. Again I ask, Why do they not meet the case? If the fact is out, why not meet it? Do they mean to deny that Captain White is dead? One would have almost supposed even that, from some remarks that have been made. Do they mean to deny the conspiracy? Or, admitting a conspiracy, do they mean to deny only that Frank Knapp, the prisoner at the bar, was abetting in the murder, being present, and so deny that he was a principal? If a conspiracy is proved, it bears closely upon every subsequent subject of inquiry. Why do they not come to the fact? Here the defence is wholly indistinct. The counsel neither take the ground, nor abandon it. They neither fly, nor light. They hover. But they must come to a closer mode of contest. They must meet the facts, and either deny or admit them. Had the prisoner at the bar, then, a knowledge of this conspiracy or not? This is the question. Instead of laying out their strength in complaining of the *manner* in which the deed is discovered, of the extraordinary pains taken to bring the prisoner's guilt to light, would it not be better to show there was no guilt? Would it not be better to show his innocence? They say, and they complain, that the community feel a great desire that he should be punished for his crimes. Would it not be better to convince you that he has committed no crime?

Gentlemen, let us now come to the case. Your first inquiry, on the evidence, will be, Was Captain White murdered in pursuance of a conspiracy, and was the defendant one of this conspiracy? If so, the second inquiry is, Was he so connected with the murder itself as that he is liable to be convicted as a *principal?* The defendant is indicted as a *principal.* If not guilty *as such,* you cannot convict him. The indictment contains three distinct classes of counts. In the first, he is charged as having done the deed with his own hand; in the second, as an aider and abettor to Richard Crowninshield, Jr., who did the deed; in the third, as an aider and abettor to some person unknown. If you believe him guilty on either of these counts, or in either of these ways, you must convict him.

It may be proper to say, as a preliminary remark, that there are two extraordinary circumstances attending this trial. One is, that Richard Crowninshield, Jr., the supposed immediate perpetrator of the murder, since his arrest, has committed suicide. He has gone to answer before a tribunal of perfect infallibility. The other is, that Joseph Knapp, the supposed originator and planner of the murder, having once made a full disclosure of the facts, under a promise of indemnity, is, nevertheless, not now a witness. Notwithstanding his disclosure and his promise of indemnity, he now refuses to testify. He chooses to return to his original state, and now stands answerable himself, when the time shall come for his trial. These circumstances it is fit you should remember, in your investigation of the case.

Your decision may affect more than the life of this defendant. If he be not convicted as principal, no one can be. Nor can any one be convicted of a participation in the crime as accessory. The Knapps and George Crowninshield will be again on the community. This shows the importance of the duty you have to perform, and serves to remind you of the care and wisdom necessary to be exercised in its performance. But certainly these considerations do not render the prisoner's guilt any clearer, nor enhance the weight of the evidence against him. No one desires you to regard consequences in that light. No one wishes any thing to be strained, or too far pressed against the prisoner. Still, it is fit you should see the full importance of the duty which devolves upon you.

And now, Gentlemen, in examining this evidence, let us begin at the beginning, and see first what we know independent of the disputed testimony. This is a case of circumstantial evidence. And these circumstances, we think, are full and satisfactory. The case mainly depends upon them, and it is common that offences of this kind must be proved in this way. Midnight assassins take no witnesses. The evidence of the facts relied on has been somewhat sneeringly denominated by the learned counsel, "circumstantial stuff," but it is not such stuff as dreams are made of. Why does he not rend this stuff? Why does he not scatter it to the winds? He dismisses it a little too summarily. It shall be my business to examine this stuff, and try its cohesion.

The letter from Palmer at Belfast, is that no more than flimsy stuff?

The fabricated letters from Knapp to the committee and to Mr. White, are they nothing but stuff?

The circumstance, that the housekeeper was away at the time the murder was committed, as it was agreed she would be, is that, too, a useless piece of the same stuff?

The facts, that the key of the chamber door was taken out and secreted; that the window was unbarred and unbolted; are these to be so slightly and so easily disposed of?

It is necessary, Gentlemen, to settle now, at the commencement, the great question of a conspiracy. If there was none, or the defendant was not a party, then there is no evidence here to convict him. If there was a conspiracy, and he is proved to have been a party, then these two facts have a strong bearing on others, and all the great points of inquiry. The defendant's counsel take no distinct ground, as I have already said, on this point, either to admit or to deny. They choose to confine themselves to a hypothetical mode of speech. They say, supposing there was a conspiracy, *non sequitur* that the prisoner is guilty as principal. Be it so. But still, if there was a conspiracy, and if he was a conspirator, and helped to plan the murder, this may shed much light on the evidence which goes to charge him with the execution of that plan.

We mean to make out the conspiracy; and that the defendant was a party to it; and then to draw all just inferences from these facts.

Let me ask your attention, then, in the first place, to those appearances, on the morning after the murder, which have a tendency to show that it was done in pursuance of a preconcerted plan of operation. What are they? A man was found murdered in his bed. No stranger had done the deed, no one unacquainted with the house had done it. It was apparent that somebody within had opened, and that somebody without had entered. There had obviously and certainly been concert and cooperation. The inmates of the house were not alarmed when the murder was perpetrated. The assassin had entered without any riot or any violence. He had found the way prepared before him. The house had been previously opened. The window was unbarred from within, and its fastening unscrewed. There was a lock on the door of the chamber in which Mr. White slept, but the key was gone. It had been taken away and secreted. The footsteps of the murderer were visible, out doors, tending toward the window. The plank by which he entered the window still remained. The road he pursued had been thus prepared for him. The victim was slain, and the murderer had escaped. Every thing indicated that somebody within had cooperated with somebody without. Every-thing proclaimed that some inmates, or somebody having access to the house, had had a hand in the murder. On the face of the circum-stances, it was apparent, therefore, that this was a premeditated, concerted murder; that there had been a conspiracy to commit it. Who, then, were the conspirators? If not now found out, we are still groping in the dark, and the whole tragedy is still a mystery.

If the Knapps and the Crowninshields were not the conspirators in this murder, then there is a whole set of conspirators not yet dis-covered. Because, independent of the testimony of Palmer and Leighton, independent of all disputed evidence, we know, from uncontroverted facts, that this murder was, and must have been, the result of concert and cooperation between two or more. We know it was not done without plan and deliberation; we see, that whoever entered the house, to strike the blow, was favored and aided by some one who had been previously in the house, without suspicion, and who had prepared the way. This is concert, this is cooperation, this is conspiracy. If the Knapps and the Crowninshields, then, were not the conspirators, who were? Joseph Knapp had a motive to desire the death of Mr. White, and that motive has been shown.

He was connected by marriage with the family of Mr. White. His wife was the daughter of Mrs. Beckford, who was the only child of a sister of the deceased. The deceased was more than eighty years old, and had no children. His only heirs were nephews and nieces. He was supposed to be possessed of a very large fortune, which would have descended, by law, to his several nephews and nieces in equal shares; or, if there was a will, then according to the will. But as he had but two branches of heirs, the children of his brother, Henry White, and of Mrs. Beckford, each of these branches, accord-ing to the common idea, would have shared one half of his property.

This popular idea is not legally correct. But it is common, and very probably was entertained by the parties. According to this idea, Mrs. Beckford, on Mr. White's death without a will, would have been entitled to one half of his ample fortune; and Joseph Knapp had married one of her three children. There was a will, and this will gave the bulk of the property to others; and we learn from Palmer that one part of the design was to destroy the will before the murder was committed. There had been a previous will, and that previous will was known or believed to have been more favorable than the other to the Beckford family. So that, by destroying the last will, and destroying the life of the testator at the same time, either the first and more favorable will would be set up, or the deceased would have no will, which would be, as was supposed, still more favorable. But the conspirators not having succeeded in obtaining and destroying the last will, though they accomplished the murder, that will being found in existence and safe, and that will bequeathing the mass of the property to others, it seemed at the time impossible for Joseph Knapp, as for any one else, indeed, but the principal devisee, to have any motive which should lead to the murder. The key which unlocks the whole mystery is the knowledge of the intention of the conspirators to steal the will. This is derived from Palmer, and it explains all. It solves the whole marvel. It shows the motive which actuated those, against whom there is much evidence, but who, without the knowledge of this intention, were not seen to have had a motive. This intention is proved, as I have said, by Palmer; and it is so congruous with all the rest of the case, it agrees so well with all facts and circumstances, that no man could well withhold his belief, though the facts were stated by a still less credible witness. If one desirous of opening a lock turns over and tries a bunch of keys till he finds one that will open it, he naturally supposes he has found *the* key of *that* lock. So, in explaining circumstances of evidence which are apparently irreconcilable or unaccountable, if a fact be suggested which at once accounts for all, and reconciles all, by whomsoever it may be stated, it is still difficult not to believe that such fact is the true fact belonging to the case. In this respect, Palmer's testimony is singularly confirmed. If it were false, his ingenuity could not furnish us such clear exposition of strange appearing circumstances. Some truth not before known can alone do that.

When we look back, then, to the state of things immediately on the discovery of the murder, we see that suspicion would naturally turn at once, not to the heirs at law, but to those principally benefited by the will. They, and they alone, would be supposed or seem to have a direct object for wishing Mr. White's life to be terminated. And, strange as it may seem, we find counsel now insisting, that, if no apology, it is yet mitigation of the atrocity of the Knapps' conduct in attempting to charge this foul murder on Mr. White, the nephew and principal devisee, that public suspicion was already so directed! As if assassination of character were excusable in proportion as circumstances may render it easy. Their endeavors, when they knew they were suspected themselves, to fix the charge on others, by foul means and by falsehood, are fair and strong proof of their own guilt. But more of that hereafter.

The counsel say that they might safely admit that Richard Crowninshield, Jr., was the perpetrator of this murder.

But how could they safely admit that? If that were admitted, every thing else would follow. For why should Richard Crowninshield, Jr., kill Mr. White? He was not his heir, nor his devisee; nor was he his enemy. What could be his motive? If Richard Crowninshield, Jr., killed Mr. White, he did it at some one's procurement who himself had a motive. And who, having any motive, is shown to have had any intercourse with Richard Crowninshield, Jr., but Joseph Knapp, and this principally through the agency of the prisoner at the bar? It is the infirmity, the distressing difficulty of the prisoner's case, that his counsel cannot and dare not admit what they yet cannot disprove, and what all must believe. He who believes, on this evidence, that Richard Crowninshield, Jr., was the immediate murderer, cannot doubt that both the Knapps were conspirators in that murder. The counsel, therefore, are wrong, I think, in saying they might safely admit this. The admission of so important and so connected a fact would render it impossible to contend further against the proof of the entire conspiracy, as we state it.

What, then, was this conspiracy? J. J. Knapp, Jr., desirous of destroying the will, and of taking the life of the deceased, hired a ruffian, who, with the aid of other ruffians, was to enter the house, and murder him in his bed.

As far back as January this conspiracy began. Endicott testifies to a conversation with J. J. Knapp at that time, in which Knapp told him that Captain White had made a will, and given the principal part of his property to Stephen White. When asked how he knew, he said, "Black and white don't lie." When asked if the will was not locked up, he said, "There is such a thing as two keys to the same lock." And speaking of the then late illness of Captain White, he said, that Stephen White would not have been sent for if *he* had been there.

Hence it appears, that as early as January Knapp had a knowledge of the will, and that he had access to it by means of false keys. This knowledge of the will, and an intent to destroy it, appear also from Palmer's testimony, a fact disclosed to him by the other conspirators. He says that he was informed of this by the Crowninshields on the 2d of April. But then it is said that Palmer is not to be credited; that by his own confession he is a felon; that he has been in the State prison in Maine; and, above all, that he was intimately associated with these conspirators themselves. Let us admit these facts. Let us admit him to be as bad as they would represent him to be; still, in law, he is a competent witness. How else are the secret designs of the wicked to be proved, but by their wicked companions, to whom they have disclosed them? The government does not select its witnesses. The conspirators themselves have chosen Palmer. He was the confidant of the prisoners. The fact, however, does not depend on his testimony alone. It is corroborated by other proof; and, taken in connection with the other circumstances, it has strong probability. In regard to the testimony of Palmer, generally, it may be said that it is less contradicted, in all parts of it, either by himself or others, than that of any other material witness, and that every thing he has told is corroborated by other evidence, so far as it is susceptible of confirmation. An attempt has been made to impair his testimony, as to his being at the Half-way House on the night of the murder; you have seen with what success. Mr. Babb is called to contradict him. You have seen how little he knows, and even that not certainly; for he himself is proved to have been in an error by supposing Palmer to have been at the Half-way House on the evening of the 9th of April. At that time he is proved to have been at Dustin's, in Danvers. If, then, Palmer, bad as he is, has disclosed the secrets of the conspiracy, and has told the truth, there is no reason why it should not be believed. Truth is truth, come whence it may.

The facts show that this murder had been long in agitation; that it was not a new proposition on the 2d of April; that it had been contemplated for five or six weeks. Richard Crowninshield was at Wenham in the latter part of March, as testified by Starrett. Frank Knapp was at Danvers in the latter part of February, as testified by Allen. Richard Crowninshield inquired whether Captain Knapp was about home, when at Wenham. The probability is, that they would open the case to Palmer as a new project. There are other circumstances that show it to have been some weeks in agitation. Palmer's testimony as to the transactions on the 2d of April is corroborated by Allen, and by Osborn's books. He says that Frank Knapp came there in the afternoon, and again in the evening. So the book shows. He says that Captain White had gone out to his farm on that day. So others prove. How could this fact, or these facts, have been known to Palmer, unless Frank Knapp had brought the knowledge? And was it not the special object of this visit to give information of this fact, that they might meet him and execute their purpose on his return from his farm? The letter of Palmer, written at Belfast, bears intrinsic marks of genuineness. It was mailed at Belfast, May 13th. It states facts that he could not have known, unless his testimony be true. This letter was not an afterthought; it is a genuine narrative. In fact, it says, "I know the business your brother Frank was transacting on the 2d of April." How could he have possibly known this, unless he had been there? The "one thousand dollars that was to be paid"; where could he have obtained this knowledge? The testimony of Endicott, of Palmer, and these facts, are to be taken together; and they most clearly show that the death of Captain White was caused by somebody interested in putting an end to his life.

As to the testimony of Leighton, as far as manner of testifying goes, he is a bad witness; but it does not follow from this that he is not to be believed. There are some strange things about him. It is strange, that he should make up a story against Captain Knapp, the person with whom he lived; that he never voluntarily told any thing; all that he has said was screwed out of him. But the story could not have been invented by him; his character for truth is unimpeached; and he intimated to another witness, soon after the murder happened, that he knew something he should not tell. There is not the least contradiction in his testimony, though he gives a poor account of withholding it. He says that he was extremely *bothered* by those who questioned him. In the main story that he relates, he is entirely consistent with himself. Some things are for him, and some against him. Examine the intrinsic probability of what he says. See if some allowance is not to be made for him, on account of his ignorance of things of this kind. It is said to be extraordinary, that he should have heard just so much of the conversation, and no more; that he should have heard just what was necessary to be proved, and nothing else. Admit that this is extraordinary; still, this does not prove it untrue. It is extraordinary that you twelve gentlemen should be called upon, out of all the men in the county, to decide this case; no one could have foretold this three weeks since. It is extraordinary that the first clew to this conspiracy should have been derived from information given by the father of the prisoner at the bar. And in every case that comes to trial there are many things extraordinary. The murder itself is a most extraordinary one; but still we do not doubt its reality.

It is argued, that this conversation between Joseph and Frank could not have been as Leighton has testified, because they had been together for several hours before; this subject must have been uppermost in their minds, whereas this appears to have been the commencement of their conversation upon it. Now this depends altogether upon the tone and manner of the expression; upon the particular word in the sentence which was emphatically spoken. If he had said, "When did you *see* Dick, Frank?" this would not seem to be the beginning of the conversation. With what emphasis it was uttered, it is not possible to learn; and therefore nothing can be made of this argument. If this boy's testimony stood alone, it should be received with caution. And the same may be said of the testimony of Palmer. But they do not stand alone. They furnish a clew to numerous other circumstances, which, when known, mutually confirm what would have been received with caution without such corroboration. How could Leighton have made up this conversation? "When did you see Dick?" "I saw him this morning." "When is he going to kill the old man?" "I don't know." "Tell him, if he don't do it soon, I won't pay him." Here is a vast amount in a few words. Had he wit enough to invent this? There is nothing so powerful as truth; and often nothing so strange. It is not even suggested that the story was made for him. There is nothing so extraordinary in the whole matter, as it would have been for this ignorant country boy to invent this story.

The acts of the parties themselves furnish strong presumption of their guilt. What was done on the receipt of the letter from Maine? This letter was signed by Charles Grant, Jr., a person not known to either of the Knapps, nor was it known to them that any other person beside the Crowninshields knew of the conspiracy. This letter, by the accidental omission of the word Jr., fell into the hands of the father, when intended for the son. The father carried it to Wenham where both the sons were. They both read it. Fix your eye steadily on this part of the *circumstantial stuff* which is in the case, and see what can be made of it. This was shown to the two brothers on Saturday, the 15th of May. Neither of them knew Palmer. And if they had known him, they could not have known him to have been the writer of this letter. It was mysterious to them how any one at Belfast could have had knowledge of this affair. Their conscious guilt prevented due circumspection. They did not see the bearing of its publication. They advised their father to carry it to the Committee of Vigilance, and it was so carried. On the Sunday following, Joseph began to think there might be something in it. Perhaps, in the mean time, he had seen one of the Crowninshields. He was apprehensive that they might be suspected; he was anxious to turn attention from their family. What course did he adopt to effect this? He addressed one letter, with a false name, to Mr. White, and another to the committee; and to complete the climax of his folly, he signed the letter addressed to the committee, "Grant," the same name as that which was signed to the letter received from Belfast. It was in the knowledge of the committee, that no person but the Knapps had seen this letter from Belfast; and that no other person knew its signature. It therefore must have been irresistibly plain to them that one of the Knapps was the writer of the letter received by the committee, charging the murder on Mr. White. Add to this the fact of its having been dated at Lynn, and mailed at Salem four days after it was dated, and who could doubt respecting it? Have you ever read or known of folly equal to this? Can you conceive of crime more odious and abominable? Merely to explain the apparent mysteries of the letter from Palmer, they excite the basest suspicions against a man, whom, if they were innocent, they had no reason to believe guilty; and whom, if they were guilty, they most certainly knew to be innocent. Could they have adopted a more direct method of exposing their own infamy? The letter to the committee has intrinsic marks of a knowledge of this transaction. It tells the *time* and the *manner* in which the murder was committed. Every line speaks the writer's condemnation. In attempting to divert attention from his family, and to charge the guilt upon another, he indelibly fixes it upon himself.

Joseph Knapp requested Allen to put these letters into the post-office, because, said he, "I wish to nip this silly affair in the bud." If there were not the order of an overruling Providence, I should say that it was the silliest piece of folly that was ever practised. Mark the destiny of crime. It is ever obliged to resort to such subterfuges; it trembles in the broad light; it betrays itself in seeking conceal-ment. He alone walks safely who walks uprightly. Who for a mo-ment can read these letters and doubt of Joseph Knapp's guilt? The constitution of nature is made to inform against him. There is no corner dark enough to conceal him. There is no turnpike-road broad enough or smooth enough for a man so guilty to walk in without stumbling. Every step proclaims his secret to every passenger. His own acts come out to fix his guilt. In attempting to charge another with his own crime, he writes his own confession. To do away the effect of Palmer's letter, signed Grant, he writes a letter himself and affixes to it the name of Grant. He writes in a disguised hand; but how could it happen that the same Grant should be in Salem that was at Belfast? This has brought the whole thing out. Evidently he did it, because he has adopted the same style. Evidently he did it, because he speaks of the price of blood, and of other circumstances connected with the murder, that no one but a conspirator could have known.

Palmer says he made a visit to the Crowninshields, on the 9th of April. George then asked him whether he had heard of the murder. Richard inquired whether he had heard the music at Salem. They said that they were suspected, that a committee had been appointed to search houses; and that they had melted up the dagger, the day after the murder, because it would be a suspicious circumstance to have it found in their possession. Now this committee was not appointed, in fact, until Friday evening. But this proves nothing against Palmer; it does not prove that George did not tell him so; it only proves that he gave a false reason for a fact. They had heard that they were suspected; how could they have heard this unless it were from the whisperings of their own consciences? Surely this rumor was not then public.

About the 27th of April, another attempt was made by the Knapps to give a direction to public suspicion. They reported themselves to have been robbed, in passing from Salem to Wenham, near Wenham Pond. They came to Salem and stated the particulars of the adventure. They described persons, their dress, size, and appearance, who had been suspected of the murder. They would have it understood that the community was infested by a band of ruffians, and that they themselves were the particular objects of their vengeance. Now this turns out to be all fictitious, all false. Can you conceive of any thing more enormous, any wickedness greater, than the circulation of such reports? than the allegation of crimes, if committed, capital? If no such crime had been committed, then it reacts with double force upon themselves, and goes very far to show their guilt. How did they conduct themselves on this occasion? Did they make hue and cry? Did they give information that they had been assaulted that night at Wenham? No such thing. They rested quietly that night; they waited to be called on for the particulars of their adventure; they made no attempt to arrest the offenders; this was not their object. They were content to fill the thousand mouths of rumor, to spread abroad false reports, to divert the attention of the public from themselves; for they thought every man suspected them, because they knew they ought to be suspected.

The manner in which the compensation for this murder was paid is a circumstance worthy of consideration. By examining the facts and dates, it will satisfactorily appear that Joseph Knapp paid a sum of money to Richard Crowninshield, in five-franc pieces, on the 24th of April. On the 21st of April, Joseph Knapp received five hundred five-franc pieces, as the proceeds of an adventure at sea. The remainder of this species of currency that came home in the vessel was deposited in a bank at Salem. On Saturday, the 24th of April, Frank and Richard rode to Wenham. They were there with Joseph an hour or more, and appeared to be negotiating private business. Richard continued in the chaise; Joseph came to the chaise and conversed with him. These facts are proved by Hart and Leighton, and by Osborn's books. On Saturday evening, about this time, Richard Crowninshield is proved, by Lummus, to have been at Wenham, with another person whose appearance corresponds with Frank's. Can any one doubt this being the same evening? What had Richard Crowninshield to do at Wenham, with Joseph, unless it were this business? He was there before the murder; he was there after the murder; he was there clandestinely, unwilling to be seen. If it were not upon this business, let it be told what it was for. Joseph Knapp could explain it; Frank Knapp might explain it. But they do not explain it; and the inference is against them.

Immediately after this, Richard passes five-franc pieces; on the same evening, one to Lummus, five to Palmer; and near this time George passes three or four in Salem. Here are nine of these pieces passed by them in four days; this is extraordinary. It is an unusual currency; in ordinary business, few men would pass nine such pieces in the course of a year. If they were not received in this way, why not explain how they came by them? Money was not so flush in their pockets that they could not tell whence it came, if it honestly came

there. It is extremely important to them to explain whence this
money came, and they would do it if they could. If, then, the price
of blood was paid at this time, in the presence and with the knowledge of this defendant, does not this prove him to have been connected with this conspiracy?

Observe, also, the effect on the mind of Richard, of Palmer's being
arrested and committed to prison; the various efforts he makes to
discover the fact; the lowering, through the crevices of the rock, the
pencil and paper for him to write upon; the sending two lines of
poetry, with the request that he would return the corresponding
lines; the shrill and peculiar whistle; the inimitable exclamations of
"Palmer! Palmer! Palmer!" All these things prove how great was his
alarm; they corroborate Palmer's story, and tend to establish the
conspiracy.

Joseph Knapp had a part to act in this matter. He must have
opened the window, and secreted the key; he had free access to
every part of the house; he was accustomed to visit there; he went
in and out at his pleasure; he could do this without being suspected.
He is proved to have been there the Saturday preceding.

If all these things, taken in connection, do not prove that Captain
White was murdered in pursuance of a conspiracy, then the case is
at an end.

Savary's testimony is wholly unexpected. He was called for a different purpose. When asked who the person was that he saw come
out of Captain White's yard between three and four o'clock in the
morning, he answered, Frank Knapp. It is not clear that this is not
true. There may be many circumstances of importance connected
with this, though we believe the murder to have been committed
between ten and eleven o'clock. The letter to Dr. Barstow states it
to have been done about eleven o'clock; it states it to have been done
with a blow on the head, from a weapon loaded with lead. Here is
too great a correspondence with the reality not to have some meaning in it. Dr. Peirson was always of the opinion, that the two classes
of wounds were made with different instruments, and by different
hands. It is possible that one class was inflicted at one time, and the
other at another. It is possible that on the last visit the pulse might

not have entirely ceased to beat; and then the finishing stroke was given. It is said, that, when the body was discovered, some of the wounds wept, while the others did not. They may have been inflicted from mere wantonness. It was known that Captain White was accustomed to keep specie by him in his chamber; this perhaps may explain the last visit. It is proved, that this defendant was in the habit of retiring to bed, and leaving it afterwards, without the knowledge of his family; perhaps he did so on this occasion. We see no reason to doubt the fact; and it does not shake our belief that the murder was committed early in the night.

What are the probabilities as to the time of the murder? Mr. White was an aged man; he usually retired to bed at about half past nine. He slept soundest in the early part of the night; usually awoke in the middle and latter part; and his habits were perfectly well known. When would persons, with a knowledge of these facts, be most likely to approach him? Most certainly, in the first hour of his sleep. This would be the safest time. If seen then going to or from the house, the appearance would be least suspicious. The earlier hour would then have been most probably selected.

Gentlemen, I shall dwell no longer on the evidence which tends to prove that there was a conspiracy, and that the prisoner was a conspirator. All the circumstances concur to make out this point. Not only Palmer swears to it, in effect, and Leighton, but Allen mainly supports Palmer, and Osborn's books lend confirmation, so far as possible, from such a source. Palmer is contradicted in nothing, either by any other witness, or any proved circumstance or occurrence. Whatever could be expected to support him does support him. All the evidence clearly manifests, I think, that there was a conspiracy; that it originated with Joseph Knapp; that defendant became a party to it, and was one of its conductors, from first to last. One of the most powerful circumstances is Palmer's letter from Belfast. The amount of this is a direct charge on the Knapps of the authorship of this murder. How did they treat this charge; like honest men, or like guilty men? We have seen how it was treated. Joseph Knapp fabricated letters, charging another person, and caused them to be put into the post-office.

I shall now proceed on the supposition, that it is proved that there was a conspiracy to murder Mr. White, and that the prisoner was party to it.

The second and the material inquiry is, Was the prisoner present at the murder, aiding and abetting therein?

This leads to the legal question in the case. What does the law mean, when it says, that, in order to charge him as a principal, "he must be present aiding and abetting in the murder"?

In the language of the late Chief Justice, "It is not required that the abettor shall be actually upon the spot when the murder is committed, or even in sight of the more immediate perpetrator of the victim, to make him a principal. If he be at a distance, cooperating in the act, by watching to prevent relief, or to give an alarm, or to assist his confederate in escape, having knowledge of the purpose and object of the assassin, this in the eye of the law is being present, aiding and abetting, so as to make him a principal in the murder."

"If he be at a distance cooperating." This is not a distance to be measured by feet or rods; if the intent to lend aid combine with a knowledge that the murder is to be committed, and the person so intending be so situate that he can by any possibility lend this aid in any manner, then he is present in legal contemplation. He need not lend any actual aid; to be ready to assist is assisting.

There are two sorts of murder; the distinction between them it is of essential importance to bear in mind: 1. Murder in an affray, or upon sudden and unexpected provocation. 2. Murder secretly, with a deliberate, predetermined intention to commit the crime. Under the first class, the question usually is, whether the offence be murder or manslaughter, in the person who commits the deed. Under the second class, it is often a question whether others than he who actually did the deed were present, aiding and assisting therein. Offences of this kind ordinarily happen when there is nobody present except those who go on the same design. If a riot should happen in the court-house, and one should kill another, this may be murder, or it may not, according to the intention with which it was done; which is always matter of fact, to be collected from the circumstances at the time. But in secret murders, premeditated and determined on, there can be no doubt of the murderous intention; there can be no doubt if a person be present, knowing a murder is to be done, of his concurring in the act. His being there is a proof of his intent to aid and abet; else, why is he there?

It has been contended, that proof must be given that the person accused did actually afford aid, did lend a hand in the murder itself; and without this proof, although he may be near by, he may be presumed to be there for an innocent purpose; he may have crept silently there to hear the news, or from mere curiosity to see what was going on. Preposterous, absurd! Such an idea shocks all common sense. A man is found to be a conspirator to commit a murder; he has planned it; he has assisted in arranging the time, the place, and the means; and he is found in the place, and at the time, and yet it is suggested that he might have been there, not for cooperation and concurrence, but from curiosity! Such an argument deserves no answer. It would be difficult to give it one, in decorous terms. Is it not to be taken for granted, that a man seeks to accomplish his own purposes? When he has planned a murder, and is present at its execution, is he there to forward or to thwart his own design? is he there to assist, or there to prevent? But "curiosity"! He may be there from mere "curiosity"! Curiosity to witness the success of the execution of his own plan of murder! The very walls of a court-house ought not to stand, the ploughshare should run through the ground it stands on, where such an argument could find toleration.

It is not necessary that the abettor should actually lend a hand, that he should take a part in the act itself; if he be present ready to assist, that is assisting. Some of the doctrines advanced would acquit the defendant, though he had gone to the bedchamber of the deceased, though he had been standing by when the assassin gave the blow. This is the argument we have heard to-day.

[The court here said, they did not so understand the argument of the counsel for defendant. Mr. Dexter said, "The intent and power alone must cooperate."]

No doubt the law is, that being ready to assist is assisting, if the party has the power to assist, in case of need. It is so stated by Fos-

ter, who is a high authority. "If A happeneth to be present at a murder, for instance, and taketh no part in it, nor endeavoreth to prevent
it, nor apprehendeth the murderer, nor levyeth hue and cry after him,
this strange behavior of his, though highly criminal, will not of itself
render him either principal or accessory." "But if a fact amounting to
murder should be committed in prosecution of some unlawful purpose, though it were but a bare trespass, to which A in the case last
stated had consented, and he had gone in order to give assistance, if
need were, for carrying it into execution, this would have amounted
to murder in him, and in every person present and joining with him."
"If the fact was committed in prosecution of the original purpose
which was unlawful, the whole party will be involved in the guilt of
him who gave the blow. For in combinations of this kind, the mortal
stroke, though given by one of the party, is considered in the eye of
the law, and of sound reason too, as given by every individual present and abetting. The person actually giving the stroke is no more
than the hand or instrument by which the others strike." The author,
in speaking of being present, means actual presence; not actual in
opposition to constructive, for the law knows no such distinction.
There is but one presence, and this is the situation from which aid,
or supposed aid, may be rendered. The law does not say where the
person is to go, or how near he is to go, but that he must be where
he may give assistance, or where the perpetrator may believe that he
may be assisted by him. Suppose that he is acquainted with the
design of the murderer, and has a knowledge of the time when it is
to be carried into effect, and goes out with a view to render assistance, if need be; why, then, even though the murderer does not know
of this, the person so going out will be an abettor in the murder.

It is contended that the prisoner at the bar could not be a principal,
he being in Brown Street, because he could not there render assistance; and you are called upon to determine this case, according as
you may be of opinion whether Brown Street was, or was not, a
suitable, convenient, well-chosen place to aid in this murder. This
is not the true question. The inquiry is not whether you would have
selected this place in preference to all others, or whether you would
have selected it at all. If the parties chose it, why should we doubt

about it? How do we know the use they intended to make of it, or the kind of aid that he was to afford by being there? The question for you to consider is, Did the defendant go into Brown Street in aid of this murder? Did he go there by agreement, by appointment with the perpetrator? If so, every thing else follows. The main thing, indeed the only thing, is to inquire whether he was in Brown Street by appointment with Richard Crowninshield. It might be to keep general watch; to observe the lights, and advise as to time of access; to meet the murderer on his return, to advise him as to his escape; to examine his clothes, to see if any marks of blood were upon them; to furnish exchange of clothes, or new disguise, if necessary; to tell him through what streets he could safely retreat, or whether he could deposit the club in the place designed; or it might be without any distinct object, but merely to afford that encouragement which would proceed from Richard Crowninshield's consciousness that he was near. It is of no consequence whether, in your opinion, the place was well chosen or not, to afford aid; if it was so chosen, if it was by appointment that he was there, it is enough. Suppose Richard Crowninshield, when applied to commit the murder, had said, "I won't do it unless there can be some one near by to favor my escape; I won't go unless you will stay in Brown Street." Upon the gentleman's argument, he would not be an aider and abettor in the murder, because the place was not well chosen; though it is apparent that the being in the place chosen was a condition, without which the murder would never have happened.

You are to consider the defendant as one in the league, in the combination to commit the murder. If he was there by appointment with the perpetrator, he is an abettor. The concurrence of the perpetrator in his being there is proved by the previous evidence of the conspiracy. If Richard Crowninshield, for any purpose whatsoever, made it a condition of the agreement, that Frank Knapp should stand as backer, then Frank Knapp was an aider and abettor; no matter what the aid was, or what sort it was, or degree, be it ever so little; even if it were to judge of the hour when it was best to go, or to see when the lights were extinguished, or to give an alarm if any one approached. Who better calculated to judge of these things than the murderer himself? and if he so determined them, that is sufficient.

Now as to the facts. Frank Knapp knew that the murder was that night to be committed; he was one of the conspirators, he knew the object, he knew the time. He had that day been to Wenham to see Joseph, and probably to Danvers to see Richard Crowninshield, for he kept his motions secret. He had that day hired a horse and chaise of Osborn, and attempted to conceal the purpose for which it was used; he had intentionally left the *place* and the *price* blank on Osborn's books. He went to Wenham by the way of Danvers; he had been told the week before to hasten Dick; he had seen the Crowninshields several times within a few days; he had a saddle-horse the Saturday night before; he had seen Mrs. Beckford at Wenham, and knew she would not return that night. She had not been away before for six weeks, and probably would not soon be again. He had just come from Wenham. Every day, for the week previous, he had visited one or another of these conspirators, save Sunday, and then probably he saw them in town. When he saw Joseph on the 6th, Joseph had prepared the house, and would naturally tell him of it; there were constant communications between them; daily and nightly visitation; too much knowledge of these parties and this transaction, to leave a particle of doubt on the mind of any one, that Frank Knapp knew the murder was to be committed this night. The hour was come, and he knew it; if so, and he was in Brown Street, without explaining why he was there, can the jury for a moment doubt whether he was there to countenance, aid, or support; or for curiosity alone; or to learn how the wages of sin and death were earned by the perpetrator.

[Here Mr. Webster read the law from Hawkins. 1 Hawk. 204, Lib. 1, ch. 32, sec. 7.]

The perpetrator would derive courage, and strength, and confidence from the knowledge that one of his associates was near by. If he was in Brown Street, he could have been there for no other purpose. If there for this purpose, then he was in the language of the law, *present,* aiding and abetting in the murder.

His interest lay in being somewhere else. If he had nothing to do with the murder, no part to act, why not stay at home? Why should he jeopard his own life, if it was not agreed that he should be there? He would not voluntarily go where the very place would cause him to swing if detected. He would not voluntarily assume the place of danger. His taking this place proves that he went to give aid. His staying away would have made an *alibi*. If he had nothing to do with the murder, he would be at home, where he could prove his *alibi*. He knew he was in danger, because he was guilty of the conspiracy, and, if he had nothing to do, would not expose himself to suspicion or detection.

Did the prisoner at the bar countenance this murder? Did he concur, or did he non-concur, in what the perpetrator was about to do? Would he have tried to shield him? Would he have furnished his cloak for protection? Would he have pointed out a safe way of retreat? As you would answer these questions, so you should answer the general question, whether he was there consenting to the murder, or whether he was there as a spectator only.

One word more on this presence, called constructive presence. What aid is to be rendered? Where is the line to be drawn, between acting, and omitting to act? Suppose he had been in the house, suppose he had followed the perpetrator to the chamber, what could he have done? This was to be a murder by stealth; it was to be a secret assassination. It was not their purpose to have an open combat; they were to approach their victim unawares, and silently give the fatal blow. But if he had been in the chamber, no one can doubt that he would have been an abettor; because of his presence, and ability to render services, if needed. What service could he have rendered, if there? Could he have helped him to fly? Could he have aided the silence of his movements? Could he have facilitated his retreat, on the first alarm? Surely, this was a case where there was more of safety in going alone than with another; where company would only embarrass. Richard Crowninshield would prefer to go alone. He knew his errand too well. His nerves needed no collateral support. He was not the man to take with him a trembling companion. He would prefer to have his aid at a distance. He would not

wish to be encumbered by his presence. He would prefer to have
him out of the house. He would prefer that he should be in Brown
Street. But whether in the chamber, in the house, in the garden,
or in the street, whatsoever is aiding in *actual presence* is *constructive presence;* any thing that is aid in one case is aid in the other.

If, then, the aid be anywhere, so as to embolden the perpetrator,
to afford him hope or confidence in his enterprise, it is the same as
though the person stood at his elbow with his sword drawn. His
being there ready to act, with the power to act, is what makes him
an abettor.

[Here Mr. Webster referred to the cases of Kelly, of Hyde, and others,
cited by counsel for the defendant, and showed that they did not militate
with the doctrine for which he contended. The difference is, in those cases
there was open violence; this was a case of secret assassination. The aid
must meet the occasion. Here no *acting* was necessary, but watching, concealment of escape, management.]

What are the *facts* in relation to this presence? Frank Knapp is
proved to have been a conspirator, proved to have known that the
deed was now to be done. Is it not probable that he was in Brown
Street to concur in the murder? There were four conspirators. It was
natural that some one of them should go with the perpetrator.
Richard Crowninshield was to be the perpetrator; he was to give
the blow. There is no evidence of any casting of the parts for the
others. The defendant would probably be the man to take the second part. He was fond of exploits, he was accustomed to the use
of sword-canes and dirks. If any aid was required, he was the man
to give it. At least, there is no evidence to the contrary of this.

Aid could not have been received from Joseph Knapp, or from
George Crowninshield. Joseph Knapp was at Wenham, and took
good care to prove that he was there. George Crowninshield has
proved satisfactorily where he was; that he was in other company,
such as it was, until eleven o'clock. This narrows the inquiry. This
demands of the prisoner to show, if he was not in this place, where
he was. It calls on him loudly to show this, and to show it truly. If
he could show it, he would do it. If he does not tell, and that truly,
it is against him. The defence of an *alibi* is a double-edged sword.

He knew that he was in a situation where he might be called upon to account for himself. If he had had no particular appointment or business to attend to, he would have taken care to be able so to account. He would have been out of town, or in some good company. Has he accounted for himself on that night to your satisfaction?

The prisoner has attempted to prove an *alibi*, in two ways. In the first place, by four young men with whom he says he was in company, on the evening of the murder, from seven o'clock till near ten o'clock. This depends upon the certainty of the night. In the second place, by his family, from ten o'clock afterwards. This depends upon the certainty of the time of the night. These two classes of proof have no connection with each other. One may be true, and the other false; or they may both be true, or both be false. I shall examine this testimony with some attention, because, on a former trial, it made more impression on the minds of the court than on my own mind. I think, when carefully sifted and compared, it will be found to have in it more of plausibility than reality.

Mr. Page testifies, that on the evening of the 6th of April he was in company with Burchmore, Balch, and Forrester, and that he met the defendant about seven o'clock, near the Salem Hotel; that he afterwards met him at Remond's, about nine o'clock, and that he was in company with him a considerable part of the evening. This young gentleman is a member of college, and says that he came to town the Saturday evening previous; that he is now able to say that it was the night of the murder when he walked with Frank Knapp, from the recollection of the fact, that he called himself to an account, on the morning after the murder, as it is natural for men to do when an extraordinary occurrence happens. Gentlemen, this kind of evidence is not satisfactory; general impressions as to time are not to be relied on. If I were called on to state the particular day on which any witness testified in this cause, I could not do it. Every man will notice the same thing in his own mind. There is no one of these young men that could give an account of himself for any other day in the month of April. They are made to remember the fact, and then they think they remember the time. The witness has no means of knowing it was Tuesday rather than any other time.

He did not know it at first; he could not know it afterwards. He says he called himself to an account. This has no more to do with the murder than with the man in the moon. Such testimony is not worthy to be relied on in any forty-shilling cause. What occasion had he to call himself to an account? Did he suppose that he should be suspected? Had he any intimation of this conspiracy?

Suppose, Gentlemen, you were either of you asked where you were, or what you were doing, on the fifteenth day of June; you could not answer this question without calling to mind some events to make it certain. Just as well may you remember on what you dined each day of the year past. Time is identical. Its subdivisions are all alike. No man knows one day from another, or one hour from another, but by some fact connected with it. Days and hours are not visible to the senses, nor to be apprehended and distinguished by the understanding. The flow of time is known only by something which marks it; and he who speaks of the date of occurrences with nothing to guide his recollection speaks at random, and is not to be relied on. This young gentleman remembers the facts and occurrences; he knows nothing why they should not have happened on the evening of the 6th; but he knows no more. All the rest is evidently conjecture or impression.

Mr. White informs you, that he told him he could not tell what night it was. The first thoughts are all that are valuable in such case. They miss the mark by taking second aim.

Mr. Balch believes, but is not sure, that he was with Frank Knapp on the evening of the murder. He has given different accounts of the time. He has no means of making it certain. All he knows is, that it was some evening before Fast-day. But whether Monday, Tuesday, or Saturday, he cannot tell.

Mr. Burchmore says, to the best of his belief, it was the evening of the murder. Afterwards he attempts to speak positively, from recollecting that he mentioned the circumstance to William Peirce, as he went to the Mineral Spring on Fast-day. Last Monday morning he told Colonel Putnam he could not fix the time. This witness stands in a much worse plight than either of the others. It is difficult to reconcile all he has said with any belief in the accuracy of his recollections.

Mr. Forrester does not speak with any certainty as to the night; and it is very certain that he told Mr. Loring and others, that he did not know what night it was.

Now, what does the testimony of these four young men amount to? The only circumstance by which they approximate to an identifying of the night is, that three of them say it was cloudy; they think their walk was either on Monday or Tuesday evening, and it is admitted that Monday evening was clear, whence they draw the inference that it must have been Tuesday.

But, fortunately, there is one *fact* disclosed in their testimony that settles the question. Balch says, that on the evening, whenever it was, he saw the prisoner; the prisoner told him he was going out of town on horseback, for a distance of about twenty minutes' drive, and that he was going to get a horse at Osborn's. This was about seven o'clock. At about nine, Balch says he saw the prisoner again, and was then told by him that he had had his ride, and had returned. Now it appears by Osborn's books, that the prisoner had a saddle-horse from his stable, not on Tuesday evening, the night of the murder, but on the Saturday evening previous. This fixes the time about which these young men testify, and is a complete answer and refutation of the attempted *alibi* on Tuesday evening.

I come now to speak of the testimony adduced by the defendant to explain where he was after ten o'clock on the night of the murder. This comes chiefly from members of the family; from his father and brothers.

It is agreed that the affidavit of the prisoner should be received as evidence of what his brother, Samuel H. Knapp, would testify if present. Samuel H. Knapp says, that, about ten minutes past ten o'clock, his brother, Frank Knapp, on his way to bed, opened his chamber door, made some remarks, closed the door, and went to his chamber; and that he did not hear him leave it afterwards. How is this witness able to fix the time at ten minutes past ten? There is no circumstance mentioned by which he fixes it. He had been in bed, probably asleep, and was aroused from his sleep by the open-

ing of the door. Was he in a situation to speak of time with precision? Could he know, under such circumstances, whether it was
ten minutes past ten, or ten minutes before eleven, when his brother
spoke to him? What would be the natural result in such a case? But
we are not left to this result. We have positive testimony on this
point. Mr. Webb tells you that Samuel told him, on the 8th of June,
"that he did not know what time his brother Frank came home, and
that he was not at home when *he* went to bed." You will consider
this testimony of Mr. Webb as indorsed upon this affidavit; and
with this indorsement upon it, you will give it its due weight. This
statement was made to him after Frank was arrested.

I come to the testimony of the father. I find myself incapable of
speaking of him or his testimony with severity. Unfortunate old
man! Another Lear, in the conduct of his children; another Lear, I
apprehend, in the effect of his distress upon his mind and understanding. He is brought here to testify, under circumstances that
disarm severity, and call loudly for sympathy. Though it is impossible not to see that his story cannot be credited, yet I am unable
to speak of him otherwise than in sorrow and grief. Unhappy father!
he strives to remember, perhaps persuades himself that he does
remember, that on the evening of the murder he was himself at
home at ten o'clock. He thinks, or seems to think, that his son came
in at about five minutes past ten. He fancies that he remembers his
conversation; he thinks he spoke of bolting the door; he thinks he
asked the time of night; he seems to remember his then going to his
bed. Alas! these are but the swimming fancies of an agitated and
distressed mind. Alas! they are but the dreams of hope, its uncertain
lights, flickering on the thick darkness of parental distress. Alas! the
miserable father knows nothing, in reality, of all these things.

Mr. Shepard says that the first conversation he had with Mr.
Knapp was soon after the murder, and *before* the arrest of his sons.
Mr. Knapp says it was *after* the arrest of his sons. His own fears led
him to say to Mr. Shepard, that his "son Frank was at home that
night; and so Phippen told him," or "as Phippen told him." Mr.
Shepard says that he was struck with the remark at the time; that it
made an unfavorable impression on his mind; he does not tell you

what that impression was, but when you connect it with the previous inquiry he had made, whether Frank had continued to associate with the Crowninshields, and recollect that the Crowninshields were then known to be suspected of this crime, can you doubt what this impression was? can you doubt as to the fears he then had?

This poor old man tells you, that he was greatly perplexed at the time; that he found himself in embarrassed circumstances; that on this very night he was engaged in making an assignment of his property to his friend, Mr. Shepard. If ever charity should furnish a mantle for error, it should be here. Imagination cannot picture a more deplorable, distressed condition.

The same general remarks may be applied to his conversation with Mr. Treadwell, as have been made upon that with Mr. Shepard. He told him, that he believed Frank was at home about the usual time. In his conversations with either of these persons, he did not pretend to know, of his own knowledge, the time that he came home. He now tells you positively that he recollects the time, and that he so told Mr. Shepard. He is directly contradicted by both these witnesses, as respectable men as Salem affords.

This idea of an *alibi* is of recent origin. Would Samuel Knapp have gone to sea if it were then thought of? His testimony, if true, was too important to be lost. If there be any truth in this part of the *alibi*, it is so near in point of time that it cannot be relied on. The mere variation of half an hour would avoid it. The mere variations of different time-pieces would explain it.

Has the defendant proved where he was on that night? If you doubt about it, there is an end of it. The burden is upon him to satisfy you beyond all reasonable doubt. Osborn's books, in connection with what the young men state, are conclusive, I think, on this point. He has not, then, accounted for himself; he has attempted it, and has failed. I pray you to remember, Gentlemen, that this is a case in which the prisoner would, more than any other, be rationally able to account for himself on the night of the murder, if he could do so. He was in the conspiracy, he knew the murder was then to be committed, and if he himself was to have no hand in its actual execution, he would of course, as a matter of safety and precaution, be somewhere else, and be able to prove afterwards that he had been somewhere else. Having this motive to prove himself elsewhere, and the power to do it if he were elsewhere, his failing in such proof must necessarily leave a very strong inference against him.

But, Gentlemen, let us now consider what is the evidence produced on the part of the government to prove that John Francis Knapp, the prisoner at the bar, was in Brown Street on the night of the murder. This is a point of vital importance in this cause. Unless this be made out, beyond reasonable doubt, the law of *presence* does not apply to the case. The government undertake to prove that he was present aiding in the murder, by proving that he was in Brown Street for this purpose. Now, what are the undoubted facts? They are, that two persons were seen in that street, several times during that evening, under suspicious circumstances; under such circumstances as induced those who saw them to watch their movements. Of this there can be no doubt. Mirick saw a man standing at the post opposite his store from fifteen minutes before nine until twenty minutes after, dressed in a full frock-coat, glazed cap, and so forth, in size and general appearance answering to the prisoner at the bar. This person was waiting there; and whenever any one approached him, he moved to and from the corner, as though he would avoid being suspected or recognized. Afterwards, two persons were seen by Webster walking in Howard Street, with a slow, deliberate movement that attracted his attention. This was about half past nine. One of these he took to be the prisoner at the bar, the other he did not know.

About half past ten a person is seen sitting on the ropewalk steps, wrapped in a cloak. He drops his head when passed, to avoid being known. Shortly after, two persons are seen to meet in this street, without ceremony or salutation, and in a hurried manner to converse for a short time; then to separate, and run off with great speed. Now, on this same night a gentleman is slain, murdered in his bed, his house being entered by stealth from without; and his house situated within three hundred feet of this street; a weapon of death is afterwards found in a place where these persons were seen to pass, in a retired place, around which they had been seen lingering. It is now known that this murder was committed by four persons, conspiring together for this purpose. No account is given who these suspected persons thus seen in Brown Street and its neighborhood were. Now, I ask, Gentlemen, whether you or any man can doubt that this murder was committed by the persons who were thus in and about Brown Street. Can any person doubt that they were there for purposes connected with this murder? If not for this purpose, what were they there for? When there is a cause so near at hand, why wander into conjecture for an explanation? Common sense requires you to take the nearest adequate cause for a known effect. Who were these suspicious persons in Brown Street? There was something extraordinary about them; something noticeable, and noticed at the time; something in their appearance that aroused suspicion. And a man is found the next morning murdered in the near vicinity.

Now, so long as no other account shall be given of those suspicious persons, so long the inference must remain irresistible that they were the murderers. Let it be remembered, that it is already shown that this murder was the result of conspiracy and of concert; let it be remembered, that the house, having been opened from within, was entered by stealth from without. Let it be remembered that Brown Street, where these persons were repeatedly seen under such suspicious circumstances, was a place from which every occupied room in Mr. White's house is clearly seen; let it be remembered, that the place, though thus very near to Mr. White's house, is a retired and lonely place; and let it be remembered that the instrument of death was afterwards found concealed very near the same spot.

Must not every man come to the conclusion, that these persons thus seen in Brown Street were the murderers? Every man's own judgment, I think, must satisfy him that this must be so. It is a plain deduction of common sense. It is a point on which each one of you may reason like a Hale or a Mansfield. The two occurrences explain each other. The murder shows why these persons were thus lurking, at that hour, in Brown Street; and their lurking in Brown Street shows who committed the murder.

If, then, the persons in and about Brown Street were the plotters and executers of the murder of Captain White, we know who they were, and you know that *there* is one of them.

This fearful concatenation of circumstances puts him to an account. He was a conspirator. He had entered into this plan of murder. The murder is committed, and he is known to have been within three minutes' walk of the place. He must account for himself. He has attempted this, and failed. Then, with all these general reasons to show he was actually in Brown Street, and his failures in his *alibi*, let us see what is the direct proof of his being there. But first, let me ask, is it not very remarkable that there is no attempt to show where Richard Crowninshield, Jr., was on that night? We hear nothing of him. He was seen in none of his usual haunts about the town. Yet, if he was the actual perpetrator of the murder, which nobody doubts, he was in the town somewhere. Can you, therefore, entertain a doubt that he was one of the persons seen in Brown Street? And as to the prisoner, you will recollect, that, since the testimony of the young men has failed to show where he was on that evening, the last we hear or know of him, on the day preceding the murder, is, that at four o'clock, P.M., he was at his brother's in Wenham. He had left home, after dinner, in a manner doubtless designed to avoid observation, and had gone to Wenham, probably by way of Danvers. As we hear nothing of him after four o'clock, P.M., for the remainder of the day and evening; as he was one of the conspirators; as Richard Crowninshield, Jr., was another; as Richard Crowninshield, Jr., was in town in the evening and yet seen in no usual place of resort; the inference is very fair, that Richard Crowninshield, Jr., and the prisoner were together, acting in execution of their conspiracy. Of the four conspirators, J. J. Knapp, Jr., was at Wenham, and George Crowninshield has been accounted for; so that if the persons seen in Brown Street were the murderers, one of them must have been Richard Crowninshield, Jr., and the other must have been the prisoner at the bar.

Now, as to the proof of his identity with one of the persons seen in Brown Street. Mr. Mirick, a cautious witness, examined the person he saw, closely, in a light night, and says that he thinks the prisoner at the bar is the person; and that he should not hesitate at all, if he were seen in the same dress. His opinion is formed partly from his own observation, and partly from the description of others. But this description turns out to be only in regard to the dress. It is said, that he is now more confident than on the former trial. If he has varied in his testimony, make such allowance as you may think proper. I do not perceive any material variance. He thought him the same person, when he was first brought to court, and as he saw him get out of the chaise. This is one of the cases in which a witness is permitted to give an opinion. This witness is as honest as yourselves, neither willing nor swift; but he says, he believes it was the man. His words are, "This is my opinion"; and this opinion it is proper for him to give. If partly founded on what he has *heard,* then this opinion is not to be taken; but if on what he *saw,* then you can have no better evidence. I lay no stress on similarity of dress. No man will ever lose his life by my voice on such evidence. But then it is proper to notice, that no inferences drawn from any *dissimilarity* of dress can be given in the prisoner's favor; because, in fact, the person seen by Mirick was dressed like the prisoner.

The description of the person seen by Mirick answers to that of the prisoner at the bar. In regard to the supposed discrepancy of statements, before and now, there would be no end to such minute inquiries. It would not be strange if witnesses should vary. I do not think much of slight shades of variation. If I believe the witness is honest, that is enough. If he has expressed himself more strongly now than then, this does not prove him false.

Peter E. Webster saw the prisoner at the bar, as he then thought, and still thinks, walking in Howard Street at half past nine o'clock. He then thought it was Frank Knapp, and has not altered his opinion since. He knew him well; he had long known him. If he then thought it was he, this goes far to prove it. He observed him the more, as it was unusual to see gentlemen walk there at that hour. It was a retired, lonely street. Now, is there reasonable doubt that Mr. Webster did see him there that night? How can you have more proof than this? He judged by his walk, by his general appearance, by his deportment. We all judge in this manner. If you believe he is right, it goes a great way in this case. But then this person, it is said, had a cloak on, and that he could not, therefore, be the same person that Mirick saw. If he were treating of men that had no occasion to disguise themselves or their conduct, there might be something in this argument. But as it is there is little in it. It may be presumed that they would change their dress. This would help their disguise. What is easier than to throw off a cloak, and again put it on? Perhaps he was less fearful of being known when alone, than when with the perpetrator.

Mr. Southwick swears all that a man can swear. He has the best means of judging that could be had at the time. He tells you that he left his father's house at half past ten o'clock, and as he passed to his own house in Brown Street, he saw a man sitting on the steps of the ropewalk; that he passed him three times, and each time he held down his head, so that he did not see his face. That the man had on a cloak, which was not wrapped around him, and a glazed cap. That he took the man to be Frank Knapp at the time; that, when he went into his house, he told his wife that he thought it was Frank Knapp; that he knew him well, having known him from a boy. And his wife swears that he did so tell her when he came home. What could mislead this witness at the time? He was not then suspecting Frank Knapp of anything. He could not then be influenced by any prejudice. If you believe that the witness saw Frank Knapp in this position at this time, it proves the case. Whether you believe it or not depends upon the credit of the witness. He swears it. If true, it is solid evidence. Mrs. Southwick supports her husband. Are they true? Are they worthy of belief? If he deserves the epithets applied to him, then he ought to be believed. In this fact they cannot be mistaken; they are right, or they are perjured. As to his not speaking to Frank Knapp, that depends upon their intimacy. But a very good reason is, Frank chose to disguise himself. This makes nothing against his credit. But it is said that he should not be believed. And why? Because, it is said, he himself now tells you, that, when he testified before the grand jury at Ipswich, he did not then say that he thought the person he saw in Brown Street was Frank Knapp, but that "the person was about the size of Selman." The means of attacking him, therefore, come from himself. If he is a false man, why should he tell truths against himself? They rely on his veracity to prove that he is a liar. Before you can come to this conclusion, you will consider whether all the circumstances are now known, that should have a bearing on this point. Suppose that, when he was before the grand jury, he was asked by the attorney this question, "Was the person you saw in Brown Street about the size of Selman?" and he answered, Yes. This was all true. Suppose, also, that he expected to be inquired of further, and no further questions were put to him? Would it not be extremely hard to impute to him perjury for this? It is not uncommon for witnesses to think that they have done all their duty, when they have answered the questions put to them. But suppose that we admit that he did not tell all he knew, this does not affect the *fact* at all; because he did tell, at the time, in the hearing of others, that the person he saw was Frank Knapp. There is not the slightest suggestion against the veracity or accuracy of Mrs. Southwick. Now she swears positively, that her husband came into the house and told her that he had seen a person on the ropewalk steps, and believed it was Frank Knapp.

It is said that Mr. Southwick is contradicted, also, by Mr. Shillaber. I do not so understand Mr. Shillaber's testimony. I think what they both testify is reconcilable, and consistent. My learned brother said, on a similar occasion, that there is more probability, in such cases, that the persons hearing should misunderstand, than that the person speaking should contradict himself. I think the same remark applicable here.

You have all witnessed the uncertainty of testimony, when witnesses are called to testify what other witnesses said. Several respectable counsellors have been summoned, on this occasion, to give testimony of that sort. They have, every one of them, given different versions. They all took minutes at the time, and without doubt intend to state the truth. But still they differ. Mr. Shillaber's version is different from every thing that Southwick has stated elsewhere. But little reliance is to be placed on slight variations in testimony, unless they are manifestly intentional. I think that Mr. Shillaber must be satisfied that he did not rightly understand Mr. Southwick. I confess I misunderstood Mr. Shillaber on the former trial, if I now rightly understand him. I, therefore, did not then recall Mr. Southwick to the stand. Mr. Southwick, as I read it, understood Mr. Shillaber as asking him about a person coming out of Newbury Street, and whether, for aught he knew, it might not be Richard Crowninshield, Jr. He answered, that he could not tell. He did not understand Mr. Shillaber as questioning him as to the person whom he saw sitting on the steps of the ropewalk. Southwick, on this trial, having heard Mr. Shillaber, has been recalled to the stand, and states that Mr. Shillaber entirely misunderstood him. This is certainly most probable, because the controlling fact in the case is not controverted; that is, that Southwick did tell his wife, at the very moment he entered his house, that he had seen a person on the ropewalk steps, whom he believed to be Frank Knapp. Nothing can prove with more certainty than this, that Southwick, at the time, *thought* the person whom he thus saw to be the prisoner at the bar.

Mr. Bray is an acknowledged accurate and intelligent witness. He was highly complimented by my brother on the former trial, although he now charges him with varying his testimony. What could be his motive? You will be slow in imputing to him any design of this kind. I deny altogether that there is any contradiction. There may be differences, but not contradiction. These arise from the difference in the questions put; the difference between believing and knowing. On the first trial, he said he did not know the person, and now says the same. Then, we did not do all we had a right to do. We did not ask him who he thought it was. Now, when so asked, he says he believes it was the prisoner at the bar. If he had then been asked this question, he would have given the same answer. That he has expressed himself more strongly, I admit; but he has not contradicted himself. He is more confident now; and that is all. A man may not assert a thing, and still may have no doubt upon it. Cannot every man see this distinction to be consistent? I leave him in that attitude; that only is the difference. On questions of identity, opinion is evidence. We may ask the witness, either if he knew who the person seen was, or who he thinks he was. And he may well answer, as Captain Bray has answered, that he does not know who it was, but that he thinks it was the prisoner.

We have offered to produce witnesses to prove, that, as soon as Bray saw the prisoner, he pronounced him the same person. We are not at liberty to call them to corroborate our own witness. How, then, could this fact of the prisoner's being in Brown Street be better proved? If ten witnesses had testified to it, it would be no better. Two men, who knew him well, took it to be Frank Knapp, and one of them so said, when there was nothing to mislead them. Two others, who examined him closely, now swear to their opinion that he is the man.

Miss Jaqueth saw three persons pass by the ropewalk, several evenings before the murder. She saw one of them pointing towards Mr. White's house. She noticed that another had something which appeared to be like an instrument of music; that he put it behind him and attempted to conceal it. Who were these persons? This was but a few steps from the place where this apparent instrument of music (of *music* such as Richard Crowninshield, Jr., spoke of to Palmer) was afterwards found. These facts prove this point of rendezvous for these parties. They show Brown Street to have been the place for consultation and observation; and to this purpose it was well suited.

Mr. Burns' testimony is also important. What was the defendant's object in his private conversation with Burns? He knew that Burns was out that night; that he lived near Brown Street, and that he had probably seen him; and he wished him to say nothing. He said to Burns, "If you saw any of your friends out that night, say nothing about it; my brother Joe and I are your friends." This is plain proof that he wished to say to him, if you saw me in Brown Street that night, say nothing about it.

But it is said that Burns ought not to be believed, because he mistook the color of the dagger, and because he has varied in his description of it. These are slight circumstances, if his general character be good. To my mind they are of no importance. It is for you to make what deduction you may think proper, on this account, from the weight of his evidence. His conversation with Burns, if Burns is believed, shows two things; first, that he desired Burns not to mention it, if he had seen him on the night of the murder; second, that he wished to fix the charge of murder on Mr. Stephen White. Both of these prove his own guilt.

I think you will be of opinion, that Brown Street was a probable place for the conspirators to assemble, and for an aid to be stationed. If we knew their whole plan, and if we were skilled to judge in such a case, then we could perhaps determine on this point better. But it is a retired place, and still commands a full view of the house; a lonely place, but still a place of observation. Not so lonely that a person would excite suspicion to be seen walking there in an ordinary manner; not so public as to be noticed by many. It is near enough to the scene of action in point of law. It was their point of centrality. The club was found near the spot, in a place provided for it, in a place that had been previously hunted out, in a con- certed place of concealment. *Here was their point of rendezvous.* Here might the lights be seen. Here might an aid be secreted. Here was he within call. Here might he be aroused by the sound of the whistle. Here might he carry the weapon. Here might he receive the murderer after the murder.

Then, Gentlemen, the general question occurs, Is it satisfactorily proved, by all these facts and circumstances, that the defendant was in and about Brown Street on the night of the murder? Considering that the murder was effected by a conspiracy; considering that he was one of the four conspirators; considering that two of the con- spirators have accounted for themselves on the night of the murder, and were not in Brown Street; considering that the prisoner does not account for himself, nor show where he was; considering that Richard Crowninshield, the other conspirator and the perpetrator, is not accounted for, nor shown to be elsewhere; considering that it is now past all doubt that two persons were seen lurking in and about Brown Street at different times, avoiding observation, and exciting so much suspicion that the neighbors actually watched them; considering that, if these persons thus lurking in Brown Street at that hour were not the murderers, it remains to this day wholly unknown who they were or what their business was; considering the testimony of Miss Jaqueth, and that the club was afterwards found near this place; considering, finally, that Webster and Southwick saw these persons, and then took one of them for the defendant, and that Southwick then told his wife so, and that Bray and Mirick examined them closely, and now swear to their belief that the prisoner was one of them; it is for you to say, putting these considerations together, whether you believe the prisoner was actually in Brown Street at the time of the murder.

By the counsel for the prisoner, much stress has been laid upon the question, whether Brown Street was a place in which aid could be given, a place in which actual assistance could be rendered in this transaction. This must be mainly decided by their own opinion who selected the place; by what they thought at the time, according to their plan of operation.

If it was agreed that the prisoner should be there to assist, it is enough. If they thought the place proper for their purpose, according to their plan, it is sufficient. Suppose we could prove expressly that they agreed that Frank should be there, and he was there, and you should think it not a well-chosen place for aiding and abetting, must he be acquitted? No! It is not what *I* think or *you* think of the appropriateness of the place; it is what *they* thought *at the time.* If the prisoner was in Brown Street by appointment and agreement with the perpetrator, for the purpose of giving assistance if assistance should be needed, it may safely be presumed that the place was suited to such assistance as it was supposed by the parties might chance to become requisite.

If in Brown Street, was he there by appointment? was he there to aid, if aid was necessary? was he there for, or against, the murderer? to concur, or to oppose? to favor, or to thwart? Did the perpetrator know he was there, there waiting? If so, then it follows that he was there by appointment. He was at the post half an hour; he was waiting for somebody. This proves appointment, arrangement, previous agreement; then it follows that he was there to aid, to encourage, to embolden the perpetrator; and that is enough. If he were in such a situation as to afford aid, or that he was relied upon for aid, then he was aiding and abetting. It is enough that the conspirator desired to have him there. Besides, it may be well said, that he could afford just as much aid there as if he had been in Essex Street, as if he had been standing even at the gate, or at the window. It was not an act of power against power that was to be done; it was a secret act, to be done by stealth. The aid was to be placed in a position secure from observation. It was important to the security of both that he should be in a lonely place. Now it is obvious that there are many purposes for which he might be in Brown Street.

1. Richard Crowninshield might have been secreted in the garden, and waiting for a signal;

2. Or he might be in Brown Street to advise him as to the time of making his entry into the house;

3. Or to favor his escape;

4. Or to see if the street was clear when he came out;

5. Or to conceal the weapon or the clothes;

6. To be ready for any unforeseen contingency.

Richard Crowninshield lived in Danvers. He would retire by the most secret way. Brown Street is that way. If you find him there, can you doubt why he was there?

If, Gentlemen, the prisoner went into Brown Street, by appointment with the perpetrator, to render aid or encouragement in any of these ways, he was *present,* in legal contemplation, aiding and abetting in this murder. It is not necessary that he should have done any thing; it is enough that he was ready to act, and in a place to act. If his being in Brown Street, by appointment, at the time of the murder, emboldened the purpose and encouraged the heart of the murderer, by the hope of instant aid, if aid should become necessary, then, without doubt, he was present, aiding and abetting, and was a principal in the murder.

I now proceed, Gentlemen, to the consideration of the testimony of Mr. Colman. Although this evidence bears on every material part of the cause, I have purposely avoided every comment on it till the present moment, when I have done with the other evidence in the case. As to the admission of this evidence, there has been a great struggle, and its importance demanded it. The general rule of law is, that confessions are to be received as evidence. They are entitled to great or to little consideration, according to the circumstances under which they are made. Voluntary, deliberate confessions are the most important and satisfactory evidence, but confessions hastily made, or improperly obtained, are entitled to little or no consideration. It is always to be inquired, whether they were purely voluntary, or were made under any undue influence of hope or fear; for, in general, if any influence were exerted on the mind of the person confessing, such confessions are not to be submitted to a jury.

Who is Mr. Colman? He is an intelligent, accurate, and cautious witness; a gentleman of high and well-known character, and of unquestionable veracity; as a clergyman, highly respectable; as a man, of fair name and fame.

Why was Mr. Colman with the prisoner? Joseph J. Knapp was his parishioner; he was the head of the family, and had been married by Mr. Colman. The interests of that family were dear to him. He felt for their afflictions, and was anxious to alleviate their sufferings. He went from the purest and best of motives to visit Joseph Knapp. He came to save, not to destroy; to rescue, not to take away life. In this family, he thought there might be a chance to save one. It is a misconstruction of Mr. Colman's motives, at once the most strange and the most uncharitable, a perversion of all just views of his conduct and intentions the most unaccountable, to represent him as acting, on this occasion, in hostility to any one, or as desirous of injuring or endangering any one. He has stated his own motives, and his own conduct, in a manner to command universal belief and universal respect. For intelligence, for consistency, for accuracy, for caution, for candor, never did witness acquit himself better, or stand fairer. In all that he did as a man, and all he has said as a witness, he has shown himself worthy of entire regard.

Now, Gentlemen, very important confessions made by the prisoner are sworn to by Mr. Colman. They were made in the prisoner's cell, where Mr. Colman had gone with the prisoner's brother, N.

Phippen Knapp. Whatever conversation took place was in the presence of N. P. Knapp. Now, on the part of the prisoner, two things are asserted; first, that such inducements were suggested to the prisoner, in this interview that no confessions made by him ought to be received; second, that, in point of fact, he made no such confessions as Mr. Colman testifies to, nor, indeed, any confessions at all. These two propositions are attempted to be supported by the testimony of N. P. Knapp. These two witnesses, Mr. Colman and N. P. Knapp, differ entirely. There is no possibility of reconciling them. No charity can cover both. One or the other has sworn falsely. If N. P. Knapp be believed, Mr. Colman's testimony must be wholly disregarded. It is, then, a question of credit, a question of belief between the two witnesses. As you decide between these, so you will decide on all this part of the case.

Mr. Colman has given you a plain narrative, a consistent account, and has uniformly stated the same things. He is not contradicted, except by the testimony of Phippen Knapp. He is influenced, as far as we can see, by no bias, or prejudice, any more than other men, except so far as his character is now at stake. He has feelings on this point, doubtless, and ought to have. If what he has stated be not true, I cannot see any ground for his escape. If he be a true man, he must have heard what he testifies. No treachery of memory brings to memory things that never took place. There is no reconciling his evidence with good intention, if the facts are not as he states them. He is on trial as to his veracity.

The relation in which the other witness stands deserves your careful consideration. He is a member of the family. He has the lives of two brothers depending, as he may think, on the effect of his evidence; depending on every word he speaks. I hope he has not another responsibility resting upon him. By the advice of a friend, and that friend Mr. Colman, J. Knapp made a full and free confession, and obtained a promise of pardon. He has since, as you know, probably by the advice of other friends, retracted that confession, and rejected the offered pardon. Events will show who of these friends and advisers advised him best, and befriended him most. In the mean time, if this brother, the witness, be one of these advisers, and advised the retraction he has, most emphatically, the lives of his brothers resting upon his evidence and upon his conduct. Compare the situation of these two witnesses. Do you not see mighty motive enough on the one side, and want of all motive on the other? I would gladly find an apology for that witness, in his agonized feelings, in his distressed situation; in the agitation of that hour, or of this. I would gladly impute it to error, or to want of recollection, to confusion of mind, or disturbance of feeling. I would gladly impute to any pardonable source that which cannot be reconciled to facts and to truth; but, even in a case calling for so much sympathy, justice must yet prevail, and we must come to the conclusion, however reluctantly, which that demands from us.

It is said, Phippen Knapp was probably correct, because he knew he should probably be called as a witness. Witness to what? When he says there was no confession, what could he expect to bear witness of? But I do not put it on the ground that he did not hear; I am compelled to put it on the other ground, that he did hear, and does not now truly tell what he heard.

If Mr. Colman were out of the scene, there are other reasons why the story of Phippen Knapp should not be believed. It has in it inherent improbabilities. It is unnatural, and inconsistent with the accompanying circumstances. He tells you that they went "to the cell of Frank, to see if he had any objection to taking a trial, and suffering his brother to accept the offer of pardon"; in other words, to obtain Frank's consent to Joseph's making a confession; and in case this consent was not obtained, that the pardon would be offered to Frank. Did they bandy about the chance of life, between these two, in this way? Did Mr. Colman, after having given this pledge to Joseph, and after having received a disclosure from Joseph, go to the cell of Frank for such a purpose as this? It is impossible; it cannot be so.

Again, we know that Mr. Colman found the club the next day; that he went directly to the place of deposit, and found it at the first attempt, exactly where he says he had been informed it was. Now Phippen Knapp says, that Frank had stated nothing respecting the club; that it was not mentioned in that conversation. He says, also, that he was present in the cell of Joseph all the time that Mr. Colman was there; that he believes he heard all that was said in Joseph's cell; and that he did not himself know where the club was, and never had known where it was, until he heard it stated in court. Now it is certain that Mr. Colman says he did not learn the particular place of deposit of the club from Joseph; that he only learned from him that it was deposited under the steps of the Howard Street meeting-house, without defining the particular steps. It is certain, also, that he had more knowledge of the position of the club than this; else how could he have placed his hand on it so readily? and where else could he have obtained this knowledge, except from Frank?

[Here Mr. Dexter said that Mr. Colman had had other interviews with Joseph, and might have derived the information from him at previous visits. Mr. Webster replied, that Mr. Colman has testified that he learned nothing in relation to the club until this visit. Mr. Dexter denied there being any such testimony. Mr. Colman's evidence was read, from the notes of the judges, and several other persons, and Mr. Webster then proceeded.]

My point is to show that Phippen Knapp's story is not true, is not consistent with itself; that, taking it for granted, as he says, that he heard all that was said to Mr. Colman in both cells, by Joseph and by Frank; and that Joseph did not state particularly where the club was deposited; and that he knew as much about the place of deposit of the club as Mr. Colman knew; why, then, Mr. Colman must either have been miraculously informed respecting the club, or Phippen Knapp has not told you the whole truth. There is no reconciling this, without supposing that Mr. Colman has misrepresented what took place in Joseph's cell, as well as what took place in Frank's cell.

Again, Phippen Knapp is directly contradicted by Mr. Wheatland. Mr. Wheatland tells the same story, as coming from Phippen Knapp, that Colman now tells. Here there are two against one. Phippen Knapp says that Frank made no confessions, and that he said he had none to make. In this he is contradicted by Wheatland. He, Phippen Knapp, told Wheatland, that Mr. Colman did ask Frank some questions, and that Frank answered them. He told him also what these answers were. Wheatland does not recollect the questions or answers, but recollects his reply; which was, "Is not this *premature?* I think this answer is sufficient to make Frank a principal." Here Phippen Knapp opposes himself to Wheatland, as well as to Mr. Colman. Do you believe Phippen Knapp against these two respectable witnesses, or them against him?

Is not Mr. Colman's testimony credible, natural, and proper? To judge of this you must go back to that scene.

The murder had been committed; the two Knapps were now arrested; four persons were already in jail supposed to be concerned in it, the Crowninshields, and Selman, and Chase. Another person at the Eastward was supposed to be in the plot; it was important to learn the facts. To do this, some one of those suspected must be admitted to turn state's witness. The contest was, Who should have this privilege? It was understood that it was about to be offered to Palmer, then in Maine; there was no good reason why he should have the preference. Mr. Colman felt interested for the family of the Knapps, and particularly for Joseph. He was a young man who had hitherto maintained a fair standing in society; he was a husband. Mr. Colman was particularly intimate with his family. With these views he went to the prison. He believed that he might safely converse with the prisoner, because he thought confessions made to a clergyman were sacred, and that he could not be called upon to disclose them. He went, the first time, in the morning, and was requested to come again. He went again at three o'clock; and was requested to call again at five o'clock. In the mean time he saw the father and Phippen, and they wished he would not go again, because it would be said the prisoners were making confession. He said he had engaged to go again at five o'clock; but would not, if Phippen would excuse him to Joseph. Phippen engaged to do this, and to meet him at his office at five o'clock. Mr. Colman went to the office at the time, and waited; but, as Phippen was not there, he walked down street, and saw him coming from the jail. He met him, and while in conversation near the church, he saw Mrs. Beckford and Mrs. Knapp going in a chaise towards the jail. He hastened to meet them, as he thought it not proper for them to go in at that time.

While conversing with them near the jail, he received two distinct messages from Joseph, that he wished to see him. He thought it proper to go; and accordingly went to Joseph's cell, and it was while there that the disclosures were made. Before Joseph had finished his statement, Phippen came to the door; he was soon after admitted. A short interval ensued, and they went together to the cell of Frank. Mr. Colman went in by invitation of Joseph, where he had for the first time learned the incidents of the tragedy. He was incredulous as to some of the facts which he had learned, they were so different from his previous impressions. He was desirous of knowing whether he could place confidence in what Joseph had told him. He, therefore, put the questions to Frank, as he has testified before you; in answer to which Frank Knapp informed him,—

1. "That the murder took place between ten and eleven o'clock."

2. "That Richard Crowninshield was alone in the house."

3. "That he, Frank Knapp, went home afterwards."

4. "That the club was deposited under the steps of the Howard Street meeting-house, and under the part nearest the burying-ground, in a rat hole."

5. "That the dagger or daggers had been worked up at the factory."

It is said that these five answers just fit the case; that they are just what was wanted, and neither more nor less. True, they are; but the reason is, because truth always fits. Truth is always congruous, and agrees with itself; every truth in the universe agrees with every other truth in the universe; whereas falsehoods not only disagree with truths, but usually quarrel among themselves. Surely Mr. Colman is influenced by no bias, no prejudice; he has no feeling to warp him, except, now that he is contradicted, he may feel an interest to be believed.

If you believe Mr. Colman, then the evidence is fairly in the case.

I shall now proceed on the ground that you do believe Mr. Colman.

When told that Joseph had determined to confess, the defendant said, "It is hard, or unfair, that Joseph should have the benefit of confessing, since the thing was done for his benefit." What thing was done for his benefit? Does not this carry an implication of the guilt of the defendant? Does it not show that he had a knowledge of the object and history of the murder?

The defendant said, "I told Joseph, when he proposed it, that it was a silly business, and would get us into trouble." He knew, then, what this business was; he knew that Joseph proposed it, and that he agreed to it, else he could not get *us* into trouble; he understood its bearing and its consequences. Thus much was said, under circumstances that make it clearly evidence against him, before there is any pretence of an inducement held out. And does this prove him to have a knowledge of the conspiracy?

He knew the daggers had been destroyed, and he knew who committed the murder. How could he have innocently known these facts? Why, if by Richard's story, this shows him guilty of a knowledge of the murder, and of the conspiracy. More than all, he knew when the deed was done, and that he went home afterwards. This shows his participation in that deed. "Went home afterwards!" Home, from what scene? home, from what fact? home, from what transaction? home, from what place? This confirms the supposition that the prisoner was in Brown Street for the purposes ascribed to him. These questions were directly put, and directly answered. He does not intimate that he received the information from another. Now, if he knows the time, and went home afterwards, and does not excuse himself, is not this an admission that he had a hand in this murder? Already proved to be a conspirator in the murder, he now confesses that he knew who did it, at what time it was done, that he was himself out of his own house at the time, and went home afterwards. Is not this conclusive, if not explained? Then comes the club. He told where it was. This is like possession of stolen goods. He is charged with the guilty knowledge of this concealment. He must show, not say, how he came by this knowledge. If a man be found with stolen goods, he must prove how he came by them. The place of deposit of the club was premeditated and selected, and he knew where it was.

Joseph Knapp was an accessory, and an accessory only; he knew only what was told him. But the prisoner knew the particular spot in which the club might be found. This shows his knowledge something more than that of an accessory. This presumption must be rebutted by evidence, or it stands strong against him. He has too much knowledge of this transaction to have come innocently by it. It must stand against him until he explains it.

This testimony of Mr. Colman is represented as new matter, and therefore an attempt has been made to excite a prejudice against it. It is not so. How little is there in it, after all, that did not appear from other sources? It is mainly confirmatory. Compare what you learn from this confession with what you before knew.

As to its being proposed by Joseph, was not that known?

As to Richard's being alone in the house, was not that known?

As to the daggers, was not that known?

As to the time of the murder, was not that known?

As to his being out that night, was not that known?

As to his returning afterwards, was not that known?

As to the club, was not that known?

So this information confirms what was known before, and fully confirms it.

One word as to the interview between Mr. Colman and Phippen Knapp on the turnpike. It is said that Mr. Colman's conduct in this matter is inconsistent with his testimony. There does not appear to me to be any inconsistency. He tells you that his object was to save Joseph, and to hurt no one, and least of all the prisoner at the bar. He had probably told Mr. White the substance of what he heard at the prison. He had probably told him that Frank confirmed what Joseph had confessed. He was unwilling to be the instrument of harm to Frank. He therefore, at the request of Phippen Knapp, wrote a note to Mr. White, requesting him to consider Joseph as authority for the information he had received. He tells you that this is the only thing he has to regret; as it may seem to be an evasion, as he doubts whether it was entirely correct. If it was an evasion, if it was a deviation, if it was an error, it was an error of mercy, an error of kindness; an error that proves he had no hostility to the prisoner at the bar. It does not in the least vary his testimony, or affect its correctness. Gentlemen, I look on the evidence of Mr.

Colman as highly important; not as bringing into the cause new facts, but as confirming, in a very satisfactory manner, other evidence. It is incredible that he can be false, and that he is seeking the prisoner's life through false swearing. If he is true, it is incredible that the prisoner can be innocent.

Gentlemen, I have gone through with the evidence in this case, and have endeavored to state it plainly and fairly before you. I think there are conclusions to be drawn from it, the accuracy of which you cannot doubt. I think you cannot doubt that there was a conspiracy formed for the purpose of committing this murder, and who the conspirators were:

That you cannot doubt that the Crowninshields and the Knapps were the parties in this conspiracy:

That you cannot doubt that the prisoner at the bar knew that the murder was to be done on the night of the 6th of April:

That you cannot doubt that the murderers of Captain White were the suspicious persons seen in and about Brown Street on that night:

That you cannot doubt that Richard Crowninshield was the perpetrator of that crime:

That you cannot doubt that the prisoner at the bar was in Brown Street on that night.

If there, then it must be by agreement, to countenance, to aid the perpetrator. And if so, then he is guilty as PRINCIPAL.

Gentlemen, your whole concern should be to do your duty, and leave consequences to take care of themselves. You will receive the law from the court. Your verdict, it is true, may endanger the prisoner's life, but then it is to save other lives. If the prisoner's guilt has been shown and proved beyond all reasonable doubt, you will convict him. If such reasonable doubts of guilt still remain, you will acquit him. You are the judges of the whole case. You owe a duty to the public, as well as to the prisoner at the bar. You cannot presume to be wiser than the law. Your duty is a plain, straight-forward one. Doubtless we would all judge him in mercy. Towards him, as an individual, the law inculcates no hostility; but towards him, if proved to be a murderer, the law, and the oaths you have taken, and public justice, demand that you do your duty.

With consciences satisfied with the discharge of duty, no consequences can harm you. There is no evil that we cannot either face or fly from, but the consciousness of duty disregarded. A sense of duty pursues us ever. It is omnipresent, like the Deity. If we take to ourselves the wings of the morning, and dwell in the uttermost parts of the sea, duty performed, or duty violated, is still with us, for our happiness or our misery. If we say the darkness shall cover us, in the darkness as in the light our obligations are yet with us. We cannot escape their power, nor fly from their presence. They are with us in this life, will be with us at its close; and in that scene of inconceivable solemnity, which lies yet farther onward, we shall still find ourselves surrounded by the consciousness of duty, to pain us wherever it has been violated, and to console us so far as God may have given us grace to perform it.

Daniel Webster

SECOND SPEECH ON FOOTE'S RESOLUTION—

REPLY TO HAYNE

❡ WEBSTER's famous "Reply to Hayne" was part of a debate that ran through five months in the Senate and covered a wide range of subjects. The resolution of Senator Foote of Connecticut, introduced in December, 1829, was opposed by Senator Benton of Missouri as an attempt of the East to check the progress of the West. Senator Hayne of South Carolina supported him, declaring that the real enemies of the Union were those who favored "consolidation," the constant siphoning off of power from the states to the federal government. He argued that the states had a right to nullify acts of Congress that they deemed unconstitutional. Hayne's second speech on this theme, January 24 and 25, was followed by Webster's second reply, January 26 and 27. He spoke before a packed Senate chamber with only such preparation as he could crowd into the intervening nights. This was the high point of the debate, though followed by Hayne's third speech and Webster's third reply. Henry Cabot Lodge says it was the highest point attained by Webster in his long career. The speech was taken down in shorthand and later corrected by Mr. Webster.

M R. PRESIDENT,—When the mariner has been tossed for many days in thick weather, and on an unknown sea, he naturally avails himself of the first pause in the storm, the earliest glance of the sun, to take his latitude, and ascertain how far the elements have driven him from his true course. Let us imitate this prudence, and, before we float farther on the waves of this debate, refer to the point from which we departed, that we may at least be able to conjecture where we now are. I ask for the reading of the resolution before the Senate.

[The Secretary read the resolution, as follows:—
"Resolved, That the Committee on Public Lands be instructed to inquire and report the quantity of public lands remaining unsold within each State and Territory, and whether it be expedient to limit for a certain period the sales of the public lands to such lands only as have heretofore been offered for sale, and are now subject to entry at the minimum price. And, also, whether the office of Surveyor-General, and some of the land offices, may not be abolished without detriment to the public interest; or whether it be expedient to adopt measures to hasten the sales and extend more rapidly the surveys of the public lands."]

We have thus heard, Sir, what the resolution is which is actually before us for consideration; and it will readily occur to every one, that it is almost the only subject about which something has not been said in the speech, running through two days, by which the Senate has been entertained by the gentleman from South Carolina. Every topic in the wide range of our public affairs, whether past or present,—every thing, general or local, whether belonging to national politics or party politics,—seems to have attracted more or less of the honorable member's attention, save only the resolution before the Senate. He has spoken of every thing but the public lands; they have escaped his notice. To that subject, in all his excursions, he has not paid even the cold respect of a passing glance.

When this debate, Sir, was to be resumed, on Thursday morning, it so happened that it would have been convenient for me to be elsewhere. The honorable member, however, did not incline to put off the discussion to another day. He had a shot, he said, to return, and he wished to discharge it. That shot, Sir, which he thus kindly informed us was coming, that we might stand out of the way, or prepare ourselves to fall by it and die with decency, has now been received. Under all advantages, and with expectation awakened by the tone which preceded it, it has been discharged, and has spent its force. It may become me to say no more of its effect, than that, if nobody is found, after all, either killed or wounded, it is not the first time, in the history of human affairs, that the vigor and success of the war have not quite come up to the lofty and sounding phrase of the manifesto.

The gentleman, Sir, in declining to postpone the debate, told the Senate, with the emphasis of his hand upon his heart, that there was something rankling *here*, which he wished to relieve. (Mr. Hayne rose, and disclaimed having used the word *rankling*.) It would not, Mr. President, be safe for the honorable member to appeal to those around him, upon the question whether he did in fact make use of that word. But he may have been unconscious of it. At any rate, it is enough that he disclaims it. But still, with or without the use of that particular word, he had yet something *here*, he said, of which he wished to rid himself by an immediate reply. In this respect, Sir, I have a great advantage over the honorable gentleman. There is nothing *here*, Sir, which gives me the slightest uneasiness; neither fear, nor anger, nor that which is sometimes more troublesome than either, the consciousness of having been in the wrong. There is nothing, either originating *here*, or now received *here* by the gentleman's shot. Nothing originating here, for I had not the slightest feeling of unkindness towards the honorable member. Some passages, it is true, had occurred since our acquaintance in this body, which I could have wished might have been otherwise; but I had used philosophy and forgotten them. I paid the honorable member the attention of listening with respect to his first speech; and when he sat down, though surprised, and I must even say astonished, at some of his opinions, nothing was farther from my intention than to commence any personal warfare. Through the whole of the few remarks I made in answer, I avoided, studiously and carefully, every thing which I thought possible to be construed into disrespect. And, Sir, while there is thus nothing originating *here* which I have wished at any time, or now wish, to discharge, I must repeat, also, that nothing has been received *here* which *rankles*, or in any way gives me annoyance. I will not accuse the honorable member of violating the rules of civilized war; I will not say, that he poisoned his arrows. But whether his shafts were, or were not, dipped in that which would have caused rankling if they had reached their destination, there was not, as it happened, quite strength enough in the bow to bring them to their mark. If he wishes now to gather up those shafts, he must look for them elsewhere; they will not be found fixed and quivering in the object at which they were aimed.

The honorable member complained that I had slept on his speech. I must have slept on it, or not slept at all. The moment the honorable member sat down, his friend from Missouri rose, and, with much honeyed commendation of the speech, suggested that the impressions which it had produced were too charming and delightful to be disturbed by other sentiments or other sounds, and proposed that the Senate should adjourn. Would it have been quite amiable in me, Sir, to interrupt this excellent good feeling? Must I not have been absolutely malicious, if I could have thrust myself forward, to destroy sensations thus pleasing? Was it not much better and kinder, both to sleep upon them myself, and to allow others also the pleasure of sleeping upon them? But if it be meant, by sleeping upon his speech, that I took time to prepare a reply to it, it is quite a mistake. Owing to other engagements, I could not employ even the interval between the adjournment of the Senate and its meeting the next morning, in attention to the subject of this debate. Nevertheless, Sir, the mere matter of fact is undoubtedly true. I did sleep on the gentleman's speech, and slept soundly. And I slept equally well on his speech of yesterday, to which I am now replying. It is quite possible that in this respect, also, I possess some advantage over the honorable member, attributable, doubtless, to a cooler temperament on my part; for, in truth, I slept upon his speeches remarkably well.

But the gentleman inquires why *he* was made the object of such a reply. Why was *he* singled out? If an attack has been made on the East, he, he assures us, did not begin it; it was made by the gentleman from Missouri. Sir, I answered the gentleman's speech because I happened to hear it; and because, also, I chose to give an answer to that speech, which, if unanswered, I thought most likely to produce injurious impressions. I did not stop to inquire who was the original drawer of the bill. I found a responsible indorser before me, and it was my purpose to hold him liable, and to bring him to his just responsibility, without delay. But, Sir, this interrogatory of the honorable member was only introductory to another. He proceeded to ask me whether I had turned upon him, in this debate, from the consciousness that I should find an overmatch, if I ventured on a contest with his friend from Missouri. If, Sir, the honorable member, *modestiae gratia,* had chosen thus to defer to his friend, and to pay him a compliment, without intentional disparagement to others, it would have been quite according to the friendly courtesies of debate, and not at all ungrateful to my own feelings. I am not one of those, Sir, who esteem any tribute of regard, whether light and occasional, or more serious and deliberate, which may be bestowed on others, as so much unjustly withholden from themselves. But the tone and manner of the gentleman's question forbid me thus to interpret it. I am not at liberty to consider it as nothing more than a civility to his friend. It had an air of taunt and disparagement, something of the loftiness of asserted superiority, which does not allow me to pass it over without notice. It was put as a question for me to answer, and so put as if it were difficult for me to answer, whether I deemed the member from Missouri an overmatch for myself, in debate here. It seems to me, Sir, that this is extraordinary language, and an extraordinary tone, for the discussions of this body.

Matches and overmatches! Those terms are more applicable elsewhere than here, and fitter for other assemblies than this. Sir, the gentleman seems to forget where and what we are. This is a Senate, a Senate of equals, of men of individual honor and personal character, and of absolute independence. We know no masters, we acknowledge no dictators. This is a hall for mutual consultation and discussion; not an arena for the exhibition of champions. I offer myself, Sir, as a match for no man; I throw the challenge of debate at no man's feet. But then, Sir, since the honorable member has put the question in a manner that calls for an answer, I will give him an answer; and I tell him, that, holding myself to be the humblest of the members here, I yet know nothing in the arm of his friend from Missouri, either alone or when aided by the arm of *his* friend from South Carolina, that need deter even me from espousing whatever opinions I may choose to espouse, from debating whenever I may choose to debate, or from speaking whatever I may see fit to say, on the floor of the Senate. Sir, when uttered as matter of commendation or compliment, I should dissent from nothing which the honorable member might say of his friend. Still less do I put forth any pretensions of my own. But when put to me as matter of taunt, I throw it back, and say to the gentleman, that he could possibly say nothing less likely than such a comparison to wound my pride of personal character. The anger of its tone rescued the remark from intentional irony, which otherwise, probably, would have been its general acceptation. But, Sir, if it be imagined that by this mutual quotation and commendation; if it be supposed that, by casting the characters of the drama, assigning to each his part, to one the attack, to another the cry of onset; or if it be thought that, by a loud and empty vaunt of anticipated victory, any laurels are to be won here; if it be imagined, especially, that any, or all these things will shake any purpose of mine, I can tell the honorable member, once for all, that he is greatly mistaken, and that he is dealing with one of whose temper and character he has yet much to learn. Sir, I shall not allow myself, on this occasion, I hope on no occasion, to be betrayed into any loss of temper; but if provoked, as I trust I never shall be, into crimination and recrimination, the honorable member may perhaps find that, in that contest, there will be blows to take as well as blows to give; that others can state comparisons as significant, at least, as his own, and that his impunity may possibly demand of him whatever powers of taunt and sarcasm he may possess. I commend him to a prudent husbandry of his resources.

But, Sir, the Coalition! Ay, "the murdered Coalition!" The gentleman asks, if I were led or frightened into this debate by the spectre of the Coalition. "Was it the ghost of the murdered Coalition," he exclaims, "which haunted the member from Massachusetts; and which, like the ghost of Banquo, would never down?" "The murdered Coalition." Sir, this charge of a coalition, in reference to the late administration, is not original with the honorable member. It did not spring up in the Senate. Whether as a fact, as an argument, or as an embellishment, it is all borrowed. He adopts it, indeed, from a very low origin, and a still lower present condition. It is one of the thousand calumnies with which the press teemed, during an excited political canvass. It was a charge, of which there was not only no proof or probability, but which was in itself wholly impossible to be true. No man of common information ever believed a syllable of it. Yet it was of that class of falsehoods, which, by continued repetition, through all the organs of detraction and abuse, are capable of misleading those who are already far misled, and of further fanning passion already kindling into flame. Doubtless it served in its day, and in greater or less degree, the end designed by it. Having done that, it has sunk into the general mass of stale and loathed calumnies. It is the very cast-off slough of a polluted and shameless press. Incapable of further mischief, it lies in the sewer, lifeless and despised. It is not now, Sir, in the power of the honorable member to give it dignity or decency, by attempting to elevate it, and to introduce it into the Senate. He cannot change it from what it is, an object of general disgust and scorn. On the contrary, the contact, if he choose to touch it, is more likely to drag him down, down, to the place where it lies itself.

But, Sir, the honorable member was not, for other reasons, entirely happy in his allusion to the story of Banquo's murder and Banquo's ghost. It was not, I think, the friends, but the enemies of the murdered Banquo, at whose bidding his spirit would not *down*. The honorable gentleman is fresh in his reading of the English classics, and can put me right if I am wrong; but, according to my poor recollection, it was at those who had begun with caresses and ended with foul and treacherous murder that the gory locks were shaken. The ghost of Banquo, like that of Hamlet, was an honest ghost. It disturbed no innocent man. It knew where its appearance would strike terror, and who would cry out, A ghost! It made itself visible in the right quarter, and compelled the guilty and the conscience-smitten, and none others, to start, with,

> "Pr'ythee, see there! behold!—look! lo
> If I stand here, I saw him!"

Their eyeballs were seared (was it not so, Sir?) who had thought to shield themselves by concealing their own hand, and laying the imputation of the crime on a low and hireling agency in wickedness; who had vainly attempted to stifle the workings of their own coward consciences by ejaculating through white lips and chattering teeth, "Thou canst not say I did it!" I have misread the great poet if those who had no way partaken in the deed of the death, either found that they were, or *feared that they should be,* pushed from their stools by the ghost of the slain, or exclaimed to a spectre created by their own fears and their own remorse, "Avaunt! and quit our sight!"

There is another particular, Sir, in which the honorable member's quick perception of resemblances might, I should think, have seen something in the story of Banquo, making it not altogether a subject of the most pleasant contemplation. Those who murdered Banquo, what did they win by it? Substantial good? Permanent power? Or disappointment, rather, and sore mortification; dust and ashes, the common fate of vaulting ambition overleaping itself? Did not even-handed justice ere long commend the poisoned chalice to their own lips? Did they not soon find that for another they had "filed their mind"? that their ambition, though apparently for the moment successful, had but put a barren sceptre in their grasp? Ay, Sir,

> "a barren sceptre in their gripe,
> Thence to be wrenched with an unlineal hand,
> No son of theirs succeeding."

Sir, I need pursue the allusion no farther. I leave the honorable gentleman to run it out at his leisure, and to derive from it all the gratification it is calculated to administer. If he finds himself pleased with the associations, and prepared to be quite satisfied, though the parallel should be entirely completed, I had almost said, I am satisfied also, but that I shall think of. Yes, Sir, I will think of that.

In the course of my observations the other day, Mr. President, I paid a passing tribute of respect to a very worthy man, Mr. Dane of Massachusetts. It so happened that he drew the Ordinance of 1787, for the government of the Northwestern Territory. A man of so much ability, and so little pretence; of so great a capacity to do good, and so unmixed a disposition to do it for its own sake; a gentleman who had acted an important part, forty years ago, in a measure the

influence of which is still deeply felt in the very matter which was
the subject of debate, might, I thought, receive from me a commen-
datory recognition. But the honorable member was inclined to be
facetious on the subject. He was rather disposed to make it matter of
ridicule, that I had introduced into the debate the name of one
Nathan Dane, of whom he assures us he had never before heard.
Sir, if the honorable member had never before heard of Mr. Dane, I
am sorry for it. It shows him less acquainted with the public men
of the country than I had supposed. Let me tell him, however, that
a sneer from him at the mention of the name of Mr. Dane is in bad
taste. It may well be a high mark of ambition, Sir, either with the
honorable gentleman or myself, to accomplish as much to make our
names known to advantage, and remembered with gratitude, as Mr.
Dane has accomplished. But the truth is, Sir, I suspect, that Mr.
Dane lives a little too far north. He is of Massachusetts, and too near
the north star to be reached by the honorable gentleman's telescope.
If his sphere had happened to range south of Mason and Dixon's
line, he might, probably, have come within the scope of his vision.

I spoke, Sir, of the Ordinance of 1787, which prohibits slavery, in
all future times, northwest of the Ohio, as a measure of great wisdom
and foresight, and one which had been attended with highly beneficial and permanent consequences. I supposed that, on this point,
no two gentlemen in the Senate could entertain different opinions.
But the simple expression of this sentiment has led the gentleman,
not only into a labored defence of slavery, in the abstract, and on
principle, but also into a warm accusation against me, as having
attacked the system of domestic slavery now existing in the Southern
States. For all this, there was not the slightest foundation, in any thing
said or intimated by me. I did not utter a single word which any
ingenuity could torture into an attack on the slavery of the South. I
said, only, that it was highly wise and useful, in legislating for the
Northwestern country while it was yet a wilderness, to prohibit the
introduction of slaves; and I added, that I presumed there was no
reflecting and intelligent person, in the neighboring State of Kentucky, who would doubt that, if the same prohibition had been
extended, at the same early period, over that commonwealth, her

strength and population would, at this day, have been far greater than they are. If these opinions be thought doubtful, they are nevertheless, I trust, neither extraordinary nor disrespectful. They attack nobody and menace nobody. And yet, Sir, the gentleman's optics have discovered, even in the mere expression of this sentiment, what he calls the very spirit of the Missouri question! He represents me as making an onset on the whole South, and manifesting a spirit which would interfere with, and disturb, their domestic condition!

Sir, this injustice no otherwise surprises me, than as it is committed here, and committed without the slightest pretence of ground for it. I say it only surprises me as being done here; for I know full well, that it is, and has been, the settled policy of some persons in the South, for years, to represent the people of the North as disposed to interfere with them in their own exclusive and peculiar concerns. This is a delicate and sensitive point in Southern feeling; and of late years it has always been touched, and generally with effect, whenever the object has been to unite the whole South against Northern men or Northern measures. This feeling, always carefully kept alive, and maintained at too intense a heat to admit discrimination or reflection, is a lever of great power in our political machine. It moves vast bodies, and gives to them one and the same direction. But it is without adequate cause, and the suspicion which exists is wholly groundless. There is not, and never has been, a disposition in the North to interfere with these interests of the South. Such interference has never been supposed to be within the power of government; nor has it been in any way attempted. The slavery of the South has always been regarded as a matter of domestic policy, left with the States themselves, and with which the federal government had nothing to do. Certainly, Sir, I am, and ever have been, of that opinion. The gentleman, indeed, argues that slavery, in the abstract, is no evil. Most assuredly I need not say I differ with him, altogether and most widely, on that point. I regard domestic slavery as one of the greatest evils, both moral and political. But whether it be a malady, and whether it be curable, and if so, by what means; or, on the other hand, whether it be the *vulnus immedicabile* of the social system, I leave it to those whose right and duty it is to inquire and to decide.

And this I believe, Sir, is, and uniformly has been, the sentiment of the North. Let us look a little at the history of this matter.

When the present Constitution was submitted for the ratification of the people, there were those who imagined that the powers of the government which it proposed to establish might, in some possible mode, be exerted in measures tending to the abolition of slavery. This suggestion would of course attract much attention in the Southern conventions. In that of Virginia, Governor Randolph said:—

"I hope there is none here, who, considering the subject in the calm light of philosophy, will make an objection dishonorable to Virginia; that, at the moment they are securing the rights of their citizens, an objection is started, that there is a spark of hope that those unfortunate men now held in bondage may, by the operation of the general government, be made free."

At the very first Congress, petitions on the subject were presented, if I mistake not, from different States. The Pennsylvania society for promoting the abolition of slavery took a lead, and laid before Congress a memorial, praying Congress to promote the abolition by such powers as it possessed. This memorial was referred, in the House of Representatives, to a select committee, consisting of Mr. Foster, of New Hampshire, Mr. Gerry of Massachusetts, Mr. Huntington of Connecticut, Mr. Lawrence of New York, Mr. Sinnickson of New Jersey, Mr. Hartley of Pennsylvania, and Mr. Parker of Virginia; all of them, Sir, as you will observe, Northern men but the last. This committee made a report, which was referred to a committee of the whole House, and there considered and discussed for several days; and being amended, although without material alteration, it was made to express three distinct propositions, on the subject of slavery and the slave-trade. First, in the words of the Constitution, that Congress could not, prior to the year 1808, prohibit the migration or importation of such persons as any of the States then existing should think proper to admit; and secondly, that Congress had authority to restrain the citizens of the United States from carrying on the African slave-trade, for the purpose of supplying foreign countries. On this proposition, our early laws against those who engage in that traffic are founded. The third proposition, and that which bears on the present question, was expressed in the following terms:—

"*Resolved,* That Congress have no authority to interfere in the emancipation of slaves, or in the treatment of them in any of the States; it remaining with the several States alone to provide rules and regulations therein which humanity and true policy may require."

This resolution received the sanction of the House of Representatives so early as March, 1790. And now, Sir, the honorable member will allow me to remind him, that not only were the select committee who reported the resolution, with a single exception, all Northern men, but also that, of the members then composing the House of Representatives, a large majority, I believe nearly two thirds, were Northern men also.

The House agreed to insert these resolutions in its journal, and from that day to this it has never been maintained or contended at the North, that Congress had any authority to regulate or interfere with the condition of slaves in the several States. No Northern gentleman, to my knowledge, has moved any such question in either House of Congress.

The fears of the South, whatever fears they might have entertained, were allayed and quieted by this early decision; and so remained till they were excited afresh, without cause, but for collateral and indirect purposes. When it became necessary, or was thought so, by some political persons, to find an unvarying ground for the exclusion of Northern men from confidence and from lead in the affairs of the republic, then, and not till then, the cry was raised, and the feeling industriously excited, that the influence of Northern men in the public counsels would endanger the relation of master and slave. For myself, I claim no other merit than that this gross and enormous injustice towards the whole North has not wrought upon me to change my opinions or my political conduct. I hope I am above violating my principles, even under the smart of injury and false imputations. Unjust suspicions and undeserved reproach, whatever pain I may experience from them, will not induce me, I trust, to overstep the limits of constitutional duty, or to encroach on the rights of others. The domestic slavery of the Southern States I leave where I find it,—in the hands of their own governments. It is their affair, not mine. Nor do I complain of the peculiar effect which the magnitude of that population has had in the distribution of power under this federal government. We know, Sir, that the representation of the States in the other house is not equal. We know that great advantage in that respect is enjoyed by the slave-holding States; and we know, too, that the intended equivalent for that advantage, that is to say, the imposition of direct taxes in the same ratio, has become merely nominal, the habit of the government being almost invariably to collect its revenue from other sources and in other modes. Nevertheless, I do not complain; nor would I countenance any movement to alter this arrangement of representation. It is the original bargain, the compact; let it stand; let the advantage of it be fully enjoyed. The Union itself is too full of benefit to be hazarded in propositions for changing its original basis. I go for the Constitution as it is, and for the Union as it is. But I am resolved not to submit in silence to accusations, either against myself individually or against the North, wholly unfounded and unjust; accusations which impute to us a disposition to evade the constitutional compact, and to extend the power of the government over the internal laws and domestic condition of the States. All such accusations, wherever and whenever made, all insinuations of the existence of any such purposes, I know and feel to be groundless and injurious. And we must confide in Southern gentlemen themselves; we must trust to those whose integrity of heart and magnanimity of feeling will lead them to a desire to maintain and disseminate truth, and who possess the means of its diffusion with the Southern public; we must leave it to them to disabuse that public of its prejudices. But in the mean time, for my own part, I shall continue to act justly, whether those towards whom justice is exercised receive it with candor or with contumely.

Having had occasion to recur to the Ordinance of 1787, in order to defend myself against the inferences which the honorable member has chosen to draw from my former observations on that subject, I am not willing now entirely to take leave of it without another remark. It need hardly be said, that that paper expresses just senti-

ments on the great subject of civil and religious liberty. Such sentiments were common, and abound in all our state papers of that day.
But this Ordinance did that which was not so common, and which is
not even now universal; that is, it set forth and declared it to be a
high and binding duty of government itself to support schools and
advance the means of education, on the plain reason that religion,
morality, and knowledge are necessary to good government, and to
the happiness of mankind. One observation further. The important
provision incorporated into the Constitution of the United States,
and into several of those of the States, and recently, as we have seen,
adopted into the reformed constitution of Virginia, restraining legislative power in questions of private right, and from impairing the
obligation of contracts, is first introduced and established, as far as
I am informed, as matter of express written constitutional law, in
this Ordinance of 1787. And I must add, also, in regard to the author
of the Ordinance, who has not had the happiness to attract the
gentleman's notice heretofore, nor to avoid his sarcasm now, that
he was chairman of that select committee of the old Congress, whose
report first expressed the strong sense of that body, that the old
Confederation was not adequate to the exigencies of the country
and recommended to the States to send delegates to the convention
which formed the present Constitution.

An attempt has been made to transfer from the North to the South
the honor of this exclusion of slavery from the Northwestern Territory. The journal, without argument or comment, refutes such attempts. The cession by Virginia was made in March, 1784. On the
19th of April following, a committee, consisting of Messrs. Jefferson,
Chase, and Howell, reported a plan for a temporary government of
the territory, in which was this article: "That, after the year 1800,
there shall be neither slavery nor involuntary servitude in any of the
said States, otherwise than in punishment of crimes, whereof the
party shall have been convicted." Mr. Spaight of North Carolina
moved to strike out this paragraph. The question was put, according
to the form then practised, "Shall these words stand as a part of the
plan?" New Hamphire, Massachusetts, Rhode Island, Connecticut,
New York, New Jersey, and Pennsylvania, seven States, voted in the

affirmative; Maryland, Virginia, and South Carolina, in the negative. North Carolina was divided. As the consent of nine States was necessary, the words could not stand, and were struck out accordingly. Mr. Jefferson voted for the clause, but was overruled by his colleagues.

In March of the next year (1785), Mr. King of Massachusetts, seconded by Mr. Ellery of Rhode Island, proposed the formerly rejected article, with this addition: "And that this regulation shall be an article of compact, and remain a fundamental principle of the constitutions between the thirteen original States, and each of the States described in the resolve." On this clause, which provided the adequate and thorough security, the eight Northern States at that time voted affirmatively, and the four Southern States negatively. The votes of nine States were not yet obtained, and thus the provision was again rejected by the Southern States. The perseverance of the North held out, and two years afterwards the object was attained. It is no derogation from the credit, whatever that may be, of drawing the Ordinance, that its principles had before been prepared and discussed, in the form of resolutions. If one should reason in that way, what would become of the distinguished honor of the author of the Declaration of Independence? There is not a sentiment in that paper which had not been voted and resolved in the assemblies, and other popular bodies in the country, over and over again.

But the honorable member has now found out that this gentleman, Mr. Dane, was a member of the Hartford Convention. However uninformed the honorable member may be of characters and occurrences at the North, it would seem that he has at his elbow, on this occasion, some high-minded and lofty spirit, some magnanimous and true-hearted monitor, possessing the means of local knowledge, and ready to supply the honorable member with every thing, down even to forgotten and moth-eaten two-penny pamphlets, which may be used to the disadvantage of his own country. But as to the Hartford Convention, Sir, allow me to say, that the proceedings of that body seem now to be less read and studied in New England than farther South. They appear to be looked to, not in New England, but elsewhere, for the purpose of seeing how far they may serve as a precedent. But they will not answer the purpose, they are quite too tame. The latitude in which they originated was too cold. Other conventions, of more recent existence, have gone a whole bar's length beyond it. The learned doctors of Colleton and Abbeville have pushed their commentaries on the Hartford collect so far, that the original text-writers are thrown entirely into the shade. I have nothing to do, Sir, with the Hartford Convention. Its journal, which the gentleman has quoted, I never read. So far as the honorable member may discover in its proceedings a spirit in any degree resembling that which was avowed and justified in those other conventions to which I have alluded, or so far as those proceedings can be shown to be disloyal to the Constitution, or tending to disunion, so far I shall be as ready as any one to bestow on them reprehension and censure.

Having dwelt long on this convention, and other occurrences of that day, in the hope, probably, (which will not be gratified), that I should leave the course of this debate to follow him at length in those excursions, the honorable member returned, and attempted another object. He referred to a speech of mine in the other house, the same which I had occasion to allude to myself, the other day; and has quoted a passage or two from it, with a bold, though uneasy and laboring, air of confidence, as if he had detected in me an inconsistency. Judging from the gentleman's manner, a stranger to the course of the debate and to the point in discussion would have imagined, from so triumphant a tone, that the honorable member was about to overwhelm me with a manifest contradiction. Any one who heard him, and who had not heard what I had, in fact, previously said, must have thought me routed and discomfited, as the gentleman had promised. Sir, a breath blows all this triumph away. There is not the slightest difference in the purport of my remarks on the two occasions. What I said here on Wednesday is in exact accordance with the opinion expressed by me in the other house in 1825. Though the gentleman had the metaphysics of Hudibras, though he were able

"to sever and divide
A hair 'twixt north and northwest side,"

he yet could not insert his metaphysical scissors between the fair reading of my remarks in 1825, and what I said here last week. There is not only no contradiction, no difference, but, in truth, too exact a similarity, both in thought and language, to be entirely in just taste. I had myself quoted the same speech; had recurred to it, and spoke with it open before me; and much of what I said was little more than a repetition from it. In order to make finishing work with this alleged contradiction, permit me to recur to the origin of this debate, and review its course. This seems expedient, and may be done as well now as at any time.

Well, then, its history is this. The honorable member from Connecticut moved a resolution, which constitutes the first branch of that which is now before us; that is to say, a resolution, instructing the committee on public lands to inquire into the expedience of limiting, for a certain period, the sales of the public lands, to such as have heretofore been offered for sale; and whether sundry offices connected with the sales of the lands might not be abolished without detriment to the public service. In the progress of the discussion which arose on this resolution, an honorable member from New Hampshire moved to amend the resolution, so as entirely to reverse its object; that is, to strike it all out, and insert a direction to the committee to inquire into the expediency of adopting measures to hasten the sales, and extend more rapidly the surveys, of the lands.

The honorable member from Maine suggested that both those propositions might well enough go for consideration to the committee; and in this state of the question, the member from South Carolina addressed the Senate in his first speech. He rose, he said, to give us his own free thoughts on the public lands. I saw him rise with pleasure, and listened with expectation, though before he concluded I was filled with surprise. Certainly, I was never more surprised, than to find him following up, to the extent he did, the sentiments and opinions which the gentleman from Missouri had put forth, and which it is known he has long entertained.

I need not repeat at large the general topics of the honorable gentleman's speech. When he said yesterday that he did not attack the Eastern States, he certainly must have forgotten, not only particular remarks, but the whole drift and tenor of his speech; unless he means by not attacking, that he did not commence hostilities, but that another had preceded him in the attack. He, in the first place, disapproved of the whole course of the government, for forty years, in regard to its disposition of the public lands; and then, turning northward and eastward, and fancying he had found a cause for alleged narrowness and niggardliness in the "accursed policy" of the tariff, to which he represented the people of New England as wedded, he went on for a full hour with remarks, the whole scope of which was to exhibit the results of this policy, in feelings and in measures unfavorable to the West. I thought his opinions unfounded and erroneous, as to the general course of the government, and ventured to reply to them.

The gentleman had remarked on the analogy of other cases, and quoted the conduct of European governments towards their own subjects settling on this continent, as in point, to show that we had been harsh and rigid in selling, when we should have given the public lands to settlers without price. I thought the honorable member had suffered his judgment to be betrayed by a false analogy; that he was struck with an appearance of resemblance where there was no real similitude. I think so still. The first settlers of North America were enterprising spirits, engaged in private adventure, or fleeing from tyranny at home. When arrived here, they were forgotten by the mother country, or remembered only to be oppressed. Carried away again by the appearance of analogy, or struck with the eloquence of the passage, the honorable member yesterday observed, that the conduct of government towards the Western emigrants, or my representation of it, brought to his mind a celebrated speech in the British Parliament. It was, Sir, the speech of Colonel Barre. On the question of the stamp act, or tea tax, I forget which, Colonel Barre had heard a member on the treasury bench argue, that the people of the United States, being British colonists, planted by the maternal care, nourished by the indulgence, and protected by the arms of England, would not grudge their mite to relieve the mother country from the heavy burden under which she groaned. The language of Colonel Barre, in reply to this, was,—"They planted by your care? Your oppression planted them in America. They fled from your tyranny, and grew by your neglect of them. So soon as you began to care for them, you showed your care by sending persons to spy out their liberties, misrepresent their character, prey upon them, and eat out their substance."

And how does the honorable gentleman mean to maintain, that language like this is applicable to the conduct of the government of the United States towards the Western emigrants, or to any representation given by me of that conduct? Were the settlers in the West driven thither by our oppression? Have they flourished only by our neglect of them? Has the government done nothing but prey upon them, and eat out their substance? Sir, this fervid eloquence of the British speaker, just when and where it was uttered, and fit to remain an exercise for the schools, is not a little out of place, when it is brought thence to be applied here, to the conduct of our own country towards her own citizens. From America to England, it may be true; from Americans to their own government, it would be strange language. Let us leave it, to be recited and declaimed by our boys against a foreign nation; not introduce it here, to recite and declaim ourselves against our own.

But I come to the point of the alleged contradiction. In my remarks on Wednesday, I contended that we could not give away gratuitously all the public lands; that we held them in trust; that the government had solemnly pledged itself to dispose of them as a common fund for the common benefit, and to sell and settle them as its discretion should dictate. Now, Sir, what contradiction does the gentleman find to this sentiment in the speech of 1825? He quotes me as having then said, that we ought not to hug these lands as a very great treasure. Very well, Sir, supposing me to be accurately reported in that expression, what is the contradiction? I have not now said, that we should hug these lands as a favorite source of pecuniary income. No such thing. It is not my view. What I have said, and what I do say, is, that they are a common fund, to be disposed of for the common benefit, to be sold at low prices for the accommodation of settlers, keeping the object of settling the lands as much in view as that of raising money from them. This I say now, and this I have always said. Is this hugging them as a favorite treasure? Is there no difference between hugging and hoarding this fund, on the one hand, as a great treasure, and, on the other, of disposing of it at low prices, placing the proceeds in the general treasury of the Union? My opinion is, that as much is to be made of the land as fairly and reasonably may be, selling it all the while at such rates as to give the fullest effect to settlement. This is not giving it all away to the States, as the gentleman would propose; nor is it hugging the fund closely and tenaciously, as a favorite treasure; but it is, in my judgment, a just and wise policy, perfectly according with all the various duties which rest on government. So much for my contradiction. And what is it? Where is the ground of the gentleman's triumph? What inconsistency in word or doctrine has he been able to detect? Sir, if this be a sample of that discomfiture with which the honorable gentleman threatened me, commend me to the word *discomfiture* for the rest of my life.

But, after all, this is not the point of the debate; and I must now bring the gentleman back to what is the point.

The real question between me and him is, Has the doctrine been advanced at the South or the East, that the population of the West should be retarded, or at least need not be hastened, on account of its effect to drain off the people from the Atlantic States? Is this doctrine, as has been alleged, of Eastern origin? That is the question. Has the gentleman found any thing by which he can make good his accusation? I submit to the Senate, that he has entirely failed; and, as far as this debate has shown, the only person who has advanced such sentiments is a gentleman from South Carolina, and a friend of the honorable member himself. The honorable gentleman has given no answer to this; there is none which can be given. The simple fact, while it requires no comment to enforce it, defies all argument to refute it. I could refer to the speeches of another Southern gentleman, in years before, of the same general character, and to the same effect, as that which has been quoted; but I will not consume the time of the Senate by the reading of them.

So then, Sir, New England is guiltless of the policy of retarding Western population, and of all envy and jealousy of the growth of the new States. Whatever there be of that policy in the country, no part of it is hers. If it has a local habitation, the honorable member has probably seen by this time where to look for it; and if it now has received a name, he has himself christened it.

[Webster next defends himself from a charge of inconsistency in his position on the public lands, and goes on to argue that the public lands may be disposed of for any project that benefits all the people. He differentiates between his construction of the powers of the government and Hayne's in matters pertaining to the "common good" and indicates that therein lies the key to their differences. He shows that New England has supported measures favorable to the West more effectively than has the South; that members from South Carolina had formerly approved measures for internal improvement by the federal government. He says he wishes to strengthen the Union, but not to extend its powers. He defends himself from the charge of inconsistency on the tariff and clarifies his position on that subject. He denies that New England has produced a disproportionate quantity of violent and reckless political argument.]

Mr. President, in carrying his warfare, such as it is, into New England, the honorable gentleman all along professes to be acting on the defensive. He chooses to consider me as having assailed South Carolina, and insists that he comes forth only as her champion, and in her defence. Sir, I do not admit that I made any attack whatever on South Carolina. Nothing like it. The honorable member, in his first speech, expressed opinions, in regard to revenue and some other topics, which I heard both with pain and with surprise. I told the gentleman I was aware that such sentiments were entertained *out* of the government, but had not expected to find them advanced in it; that I knew there were persons in the South who speak of our Union with indifference or doubt, taking pains to magnify its evils, and to say nothing of its benefits; that the honorable member himself, I was sure, could never be one of these; and I regretted the expression of such opinions as he had avowed, because I thought their obvious tendency was to encourage feelings of disrespect to the Union, and to impair its strength. This, Sir, is the sum and substance of all I said on the subject. And this constitutes the attack which called on the chivalry of the gentleman, in his own opinion, to harry us with such a foray among the party pamphlets and party proceedings of Massachusetts! If he means that I spoke with dissatisfaction or disrespect of the ebullitions of individuals in South Carolina, it is true. But if he means that I assailed the character of the State, her honor, or patriotism, that I reflected on her history or her conduct, he has not the slightest ground for any such assumption. I did not even refer, I think, in my observations, to any collection of individuals. I said nothing of the recent conventions. I spoke in the most guarded and careful manner, and only expressed my regret for the publication of opinions, which I presumed the honorable member disapproved as much as myself. In this, it seems, I was mistaken. I do not remember that the gentleman has disclaimed any sentiment, or any opinion, of a supposed anti-union tendency, which on all or any of the recent occasions has been expressed. The whole drift of his speech has been rather to prove, that, in divers times and manners, sentiments equally liable to my objection have been avowed in New England. And one would suppose that his object, in this reference to Massachusetts, was to find a precedent to justify proceedings in the South, were it not for the reproach and contumely with which he labors, all along, to load these his own chosen precedents. By way of defending South Carolina from what he chooses to think an attack on her, he first quotes the example of Massachusetts, and then denounces that example in good set terms. This twofold purpose, not very consistent, one would think, with itself, was exhibited more than once in the course of his speech. He referred, for instance, to the Hartford Convention. Did he do this for authority, or for a topic of reproach? Apparently for both, for he told us that he should find no fault with the mere fact of holding such a convention, and considering and discussing such questions as he supposes were then and there discussed; but what rendered it obnoxious was its being held at the time, and under the circumstances of the country then existing. We were in a war, he said, and the country needed all our aid; the hand of government required to be strengthened, not weakened; and patriotism should have postponed such proceedings to another day. The thing itself, then, is a precedent; the time and manner of it only, a subject of censure.

Now, Sir, I go much further, on this point, than the honorable member. Supposing, as the gentleman seems to do, that the Hartford Convention assembled for any such purpose as breaking up the Union, because they thought unconstitutional laws had been passed, or to consult on that subject, or *to calculate the value of the Union;* supposing this to be their purpose, or any part of it, then I say the meeting itself was disloyal, and was obnoxious to censure, whether held in time of peace or time of war, or under whatever circumstances. The material question is the *object.* Is dissolution the *object?* If it be, external circumstances may make it a more or less aggravated case, but cannot affect the principle. I do not hold, therefore, Sir, that the Hartford Convention was pardonable, even to the extent of the gentleman's admission, if its objects were really such as have been imputed to it. Sir, there never was a time, under any degree of excitement, in which the Hartford, or any other convention, could have maintained itself one moment in New England, if assembled for any such purpose as the gentleman says would have been an allowable purpose. To hold conventions to decide constitutional law! To try the binding validity of statutes by votes in a convention! Sir, the Hartford Convention, I presume, would not desire that the honorable gentleman should be their defender or advocate, if he puts their case upon such untenable and extravagant grounds.

Then, Sir, the gentleman has no fault to find with these recently promulgated South Carolina opinions. And certainly he need have none; for his own sentiments, as now advanced, and advanced on reflection, as far as I have been able to comprehend them, go the full length of all these opinions. I propose, Sir, to say something on these, and to consider how far they are just and constitutional. Before doing that, however, let me observe that the eulogium pronounced by the honorable gentleman on the character of the State of South Carolina, for her Revolutionary and other merits, meets my hearty concurrence. I shall not acknowledge that the honorable member goes before me in regard for whatever of distinguished talent, or distinguished character, South Carolina has produced. I claim part of the honor, I partake in the pride, of her great names. I claim them for countrymen, one and all, the Laurenses, the Rutledges, the Pinckneys, the Sumpters, the Marions, Americans all, whose fame is no more to be hemmed in by State lines, than their talents and patriotism were capable of being circumscribed within the same narrow limits. In their day and generation, they served and honored the country, and the whole country; and their renown is of the treasures of the whole country. Him whose honored name the gentleman himself bears,— does he esteem me less capable of gratitude for his patriotism, or sympathy for his sufferings, than if his eyes had first opened upon the light of Massachusetts, instead of South Carolina? Sir, does he suppose it in his power to exhibit a Carolina name so bright, as to produce envy in my bosom? No, Sir, increased gratification and delight, rather. I thank God, that, if I am gifted with little of the spirit which is able to raise mortals to the skies, I have yet none, as I trust, of that other spirit, which would drag angels down. When I shall be found, Sir, in my place here in the Senate, or elsewhere, to sneer at public merit, because it happens to spring up beyond the little limits of my own State or neighborhood; when I refuse, for any such cause, or for any cause, the homage due to American talent, to elevated patriotism, to sincere devotion to liberty and the country; or, if I see an uncommon endowment of Heaven, if I see extraordinary capacity and virtue, in any son of the South, and if, moved by local prejudice or gangrened by State jealousy, I get up here to abate the tithe of a hair from his just character and just fame, may my tongue cleave to the roof of my mouth!

Sir, let me recur to pleasing recollections; let me indulge in refreshing remembrance of the past; let me remind you that, in early times, no States cherished greater harmony, both of principle and feeling, than Massachusetts and South Carolina. Would to God that harmony might again return! Shoulder to shoulder they went through the Revolution, hand in hand they stood round the administration of Washington, and felt his own great arm lean on them for support. Unkind feeling, if it exist, alienation, and distrust are the growth, unnatural to such soils, of false principles since sown. They are weeds, the seeds of which that same great arm never scattered.

Mr. President, I shall enter on no encomium upon Massachusetts;

she needs none. There she is. Behold her, and judge for yourselves. There is her history; the world knows it by heart. The past, at least, is secure. There is Boston, and Concord, and Lexington, and Bunker Hill; and there they will remain for ever. The bones of her sons, falling in the great struggle for Independence, now lie mingled with the soil of every State from New England to Georgia; and there they will lie for ever. And, Sir, where American Liberty raised its first voice, and where its youth was nurtured and sustained, there it still lives, in the strength of its manhood and full of its original spirit. If discord and disunion shall wound it, if party strife and blind ambition shall hawk at and tear it, if folly and madness, if uneasiness under salutary and necessary restraint, shall succeed in separating it from that Union, by which alone its existence is made sure, it will stand, in the end, by the side of that cradle in which its infancy was rocked; it will stretch forth its arm with whatever of vigor it may still retain over the friends who gather round it; and it will fall at last, if fall it must, amidst the proudest monuments of its own glory, and on the very spot of its origin.

There yet remains to be performed, Mr. President, by far the most grave and important duty, which I feel to be devolved on me by this occasion. It is to state, and to defend, what I conceive to be the true principles of the Constitution under which we are here assembled. I might well have desired that so weighty a task should have fallen into other and abler hands. I could have wished that it should have been executed by those whose character and experience give weight and influence to their opinions, such as cannot possibly belong to mine. But, Sir, I have met the occasion, not sought it; and I shall proceed to state my own sentiments, without challenging for them any particular regard, with studied plainness, and as much precision as possible.

I understand the honorable gentleman from South Carolina to maintain, that it is a right of the State legislatures to interfere, whenever, in their judgment, this government transcends its constitutional limits, and to arrest the operation of its laws.

I understand him to maintain this right, as a right existing *under* the Constitution, not as a right to overthrow it on the ground of extreme necessity, such as would justify violent revolution.

I understand him to maintain an authority, on the part of the States, thus to interfere, for the purpose of correcting the exercise of power by the general government, of checking it, and of compelling it to conform to their opinion of the extent of its powers.

I understand him to maintain, that the ultimate power of judging of the constitutional extent of its own authority is not lodged exclusively in the general government, or any branch of it; but that, on the contrary, the States may lawfully decide for themselves, and each State for itself, whether, in a given case, the act of the general government transcends its power.

I understand him to insist, that, if the exigency of the case, in the opinion of any State government, require it, such State government may, by its own sovereign authority, annul an act of the general government which it deems plainly and palpably unconstitutional.

This is the sum of what I understand from him to be the South Carolina doctrine, and the doctrine which he maintains. I propose to consider it, and compare it with the Constitution. Allow me to say, as a preliminary remark, that I call this the South Carolina doctrine only because the gentleman himself has so denominated it. I do not feel at liberty to say that South Carolina, as a State, has ever advanced these sentiments. I hope she has not, and never may. That a great majority of her people are opposed to the tariff laws, is doubtless true. That a majority, somewhat less than that just mentioned, conscientiously believe these laws unconstitutional, may probably also be true. But that any majority holds to the right of direct State interference at State discretion, the right of nullifying acts of Congress by acts of State legislation, is more than I know, and what I shall be slow to believe.

That there are individuals besides the honorable gentleman who do maintain these opinions, is quite certain. I recollect the recent expression of a sentiment, which circumstances attending its utterance and publication justify us in supposing was not unpremeditated. "The sovereignty of the State,—never to be controlled, construed, or decided on, but by her own feelings of honorable justice."

[Mr. Hayne here rose and said, that, for the purpose of being clearly understood, he would state that his proposition was in the words of the Virginia resolution, as follows:—

"That this assembly doth explicitly and peremptorily declare, that it views the powers of the federal government, as resulting from the compact to which the States are parties, as limited by the plain sense and intention of the instrument constituting that compact, as no farther valid than they are authorized by the grants enumerated in that compact; and that, in case of a deliberate, palpable, and dangerous exercise of other powers, not granted by the said compact, the States who are parties thereto have the right, and are in duty bound, to interpose, for arresting the progress of the evil, and for maintaining within their respective limits the authorities, rights, and liberties appertaining to them."

Mr. Webster resumed:—]

I am quite aware, Mr. President, of the existence of the resolution which the gentleman read, and has now repeated, and that he relies on it as his authority. I know the source, too, from which it is understood to have proceeded. I need not say that I have much respect for the constitutional opinions of Mr. Madison; they would weigh greatly with me always. But before the authority of his opinion be vouched for the gentleman's proposition, it will be proper to consider what is the fair interpretation of that resolution, to which Mr. Madison is understood to have given his sanction. As the gentleman construes it, it is an authority for him. Possibly, he may not have adopted the right construction. That resolution declares, that, *in the case of the dangerous exercise of powers not granted by the general government, the States may interpose to arrest the progress of the evil.* But how interpose, and what does this declaration purport? Does it mean no more than that there may be extreme cases, in which the people, in any mode of assembling, may resist usurpation, and relieve themselves from a tyrannical government? No one will deny this. Such resistance is not only acknowledged to be just in America, but in England also. Blackstone admits as much, in the theory, and practice, too, of the English constitution. We, Sir, who oppose the Carolina doctrine, do not deny that the people may, if they choose, throw off any government when it becomes oppressive and intolerable, and erect a better in its stead. We all know that civil institutions are established for the public benefit, and that when they cease to answer the ends of their existence they may be changed. But I do not understand the doctrine now contended for to be that, which, for the sake of distinction, we may call the right of revolution. I understand the gentleman to maintain, that, without revolution, without civil commotion, without rebellion, a remedy for supposed abuse and transgression of the powers of the general government lies in a direct appeal to the interference of the State governments.

[Mr. Hayne here rose and said: He did not contend for the mere right of revolution, but for the right of constitutional resistance. What he maintained was, that in case of a plain, palpable violation of the Constitution by the general government, a State may interpose; and that this interposition is constitutional.

Mr. Webster resumed:—]

So, Sir, I understood the gentleman, and am happy to find that I did not misunderstand him. What he contends for is, that it is constitutional to interrupt the administration of the Constitution itself, in the hands of those who are chosen and sworn to administer it, by the direct interference, in form of law, of the States, in virtue of their sovereign capacity. The inherent right in the people to reform their government I do not deny; and they have another right, and that is, to resist unconstitutional laws, without overturning the government. It is no doctrine of mine that unconstitutional laws bind the people. The great question is, Whose prerogative is it to decide on the constitutionality or unconstitutionality of the laws? On that, the main debate hinges. The proposition, that, in case of a supposed violation of the Constitution by Congress, the States have a constitutional right to interfere and annul the law of Congress, is the proposition of the gentleman. I do not admit it. If the gentleman had intended no more than to assert the right of revolution for justifiable cause, he would have said only what all agree to. But I cannot conceive that there can be a middle course, between submission to the laws, when regularly pronounced constitutional, on the one hand, and open resistance, which is revolution or rebellion, on the other. I say, the right of a State to annul a law of Congress cannot be maintained, but on the ground of the inalienable right of man to resist oppression; that is to say, upon the ground of revolution. I admit that there is an ultimate violent remedy, above the Constitution and in defiance of the Constitution, which may be resorted to when a revolution is to be justified. But I do not admit, that, under the Constitution and in conformity with it, there is any mode in which a State government, as a member of the Union, can interfere and stop the progress of the general government, by force of her own laws, under any circumstances whatever.

This leads us to inquire into the origin of this government and the source of its power. Whose agent is it? Is it the creature of the State legislatures, or the creature of the people? If the government of the United States be the agent of the State governments, then they may control it, provided they can agree in the manner of controlling it; if it be the agent of the people, then the people alone can control it, restrain it, modify, or reform it. It is observable enough, that the doctrine for which the honorable gentleman contends leads him to the necessity of maintaining, not only that this general government is the creature of the States, but that it is the creature of each of the States severally, so that each may assert the power for itself of determining whether it acts within the limits of its authority. It is the servant of four-and-twenty masters, of different wills and different purposes, and yet bound to obey all. This absurdity (for it seems no less) arises from a misconception as to the origin of this government and its true character. It is, Sir, the people's Constitution, the people's government, made for the people, made by the people, and answerable to the people. The people of the United States have declared that this Constitution shall be the supreme law. We must either admit the proposition, or dispute their authority. The States are, unquestionably, sovereign, so far as their sovereignty is not affected by this supreme law. But the State legislatures, as political bodies, however sovereign, are yet not sovereign over the people. So far as the people have given power to the general government, so far the grant is unquestionably good, and the government holds of the people, and not of the State governments. We are all agents of the same supreme power, the people. The general government and the State governments derive their authority from the same source. Neither can, in relation to the other, be called primary, though one is definite and restricted, and the other general and residuary. The national government possesses those powers which it can be shown the people have conferred on it, and no more. All the rest belongs to the State governments, or to the people themselves. So far as the people have restrained State sovereignty, by the expression of their will, in the Constitution of the United States, so far, it must be admitted, State sovereignty is effectually controlled. I do not contend that it is, or ought to be, controlled farther. The sentiment to which I have referred propounds that State sovereignty is only to be controlled by its own "feeling of justice"; that is to say, it is not to be controlled at all, for one who is to follow his own feelings is under no legal control. Now, however men may think this ought to be, the fact is, that the people of the United States have chosen to impose control on State sovereignties. There are those, doubtless, who wish they had been left without restraint; but the Constitution has ordered the matter differently. To make war, for instance, is an exercise of sovereignty; but the Constitution declares that no State shall make war. To coin money is another exercise of sovereign power; but no State is at liberty to coin money. Again, the Constitution says that no sovereign State shall be so sovereign as to make a treaty. These prohibitions, it must be confessed, are a control on the State sovereignty of South Carolina, as well as of the other States, which does not arise "from her own feelings of honorable justice." The opinion referred to, therefore, is in defiance of the plainest provisions of the Constitution.

There are other proceedings of public bodies which have already been alluded to, and to which I refer again, for the purpose of ascertaining more fully what is the length and breadth of that doctrine, denominated the Carolina doctrine, which the honorable member has now stood up on this floor to maintain. In one of them I find it resolved, that "the tariff of 1828, and every other tariff designed to promote one branch of industry at the expense of others, is contrary to the meaning and intention of the federal compact; and such a dangerous, palpable, and deliberate usurpation of power, by a determined majority, wielding the general government beyond the

limits of its delegated powers, as calls upon the States which compose the suffering minority, in their sovereign capacity, to exercise
the powers which, as sovereigns, necessarily devolve upon them,
when their compact is violated."

Observe, Sir, that this resolution holds the tariff of 1828, and every
other tariff designed to promote one branch of industry at the
expense of another, to be such a dangerous, palpable, and deliberate
usurpation of power, as calls upon the States, in their sovereign
capacity, to interfere by their own authority. This denunciation, Mr.
President, you will please to observe, includes our old tariff of 1816,
as well as all others; because that was established to promote the
interest of the manufacturers of cotton, to the manifest and admitted
injury of the Calcutta cotton trade. Observe, again, that all the
qualifications are here rehearsed and charged upon the tariff, which
are necessary to bring the case within the gentleman's proposition.
The tariff is a usurpation; it is a dangerous usurpation; it is a palpable
usurpation; it is a deliberate usurpation. It is such a usurpation,
therefore, as calls upon the States to exercise their right of interference. Here is a case, then, within the gentleman's principles, and
all his qualifications of his principles. It is a case for action. The
Constitution is plainly, dangerously, palpably, and deliberately violated; and the States must interpose their own authority to arrest
the law. Let us suppose the State of South Carolina to express this
same opinion, by the voice of her legislature. That would be very
imposing; but what then? Is the voice of one State conclusive? It so
happens that, at the very moment when South Carolina resolves that
the tariff laws are unconstitutional, Pennsylvania and Kentucky
resolve exactly the reverse. *They* hold those laws to be both highly
proper and strictly constitutional. And now, Sir, how does the
honorable member propose to deal with this case? How does he
relieve us from this difficulty, upon any principle of his? His construction gets us into it; how does he propose to get us out?

In Carolina, the tariff is a palpable, deliberate usurpation; Carolina, therefore, may nullify it, and refuse to pay the duties. In Pennsylvania, it is both clearly constitutional and highly expedient; and
there the duties are to be paid. And yet we live under a government

of uniform laws, and under a Constitution too, which contains an express provision, as it happens, that all duties shall be equal in all the States. Does not this approach absurdity?

If there be no power to settle such questions, independent of either of the States, is not the whole Union a rope of sand? Are we not thrown back again, precisely, upon the old Confederation?

It is too plain to be argued. Four-and-twenty interpreters of constitutional law, each with a power to decide for itself, and none with authority to bind any body else, and this constitutional law the only bond of their union! What is such a state of things but a mere connection during pleasure, or, to use the phraseology of the times, *during feeling?* And that feeling, too, not the feeling of the people, who established the Constitution, but the feeling of the State governments.

In another of the South Carolina addresses, having premised that the crisis requires "all the concentrated energy of passion," an attitude of open resistance to the laws of the Union is advised. Open resistance to the laws, then, is the constitutional remedy, the conservative power of the State, which the South Carolina doctrines teach for the redress of political evils, real or imaginary. And its authors further say, that, appealing with confidence to the Constitution itself, to justify their opinions, they cannot consent to try their accuracy by the courts of justice. In one sense, indeed, Sir, this is assuming an attitude of open resistance in favor of liberty. But what sort of liberty? The liberty of establishing their own opinions, in defiance of the opinions of all others; the liberty of judging and of deciding exclusively themselves, in a matter in which others have as much right to judge and decide as they; the liberty of placing their own opinions above the judgment of all others, above the laws, and above the Constitution. This is their liberty, and this is the fair result of the proposition contended for by the honorable gentleman. Or, it may be more properly said, it is identical with it, rather than a result from it.

In the same publication we find the following:—"Previously to our Revolution, when the arm of oppression was stretched over New England, where did our Northern brethren meet with a braver sympathy than that which sprung from the bosoms of Carolinians? We had no extortion, no oppression, no collision with the king's ministers, no navigation interests springing up, in envious rivalry of England."

This seems extraordinary language. South Carolina no collision with the king's ministers in 1775; No extortion! No oppression! But, Sir, it is also most significant language. Does any man doubt the purpose for which it was penned? Can any one fail to see that it was designed to raise in the reader's mind the question, whether, *at this time*,—that is to say, in 1828,—South Carolina has any collision with the king's ministers, any oppression, or extortion, to fear from England? whether, in short, England is not as naturally the friend of South Carolina as New England, with her navigation interests springing up in envious rivalry of England?

Is it not strange, Sir, that an intelligent man in South Carolina, in 1828, should thus labor to prove that, in 1775, there was no hostility, no cause of war, between South Carolina and England? That she had no occasion, in reference to her own interest, or from a regard to her own welfare, to take up arms in the Revolutionary contest? Can any one account for the expression of such strange sentiments, and their circulation through the State, otherwise than by supposing the object to be what I have already intimated, to raise the question, if they had no *"collision"* (mark the expression) with the ministers of King George the Third, in 1775, what *collision* have they, in 1828, with the ministers of King George the Fourth? What is there now in the existing state of things, to separate Carolina from *Old*, more, or rather, than from *New* England?

Resolutions, Sir, have been recently passed by the legislature of South Carolina. I need not refer to them; they go no farther than the honorable gentleman himself has gone, and I hope not so far. I content myself, therefore, with debating the matter with him.

And now, Sir, what I have first to say on this subject is, that at no time, and under no circumstances, has New England, or any State in New England, or any respectable body of persons in New England, or any public man of standing in New England, put forth such a doctrine as this Carolina doctrine.

The gentleman has found no case, he can find none, to support his own opinions by New England authority. New England has studied the Constitution in other schools, and under other teachers. She looks upon it with other regards, and deems more highly and reverently both of its just authority and its utility and excellence. The history of her legislative proceedings may be traced. The ephemeral effusions of temporary bodies, called together by the excitement of the occasion, may be hunted up; they have been hunted up. The opinions and votes of her public men, in and out of Congress, may be explored. It will all be in vain. The Carolina doctrine can derive from her neither countenance nor support. She rejects it now; she always did reject it; and till she loses her senses, she always will reject it. The honorable member has referred to expressions on the subject of the embargo law, made in this place, by an honorable and venerable gentleman, now favoring us with his presence. He quotes that distinguished Senator as saying, that, in his judgment, the embargo law was unconstitutional, and that therefore, in his opinion, the people were not bound to obey it. That, Sir, is perfectly constitutional language. An unconstitutional law is not binding; *but then it does not rest with a resolution or a law of a State legislature to decide whether an act of Congress be or be not constitutional.* An unconstitutional act of Congress would not bind the people of this District, although they have no legislature to interfere in their behalf; and, on the other hand, a constitutional law of Congress does bind the citizens of every State, although all their legislatures should undertake to annul it by act or resolution. The venerable Connecticut Senator is a constitutional lawyer, of sound principles and enlarged knowledge; a statesman practised and experienced, bred in the company of Washington, and holding just views upon the nature of our governments. He believed the embargo unconstitutional, and so did others; but what then? Who did he suppose was to decide the question? The State legislatures? Certainly not. No such sentiment ever escaped his lips.

Let us follow up, Sir, this New England opposition to the embargo laws; let us trace it, till we discern the principle which controlled and governed New England throughout the whole course of that opposition. We shall then see what similarity there is between the New England school of constitutional opinions, and this modern Carolina school. The gentleman, I think, read a petition from some single individual addressed to the legislature of Massachusetts, as-serting the Carolina doctrine; that is, the right of State interference to arrest the laws of the Union. The fate of that petition shows the sentiment of the legislature. It met no favor. The opinions of Massa-chusetts were very different. They had been expressed in 1798, in answer to the resolutions of Virginia, and she did not depart from them, nor bend them to the times. Misgoverned, wronged, oppressed, as she felt herself to be, she still held fast her integrity to the Union. The gentleman may find in her proceedings much evidence of dis-satisfaction with the measures of government, and great and deep dislike to the embargo; all this makes the case so much the stronger for her; for, notwithstanding all this dissatisfaction and dislike, she still claimed no right to sever the bonds of the Union. There was heat, and there was anger in her political feeling. Be it so; but neither her heat nor her anger betrayed her into infidelity to the government. The gentleman labors to prove that she disliked the embargo as much as South Carolina dislikes the tariff, and expressed her dislike as strongly. Be it so; but did she propose the Carolina remedy? did she threaten to interfere, by State authority, to annul the laws of the Union? That is the question for the gentleman's consideration.

No doubt, Sir, a great majority of the people of New England conscientiously believed the embargo law of 1807 unconstitutional; as conscientiously, certainly, as the people of South Carolina hold that opinion of the tariff. They reasoned thus: Congress has power to regulate commerce; but here is a law, they said, stopping all com-merce, and stopping it indefinitely. The law is perpetual; that is, it is not limited in point of time, and must of course continue until it shall be repealed by some other law. It is as perpetual, therefore, as the law against treason or murder. Now, is this regulating commerce, or destroying it? Is it guiding, controlling, giving the rule to com-merce, as a subsisting thing, or is it putting an end to it altogether? Nothing is more certain, than that a majority in New England deemed this law a violation of the Constitution. The very case required by the gentleman to justify State interference had then arisen. Massachusetts believed this law to be "a deliberate, palpable, and dangerous exercise of a power not granted by the Constitution." Deliberate it was, for it was long continued; palpable she thought it, as no words in the Constitution gave the power and only a construction, in her opinion most violent, raised it; dangerous it was, since it threatened utter ruin to her most important interests. Here, then, was a Carolina case. How did Massachusetts deal with it? It was, as she thought, a plain, manifest, palpable violation of the Constitution, and it brought ruin to her doors. Thousands of families, and hundreds of thousands of individuals, were beggared by it. While she saw and felt all this, she saw and felt also, that, as a measure of national policy, it was perfectly futile; that the country was no way benefited by that which caused so much individual distress; that it was efficient only for the production of evil, and all that evil inflicted on ourselves. In such a case, under such circumstances, how did Massachusetts demean herself? Sir, she remonstrated, she memorialized, she addressed herself to the general government, not exactly "with the concentrated energy of passion," but with her own strong sense, and the energy of sober conviction. But she did not interpose the arm of her own power to arrest the law, and break the embargo. Far from it. Her principles bound her to two things; and she followed her principles, lead where they might. First, to submit to every constitutional law of Congress, and secondly, if the constitutional validity of the law be doubted, to refer that question to the decision of the proper tribunals. The first principle is vain and ineffectual without the second. A majority of us in New England believed the embargo law unconstitutional; but the great question was, and always will be in such cases, Who is to decide this? Who is to judge between the people and the government? And, Sir, it is quite plain, that the Constitution of the United States confers on the government itself, to be exercised by its appropriate department, and under its own responsibility to the people, this power of deciding ultimately and conclusively upon the just extent of its own authority. If this had not been done, we should not have advanced a single step beyond the old Confederation.

Being fully of opinion that the embargo law was unconstitutional, the people of New England were yet equally clear in the opinion, (it was a matter they did doubt upon), that the question, after all, must be decided by the judicial tribunals of the United States. Before those tribunals, therefore, they brought the question. Under the provisions of the law, they had given bonds to millions in amount, and which were alleged to be forfeited. They suffered the bonds to be sued, and thus raised the question. In the old-fashioned way of settling disputes, they went to law. The case came to hearing, and solemn argument; and he who espoused their cause, and stood up for them against the validity of the embargo act, was none other than that great man, of whom the gentleman has made honorable mention, Samuel Dexter. He was then, Sir, in the fulness of his knowledge, and the maturity of his strength. He had retired from long and distinguished public service here, to the renewed pursuit of professional duties, carrying with him all that enlargement and expansion, all the new strength and force, which an acquaintance with the more general subjects discussed in the national councils is capable of adding to professional attainment, in a mind of true greatness and comprehension. He was a lawyer, and was also a statesman. He had studied the Constitution, when he filled public station, that he might defend it; he had examined its principles that he might maintain them. More than all men, or at least as much as any man, he was attached to the general government and to the union of the States. His feelings and opinions all ran in that direction. A question of constitutional law, too, was, of all subjects, that one which was best suited to his talents and learning. Aloof from technicality, and unfettered by artificial rule, such a question gave opportunity for that deep and clear analysis, that mighty grasp of principle, which so much distinguished his higher efforts. His very statement was argument; his inference seemed demonstration. The earnestness of his own conviction wrought conviction in others. One was convinced, and believed, and assented, because it was gratifying, delightful, to think, and feel, and believe, in unison with an intellect of such evident superiority.

Mr. Dexter, Sir, such as I have described him, argued the New England cause. He put into his effort his whole heart, as well as all the powers of his understanding; for he had avowed, in the most public manner, his entire concurrence with his neighbors on the point in dispute. He argued the cause; it was lost, and New England submitted. The established tribunals pronounced the law constitutional, and New England acquiesced. Now, Sir, is not this the exact opposite of the doctrine of the gentleman from South Carolina? According to him, instead of referring to the judicial tribunals, we should have broken up the embargo by laws of our own; we should have repealed it, *quoad* New England; for we had a strong, palpable, and oppressive case. Sir, we believed the embargo unconstitutional; but still that was matter of opinion, and who was to decide it? We thought it a clear case; but, nevertheless, we did not take the law into our own hands, because we did not wish to bring about a revolution, nor to break up the Union; for I maintain, that between submission to the decision of the constituted tribunals, and revolution, or disunion, there is no middle ground; there is no ambiguous condition, half allegiance and half rebellion. And, Sir, how futile, how very futile it is, to admit the right of State interference, and then attempt to save it from the character of unlawful resistance, by adding terms of qualification to the causes and occasions, leaving all these qualifications, like the case itself, in the discretion of the State governments. It must be a clear case, it is said, a deliberate case, a palpable case, a dangerous case. But then the State is still left at liberty to decide for herself what is clear, what is deliberate, what is palpable, what is dangerous. Do adjectives and epithets avail any thing?

Sir, the human mind is so constituted, that the merits of both sides of a controversy appear very clear, and very palpable, to those who respectively espouse them; and both sides usually grow clearer as the controversy advances. South Carolina sees unconstitutionality in the tariff; she sees oppression there also, and she sees danger. Pennsylvania, with a vision not less sharp, looks at the same tariff, and sees no such thing in it; she sees it all constitutional, all useful, all safe. The faith of South Carolina is strengthened by opposition, and she now not only sees, but *resolves,* that the tariff is palpably unconstitutional, oppressive, and dangerous; but Pennsylvania, not to be behind her neighbors, and equally willing to strengthen her own faith by a confident asseveration, *resolves,* also, and gives to every warm affirmative of South Carolina, a plain, downright, Pennsylvania negative. South Carolina, to show the strength and unity of her opinion, brings her assembly to a unanimity, within seven voices; Pennsylvania, not to be outdone in this respect any more than in others, reduces her dissentient fraction to a single vote. Now, Sir, again, I ask the gentleman, What is to be done? Are these States both right? Is he bound to consider them both right? If not, which is in the wrong? or rather, which has the best right to decide? And if he, and if I, are not to know what the Constitution means, and what it is, till those two State legislatures, and the twenty-two others, shall agree in its construction, what have we sworn to, when we have sworn to maintain it? I was forcibly struck, Sir, with one reflection, as the gentleman went on in his speech. He quoted Mr. Madison's resolutions, to prove that a State may interfere, in a case of deliberate, palpable, and dangerous exercise of a power not granted. The honorable member supposes the tariff law to be such an exercise of power; and that consequently a case has arisen in which the State may, if it see fit, interfere by its own law. Now it so happens, nevertheless, that Mr. Madison deems this same tariff law quite constitutional. Instead of a clear and palpable violation, it is, in his judgment, no violation at all. So that, while they use his authority for a hypothetical case, they reject it in the very case before them. All this, Sir, shows the inherent futility, I had almost used a stronger word, of conceding this power of interference to the State, and then attempting to secure it from abuse by imposing qualifications of which the States themselves are to judge. One of two things is true; either the laws of the Union are beyond the discretion and beyond the control of the States; or else we have no constitution of general government, and are thrust back again to the days of the Federation.

Let me here say, Sir, that if the gentleman's doctrine had been received and acted upon in New England, in the times of the embargo and non-intercourse, we should probably not now have been here. The government would very likely have gone to pieces, and crumbled into dust. No stronger case can ever arise than existed under those laws; no States can ever entertain a clearer conviction than the New England States then entertained; and if they had been under the influence of that heresy of opinion, as I must call it, which the honorable member espouses, this Union would, in all probability, have been scattered to the four winds. I ask the gentleman, therefore, to apply his principles to that case; I ask him to come forth and declare, whether, in his opinion, the New England States would have been justified in interfering to break up the embargo system under the conscientious opinions which they held upon it? Had they a right to annul that law? Does he admit or deny? If what is thought palpably unconstitutional in South Carolina justifies that State in arresting the progress of the law, tell me whether that which was thought palpably unconstitutional also in Massachusetts would have justified her in doing the same thing. Sir, I deny the whole doctrine. It has not a foot of ground in the Constitution to stand on. No public man of reputation ever advanced it in Massachusetts in the warmest times, or could maintain himself upon it there at any time.

I wish now, Sir, to make a remark upon the Virginia resolutions of 1798. I cannot undertake to say how these resolutions were understood by those who passed them. Their language is not a little indefinite. In the case of the exercise by Congress of a dangerous power not granted to them, the resolutions assert the right, on the part of the State, to interfere and arrest the progress of the evil. This is susceptible of more than one interpretation. It may mean no more than that the States may interfere by complaint and remonstrance, or by proposing to the people an alteration of the Federal Constitution. This would all be quite unobjectionable. Or it may be that no more is meant than to assert the general right of revolution, as against all governments, in cases of intolerable oppression. This no one doubts, and this, in my opinion, is all that he who framed the resolutions could have meant by it; for I shall not readily believe that he was ever of opinion that a State, under the Constitution and in conformity with it, could, upon the ground of her own opinion of its unconstitutionality, however clear and palpable she might think the case, annul a law of Congress, so far as it should operate on herself, by her own legislative power.

I must now beg to ask, Sir, Whence is this supposed right of the States derived? Where do they find the power to interfere with the laws of the Union? Sir, the opinion which the honorable gentleman maintains is a notion founded in a total misapprehension, in my judgment, of the origin of this government, and of the foundation on which it stands. I hold it to be a popular government, erected by the people; those who administer it, responsible to the people; and itself capable of being amended and modified, just as the people may choose it should be. It is as popular, just as truly emanating from the people, as the State governments. It is created for one purpose; the State governments for another. It has its own powers; they have theirs. There is no more authority with them to arrest the operation of a law of Congress, than with Congress to arrest the operation of their laws. We are here to administer a Constitution emanating immediately from the people, and trusted by them to our administration. It is not the creature of the State governments. It is of no moment to the argument, that certain acts of the State legislatures are necessary to fill our seats in this body. That is not one of their original State powers, a part of the sovereignty of the State. It is a duty which the people, by the Constitution itself, have imposed on the State legislatures; and which they might have left to be performed elsewhere, if they had seen fit. So they have left the choice of President with electors; but all this does not affect the proposition that this whole government, President, Senate, and House of Representatives, is a popular government. It leaves it still all its popular character. The governor of a State (in some of the States) is chosen, not directly by the people, but by those who are chosen by the people, for the purpose of performing, among other duties, that of electing a governor. Is the government of the State, on that account, not a popular government? This government, Sir, is the independent offspring of the popular will. It is not the creature of State legislatures; nay, more, if the whole truth must be told, the people brought it into existence, established it, and have hitherto supported it, for the very purpose, amongst others, of imposing certain salutary restraints on State sovereignties. The States cannot now make war; they cannot contract alliances; they cannot make, each for itself, separate regulations of commerce; they cannot lay imposts; they cannot coin money. If this Constitution, Sir, be the creature of State legislatures, it must be admitted that it has obtained a strange control over the volition of its creators.

The people, then, Sir, erected this government. They gave it a Constitution, and in that Constitution they have enumerated the powers which they bestow on it. They have made it a limited government. They have defined its authority. They have restrained it to the exercise of such powers as are granted; and all others, they declare, are reserved to the States or the people. But, Sir, they have not stopped here. If they had, they would have accomplished but half their work. No definition can be so clear, as to avoid possibility of doubt; no limitation so precise, as to exclude all uncertainty. Who, then, shall construe this grant of the people? Who shall interpret their will, where it may be supposed they have left it doubtful? With whom do they repose this ultimate right of deciding on the powers of the government? Sir, they have settled all this in the fullest manner. They have left it with the government itself, in its appropriate branches. Sir, the very chief end, the main design, for which the whole Constitution was framed and adopted, was to establish a government that should not be obliged to act through State agency, or depend on State opinion and State discretion. The people had had quite enough of that kind of government under the Confederation. Under that system, the legal action, the application of law to individuals, belonged exclusively to the States. Congress could only recommend; their acts were not of binding force, till the States had adopted and sanctioned them. Are we in that condition still? Are we yet at the mercy of State discretion and State construction? Sir, if we are, then vain will be our attempt to maintain the Constitution under which we sit.

But, Sir, the people have wisely provided, in the Constitution itself, a proper suitable mode and tribunal for settling questions of constitutional law. There are in the Constitution grants of powers to Congress, and restrictions on these powers. There are, also, prohibitions on the States. Some authority must, therefore, necessarily exist, having the ultimate jurisdiction to fix and ascertain the interpretation of these grants, restrictions, and prohibitions. The Constitution has itself pointed out, ordained, and established that authority. How has it accomplished this great and essential end? By declaring, Sir, that *"the Constitution, and the laws of the United States made in pursuance thereof, shall be the supreme law of the land, any thing in the constitution or laws of any State to the contrary notwithstanding."*

This, Sir, was the first great step. By this the supremacy of the Constitution and laws of the United States is declared. The people so will it. No State law is to be valid which comes in conflict with the Constitution, or any law of the United States passed in pursuance of it. But who shall decide this question of interference? To whom lies the last appeal? This, Sir, the Constitution itself decides also, by declaring, *"that the judicial power shall extend to all cases arising under the Constitution and laws of the United States."* These two provisions cover the whole ground. They are, in truth, the keystone of the arch! With these it is a government; without them it is a confederation. In pursuance of these clear and express provisions, Congress established, at its very first session, in the judicial act, a mode for carrying them into full effect, and for bringing all questions of constitutional power to the final decision of the Supreme Court. It then, Sir, became a government. It then had the means of self-protection; and but for this, it would, in all probability, have been now among things which are past. Having constituted the government, and declared its powers, the people have further said, that, since somebody must decide on the extent of these powers, the government shall itself decide; subject, always, like other popular governments, to its responsibility to the people. And now, Sir, I repeat, how is it that a State legislature acquires any power to interfere? Who, or what, gives them the right to say

to the people, "We, who are your agents and servants for one purpose, will undertake to decide, that your other agents and servants,
appointed by you for another purpose, have transcended the authority you gave them!" The reply would be, I think, not impertinent,—
"Who made you a judge over another's servants? To their own
masters they stand or fall."

Sir, I deny this power of State legislatures altogether. It cannot
stand the test of examination. Gentlemen may say, that, in an
extreme case, a State government might protect the people from
intolerable oppression. Sir, in such a case, the people might protect
themselves, without the aid of the State governments. Such a case
warrants revolution. It must make, when it comes, a law for itself.
A nullifying act of a State legislature cannot alter the case, nor make
resistance any more lawful. In maintaining these sentiments, Sir, I
am but asserting the rights of the people. I state what they have
declared, and insist on their right to declare it. They have chosen to
repose this power in the general government, and I think it my duty
to support it, like other constitutional powers.

For myself, Sir, I do not admit the competency of South Carolina,
or any other State, to prescribe my constitutional duty; or to settle,
between me and the people, the validity of laws of Congress, for
which I voted. I decline her umpirage. I have not sworn to support
the Constitution according to her construction of its clauses. I have
not stipulated, by my oath of office or otherwise, to come under any
responsibility, except to the people, and those whom they have
appointed to pass upon the question, whether laws, supported by
my votes, conform to the Constitution of the country. And, Sir, if we
look to the general nature of the case, could any thing have been
more preposterous, than to make a government for the whole Union,
and yet leave its powers subject, not to one interpretation, but to
thirteen or twenty-four interpretations? Instead of one tribunal,
established by all, responsible to all, with power to decide for all,
shall constitutional questions be left to four-and-twenty popular
bodies, each at liberty to decide for itself, and none bound to respect
the decisions of others; and each at liberty, too, to give a new
construction on every new election of its own members? Would any

thing, with such a principle in it, or rather with such a destitution of all principle, be fit to be called a government? No, Sir. It should not be denominated a Constitution. It should be called, rather, a collection of topics for everlasting controversy; heads of debate for a disputatious people. It would not be a government. It would not be adequate to any practical good, or fit for any country to live under.

To avoid all possibility of being misunderstood, allow me to repeat again, in the fullest manner, that I claim no powers for the government by forced or unfair construction. I admit that it is a government of strictly limited powers; of enumerated, specified, and particularized powers; and that whatsoever is not granted, is withheld. But notwithstanding all this, and however the grant of powers may be expressed, its limit and extent may yet, in some cases, admit of doubt; and the general government would be good for nothing, it would be incapable of long existing, if some mode had not been provided in which those doubts, as they should arise, might be peaceably, but authoritatively, solved.

And now, Mr. President, let me run the honorable gentleman's doctrine a little into its practical application. Let us look at his probable *modus operandi*. If a thing can be done, an ingenious man can tell *how* it is to be done, and I wish to be informed *how* this State interference is to be put in practice, without violence, bloodshed, and rebellion. We will take the existing case of the tariff law. South Carolina is said to have made up her opinion upon it. If we do not repeal it (as we probably shall not), she will then apply to the case the remedy of her doctrine. She will, we must suppose, pass a law of her legislature, declaring the several acts of Congress, usually called the tariff laws, null and void, so far as they respect South Carolina, or the citizens thereof. So far, all is a paper transaction, and easy enough. But the collector at Charleston is collecting the duties imposed by these tariff laws. He, therefore, must be stopped. The collector will seize the goods if the tariff duties are not paid. The State authorities will undertake their rescue, the marshal, with his posse, will come to the collector's aid, and here the contest begins. The militia of the State will be called out to sustain the nullifying act. They will march, Sir, under a very gallant leader; for

I believe the honorable member himself commands the militia of that part of the State. He will raise the NULLIFYING ACT on his standard, and spread it out as his banner! It will have a preamble, setting forth, that the tariff laws are palpable, deliberate, and dangerous violations of the Constitution! He will proceed, with this banner flying, to the custom-house in Charleston,

"All the while,
Sonorous metal blowing martial sounds."

Arrived at the custom-house, he will tell the collector that he must collect no more duties under any of the tariff laws. This he will be somewhat puzzled to say, by the way, with a grave countenance, considering what hand South Carolina herself had in that of 1816. But, Sir, the collector would not, probably, desist, at his bidding. He would show him the law of Congress, the treasury instruction, and his own oath of office. He would say, he should perform his duty, come what might.

Here would ensue a pause; for they say that a certain stillness precedes the tempest. The trumpeter would hold his breath awhile, and before all this military array should fall on the custom-house, collector, clerks, and all, it is very probable some of those composing it would request of their gallant commander-in-chief to be informed a little upon the point of law; for they have, doubtless, a just respect for his opinions as a lawyer, as well as for his bravery as a soldier. They know he has read Blackstone and the Constitution, as well as Turenne and Vauban. They would ask him, therefore, something concerning their rights in this matter. They would inquire, whether it was not somewhat dangerous to resist a law of the United States. What would be the nature of their offence, they would wish to learn, if they, by military force and array, resisted the execution in Carolina of a law of the United States, and it should turn out, after all, that the law *was constitutional?* He would answer, of course, Treason. No lawyer could give any other answer. John Fries, he would tell them, had learned that, some years ago. How, then, they would ask, do you propose to defend us? We are not afraid of bullets, but treason has a way of taking people off that we do not much relish. How do you propose to defend us? "Look at my float-ing banner," he would reply; "see there the *nullifying law!*" Is it your opinion, gallant commander, they would then say, that, if we should be indicted for treason, that same floating banner of yours would make a good plea in bar? "South Carolina is a sovereign State," he would reply. That is true; but would the judge admit our plea? "These tariff laws," he would repeat, "are unconstitutional, palpably, deliberately, dangerously." That may all be so; but if the tribunal should not happen to be of that opinion, shall we swing for it? We are ready to die for our country, but it is rather an awkward business, this dying without touching the ground! After all, that is a sort of hemp tax worse than any part of the tariff.

Mr. President, the honorable gentleman would be in dilemma, like that of another great general. He would have a knot before him which he could not untie. He must cut it with his sword. He must say to his followers, "Defend yourselves with your bayonets"; and this is war,—civil war.

Direct collision, therefore, between force and force, is the un-avoidable result of that remedy for the revision of unconstitutional laws which the gentleman contends for. It must happen in the very first case to which it is applied. Is not this the plain result? To resist by force the execution of a law, generally, is treason. Can the courts of the United States take notice of the indulgence of a State to commit treason? The common saying, that a State cannot com-mit treason herself, is nothing to the purpose. Can she authorize others to do it? If John Fries had produced an act of Pennsylvania, annulling the law of Congress, would it have helped his case? Talk about it as we will, these doctrines go the length of revolution. They are incompatible with any peaceable administration of the govern-ment. They lead directly to disunion and civil commotion; and therefore it is, that at their commencement, when they are first found to be maintained by respectable men, and in a tangible form, I enter my public protest against them all.

The honorable gentleman argues, that if this government be the sole judge of the extent of its own powers, whether that right of judging be in Congress or the Supreme Court, it equally subverts

State sovereignty. This the gentleman sees, or thinks he sees, although he cannot perceive how the right of judging, in this matter, if left to the exercise of State legislatures, has any tendency to subvert the government of the Union. The gentleman's opinion may be, that the right *ought not* to have been lodged with the general government; he may like better such a constitution as we should have under the right of State interference; but I ask him to meet me on the plain matter of fact. I ask him to meet me on the Constitution itself. I ask him if the power is not found there, clearly and visibly found there?

But, Sir, what is this danger, and what are the grounds of it? Let it be remembered, that the Constitution of the United States is not unalterable. It is to continue in its present form no longer than the people who established it shall choose to continue it. If they shall become convinced that they have made an injudicious or inexpedient partition and distribution of power between the State governments and the general government, they can alter that distribution at will.

If any thing be found in the national Constitution, either by original provision or subsequent interpretation, which ought not to be in it, the people know how to get rid of it. If any construction, unacceptable to them, be established, so as to become practically a part of the Constitution, they will amend it, at their own soverign pleasure. But while the people choose to maintain it as it is, while they are satisfied with it, and refuse to change it, who has given, or who can give, to the State legislatures a right to alter it, either by interference, construction, or otherwise? Gentlemen do not seem to recollect that the people have any power to do any thing for themselves. They imagine there is no safety for them, any longer than they are under the close guardianship of the State legislatures. Sir, the people have not trusted their safety, in regard to the general Constitution, to these hands. They have required other security, and taken other bonds. They have chosen to trust themselves, first, to the plain words of the instrument, and to such construction as the government themselves, in doubtful cases, should put on their own powers, under their oaths of office, and subject to their responsibility to them; just as the people of a State trust their own State governments with a similar power. Secondly, they have reposed their trust in the efficacy of frequent elections, and in their own power to remove their own servants and agents whenever they see cause. Thirdly, they have reposed trust in the judicial power, which, in order that it might be trustworthy, they have made as respectable, as disinterested, and as independent as was practicable. Fourthly, they have seen fit to rely, in case of necessity, or high expediency, on their known and admitted power to alter or amend the Constitution, peaceably and quietly, whenever experience shall point out defects or imperfections. And, finally, the people of the United States have at no time, in no way, directly or indirectly, authorized any State legislature to construe or interpret *their* high instrument of government; much less, to interfere, by their own power, to arrest its course and operation.

If, Sir, the people in these respects had done otherwise than they have done, their constitution could neither have been preserved, nor would it have been worth preserving. And if its plain provisions shall now be disregarded, and these new doctrines interpolated in it, it will become as feeble and helpless a being as its enemies, whether early or more recent, could possibly desire. It will exist in every State but as a poor dependent on State permission. It must borrow leave to be; and will be, no longer than State pleasure, or State discretion, sees fit to grant the indulgence, and to prolong its poor existence.

But, Sir, although there are fears, there are hopes also. The people have preserved this, their own chosen Constitution, for forty years, and have seen their happiness, prosperity, and renown grow with its growth, and strengthen with its strength. They are now, generally, strongly attached to it. Overthrown by direct assault, it cannot be; evaded, undermined, NULLIFIED, it will not be, if we, and those who shall succeed us here, as agents and representatives of the people, shall conscientiously and vigilantly discharge the two great branches of our public trust, faithfully to preserve, and wisely to administer it.

Mr. President, I have thus stated the reasons of my dissent to the doctrines which have been advanced and maintained. I am conscious of having detained you and the Senate much too long. I was drawn into the debate with no previous deliberation, such as is suited to the discussion of so grave and important a subject. But it is a subject of which my heart is full, and I have not been willing to suppress the utterance of its spontaneous sentiments. I cannot, even now, persuade myself to relinquish it, without expressing once more my deep conviction, that, since it respects nothing less than the Union of the States, it is of most vital and essential importance to the public happiness. I profess, Sir, in my career hitherto, to have kept steadily in view the prosperity and honor of the whole country, and the preservation of our Federal Union. It is to that Union we owe our safety at home, and our consideration and dignity abroad. It is to that Union that we are chiefly indebted for whatever makes us most proud of our country. That Union we reached only by the discipline of our virtues in the severe school of adversity. It had its origin in the necessities of disordered finance, prostrate commerce, and ruined credit. Under its benign influences, these great interests immediately awoke, as from the dead, and sprang forth with newness of life. Every year of its duration has teemed with fresh proofs of its utility and its blessings; and although our territory has stretched out wider and wider, and our population spread farther and farther, they have not outrun its protection or its benefits. It has been to us all a copious fountain of national, social, and personal happiness.

I have not allowed myself, Sir, to look beyond the Union, to see what might lie hidden in the dark recess behind. I have not coolly weighed the chances of preserving liberty when the bonds that unite us together shall be broken asunder. I have not accustomed myself to hang over the precipice of disunion, to see whether, with my short sight, I can fathom the depth of the abyss below; nor could I regard him as a safe counsellor in the affairs of this government, whose thoughts should be mainly bent on considering, not how the Union may be best preserved, but how tolerable might be the condition of the people when it should be broken up and destroyed. While the Union lasts, we have high, exciting, gratifying prospects spread out before us, for us and our children. Beyond that I seek not to penetrate the veil. God grant that in my day, at least, that curtain may not rise! God grant that on my vision never may be opened what lies behind! When my eyes shall be turned to behold for the last time the

sun in heaven, may I not see him shining on the broken and dishonored fragments of a once glorious Union; on States dissevered,
discordant, belligerent; on a land rent with civil feuds, or drenched,
it may be, in fraternal blood! Let their last feeble and lingering
glance rather behold the gorgeous ensign of the republic, now known
and honored throughout the earth, still full high advanced, its arms
and trophies streaming in their original lustre, not a stripe erased or
polluted, nor a single star obscured, bearing for its motto, no such
miserable interrogatory as "What is all this worth?" nor those other
words of delusion and folly, "Liberty first and Union afterwards";
but everywhere, spread all over in characters of living light, blazing
on all its ample folds, as they float over the sea and over the land,
and in every wind under the whole heavens, that other sentiment,
dear to every true American heart,—Liberty *and* Union, now and for
ever, one and inseparable!

William Ellery Channing

―――――――――――

UNITARIAN CHRISTIANITY

¶ DR. WILLIAM ELLERY CHANNING (1780-1842), eminent American preacher of the nineteenth century, was born in Newport, Rhode Island, April 7th, 1780. After his graduation from Harvard College in 1798, he tutored the children of David Meade Randolph in Virginia, there imbibing a strong hatred of slavery and reading widely in the liberal writings of Rousseau, William Godwin, Mary Wollstonecraft and others. He was made pastor of the Federal Street Church in Boston in 1803 and during his long ministry there, until his death in 1842, he became the leader of the liberal Christians in America. He is known for his powerful attacks on Calvinistic dogma, his moral and humanitarian teachings, his opposition to slavery. He is often thought of as a forerunner of the Transcendentalists.

Channing's sermon on "Unitarian Christianity" was preached in Baltimore at the ordination of Jared Sparks, later biographer of George Washington, on May 5, 1819.

I Thess. v. 21: "Prove all things; hold fast that which is good."

THE PECULIAR CIRCUMSTANCES of this occasion not only justify, but seem to demand a departure from the course generally followed by preachers at the introduction of a brother into the sacred office. It is usual to speak of the nature, design, duties, and advantages of the Christian ministry; and on these topics I should now be happy to insist, did I not remember that a minister is to be given this day to a religious society, whose peculiarities of opinion have drawn upon them much remark, and may I not add, much reproach. Many good minds, many sincere Christians, I am aware, are apprehensive that the solemnities of this day are to give a degree of influence to principles which they deem false and injurious. The fears and anxieties of such men I respect; and, believing that they are grounded in part on mistake, I have thought it my duty to lay before you, as clearly as I can, some of the distinguishing opinions of that class of Christians in our country, who are known to sympathize with this religious society. I must ask your patience, for such a subject is not to be despatched in a narrow compass. I must also ask you to remember, that it is impossible to exhibit, in a single discourse, our views of every doctrine of Revelation, much less the differences of opinion which are known to subsist among ourselves. I shall confine myself to topics, on which our sentiments have been misrepresented, or which distinguish us most widely from others. May I not hope to be heard with candor? God deliver us all from prejudice and unkindness, and fill us with the love of truth and virtue.

There are two natural divisions under which my thoughts will be arranged. I shall endeavour to unfold, 1st, The principles which we adopt in interpreting the Scriptures. And 2dly, Some of the doctrines which the Scriptures, so interpreted, seem to us clearly to express.

I. We regard the Scriptures as the records of God's successive revelations to mankind, and particularly of the last and most perfect revelation of his will by Jesus Christ. Whatever doctrines seem to us to be clearly taught in the Scriptures, we receive without reserve or exception. We do not, however, attach equal importance to all the books in this collection. Our religion, we believe, lies chiefly in the New Testament. The dispensation of Moses, compared with that of Jesus, we consider as adapted to the childhood of the human race, a preparation for a nobler system, and chiefly useful now as serving to confirm and illustrate the Christian Scriptures. Jesus Christ is the only master of Christians, and whatever he taught, either during his personal ministry, or by his inspired Apostles, we regard as of divine authority, and profess to make the rule of our lives.

This authority, which we give to the Scriptures, is a reason, we conceive, for studying them with peculiar care, and for inquiring anxiously into the principles of interpretation, by which their true meaning may be ascertained. The principles adopted by the class of Christians in whose name I speak, need to be explained, because they are often misunderstood. We are particularly accused of making an unwarrantable use of reason in the interpretation of Scripture. We are said to exalt reason above revelation, to prefer our own wisdom to God's. Loose and undefined charges of this kind are circulated so freely, that we think it due to ourselves, and to the cause of truth, to express our views with some particularity.

Our leading principle in interpreting Scripture is this, that the Bible is a book written for men, in the language of men, and that its meaning is to be sought in the same manner as that of other books. We believe that God, when he speaks to the human race, conforms, if we may so say, to the established rules of speaking and writing. How else would the Scriptures avail us more, than if communicated in an unknown tongue?

Now all books, and all conversation, require in the reader or hearer the constant exercise of reason; or their true import is only to be obtained by continual comparison and inference. Human language, you well know, admits various interpretations; and every word and every sentence must be modified and explained according to the subject which is discussed, according to the purposes, feelings, circumstances, and principles of the writer, and according to the genius and idioms of the language which he uses. These are acknowledged principles in the interpretation of human writings; and a man, whose words we should explain without reference to these principles, would reproach us justly with a criminal want of candor, and an intention of obscuring or distorting his meaning.

Were the Bible written in a language and style of its own, did it consist of words which admit but a single sense, and of sentences wholly detached from each other, there would be no place for the principles now laid down. We could not reason about it, as about other writings. But such a book would be of little worth; and perhaps, of all books, the Scriptures correspond least to this description. The Word of God bears the stamp of the same hand, which we see

in his works. It has infinite connexions and dependences. Every proposition is linked with others, and is to be compared with others,
that its full and precise import may be understood. Nothing stands
alone. The New Testament is built on the Old. The Christian dispensation is a continuation of the Jewish, the completion of a vast
scheme of providence, requiring great extent of view in the reader.
Still more, the Bible treats of subjects on which we receive ideas
from other sources besides itself; such subjects as the nature, passions, relations, and duties of man; and it expects us to restrain and
modify its language by the known truths which observation and
experience furnish on these topics.

We profess not to know a book which demands a more frequent
exercise of reason than the Bible. In addition to the remarks now
made on its infinite connexions, we may observe that its style
nowhere affects the precision of science, or the accuracy of definition. Its language is singularly glowing, bold, and figurative, demanding more frequent departures from the literal sense than that
of our own age and country, and consequently demanding more
continual exercise of judgment.—We find, too, that the different
portions of this book, instead of being confined to general truths,
refer perpetually to the times when they were written, to states of
society, to modes of thinking, to controversies in the church, to feelings and usages which have passed away, and without the knowledge of which we are constantly in danger of extending to all times,
and places, what was of temporary and local application.—We find,
too, that some of these books are strongly marked by the genius and
character of their respective writers, that the Holy Spirit did not so
guide the Apostles as to suspend the peculiarities of their minds,
and that a knowledge of their feelings, and of the influences under
which they were placed, is one of the preparations for understanding
their writings. With these views of the Bible, we feel it our bounden
duty to exercise our reason upon it perpetually, to compare, to infer,
to look beyond the letter to the spirit, to seek in the nature of the
subject, and the aim of the writer, his true meaning; and, in general,
to make use of what is known, for explaining what is difficult, and
for discovering new truths.

Need I descend to particulars, to prove that the Scriptures demand the exercise of reason? Take, for example, the style in which they generally speak of God, and observe how habitually they apply to him human passions and organs. Recollect the declarations of Christ, that he came not to send peace, but a sword; that unless we eat his flesh, and drink his blood, we have no life in us; that we must hate father and mother, and pluck out the right eye; and a vast number of passages equally bold and unlimited. Recollect the unqualified manner in which it is said of Christians, that they possess all things, know all things, and can do all things. Recollect the verbal contradiction between Paul and James, and the apparent clashing of some parts of Paul's writings with the general doctrines and end of Christianity. I might extend the enumeration indefinitely; and who does not see, that we must limit all these passages by the known attributes of God, of Jesus Christ, and of human nature, and by the circumstances under which they were written, so as to give the language a quite different import from what it would require, had it been applied to different beings, or used in different connexions.

Enough has been said to show, in what sense we make use of reason in interpreting Scripture. From a variety of possible interpretations, we select that which accords with the nature of the subject and the state of the writer, with the connexion of the passage, with the general strain of Scripture, with the known character and will of God, and with the obvious and acknowledged laws of nature. In other words, we believe that God never contradicts, in one part of Scripture, what he teaches in another; and never contradicts, in revelation, what he teaches in his works and providence. And we therefore distrust every interpretation, which, after deliberate attention, seems repugnant to any established truth. We reason about the Bible precisely as civilians do about the constitution under which we live; who, you know, are accustomed to limit one provision of that venerable instrument by others, and to fix the precise import of its parts, by inquiring into its general spirit, into the intentions of its authors, and into the prevalent feelings, impressions, and circumstances of the time when it was framed. Without these principles of interpretation, we frankly acknowledge, that we cannot defend the divine authority of the Scriptures. Deny us this latitude, and we must abandon this book to its enemies.

We do not announce these principles as original, or peculiar to ourselves. All Christians occasionally adopt them, not excepting those who most vehemently decry them, when they happen to menace some favorite article of their creed. All Christians are compelled to use them in their controversies with infidels. All sects employ them in their warfare with one another. All willingly avail themselves of reason, when it can be pressed into the service of their own party, and only complain of it, when its weapons wound themselves. None reason more frequently than those from whom we differ. It is astonishing what a fabric they rear from a few slight hints about the fall of our first parents; and how ingeniously they extract, from detached passages, mysterious doctrines about the divine nature. We do not blame them for reasoning so abundantly, but for violating the fundamental rules of reasoning, for sacrificing the plain to the obscure, and the general strain of Scripture to a scanty number of insulated texts.

We object strongly to the contemptuous manner in which human reason is often spoken of by our adversaries, because it leads, we believe, to universal skepticism. If reason be so dreadfully darkened by the fall, that its most decisive judgments on religion are unworthy of trust, then Christianity, and even natural theology, must be abandoned; for the existence and veracity of God, and the divine original of Christianity, are conclusions of reason, and must stand or fall with it. If revelation be at war with this faculty, it subverts itself, for the great question of its truth is left by God to be decided at the bar of reason. It is worthy of remark, how nearly the bigot and the skeptic approach. Both would annihilate our confidence in our faculties, and both throw doubt and confusion over every truth. We honor revelation too highly to make it the antagonist of reason, or to believe that it calls us to renounce our highest powers.

We indeed grant, that the use of reason in religion is accompanied with danger. But we ask any honest man to look back on the history of the church, and say whether the renunciation of it be not still more dangerous. Besides, it is a plain fact that men reason as erroneously on all subjects as on religion. Who does not know the wild and groundless theories which have been framed in physical and political science? But who ever supposed that we must cease to exercise reason on nature and society, because men have erred for ages in explaining them? We grant that the passions continually, and sometimes fatally, disturb the rational faculty in its inquiries into revelation. The ambitious contrive to find doctrines in the Bible, which favor their love of dominion. The timid and dejected discover there a gloomy system, and the mystical and fanatical, a visionary theology. The vicious can find examples or assertions on which to build the hope of a late repentance, or of acceptance on easy terms. The falsely refined contrive to light on doctrines which have not been soiled by vulgar handling. But the passions do not distract the reason in religious, any more than in other inquiries, which excite strong and general interest; and this faculty, of consequence, is not to be renounced in religion, unless we are prepared to discard it universally. The true inference from the almost endless errors, which have darkened theology, is, not that we are to neglect and disparage our powers, but to exert them more patiently, circumspectly, uprightly. The worst errors, after all, having sprung up in that church, which proscribes reason, and demands from its members implicit faith. The most pernicious doctrines have been the growth of the darkest times, when the general credulity encouraged bad men and enthusiasts to broach their dreams and inventions, and to stifle the faint remonstrances of reason, by the menaces of everlasting perdition. Say what we may, God has given us a rational nature, and will call us to account for it. We may let it sleep, but we do so at our peril. Revelation is addressed to us as rational beings. We may wish, in our sloth, that God had given us a system, demanding no labor of comparing, limiting, and inferring. But such a system would be at variance with the whole character of our present existence; and it is the part of wisdom to take revelation as it is given to us, and to interpret it by the help of the faculties, which it everywhere supposes, and on which it is founded.

To the views now given, an objection is commonly urged from the character of God. We are told, that God being infinitely wiser than men, his discoveries will surpass human reason. In a revelation from such a teacher, we ought to expect propositions which we cannot reconcile with one another, and which may seem to contradict established truths; and it becomes us not to question or explain them away, but to believe, and adore, and to submit our weak and carnal reason to the Divine Word. To this objection, we have two short answers. We say, first, that it is impossible that a teacher of infinite wisdom should expose those, whom he would teach, to infinite error. But if once we admit that propositions, which in their literal sense appear plainly repugnant to one another, or to any known truth, are still to be literally understood and received, what possible limit can we set to the belief of contradictions? What shelter have we from the wildest fanaticism, which can always quote passages, that, in their literal and obvious sense, give support to its extravagances? How can the Protestant escape from transubstantiation, a doctrine most clearly taught us, if the submission of reason, now contended for, be a duty? How can we even hold fast the truth of revelation, for if one apparent contradiction may be true, so may another, and the proposition that Christianity is false, though involving inconsistency, may still be a verity?

We answer again, that, if God be infinitely wise, he cannot sport with the understandings of his creatures. A wise teacher discovers his wisdom in adapting himself to the capacities of his pupils, not in perplexing them with what is unintelligible, not in distressing them with apparent contradictions, not in filling them with a skeptical distrust of their own powers. An infinitely wise teacher, who knows the precise extent of our minds, and the best method of enlightening them, will surpass all other instructors in bringing down truth to our apprehension, and in showing its loveliness and harmony. We ought, indeed, to expect occasional obscurity in such a book as the Bible, which was written for past and future ages, as well as for the present. But God's wisdom is a pledge, that whatever is necessary for *us*, and necessary for salvation, is revealed too plainly to be mistaken, and too consistently to be questioned, by a sound and upright mind. It is not the mark of wisdom to use an unintelligible phraseology, to communicate what is above our capacities, to confuse and unsettle the intellect by appearances of contradiction. We honor our Heavenly Teacher too much to ascribe to him such a revelation. A revelation is a gift of light. It cannot thicken our darkness, and multiply our perplexities.

II. Having thus stated the principles according to which we interpret Scripture, I now proceed to the second great head of this discourse, which is, to state some of the views which we derive from that sacred book, particularly those which distinguish us from other Christians.

1. In the first place, we believe in the doctrine of God's UNITY, or that there is one God, and one only. To this truth we give infinite importance, and we feel ourselves bound to take heed, lest any man spoil us of it by vain philosophy. The proposition that there is one God, seems to us exceedingly plain. We understand by it, that there is one being, one mind, one person, one intelligent agent, and one only, to whom underived and infinite perfection and dominion belong. We conceive that these words could have conveyed no other meaning to the simple and uncultivated people, who were set apart to be the depositaries of this great truth, and who were utterly incapable of understanding those hair-breadth distinctions between being and person, which the sagacity of later ages has discovered. We find no intimation that this language was to be taken in an unusual sense, or that God's unity was a quite different thing from the oneness of other intelligent beings.

We object to the doctrine of the Trinity, that, whilst acknowledging in words, it subverts in effect, the unity of God. According to this doctrine, there are three infinite and equal persons, possessing supreme divinity, called the Father, Son, and Holy Ghost. Each of these persons, as described by theologians, has his own particular consciousness, will, and perceptions. They love each other, converse with each other, and delight in each other's society. They perform different parts in man's redemption, each having his appropriate office, and neither doing the work of the other. The Son is mediator and not the Father. The Father sends the Son, and is not himself sent; nor is he conscious, like the Son, of taking flesh. Here, then, we have three intelligent agents, possessed of different consciousnesses, different wills, and different perceptions, performing different acts, and sustaining different relations; and if these things do not imply and constitute three minds or beings, we are utterly at a loss to know how three minds or beings are to be formed. It is difference of properties, and acts, and consciousness, which leads us to the belief of different intelligent beings, and, if this mark fails us, our whole knowledge falls; we have no proof that all the agents and persons in the universe are not one and the same mind. When we attempt to conceive of three Gods, we can do nothing more than represent to ourselves three agents, distinguished from each other by similar marks and peculiarities to those which separate the persons of the Trinity; and when common Christians hear these persons spoken of as conversing with each other, loving each other, and performing different acts, how can they help regarding them as different beings, different minds?

We do, then, with all earnestness, though without reproaching our brethren, protest against the irrational and unscriptural doctrine of the Trinity. "To us," as to the Apostle and the primitive Christians, "there is one God, even the Father." With Jesus, we worship the Father, as the only living and true God. We are astonished that any man can read the New Testament, and avoid the conviction that the Father alone is God. We hear our Saviour continually appropriating this character to the Father. We find the Father continually distinguished from Jesus by this title. "God sent his Son." "God anointed Jesus." Now, how singular and inexplicable is this phraseology, which fills the New Testament, if this title belong equally to Jesus, and if a principal object of this book is to reveal him as God, as partaking equally with the Father in supreme divinity! We challenge our opponents to adduce one passage in the New Testament, where the word God means three persons, where it is not limited to one person, and where, unless turned from its usual sense by the connexion, it does not mean the Father. Can stronger proof be given, that the doctrine of three persons in the Godhead is not a fundamental doctrine of Christianity?

This doctrine, were it true, must, from its difficulty, singularity, and importance, have been laid down with great clearness, guarded with great care, and stated with all possible precision. But where does this statement appear? From the many passages which treat of God, we ask for one, one only, in which we are told, that he is a threefold being, or that he is three persons, or that he is Father, Son, and Holy Ghost. On the contrary, in the New Testament, where, at least, we might expect many express assertions of this nature, God is declared to be one, without the least attempt to prevent the acceptation of the words in their common sense; and he is always spoken of and addressed in the singular number, that is, in language which was universally understood to intend a single person, and to which no other idea could have been attached, without an express admonition. So entirely do the Scriptures abstain from stating the Trinity, that when our opponents would insert it into their creeds and doxologies, they are compelled to leave the Bible, and to invent forms of words altogether unsanctioned by Scriptural phraseology. That a doctrine so strange, so liable to misapprehension, so fundamental as this is said to be, and requiring such careful exposition, should be left so undefined and unprotected, to be made out by inference, and to be hunted through distant and detached parts of Scripture, this is a difficulty, which, we think, no ingenuity can explain.

We have another difficulty. Christianity, it must be remembered, was planted and grew up amidst sharp-sighted enemies, who overlooked no objectionable part of the system, and who must have fastened with great earnestness on a doctrine involving such apparent contradictions as the Trinity. We cannot conceive an opinion against which the Jews, who prided themselves on an adherence to God's unity, would have raised an equal clamor. Now, how happens it that in the apostolic writings, which relate so much to objections against Christianity, and to the controversies which grew out of this religion, not one word is said implying that objections were brought against the Gospel from the doctrine of the Trinity, not one word is uttered in its defence and explanation, not a word to rescue it from reproach and mistake? This argument has almost the force of demonstration. We are persuaded that had three divine persons been announced by the first preachers of Christianity, all equal, and all infinite, one of whom was the very Jesus who had lately died on a cross, this peculiarity of Christianity would have almost absorbed every other, and the great labor of the Apostles would have been to repel the continual assaults which it would have awakened. But the fact is that not a whisper of objection to Christianity, on that account, reaches our ears from the apostolic age. In the Epistles we see not a trace of controversy called forth by the Trinity.

We have further objections to this doctrine, drawn from its practical influence. We regard it as unfavorable to devotion, by dividing and distracting the mind in its communion with God. It is a great excellence of the doctrine of God's unity, that it offers to us ONE OBJECT of supreme homage, adoration, and love, One Infinite Father, one Being of beings, one original and fountain, to whom we may refer all good, in whom all our powers and affections may be concentrated, and whose lovely and venerable nature may pervade all our thoughts. True piety, when directed to an undivided Deity, has a chasteness, a singleness, most favorable to religious awe and love. Now, the Trinity sets before us three distinct objects of supreme adoration; three infinite persons, having equal claims on our hearts; three divine agents, performing different offices, and to be acknowledged and worshipped in different relations. And is it possible, we ask, that the weak and limited mind of man can attach itself to these with the same power and joy, as to One Infinite Father, the only First Cause, in whom all the blessings of nature and redemption meet as their centre and source? Must not devotion be distracted by the equal and rival claims of three equal persons, and must not the worship of the conscientious, consistent Christian be disturbed by an apprehension, lest he withhold from one or another of these his due proportion of homage?

We also think that the doctrine of the Trinity injures devotion not only by joining to the Father other objects of worship, but by taking from the Father the supreme affection which is his due, and transferring it to the Son. This is a most important view. That Jesus Christ, if exalted into the infinite Divinity, should be more interesting than the Father, is precisely what might be expected from history, and from the principles of human nature. Men want an object of worship like themselves, and the great secret of idolatry lies in this propensity. A God, clothed in our form, and feeling our wants and sorrows, speaks to our weak nature more strongly, than a Father in heaven, a pure spirit, invisible and unapproachable, save by the reflecting and purified mind.—We think, too, that the peculiar offices ascribed to Jesus by the popular theology, make him the most attractive person in the Godhead. The Father is the depositary of the justice, the vindicator of the rights, the avenger of the laws of the Divinity. On the other hand, the Son, the brightness of the divine mercy, stands between the incensed Deity and guilty humanity, exposes his meek head to the storms, and his compassionate breast to the sword of the divine justice, bears our whole load of punishment, and purchases with his blood every blessing which descends from heaven. Need we state the effect of these representations, especially on common minds, for whom Christianity was chiefly designed, and whom it seeks to bring to the Father as the loveliest being? We do believe that the worship of a bleeding, suffering God, tends strongly to absorb the mind, and to draw it from other objects, just as the human tenderness of the Virgin Mary has given her so conspicuous a place in the devotions of the Church of Rome. We believe, too, that this worship, though attractive, is not most fitted to spiritualize the mind, that it awakens human transport, rather than that deep veneration of the moral perfections of God which is the essence of piety.

2. Having thus given our views of the unity of God, I proceed in the second place to observe, that we believe in the unity of Jesus Christ. We believe that Jesus is one mind, one soul, one being, as truly one as we are, and equally distinct from the one God. We complain of the doctrine of the Trinity, that, not satisfied with making God three beings, it makes Jesus Christ two beings, and thus introduces infinite confusion into our conceptions of his character. This corruption of Christianity, alike repugnant to common sense and to the general strain of Scripture, is a remarkable proof of the power of a false philosophy in disfiguring the simple truth of Jesus.

According to this doctrine, Jesus Christ, instead of being one mind, one conscious intelligent principle, whom we can understand, consists of two souls, two minds; the one divine, the other human; the one weak, the other almighty; the one ignorant, the other omniscient. Now we maintain that this is to make Christ two beings. To denominate him one person, one being, and yet to suppose him made up of two minds, infinitely different from each other, is to abuse and confound language, and to throw darkness over all our conceptions of intelligent natures. According to the common doctrine, each of these two minds in Christ has its own consciousness, its own will, its own perceptions. They have, in fact, no common properties. The divine mind feels none of the wants and sorrows of the human, and the human is infinitely removed from the perfection and happiness of the divine. Can you conceive of two beings in the universe more distinct? We have always thought that one person was constituted and distinguished by one consciousness. The doctrine that one and the same person should have two consciousnesses, two wills, two souls, infinitely different from each other, this we think an enormous tax on human credulity.

We say that if a doctrine, so strange, so difficult, so remote from all the previous conceptions of men, be indeed a part and an essential part of revelation, it must be taught with great distinctness, and we ask our brethren to point to some plain, direct passage, where Christ is said to be composed of two minds infinitely different, yet constituting one person. We find none. Other Christians, indeed, tell us, that this doctrine is necessary to the harmony of the Scriptures, that some texts ascribe to Jesus Christ human, and others divine properties, and that to reconcile these, we must suppose two minds, to which these properties may be referred. In other words, for the purpose of reconciling certain difficult passages, which a just criticism can in a great degree, if not wholly, explain, we must invent an hypothesis vastly more difficult, and involving gross absurdity. We are to find our way out of a labyrinth by a clue which conducts us into mazes infinitely more inextricable.

Surely, if Jesus Christ felt that he consisted of two minds, and that this was a leading feature of his religion, his phraseology respecting himself would have been colored by this peculiarity. The universal language of men is framed upon the idea that one person is one person, is one mind, and one soul; and when the multitude heard this language from the lips of Jesus, they must have taken it in its usual sense, and must have referred to a single soul all which he spoke, unless expressly instructed to interpret it differently. But where do we find this instruction? Where do you meet, in the New Testament, the phraseology which abounds in Trinitarian books, and which necessarily grows from the doctrine of two natures in Jesus? Where does this divine teacher say, "This I speak as God, and this as man; this is true only of my human mind, this only of my divine"? Where do we find in the Epistles a trace of this strange phraseology? Nowhere. It was not needed in that day. It was demanded by the errors of a later age.

We believe, then, that Christ is one mind, one being, and, I add, a being distinct from the one God. That Christ is not the one God, not the same being with the Father, is a necessary inference from our former head, in which we saw that the doctrine of three persons in God is a fiction. But on so important a subject, I would add a few remarks. We wish that those from whom we differ would weigh one striking fact. Jesus, in his preaching, continually spoke of God. The word was always in his mouth. We ask, does he, by this word, ever mean himself? We say, never. On the contrary, he most plainly distinguishes between God and himself, and so do his disciples. How this is to be reconciled with the idea that the manifestation of Christ, as God, was a primary object of Christianity, our adversaries must determine.

If we examine the passages in which Jesus is distinguished from God, we shall see, that they not only speak of him as another being, but seem to labor to express his inferiority. He is continually spoken of as the Son of God, sent of God, receiving all his powers from God, working miracles because God was with him, judging justly because God taught him, having claims on our belief because he was anointed and sealed by God, and as able of himself to do nothing. The New Testament is filled with this language. Now we ask, what impression this language was fitted and intended to make? Could any, who heard it, have imagined that Jesus was the very God to whom he was so industriously declared to be inferior; the very Being by whom he was sent, and from whom he professed to have received his message and power? Let it here be remembered, that the human birth, and bodily form, and humble circumstances, and mortal sufferings of Jesus, must all have prepared men to interpret, in the most unqualified manner, the language in which his inferiority to God was declared. Why, then, was this language used so continually, and without limitation, if Jesus were the Supreme Deity, and if this truth were an essential part of his religion? I repeat it, the human condition and sufferings of Christ tended strongly to exclude from men's minds the idea of his proper Godhead; and, of course, we should expect to find in the New Testament perpetual care and effort to counteract this tendency to hold him forth as the same being with his Father, if this doctrine were, as is pretended, the soul and centre of his religion. We should expect to find the phraseology of Scripture cast into the mould of this doctrine, to hear familiarly of God the Son, of our Lord God Jesus, and to be told, that to us there is one God, even Jesus. But, instead of this, the inferiority of Christ pervades the New Testament. It is not only implied in the general phraseology, but repeatedly and decidedly expressed, and unaccompanied with any admonition to prevent its application to his whole nature. Could it, then, have been the great design of the sacred writers to exhibit Jesus as the Supreme God?

I am aware that these remarks will be met by two or three texts, in which Christ is called God, and by a class of passages, not very numerous, in which divine properties are said to be ascribed to him. To these we offer one plain answer. We say that it is one of the most established and obvious principles of criticism, that language is to be explained according to the known properties of the subject to which it is applied. Every man knows that the same words convey very different ideas when used in relation to different beings. Thus, Solomon *built* the temple in a different manner from the architect whom he employed; and God *repents* differently from man. Now we maintain that the known properties and circumstances of Christ, his birth, sufferings, and death, his constant habit of speaking of God as a distinct being from himself, his praying to God, his ascribing to God all his power and offices, these acknowledged properties of Christ, we say, oblige us to interpret the comparatively few passages which are thought to make him the Supreme God, in a manner consistent with his distinct and inferior nature. It is our duty to explain such texts by the rule which we apply to other texts in which human beings are called gods, and are said to be partakers of the divine nature, to know and possess all things, and to be filled with all God's fulness. These latter passages we do not hesitate to modify, and restrain, and turn from the most obvious sense, because this sense is opposed to the known properties of the beings to whom they relate; and we maintain, that we adhere to the same principle, and use no greater latitude, in explaining, as we do the passages which are thought to support the Godhead of Christ.

Trinitarians profess to derive some important advantages from their mode of viewing Christ. It furnishes them, they tell us, with an infinite atonement, for it shows them an infinite being suffering for their sins. The confidence with which this fallacy is repeated astonishes us. When pressed with the question whether they really believe that the infinite and unchangeable God suffered and died on the cross, they acknowledge that this is not true, but that Christ's human mind alone sustained the pains of death. How have we, then, an infinite sufferer? This language seems to us an imposition on common minds, and very derogatory to God's justice, as if this attribute could be satisfied by a sophism and a fiction.

We are also told that Christ is a more interesting object, that his love and mercy are more felt, when he is viewed as the Supreme God, who left his glory to take humanity and to suffer for men. That Trinitarians are strongly moved by this representation, we do not mean to deny; but we think their emotions altogether founded on a misapprehension of their own doctrines. They talk of the second person of the Trinity's leaving his glory and his Father's bosom, to visit and save the world. But this second person, being the unchangeable and infinite God, was evidently incapable of parting with the least degree of his perfection and felicity. At the moment of his taking flesh, he was as intimately present with his Father as before, and equally with his Father filled heaven, and earth, and immensity. This Trinitarians acknowledge; and still they profess to be touched and overwhelmed by the amazing humiliation of this immutable being! But not only does their doctrine, when fully explained, reduce Christ's humiliation to a fiction, it almost wholly destroys the impressions with which his cross ought to be viewed. According to their doctrine, Christ was comparatively no sufferer at all. It is true, his human mind suffered; but this, they tell us, was an infinitely small part of Jesus, bearing no more proportion to his whole nature, than a single hair of our heads to the whole body, or than a drop to the ocean. The divine mind of Christ, that which was most properly himself, was infinitely happy, at the very moment of the suffering of his humanity. Whilst hanging on the cross, he was the happiest being in the universe, as happy as the infinite Father; so that his pains, compared with his felicity, were nothing. This Trinitarians do, and must, acknowledge. It follows necessarily from the immutableness of the divine nature, which they ascribe to Christ; so that their system, justly viewed, robs his death of interest, weakens our sympathy with his sufferings, and is, of all others, most unfavorable to a love of Christ, founded on a sense of his sacrifices for mankind. We esteem our own views to be vastly more affecting. It is our belief that Christ's humiliation was real and entire, that the whole Saviour, and not a part of him, suffered, that his crucifixion was a scene of deep and unmixed agony. As we stand round his cross, our minds are not distracted, nor our sensibility weakened, by contemplating him as composed of incongruous and infinitely differing minds, and as having a balance of infinite felicity. We recognise in the dying Jesus but one mind. This, we think, renders his sufferings, and his patience and love in bearing them, incomparably more impressive and affecting than the system we oppose.

3. Having thus given our belief on two great points, namely, that there is one God, and that Jesus Christ is a being distinct from, and inferior to, God, I now proceed to another point, on which we lay still greater stress. We believe in the *moral perfection of God*. We consider no part of theology so important as that which treats of God's moral character; and we value our views of Christianity chiefly as they assert his amiable and venerable attributes.

It may be said, that, in regard to this subject, all Christians agree, that all ascribe to the Supreme Being infinite justice, goodness, and

holiness. We reply, that it is very possible to speak of God magnifi-
cently, and to think of him meanly; to apply to his person high-
sounding epithets, and to his government, principles which make
him odious. The Heathens called Jupiter the greatest and the best;
but his history was black with cruelty and lust. We cannot judge of
men's real ideas of God by their general language, for in all ages
they have hoped to soothe the Deity by adulation. We must inquire
into their particular views of his purposes, of the principles of his
administration, and of his disposition towards his creatures.

We conceive that Christians have generally leaned towards a very
injurious view of the Supreme Being. They have too often felt as if
he were raised, by his greatness and sovereignty, above the principles
of morality, above those eternal laws of equity and rectitude, to
which all other beings are subjected. We believe that in no being is
the sense of right so strong, so omnipotent, as in God. We believe
that his almighty power is entirely submitted to his perceptions of
rectitude; and this is the ground of our piety. It is not because he is
our Creator merely, but because he created us for good and holy
purposes; it is not because his will is irresistible, but because his will
is the perfection of virtue, that we pay him allegiance. We cannot
bow before a being, however great and powerful, who governs
tyrannically. We respect nothing but excellence, whether on earth
or in heaven. We venerate not the loftiness of God's throne, but the
equity and goodness in which it is established.

We believe that God is infinitely good, kind, benevolent, in the
proper sense of these words; good in disposition, as well as in act;
good, not to a few, but to all; good to every individual, as well as
to the general system.

We believe, too, that God is just; but we never forget that his
justice is the justice of a good being, dwelling in the same mind, and
acting in harmony, with perfect benevolence. By this attribute, we
understand God's infinite regard to virtue or moral worth, expressed
in a moral government; that is, in giving excellent and equitable
laws, and in conferring such rewards, and inflicting such punishments, as are best fitted to secure their observance. God's justice
has for its end the highest virtue of the creation, and it punishes for

this end alone, and thus it coincides with benevolence; for virtue and happiness, though not the same, are inseparably conjoined.

God's justice thus viewed, appears to us to be in perfect harmony with his mercy. According to the prevalent systems of theology, these attributes are so discordant and jarring, that to reconcile them is the hardest task, and the most wonderful achievement, of infinite wisdom. To us they seem to be intimate friends, always at peace, breathing the same spirit, and seeking the same end. By God's mercy, we understand not a blind instinctive compassion, which forgives without reflection, and without regard to the interests of virtue. This, we acknowledge, would be incompatible with justice, and also with enlightened benevolence. God's mercy, as we understand it, desires strongly the happiness of the guilty, but only through their penitence. It has a regard to character as truly as his justice. It defers punishment, and suffers long, that the sinner may return to his duty, but leaves the impenitent and unyielding to the fearful retribution threatened in God's Word.

To give our views of God in one word, we believe in his Parental character. We ascribe to him, not only the name, but the dispositions and principles of a father. We believe that he has a father's concern for his creatures, a father's desire for their improvement, a father's equity in proportioning his commands to their powers, a father's joy in their progress, a father's readiness to receive the penitent, and a father's justice for the incorrigible. We look upon this world as a place of education, in which he is training men by prosperity and adversity, by aids and obstructions, by conflicts of reason and passion, by motives to duty and temptations to sin, by various discipline suited to free and moral beings, for union with himself, and for a sublime and ever-growing virtue in heaven.

Now, we object to the systems of religion which prevail among us, that they are adverse, in a greater or less degree, to these purifying, comforting, and honorable views of God; that they take from us our Father in heaven, and substitute for him a being, whom we cannot love if we would, and whom we ought not to love if we could. We object, particularly on this ground, to that system which arrogates to itself the name of Orthodoxy, and which is now industriously propagated through our country. This system indeed takes various shapes, but in all it casts dishonor on the Creator. According to its old and genuine form, it teaches that God brings us into life wholly depraved, so that under the innocent features of our childhood is hidden a nature averse to all good and propense to all evil, a nature which exposes us to God's displeasure and wrath, even before we have acquired power to understand our duties, or to reflect upon our actions. According to a more modern exposition, it teaches that we came from the hands of our Maker with such a constitution, and are placed under such influences and circumstances, as to render certain and infallible the total depravity of every human being, from the first moment of his moral agency; and it also teaches that the offence of the child, who brings into life this ceaseless tendency to unmingled crime, exposes him to the sentence of everlasting damnation. Now, according to the plainest principles of morality, we maintain that a natural constitution of the mind, unfailingly disposing it to evil and to evil alone, would absolve it from guilt; that to give existence under this condition would argue unspeakable cruelty; and that to punish the sin of this unhappily constituted child with endless ruin, would be a wrong unparalleled by the most merciless despotism.

This system also teaches that God selects from this corrupt mass a number to be saved, and plucks them, by a special influence, from the common ruin; that the rest of mankind, though left without that special grace which their conversion requires, are commanded to repent, under penalty of aggravated woe; and that forgiveness is promised them, on terms which their very constitution infallibly disposes them to reject, and in rejecting which they awfully enhance the punishments of hell. These proffers of forgiveness and exhortations of amendment, to beings born under a blighting curse, fill our minds with a horror which we want words to express.

That this religious system does not produce all the effects on character which might be anticipated, we most joyfully admit. It is often, very often, counteracted by nature, conscience, common sense, by the general strain of Scripture, by the mild example and precepts of Christ, and by the many positive declarations of God's universal

kindness and perfect equity. But still we think that we see its unhappy influence. It tends to discourage the timid, to give excuses to
the bad, to feed the vanity of the fanatical, and to offer shelter to the
bad feelings of the malignant. By shocking, as it does, the fundamental principles of morality, and by exhibiting a severe and partial
Deity, it tends strongly to pervert the moral faculty, to form a
gloomy, forbidding, and servile religion, and to lead men to substitute censoriousness, bitterness, and persecution, for a tender and
impartial charity. We think, too, that this system, which begins with
degrading human nature, may be expected to end in pride; for pride
grows out of a consciousness of high distinctions, however obtained,
and no distinction is so great as that which is made between the
elected and abandoned of God.

The false and dishonorable views of God which have now been
stated, we feel ourselves bound to resist unceasingly. Other errors
we can pass over with comparative indifference. But we ask our
opponents to leave to us a GOD, worthy of our love and trust, in
whom our moral sentiments may delight, in whom our weaknesses
and sorrows may find refuge. We cling to the Divine perfections. We
meet them everywhere in creation, we read them in the Scriptures,
we see a lovely image of them in Jesus Christ; and gratitude, love,
and veneration call on us to assert them. Reproached, as we often
are, by men, it is our consolation and happiness, that one of our
chief offences is the zeal with which we vindicate the dishonored
goodness and rectitude of God.

4. Having thus spoken of the unity of God; of the unity of Jesus,
and his inferiority to God; and of the perfections of the Divine character; I now proceed to give our views of the mediation of Christ,
and of the purposes of his mission. With regard to the great object
which Jesus came to accomplish, there seems to be no possibility
of mistake. We believe that he was sent by the Father to effect a
moral, or spiritual deliverance of mankind; that is, to rescue men
from sin and its consequences, and to bring them to a state of everlasting purity and happiness. We believe, too, that he accomplishes
this sublime purpose by a variety of methods; by his instructions
respecting God's unity, parental character, and moral government,

which are admirably fitted to reclaim the world from idolatry and impiety, to the knowledge, love, and obedience of the Creator; by his promises of pardon to the penitent, and of divine assistance to those who labor for progress in moral excellence; by the light which he has thrown on the path of duty; by his own spotless example, in which the loveliness and sublimity of virtue shine forth to warm and quicken, as well as guide us to perfection; by his threatenings against incorrigible guilt; by his glorious discoveries of immortality; by his sufferings and death; by that signal event, the resurrection, which powerfully bore witness to his divine mission, and brought down to men's senses a future life; by his continual intercession, which obtains for us spiritual aid and blessings; and by the power with which he is invested of raising the dead, judging the world, and conferring the everlasting rewards promised to the faithful.

We have no desire to conceal the fact that a difference of opinion exists among us, in regard to an interesting part of Christ's mediation; I mean, in regard to the precise influence of his death on our forgiveness. Many suppose, that this event contributes to our pardon, as it was a principal means of confirming his religion, and of giving it a power over the mind; in other words, that it procures forgiveness by leading to that repentance and virtue, which is the great and only condition on which forgiveness is bestowed. Many of us are dissatisfied with this explanation, and think that the Scriptures ascribe the remission of sins to Christ's death, with an emphasis so peculiar, that we ought to consider this event as having a special influence in removing punishment, though the Scriptures may not reveal the way in which it contributes to this end.

Whilst, however, we differ in explaining the connexion between Christ's death and human forgiveness, a connexion which we all gratefully acknowledge, we agree in rejecting many sentiments which prevail in regard to his mediation. The idea, which is conveyed to common minds by the popular system, that Christ's death has an influence in making God placable, or merciful, in awakening his kindness towards men, we reject with strong disapprobation. We are happy to find that this very dishonorable notion is disowned by intelligent Christians of that class from which we differ. We recollect, however, that, not long ago, it was common to hear of Christ, as having died to appease God's wrath, and to pay the debt of sinners to his inflexible justice; and we have a strong persuasion that the language of popular religious books, and the common mode of stating the doctrine of Christ's mediation, still communicate very degrading views of God's character. They give to multitudes the impression, that the death of Jesus produces a change in the mind of God towards man, and that in this its efficacy chiefly consists. No error seems to us more pernicious. We can endure no shade over the pure goodness of God. We earnestly maintain that Jesus, instead of calling forth, in any way or degree, the mercy of the Father, was sent by that mercy, to be our Saviour; that he is nothing to the human race but what he is by God's appointment; that he communicates nothing but what God empowers him to bestow; that our Father in heaven is originally, essentially, and eternally placable, and disposed to forgive; and that his unborrowed, underived, and unchangeable love is the only fountain of what flows to us through his Son. We conceive that Jesus is dishonored, not glorified, by ascribing to him an influence which clouds the splendor of Divine benevolence.

We farther agree in rejecting, as unscriptural and absurd, the explanation given by the popular system, of the manner in which Christ's death procures forgiveness for men. This system used to teach as its fundamental principle, that man, having sinned against an infinite Being, has contracted infinite guilt, and is consequently exposed to an infinite penalty. We believe, however, that this reasoning, if reasoning it may be called, which overlooks the obvious maxim that the guilt of a being must be proportioned to his nature and powers, has fallen into disuse. Still the system teaches that sin, of whatever degree, exposes to endless punishment, and that the whole human race, being infallibly involved by their nature in sin, owe this awful penalty to the justice of their Creator. It teaches that this penalty cannot be remitted, in consistency with the honor of the divine law, unless a substitute be found to endure it or to suffer an equivalent. It also teaches that, from the nature of the case, no substitute is adequate to this work, save the infinite God himself; and accordingly, God, in his second person, took on him human nature, that he might pay to his own justice the debt of punishment incurred by men, and might thus reconcile forgiveness with the claims and threatenings of his law. Such is the prevalent system. Now, to us, this doctrine seems to carry on its front strong marks of absurdity; and we maintain that Christianity ought not to be encumbered with it, unless it be laid down in the New Testament fully and expressly. We ask our adversaries, then, to point to some plain passages where it is taught. We ask for one text in which we are told that God took human nature that he might make an infinite satisfaction to his own justice; for one text which tells us that human guilt requires an infinite substitute; that Christ's sufferings owe their efficacy to their being borne by an infinite being; or that his divine nature gives infinite value to the sufferings of the human. Not *one word* of this description can we find in the Scriptures; not a text which even hints at these strange doctrines. They are altogether, we believe, the fictions of theologians. Christianity is in no degree responsible for them. We are astonished at their prevalence. What can be plainer than that God cannot, in any sense, be a sufferer, or bear a penalty in the room of his creatures? How dishonorable to him is the supposition that his justice is now so severe as to exact infinite punishment for the sins of frail and feeble men, and now so easy and yielding, as to accept the limited pains of Christ's human soul as a full equivalent for the endless woes due from the world? How plain is it also, according to this doctrine, that God, instead of being plenteous in forgiveness, never forgives; for it seems absurd to speak of men as forgiven, when their whole punishment, or an equivalent to it, is borne by a substitute? A scheme more fitted to obscure the brightness of Christianity and the mercy of God, or less suited to give comfort to a guilty and troubled mind, could not, we think, be easily framed.

We believe, too, that this system is unfavorable to the character. It naturally leads men to think that Christ came to change God's mind rather than their own; that the highest object of his mission was to avert punishment, rather than to communicate holiness; and that a large part of religion consists in disparaging good works and human virtue, for the purpose of magnifying the value of Christ's vicarious sufferings. In this way, a sense of the infinite importance and indispensable necessity of personal improvement is weakened, and high-sounding praises of Christ's cross seem often to be substituted for obedience to his precepts. For ourselves, we have not so learned Jesus. Whilst we gratefully acknowledge that he came to rescue us from punishment, we believe that he was sent on a still nobler errand, namely, to deliver us from sin itself, and to form us to a sublime and heavenly virtue. We regard him as a Saviour, chiefly as he is the light, physician, and guide of the dark, diseased, and wandering mind. No influence in the universe seems to us so glorious as that over the character; and no redemption so worthy of thankfulness as the restoration of the soul to purity. Without this, pardon, were it possible, would be of little value. Why pluck the sinner from hell, if a hell be left to burn in his own breast? Why raise him to heaven, if he remains a stranger to its sanctity and love? With these impressions, we are accustomed to value the Gospel chiefly as it abounds in effectual aids, motives, excitements to a generous and divine virtue. In this virtue, as in a common centre, we see all its doctrines, precepts, promises meet; and we believe that faith in this religion is of no worth, and contributes nothing to salvation, any farther than as it uses these doctrines, precepts, promises, and the whole life, character, sufferings, and triumphs of Jesus, as the means of purifying the mind, of changing it into the likeness of his celestial excellence.

5. Having thus stated our views of the highest object of Christ's mission, that it is the recovery of men to virtue, or holiness, I shall now, in the last place, give our views of the nature of Christian virtue, or true holiness. We believe that all virtue has its foundation in the moral nature of man, that is, in conscience, or his sense of duty, and in the power of forming his temper and life according to conscience. We believe that these moral faculties are the grounds of responsibility, and the highest distinctions of human nature, and that no act is praiseworthy, any farther than it springs from their exertion. We believe that no dispositions infused into us without our own moral activity are of the nature of virtue, and therefore, we reject the doctrine of irresistible divine influence on the human

mind, moulding it into goodness, as marble is hewn into a statute. Such goodness, if this word may be used, would not be the object of moral approbation, any more than the instinctive affections of inferior animals, or the constitutional amiableness of human beings.

By these remarks, we do not mean to deny the importance of God's aid or Spirit; but by this Spirit, we mean a moral, illuminating, and persuasive influence, not physical, not compulsory, not involving a necessity of virtue. We object, strongly, to the idea of many Christians respecting man's impotence and God's irresistible agency on the heart, believing that they subvert our responsibility and the laws of our moral nature, that they make men machines, that they cast on God the blame of all evil deeds, that they discourage good minds, and inflate the fanatical with wild conceits of immediate and sensible inspiration.

Among the virtues, we give the first place to the love of God. We believe that this principle is the true end and happiness of our being, that we were made for union with our Creator, that his infinite perfection is the only sufficient object and true resting-place for the insatiable desires and unlimited capacities of the human mind, and that, without him, our noblest sentiments, admiration, veneration, hope, and love, would wither and decay. We believe, too, that the love of God is not only essential to happiness, but to the strength and perfection of all the virtues; that conscience, without the sanction of God's authority and retributive justice, would be a weak director; that benevolence, unless nourished by communion with his goodness, and encouraged by his smile, could not thrive amidst the selfishness and thanklessness of the world; and that self-government, without a sense of the divine inspection, would hardly extend beyond an outward and partial purity. God, as he is essentially goodness, holiness, justice, and virtue, so he is the life, motive, and sustainer of virtue in the human soul.

But, whilst we earnestly inculcate the love of God, we believe that great care is necessary to distinguish it from counterfeits. We think that much which is called piety is worthless. Many have fallen into the error that there can be no excess in feelings which have God for their object; and, distrusting as coldness that self-possession without which virtue and devotion lose all their dignity, they have abandoned themselves to extravagances which have brought contempt on piety. Most certainly, if the love of God be that which often bears its name, the less we have of it the better. If religion be the shipwreck of understanding, we cannot keep too far from it. On this subject, we always speak plainly. We cannot sacrifice our reason to the reputation of zeal. We owe it to truth and religion to maintain that fanaticism, partial insanity, sudden impressions, and ungovernable transports, are any thing rather than piety.

We conceive, that the true love of God is a moral sentiment, founded on a clear perception, and consisting in a high esteem and veneration of his moral perfections. Thus, it perfectly coincides, and is in fact the same thing, with the love of virtue, rectitude, and goodness. You will easily judge, then, what we esteem the surest and only decisive signs of piety. We lay no stress on strong excitements. We esteem him, and him only a pious man, who practically conforms to God's moral perfections and government; who shows his delight in God's benevolence by loving and serving his neighbour; his delight in God's justice by being resolutely upright; his sense of God's purity by regulating his thoughts, imagination, and desires; and whose conversation, business, and domestic life are swayed by a regard to God's presence and authority. In all things else men may deceive themselves. Disordered nerves may give them strange sights, and sounds, and impressions. Texts of Scripture may come to them as from Heaven. Their whole souls may be moved, and their confidence in God's favor be undoubting. But in all this there is no religion. The question is, Do they love God's commands, in which his character is fully expressed, and give up to these their habits and passions? Without this, ecstasy is a mockery. One surrender of desire to God's will, is worth a thousand transports. We do not judge of the bent of men's minds by their raptures, any more than we judge of the natural direction of a tree during a storm. We rather suspect loud profession, for we have observed that deep feeling is generally noiseless, and least seeks display.

We would not, by these remarks, be understood as wishing to exclude from religion warmth, and even transport. We honor, and highly value, true religious sensibility. We believe that Christianity is intended to act powerfully on our whole nature, on the heart as well as the understanding and the conscience. We conceive of heaven as a state where the love of God will be exalted into an unbounded fervor and joy; and we desire, in our pilgrimage here, to drink into the spirit of that better world. But we think that religious warmth is only to be valued when it springs naturally from an improved character, when it comes unforced, when it is the recompense of obedience, when it is the warmth of a mind which understands God by being like him, and when, instead of disordering, it exalts the understanding, invigorates conscience, gives a pleasure to common duties, and is seen to exist in connexion with cheerfulness, judiciousness, and a reasonable frame of mind. When we observe a fervor, called religious, in men whose general character expresses little refinement and elevation, and whose piety seems at war with reason, we pay it little respect. We honor religion too much to give its sacred name to a feverish, forced, fluctuating zeal, which has little power over the life.

Another important branch of virtue we believe to be love to Christ. The greatness of the work of Jesus, the spirit with which he executed it, and the sufferings which he bore for our salvation, we feel to be strong claims on our gratitude and veneration. We see in nature no beauty to be compared with the loveliness of his character, nor do we find on earth a benefactor to whom we owe an equal debt. We read his history with delight, and learn from it the perfection of our nature. We are particularly touched by his death, which was endured for our redemption, and by that strength of charity which triumphed over his pains. His resurrection is the foundation of our hope of immortality. His intercession gives us boldness to draw nigh to the throne of grace, and we look up to heaven with new desire, and we think that, if we follow him here, we shall there see his benignant countenance, and enjoy his friendship for ever.

I need not express to you our views on the subject of the benevolent virtues. We attach such importance to these, that we are sometimes reproached with exalting them above piety. We regard the

spirit of love, charity, meekness, forgiveness, liberality, and benefi-
cence, as the badge and distinction of Christians, as the brightest
image we can bear of God, as the best proof of piety. On this subject,
I need not, and cannot enlarge; but there is one branch of benevolence which I ought not to pass over in silence, because we think
that we conceive of it more highly and justly than many of our
brethren. I refer to the duty of candor, charitable judgment, especially towards those who differ in religious opinion. We think that
in nothing have Christians so widely departed from their religion,
as in this particular. We read with astonishment and horror, the
history of the church; and sometimes when we look back on the
fires of persecution, and on the zeal of Christians in building up
walls of separation, and in giving up one another to perdition, we
feel as if we were reading the records of an infernal, rather than a
heavenly kingdom. An enemy to every religion, if asked to describe
a Christian, would, with some show of reason, depict him as an
idolator of his own distinguishing opinions, covered with badges of
party, shutting his eyes on the virtues, and his ears on the arguments,
of his opponents, arrogating all excellence to his own sect and all
saving power to his own creed, sheltering under the name of pious
zeal the love of domination, the conceit of infallibility, and the
spirit of intolerance, and trampling on men's rights under the pretence of saving their souls.

We can hardly conceive of a plainer obligation on beings of our
frail and fallible nature, who are instructed in the duty of candid
judgment, than to abstain from condemning men of apparent con-
scientiousness and sincerity, who are chargeable with no crime but
that of differing from us in the interpretation of the Scriptures, and
differing, too, on topics of great and acknowledged obscurity. We
are astonished at the hardihood of those, who, with Christ's warn-
ings sounding in their ears, take on them the responsibility of making creeds for his church, and cast out professors of virtuous lives
for imagined errors, for the guilt of thinking for themselves. We
know that zeal for truth is the cover for his usurpation of Christ's
prerogative; but we think that zeal for truth, as it is called, is very
suspicious, except in men whose capacities and advantages, whose

patient deliberation, and whose improvements in humility, mildness, and candor, give them a right to hope that their views are more just than those of their neighbours. Much of what passes for a zeal for truth, we look upon with little respect, for it often appears to thrive most luxuriantly where other virtues shoot up thinly and feebly; and we have no gratitude for those reformers who would force upon us a doctrine which has not sweetened their own tempers, or made them better men than their neighbours.

We are accustomed to think much of the difficulties attending religious inquiries; difficulties springing from the slow developement of our minds, from the power of early impressions, from the state of society, from human authority, from the general neglect of the reasoning powers, from the want of just principles of criticism and of important helps in interpreting Scripture, and from various other causes. We find, that on no subject have men, and even good men, ingrafted so many strange conceits, wild theories, and fictions of fancy, as on religion; and remembering, as we do, that we ourselves are sharers of the common frailty, we dare not assume infallibility in the treatment of our fellow-Chrsitians, or encourage in common Christians who have little time for investigation, the habit of denouncing and contemning other denominations, perhaps more enlightened and virtuous than their own. Charity, forbearance, a delight in the virtues of different sects, a backwardness to censure and condemn, these are virtues, which, however poorly practised by us, we admire and recommend; and we would rather join ourselves to the church in which they abound, than to any other communion, however elated with the belief of its own orthodoxy, however strict in guarding its creed, however burning with zeal against imagined error.

I have thus given the distinguishing views of those Christians in whose names I have spoken. We have embraced this system, not hastily or lightly, but after much deliberation; and we hold it fast, not merely because we believe it to be true, but because we regard it as purifying truth, as a doctrine according to godliness, as able to "work mightily" and to "bring forth fruit" in them who believe. That we wish to spread it, we have no desire to conceal; but we think that we wish its diffusion, because we regard it as more friendly to practical piety and pure morals than the opposite doctrines, because it gives clearer and nobler views of duty, and stronger motives to its performance, because it recommends religion at once to the understanding and the heart, because it asserts the lovely and venerable attributes of God, because it tends to restore the benevolent spirit of Jesus to his divided and afflicted church, and because it cuts off every hope of God's favor, except that which springs from practical conformity to the life and precepts of Christ. We see nothing in our views to give offence, save their purity, and it is their purity which makes us seek and hope their extension through the world.

My friend and brother;—You are this day to take upon you important duties; to be clothed with an office which the Son of God did not disdain; to devote yourself to that religion which the most hallowed lips have preached, and the most precious blood sealed. We trust that you will bring to this work a willing mind, a firm purpose, a martyr's spirit, a readiness to toil and suffer for the truth, a devotion of your best powers to the interests of piety and virtue. I have spoken of the doctrines which you will probably preach; but I do not mean that you are to give yourself to controversy. You will remember that good practice is the end of preaching, and will labor to make your people holy livers, rather than skilful disputants. Be careful lest the desire of defending what you deem truth, and of repelling reproach and misrepresentation, turn you aside from your great business, which is to fix in men's minds a living conviction of the obligation, sublimity, and happiness of Christian virtue. The best way to vindicate your sentiments, is to show, in your preaching and life, their intimate connexion with Christian morals, with a high and delicate sense of duty, with candor towards your opposers, with inflexible integrity, and with an habitual reverence for God. If any light can pierce and scatter the clouds of prejudice, it is that of a pure example. My brother, may your life preach more loudly than your lips. Be to this people a pattern of all good works, and may your instructions derive authority from a well-grounded belief in your hearers, that you speak from the heart, that you preach from

experience, that the truth which you dispense has wrought powerfully in your own heart, that God, and Jesus, and heaven, are not
merely words on your lips, but most affecting realities to your mind,
and springs of hope and consolation, and strength, in all your trials.
Thus laboring, may you reap abundantly, and have a testimony of
your faithfulness, not only in your own conscience, but in the esteem,
love, virtues, and improvements of your people.

To all who hear me, I would say, with the Apostle, Prove all
things, hold fast that which is good. Do not, brethren, shrink from
the duty of searching God's Word for yourselves, through fear of
human censure and denunciation. Do not think that you may innocently follow the opinions which prevail around you, without investigation, on the ground that Christianity is now so purified from
errors, as to need no laborious research. There is much reason to
believe that Christianity is at this moment dishonored by gross and
cherished corruptions. If you remember the darkness which hung
over the Gospel for ages; if you consider the impure union, which
still subsists in almost every Christian country, between the church
and state, and which enlists men's selfishness and ambition on the
side of established error; if you recollect in what degree the spirit
of intolerance has checked free inquiry, not only before, but since
the Reformation; you will see that Christianity cannot have freed
itself from all the human inventions which disfigured it under the
Papal tyranny. No. Much stubble is yet to be burned; much rubbish
to be removed; many gaudy decorations which a false taste has
hung around Christianity, must be swept away; and the earth-born
fogs which have long shrouded it, must be scattered, before this
divine fabric will rise before us in its native and awful majesty, in
its harmonious proportions, in its mild and celestial splendors. This
glorious reformation in the church, we hope, under God's blessing,
from the progress of the human intellect, from the moral progress
of society, from the consequent decline of prejudice and bigotry,
and, though last but not least, from the subversion of human authority in matters of religion, from the fall of those hierarchies, and
other human institutions, by which the minds of individuals are
oppressed under the weight of numbers, and a Papal dominion is

perpetuated in the Protestant church. Our earnest prayer to God is that he will overturn, and overturn, and overturn the strong-holds of spiritual usurpation, until HE shall come whose right it is to rule the minds of men; that the conspiracy of ages against the liberty of Christians may be brought to an end; that the servile assent, so long yielded to human creeds, may give place to honest and devout inquiry into the Scriptures; and that Christianity, thus purified from error, may put forth its almighty energy, and prove itself, by its ennobling influence on the mind, to be indeed "the power of God unto salvation."

Ralph Waldo Emerson

THE AMERICAN SCHOLAR

¶ RALPH WALDO EMERSON (1803-1882), throughout his life, aspired to be a public teacher. He was born in Boston on May 25, 1803, the son of a Unitarian preacher who died when Ralph Waldo was a boy of eight. Despite the poverty of the family, Emerson attended Harvard College, being graduated in 1821. He taught school for a short time, then entered the Harvard Divinity School. In 1826 he was licensed to preach. Ill health took him to Florida in 1826 and 1827, thus preventing his entering immediately into pastoral duties. In 1829, he became assistant pastor of the Second Church of Boston, a charge he relinquished in 1832 because of reluctance to administer the sacrament of communion. On December 25, 1832, he sailed for Europe and there visited the leading literary figures of the day, Carlyle, Wordsworth, Coleridge. In 1836, Emerson published his first major essay, "Nature," a statement of his philosophy, and from then on until his death on April 27, 1882, numerous essays, poems, and lectures earned for him the reputation of being the leading American thinker of his time.

"The American Scholar" is usually considered to be Emerson's most famous speech. Oliver Wendell Holmes thought of it as "our intellectual Declaration of Independence," and noted that "young men went out from it as if a prophet had been proclaiming to them 'Thus saith the Lord.'" Across the waters, where printed copies of the oration were read with interest, Carlyle observed that "out of the West comes a clear utterance, clearly recognizable as a *man's* voice, and I *have* a kinsman and brother: God be thanked for it! I could have *wept* to read that speech."

The address was delivered August 31, 1837, in early afternoon, at the recently reconstructed First Parish Church in Cambridge, Massa-

264

chusetts, a plain wooden meetinghouse, used sometimes to serve the needs of Harvard University on anniversary occasions. The audience consisted of the Phi Beta Kappa Society of Harvard University and its guests, thus including the leading scholars, teachers, university officials, and literary men of the time.

M R. PRESIDENT AND GENTLEMEN:
I greet you on the recommencement of our literary year. Our anniversay is one of hope, and, perhaps, not enough of labor. We do not meet for games of strength or skill, for the recitation of histories, tragedies, and odes, like the ancient Greeks; for parliaments of love and poesy, like the Troubadours; nor for the advancement of science, like our contemporaries in the British and European capitals. Thus far, our holiday has been simply a friendly sign of the survival of the love of letters amongst a people too busy to give to letters any more. As such it is precious as the sign of an indestructible instinct. Perhaps the time is already come when it ought to be, and will be, something else; when the sluggard intellect of this continent will look from under its iron lids and fill the postponed expectation of the world with something better than the exertions of mechanical skill. Our day of dependence, our long apprenticeship to the learning of other lands, draws to a close. The millions that around us are rushing into life, cannot always be fed on the sere remains of foreign harvests. Events, actions arise, that must be sung, that will sing themselves. Who can doubt that poetry will revive and lead in a new age, as the star in the constellation Harp, which now flames in our zenith, astronomers announce, shall one day be the pole-star for a thousand years?

In this hope I accept the topic which not only usage but the nature of our association seem to prescribe to this day,—the American Scholar. Year by year we come up hither to read one more chapter of his biography. Let us inquire what light new days and events have thrown on his character and his hopes.

It is one of those fables which out of an unknown antiquity convey an unlooked-for wisdom, that the gods, in the beginning, divided Man into men, that he might be more helpful to himself;

just as the hand was divided into fingers, the better to answer its end.

The old fable covers a doctrine ever new and sublime; that there is One Man,—present to all particular men only partially, or through one faculty; and that you must take the whole society to find the whole man. Man is not a farmer, or a professor, or an engineer, but he is all. Man is priest, and scholar, and statesman, and producer, and soldier. In the *divided* or social state these functions are parcelled out to individuals, each of whom aims to do his stint of the joint work, whilst each other performs his. The fable implies that the individual, to possess himself, must sometimes return from his own labor to embrace all the other laborers. But, unfortunately, this original unit, this fountain of power, has been so distributed to multitudes, has been so minutely subdivided and peddled out, that it is spilled into drops, and cannot be gathered. The state of society is one in which the members have suffered amputation from the trunk, and strut about so many walking monsters,—a good finger, a neck, a stomach, an elbow, but never a man.

Man is thus metamorphosed into a thing, into many things. The planter, who is Man sent out into the field to gather food, is seldom cheered by any idea of the true dignity of his ministry. He sees his bushel and his cart, and nothing beyond, and sinks into the farmer, instead of Man on the farm. The tradesman scarcely ever gives an ideal worth to his work, but is ridden by the routine of his craft, and the soul is subject to dollars. The priest becomes a form; the attorney a statute-book; the mechanic a machine; the sailor a rope of the ship.

In this distribution of functions the scholar is the delegated intellect. In the right state he is *Man Thinking*. In the degenerate state, when the victim of society, he tends to become a mere thinker, or still worse, the parrot of other men's thinking.

In this view of him, as Man Thinking, the theory of his office is contained. Him Nature solicits with all her placid, all her monitory pictures; him the past instructs; him the future invites. Is not indeed every man a student, and do not all things exist for the student's behoof? And, finally, is not the true scholar the only true master?

But the old oracle said, "All things have two handles: beware of the wrong one." In life, too often, the scholar errs with mankind and forfeits his privilege. Let us see him in his school, and consider him in reference to the main influences he receives.

I. The first in time and the first in importance of the influences upon the mind is that of nature. Every day, the sun; and, after sunset, Night and her stars. Ever the winds blow; ever the grass grows. Every day, men and women, conversing—beholding and beholden. The scholar is he of all men whom this spectacle most engages. He must settle its value in his mind. What is nature to him? There is never a beginning, there is never an end, to the inexplicable continuity of this web of God, but always circular power returning into itself. Therein it resembles his own spirit, whose beginning, whose ending, he never can find,—so entire, so boundless. Far too as her splendors shine, system on system shooting like rays, upward, downward, without centre, without circumference,— in the mass and in the particle, Nature hastens to render account of herself to the mind. Classification begins. To the young mind every thing is individual, stands by itself. By and by, it finds how to join two things and see in them one nature; then three, then three thousand; and so, tyrannized over by its own unifying instinct, it goes on tying things together, diminishing anomalies, .discovering roots running under ground whereby contrary and remote things cohere and flower out from one stem. It presently learns that since the dawn of history there has been a constant accumulation and classifying of facts. But what is classification but the perceiving that these objects are not chaotic, and are not foreign, but have a law which is also a law of the human mind? The astronomer discovers that goeometry, a pure abstraction of the human mind, is the measure of planetary motion. The chemist finds proportions and intelligible method throughout matter; and science is nothing but the finding of analogy, identity, in the most remote parts. The ambitious soul sits down before each refractory fact; one after another reduces all strange constitutions, all new powers, to their class and their law, and goes on forever to animate the last fibre of organization, the outskirts of nature, by insight.

Thus to him, to his schoolboy under the bending dome of day, is suggested that he and it proceed from one root; one is leaf and one is flower; relation, sympathy, stirring in every vein. And what is that root? Is not that the soul of his soul? A thought too bold; a dream too wild. Yet when this spiritual light shall have revealed the law of more earthly natures,—when he has learned to worship the soul, and to see that the natural philosophy that now is, is only the first gropings of its gigantic hand, he shall look forward to an ever expanding knowledge as to a becoming creator. He shall see that nature is the opposite of the soul, answering to it part for part. One is seal and one is print. Its beauty is the beauty of his own mind. Its laws are the laws of his own mind. Nature then becomes to him the measure of his attainments. So much of nature as he is ignorant of, so much of his own mind does he not yet possess. And, in fine, the ancient precept, "Know thyself," and the modern precept, "Study nature," become at last one maxim.

II.   The next great influence into the spirit of the scholar is the mind of the Past,—in whatever form, whether of literature, of art, of institutions, that mind is inscribed. Books are the best type of the influence of the past, and perhaps we shall get at the truth,—learn the amount of this influence more conveniently,—by considering their value alone.

The theory of books is noble. The scholar of the first age received into him the world around; brooded thereon; gave it the new arrangement of his own mind, and uttered it again. It came into him life; it went out from him truth. It came to him short-lived actions; it went out from him immortal thoughts. It came to him business; it went from him poetry. It was dead fact; now, it is quick thought. It can stand, and it can go. It now endures, it now flies, it now inspires. Precisely in proportion to the depth of mind from which it issued, so high does it soar, so long does it sing.

Or, I might say, it depends on how far the process had gone, of transmuting life into truth. In proportion to the completeness of the distillation, so will the purity and imperishableness of the product be. But none is quite perfect. As no air-pump can by any means make a perfect vacuum, so neither can any artist entirely exclude the conventional, the local, the perishable from his book, or write a book of pure thought, that shall be as efficient, in all respects, to a remote posterity, as to contemporaries, or rather to the second age. Each age, it is found, must write its own books; or rather, each generation for the next succeeding. The books of an older period will not fit this.

Yet hence arises a grave mischief. The sacredness which attaches to the act of creation, the act of thought, is transferred to the record. The poet chanting was felt to be a divine man: henceforth the chant is divine also. The writer was a just and wise spirit: henceforward it is settled the book is perfect; as love of the hero corrupts into worship of his statue. Instantly the book becomes noxious: the guide is a tyrant. The sluggish and perverted mind of the multitude, slow to open to the incursions of Reason, having once so opened, having once received this book, stands upon it, and makes an outcry if it is disparaged. Colleges are built on it. Books are written on it by thinkers, not by Man Thinking; by men of talent, that is, who start wrong, who set out from accepted dogmas, not from their own sight of principles. Meek young men grow up in libraries, believing it their duty to accept the views which Cicero, which Locke, which Bacon, have given; forgetful that Cicero, Locke, and Bacon were only young men in libraries when they wrote these books.

Hence, instead of Man Thinking, we have the bookworm. Hence the book-learned class, who value books, as such; not as related to nature and the human constitution, but as making a sort of Third Estate with the world and the soul. Hence the restorers of readings, the emendators, the bibliomaniacs of all degrees.

Books are the best of things, well used; abused, among the worst. What is the right use? What is the one end which all means go to effect? They are for nothing but to inspire. I had better never see a book than to be warped by its attraction clean out of my own orbit, and made a satellite instead of a system. The one thing in the world, of value, is the active soul. This every man is entitled to; this every man contains within him, although in almost all men obstructed and as yet unborn. The soul active sees absolute truth and utters truth, or creates. In this action it is genius; not the privilege of here and there a favorite, but the sound estate of every man. In its essence it is progressive. The book, the college, the school of art, the institution of any kind, stop with some past utterance of genius. This is good, say they,—let us hold by this. They pin me down. They look backward and not forward. But genius looks forward: the eyes of man are set in his forehead, not in his hindhead: man hopes: genius creates. Whatever talents may be, if the man create not, the pure efflux of the Deity is not his;—cinders and smoke there may be, but not yet flame. There are creative manners, there are creative actions, and creative words; manners, actions, words, that is, indicative of no custom or authority, but springing spontaneous from the mind's own sense of good and fair.

On the other part, instead of being its own seer, let it receive from another mind its truth, though it were in torrents of light, without periods of solitude, inquest, and self-recovery, and a fatal disservice is done. Genius is always sufficiently the enemy of genius by over-influence. The literature of every nation bears me witness. The English dramatic poets have Shakspearized now for two hundred years.

Undoubtedly there is a right way of reading, so it be sternly subordinated. Man Thinking must not be subdued by his instruments. Books are for the scholar's idle times. When he can read God directly, the hour is too precious to be wasted in other men's transcripts of their readings. But when the intervals of darkness come, as come they must,—when the sun is hid and the stars withdraw their shining,—we repair to the lamps which were kindled by their ray, to guide our steps to the East again, where the dawn is. We hear, that we may speak. The Arabian proverb says, "A fig tree, looking on a fig tree, becometh fruitful."

It is remarkable, the character of the pleasure we derive from the best books. They impress us with the conviction that one nature wrote and the same reads. We read the verses of one of the great English poets, of Chaucer, of Marvell, of Dryden, with the most modern joy,—with a pleasure, I mean, which is in great part caused by the abstraction of all *time* from their verses. There is some awe mixed with the joy of our surprise, when this poet, who lived in some past world, two or three hundred years ago, says that which lies close to my own soul, that which I also had well-nigh thought and said. But for the evidence thence afforded to the philosophical doctrine of the identity of all minds, we should suppose some pre-established harmony, some foresight of souls that were to be, and some preparation of stores for their future wants, like the fact observed in insects, who lay up food before death for the young grub they shall never see.

I would not be hurried by any love of system, by any exaggeration of instincts, to underrate the Book. We all know, that as the human body can be nourished on any food, though it were boiled grass and the broth of shoes, so the human mind can be fed by any knowledge. And great and heroic men have existed who had almost no other information than by the printed page. I only would say that it needs a strong head to bear that diet. One must be an inventor to read well. As the proverb says, "He that would bring home the wealth of the Indies, must carry out the wealth of the Indies." There is then creative reading as well as creative writing. When the mind is braced by labor and invention, the page of whatever book we read becomes luminous with manifold allusion. Every sentence is doubly significant, and the sense of our author is as broad as the world. We then see, what is always true, that as the seer's hour of vision is short and rare among heavy days and months, so is its record, perchance, the least part of his volume. The discerning will read, in his Plato or Shakspeare, only that least part,—only the authentic utterances of the oracle;—all the rest he rejects, were it never so many times Plato's and Shakspeare's.

Of course there is a portion of reading quite indispensable to a wise man. History and exact science he must learn by laborious reading. Colleges, in like manner, have their indispensable office,—to teach elements. But they can only highly serve us when they aim not to drill, but to create; when they gather from far every ray of various genius to their hospitable halls, and by the concentrated fires, set the hearts of their youth on flame. Thought and knowledge are natures in which apparatus and pretension avail nothing. Gowns and pecuniary foundations, though of towns of gold, can never countervail the least sentence or syllable of wit. Forget this, and our American colleges will recede in their public importance, whilst they grow richer every year.

III. There goes in the world a notion that the scholar should be a recluse, a valetudinarian,—as unfit for any handiwork or public labor as a penknife for an axe. The so-called "practical men" sneer at speculative men, as if, because they speculate or *see,* they could do nothing. I have heard it say that the clergy,—who are always, more universally than any other class, the scholars of their day,—are addressed as women; that the rough, spontaneous conversation of men they do not hear, but only a mincing and diluted speech. They are often virtually disfranchised; and indeed there are advocates for their celibacy. As far as this is true of the studious classes, it is not just and wise. Action is with the scholar subordinate, but it is essential. Without it he is not yet man. Without it thought can never ripen into truth. Whilst the world hangs before the eye as a cloud of beauty, we cannot even see its beauty. Inaction is cowardice, but there can be no scholar without the heroic mind. The preamble of thought, the transition through which it passes from the unconscious to the conscious, is action. Only so much do I know, as I have lived. Instantly we know whose words are loaded with life, and whose not.

The world,—this shadow of the soul, or *other me,*—lies wide around. Its attractions are the keys which unlock my thoughts and make me acquainted with myself. I run eagerly into this resounding tumult. I grasp the hands of those next me, and take my place in the ring to suffer and to work, taught by an instinct that so shall the dumb abyss be vocal with speech. I pierce its order; I dissipate its fear; I dispose of it within the circuit of my expanding life. So much only of life as I know by experience, so much of the wilderness have I vanquished and planted, or so far have I extended my being, my dominion. I do not see how any man can afford, for the sake of his nerves and his nap, to spare any action in which he can partake. It is pearls and rubies to his discourse. Drudgery, calamity, exasperation, want, are instructors in eloquence and wisdom. The true scholar grudges every opportunity of action past by, as a loss of power. It is the raw material out of which the intellect moulds her splendid products. A strange process too, this by which experience is converted into thought, as a mulberry leaf is converted into satin. The manufacture goes forward at all hours.

The actions and events of our childhood and youth are now matters of calmest observation. They lie like fair pictures in the air. Not so with our recent actions,—with the business which we now have in hand. On this we are quite unable to speculate. Our affections as yet circulate through it. We no more feel or know it than we feel the feet, or the hand, or the brain of our body. The new deed is yet a part of life,—remains for a time immersed in our unconscious life. In some contemplative hour it detaches itself from the life like a ripe fruit, to become a thought of the mind. Instantly it is raised, transfigured; the corruptible has put on incorruption. Henceforth it is an object of beauty, however base its origin and neighborhood. Observe too the impossibility of antedating this act. In its grub state, it cannot fly, it cannot shine, it is a dull grub. But suddenly, without observation, the selfsame thing unfurls beautiful wings, and is an angel of wisdom. So is there no fact, no event, in our private history, which shall not, sooner or later, lose its adhesive, inert form, and astonish us by soaring from our body into the empyrean. Cradle and infancy, school and playground, the fear of boys, and dogs, and ferules, the love of little maids and berries, and many another fact that once filled the whole sky, are gone already; friend and relative, profession and party, town and country, nation and world, must also soar and sing.

Of course, he who has put forth his total strength in fit actions has the richest return of wisdom. I will not shut myself out of this globe of action, and transplant an oak into a flowerpot, there to hunger and pine; nor trust the revenue of some single faculty, and exhaust one vein of thought, much like those Savoyards, who, getting their livelihood by carving shepherds, shepherdesses, and smoking Dutchmen, for all Europe, went out one day to the mountain to find stock, and discovered that they had whittled up the last of their pine trees. Authors we have, in numbers, who have written out their vein, and who, moved by a commendable prudence, sail for Greece or Palestine, follow the trapper into the prairie, or ramble round Algiers, to replenish their merchantable stock.

If it were only for a vocabulary, the scholar would be covetous of action. Life is our dictionary. Years are well spent in country labors; in town; in the insight into trades and manufactures; in frank intercourse with many men and women; in science; in art; to the one end of mastering in all their facts a language by which to illustrate and embody our perceptions. I learn immediately from any speaker how much he has already lived, through the poverty or the splendor of his speech. Life lies behind us as the quarry from whence we get tiles and copestones for the masonry of to-day. This is the way to learn grammar. Colleges and books only copy the language which the field and the work-yard made.

But the final value of action, like that of books, and better than books, is that it is a resource. That great principle of Undulation in nature, that shows itself in the inspiring and expiring of the breath; in desire and satiety; in the ebb and flow of the sea; in day and night; in heat and cold; and, as yet more deeply ingrained in every atom and every fluid, is known to us under the name of Polarity,— these "fits of easy transmission and reflection," as Newton called them, are the law of nature because they are the law of spirit.

The mind now thinks, now acts, and each fit reproduces the other. When the artist has exhausted his materials, when the fancy no longer paints, when thoughts are no longer apprehended and books are a weariness,—he has always the resource *to live*. Character is higher than intellect. Thinking is the function. Living is the functionary. The stream retreats to its source. A great soul will be strong to live, as well as strong to think. Does he lack organ or medium to impart his truths? He can still fall back on this elemental force of living them. This is a total act. Thinking is a partial act. Let the grandeur of justice shine in his affairs. Let the beauty of affection cheer his lowly roof. Those "far from fame," who dwell and act with him, will feel the force of his constitution in the doings and passages of the day better than it can be measured by any public and designed display. Time shall teach him that the scholar loses no hour which the man lives. Herein he unfolds the sacred germ of his instinct, screened from influence. What is lost in seemliness is gained in strength. Not out of those on whom systems of education have exhausted their culture, comes the helpful giant to destroy the old or to build the new, but out of unhandselled savage nature; out of terrible Druids and Berserkers come at last Alfred and Shakspeare.

I hear therefore with joy whatever is beginning to be said of the dignity and necessity of labor to every citizen. There is virtue yet in the hoe and the spade, for learned as well as for unlearned hands. And labor is everywhere welcome; always we are invited to work; only be this limitation observed, that a man shall not for the sake of wider activity sacrifice any opinion to the popular judgments and modes of action.

I have now spoken of the education of the scholar by nature, by books, and by action. It remains to say somewhat of his duties.

They are such as become Man Thinking. They may all be comprised in self-trust. The office of the scholar is to cheer, to raise, and to guide men by showing them facts amidst appearances. He plies the slow, unhonored, and unpaid task of observation. Flamsteed and Herschel, in their glazed observatories, may catalogue the stars with the praise of all men, and the results being splendid and useful, honor is sure. But he, in his private observatory, cataloguing obscure and nebulous stars of the human mind, which as yet no man has thought of as such,—watching days and months sometimes for a few facts; correcting still his old records;—must relinquish display and immediate fame. In the long period of his preparation he must betray often an ignorance and shiftlessness in popular arts, incurring the disdain of the able who shoulder him aside. Long he must stammer in his speech; often forego the living for the dead. Worse yet, he must accept—how often!—poverty and solitude. For the ease and pleasure of treading the old road, accepting the fashions, the education, the religion of society, he takes the cross of making his own, and, of course, the self-accusation, the faint heart, the frequent uncertainty and loss of time, which are the nettles and tangling vines in the way of the self-relying and self-directed; and the state of virtual hostility in which he seems to stand to society, and especially to educated society. For all this loss and scorn, what offset? He is to find consolation in exercising the highest functions of human nature. He is one who raises himself from private considerations and breathes and lives on public and illustrious thoughts. He is the world's eye. He is the world's heart. He is to resist the vulgar prosperity that retrogrades ever to barbarism, by preserving and communicating heroic sentiments, noble biographies, melodious verse, and the conclusions of history. Whatsoever oracles the human heart, in all emergencies, in all solemn hours, has uttered as its commentary on the world of actions,—these he shall receive and impart. And whatsoever new verdict Reason from her inviolable seat pronounces on the passing men and events of to-day,—this he shall hear and promulgate.

These being his functions, it becomes him to feel all confidence in himself, and to defer never to the popular cry. He and he only knows the world. The world of any moment is the merest appearance. Some great decorum, some fetish of a government, some ephemeral trade, or war, or man, is cried up by half mankind and cried down by the other half, as if all depended on this particular up or down. The odds are that the whole question is not worth the poorest thought which the scholar has lost in listening to the controversy. Let him not quit his belief that a popgun is a popgun, though the ancient and honorable of the earth affirm it to be the crack of doom. In silence, in steadiness, in severe abstraction, let him hold by himself; add observation to observation, patient of neglect, patient of reproach, and bide his own time—happy enough if he can satisfy himself alone that this day he has seen something truly. Success treads on every right step. For the instinct is sure, that prompts him to tell his brother what he thinks. He then learns that in going down into the secrets of his own mind he has descended into the secrets of all minds. He learns that he who has mastered any law in his private thoughts, is master to that extent of all men whose language he speaks, and of all into whose language his own can be translated. The poet, in utter solitude remembering his spontaneous thoughts and recording them, is found to have recorded that which men in crowded cities find true for them also. The orator distrusts at first the fitness of his frank confessions, his want of knowledge of the persons he addresses, until he finds that he is the complement of his hearers;—that they drink his words because he fulfils for them their own nature; the deeper he dives into his privatest, secretest presentiment, to his wonder he finds this is the most acceptable, most public, and universally true. The people delight in it; the better part of every man feels, This is my music; this is myself.

In self-trust all the virtues are comprehended. Free should the scholar be,—free and brave. Free even to the definition of freedom, "without any hindrance that does not arise out of his own constitution." Brave; for fear is a thing which a scholar by his very function puts behind him. Fear always springs from ignorance. It is a shame to him if his tranquillity, amid dangerous times, arise from the presumption that like children and women his is a protected class; or if he seeks a temporary peace by the diversion of his thoughts from politics or vexed questions, hiding his head like an ostrich in the flowering bushes, peeping into microscopes, and turning rhymes, as a boy whistles to keep his courage up. So is the danger a danger still; so is the fear worse. Manlike let him turn and face it. Let him look into its eye and search its nature, inspect its origin,—see the whelping of this lion—which lies no great way back; he will then find in himself a perfect comprehension of its nature and extent; he will have made his hands meet on the other side, and can henceforth defy it and pass on superior. The world is his who can see through its pretension. What deafness, what stone-blind custom, what overgrown error you behold is there only by sufferance,—by your sufferance. See it to be a lie, and you have already dealt it its mortal blow.

Yes, we are the cowed,—we the trustless. It is a mischievous notion that we are come late into nature; that the world was finished a long time ago. As the world was plastic and fluid in the hands of God, so it is ever to so much of his attributes as we bring to it. To ignorance and sin, it is flint. They adapt themselves to it as they may; but in proportion as a man has any thing in him divine, the firmament flows before him and takes his signet and form. Not he is great who can alter matter, but he who can alter my state of mind.

They are the kings of the world who give the color of their present thought to all nature and all art, and persuade men by the cheerful serenity of their carrying the matter, that this thing which they do is the apple which the ages have desired to pluck, now at last ripe, and inviting nations to the harvest. The great man makes the great thing. Wherever Macdonald sits, there is the head of the table. Linnaeus makes botany the most alluring of studies, and wins it from the farmer and the herb-woman; Davy, chemistry; and Cuvier, fossils. The day is always his who works in it with serenity and great aims. The unstable estimates of men crowd to him whose mind is filled with a truth, as the heaped waves of the Atlantic follow the moon.

For this self-trust, the reason is deeper than can be fathomed,— darker than can be enlightened. I might not carry with me the feeling of my audience in stating my own belief. But I have already shown the ground of my hope, in adverting to the doctrine that man is one. I believe man has been wronged; he has wronged himself. He has almost lost the light that can lead him back to his pre-rogatives. Men are become of no account. Men in history, men in the world of to-day, are bugs, are spawn, and are called "the mass" and "the herd." In a century, in a millennium, one or two men; that is to say, one or two approximations to the right state of every man. All the rest behold in the hero or the poet their own green and crude being,—ripened; yes, and are content to be less, so *that* may attain to its full stature. What a testimony, full of grandeur, full of pity, is borne to the demands of his own nature, by the poor clans-man, the poor partisan, who rejoices in the glory of his chief. The poor and the low find some amends to their immense moral capacity, for their acquiescence in a political and social inferiority. They are content to be brushed like flies from the path of a great person, so that justice shall be done by him to that common nature which it is dearest desire of all to see enlarged and glorified. They sun them-selves in the great man's light, and feel it to be their own element. They cast the dignity of man from their downtrod selves upon the shoulders of a hero, and will perish to add one drop of blood to make that great heart beat, those giant sinews combat and conquer. He lives for us, and we live in him.

Men, such as they are, very naturally seek money or power; and power because it is as good as money,—the "spoils," so called, "of office." And why not? for they aspire to the highest, and this, in their sleep-walking, they dream is highest. Wake them and they shall quit the false good and leap to the true, and leave governments to clerks and desks. This revolution is to be wrought by the gradual domestication of the idea of Culture. The main enterprise of the world for splendor, for extent, is the upbuilding of a man. Here are the materials strewn along the ground. The private life of one man shall be a more illustrious monarchy, more formidable to its enemy, more sweet and serene in its influence to its friend, than any kingdom in history. For a man, rightly viewed, comprehendeth the particular natures of all men. Each philosopher, each bard, each actor has only done for me, as by a delegate, what one day I can do for myself. The books which once we valued more than the apple of the eye, we have quite exhausted. What is that but saying that we have come up with the point of view which the universal mind took through the eyes of one scribe; we have been that man, and have passed on. First, one, then another, we drain all cisterns, and waxing greater by all these supplies, we crave a better and more abundant food. The man has never lived that can feed us ever. The human mind cannot be enshrined in a person who shall set a barrier on any one side to this unbounded, unboundable empire. It is one central fire, which, flaming now out of the lips of Etna, lightens the capes of Sicily, and now out of the throat of Vesuvius, illuminates the towers and vineyards of Naples. It is one light which beams out of a thousand stars. It is one soul which animates all men.

But I have dwelt perhaps tediously upon this abstraction of the Scholar. I ought not to delay longer to add what I have to say of nearer reference to the time and to this country.

Historically, there is thought to be a difference in the ideas which predominate over successive epochs, and there are data for marking the genius of the Classic, of the Romantic, and now of the Reflective or Philosophical age. With the views I have intimated of the oneness or the identity of the mind through all individuals, I do not much dwell on these differences. In fact, I believe each individual passes through all three. The boy is a Greek; the youth, romantic; the adult, reflective. I deny not, however, that a revolution in the leading idea may be distinctly enough traced.

Our age is bewailed as the age of Introversion. Must that needs be evil? We, it seems, are critical; we are embarrassed with second thoughts; we cannot enjoy any thing for hankering to know whereof the pleasure consists; we are lined with eyes; we see with our feet; the time is infected with Hamlet's unhappiness,—

"Sicklied o'er with the pale cast of thought."

It is so bad then? Sight is the last thing to be pitied. Would we be blind? Do we fear lest we should outsee nature and God, and drink truth dry? I look upon the discontent of the literary class as a mere announcement of the fact that they find themselves not in the state of mind of their fathers, and regret the coming state as untried; as a boy dreads the water before he has learned that he can swim. If there is any period one would desire to be born in, is it not the age of Revolution; when the old and the new stand side by side and admit of being compared; when the energies of all men are searched by fear and by hope; when the historic glories of the old can be compensated by the rich possibilities of the new era? This time, like all times, is a very good one, if we but know what to do with it.

I read with some joy of the auspicious signs of the coming days, as they glimmer already through poetry and art, through philosophy and science, through church and state.

One of these signs is the fact that the same movement which effected the elevation of what was called the lowest class in the state, assumed in literature a very marked and as benign an aspect. Instead of the sublime and beautiful, the near, the low, the common, was explored and poetized. That which had been negligently trodden under foot by those who were harnessing and provisioning themselves for long journeys into far countries, is suddenly found to be richer than all foreign parts. The literature of the poor, the feelings of the child, the philosophy of the street, the meaning of household life, are the topics of the time. It is a great stride. It is a sign—is it not?—of new vigor when the extremities are made active, when currents of warm life run into the hands and the feet. I ask not for the great, the remote, the romantic; what is doing in Italy or Arabia; what is Greek art, or Provencal minstrelsy; I embrace the common, I explore and sit at the feet of the familiar, the low. Give me insight into to-day, and you may have the antique and future worlds. What would we really know the meaning of? The meal in the firkin; the milk in the pan; the ballad in the street; the news of the boat; the glance of the eye; the form and the gait of the body;— show me the ultimate reason of these matters; show me the sublime presence of the highest spiritual cause lurking, as always it does lurk, in these suburbs and extremities of nature; let me see every trifle bristling with the polarity that ranges it instantly on an eternal law; and the shop, the plough, and the ledger referred to the like cause by which light undulates and poets sing;—and the world lies no longer a dull miscellany and lumber-room, but has form and order; there is no trifle, there is no puzzle, but one design unites and animates the farthest pinnacle and the lowest trench.

This idea has inspired the genius of Goldsmith, Burns, Cowper, and, in a newer time, of Goethe, Wordsworth, and Carlyle. This idea they have differently followed and with various success. In contrast with their writing, the style of Pope, of Johnson, of Gibbon, looks cold and pedantic. This writing is blood-warm. Man is surprised to find that things near are not less beautiful and wondrous than things remote. The near explains the far. The drop is a small ocean. A man is related to all nature. This perception of the worth of the vulgar is fruitful in discoveries. Goethe, in this very thing the most modern of the moderns, has shown us, as none ever did, the genius of the ancients.

There is one man of genius who has done much for this philosophy of life, whose literary value has never yet been rightly estimated;—I mean Emanuel Swedenborg. The most imaginative of men, yet writing with the precision of a mathematician, he endeavored to engraft a purely philosophical Ethics on the popular Christianity of his time. Such an attempt of course must have difficulty which no genius could surmount. But he saw and showed the connection between nature and the affections of the soul. He pierced the emblematic or spiritual character of the visible, audible, tangible world. Especially did his shade-loving muse hover over and interpret the lower parts of nature; he showed the mysterious bond that allies moral evil to the foul material forms, and has given in epical parables a theory of insanity, of beasts, of unclean and fearful things.

Another sign of our times, also marked by an analogous political movement, is the new importance given to the single person. Every thing that tends to insulate the individual,—to surround him with barriers of natural respect, so that each man shall feel the world is his, and man shall treat with man as a sovereign state with a sovereign state,—tends to true union as well as greatness. "I learned," said the melancholy Pestalozzi, "that no man in God's wide earth is either willing or able to help any other man." Help must come from the bosom alone. The scholar is that man who must take up into himself all the ability of the time, all the contributions of the past, all the hopes of the future. He must be an university of knowledges. If there be one lesson more than another which should pierce his ear, it is, The world is nothing, the man is all; in yourself is the law of all nature, and you know not yet how a globule of sap ascends; in yourself slumbers the whole of Reason; it is for you to know all; it is for you to dare all. Mr. President and Gentlemen, this confidence in the unsearched might of man belongs, by all motives, by all prophecy, by all preparation, to the American Scholar. We have listened too long to the courtly muses of Europe. The spirit of the American freeman is already suspected to be timid, imitative, tame. Public and private avarice make the air we breathe thick and fat. The scholar is decent, indolent, complaisant. See already the tragic consequence. The mind of this country, taught to aim at low objects, eats upon itself. There is no work for any but the decorous and the complaisant. Young men of the fairest promise, who begin life upon our shores, inflated by the mountain winds, shined upon by all the stars of God, find the earth below not in unison with these, but are hindered from action by the disgust which the principles on which business is managed inspire, and turn drudges, or die of disgust, some of them suicides. What is the remedy? They did not yet see, and thousands of young men as hopeful now crowding to the barriers for the career do not yet see, that if the single man plant himself indomitably on his instincts, and there abide, the huge world will come round to him. Patience,—patience; with the shades of all the good and great for company; and for solace the perspective of your own infinite life; and for work the study and the communication of principles, the making those instincts prevalent, the conversion of the world. Is it not the chief disgrace in the world, not to be an unit;—not to be reckoned one character;—not to yield that peculiar fruit which each man was created to bear, but to be reckoned in the gross, in the hundred, or the thousand, of the party, the section, to which we belong; and our opinion predicted geographically, as the north, or the south? Not so, brothers and friends—please God, ours shall not be so. We will walk on our own feet; we will work with our own hands; we will speak our own minds. The study of letters shall be no longer a name for pity, for doubt, and for sensual indulgence. The dread of man and the love of man shall be a wall of defence and a wreath of joy around all. A nation of men will for the first time exist, because each believes himself inspired by the Divine Soul which also inspires all men.

Abraham Lincoln

ADDRESS AT COOPER UNION

¶ ABRAHAM LINCOLN (1809-1865) was born near Hodgens-ville, Kentucky, February 12, 1809. The family moved to Indiana in 1816 and to Illinois in 1830. Lincoln's schooling in Kentucky and Indiana was brief, amounting to about a year in all. He was elected to the Illinois Legislature in 1834 and served there until 1842; admitted to the bar in 1837; served as a member of the House of Representatives, 1847-49; was nominated for the United States Senate by the Republicans in 1858, but lost to his Democratic opponent, Stephen A. Douglas, with whom he engaged in a series of debates during the campaign. He was elected President of the United States in 1860, and re-elected in 1864. His death occurred, as a result of an assassin's bullet, on April 15, 1865.

After the Lincoln-Douglas debates of 1858, Lincoln was recognized to be a leader among Republicans and a very popular orator. In 1860 the Young Men's Republican Union of New York invited him to address them. At the Cooper Union in New York, before a crowd estimated at fifteen hundred, Lincoln delivered what is sometimes considered to be his "president-making" address. The speech was delivered on February 27, 1860. William Cullen Bryant presided at the meeting. (The text of the address is from the revised and annotated edition published by the Young Men's Republican Union under the editorship of Charles C. Nott and Cephas Brainerd in September, 1860. Lincoln authorized the text. A reprint of the address is to be found in *Abraham Lincoln: His Speeches and Writings*, edited by Roy P. Basler, 1946.)

M R. PRESIDENT and fellow citizens of New York:—
The facts with which I shall deal this evening are mainly old and familiar; nor is there anything new in the general use I shall make of them. If there shall be any novelty, it will be in the mode of presenting the facts, and the inferences and observations following that presentation.

In his speech last autumn, at Columbus, Ohio, as reported in "The New York Times," Senator Douglas said:

"Our fathers, when they framed the Government under which we live, understood this question just as well, and even better, than we do now."

I fully indorse this, and I adopt it as a text for this discourse. I so adopt it because it furnishes a precise and an agreed starting point for a discussion between Republicans and that wing of the Democracy headed by Senator Douglas. It simply leaves the inquiry: *"What was the understanding those fathers had of the question mentioned?"*

What is the frame of government under which we live?

The answer must be: "The Constitution of the United States." That Constitution consists of the original, framed in 1787, (and under which the present government first went into operation,) and twelve subsequently framed amendments, the first ten of which were framed in 1789.

Who were our fathers that framed the Constitution? I suppose the "thirty-nine" who signed the original instrument may be fairly called our fathers who framed that part of the present Government. It is almost exactly true to say they framed it, and it is altogether true to say they fairly represented the opinion and sentiment of the whole nation at that time. Their names, being familiar to nearly all, and accessible to quite all, need not now be repeated.

I take these "thirty-nine," for the present, as being "our fathers who framed the Government under which we live."

What is the question which, according to the text, those fathers understood "just as well, and even better than we do now?"

It is this: Does the proper division of local from federal authority, or anything in the Constitution, forbid our *Federal Government* to control as to slavery in *our Federal Territories?*

Upon this, Senator Douglas holds the affirmative, and Republicans the negative. This affirmation and denial form an issue; and this issue—this question—is precisely what the text declares our fathers understood "better than we."

Let us now inquire whether the "thirty-nine," or any of them, ever acted upon this question; and if they did, how they acted upon it— how they expressed that better understanding?

In 1784, three years before the Constitution—the United States then owning the Northwestern Territory, and no other, the Congress of the Confederation had before them the question of prohibiting slavery in that Territory; and four of the "thirty-nine" who afterward framed the Constitution, were in that Congress, and voted on that question. Of these, Roger Sherman, Thomas Mifflin, and Hugh Williamson voted for the prohibition, thus showing that, in their understanding, no line dividing local from federal authority, nor anything else, properly forbade the Federal Government to control as to slavery in federal territory. The other of the four—James M'Henry—voted against the prohibition, showing that, for some cause, he thought it improper to vote for it.

In 1787, still before the Constitution, but while the Convention was in session framing it, and while the Northwestern Territory still was the only territory owned by the United States, the same question of prohibiting slavery in the territory again came before the Congress of the Confederation; and two more of the "thirty-nine" who afterward signed the Constitution, were in that Congress, and voted on the question. They were William Blount and William Few; and they both voted for the prohibition—thus showing that, in their understanding, no line dividing local from federal authority, nor anything else, properly forbids the Federal Government to control as to slavery in Federal territory. This time the prohibition became a law, being part of what is now well known as the Ordinance of '87.

The question of federal control of slavery in the territories, seems not to have been directly before the Convention which framed the original Constitution; and hence it is not recorded that the "thirty-nine," or any of them, while engaged on that instrument, expressed any opinion on that precise question.

In 1789, by the first Congress which sat under the Constitution, an act was passed to enforce the Ordinance of '87, including the prohibition of slavery in the Northwestern Territory. The bill for this act was reported by one of the "thirty-nine," Thomas Fitzsimmons, then a member of the House of Representatives from Pennsylvania. It went through all its stages without a word of opposition, and finally passed both branches without yeas and nays, which is equivalent to an unanimous passage. In this Congress there were sixteen of the thirty-nine fathers who framed the original Constitution. They were John Langdon, Nicholas Gilman, Wm. S. Johnson, Roger Sherman, Robert Morris, Thos. Fitzsimmons, William Few, Abraham Baldwin, Rufus King, William Paterson, George Clymer, Richard Bassett, George Read, Pierce Butler, Daniel Carroll, James Madison.

This shows that, in their understanding, no line dividing local from federal authority, nor anything in the Constitution, properly forbade Congress to prohibit slavery in the federal territory; else both their fidelity to correct principle, and their oath to support the Constitution, would have constrained them to oppose the prohibition.

Again, George Washington, another of the "thirty-nine," was then President of the United States, and, as such approved and signed the bill; thus completing its validity as a law, and thus showing that, in his understanding, no line dividing local from federal authority, nor anything in the Constitution, forbade the Federal Government, to control as to slavery in federal territory.

No great while after the adoption of the original Constitution, North Carolina ceded to the Federal Government the country now constituting the State of Tennessee; and a few years later Georgia ceded that which now constitutes the States of Mississippi and Alabama. In both deeds of cession it was made a condition by the ceding States that the Federal Government should not prohibit slavery in the ceded country. Besides this, slavery was then actually

in the ceded country. Under these circumstances, Congress, on taking charge of these countries, did not absolutely prohibit slavery
within them. But they did interfere with it—take control of it—even
there, to a certain extent. In 1798, Congress organized the Territory
of Mississippi. In the act of organization, they prohibited the bringing of slaves into the Territory, from any place without the United
States, by fine, and giving freedom to slaves so brought. This act
passed both branches of Congress without yeas and nays. In that
Congress were three of the "thirty-nine" who framed the original
Constitution. They were John Langdon, George Read and Abraham
Baldwin. They all, probably, voted for it. Certainly they would have
placed their opposition to it upon record, if, in their understanding,
any line dividing local from federal authority, or anything in the
Constitution, properly forbade the Federal Government to control
as to slavery in federal territory.

In 1803, the Federal Government purchased the Louisiana country.
Our former territorial acquisitions came from certain of our own
States; but this Louisiana country was acquired from a foreign
nation. In 1804, Congress gave a territorial organization to that part
of it which now constitutes the State of Louisiana. New Orleans,
lying within that part, was an old and comparatively large city. There
were other considerable towns and settlements, and slavery was
extensively and thoroughly intermingled with the people. Congress
did not, in the Territorial Act, prohibit slavery; but they did interfere with it—take control of it—in a more marked and extensive way
than they did in the case of Mississippi. The substance of the provision therein made, in relation to slaves, was:

First. That no slave should be imported into the territory from
foreign parts.

Second. That no slave should be carried into it who had been
imported into the United States since the first day of May, 1798.

Third. That no slave should be carried into it, except by the owner,
and for his own use as a settler; the penalty in all the cases being a
fine upon the violator of the law, and freedom to the slave.

This act also was passed without yeas and nays. In the Congress which passed it, there were two of the "thirty-nine." They were Abraham Baldwin and Jonathan Dayton. As stated in the case of Mississippi, it is probable they both voted for it. They would not have allowed it to pass without recording their opposition to it, if, in their understanding, it violated either the line properly dividing local from federal authority, or any provision of the Constitution.

In 1819-20, came and passed the Missouri question. Many votes were taken, by yeas and nays, in both branches of Congress, upon the various phases of the general question. Two of the "thirty-nine"— Rufus King and Charles Pinckney—were members of that Congress. Mr. King steadily voted for slavery prohibition and against all compromises, while Mr. Pinckney as steadily voted against slavery prohibition and against all compromises. By this, Mr. King showed that, in his understanding, no line dividing local from federal authority, nor anything in the Constitution, was violated by Congress prohibiting slavery in federal territory; while Mr. Pinckney, by his votes, showed that, in his understanding, there was some sufficient reason for opposing such prohibition in that case.

The cases I have mentioned are the only acts of the "thirty-nine," or of any of them, upon the direct issue, which I have been able to discover.

To enumerate the persons who thus acted, as being four in 1784, two in 1787, seventeen in 1789, three in 1798, two in 1804, and two in 1819-20—there would be thirty of them. But this would be counting John Langdon, Roger Sherman, William Few, Rufus King, and George Read each twice, and Abraham Baldwin, three times. The true number of those of the "thirty-nine" whom I have shown to have acted upon the question, which, by the text, they understood better than we, is twenty-three, leaving sixteen not shown to have acted upon it in any way.

Here, then, we have twenty-three out of our thirty-nine fathers "who framed the government under which we live," who have, upon their official responsibility and their corporal oaths, acted upon the very question which the text affirms they "understood just as well, and even better than we do now;" and twenty-one of them—a clear majority of the whole "thirty-nine"—so acting upon it as to make them guilty of gross political impropriety and wilful perjury, if, in their understanding, any proper division between local and federal authority, or anything in the Constitution they had made themselves, and sworn to support, forbade the Federal Government to control as to slavery in the federal territories. Thus the twenty-one acted; and, as actions speak louder than words, so actions, under such responsibility, speak still louder.

Two of the twenty-three voted against Congressional prohibition of slavery in the federal territories, in the instances in which they acted upon the question. But for what reasons they so voted is not known. They may have done so because they thought a proper division of local from federal authority, or some provision or principle of the Constitution, stood in the way; or they may, without any such question, have voted against the prohibition, on what appeared to them to be sufficient grounds of expediency. No one who has sworn to support the Constitution can conscientiously vote for what he understands to be an unconstitutional measure, however expedient he may think it; but one may and ought to vote against a measure which he deems constitutional, if, at the same time, he deems it inexpedient. It, therefore, would be unsafe to set down even the two who voted against the prohibition, as having done so because, in their understanding, any proper division of local from federal authority, or anything in the Constitution, forbade the Federal Government to control as to slavery in federal territory.

The remaining sixteen of the "thirty-nine," so far as I have discovered, have left no record of their understanding upon the direct question of federal control of slavery in the federal territories. But there is much reason to believe that their understanding upon that question would not have appeared different from that of their twenty-three compeers, had it been manifested at all.

For the purpose of adhering rigidly to the text, I have purposely omitted whatever understanding may have been manifested by any person, however distinguished, other than the thirty-nine fathers who framed the original Constitution; and, for the same reason, I have also omitted whatever understanding may have been manifested by any of the "thirty-nine" even, on any other phase of the general question of slavery. If we should look into their acts and declarations on those other phases, as the foreign slave trade, and the morality and policy of slavery generally, it would appear to us that on the direct question of federal control of slavery in federal territories, the sixteen, if they had acted at all, would probably have acted just as the twenty-three did. Among that sixteen were several of the most noted anti-slavery men of those times—as Dr. Franklin, Alexander Hamilton and Gouverneur Morris—while there was not one now known to have been otherwise, unless it may be John Rutledge, of South Carolina.

The sum of the whole is, that of our thirty-nine fathers who framed the original Constitution, twenty-one—a clear majority of the whole—certainly understood that no proper division of local from federal authority, nor any part of the Constitution, forbade the Federal Government to control slavery in the federal territories; while all the rest probably had the same understanding. Such, unquestionably, was the understanding of our fathers who framed the original Constitution; and the text affirms that they understood the question "better than we."

But, so far, I have been considering the understanding of the question manifested by the framers of the original Constitution. In and by the original instrument, a mode was provided for amending it; and, as I have already stated, the present frame of "the Government under which we live" consists of that original, and twelve amendatory articles framed and adopted since. Those who now insist that federal control of slavery in federal territories violates the Constitution, point us to the provisions which they suppose it thus violates; and, as I understand, that all fix upon provisions in these amendatory articles, and not in the original instrument. The Supreme Court, in the Dred Scott case, plant themselves upon the fifth amendment, which provides that no person shall be deprived of "life, liberty or property without due process of law;" while Senator Douglas and his peculiar adherents plant themselves upon the tenth amendment, providing that "the powers not delegated to the United States by the Constitution" "are reserved to the States respectively, or to the people."

Now, it so happens that these amendments were framed by the first Congress which sat under the Constitution—the identical Congress which passed the act already mentioned, enforcing the prohibition of slavery in the Northwestern Territory. Not only was it the same Congress, but they were the identcial, same individual men who, at the same session, and at the same time within the session, had under consideration, and in progress toward maturity, these Constitutional amendments, and this act prohibiting slavery in all the territory the nation then owned. The Constitutional amendments were introduced before, and passed after the act enforcing the Ordinance of '87; so that, during the whole pendency of the act to enforce the Ordinance, the Constitutional amendments were also pending.

The seventy-six members of that Congress, including sixteen of the framers of the original Constitution, as before stated, were pre-eminently our fathers who framed that part of "the Government under which we live," which is now claimed as forbidding the Federal Government to control slavery in the federal territories.

Is it not a little presumptuous in any one at this day to affirm that the two things which that Congress deliberately framed, and carried to maturity at the same time, are absolutely inconsistent with each other? And does not such affirmation become impudently absurd when coupled with the other affirmation from the same mouth, that those who did the two things, alleged to be inconsistent, understood whether they really were inconsistent better than we—better than he who affirms that they are inconsistent?

It is surely safe to assume that the thirty-nine framers of the original Constitution, and the seventy-six members of the Congress which framed the amendments thereto, taken together, do certainly include those who may be fairly called "our fathers who framed the Government under which we live." And so assuming, I defy any man to show that any one of them ever, in his whole life, declared that, in his understanding, any proper division of local from federal authority, or any part of the Constitution, forbade the Federal Government to control as to slavery in the federal territories. I go a step further. I defy any one to show that any living man in the whole world ever did, prior to the beginning of the present century, (and I might almost say prior to the beginning of the last half of the present century,) declare that, in his understanding, any proper division of local from federal authority, or any part of the Constitution, forbade the Federal Government to control as to slavery in the federal territories. To those who now so declare, I give, not only "our fathers who framed the Government under which we live," but with them all other living men within the century in which it was framed, among whom to search, and they shall not be able to find the evidence of a single man agreeing with them.

Now, and here, let me guard a little against being misunderstood. I do not mean to say we are bound to follow implicitly in whatever our fathers did. To do so, would be to discard all the lights of current experience—to reject all progress—all improvement. What I do say is, that if we would supplant the opinions and policy of our fathers in any case, we should do so upon evidence so conclusive, and argument so clear, that even their great authority, fairly considered and weighed, cannot stand; and most surely not in a case whereof we ourselves declare they understood the question better than we.

If any man at this day sincerely believes that a proper division of local from federal authority, or any part of the Constitution, forbids the Federal Government to control as to slavery in the federal territories, he is right to say so, and to enforce his position by all truthful evidence and fair argument which he can. But he has no right to mislead others, who have less access to history, and less leisure to study it, into the false belief that "our fathers who framed the Government under which we live" were of the same opinion—thus substituting falsehood and deception for truthful evidence and fair argument. If any man at this day sincerely believes "our fathers who framed the Government under which we live," used and applied principles, in other cases, which ought to have led them to understand that a proper division of local from federal authority or some part of the Constitution, forbids the Federal Government to control as to slavery in the federal territories, he is right to say so. But he should, at the same time, brave the responsibility of declaring that, in his opinion, he understands their principles better than they did themselves; and especially should he not shirk that responsibility by asserting that they "understood the question just as well, and even better, than we do now."

But enough! *Let all who believe that "our fathers, who framed the Government under which we live, understood this question just as well, and even better, than we do now," speak as they spoke, and act as they acted upon it. This is all Republicans ask—all Republicans desire—in relation to slavery. As those fathers marked it, so let it be again marked, as an evil not to be extended, but to be tolerated and protected only because of and so far as its actual presence among us makes that toleration and protection a necessity. Let all the guaranties those fathers gave it, be, not grudgingly, but fully and fairly, maintained.* For this Republicans contend, and with this, so far as I know or believe, they will be content.

And now, if they would listen—as I suppose they will not—I would address a few words to the Southern people.

I would say to them:—You consider yourselves a reasonable and a just people; and I consider that in the general qualities of reason and justice you are not inferior to any other people. Still, when you speak of us Republicans, you do so only to denounce us as reptiles, or, at the best, as no better than outlaws. You will grant a hearing to pirates or murderers, but nothing like it to "Black Republicans." In all your contentions with one another, each of you deems an unconditional condemnation of "Black Republicanism" as the first thing to be attended to. Indeed, such condemnation of us seems to be an indispensable prerequisite—license, so to speak—among you to be admitted or permitted to speak at all. Now, can you, or not, be prevailed upon to pause and to consider whether this is quite just to us, or even to yourselves? Bring forward your charges and specifications, and then be patient long enough to hear us deny or justify.

You say we are sectional. We deny it. That makes an issue; and the burden of proof is upon you. You produce your proof; and what is it? Why, that our party has no existence in your section—gets no votes in your section. The fact is substantially true; but does it prove the issue? If it does, then in case we should, without change of principle, begin to get votes in your section, we should thereby cease to be sectional. You cannot escape this conclusion; and yet, are you willing to abide by it? If you are, you will probably soon find that we have ceased to be sectional, for we shall get votes in your section this very year. You will then begin to discover, as the truth plainly is, that your proof does not touch the issue. The fact that we get no votes in your section, is a fact of your making, and not of ours. And if there be fault in that fact, that fault is primarily yours, and remains until you show that we repel you by some wrong principle or practice. If we do repel you by any wrong principle or practice, the fault is ours; but this brings you to where you ought to have started—to a discussion of the right or wrong of our principle. If our principle, put in practice, would wrong your section for the benefit of ours, or for any other object, then our principle, and we with it, are sectional, and are justly opposed and denounced as such. Meet us, then, on the question of whether our principle, put in practice, would wrong your section; and so meet it as if it were possible that something may be said on our side. Do you accept the challenge? No! Then you really believe that the principle which "our fathers who framed the Government under which we live" thought so clearly right as to adopt it, and indorse it again and again, upon their official oaths, is in fact so clearly wrong as to demand your condemnation without a moment's consideration.

Some of you delight to flaunt in our faces the warning against sectional parties given by Washington in his Farewell Address. Less than eight years before Washington gave that warning, he had, as President of the United States, approved and signed an act of Congress, enforcing the prohibition of slavery in the Northwestern Territory, which act embodied the policy of the Government upon that subject up to and at the very moment he penned that warning; and about one year after he penned it, he wrote LaFayette that he considered that prohibition a wise measure, expressing in the same connection his hope that we should at some time have a confederacy of free States.

Bearing this in mind, and seeing that sectionalism has since arisen upon this same subject, is that warning a weapon in your hands against us, or in our hands against you? Could Washington himself speak, would he cast the blame of that sectionalism upon us, who sustain his policy, or upon you who repudiate it? We respect that warning of Washington, and we commend it to you, together with his example pointing to the right application of it.

But you say you are conservative—eminently conservative—while we are revolutionary, destructive, or something of the sort. What is conservatism? Is it not adherence to the old and tried, against the new and untried? We stick to, contend for, the identical old policy on the point in controversy which was adopted by "our fathers who framed the Government under which we live," while you with one accord reject, and scout, and spit upon that old policy, and insist upon substituting something new. True, you disagree among yourselves as to what that substitute shall be. You are divided on new propositions and plans, but you are unanimous in rejecting and denouncing the old policy of the fathers. Some of you are for reviving the foreign slave trade; some for a Congressional Slave-Code for the Territories; some for Congress forbidding the Territories to prohibit Slavery within their limits; some for maintaining Slavery in the Territories through the judiciary; some for the "gur-reat pur-inciple" that "if one man would enslave another, no third man should object," fantastically called "Popular Soverignty;" but never a man among you is in favor of federal prohibition of slavery in federal territories, according to the practice of "our fathers who framed the Government under which we live." Not one of all your various plans can show a precedent or an advocate in the century within which our Government originated. Consider, then, whether your claim of conservatism for yourselves, and your charge of destructiveness against us, are based on the most clear and stable foundations.

Again, you say we have made the slavery question more prominent than it formerly was. We deny it. We admit that it is more prominent, but we deny that we made it so. It was not we, but you, who discarded the old policy of the fathers. We resisted, and still resist, your innovation; and thence comes the greater prominence of the question. Would you have that question reduced to its former proportions? Go back to that old policy. What has been will be again, under the same conditions. If you would have the peace of the old times, readopt the precepts and policy of the old times.

You charge that we stir up insurrections among your slaves. We deny it; and what is your proof? Harper's Ferry! John Brown!! John Brown was no Republican; and you have failed to implicate a single Republican in his Harper's Ferry enterprise. If any member of our party is guilty in that matter, you know it or you do not know it. If you do know it, you are inexcusable for not designating the man and proving the fact. If you do not know it, you are inexcusable for asserting it, and especially for persisting in the assertion after you have tried and failed to make the proof. You need not be told that persisting in a charge which one does not know to be true, is simply malicious slander.

Some of you admit that no Republican designedly aided or encouraged the Harper's Ferry affair, but still insist that our doctrines and declarations necessarily lead to such results. We do not believe it. We know we hold to no doctrine, and make no declaration, which were not held to and made by "our fathers who framed the Government under which we live." You never dealt fairly by us in relation to this affair. When it occurred, some important State elections were near at hand, and you were in evident glee with the belief that, by charging the blame upon us, you could get an advantage of us in those elections. The elections came, and your expectations were not quite fulfilled. Every Republican man knew that, as to himself at least, your charge was a slander, and he was not much inclined by it to cast his vote in your favor. Republican doctrines and declarations are accompanied with a continual protest against any interference whatever with your slaves, or with you about your slaves. Surely, this does not encourage them to revolt. True, we do, in common with "our fathers, who framed the Government under which we live," declare our belief that slavery is wrong; but the slaves do not hear us declare even this. For anything we say or do, the slaves would scarcely know there is a Republican party. I believe they would not, in fact, generally know it but for your misrepresentations of us, in their hearing. In your political contests among yourselves, each faction charges the other with sympathy with Black Republicanism; and then, to give point to the charge, defines Black Republicanism to simply be insurrection, blood and thunder among the slaves.

Slave insurrections are no more common now than they were before the Republican party was organized. What induced the Southampton insurrection, twenty-eight years ago, in which, at least three times as many lives were lost as at Harper's Ferry? You can scarcely stretch your very elastic fancy to the conclusion that Southampton was "got up by Black Republicanism." In the present state of things in the United States, I do not think a general, or even a very extensive slave insurrection is possible. The indispensable concert of action cannot be attained. The slaves have no means of rapid communication; nor can incendiary freemen, black or white, supply it. The explosive materials are everywhere in parcels; but there neither are, nor can be supplied, the indispensable connecting trains.

Much is said by Southern people about the affection of slaves for their masters and mistresses; and a part of it, at least, is true. A plot for an uprising could scarcely be devised and communicated to twenty individuals before some one of them, to save the life of a favorite master or mistress, would divulge it. This is the rule; and the slave revolution in Hayti was not an exception to it, but a case occurring under peculiar circumstances. The gunpowder plot of British history, though not connected with slaves, was more in point. In that case, only about twenty were admitted to the secret; and yet one of them, in his anxiety to save a friend, betrayed the plot to that friend, and, by consequence, averted the calamity. Occasional poisonings from the kitchen, and open or stealthy assassinations in the field, and local revolts extending to a score or so, will continue to occur as the natural results of slavery; but no general insurrection of slaves, as I think, can happen in this country for a long time. Whoever much fears, or much hopes for such an event, will be alike . disappointed.

In the language of Mr. Jefferson, uttered many years ago, "It is still in our power to direct the process of emancipation, and deportation, peaceably, and in such slow degrees, as that the evil will wear off insensibly; and their places be, *pari passu,* filled up by free white laborers. If, on the contrary, it is left to force itself on, human nature must shudder at the prospect held up."

Mr. Jefferson did not mean to say, nor do I, that the power of emancipation is in the Federal Government. He spoke of Virginia; and, as to the power of emancipation, I speak of the slaveholding States only. The Federal Government, however, as we insist, has the power of restraining the extension of the institution—the power to insure that a slave insurrection shall never occur on any American soil which is now free from slavery.

John Brown's effort was peculiar. It was not a slave insurrection. It was an attempt by white men to get up a revolt among slaves, in which the slaves refused to participate. In fact, it was so absurd that the slaves, with all their ignorance, saw plainly enough it could not succeed. That affair, in its philosophy, corresponds with the many attempts, related in history, at the assassination of kings and emperors. An enthusiast broods over the oppression of a people till he fancies himself commissioned by Heaven to liberate them. He ventures the attempt, which ends in little else than his own execution. Orsini's attempt on Louis Napoleon, and John Brown's attempt at Harper's Ferry were, in their philosophy, precisely the same. The eagerness to cast blame on old England in the one case, and on New England in the other, does not disprove the sameness of the two things.

And how much would it avail you, if you could, by the use of John Brown, Helper's Book, and the like, break up the Republican organization? Human action can be modified to some extent, but human nature cannot be changed. There is a judgment and a feeling against slavery in this nation, which cast at least a million and a half of votes. You cannot destroy that judgment and feeling—that sentiment —by breaking up the political organization which rallies around it. You can scarcely scatter and disperse an army which has been formed into order in the face of your heaviest fire; but if you could, how much would you gain by forcing the sentiment which created it out of the peaceful channel of the ballot-box, into some other channel? What would that other channel probably be? Would the number of John Browns be lessened or enlarged by the operation?

But you will break up the Union rather than submit to a denial of your Constitutional rights.

That has a somewhat reckless sound; but it would be palliated, if not fully justified, were we proposing, by the mere force of numbers, to deprive you of some right, plainly written down in the Constitution. But we are proposing no such thing.

When you make these declarations, you have a specific and well-understood allusion to an assumed Constitutional right of yours, to take slaves into the federal territories, and to hold them there as property. But no such right is specifically written in the Constitution. That instrument is literally silent about any such right. We, on the contrary, deny that such a right has any existence in the Constitution, even by implication.

Your purpose, then, plainly stated, is that you will destroy the Government, unless you be allowed to construe and enforce the Constitution as you please, on all points in dispute between you and us. You will rule or ruin in all events.

This, plainly stated, is your language. Perhaps you will say the Supreme Court has decided the disputed Constitutional question in your favor. Not quite so. But waiving the lawyer's distinction between dictum and decision, the Court have decided the question for you in a sort of way. The Court have substantially said, it is your Constitutional right to take slaves into the federal territories, and to hold them there as property. When I say the decision was made in a sort of way, I mean it was made in a divided Court, by a bare majority of the Judges, and they not quite agreeing with one another in the reasons for making it; that it is so made as that its avowed supporters disagree with one another about its meaning, and that it was mainly based upon a mistaken statement of fact—the statement in the opinion that "the right of property in a slave is distinctly and expressly affirmed in the Constitution."

An inspection of the Constitution will show that the right of property in a slave is not "*distinctly* and *expressly* affirmed" in it. Bear in mind, the Judges do not pledge their judicial opinion that such right is *impliedly* affirmed in the Constitution; but they pledge their veracity that it is "*distinctly* and *expressly*" affirmed there—"distinctly," that is, not mingled with anything else—"expressly," that is, in words meaning just that, without the aid of any inference, and susceptible of no other meaning.

If they had only pledged their judicial opinion that such right is affirmed in the instrument by implication, it would be open to others to show that neither the word "slave" nor "slavery" is to be found in the Constitution, nor the word "property" even, in any connection with language alluding to the things slave, or slavery; and that wherever in that instrument the slave is alluded to, he is called a "person;"—and wherever his master's legal right in relation to him is alluded to, it is spoken of as "service or labor which may be due,"— as a debt payable in service or labor. Also, it would be open to show, by contemporaneous history, that this mode of alluding to slaves and slavery, instead of speaking of them, was employed on purpose to exclude from the Constitution the idea that there could be property in man.

To show all this, is easy and certain.

When this obvious mistake of the Judges shall be brought to their notice, is it not reasonable to expect that they will withdraw the mistaken statement, and reconsider the conclusion based upon it?

And then it is to be remembered that "our fathers, who framed the Government under which we live"—the men who made the Constitution—decided this same Constitutional question in our favor, long ago—decided it without division among themselves, when making the decision; without division among themselves about the meaning of it after it was made, and, so far as any evidence is left, without basing it upon any mistaken statement of facts.

Under all these circumstances, do you really feel yourselves justified to break up this Government unless such a court decision as yours is, shall be at once submitted to as a conclusive and final rule of political action? But you will not abide the election of a Republican president! In that supposed event, you say, you will destroy the Union; and then, you say, the great crime of having destroyed it will be upon us! That is cool. A highwayman holds a pistol to my ear, and mutters through his teeth, "Stand and deliver, or I shall kill you, and then you will be a murderer!"

To be sure, what the robber demanded of me—my money—was my own; and I had a clear right to keep it; but it was no more my own than my vote is my own; and the threat of death to me, to extort my money, and the threat of destruction to the Union, to extort my vote, can scarcely be distinguished in principle.

A few words now to Republicans. *It is exceedingly desirable that all parts of this great Confederacy shall be at peace, and in harmony, one with another. Let us Republicans do our part to have it so. Even though much provoked, let us do nothing through passion and ill temper. Even though the southern people will not so much as listen to us, let us calmly consider their demands, and yield to them if, in our deliberate view of our duty, we possibly can.* Judging by all they say and do, and by the subject and nature of their controversy with us, let us determine, if we can, what will satisfy them.

Will they be satisfied if the Territories be unconditionally surrendered to them? We know they will not. In all their present complaints against us, the Territories are scarcely mentioned. Invasions and insurrections are the rage now. Will it satisfy them, if, in the future, we have nothing to do with invasions and insurrections? We know it will not. We so know, because we know we never had anything to do with invasions and insurrections; and yet this total abstaining does not exempt us from the charge and the denunciation.

The question recurs, what will satisfy them? Simply this: We must not only let them alone, but we must somehow, convince them that we do let them alone. This, we know by experience, is no easy task. We have been so trying to convince them from the very beginning of our organization, but with no success. In all our platforms and speeches we have constantly protested our purpose to let them alone; but this has had no tendency to convince them. Alike unavailing to convince them, is the fact that they have never detected a man of us in any attempt to disturb them.

These natural, and apparently adequate means all failing, what will convince them? This, and this only: cease to call slavery *wrong*, and join them in calling it *right*. And this must be done thoroughly —done in *acts* as well as in *words*. Silence will not be tolerated—we must place ourselves avowedly with them. Senator Douglas's new sedition law must be enacted and enforced, suppressing all declarations that slavery is wrong, whether made in politics, in presses, in pulpits, or in private. We must arrest and return their fugitive slaves with greedy pleasure. We must pull down our Free State constitutions. The whole atmosphere must be disinfected from all taint of opposition to slavery, before they will cease to believe that all their troubles proceed from us.

I am quite aware they do not state their case precisely in this way. Most of them would probably say to us, "Let us alone, do nothing to us, and say what you please about slavery." But we do let them alone—have never disturbed them—so that, after all, it is what we say, which dissatisfies them. They will continue to accuse us of doing, until we cease saying.

I am also aware they have not, as yet, in terms, demanded the overthrow of our Free-State Constitutions. Yet those Constitutions declare the wrong of slavery, with more solemn emphasis, than do all other sayings against it; and when all these other sayings shall have been silenced, the overthrow of these Constitutions will be demanded, and nothing be left to resist the demand. It is nothing to the contrary, that they do not demand the whole of this just now. Demanding what they do, and for the reason they do, they can voluntarily stop nowhere short of this consummation. Holding, as they do, that slavery is morally right, and socially elevating, they cannot cease to demand a full national recognition of it, as a legal right, and a social blessing.

Nor can we justifiably withhold this, on any ground save our conviction that slavery is wrong. If slavery is right, all words, acts, laws, and constitutions against it, are themselves wrong, and should be silenced, and swept away. If it is right, we cannot justly object to its nationality—its universality; if it is wrong, they cannot justly insist upon its extension—its enlargement. All they ask, we could readily grant, if we thought slavery right; all we ask, they could as readily grant, if they thought it wrong. Their thinking it right, and our thinking it wrong, is the precise fact upon which depends the whole controversy. Thinking it right, as they do, they are not to blame for desiring its full recognition, as being right; but, thinking it wrong, as we do, can we yield to them? Can we cast our votes with their view, and against our own? In view of our moral, social, and political responsibilities, can we do this?

Wrong as we think slavery is, we can yet afford to let it alone where it is, because that much is due to the necessity arising from its actual presence in the nation; but can we, while our votes will prevent it, allow it to spread into the National Territories, and to overrun us here in these Free States? If our sense of duty forbids this, then let us stand by our duty, fearlessly and effectively. Let us be diverted by none of those sophistical contrivances wherewith we are so industriously plied and belabored—contrivances such as groping for some middle ground between the right and the wrong, vain as the search for a man who should be neither a living man nor a dead man—such as a policy of "don't care" on a question about which all true men do care—such as Union appeals beseeching true Union men to yield to Disunionists, reversing the divine rule, and calling, not the sinners, but the righteous to repentance—such as invocations to Washington, imploring men to unsay what Washington said, and undo what Washington did.

Neither let us be slandered from our duty by false accusations against us, nor frightened from it by menaces of destruction to the Government nor of dungeons to ourselves. *Let us have faith that right makes might, and in that faith, let us, to the end, dare to do our duty as we understand it.*

Abraham Lincoln

FAREWELL ADDRESS AT SPRINGFIELD

¶ LINCOLN left Springfield on February 11, 1861, to go to Washington to take up the duties of the presidency. As he left Springfield, friends and neighbors gathered at the railroad station to bid him good-by. His farewell remarks were delivered from the rear of the train just as he was ready to leave. Both Lincoln and the audience were deeply moved by the occasion. (The text of this address is from *The Complete Works of Abraham Lincoln;* other versions are reprinted in *Abraham Lincoln: His Speeches and Writings,* edited by Roy P. Basler, 1946.)

MY FRIENDS:
No one, not in my situation, can appreciate my feeling of sadness at this parting. To this place, and the kindness of these people, I owe everything. Here I have lived a quarter of a century, and have passed from a young to an old man. Here my children have been born, and one is buried. I now leave, not knowing when or whether ever I may return, with a task before me greater than that which rested upon Washington. Without the assistance of that Divine Being who ever attended him, I cannot succeed. With that assistance, I cannot fail. Trusting in Him who can go with me, and remain with you, and be everywhere for good, let us confidently hope that all will yet be well. To His care commending you, as I hope in your prayers you will commend me, I bid you an affectionate farewell.

Abraham Lincoln

ADDRESS AT THE DEDICATION OF THE

CEMETERY AT GETTYSBURG

¶ THE BATTLE OF GETTYSBURG took place on July 1, 2, and 3, 1863. It was recognized to be a turning point of the war. The states having soldiers in the Army of the Potomac who were killed at the battle of Gettysburg, or died at various hospitals, procured grounds on a prominent part of the battlefield for a cemetery and had the dead removed to them and properly buried. The grounds were consecrated by a solemn ceremony on November 19, 1863. Edward Everett, the outstanding orator of the era, was asked to give the principal oration for the occasion. Lincoln was asked to deliver a "few appropriate remarks" in dedicating the grounds. (The text is that of the final manuscript, known as "the Bliss copy," which Lincoln prepared for Colonel Alexander Bliss for publication as a lithograph facsimile, and is reprinted in *Abraham Lincoln: His Speeches and Writings,* edited by Roy P. Basler, 1946.)

FOUR SCORE and seven years ago our fathers brought forth on this continent, a new nation, conceived in Liberty, and dedicated to the proposition that all men are created equal.

Now we are engaged in a great civil war, testing whether that nation, or any nation so conceived and so dedicated, can long endure. We are met on a great battle-field of that war. We have come to dedicate a portion of that field, as a final resting place for those who here gave their lives that that nation might live. It is altogether fitting and proper that we should do this.

But, in a larger sense, we can not dedicate—we can not consecrate —we can not hallow—this ground. The brave men, living and dead, who struggled here, have consecrated it, far above our poor power to add or detract. The world will little note, nor long remember what we say here, but it can never forget what they did here. It is for us the living, rather, to be dedicated here to the unfinished work which they who fought here have thus far so nobly advanced. It is rather for us to be here dedicated to the great task remaining before us— that from these honored dead we take increased devotion to that cause for which they gave the last full measure of devotion—that we here highly resolve that these dead shall not have died in vain—that this nation, under God, shall have a new birth of freedom—and that government of the people, by the people, for the people, shall not perish from the earth.

Abraham Lincoln

SECOND INAUGURAL ADDRESS

¶ IN 1864, Lincoln was re-elected to the presidency by an over-whelming majority, despite opposition in the North to the conduct of the war. As the time of the inauguration drew near, the war appeared to be nearing its close. Richmond was to fall within a month. A crowd estimated at fifty thousand assembled to witness Lincoln's inauguration. The Second Inaugural was delivered March 4, 1865, and stands as one of Lincoln's most sublime and moving addresses. (The text is from *Abraham Lincoln: His Speeches and Writings*, edited by Roy P. Basler, 1946.)

AT THIS SECOND appearing to take the oath of the presidential office, there is less occasion for an extended address than there was at the first. Then a statement, somewhat in detail, of a course to be pursued, seemed fitting and proper. Now, at the expiration of four years, during which public declarations have been constantly cailed forth on every point and phase of the great contest which still absorbs the attention, and engrosses the energies of the nation, little that is new could be presented. The progress of our arms, upon which all else chiefly depends, is as well known to the public as to myself; and it is, I trust, reasonably satisfactory and encouraging to all. With high hope for the future, no prediction in regard to it is ventured.

On the occasion corresponding to this four years ago, all thoughts were anxiously directed to an impending civil war. All dreaded it—all sought to avert it. While the inaugural address was being delivered from this place, devoted altogether to *saving* the Union without war, insurgent agents were in the city seeking to *destroy* it without war—seeking to dissolve the Union, and divide effects, by negotiation. Both parties deprecated war; but one of them would *make* war rather than let the nation survive; and the other would *accept* war rather than let it perish. And the war came.

One eighth of the whole population were colored slaves, not distributed generally over the Union, but localized in the Southern part of it. These slaves constituted a peculiar and powerful interest. All knew that this interest was, somehow, the cause of the war. To strengthen, perpetuate, and extend this interest was the object for which the insurgents would rend the Union, even by war; while the government claimed no right to do more than to restrict the territorial enlargement of it. Neither party expected for the war, the magniture, or the duration, which it has already attained. Neither anticipated that the *cause* of the conflict might cease with, or even before, the conflict itself should cease. Each looked for an easier triumph, and a result less fundamental and astounding. Both read the same Bible, and pray to the same God; and each invokes His aid against the other. It may seem strange that any men should dare to ask a just God's assistance in wringing their bread from the sweat of other men's faces; but let us judge not that we be not judged. The prayers of both could not be answered; that of neither has been answered fully. The Almighty has his own purposes. "Woe unto the world because of offences! for it must needs be that offences come; but woe to that man by whom the offence cometh!" If we shall suppose that American Slavery is one of those offences which, in the providence of God, must needs come, but which, having continued through His appointed time, He now wills to remove, and that He gives to both North and South, this terrible war, as the woe due to those by whom the offence came, shall we discern therein any departure from those divine attributes which the believers in a Living God always ascribe to Him? Fondly do we hope—fervently do we pray—that this mighty scourge of war may speedily pass away. Yet, if God wills that it continue, until all the wealth piled by the bondman's two hundred and fifty years of unrequited toil shall be sunk, and until every drop of blood drawn with the lash, shall be paid by another drawn with the sword, as was said three thousand years ago, so still it must be said "the judgments of the Lord, are true and righteous altogether."

With malice toward none; with charity for all; with firmness in the right, as God gives us to see the right, let us strive on to finish the work we are in; to bind up the nation's wounds; to care for him who shall have borne the battle, and for his widow, and his orphan— to do all which may achieve and cherish a just and lasting peace, among ourselves, and with all nations.

Wendell Phillips

TOUSSAINT L'OUVERTURE

¶ WENDELL PHILLIPS (1811-1884), member of a prominent
Boston family, was graduated from Harvard College and Harvard
Law School. He early became absorbed in the anti-slavery movement and for twenty-five years spent his extraordinary talents as an
orator and agitator in stirring the public conscience against slavery.
His intense feeling led him to curse the Constitution of the United
States, to oppose voting or holding office under it, and to advocate
the breaking up of the Union. In this cause he endured public
ostracism and personal danger from mob violence. After the Civil
War he turned his attention to women's rights, temperance, Irish
freedom, labor, and other reforms.

His eulogy of Toussaint L'Ouverture was one of several lectures
that he delivered many times before various audiences, beginning
probably in 1860. (The text here given is as Phillips revised it for
publication in his *Speeches, Lectures, and Letters,* 1863.)

LADIES AND GENTLEMEN: I have been requested to offer
you a sketch made some years since, of one of the most remarkable men of the last generation,—the great St. Domingo chief,
Toussaint L'Ouverture, an unmixed negro, with no drop of white
blood in his veins. My sketch is at once a biography and an argument,—a biography, of course very brief, of a negro soldier and
statesman, which I offer you as an argument in behalf of the race
from which he sprung. I am about to compare and weigh races;
indeed I am engaged to-night in what you will think the absurd
effort to convince you that the negro race, instead of being that

object of pity or contempt which we usually consider it, is entitled, judged by the facts of history, to a place close by the side of the Saxon. Now races love to be judged in two ways—by the great men they produce and by the average merit of the mass of the race. We Saxons are proud of Bacon, Shakespeare, Hampden, Washington, Franklin, the stars we have lent to the galaxy of history; and then we turn with equal pride to the average merit of Saxon blood, since it streamed from its German home. So, again, there are three tests by which races love to be tried. The first, the basis of all, is courage,— the element which says, here and to-day, "This continent is mine, from the Lakes to the Gulf: let him beware who seeks to divide it!" [*Cheers.*] And the second is the recognition that force is doubled by purpose; liberty regulated by law is the secret of Saxon progress. And the third element is persistency, endurance; first a purpose, then death or success. Of these three elements is made that Saxon pluck which has placed our race in the van of modern civilization.

In the hour you lend me to-night, I attempt the Quixotic effort to convince you that the negro blood, instead of standing at the bottom of the list, is entitled, if judged either by its great men or its masses, either by its courage, its purpose, or its endurance, to a place as near ours as any other blood known in history. And, for the purpose of my argument, I take an island, St. Domingo, about the size of South Carolina, the third spot in America upon which Columbus placed his foot. Charmed by the magnificence of its scenery and fertility of its soil, he gave it the fondest of all names, Hispaniola, Little Spain. His successor, more pious, rebaptized it from St. Dominic, St. Domingo; and when the blacks, in 1803, drove our white blood from its surface, they drove our names with us, and began the year 1804 under the old name, Hayti, the land of mountains. It was originally tenanted by filibusters, French and Spanish, of the early commercial epochs, the pirates of that day as of ours. The Spanish took the eastern two-thirds, the French the western third of the island, and they gradually settled into colonies. The French, to whom my story belongs, became the pet colony of the mother land. Guarded by peculiar privileges, enriched by the scions of wealthy houses, aided by the unmatched fertility of the soil, it soon was the richest gem in the Bourbon crown; and at the period to which I call your attention, about the era of our Constitution, 1789, its wealth was almost incredible. The effeminacy of the white race rivalled that of the Sybarite of antiquity, while the splendour of their private life outshone Versailles, and their luxury found no mate but in the mad prodigality of the Caesars. At this time the island held about thirty thousand whites, twenty or thirty thousand mulattoes, and five hundred thousand slaves. The slave trade was active. About twenty-five thousand slaves were imported annually; and this only sufficed to fill the gap which the murderous culture of sugar annually produced. The mulattoes, as with us, were children of the slaveholders, but, unlike us, the French slaveholder never forgot his child by a bondswoman. He gave him everything but his name,—wealth, rich plantations, gangs of slaves; sent him to Paris for his education, summoned the best culture of France for the instruction of his daughters, so that in 1790 the mulatto race held one-third of the real estate and one-quarter of the personal estate of the island. But though educated and rich, he bowed under the same yoke as with us. Subjected to special taxes, he could hold no public office, and, if convicted of any crime, was punished with double severity. His son might not sit on the same seat at school with a white boy; he might not enter a church where a white man was worshipping; if he reached a town on horseback, he must dismount and lead his horse by the bridle; and when he died, even his dust could not rest in the same soil with a white body. Such was the white race and the mulatto,—the thin film of a civilization beneath which surged the dark mass of five hundred thousand slaves.

It was over such a population,—the white man melted in sensuality; the mulatto feeling all the more keenly his degradation from the very wealth and culture he enjoyed; the slave, sullen and indifferent, heeding not the quarrels or the changes of the upper air,—it was over this population that there burst, in 1789, the thunder-storm of the French Revolution. The first words which reached the island were the motto of the Jacobin Club,—"Liberty, Equality." The white man heard them aghast. He had read of the streets of Paris running blood. The slave heard them with indifference; it was a quarrel in the upper air, between other races, which did not concern him. The mulatto heard them with a welcome which no dread of other classes could quell. Hastily gathered into conventions, they sent to Paris a committee of the whole body, laid at the feet of the National Convention the free gift of six millions of francs, pledged one-fifth of their annual rental toward the payment of the national debt, and only asked in return that this yoke of civil and social contempt should be lifted from their shoulders.

You may easily imagine the temper in which Mirabeau and Lafayette welcomed this munificent gift of the free mulattoes of the West Indies, and in which the petition for equal civil rights was received by a body which had just resolved that all men were equal. The Convention hastened to express its gratitude, and issued a decree which commences thus: "All freeborn French citizens are equal before the law." Ogé was selected—the friend of Lafayette, a lieutenant-colonel in the Dutch service, the son of a wealthy mulatto woman, educated in Paris, the comrade of all the leading French Republicans—to carry the decree and the message of French Democracy to the island. He landed. The decree of the National Convention was laid on the table of the General Assembly of the island. One old planter seized it, tore it in fragments, and trampled it under his feet, swearing by all the saints in the calendar that the island might sink before they would share their rights with bastards. They took an old mulatto, worth a million, who had simply asked for his rights under that decree, and hung him. A white lawyer of seventy, who drafted the petition, they hung at his side. They took Ogé, broke him on the wheel, ordered him to be drawn and quartered, and one quarter of his body to be hung up in each of the four principal cities of the island; and then they adjourned.

You can conceive better than I can describe the mood in which Mirabeau and Danton received the news that their decree had been torn in pieces and trampled under foot by the petty legislature of an island colony and their comrade drawn and quartered by the orders of its Governor. Robespierre rushed to the tribune and shouted, "Perish the colonies rather than sacrifice one iota of our principles!"

The Convention reaffirmed their decree and sent it out a second time to be executed.

But it was not then as now, when steam has married the continents. It took months to communicate; and while this news of the death of Ogé and the defiance of the National Convention was going to France, and the answer returning, great events had taken place in the island itself. The Spanish, or the eastern section, perceiving these divisions, invaded the towns of the western, and conquered many of its cities. One-half of the slaveholders were Republicans, in love with the new constellation which had just gone up in our Northern sky, seeking to be admitted a State in this Republic, plotting for annexation. The other half were Loyalists, anxious, deserted as they supposed themselves by the Bourbons, to make alliance with George III. They sent to Jamaica, and entreated its Governor to assist them in their intrigue. At first, he lent them only a few hundred soldiers. Some time later, General Howe and Admiral Parker were sent with several thousand men, and finally, the English government entering more seriously into the plot, General Maitland landed with four thousand Englishmen on the north side of the island, and gained many successes. The mulattoes were in the mountains, awaiting events. They distrusted the government, which a few years before they had assisted to put down an insurrection of the whites, and which had forfeited its promise to grant them civil privileges. Deserted by both sections, Blanchelande, the Governor, had left the capital and fled for refuge to a neighboring city.

In this state of affairs, the second decree reached the island. The whites forgot their quarrel, sought out Blanchelande, and obliged him to promise that he never would publish the decree. Affrighted, the Governor consented to that course, and they left him. He then began to reflect that in reality he was deposed, that the Bourbons had lost the sceptre of the island. He remembered his successful appeal to the mulattoes, five years before, to put down an insurrection. Deserted now by the whites and by the mulattoes, only one force was left him in the island,—that was the blacks: they had always remembered with gratitude the *code noir*, black code, of Louis XIV, the first interference of any power in their behalf. To the blacks

Blanchelande appealed. He sent a deputation to the slaves. He was aided by the agents of Comte d'Artois, afterwards Charles X, who was seeking to do in St. Domingo what Charles II did in Virginia, (whence its name of Old Dominion,) institute a reaction against the rebellion at home. The two joined forces, and sent first to Toussaint. Nature made him a Metternich, a diplomatist. He probably wished to avail himself of this offer, foreseeing advantage to his race, but to avail himself of it so cautiously as to provide against failure, risking as little as possible till the intentions of the other party had been tested, and so managing as to be able to go on or withdraw as the best interest of his race demanded. He had practised well the Greek rule, "Know thyself," and thoroughly studied his own part. Later in life, when criticising his great mulatto rival, Rigaud, he showed how well he knew himself. "I know Rigaud," he said, "he drops the bridle when he gallops, he shows his arm when he strikes. For me, I gallop also, but know where to stop: when I strike I am felt, not seen. Rigaud works only by blood and massacre. I know how to put the people in movement: but when I appear, all must he calm."

He said, therefore, to the envoys, "Where are your credentials?" "We have none." "I will have nothing to do with you." They then sought Francois and Biassou, two other slaves of strong passions, considerable intellect, and great influence over their fellow-slaves, and said, "Arm, assist the goverment, put down the English on the one hand, and the Spanish on the other;" and on the 21st of August, 1791, fifteen thousand blacks, led by Francois and Biassou, supplied with arms from the arsenal of the government, appeared in the midst of the colony. It is believed that Toussaint, unwilling himself to head the movement, was still desirous that it should go forward, trusting, as proved the case, that it would result in benefit to his race. He is supposed to have advised Francois in his course,—saving himself for a more momentous hour.

This is what Edward Everett calls the Insurrection of St. Domingo. It bore for its motto on one side of its banner, "Long live the King;" and on the other, "We claim the Old Laws." Singular mottoes for a rebellion! In fact it was the *posse comitatus;* it was the only French army on the island; it was the only force that had a right to bear arms; and what it undertook, it achieved. It put Blanchelande in his seat; it put the island beneath his rule. When it was done, the blacks said to the Governor they had created, "Now, grant us one day in seven; give us one day's labor; we will buy another, and with the two buy a third,"—the favorite method of emancipation at that time. Like the Blanchelande of five years before, he refused. He said, "Disarm, disperse!" and the blacks answered, "The right hand that has saved you, the right hand that has saved the island for the Bourbons, may perchance clutch some of our own rights;" and they stood still. [*Cheering.*] This is the first insurrection, if any such there were in San Domingo,—the first determined purpose on the part of the negro, having saved the government, to save himself.

Now let me stop a moment to remind you of one thing. I am about to open to you a chapter of bloody history,—no doubt of it. Who set the example? Who dug up from its grave of a hundred years the hideous punishment of the wheel, and broke Ogé, every bone, a living man? Who flared in the face of indignant and astonished Europe the forgotten barbarity of quartering the yet palpitating body? Our race. And if the black man learned the lesson but too well, it does not lie in our lips to complain. During this whole struggle, the record is,—written, mark you, by the white man,—the whole picture from the pencil of the white race,—that for one life the negro took in battle, in hot and bloody fight, the white race took, in the cool malignity of revenge, three to answer for it. Notice, also, that up to this moment the slave had taken no part in the struggle, except at the bidding of the government; and even then, not for himself, but only to sustain the laws.

At this moment, then, the island stands thus: The Spaniard is on the east, triumphant; the Englishman is on the northwest, entrenched; the mulattoes are in the mountains, waiting; the blacks are in the valleys, victorious; one-half the French slaveholding element is republican, the other half royalist; the white race against the mulatto and the black; the black against both; the Frenchman against the English and Spaniard; the Spaniard against both. It is a war of races and a war of nations. At such a moment Toussaint L'Ouverture appeared.

He had been born a slave on a plantation in the north of the island,—an unmixed negro,—his father stolen from Africa. If anything, therefore, that I say of him to-night moves your admiration, remember, the black race claims it all,—we have no part nor lot in it. He was fifty years old at this time. An old negro had taught him to read. His favorite books were Epictetus, Raynal, Military Memoirs, Plutarch. In the woods he learned some of the qualities of herbs, and was village doctor. On the estate, the highest place he ever reached was that of coachman. At fifty, he joined the army as physician. Before he went, he placed his master and mistress on shipboard, freighted the vessel with a cargo of sugar and coffee, and sent them to Baltimore, and never afterwards did he forget to send them, year by year, ample means of support. And I might add, that of all the leading negro generals, each one saved the man under whose roof he was born, and protected the family. [*Cheering.*]

Let me add another thing. If I stood here to-night to tell the story of Napoleon, I should take it from the lips of Frenchmen, who find no language rich enough to paint the great captain of the nineteenth century. Were I here to tell you the story of Washington, I should take it from your hearts,—you, who think no marble white enough on which to carve the name of the Father of his Country. [*Applause.*] I am about to tell you the story of a negro who has left hardly one written line. I am to glean it from the reluctant testimony of Britons, Frenchmen, Spaniards,—men who despised him as a negro and a slave, and hated him because he had beaten them in many a battle. All the materials for his biography are from the lips of his enemies.

The second story told of him is this. About the time he reached the camp, the army had been subjected to two insults. First, their commissioners, summoned to meet the French Committee were ignominiously and insultingly dismissed; and when, afterwards, François, their general, was summoned to a second conference, and went to it on horseback, accompanied by two officers, a young lieutenant, who had known him as a slave, angered at seeing him in the uniform of an officer raised his riding-whip and struck him over the shoulders. If he had been the savage which the negro is painted to us, he had only to breathe the insult to his twenty-five thousand soldiers, and they would have trodden out the Frenchman in blood. But the indignant chief rode back in silence to his tent, and it was twenty-four hours before his troops heard of this insult to their general. Then the word went forth, "Death to every white man!" They had fifteen hundred prisoners. Ranged in front of the camp, they were about to be shot. Toussaint, who had a vein of religious fanaticism, like most great leaders,—like Mohammed, like Napoleon, like Cromwell, like John Brown [*Cheers*],—he could preach as well as fight,—mounting a hillock, and getting the ear of the crowd, exclaimed: "Brothers, this blood will not wipe out the insult to our chief; only the blood in yonder French camp can wipe it out. To shed that is courage; to shed this is cowardice and cruelty besides;" —and he saved fifteen hundred lives. [*Applause.*]

I cannot stop to give in detail every one of his efforts. This was in 1793. Leap with me over seven years; come to 1800; what has he achieved? He has driven the Spaniard back into his own cities, conquered him there, and put the French banner over every Spanish town; and for the first time, and almost the last, the island obeys one law. He has put the mulatto under his feet. He has attacked Maitland, defeated him in pitched battles, and permitted him to retreat to Jamaica; and when the French army rose upon Laveaux, their general, and put him into chains, Toussaint defeated them, took Laveaux out of prison, and put him at the head of his own troops. The grateful French in return named him General-in-Chief. *Cet homme fait l'ouverture partout*, said one,—"This man makes an opening everywhere,"—hence his soldiers named him L'Ouverture, *the opening.*

This was the work of seven years. Let us pause a moment, and find something to measure him by. You remember Macaulay says, comparing Cromwell with Napoleon, that Cromwell showed the greater military genius, if we consider that he never saw an army till he was forty; while Napoleon was educated from a boy in the best military schools in Europe. Cromwell manufactured his own army; Napoleon at the age of twenty-seven was placed at the head of the best troops Europe ever saw. They were both successful; but, says Macaulay, with such disadvantages, the Englishman showed the greater genius. Whether you allow the inference or not, you will at least grant that it is a fair mode of measurement. Apply it to Toussaint. Cromwell never saw an army till he was forty; this man never saw a soldier till he was fifty. Cromwell manufactured his own army—out of what? Englishmen,—the best blood in Europe. Out of the middle class of Englishmen,—the best blood of the island. And with it he conquered what? Englishmen,—their equals. This man manufactured his army out of what? Out of what you call the despicable race of negroes, debased, demoralized by two hundred years of slavery, one hundred thousand of them imported into the island within four years, unable to speak a dialect intelligible even to each other. Yet out of this mixed, and, as you say, despicable mass, he forged a thunderbolt and hurled it at what? At the proudest blood in Europe, the Spaniard, and sent him home conquered [*cheers*]; at the most warlike blood in Europe, the French, and put them under his feet; at the pluckiest blood in Europe, the English, and they skulked home to Jamaica. [*Applause.*] Now if Cromwell was a general, at least this man was a soldier. I know it was a small territory; it was not as large as the continent; but it was as large as that Attica, which, with Athens for a capital, has filled the earth with its fame for two thousand years. We measure genius by quality, not by quantity.

Further,—Cromwell was only a soldier; his fame stops there. Not one line in the statute book of Britain can be traced to Cromwell; not one step in the social life of England finds its motive power in his brain. The state he founded went down with him to his grave. But this man no sooner put his hand on the helm of State, than the ship steadied with an upright keel, and he began to evince a statesmanship as marvellous as his military genius. History says that the most statesmanlike act of Napoleon was his proclamation of 1802, at the peace of Amiens, when, believing that the indelible loyalty of a native-born heart is always a sufficient basis on which to found an empire, he said: "Frenchmen come home. I pardon the crimes of the last twelve years; I blot out its parties; I found my throne on the hearts of all Frenchmen;"—and twelve years of unclouded success showed how wisely he judged. That was in 1802. In 1800 this negro made a proclamation; it runs thus: "Sons of St. Domingo, come home. We never meant to take your houses or your lands. The negro only asked that liberty which God gave him. Your houses wait for you; your lands are ready; come and cultivate them;" and from Madrid and Paris, from Baltimore and New Orleans, the emigrant planters crowded home to enjoy their estates, under the pledged word that was never broken of a victorious slave. [*Cheers.*]

Again, Carlyle has said, "The natural king is one who melts all wills into his own." At this moment he turned to his armies,—poor, ill-clad and half-starved,—and said to them: "Go back and work on those estates you have conquered; for an empire can be founded only on order and industry, and you can learn these virtues only there." And they went. The French Admiral, who witnessed the scene, said that in a week his army melted back into peasants.

It was 1800. The world waited fifty years before, in 1846, Robert Peel dared to venture, as a matter of practical statesmanship, the theory of free trade. Adam Smith theorized, the French statesmen dreamed, but no man at the head of affairs had ever dared to risk it as a practical measure. Europe waited till 1846 before the most practical intellect in the world, the English, adopted the great economic formula of unfettered trade. But in 1800 this black, with the instinct of statesmanship, said to the committee who were drafting for him a Constitution: "Put at the head of the chapter of commerce that the ports of St. Domingo are open to the trade of the world." [*Cheers.*] With lofty indifference to race, superior to all envy or prejudice, Toussaint had formed this committee of eight white proprietors and one mulatto—not a soldier or a negro on the list, although Haytien history proves that, with the exception of Rigaud, the rarest genius has always been shown by pure negroes.

Again, it was 1800, at the time when England was poisoned on every page of her statute-book with religious intolerance, when a man could not enter the House of Commons without taking an Episcopal communion, when every state in the Union, except Rhode

Island, was full of the intensest religious bigotry. This man was a negro. You say that is a superstitious blood. He was uneducated. You say that makes a man narrow-minded. He was a Catholic. Many say that is but another name for intolerance. And yet—negro, Catholic, slave—he took his place by the side of Roger Williams, and said to his committee: "Make it the first line of my Constitution that I know no difference between religious beliefs." [*Applause.*]

Now, blue-eyed Saxon, proud of your race, go back with me to the commencement of the century, and select what statesman you please. Let him be either American or European; let him have a brain the result of six generations of culture; let him have the ripest training of university routine; let him add to it the better education of practical life; crown his temples with the silver of seventy years; and show me the man of Saxon lineage for whom his most sanguine admirer will wreathe a laurel rich as embittered foes have placed on the brow of this negro,—rare military skill, profound knowledge of human nature, content to blot out all party distinctions, and trust a state to the blood of its sons,—anticipating Sir Robert Peel fifty years, and taking his station by the side of Roger Williams before any Englishman or American had won the right; and yet this is the record which the history of rival states makes up for this inspired black of St. Domingo. [*Cheers.*]

It was 1801. The Frenchmen who lingered on the island described its prosperity and order as almost incredible. You might trust a child with a bag of gold to go from Samana to Port-au-Prince without risk. Peace was in every household; the valleys laughed with fertility; culture climbed the mountains; the commerce of the world was represented in its harbors. At this time Europe concluded the Peace of Amiens, and Napoleon took his seat on the throne of France. He glanced his eyes across the Atlantic, and, with a single stroke of his pen, reduced Cayenne and Martinique back into chains. He then said to his Council, "What shall I do with St. Domingo?" The slaveholders said, "Give it to us." Napoleon turned to the Abbé Grégoire, "What is your opinion?" "I think those men would change their opinions, if they changed their skins." Colonel Vincent, who had been private secretary to Toussaint, wrote a letter to Napoleon, in which he said: "Sire, leave it alone; it is the happiest spot in your dominions; God raised this man to govern; races melt under his hand. He has saved you this island; for I know of my own knowledge that, when the Republic could not have lifted one finger to prevent it, George III offered him any title and any revenue if he would hold the island under the British crown. He refused, and saved it for France." Napoleon turned away from his Council, and is said to have remarked, "I have sixty thousand idle troops; I must find them something to do." He meant to say, "I am about to seize the crown; I dare not do it in the faces of sixty thousand republican soldiers: I must give them work at a distance to do." The gossip of Paris gives another reason for his expedition against St. Domingo. It is said that the satirists of Paris had christened Toussaint, the Black Napoleon; and Napoleon hated his black shadow. Toussaint had unfortunately once addressed him a letter, "The first of the blacks to the first of the whites." He did not like the comparison. You would think it too slight a motive. But let me remind you of the present Napoleon, that when the epigrammatists of Paris christened his wasteful and taste-less expense at Versailles, *Soulouquerie,* from the name of Soulouque, the Black Emperor, he deigned to issue a specific order forbidding the use of the word. The Napoleon blood is very sensitive. So Na-poleon resolved to crush Toussaint from one motive or another, from the prompting of ambition, or dislike of this resemblance,— which was very close. If either imitated the other, it must have been the white, since the negro preceded him several years. They were very much alike, and they were very French,—French even in vanity, common to both. You remember Bonaparte's vainglorious words to his soldiers at the Pyramids: "Forty centuries look down upon us." In the same mood Toussaint said to the French captain who urged him to go to France in his frigate, "Sir, your ship is not large enough to carry me." Napoleon, you know, could never bear the military uniform. He hated the restraint of his rank; he loved to put on the gray coat of the Little Corporal, and wander in the camp. Toussaint also never could bear a uniform. He wore a plain coat, and often the yellow Madras handkerchief of the slaves. A French lieutenant once called him a maggot in a yellow handkerchief. Toussaint took him prisoner next day, and sent him home to his mother. Like Napoleon, he could fast many days; could dictate to three secretaries at once; could wear out four or five horses. Like Napoleon, no man ever divined his purpose or penetrated his plan. He was only a negro, and so, in him, they called it hypocrisy. In Bonaparte we style it diplomacy. For instance, three attempts made to assassinate him all failed, from not firing at the right spot. If they thought he was in the north in a carriage, he would be in the south on horseback; if they thought he was in the city in a house, he would be in the field in a tent. They once riddled his carriage with bullets; he was on horseback on the other side. The seven Frenchmen who did it were arrested. They expected to be shot. The next day was some saint's day; he ordered them to be placed before the high altar, and, when the priest reached the prayer for forgiveness, came down from his high seat, repeated it with him, and permitted them to go unpunished. [*Cheers.*] He had that wit common to all great commanders, which makes its way in a camp. His soldiers getting disheartened, he filled a large vase with powder, and, scattering six grains of rice in it, shook them up, and said: "See, there is the white, there is the black; what are you afraid of?" So when people came to him in great numbers for office, as it is reported they do sometimes even in Washington, he learned the first words of a Catholic prayer in Latin, and, repeating it, would say, "Do you understand that?" "No, sir." "What! want an office and not know Latin? Go home and learn it!"

Then, again, like Napoleon,—like genius always,—he had confidence in his power to rule men. You remember when Bonaparte returned from Elba, and Louis XVIII sent an army against him, Bonaparte descended from his carriage, opened his coat, offering his breast to their muskets, and saying, "Frenchmen, it is the Emperor!" and they ranged themselves behind him, *his* soldiers, shouting "*Vive l'Empereur!*" That was in 1815. Twelve years before, Toussaint, finding that four of his regiments had deserted and gone to Leclerc, drew his sword, flung it on the grass, went across the field to them, and said, "Children, can you point a bayonet at me?" The blacks fell on their knees, praying his pardon. His bitterest enemies watched him, and none of them charged him with love of money, sensuality or cruel use of power. The only instance in which his sternest critic has charged him with severity is this. During a tumult, a few white proprietors who had returned, trusting his proclamation, were killed. His nephew, General Moise, was accused of indecision in quelling the riot. He assembled a court-martial, and, on its verdict, ordered his own nephew to be shot, sternly Roman in thus keeping his promise of protection to the whites. Above the lust of gold, pure in private life, generous in the use of his power, it was against such a man that Napoleon sent his army, giving to General Leclerc, the husband of his beautiful sister Pauline, thirty thousand of his best troops, with orders to reintroduce slavery. Among these soldiers came all of Toussaint's old mulatto rivals and foes.

Holland lent sixty ships. England promised by special message to be neutral; and you know neutrality means sneering at freedom, and sending arms to tyrants. [*Loud and long-continued applause.*] England promised neutrality, and the black looked out on the whole civilized world marshalled against him. America, full of slaves, of course was hostile. Only the Yankee sold him poor muskets at a very high price. [*Laughter.*] Mounting his horse, and riding to the eastern end of the island, Samana, he looked out on a sight such as no native had ever seen before. Sixty ships of the line, crowded by the best soldiers of Europe, rounded the point. They were soldiers who had never yet met an equal, whose tread, like Caesar's, had shaken Europe,—soldiers who had scaled the pyramids, and planted the French banners on the walls of Rome. He looked a moment, counted the flotilla, let the reins fall on the neck of his horse, and turning to Christophe, exclaimed: "All France is come to Hayti; they can only come to make us slaves; and we are lost!" He then recognized the only mistake of his life,—his confidence in Bonaparte, which had led him to disband his army.

Returning to the hills, he issued the only proclamation which bears his name and breathes vengeance: "My children, France comes to make us slaves. God gave us liberty; France has no right to take it away. Burn the cities, destroy the harvests, tear up the roads with cannon, poison the wells, show the white man the hell he comes to make;" and he was obeyed. [*Applause.*] When the great William of Orange saw Louis XIV cover Holland with troops, he said, "Break down the dykes, give Holland back to ocean;" and Europe said "Sublime!" When Alexander saw the armies of France descend upon Russia, he said, "Burn Moscow, starve back the invaders;" and Europe said "Sublime!" This black saw all Europe marshalled to crush him and gave to his people the same heroic example of defiance.

It is true the scene grows bloodier as we proceed. But, remember, the white man fitly accompanied his infamous attempt to *reduce freemen to slavery* with every bloody and cruel device that bitter and shameless hate could invent. Aristocracy is always cruel. The black man met the attempt, as every such attempt should be met, with war to the hilt. In his first struggle to gain his freedom, he had been generous and merciful, saved lives and pardoned enemies, as the people in every age and clime have always done when rising against aristocrats. Now, to save his liberty, the negro exhausted every means, seized every weapon, and turned back the hateful invaders with a vengeance as terrible as their own, though even now he refused to be cruel.

Leclerc sent word to Christophe that he was about to land at Cape City. Christophe said, "Toussaint is governor of the island. I will send to him for permission. If without it a French soldier sets foot on shore, I will burn the town, and fight over its ashes."

Leclerc landed. Christophe took two thousand *white* men, women, and children, and carried them to the mountains in safety, then with his own hands set fire to the splendid palace which French architects had just finished for him, and in forty hours the place was in ashes. The battle was fought in its streets and the French driven back to their boats. [*Cheers.*] Wherever they went they were met with fire and sword. Once, resisting an attack, the blacks, Frenchmen born, shouted the Marseilles hymn, and the French soldiers stood still; they could not fight the Marseillaise. And it was not till their officers sabred them on that they advanced, and then they were beaten. Beaten in the field, the French then took to lies. They issued proclamations, saying, "We do not come to make you slaves; this man Toussaint tells you lies. Join us, and you shall have the rights you claim." They cheated every one of his officers, except Christophe and Dessalines, and his own brother Pierre, and finally these also deserted him, and he was left alone. He then sent word to Leclerc, "I will submit. I could continue the struggle for years,—could prevent a single Frenchman from safely quitting your camp. But I hate bloodshed. I have fought only for the liberty of my race. Guarantee that, I will submit and come in." He took the oath to be a faithful citizen; and on the same crucifix Leclerc swore that he should be faithfully protected and that the island should be free. As the French general glanced along the line of his splendidly equipped troops, and saw, opposite, Toussaint's ragged, ill-armed followers he said to him, "L'Ouverture, had you continued the war, where could you have got arms?" "I would have taken yours," was the Spartan reply. [*Cheers.*] He went down to his house in peace; it was summer. Leclerc remembered that the fever months were coming, when his army would be in hospitals, and when one motion of that royal hand would sweep his troops into the sea. He was too dangerous to be left at large. So they summoned him to attend a council; and here is the only charge made against him,—the only charge. They say he was fool enough to go. Grant it; what was the record? The white man lies shrewdly to cheat the negro. Knight errantry was truth. The foulest insult you can offer a man since the Crusades is, You lie. Of Toussaint, Hermona, the Spanish general, who knew him well, said, "He was the purest soul God ever put into a body." Of him history bears witness, "He never broke his word." Maitland was travelling in the depths of the woods to meet Toussaint, when he was met by a messenger, and told that he was betrayed. He went on, and met Toussaint, who showed him two letters, —one from the French general, offering him any rank if he would put Maitland in his power, and the other his reply. It was, "Sir, I have promised the Englishman that he shall go back." [*Cheers.*] Let it stand, therefore, that the negro, truthful as a knight of old, was cheated by his lying foe. Which race has reason to be proud of such a record?

But he was not cheated. He was under espionage. Suppose he had refused: the government would have doubted him,—would have found some cause to arrest him. He probably reasoned thus: "If I go willingly I shall be treated accordingly;" and he went. The moment he entered the room, the officers drew their swords and told him he was a prisoner; and one young lieutenant who was present says, "He was not at all surprised, but seemed very sad." They put him on shipboard, and weighed anchor for France. As the island faded from his sight, he turned to the captain, and said, "You think you have rooted up the tree of liberty, but I am only a branch; I have planted the tree so deep that all France can never root it up." [*Cheers.*] Arrived in Paris, he was flung into jail, and Napoleon sent his secretary, Caffarelli, to him, supposing he had buried large treasures. He listened awhile, then replied, "Young man, it is true I have lost treasures, but they are not such as you come to seek." He was then sent to the Castle of St. Joux, to a dungeon twelve feet by twenty, built wholly of stone, with a narrow window, high up on the side, looking out on the snows of Switzerland. In winter, ice covers the floor; in summer, it is damp and wet. In this living tomb the child of the sunny tropics was left to die. From this dungeon he wrote two letters to Napoleon. One of them ran thus:—"Sire, I am a French citizen. I never broke a law. By the grace of God, I have saved for you the best island of your realm. Sire, of your mercy grant me justice."

Napoleon never answered the letters. The commandant allowed him five francs a day for food and fuel. Napoleon heard of it, and reduced the sum to three. The luxurious usurper who complained that the English government was stingy because it allowed him only six thousand dollars a month, stooped from his throne to cut down a dollar to a half, and still Toussaint did not die quick enough.

This dungeon was a tomb. The story is told that, in Josephine's time, a young French Marquis was placed there, and the girl to whom he was betrothed went to the Empress and prayed for his release. Said Josephine to her, "Have a model of it made, and bring it to me." Josephine placed it near Napoleon. He said, "Take it away —it is horrible!" She put it on his footstool, and he kicked it from him. She held it to him for the third time, and said, "Sire, in this horrible dungeon you have put a man to die." "Take him out," said Napoleon, and the girl saved her lover. In this tomb Toussaint was buried, but he did not die fast enough. Finally, the commandant was told to go into Switzerland, to carry the keys of the dungeon with him, and to stay four days; when he returned, Toussaint was found starved to death. That imperial assassin was taken twelve years after to his prison at St. Helena, planned for a tomb, as he had planned that of Toussaint, and there he whined away his dying hours in pitiful complaints of curtains and titles, of dishes and rides. God grant that when some future Plutarch shall weigh the great men of our epoch, the whites against the blacks, he do not put that whining child at St. Helena into one scale and into the other the negro meeting death like a Roman, without a murmur, in the solitude of his icy dungeon!

From the moment he was betrayed, the negroes began to doubt the French, and rushed to arms. Soon every negro but Maurepas deserted the French. Leclerc summoned Maurepas to his side. He came, loyally bringing with him five hundred soldiers. Leclerc spiked his epaulettes to his shoulders, shot him, and flung him into the sea. He took his five hundred soldiers on shore, shot them on the edge of a pit and tumbled them in. Desslaines from the mountain saw it, and, selecting five hundred French officers from his prisons, hung them on separate trees in sight of Leclerc's camp; and born, as I was, not far from Bunker Hill, I have yet found no reason to think he did wrong. [*Cheers.*] They murdered Pierre Toussaint's wife at his own door and after such treatment that it was mercy when they killed her. The maddened husband, who had but a year before saved the lives of twelve hundred white men, carried his next thousand prisoners and sacrificed them on her grave.

The French exhausted every form of torture. The negroes were bound and thrown into the sea; anyone who floated was shot,—others sunk with cannon-balls tied to their feet; some smothered with sulphur fumes,—others strangled, scourged to death, gibbeted; sixteen of Toussaint's officers were chained to rocks in desert islands, —others in marshes, and left to be devoured by poisonous reptiles and insects. Rochambeau sent to Cuba for bloodhounds. When they arrived the young girls went down to the wharf, decked the hounds with ribbons and flowers, kissed their necks, and, seated in the amphitheatre, the women clapped their hands to see a negro thrown to these dogs, previously starved to rage. But the negroes besieged this very city so closely that these same girls, in their misery, ate the very hounds they had welcomed.

Then flashed forth that defying courage and sublime endurance which show how alike all races are when tried in the same furnace. The Roman wife, whose husband faltered when Nero ordered him to kill himself, seized the dagger, and, mortally wounding her own body, cried, "Poetus, it is not hard to die." The world records it with proud tears. Just in the same spirit, when a negro colonel was ordered to execution, and trembled, his wife seized his sword, and, giving herself a death-wound, said, "Husband, death is sweet when liberty is gone."

The war went on. Napoleon sent over thirty thousand more soldiers. But disaster still followed his efforts. What the sword did not devour, the fever ate up. Leclerc died. Pauline carried his body back to France. Napoleon met her at Bordeau, saying, "Sister, I gave you an army,—you bring me back ashes." Rochambeau—the Rochambeau of our history—left in command of eight thousand troops, sent word to Dessalines: "When I take you, I will not shoot you like a soldier, or hang you like a white man, I will whip you to death like a slave." Dessalines chased him from battle-field to battle-field, from fort to fort, and finally shut him up in Samana. Heating cannon balls to destroy his fleet, Dessalines learned that Rochambeau had begged of the British Admiral to cover his troops with the English flag, and the generous negro suffered the boaster to embark undisturbed.

Some doubt the courage of the negro. Go to Hayti, and stand on those fifty thousand graves of the best soldiers France ever had, and ask them what they think of the negro's sword. And if that does not satisfy you, go to France, to the splendid mausoleum of the Counts of Rochambeau, and to the eight thousand graves of Frenchmen who skulked home under the English flag, and ask them. And if that does not satisfy you, come home, and if it had been October, 1859, you might have come by way of quaking Virginia, and asked her what she thought of negro courage.

You may also remember this,—that we Saxons were slaves about four hundred years, sold with the land, and our fathers never raised a finger to end that slavery. They waited till Christianity and civilization, till commerce and the discovery of America, melted away their chains. Spartacus in Italy led the slaves of Rome against the Empress of the world. She murdered him and crucified them. There never was a slave rebellion successful but once, and that was in St. Domingo. Every race has been, some time or other, in chains. But there never was a race that, weakened and degraded by such chattel slavery, unaided, tore off its own fetters, forged them into swords, and won its liberty on the battle-field, but one, and that was the black race of St. Domingo. God grant that the wise vigor of our government may avert that necessity from our land,—may raise into peaceful liberty the four million committed to our care, and show under democratic institutions a statesmanship as farsighted as that of England, as brave as the negro of Hayti!

So much for the courage of the negro. Now look at his endurance. In 1805 he said to the white men, "This island is ours; not a white foot shall touch it." Side by side with him stood the South American republics, planted by the best blood of the countrymen of Lope de Vega and Cervantes. They topple over so often that you could no more daguerreotype their crumbling fragments than you could the waves of the ocean. And yet, at their side, the negro has kept his island sacredly to himself. It is said that at first, with rare patriotism, the Haytien government ordered the destruction of all the sugar plantations remaining, and discouraged its culture, deeming that the temptation which lured the French back again to attempt their enslavement. Burn over New York to-night, fill up her canals, sink every ship, destroy her railroads, blot out every remnant of education from her sons, let her be ignorant and penniless, with nothing but her hands to begin the world again,—how much could she do in sixty years? And Europe, too, would lend you money, but she will not lend Hayti a dollar. Hayti, from the ruins of her colonial dependence, is become a civilized state, the seventh nation in the catalogue of commerce with this country, inferior in morals and education to none of the West Indian isles. Foreign merchants trust her courts as willingly as they do our own. Thus far, she has foiled the ambition of Spain, the greed of England, and the malicious statesmanship of Calhoun. Toussaint made her what she is. In this work there was grouped around him a score of men, mostly of pure negro blood, who ably seconded his efforts. They were able in war and skillful in civil affairs, but not, like him, remarkable for that rare mingling of high qualities which alone makes true greatness, and insures a man leadership among those otherwise almost his equals. Toussaint was indisputably their chief. Courage, purpose, endurance,—these are the tests. He did plant a state so deep that all the world has not been able to root it up.

I would call him Napoleon, but Napoleon made his way to empire over broken oaths and through a sea of blood. This man never broke his word. "No Retaliation" was his great motto and the rule of his life; and the last words uttered to his son in France were these: "My boy, you will one day go back to St. Domingo; forget that France murdered your father." I would call him Cromwell, but Cromwell was only a soldier and the state he founded went down with him into his grave. I would call him Washington, but the great Virginian held slaves. This man risked his empire rather than permit the slave-trade in the humblest village of his dominions.

You think me a fanatic to-night, for you read history not with your eyes, but with your prejudices. But fifty years hence, when Truth gets a hearing, the Muse of History will put Phocian for the Greek, and Brutus for the Roman, Hampden for England, Fayette for France, choose Washington as the bright consummate flower of our earlier civilization, and John Brown the ripe fruit of our noonday [*Thunders of applause*], then, dipping her pen in the sunlight, will write in the clear blue, above them all, the name of the soldier, the statesman, the martyr, Toussaint L'Ouverture. [*Long continued applause.*]

Wendell Phillips

THE SCHOLAR IN A REPUBLIC

¶ PHILLIPS's career as an agitator for unpopular causes had not endeared him to the conservative elements in Boston; it was therefore a little surprising that in 1881 he was asked to give the annual Phi Beta Kappa address at Harvard. He was seventy years old. Hitherto he had generally spoken before popular audiences, but now he was to address scholars. His speech satisfied the requirements of the academic occasion, but he did not miss the opportunity to rebuke Harvard scholarship for its apathy. His magnetic eloquence made his conservative audience applaud to the echo sentiments that they could not really have approved, justifying the comment of an earlier critic that he was "an infernal machine set to music." Longfellow said, "It was marvelous and delightful, but preposterous from beginning to end." Thomas Wentworth Higginson reported, "He had never seemed more at his ease, more colloquial, more thoroughly extemporaneous . . . yet it had all been sent to the Boston daily papers in advance and appeared with scarcely a word's variation, except where he had been compelled to omit some passages for want of time."

MR. PRESIDENT and Brothers of the P.B.K.: A hundred years ago our society was planted,—a slip from the older root in Virginia. The parent seed, tradition says, was French,—part of that conspiracy for free speech whose leaders prated democracy in the *salons*, while they carefully held on to the flesh-pots of society by crouching low to kings and their mistresses, and whose final object of assault was Christianity itself. Voltaire gave the watchword,—

333

"Crush the wretch."
"Écrasez l'infame."

No matter how much or how little truth there may be in the tradition; no matter what was the origin or what was the object of our
society, if it had any special one,—both are long since forgotten. We
stand now simply a representative of free, brave, American scholarship. I emphasize *American* scholarship.

In one of those glowing, and as yet unequalled pictures which
Everett drew for us, here and elsewhere, of Revolutionary scenes, I
remember his saying, that the independence we then won, if taken
in its literal and narrow sense, was of no interest and little value; but,
construed in the fulness of its real meaning, it bound us to a distinctive American character and purpose, to a keen sense of large responsibility, and to a generous self-devotion. It is under the shadow of
such unquestioned authority that I use the term "American scholarship."

Our society was, no doubt, to some extent, a protest against the
sombre theology of New England, where, a hundred years ago, the
atmosphere was black with sermons, and where religious speculation
beat uselessly against the narrowest limits.

The first generation of Puritans—though Lowell does let Cromwell
call them "a small colony of pinched fanatics"—included some men,
indeed not a few, worthy to walk close to Roger Williams and Sir
Harry Vane,—the two men deepest in thought and bravest in speech
of all who spoke English in their day, and equal to any in practical
statesmanship. Sir Harry Vane, in my judgment the noblest human
being who ever walked the streets of yonder city,—I do not forget
Franklin or Sam Adams, Washington or Fayette, Garrison or John
Brown,—but Vane dwells an arrow's flight above them all, and his
touch consecrated the continent to measureless tolerance of opinion
and entire equality of rights. We are told we can find in Plato "all
the intellectual life of Europe for two thousand years;" so you can
find in Vane the pure gold of two hundred and fifty years of American civilization, with no particle of its dross. Plato would have welcomed him to the Academy, and Fenelon kneeled with him at the

altar. He made Somers and John Marshall possible; like Carnot, he organized victory; and Milton pales before him in the stainlessness of his record. He stands among English statesmen pre-eminently the representative, in practice and in theory, of serene faith in the safety of trusting truth wholly to her own defence. For other men we walk backward, and throw over their memories the mantle of charity and excuse, saying reverently, "Remember the temptation and the age." But Vane's ermine has no stain; no act of his needs explanation or apology; and in thought he stands abreast of our age,—like pure intellect, belongs to all time.

Carlyle said, in years when his words were worth heeding, "Young men, close your Byron, and open your Goethe." If my counsel had weight in these halls, I should say, "Young men, close your John Winthrop and Washington, your Jefferson and Webster, and open Sir Harry Vane." The generation that knew Vane gave to our Alma Mater for a seal the simple pledge,—*Veritas*.

But the narrowness and poverty of colonial life soon starved out this element. Harvard was rededicated *Christo et Ecclesiae;* and up to the middle of the last century, free thought in religion meant Charles Chauncy and the Brattle-Street Church protest, while free thought hardly existed anywhere else. But a single generation changed all this. A hundred years ago there were pulpits that led the popular movement; while outside of religion and of what called itself literature, industry and a jealous sense of personal freedom obeyed, in their rapid growth, the law of their natures. English common-sense and those municipal institutions born of the common law, and which had saved and sheltered it, grew inevitably too large for the eggshell of English dependence, and allowed it to drop off as naturally as the chick does when she is ready. There was no change of law, nothing that could properly be called revolution, only noise-less growth, the seed bursting into flower, infancy becoming man-hood. It was life, in its omnipotence, rending whatever dead matter confined it. So have I seen the tiny weeds of a luxuriant Italian spring upheave the colossal foundations of the Caesars' palace, and leave it a mass of ruins.

But when the veil was withdrawn, what stood revealed astonished the world. It showed the undreamt power, the serene strength of simple manhood, free from the burden and restraint of absurd institutions in Church and State. The grandeur of this new Western constellation gave courage to Europe, resulting in the French Revolution, the greatest, the most unmixed, the most unstained and wholly perfect blessing Europe has had in modern times, unless we may possibly except the Reformation and the invention of printing.

What precise effect that giant wave had when it struck our shore we can only guess. History is, for the most part, an idle amusement, the day-dream of pedants and triflers. The details of events, the actors' motives, and their relation to each other are buried with them. How impossible to learn the exact truth of what took place yesterday under your next neighbor's roof! Yet, we complacently argue and speculate about matters a thousand miles off, and a thousand years ago, as if we knew them. When I was a student here, my favorite study was history. The world and affairs have shown me that one half of history is loose conjecture, and much of the rest is the writer's opinion. But most men see facts, not with their eyes, but with their prejudices. Anyone familiar with courts will testify how rare it is for an honest man to give a perfectly correct account of a transaction. We are tempted to see facts as we think they ought to be, or wish they were. And yet journals are the favorite original sources of history. Tremble, my good friend, if your sixpenny neighbor keeps a journal. "It adds a new terror to death." You shall go down to your children not in your fair lineaments and proportions, but with the smirks, elbows, and angles he sees you with. Journals are excellent to record the depth of the last snow and the date when the May-flower opens; but when you come to men's motives and characters, journals are the magnets that get near the chronometer of history and make all its records worthless. You can count on the fingers of your two hands all the robust minds that ever kept journals. Only milksops and fribbles indulge in that amusement, except now and then a respectable mediocrity. One such journal nightmares New England annals, emptied into history by respectable middle-aged gentlemen who fancy that narrowness and spleen, like poor wine, mellow into truth when they get to be a century old. But you might

as well cite the *Daily Advertiser* of 1850 as authority on one of Garrison's actions.

And, after all, of what value are these minutiae? Whether Luther's
zeal was partly kindled by lack of gain from the sale of indulgences,
whether Boston rebels were half smugglers and half patriots, what
matters it now? Enough that he meant to wrench the gag from
Europe's lips, and that they were content to suffer keenly, that we
might have an untrammelled career. We can only hope to discover
the great currents and massive forces which have shaped our lives;
all else is trying to solve a problem of whose elements we know
nothing. As the poet-historian of the last generation says so plain-
tively, "History comes like a beggarly gleaner in the field, after
Death, the great lord of the domain, has gathered the harvest, and
lodged it in his garner, which no man may open."

But we may safely infer that French debate and experience broad-
ened and encouraged our fathers. To that we undoubtedly owe, in
some degree, the theoretical perfection, ingrafted on English practical sense and old forms, which marks the foundation of our republic. English civil life, up to that time, grew largely out of custom,
rested almost wholly on precedent. For our model there was no authority in the record, no precedent on the file; unless you find it,
perhaps, partially in that Long Parliament bill with which Sir Harry
Vane would have outgeneralled Cromwell, if the shameless soldier
had not crushed it with his muskets.

Standing on Saxon foundations, and inspired, perhaps in some
degree by Latin example, we have done what no race, no nation, no
age, had before dared even to try. We have founded a republic on
the unlimited suffrage of the millions. We have actually worked out
the problem that man, as God created him, may be trusted with self-
government. We have shown the world that a Church without a
bishop, and a State without a king, is an actual, real, everyday possibility. Look back over the history of the race; where will you find a
chapter that precedes us in that achievement? Greece had her republics, but they were the republics of a few freemen and subjects and
many slaves; and "the battle of Marathon was fought by slaves,
unchained from the door-posts of their masters' houses." Italy had

her republics: they were the republics of wealth and skill and family, limited and aristocratic. The Swiss republics were groups of cousins. Holland had her republic, a republic of guilds and land-holders, trusting the helm of state to property and education. And all these, which at their best held but a million or two within their narrow limits, have gone down in the ocean of time.

A hundred years ago our fathers announced this sublime, and, as it seemed then, foolhardy declaration,—that God intended all men to be free and equal: all men, without restriction, without qualifications, without limit. A hundred years have rolled away since that venturous declaration; and to-day, with a territory that joins ocean to ocean, with fifty millions of people, with two wars behind her, with the grand achievement of having grappled with the fearful disease that threatened her central life and broken four millions of fetters, the great Republic, stronger than ever, launches into the second century of her existence. The history of the world has no such chapter in its breath, its depth, its significance, or its bearing on future history.

What Wycliffe did for religion, Jefferson and Sam Adams did for the State,—they trusted it to the people. He gave the masses the Bible, the right to think. Jefferson and Sam Adams gave them the ballot, the right to rule. His intrepid advance contemplated theirs as its natural, inevitable result. Their serene faith completed the gift which the Anglo-Saxon race makes to humanity. We have not only established a new measure of the possibilities of the race; we have laid on strength, wisdom, and skill a new responsibility. Grant that each man's relations to God and his neighbor are exclusively his own concern, and that he is entitled to all the aid that will make him the best judge of these relations; that the people are the source of all power, and their measureless capacity, the lever of all progress; their sense of right, the court of final appeal in civil affairs; the institutions they create the only ones any power has a right to impose; that the attempt of one class to prescribe the law, the religion, the morals, or the trade of another is both unjust and harmful,—and the Wycliffe and Jefferson of history mean this if they mean anything,—then, when in 1867, Parliament doubled the English franchise, Robert Lowe was right in affirming, amid the cheers of the House, "Now the first interest and duty of every Englishman is to educate the masses—our masters." Then, whoever sees farther than his neighbor is that neighbor's servant to lift him to such higher level. Then, power, ability, influence, character, virtue, are only trusts with which to serve our time.

We all agree in the duty of scholars to help those less favored in life, and that this duty of scholars to educate the masses is still more imperative in a republic, since a republic trusts the State wholly to the intelligence and moral sense of the people. The experience of the last forty years shows every man that law has no atom of strength, either in Boston or New Orleans, unless, and only so far as, public opinion indorses it, and that your life, goods, and good name rest on the moral sense, self-respect, and law-abiding mood of the men that walk the streets, and hardly a whit on the provisions of the statute-book. Come, any one of you, outside of the ranks of popular men, and you will not fail to find it so. Easy men dream that we live under a government of law. Absurd mistake! We live under a government of men and newspapers. Your first attempt to stem dominant and keenly-cherished opinions will reveal this to you.

But what is education? Of course it is not book-learning. Book-learning does not make five per cent of that mass of common sense that "runs" the world, transacts its business, secures its progress, trebles its power over Nature, works out in the long run a rough average justice, wears away the world's restraints, and lifts off its burdens. The ideal Yankee, who "has more brains in his hand than others have in their skulls," is not a scholar; and two thirds of the inventions that enable France to double the world's sunshine, and make Old and New England the workshops of the world, did not come from colleges or from minds trained in the schools of science, but struggled up, forcing their way against giant obstacles, from the irrepressible instinct of untrained natural power. Her workshops, not her colleges, made England, for a while, the mistress of the world; and the hardest job her workman had was to make Oxford willing he should work his wonders.

So of moral gains. As shrewd an observer as Governor Marcy, of

New York, often said he cared nothing for the whole press of the sea-board, representing wealth and education (he meant book-learning), if it set itself against the instincts of the people. Lord Brougham, in a remarkable comment on the life of Romilly, enlarges on the fact that the great reformer of the penal law found all the legis-lative and all the judicial power of England, its colleges and its bar, marshalled against him, and owed his success, *as all such reforms do*, says his lordship, to public meetings and popular instinct. It would be no exaggeration to say that government itself began in usurpation, in the feudalism of the soldier and the bigotry of the priest; that liberty and civilization are only fragments of rights wrung from the strong hands of wealth and book-learning. Almost all the great truths relating to society were not the result of scholarly meditation, "hiv-ing up wisdom with each curious year," but have been first heard in the solemn protests of martyred patriotism and the loud cries of crushed and starving labor. When common sense and the common people have stereotyped a principle into a statute, then book-men come to explain how it was discovered and on what ground it rests. The world makes history, and scholars write it,—one half truly, and the other half as their prejudices blur and distort it.

New England learned more of the principle of toleration from a lyceum committee doubting the dicta of editors and bishops when they forbade it to put Theodore Parker on its platform; more from a debate whether the Antislavery cause should be so far countenanced as to invite one of its advocates to lecture; from Sumner and Emer-son, George William Curtis, and Edwin Whipple, refusing to speak unless a negro could buy his way into their halls as freely as any other,—New England has learned more from these lessons than she has or could have done from all the treatises on free printing from Milton and Roger Williams through Locke down to Stuart Mill.

Selden, the profoundest scholar of his day, affirmed, "No man is wiser for his learning;" and that was only an echo of the Saxon proverb, "No fool is a perfect fool until he learns Latin." Bancroft says of our fathers that "the wildest theories of the human reason were reduced to practice by a community so humble that no states-man condescended to notice it, and a legislation without precedent

was produced off-hand by the instincts of the people." And Wordsworth testifies, that, while German schools might well blush for their
subserviency,—

> "A few strong instincts and a few plain rules,
> Among the herdsmen of the Alps, have wrought
> More for mankind at this unhappy day
> Than all the pride of intellect and thought."

Wycliffe was, no doubt, a learned man. But the learning of his day
would have burned him, had it dared, as it did burn his dead body
afterwards. Luther and Melanchthon were scholars, but they were
repudiated by the scholarship of their time, which followed Erasmus,
trying "all his life to tread on eggs without breaking them;" he who
proclaimed that "peaceful error was better than tempestuous truth."
What would college-graduate Seward weigh, in any scale, against
Lincoln bred in affairs?

Hence, I do not think the greatest things have been done for the
world by its book-men. Education is not the chips of arithmetic and
grammar,—nouns, verbs, and the multiplication table; neither is it
that last year's almanac of dates, or series of lies agreed upon, which
we so often mistake for history. Education is not Greek and Latin
and the air-pump. Still, I rate at its full value the training we get
in these walls. Though what we actually carry away is little enough,
we do get some training of our powers, as the gymnast or the fencer
does of his muscles; we go hence also with such general knowledge
of what mankind has agreed to consider proved and settled, that we
know where to reach for the weapon when we need it.

I have often thought the motto prefixed to his college library catalogue by the father of the late Professor Peirce,—Professor Peirce, the
largest natural genius, the man of the deepest reach and firmest grasp
and widest sympathy, that God has given to Harvard in our day,
whose presence made you the loftiest peak and farthest outpost of
more than mere scientific thought, the magnet who, with his twin
Agassiz, made Harvard for forty years the intellectual Mecca of
forty States,—his father's catalogue bore for a motto, *Scire ubi aliquid
invenias magna pars eruditionis est;* and that always seemed to me
to gauge very nearly all we acquired at college, except facility in the

use of our powers. Our influence in the community does not really spring from superior attainments, but from this thorough training of faculties, and more even, perhaps, from the deference men accord to us.

Gibbon says we have two educations,—one from teachers, and the other we give ourselves. This last is the real and only education of the masses,—one gotten from life, from affairs, from earning one's bread; necessity, the mother of invention; responsibility, that teaches prudence, and inspires respect for right. Mark the critic out of office: how reckless in assertion, how careless of consequences; and then the caution, forethought, and fair play of the same man charged with administration. See that young, thoughtless wife suddenly widowed; how wary and skilful, what ingenuity in guarding her child and saving his rights! Any one who studied Europe forty or fifty years ago could not but have marked the level of talk there, far below that of our masses. It was of crops and rents, markets and marriages, scandal and fun. Watch men here, and how often you listen to the keenest discussions of right and wrong, this leader's honesty, that party's justice, the fairness of this law, the impolicy of that measure, —lofty, broad topics, training morals, widening views. Niebuhr said of Italy, sixty years ago, "No one feels himself a citizen. Not only are the people destitute of hope, but they have not even wishes touching the world's affairs; and hence all the springs of great and noble thoughts are choked up."

In this sense the Frémont campaign of 1856 taught Americans more than a hundred colleges; and John Brown's pulpit at Harper's Ferry was equal to any ten thousand ordinary chairs. God lifted a million of hearts to his gibbet, as the Roman cross lifted a world to itself in that divine sacrifice of two thousand years ago. As much as statesmanship had taught in our previous eighty years, that one week of intellectual watching and weighing and dividing truth taught twenty millions of people. Yet how little, brothers, can we claim for bookmen in that uprising and growth of 1856! And, while the first of American scholars could hardly find in the rich vocabulary of Saxon scorn words enough to express, amid the plaudits of his class, his loathing and contempt for John Brown, Europe thrilled to him as proof that our institutions had not lost all their native and distinctive life. She had grown tired of our parrot note and cold moonlight reflection of older civilizations. Lansdowne and Brougham could confess to Sumner that they had never read a page of their contemporary, Daniel Webster; and you spoke to vacant eyes when you named Prescott, fifty years ago, to average Europeans; while Vienna asked, with careless indifference, "Seward, who is he?" But long before our ranks marched up State Street to the John Brown song, the banks of the Seine and of the Danube hailed the new life which had given us another and nobler Washington. Lowell foresaw him when, forty years ago, he sang of,—

> "Truth forever on the scaffold,
> Wrong forever on the throne;
> Yet that scaffold sways the future,
> And behind the dim unknown
> Standeth God, within the shadow,
> Keeping watch above His own."

And yet the book-men, as a class, have not yet acknowledged him.

It is here that letters betray their lack of distinctive American character. Fifty millions of men God gives us to mould; burning questions, keen debate, great interests trying to vindicate their right to be, sad wrongs brought to the bar of public judgment,—these are the people's schools. Timid scholarship either shrinks from sharing in these agitations, or denounces them as vulgar and dangerous interference by incompetent hands with matters above them. A chronic distrust of the people pervades the book-educated class of the North; they shrink from that free speech which is God's normal school for educating men, throwing upon them the grave responsibility of deciding great questions, and so lifting them to a higher level of intellectual and moral life. Trust the people—the wise and the ignorant, the good and the bad—with the gravest questions, and in the end you educate the race. At the same time you secure, not perfect institutions, not necessarily good ones, but the best institutions possible while human nature is the basis and the only material to build with. Men are educated and the State uplifted by allowing all—every one—to broach all their mistakes and advocate all their errors. The community that will not protect its most ignorant and unpopular member in the free utterance of his opinion, no matter how false or hateful, is only a gang of slaves!

Anacharsis went into the Archon's court at Athens, heard a case argued by the great men of that city, and saw the vote by five hundred men. Walking in the streets, someone asked him, "What do you think of Athenian liberty?" "I think," said he, "wise men argue cases, and fools decide them." Just what that timid scholar, two thousand years ago, said in the streets of Athens, that which calls itself scholarship here says to-day of popular agitation,—that it lets wise men argue questions and fools decide them. But that Athens where fools decided the gravest questions of policy and of right and wrong, where property you had gathered wearily to-day might be wrung from you by the caprice of the mob to-morrow,—that very Athens probably secured, for its era, the greatest amount of human happiness and nobleness, invented art, and sounded for us the depths of philosophy. God lent to it the largest intellects, and it flashes to-day the torch that gilds yet the mountain peaks of the Old World. While Egypt, the hunker conservative of antiquity, where nobody dared to differ from the priest or to be wiser than his grandfather; where men pretended to be alive, though swaddled in the grave-clothes of creed and custom as close as their mummies were in linen,—that Egypt is hid in the tomb it inhabited, and the intellect Athens has trained for us digs to-day those ashes to find out how buried and forgotten hunkerism lived and acted.

I know a signal instance of this disease of scholar's distrust, and the cure was as remarkable. In boyhood and early life I was honored with the friendship of Lothrop Motley. He grew up in the thin air of Boston provincialism, and pined on such weak diet. I remember sitting with him once in the State House when he was a member of our legislature. With biting words and a keen crayon he sketched the ludicrous points in the minds and persons of his fellow-members, and tearing up the pictures, said scornfully, "What can become of a country with such fellows as these making its laws? No safe investments; your good name lied away any hour, and little worth keeping if it were not." In vain I combated the folly. He went to Europe;

spent four or five years. I met him the day he landed on his return. As if our laughing talk in the State House had that moment ended, he took my hand with the sudden exclamation, "You were all right; I was all wrong! It *is* a country worth dying for; better still, worth living and working for, to make it all it can be!" Europe made him one of the most American of all Americans. Some five years later, when he sounded the bugle-note in his letter to the London *Times*, some critics who knew his early mood, but not its change, suspected there might be a taint of ambition in what they thought so sudden a conversion. I could testify that the mood was five years old,—years before the slightest shadow of political expectation had dusked the clear mirror of his scholar life.

This distrust shows itself in the growing dislike of universal suffrage, and the efforts to destroy it made of late by all our easy classes. The white South hates universal suffrage; the so-called cultivated North distrusts it. Journal and college, social-science convention and the pulpit, discuss the propriety of restraining it. Timid scholars tell their dread of it. Carlyle, that bundle of sour prejudices, flouts universal suffrage with a blasphemy that almost equals its ignorance. See his words: "Democracy will prevail when men believe the vote of Judas as good as that of Jesus Christ." No democracy ever claimed that the vote of ignorance and crime was as good in any sense as that of wisdom and virtue. It only asserts that crime and ignorance have the same right to vote that virtue has. Only by allowing that right, and so appealing to their sense of justice, and throwing upon them the burden of their full responsibility, can we hope ever to raise crime and ignorance to the level of self-respect. The right to choose your governor rests on precisely the same foundation as the right to choose your religion; and no more arrogant or ignorant arraignment of all that is noble in the civil and religious Europe of the last five hundred years ever came from the triple crown on the Seven Hills than this sneer of the bigot Scotsman. Protestantism holds up its hands in holy horror, and tells us that the Pope scoops out the brains of his churchmen, saying, "I'll think for you; you need only obey." But the danger is, you meet such popes far away from the Seven Hills; and it is sometimes difficult at first to recognize them, for they do not by any means always wear the triple crown.

Evarts and his committee, appointed to inquire why the New York City government is a failure, were not wise enough, or did not dare, to point out the real cause,—the tyranny of that tool of the demagogue, the corner grog shop; but they advised taking away the ballot from the poor citizen. But this provision would not reach the evil. Corruption does not so much rot the masses; it poisons Congress. Credit-Mobilier and money rings are not housed under thatched roofs; they flaunt at the Capitol. As usual in chemistry, the scum floats uppermost. The railway king disdained canvassing for voters: "It is cheaper," he said, "to buy legislatures."

It is not the masses who have most disgraced our political annals. I have seen many mobs between the seaboard and the Mississippi. I never saw or heard of any but well-dressed mobs, assembled and countenanced, if not always led in person, by respectability and what called itself education. That unrivalled scholar, the first and greatest New England ever lent to Congress, signalled his advent by quoting the original Greek of the New Testament in support of slavery, and offering to shoulder his musket in its defence; and forty years later the last professor who went to quicken and lift the moral mood of those halls is found advising a plain, blunt, honest witness to forge and lie, that this scholarly reputation might be saved from wreck. Singular comment on Landor's sneer, that there is a spice of the scoundrel in most of our literary men. But no exacting level of property qualification for a vote would have saved those stains. In those cases Judas did not come from the unlearned class.

Grown gray over history, Macaulay prophesied twenty years ago that soon in these States the poor, worse than another inroad of Goths and Vandals, would begin a general plunder of the rich. It is enough to say that our national funds sell as well in Europe as English consols; and the universal-suffrage Union can borrow money as cheaply as Great Britain, ruled, one half by Tories, and the other half by men not certain that they dare call themselves Whigs. Some men affected to scoff at democracy as no sound basis for national debt, doubting the payment of ours. Europe not only wonders at its rapid payment, but the only taint of fraud that touches even the hem of our garment is the fraud of the capitalist cunningly adding to its burdens, and increasing unfairly the value of his bonds; not the first hint from the people of repudiating an iota even of its unjust additions.

Yet the poor and the unlearned class is the one they propose to punish by disfranchisement.

No wonder the humbler class looks on the whole scene with alarm. They see their dearest right in peril. When the easy class conspires to steal, what wonder the humbler class draws together to defend itself? True, universal suffrage is a terrible power; and with all the great cities brought into subjection to the dangerous classes by grog, and Congress sitting to register the decrees of capital, both sides may well dread the next move. Experience proves that popular governments are the best protectors of life and property. But suppose they were not, Bancroft allows that "the fears of one class are no measure of the rights of another."

Suppose that universal suffrage endangered peace and threatened property. There is something more vlauable than wealth, there is something more sacred than peace. As Humboldt says, "The finest fruit earth holds up to its Maker is man." To ripen, lift, and educate a man is the first duty. Trade, law, learning, science, and religion are only the scaffolding wherewith to build a man. Despotism looks down into the poor man's cradle, and knows it can crush resistance and curb ill-will. Democracy sees the ballot in that baby-hand; and selfishness bids her put integrity on one side of those baby footsteps and intelligence on the other, lest her own hearth be in peril. Thank God for His method of taking bonds of wealth and culture to share all their blessings with the humblest soul He gives to their keeping! The American should cherish as serene a faith as his fathers had. Instead of seeking a coward safety by battening down the hatches and putting man back into chains, he should recognize that God places him in this peril that he may work out a noble security by concentrating all moral forces to lift this weak, rotting, and danger- ous mass into sunlight and health. The fathers touched their highest level when, with stout-hearted and serene faith, they trusted God that it was safe to leave men with all the rights he gave them. Let us be worthy of their blood, and save this sheet-anchor of the race,—universal suffrage,—God's church, God's school, God's method of gently binding men into commonwealths in order that they may at last melt into brothers.

I urge on college-bred men, that, as a class, they fail in republican duty when they allow others to lead in the agitation of the great social questions which stir and educate the age. Agitation is an old word with a new meaning. Sir Robert Peel, the first English leader who felt himself its tool, defined it to be "marshalling the conscience of a nation to mould its laws." Its means are reason and argument,—no appeal to arms. Wait patiently for the growth of public opinion. That secured, then every step taken is taken forever. An abuse once removed never reappears in history. The freer a nation becomes, the more utterly democratic in its form, the more need of this outside agitation. Parties and sects laden with the burden of securing their own success cannot afford to risk new ideas. "Predominant opinions," said Disraeli, "are the opinions of a class that is vanishing." The agitator must stand outside of organizations, with no bread to earn, no candidate to elect, no party to save, no object but truth,—to tear a question open and riddle it with light.

In all modern constitutional governments, agitation is the only peaceful method of progress. Wilberforce and Clarkson, Rowland Hill and Romilly, Cobden and John Bright, Garrison and O'Connell, have been the master-spirits in this new form of crusade. Rarely in this country have scholarly men joined, as a class, in these great popular schools, in these social movements which make the great interests of society "crash and jostle against each other like frigates in a storm."

It is not so much that the people need us, or will feel any lack from our absence. They can do without us. By sovereign and super-abundant strength they can crush their way through all obstacles.

> "They will march prospering,—not through our presence;
> Songs will inspirit them,—not from our lyre;
> Deeds will be done,—while we boast our quiescence,
> Still bidding crouch whom the rest bid aspire."

The misfortune is, we lose a God-given opportunity of making the change an unmixed good, or with the slightest possible share of evil, and are recreant besides to a special duty. These "agitations" are the opportunities and the means God offers us to refine the taste, mould the character, lift the purpose, and educate the moral sense of the masses on whose intelligence and self-respect rests the State. God furnishes these texts. He gathers for us this audience, and only asks of our coward lips to preach the sermons.

There have been four or five of these great opportunities. The crusade against slavery—that grand hypocrisy which poisoned the national life of two generations—was one,—a conflict between two civilizations which threatened to rend the Union. Almost every element among us was stirred to take a part in the battle. Every great issue, civil and moral, was involved,—toleration of opinion, limits of authority, relation of citizen to law, place of the Bible, priest and layman, sphere of woman, question of race, State rights and nationality; and Channing testified that free speech and free printing owed their preservation to the struggle. But the pulpit flung the Bible at the reformer; law visited him with its penalties; society spewed him out of its mouth; bishops expurgated the pictures of their Common Prayer Books; and editors omitted pages in re-publishing English history; even Pierpont emasculated his Class-book; Bancroft remodelled his chapters; and Everett carried Washington through thirty States, remembering to forget the brave words the wise Virginian had left on record warning his countrymen of this evil. Amid this battle of the giants, scholarship sat dumb for thirty years until imminent deadly peril convulsed it into action, and colleges, in their despair, gave to the army that help they had refused to the market-place and the rostrum.

There was here and there an exception. That earthquake scholar at Concord, whose serene word, like a whisper among the avalanches, topples down superstitions and prejudices, was at his post, and with half a score of others, made the exception that proved the rule. Pulpits, just so far as they could not boast of culture, and nestled closest down among the masses, were infinitely braver than the "spires and antique towers" of stately collegiate institutions.

Then came reform of penal legislation,—the effort to make law mean justice, and substitute for its barbarism Christianity and civilization. In Massachusetts, Rantoul represents Beccaria and Livingston, Mackintosh and Romilly. I doubt if he ever had one word of encouragement from Massachusetts letters; and with a single exception, I have never seen, till within a dozen years, one that could be called a scholar active in moving the legislature to reform its code.

The London *Times* proclaimed, twenty years ago, that intemperance produced more idleness, crime, disease, want, and misery, than all other causes put together; and the Westminster *Review* calls it a "curse that far eclipses every other calamity under which we suffer." Gladstone, speaking as prime minister, admitted that "greater calamities are inflicted on mankind by intemperance than by the three great historical scourges,—war, pestilence, and famine." De Quincey says, "The most remarkable instance of a combined movement in society which history, perhaps, will be summoned to notice, is that which, in our day, has applied itself to the abatement of intemperance. Two vast movements are hurrying into action by velocities continually accelerated,—the great revolutionary movement from *political* causes, concurring with the great *physical* movement in locomotion and social intercourse from the gigantic power of steam. At the opening of such a crisis, had no *third movement arisen of resistance to intemperate habits,* there would have been ground of despondency as to the melioration of the human race." These are English testimonies, where the State rests more than half on bayonets. Here we are trying to rest the ballot-box on a drunken people. "We can rule a great city," said Sir Robert Peel, "America cannot;" and he cited the mobs of New York as sufficient proof of his assertion.

Thoughtful men see that up to this hour the government of great cities has been with us a failure; that worse than the dry rot of legislative corruption, than the rancor of party spirit, than Southern barbarism, than even the tyranny of incorporated wealth, is the giant burden of intemperance, making universal suffrage a failure and a curse in every great city. Scholars who play statesmen, and editors who masquerade as scholars, can waste much excellent anxiety that clerks shall get no office until they know the exact date of

Caesar's assassination, as well as the latitude of Pekin, and the Rule of Three. But while this crusade—the Temperance movement—has been, for sixty years, gathering its facts and marshalling its arguments, rallying parties, besieging legislatures, and putting great States on the witness-stand as evidence of the soundness of its methods, scholars have given it nothing but a sneer. But if universal suffrage ever fails here for a time,—permanently it cannot fail,—it will not be incapable civil service, nor an ambitious soldier, nor Southern vandals, nor venal legislatures, nor the greed of wealth, nor boy statesmen rotten before they are ripe, that will put universal suffrage into eclipse: it will be rum intrenched in great cities and commanding every vantage ground.

Social science affirms that woman's place in society marks the level of civilization. From its twilight in Greece, through the Italian worship of the Virgin, the dreams of chivalry, the justice of the civil law, and the equality of French society, we trace her gradual recognition; while our common law, as Lord Brougham confessed, was, with relation to women, the opprobrium of the age and of Christianity. For forty years plain men and women, working noiselessly, have washed away that opprobrium; the statute-books of thirty States have been remodelled, and woman stands to-day almost face to face with her last claim,—the ballot. It has been a weary and thankless, though successful, struggle. But if there be any refuge from that ghastly curse,—the vice of great cities, before which social science stands palsied and dumb,—it is in this more equal recognition of woman. If, in this critical battle for universal suffrage—our fathers' noblest legacy to us, and the greatest trust God leaves in our hands, —there be any weapon, which once taken from the armory will make victory certain, it will be, as it has been in art, literature, and society, summoning woman into the political arena.

But at any rate, up to this point, putting suffrage aside, there can be no difference of opinion; everything born of Christianity, or allied to Grecian culture or Saxon law, must rejoice in the gain. The literary class, until within half a dozen years, has taken note of this great uprising only to fling every obstacle in its way. The first glimpse we get of Saxon blood in history is that line of Tacitus in his "Germany," which reads, "In all grave matters they consult their women." Years hence, when robust Saxon sense has flung away Jewish superstition and Eastern prejudice, and put under its foot fastidious scholarship and squeamish fashion, some second Tacitus, from the valley of the Mississippi, will answer to him of the Seven Hills, "In all grave questions we consult our women."

I used to think that then we could say to letters as Henry of Navarre wrote to the Sir Philip Sidney of his realm, Crillon, "the bravest of the brave," "We have conquered at Arques, *et tu n'y étais pas, Crillon,*"—"You were not there, my Crillon." But a second thought reminds me that what claims to be literature has been always present in that battlefield, and always in the ranks of the foe.

Ireland is another touchstone which reveals to us how absurdly we masquerade in democratic trappings while we have gone to seed in Tory distrust of the people; false to every duty, which, as eldest-born of democratic institutions, we owe to the oppressed, and careless of the lesson every such movement may be made in keeping public thought, clear, keen, and fresh as to principles which are the essence of our civilization, the groundwork of all education in republics.

Sydney Smith said, "The moment Ireland is mentioned the English seem to bid adieu to common-sense, and to act with the barbarity of tyrants and the fatuity of idiots. . . . As long as the patient will suffer, the cruel will kick. . . . If the Irish go on withholding and forbearing, and hesitating whether this is the time for discussion or that is the time, they will be laughed at another century as fools, and kicked for another century as slaves." Byron called England's Union with Ireland "the union of the shark with his prey." Bentham's conclusion, from a survey of five hundred years of European history, was, "Only by making the ruling few uneasy can the oppressed many obtain a particle of relief." Edmund Burke—Burke, the noblest figure in the Parliamentary history of the last hundred years, greater than Cicero in the senate and almost Plato in the academy—Burke affirmed, a century ago, "Ireland has learned at last that justice is to be had from England only when demanded at the sword's point."

And a century later, only last year, Gladstone himself proclaimed in a public address in Scotland, "England never concedes anything to Ireland except when moved to do so by fear."

When we remember these admissions, we ought to clap our hands at every fresh Irish "outrage," as a parrot-press styles it, aware that it is only a far-off echo of the musket-shots that rattled against the Old State House on the 5th of March, 1770, and of the war-whoop that made the tiny spire of the Old South tremble when Boston rioters emptied the three India teaships into the sea,—welcome evidence of living force and rare intelligence in the victim, and a sign that the day of deliverance draws each hour nearer. Cease ringing endless changes of eulogy on the men who made North's Boston port-bill a failure, while every leading journal sends daily over the water wishes for the success of Gladstone's copy of the bill for Ireland. If all rightful government rests on consent,—if, as the French say, you "can do almost anything with a bayonet except sit on it,"—be at least consistent, and denounce the man who covers Ireland with regiments to hold up a despotism which, within twenty months, he has confessed rests wholly upon fear.

Then note the scorn and disgust with which we gather up our garments about us and disown the Sam Adams and William Prescott, the George Washington and John Brown, of St. Petersburg, the spiritual descendants, the living representatives of those who make our history worth anything in the world's annals,—the Nihilists.

Nihilism is the righteous and honorable resistance of a people crushed under an iron rule. Nihilism is evidence of life. When "order reigns in Warsaw," it is a spiritual death. Nihilism is the last weapon of victims choked and manacled beyond all other resistance. It is crushed humanity's only means of making the oppressor tremble. God means that unjust power shall be insecure; and every move of the giant, prostrate in chains, whether it be to lift a single dagger, or stir a city's revolt, is a lesson in justice. One might well tremble for the future of the race if such a despotism could exist without provoking the bloodiest resistance. I honor Nihilism, since it redeems human nature from the suspicion of being utterly vile, made up only of heartless oppressors and contented slaves. Every line in our history, every interest of civilization, bids us rejoice when the tyrant grows pale and the slave rebellious. We cannot but pity the suffering of any human being, however richly deserved; but such pity must not confuse our moral sense. Humanity gains. Chatham rejoiced when our fathers rebelled. For every single reason they alleged, Russia counts a hundred, each one ten times bitterer than any Hancock or Adams could give. Sam Johnson's standing toast in Oxford port was, "Success to the first insurrection of slaves in Jamaica,"— a sentiment Southey echoed. "Eschew cant," said that old moralist. But of all the cants that are canted in this canting world, though the cant of piety may be the worst, the cant of Americans bewailing Russian Nihilism is the most disgusting.

I know what reform needs, and all it needs, in a land where discussion is free, the press untrammelled, and where public halls protect debate. There, as Emerson says, "What the tender and poetic youth dreams to-day, and conjures up with inarticulate speech, is to-morrow the vociferated result of public opinion, and the day after is the charter of nations." Lieber said, in 1870, "Bismarck proclaims to-day in the Diet the very principles for which we were hunted and exiled fifty years ago." Submit to risk your daily bread, expect social ostracism, count on a mob now and then, "be in earnest, don't equivocate, don't excuse, don't retreat a single inch," and you will finally be heard. No matter how long and weary the waiting, at last,—

> "Ever the truth comes uppermost,
>   And ever is justice done;
> For Humanity sweeps onward:
>   Where to-day the martyr stands
> On the morrow crouches Judas,
>   With the silver in his hands;
>
> "Far in front the cross stands ready,
>   And the crackling fagots burn,
> While the hooting mob of yesterday
>   In silent awe return
> To glean up the scattered ashes
>   Into History's golden urn."

In such a land he is doubly and trebly guilty who, except in some most extreme case, disturbs the sober rule of law and order.

But such is not Russia. In Russia there is no press, no debate, no explanation of what government does, no remonstrance allowed, no agitation of public issues. Dead silence, like that which reigns at the summit of Mont Blanc, freezes the whole empire, long ago described as "a despotism tempered by assassination." Meanwhile, such despotism has unsettled the brains of the ruling family, as unbridled power doubtless made some of the twelve Caesars insane, —a madman sporting with the lives and comfort of a hundred millions of men. The young girl whispers in her mother's ear, under a ceiled roof, her pity for a brother knouted and dragged half dead into exile for his opinions. The next week she is stripped naked and flogged to death in the public square. No inquiry, no explanation, no trial, no protest; one dead uniform silence,—the law of the tyrant. Where is there ground for any hope of peaceful change? Where the fulcrum upon which you can plant any possible lever?

Machiavelli's sorry picture of poor human nature would be fulsome flattery if men could keep still under such oppression. No, no! in such a land dynamite and the dagger are the necessary and proper substitutes for Faneuil Hall and the *Daily Advertiser*. Anything that will make the madman quake in his bedchamber, and rouse his victims into reckless and desperate resistance. This is the only view an American, the child of 1620 and 1776, can take of Nihilism. Any other unsettles and perplexes the ethics of our civilization.

Born within sight of Bunker Hill, in a commonwealth which adopts the motto of Algernon Sydney, *sub libertate quietem* ("accept no peace without liberty"); son of Harvard, whose first pledge was "Truth;" citizen of a republic based on the claim that no government is rightful unless resting on the consent of the people, and which assumes to lead in asserting the rights of humanity,—I at least can say nothing else and nothing less; no, not if every tile on Cambridge roofs were a devil hooting my words!

I shall bow to any rebuke from those who hold Christianity to command entire non-resistance. But criticism from any other quarter is only that nauseous hypocrisy which, stung by threepenny tea-tax, piles Bunker Hill with granite and statues, prating all the time of patriotism and broadswords, while, like another Pecksniff, it recommends a century of dumb submission and entire non-resistance to the Russians, who for a hundred years have seen their sons by thousands dragged to death or exile, no one knows which, in this worse than Venetian mystery of police, and their maidens flogged to death in the market-place, and who share the same fate if they presume to ask the reason why.

"It is unfortunate," says Jefferson, "that the efforts of mankind to secure the freedom of which they have been deprived, should be accompanied with violence and even with crime. But while we weep over the means, we must pray for the end." Pray fearlessly for such ends; there is no risk! "Men are all tories by nature," says Arnold, "when tolerably well off; only monstrous injustice and atrocious cruelty can rouse them." Some talk of the rashness of the uneducated classes. Alas! ignorance is far oftener obstinate than rash. Against one French Revolution—that scarecrow of the ages—weigh Asia, "carved in stone," and a thousand years of Europe, with her half-dozen nations meted out and trodden down to be the dull and contented footstools of priests and kings. The customs of a thousand years ago are the sheet-anchor of the passing generation, so deeply buried, so fixed, that the most violent efforts of the maddest fanatic can drag it but a hand's-breadth.

Before the war, Americans were like the crowd in that terrible hall of Eblis which Beckford painted for us,—each man with his hand pressed on the incurable sore in his bosom, and pledged not to speak of it; compared with other lands, we were intellectually and morally a nation of cowards.

When I first entered the Roman States, a custom-house official seized all my French books. In vain I held up to him a treatise by Fenelon, and explained that it was by a Catholic archbishop of Cambray. Gruffly he answered, "It makes no difference; *it is French.*" As I surrendered the volume to his remorseless grasp, I could not but honor the nation which had made its revolutionary purpose so definite that despotism feared its very language. I only wished that injustice and despotism everywhere might one day have as good cause to hate and to fear everything American.

At last that disgraceful seal of slave complicity is broken. Let us inaugurate a new departure, recognize that we are afloat on the current of Niagara, eternal vigilance the condition of our safety, that we are irrevocably pledged to the world not to go back to bolts and bars,—could not if we would, and would not if we could. Never again be ours the fastidious scholarship that shrinks from rude contact with the masses. Very pleasant it is to sit high up in the world's theatre and criticise the ungraceful struggles of the gladiators, shrug one's shoulders at the actors' harsh cries, and let everyone know that but for "this villainous saltpetre you would yourself have been a soldier." But Bacon says, "In the theatre of man's life, God and his angels only should be lookers-on." "Sin is not taken out of man as Eve was out of Adam, by putting him to sleep." "Very beautiful," says Richter, "is the eagle when he floats with outstretched wings aloft in the clear blue; but sublime when he plunges down through the tempest to his eyry on the cliff, where his unfledged young ones dwell and are starving." Accept proudly the analysis of Fisher Ames: "A monarchy is a man-of-war, stanch, iron-ribbed, and resistless when under full sail; yet a single hidden rock sends her to the bottom. Our republic is a raft, hard to steer, and your feet always wet; but nothing can sink her." If the Alps, piled in cold and silence, be the emblem of despotism, we joyfully take the ever-restless ocean for ours,—only pure because never still.

Journalism must have more self-respect. Now it praises good and bad men so indiscriminately that a good word from nine tenths of our journals is worthless. In burying our Aaron Burrs, both political parties—in order to get the credit of magnanimity—exhaust the vocabulary of eulogy so thoroughly that there is nothing left with which to distinguish our John Jays. The love of a good name in life and a fair reputation to survive us—that strong bond to well-doing—is lost where every career, however stained, is covered with the same fulsome flattery, and where what men say in the streets is the exact opposite of what they say to each other. *De mortuis nil nisi bonum*, most men translate, "Speak only good of the dead." I prefer to construe it, "Of the dead say nothing unless you can tell something good." And if the sin and the recreancy have been marked and far reaching in their evil, even the charity of silence is not permissible.

To be as good as our fathers we must be better. They silenced their fears and subdued their prejudices, inaugurating free speech and equality with no precedent on the file. Europe shouted "Madmen!" and gave us forty years for the shipwreck. With serene faith they persevered. Let us rise to their level. Crush appetite, and prohibit temptation if it rots great cities. Intrench labor in sufficient bulwarks against that wealth which, without the tenfold strength of modern incorporation, wrecked the Grecian and Roman States; and with a sterner effort still, summon women into civil life as reinforcement to our laboring ranks in the effort to make our civilization a success.

Sit not, like the figure on our silver coin, looking ever backward.

"New occasions teach new duties;
 Time makes ancient good uncouth;
 They must upward still, and onward,
 Who would keep abreast of Truth.
 Lo! before us gleam her camp-fires!
 We ourselves must Pilgrims be,
 Launch our Mayflower, and steer boldly
 Through the desperate winter sea,
 Nor attempt the Future's portal
 With the Past's blood-rusted key."

George William Curtis

THE PURITAN PRINCIPLE—

LIBERTY UNDER THE LAW

¶ GEORGE WILLIAM CURTIS (1824-1892) was born in Providence, Rhode Island. Though without college training, he became a scholarly man of letters, contributing to various newspapers and magazines many reports, essays, criticisms, and reviews. During two years' residence at Brook Farm, and later, he was strongly influenced by Emerson. In 1846 he left for a tour of several years' duration in Europe, Egypt, and Syria, contributing while abroad many letters on men and events to the *New York Tribune*. After his return he published several books, and in 1863 became editor of *Harper's Weekly*. He took an active interest in politics and reform and was influential in the overthrow of the infamous Tweed ring. Though a leader in the Republican party, he never held public office. His first notable speech, delivered at Wesleyan University in 1856, was on "The Duty of the American Scholar to Politics and the Times," and this was the theme that dominated much of his writing and speaking throughout his life. He became an active and effective advocate of civil service reform. On this and other issues of the day he was the voice of the public conscience.

"Liberty under the Law" was delivered at a dinner of the New England Society of the City of New York, December 22, 1876. The country was torn by the controversy about whether Hayes or Tilden had been elected President and there was loose talk of starting another civil war to settle the matter. Edward Everett Hale believed that this speech saved the nation from that "terrible calamity." He said, "Those three hundred men of mark in New York went home that night, and went to their business the next day, to say that a court of arbitration must be established to settle that controversy. In that moment of Mr. Curtis's triumph, as I believe, it was settled." (The text that follows is from *Orations and Addresses of George William Curtis,* New York, 1894, where the speech is reprinted from the pamphlet report of the occasion issued by the New England Society.)

MR. PRESIDENT AND GENTLEMEN OF THE NEW ENGLAND SOCIETY:—It was Izaak Walton, in his "Angler," who said that Dr. Botelier was accustomed to remark "that doubtless God might have made a better berry than the strawberry, but doubtless he never did." And I suppose I speak the secret feeling of this festive company when I say that doubtless there might have been a better place to be born in than New England, but doubtless no such place exists. [*Applause and laughter.*] And if any sceptic should reply that our very presence here would seem to indicate that doubtless, also, New England is as good a place to leave as to stay in [*Laughter*], I should reply to him that, on the contrary, our presence is but an added glory of our mother. It is an illustration of the devout missionary spirit, of the willingness in which she has trained us to share with others the blessings that we have received, and to circle the continent, to girdle the globe, with the strength of New England character and the purity of New England principles. [*Applause.*] Even the Knickerbockers, Mr. President—in whose stately and splendid city we are at this moment assembled, and assembled of right because it is our home—even they would doubtless concede that much of the state and splendor of this city is due to the enterprise, the industry, and the genius of those whom their first historian describes as "losel Yankees." [*Laughter.*] Sir, they grace our feast with their presence; they will enliven it, I am sure, with their eloquence and wit. Our tables are rich with the flowers grown in their soil; but there is one flower that we do not see, one flower whose perfume fills a continent, which has blossomed for more than two centuries and a half with ever-increasing and deepening beauty—a flower which blooms at this moment, on this wintry night, in never-fading freshness in a million of true hearts, from the snow-clad Katahdin to the warm Golden Gate of the South Sea, and over its waters to the isles of the East and the land of Prester John—the flower of flowers, the Pilgrim's Mayflower. [*Applause.*]

Well, sir, holding that flower in my hand at this moment, I say that the day we celebrate commemorates the introduction upon this continent of the master principle of its civilization. I do not forget that we are a nation of many nationalities. I do not forget that there are gentlemen at this board who wear the flower of other nations close upon their hearts. I remember the forget-me-nots of Germany, and I know that the race which keeps "watch upon the Rhine" keeps watch also upon the Mississippi and the Lakes. I recall—how could I forget?—the delicate shamrock; for

"There came to this beach a poor exile of Erin,"

and on this beach, with his native modesty,

"He still sings his bold anthem of Erin-go-Bragh."

[*Applause.*] I remember surely, sir, the lily—too often the tiger-lily—of France [*laughter and applause*] and the thistle of Scotland; I recall the daisy and the rose of England; and, sir, in Switzerland, high upon the Alps, on the very edge of the glacier, the highest flower that grows in Europe, is the rare *edelweiss*. It is in Europe; we are in America. And here in America, higher than shamrock or thistle, higher than rose, lily, or daisy, higher than the highest, blooms the perennial Mayflower. [*Applause.*] For, sir and gentlemen, it is the English-speaking race that has moulded the destiny of this continent; and the Puritan influence is the strongest influence that has acted upon it. [*Applause.*]

I am surely not here to assert that the men who have represented that influence have always been men whose spirit was blended of sweetness and light. I confess truly their hardness, their prejudice, their narrowness. All this I know: Charles Stuart could bow more blandly, could dance more gracefully than John Milton; and the Cavalier king looks out from the canvas of Vandyck with a more romantic beauty of flowing love-locks than hung upon the brows of Edward Winslow, the only Pilgrim father whose portrait comes down to us. [*Applause.*] But, sir, we estimate the cause beyond the man. Not even is the gracious spirit of Christianity itself measured by its confessors. If we could see the actual force, the creative power of the Pilgrim principle, we are not to look at the company who came over in the cabin of the *Mayflower;* we are to look upon the forty millions who fill this continent from sea to sea. [*Applause.*] The *Mayflower,* sir, brought seed and not a harvest. In a century and a half the religious restrictions of the Puritans had grown into absolute religious liberty, and in two centuries it had burst beyond the limits of New England, and John Carver of the *Mayflower* had ripened into Abraham Lincoln of the Illinois prairie. [*Great and prolonged applause.*] Why, gentlemen, if you would see the most conclusive proof of the power of this principle, you have but to observe that the local distinctive title of New-Englanders has now become that of every man in the country. Every man who hears me, from whatever State in the Union, is, to Europe, a Yankee, and to-day the United States are but the "universal Yankee nation." [*Applause.*]

Do you ask me, then, what is this Puritan principle? Do you ask me whether it is as good for to-day as for yesterday; whether it is good for every national emergency; whether it is good for the situation of this hour? I think we need neither doubt nor fear. The Puritan principle in its essence is simply individual freedom. From that spring religious liberty and political equality. The free State, the free Church, the free School—these are the triple armor of American nationality, of American security. [*Applause.*] But the Pilgrims, while they have stood above all men for their idea of liberty, have always asserted liberty *under law* and never separated it from law. John Robinson, in the letter that he wrote the Pilgrims when they sailed, said these words, that well, sir, might be written in gold around the cornice of that future banqueting-hall to which you have alluded, "You know that the image of the Lord's dignity and authority which the magistry beareth is honorable in how mean person soever." [*Applause.*] This is the Puritan principle. Those men stood for liberty *under the law.* They had tossed long upon a wintry sea; their minds were full of images derived from their voyage; they knew that the will of the people alone is but a gale smiting a rudderless and sailless ship, and hurling it, a mass of wreck, upon the rocks. But the will of the people, subject to law, is the same gale filling the trim canvas of a ship that minds the helm, bearing it over yawning and awful abysses of ocean safety to port. [*Loud applause.*]

Now, gentlemen, in this country the Puritan principle in its development has advanced to this point, that it provides us a lawful remedy for every emergency that may arise. [*Cheers.*] I stand here as a son of New England. In every fibre of my being am I a child of the Pilgrims. [*Applause.*] The most knightly of all the gentlemen at Elizabeth's court said to the young poet, when he would write an immortal song, "Look into thy heart and write." And I, sir and brothers, if, looking into my own heart at this moment, I might dare to think that what I find written there is written also upon the heart of my mother, clad in her snows at home, her voice in this hour would be a message spoken from the land of the Pilgrims to the capital of this nation—a message like that which Patrick Henry sent from Virginia to Massachusetts when he heard of Concord and Lexington: "I am not a Virginian, I am an American." [*Great applause.*] And so, gentlemen, at this hour, we are not Republicans, we are not Democrats, we are Americans. [*Tremendous applause.*]

The voice of New England, I believe, going to the capital, would be this, that neither is the Republican Senate to insist upon its exclusive partisan way, nor is the Democratic House to insist upon its exclusive partisan way, but Senate and House, representing the American people and the American people only, in the light of the Constitution and by the authority of the law, are to provide a way over which a President, be he Republican or be he Democrat, shall pass unchallenged to his chair. [*Vociferous applause, the company rising to their feet.*] Ah, gentlemen [*Renewed applause*]—think not, Mr. President, that I am forgetting the occasion or its amenities. [*Cries of "No, no," and "Go on."*] I am remembering the Puritans; I am remembering Plymouth Rock, and the virtues that made it illustrious. [*A voice—"Justice."*] But we, gentlemen, are to imitate those virtues, as our toast says, only by being greater than the men who stood upon that rock. [*Applause.*] As this gay and luxurious banquet to their scant and severe fare, so must our virtues, to be worthy of them, be greater and richer than theirs. And as we are three centuries older, so should we be three centuries wiser than they. [*Applause.*] Sons of the Pilgrims, you are not to level forests, you are not to war with savage men and savage beasts, you are not to tame a continent nor even found a State. Our task is nobler, is diviner. Our task, sir, is to reconcile a nation. It is to curb the fury of party spirit. It is to introduce a loftier and manlier tone everywhere into our political life. It is to educate every boy and every girl, and then leave them perfectly free to go from any school-house to any church. [*Cries of "Good," and cheers.*] Above all, sir, it is to protect absolutely the equal rights of the poorest and the richest, of the most ignorant and the most intelligent citizen, and it is to stand forth, brethren, as a triple wall of brass around our native land, against the mad blows of violence or the fatal dry-rot of fraud. [*Loud applause.*] And at this moment, sir, the grave and august shades of the forefathers whom we invoke bend over us in benediction as they call us to this sublime task. This, brothers and friends, this is to imitate the virtues of our forefathers; this is to make our day as glorious as theirs. [*Great applause, followed by three cheers for the distinguished speaker.*]

George William Curtis

THE PUBLIC DUTY OF

EDUCATED MEN

¶ THIS IS one of Curtis' numerous addresses before academic institutions. It was delivered at the commencement exercises of Union
College, June 27, 1877. The theme was a favorite one with Curtis—
education as a power in human affairs.

IT IS with diffidence that I rise to add any words of mine to the
music of these younger voices. This day, gentlemen of the graduating class, is especially yours. It is a day of high hope and expectation, and the counsels that fall from older lips should be carefully
weighed, lest they chill the ardor of a generous enthusiasm or stay
the all-conquering faith of youth that moves the world. To those who,
constantly and actively engaged in a thousand pursuits, are still persuaded that educated intelligence moulds States and leads mankind,
no day in the year is more significant, more inspiring, than this of
the College Commencement. It matters not at what college it may
be celebrated. It is the same at all. We stand here indeed beneath
these college walls, beautiful for situation, girt at this moment with
the perfumed splendor of midsummer, and full of tender memories
and joyous associations to those who hear me. But on this day, and
on other days, at a hundred other colleges, this summer sun beholds
the same spectacle of eager and earnest throngs. The faith that we
hold, they also cherish. It is the same God that is worshipped at the

different altars. It is the same benediction that descends upon every reverent head and believing heart. In this annual celebration of faith in the power and the responsibility of educated men, all the colleges in this country, in whatever State, of whatever age, of whatever religious sympathy or direction, form but one great Union University.

But the interest of the day is not that of mere study, of sound scholarship as an end, of good books for their own sake, but of education as a power in human affairs, of educated men as an influence in the commonwealth. "Tell me," said an American scholar of Goethe, the many-sided, "what did he ever do for the cause of man?" The scholar, the poet, the philosopher, are men among other men. From these unavoidable social relations spring opportunities and duties. How do they use them? How do they discharge them? Does the scholar show in his daily walk that he has studied the wisdom of ages in vain? Does the poet sing of angelic purity and lead an unclean life? Does the philosopher peer into other worlds and fail to help this world upon its way? Four years before our civil war the same scholar—it was Theodore Parker—said sadly, "If our educated men had done their duty, we should not now be in the ghastly condition we bewail." The theme of to-day seems to me to be prescribed by the occasion. It is the festival of the departure of a body of educated young men into the world. This company of picked recruits marches out with beating drums and flying colors to join the army. We who feel that our fate is gracious which allowed a liberal training, are here to welcome and to advise. On your behalf, Mr. President and gentlemen, with your authority, and with all my heart, I shall say a word to them and to you of the public duty of educated men in America.

I shall not assume, gentlemen graduates, for I know that it is not so, that what Dr. Johnson says of the teachers of Rasselas and the princes of Abyssinia can be truly said of you in your happy valley—"The sages who instructed them told them of nothing but the miseries of public life, and described all beyond the mountains as regions of calamity where discord was always raging, and where man preyed upon man." The sages who have instructed you are

American citizens. They know that patriotism has its glorious opportunities and its sacred duties. They have not shunned the one, and they have well performed the other. In the sharpest stress of our awful conflict, a clear voice of patriotic warning was heard from these peaceful academic shades, the voice of the venerated teacher whom this University still freshly deplores,[1] drawing from the wisdom of experience stored in his ample learning a lesson of startling cogency and power from the history of Greece for the welfare of America.

This was the discharge of a public duty by an educated man. It illustrated an indispensable condition of a progressive republic, the active, practical interest in politics of the most intelligent citizens. Civil and religious liberty in this country can be preserved only through the agency of our political institutions. But those institutions alone will not suffice. It is not the ship so much as the skillful sailing that assures the prosperous voyage. American institutions presuppose not only general honesty and intelligence in the people, but their constant and direct application to public affairs. Our system rests upon all the people, not upon a part of them, and the citizen who evades his share of the burden betrays his fellows. Our safety lies not in our institutions, but in ourselves. It was under the forms of the republic that Julius Caesar made himself emperor of Rome. It was while professing reverence for the national traditions that James II was destroying religious liberty in England. To labor, said the old monks, is to pray. What we earnestly desire we earnestly toil for. That she may be prized more truly, heaven-eyed Justice flies from us, like the Tartar maid from her lovers, and she yields her embrace at last only to the swiftest and most daring of her pursuers.

By the words public duty I do not necessarily mean official duty, although it may include that. I mean simply that constant and active practical participation in the details of politics without which, upon the part of the most intelligent citizens, the conduct of public affairs falls under the control of selfish and ignorant, or crafty and venal men. I mean that personal attention—which, as it must be incessant,

[1] Professor Tayler Lewis died on May 11, 1877. The work referred to was his "Heroic Periods in a Nation's History."

is often wearisome and even repulsive—to the details of politics, attendance at meetings, service upon committees, care and trouble and expense of many kinds, patient endurance of rebuffs, chagrins, ridicules, disappointments, defeats—in a word, all those duties and services which, when selfishly and meanly performed, stigmatize a man as a mere politician; but whose constant, honorable, intelligent, and vigilant performance is the gradual building, stone by stone and layer by layer, of that great temple of self-restrained liberty which all generous souls mean that our government shall be.

Public duty in this country is not discharged, as is so often supposed, by voting. A man may vote regularly and still fail essentially of his political duty, as the Pharisee, who gave tithes of all that he possessed and fasted three times in the week, yet lacked the very heart of religion. When an American citizen is content with voting merely, he consents to accept what is often a doubtful alternative. His first duty is to help shape the alternative. This, which was formerly less necessary, is now indispensable. In a rural community such as this country was a hundred years ago, whoever was nominated for office was known to his neighbors, and the consciousness of that knowledge was a conservative influence in determining nominations. But in the local elections of the great cities of to-day, elections that control taxation and expenditure, the mass of the voters vote in absolute ignorance of the candidates. The citizen who supposes that he does all his duty when he votes places a premium upon political knavery. Thieves welcome him to the polls and offer him a choice, which he has done nothing to prevent, between Jeremy Diddler and Dick Turpin. The party-cries for which he is responsible are, "Turpin and Honesty," "Diddler and Reform." And within a few years, as a result of this indifference to the details of public duty, the most powerful politician in the Empire State of the Union was Jonathan Wild the Great, the captain of a band of plunderers. I know it is said that the knaves have taken the honest men in a net, and have contrived machinery which will inevitably grind only the grist of rascals. The answer is, that when honest men did once what they ought to do always, the thieves were netted and their machine was broken. To say that in this country the rogues must rule, is to defy history and to despair of the republic. It is to repeat the imbecile executive cries of sixteen years ago, "Oh, dear! the States have no right to go?" and, "Oh, dear! the nation has no right to help itself." Let the Union, stronger than ever and unstained with national wrong, teach us the power of patriotic virtue—and Ludlow Street jail console those who suppose that American politics must necessarily be a game of thieves and bullies.

If ignorance and corruption and intrigue control the primary meeting and manage the convention and dictate the nomination, the fault is in the honest and intelligent workshop and office, in the library and the parlor, in the church and the school. When these are as constant and faithful to their political rights as the slums and the grog-shops, the pool-rooms and the kennels; when the educated, industrious, temperate, thirfty citizens are as zealous and prompt and unfailing in political activity as the ignorant and venal and mischievous, or when it is plain that they cannot be roused to their duty, then, but not until then—if ignorance and corruption always carry the day—there can be no honest question that the republic has failed. But let us not be deceived. While good men sit at home, not knowing that there is anything to be done, nor caring to know; cultivating a feeling that politics are tiresome and dirty, and politicians vulgar bullies and bravòes; half persuaded that a republic is the contemptible rule of a mob, and secretly longing for a splendid and vigorous despotism—then remember it is not a government mastered by ignorance, it is a government betrayed by intelligence; it is not the victory of the slums, it is the surrender of the schools; it is not that bad men are brave, but that good men are infidels and cowards.

But, gentlemen, when you come to address yourselves to these primary public duties, your first surprise and dismay will be the discovery that, in a country where education is declared to be the hope of its institutions, the higher education is often practically held to be almost a disadvantage. You will go from these halls to hear a very common sneer at college-bred men; to encounter a jealousy of education, as making men visionary and pedantic and impracticable; to confront a belief that there is something enfeebling in the higher education, and that self-made men, as they are called, are the sure stay of the State. But what is really meant by a self-made man? It is a man of native sagacity and strong character, who was taught, it is proudly said, only at the plough or the anvil or the bench. He was schooled by adversity, and was polished by hard attrition with men. He is Benjamin Franklin, the printer's boy, or Abraham Lincoln, the rail-splitter. They never went to college, but nevertheless, like Agamemnon, they were kings of men, and the world blesses their memory.

So it does; but the sophistry here is plain enough, although it is not always detected. Great genius and force of character undoubtedly make their own career. But because Walter Scott was dull at school, is a parent to see with joy that his son is a dunce? Because Lord Chatham was of a towering conceit, must we infer that pompous vanity portends a comprehensive statesmanship that will fill the world with the splendor of its triumphs? Because Sir Robert Walpole gambled and swore and boozed at Houghton, are we to suppose that gross sensuality and coarse contempt of human nature are the essential secrets of a power that defended liberty against Tory intrigue and priestly politics? Was it because Benjamin Franklin was not college-bred that he drew the lightning from heaven and tore the sceptre from the tyrant? Was it because Abraham Lincoln had little schooling that his great heart beat true to God and man, lifting him to free a race and die for his country? Because men naturally great have done great service in the world without advantages, does it follow that lack of advantage is the secret of success? Was Pericles a less sagacious leader of the State, during forty years of Athenian glory, because he was thoroughly accomplished in every grace of learning? Or, swiftly passing from the Athenian agora to the Boston town-meeting, behold Samuel Adams, tribune of New England against Old England, of America against Europe, of liberty against despotism. Was his power enfeebled, his fervor chilled, his patriotism relaxed, by his college education? No, no; they were strengthened, kindled, confirmed. Taking his Master's degree one hundred and thirty-four years ago, thirty-three years before the Declaration of Independence, Samuel Adams, then twenty-one years old, declared in a Latin discourse—the first flashes of the fire that blazed afterwards in Faneuil Hall and kindled America—that it is lawful to resist the supreme magistrate if the commonwealth cannot otherwise be preserved. In the very year that Jefferson was born, the college boy, Samuel Adams, on a Commencement day like this, on an academical platform like this on which we stand, struck the key-note of American independence, which still stirs the heart of man with its music.

Or, within our own century, look at the great modern statesmen who have shaped the politics of the world. They were educated men; were they therefore visionary, pedantic, impracticable? Cavour, whose monument is United Italy—one from the Alps to Tarentum, from the lagoons of Venice to the gulf of Salerno; Bismarck, who has raised the German empire from a name to a fact; Gladstone, to-day the incarnate heart and conscience of England—they are the perpetual refutation of the sneer that high education weakens men for practical affairs. Trained themselves, such men know the value of training. All countries, all ages, all men, are their teachers. The broader their education, the wider the horizon of their thought and observation; the more affluent their resources, the more humane their policy. Would Samuel Adams have been a truer popular leader had he been less an educated man? Would Walpole the less truly have served his country had he been, with all his capacities, a man whom England could have revered and loved? Could Gladstone so sway England with his fervent eloquence, as the moon the tides, were he a gambling, swearing, boozing squire like Walpole? There is no sophistry more poisonous to the State, no folly more stupendous and demoralizing, than the notion that the purest character and the highest education are incompatible with the most commanding mastery of men and the most efficient administration of affairs.

Undoubtedly a practical and active interest in politics will lead you to party association and co-operation. Great public results—the repeal of the corn-laws in England, the abolition of slavery in America—are due to that organization of effort and concentration of aim which arouse, instruct, and inspire the popular heart and will. This is the spring of party, and those who earnestly seek practical results instinctively turn to this agency of united action. But in this tendency, useful in the State as the fire upon the household hearth, lurks, as in that fire, the deadliest peril. Here is our republic —it is a ship with towering canvas spread, sweeping before the prosperous gale over a foaming and sparkling sea; it is a lightning train darting with awful speed along the edge of dizzy abysses and across bridges that quiver over unsounded gulfs. Because we are Americans, we have no peculiar charm, no magic spell, to stay the eternal laws. Our safety lies alone in cool self-possession, directing the forces of wind and wave and fire. If once the madness to which the excitement tends usurps control, the catastrophe is inevitable. And so deep is the conviction that sooner or later this madness must seize every republic that the most plausible suspicion of the per-manence of the American government is founded in the belief that party spirit cannot be restrained. It is indeed a master passion, but its control is the true conservatism of the republic and of happy human progress; and it is men made familiar by education with the history of its ghastly catastrophes, men with the proud courage of independence, who are to temper by lofty action, born of that knowl-edge, the ferocity of party spirit.

The first object of concerted political action is the highest welfare of the country. But the conditions of party association are such that the means are constantly and easily substituted for the end. The sophistry is subtle and seductive. Holding the ascendency of his party essential to the national welfare, the zealous partisan merges patriotism in party. He insists that not to sustain the party is to betray the country, and against all honest doubt and reasonable hesitation and reluctance he vehemently urges that quibbles of con-science must be sacrificed to the public good; that wise and practical men will not be squeamish; that every soldier in the army cannot indulge his own whims; and that if the majority may justly prevail in determining the government, it must not be questioned in the control of a party.

This spirit adds moral coercion to sophistry. It denounces as a traitor him who protests against party tyranny, and it makes un-flinching adherence to what is called regular party action the condition of the gratification of honorable political ambition. Because a man who sympathizes with the party aims refuses to vote for a thief, this spirit scorns him as a rat and a renegade. Because he holds to principle and law against party expediency and dictation, he is proclaimed as the betrayer of his country, justice, and humanity. Because he tranquilly insists upon deciding for himself when he must dissent from his party, he is reviled as a popinjay and a visionary fool. Seeking with honest purpose only the welfare of his country, the hot air around him hums with the cry of "the grand old party," "the traditions of the party," "loyalty to the party," "future of the party," "servant of the party;" and he sees and hears the gorged and portly money-changers in the temple usurping the very divinity of the God. Young hearts! be not dismayed. If ever any one of you shall be the man so denounced, do not forget that your own individual convictions are the whip of small cords which God has put into your hands to expel the blasphemers.

The same party spirit naturally denies the patriotism of its opponents. Identifying itself with the country, it regards all others as public enemies. This is substantially revolutionary politics. It is the condition of France, where, in its own words, the revolution is permanent. Instead of regarding the other party as legitimate opponents—in the English phrase, His Majesty's Opposition—lawfully seeking a different policy under the government, it decries that party as a conspiracy plotting the overthrow of the government itself. History is lurid with the wasting fires of this madness. We need not look to that of other lands. Our own is full of it. It is painful to turn to the opening years of the Union, and see how the great men whom we are taught to revere, and to whose fostering care the beginning of the republic was intrusted, fanned their hatred and suspicion of each other. Do not trust the flattering voices that whisper of a Golden Age behind us, and bemoan our own as a degenerate day. The castles of hope always shine along the horizon. Our fathers saw theirs where we are standing. We behold ours where our fathers stood. But pensive regret for the heroic past, like eager anticipation of the future, shows only that the vision of a loftier life forever allures the human soul. We think our fathers to have been wiser than we, and their day more enviable. But eighty years ago the Federalists abhorred their opponents as Jacobins, and thought Robespierre and Marat no worse than Washington's Secretary of State. Their opponents retorted that the Federalists were plotting to establish a monarchy by force of arms. The New England pulpit anathematized Tom Jefferson as an atheist and a satyr. Jefferson denounced John Jay as a rogue, and the chief newspaper of the opposition, on the morning that Washington retired from the Presidency, thanked God that the country was now rid of the man who was the source of all its misfortunes. There is no mire in which party spirit wallows to-day with which our fathers were not befouled; and how little sincere the vituperation was, how shallow a fury, appears when Jefferson and Adams had retired from public life. Then they corresponded placidly and familiarly, each at last conscious of the other's fervent patriotism; and when they died, they were lamented in common by those who in their names had flown at each other's throat, as the patriarchal Castor and Pollux of the pure age of our politics, now fixed as a constellation of hope in our heaven.

The same brutal spirit showed itself at the time of Andrew Johnson's impeachment. Impeachment is a proceeding to be instituted only for great public reasons, which should presumptively, command universal support. To prostitute the power of impeachment to a mere party purpose would readily lead to the reversal of the result of an election. But it was made a party measure. The party was to be whipped into its support; and when certain senators broke the party yoke upon their necks, and voted according to their convictions, as honorable men always will whether the party whips like it or not, one of the whippers-in exclaimed of a patriotism, the struggle of obedience to which cost one senator, at least, his life, "If there is anything worse than the treachery, it is the cant which pretends that it is the result of conscientious conviction; the pretence of a conscience is quite unbearable." This was the very acridity of bigotry, which in other times and countries raised the cruel tribunal of the Inquisition and burned opponents for the glory of God. The party madness that dictated these words, and the sympathy that approved them, were treason not alone to the country, but to well-ordered human society. Murder may destroy great statesmen, but corruption makes great States impossible, and this was an attempt at the most insidious corruption. The man who attempts to terrify a senator of the United States into casting a dishonest vote, by stigmatizing him as a hypocrite and devoting him to party hatred, is only a more plausible rascal than his opponent who gives Pat O'Flanagan a fraudulent naturalization paper or buys his vote with a dollar or a glass of whiskey. Whatever the offences of the President may have been, they were as nothing when compared with the party spirit which declared that it was tired of the intolerable cant of honesty. So the sneering Cavalier was tired of the cant of the Puritan conscience; but the conscience of which plumed Injustice and coroneted Privilege were tired has been for three centuries the invincible body-guard of civil and religious liberty.

Gentlemen, how dire a calamity the same party spirit was preparing for the country within a few months we can now perceive with amazement and with hearty thanksgiving for a great deliverance. The ordeal of last winter was the severest strain ever yet applied to republican institutions. It was a mortal strain along the very fibre of our system. It was not a collision of sections, nor a conflict of principles of civilization. It was a supreme and triumphant test of American patroitism. Greater than the declaration of independence by colonies hopelessly alienated from the crown and already in arms; greater than emancipation, as a military expedient, amid the throes of civil war, was the peaceful and reasonable consent of two vast parties—in a crisis plainly foreseen and criminally neglected, a crisis in which each party asserted its solution to be indisputable—to devise a lawful settlement of the tremendous contest, a settlement which, through furious storms of disappointment and rage, has been religiously respected. We are told that our politics are mean —that already, in its hundredth year, the decadence of the American republic appears and the hope of the world is clouded. But tell me, scholars, in what high hour of Greece, when, as De Witt Clinton declared, "the herb-woman of Athens could criticise the phraseology of Demosthenes, and the meanest artisan could pronounce judgement on the works of Apelles and Phidias," or at what proud epoch of imperial Rome, or millennial moment of the fierce Italian republics, was ever so momentous a party difference so wisely, so peacefully, so humanely composed? Had the sophistry of party prevailed; had each side resolved that not to insist upon its own claim at every hazard was what the mad party spirit of each side declared it to be—a pusillanimous surrender; had the spirit of Marius mastered one party and that of Sylla the other, this waving valley of the Mohawk would not to-day murmur with the music of industry, these tranquil voices of scholars blending with its happy harvest-song; it would have smoked and roared with fraternal war, and this shuddering river would have run red through desolated meadows and by burning homes.

It is because these consequences are familiar to the knowledge of educated and thoughtful men that such men are constantly to assuage this party fire and to take care that party is always subordinated to patriotism. Perfect party discipline is the most dangerous weapon of party spirit, for it is the abdication of the individual judgment; it is the application to political parties of the Jesuit principle of implicit obedience.

It is for you to help break this withering spell. It is for you to assert the independence and the dignity of the individual citizen, and to prove that party was made for the voter, not the voter for party. When you are angrily told that if you erect your personal whim against the regular party behest, you make representative government impossible by refusing to accept its conditions, hold fast by your own conscience and let the party go. There is not an American merchant who would send a ship to sea under the command of Captain Kidd, however skilful a sailor he might be. Why should he vote to send Captain Kidd to the legislature or to put him in command of the ship of state because his party directs? The party which to-day nominates Captain Kidd will to-morrow nominate Judas Iscariot, and to-morrow, as to-day, party spirit will spurn you as a traitor for refusing to sell your master. "I tell you," said an ardent and well-meaning partisan, speaking of a closely contested election in another State—"I tell you it is a nasty State, and I hope we have done nasty work enough to carry it." But if your

State has been carried by nasty means this year, success will require nastier next year, and the nastiest means will always carry it. The party may win, but the State will have been lost, for there are successes which are failures. When a man is sitting upon the bough of a tree and diligently sawing it off between himself and the trunk, he may succeed, but his success will break his neck.

The remedy for the constant excess of party spirit lies, and lies alone, in the courageous independence of the individual citizen. The only way, for instance, to procure the party nomination of good men, is for every self-respecting voter to refuse to vote for bad men. In the mediaeval theology the devils feared nothing so much as the drop of holy water and the sign of the cross, by which they were exorcised. The evil spirits of party fear nothing so much as bolting and scratching. *In hoc signo vinces.* If a farmer would reap a good crop, he scratches the weeds out of his field. If we would have good men upon the ticket, we must scratch bad men off. If the scratching breaks down the party, let it break; for the success of the party by such means would break down the country. The evil spirits must be taught by means that they can understand. "Them fellers," said the captain of a canal-boat of his men—"them fellers never think you mean a thing until you kick 'em. They feel that, and understand."

It is especially necessary for us to perceive the vital relation of individual courage and character to the common welfare, because ours is a government of public opinion, and public opinion is but the aggregate of individual thought. We have the awful responsibility as a community of doing what we choose, and it is of the last importance that we choose to do what is wise and right. In the early days of the antislavery agitation a meeting was called at Faneuil Hall, in Boston, which a good-natured mob of sailors was hired to suppress. They took possession of the floor and danced breakdowns and shouted choruses and refused to hear any of the orators upon the platform. The most eloquent pleaded with them in vain. They were urged by the memories of the Cradle of Liberty, for the honor of Massachusetts, for their own honor as Boston boys, to respect liberty of speech. But they still laughed and sang and danced, and were proof aganist every appeal. At last a man suddenly arose from among themselves and began to speak. Struck by his tone and quaint appearance, and with the thought that he might be one of themselves, the mob became suddenly still. "Well, fellow-citizens," he said, "I wouldn't be quiet if I didn't want to." The words were greeted with a roar of delight from the mob, which supposed it had found its champion, and the applause was unceasing for five minutes, during which the strange orator tranquilly awaited his chance to continue. The wish to hear more hushed the tumult, and when the hall was still he resumed, "No, I certainly wouldn't stop if I hadn't a mind to; but then, if I were you, I *would* have a mind to!" The oddity of the remark and the earnestness of the tone held the crowd silent, and the speaker continued: "Not because this is Faneuil Hall, nor for the honor of Massachusetts, nor because you are Boston boys, but because you are men, and because honorable and generous men always love fair play." The mob was conquered. Free speech and fair play were secured. Public opinion can do what it has a mind to in this country. If it be debased and demoralized, it is the most odious of tyrants. It is Nero and Caligula multiplied by millions. Can there then be a more stringent public duty for every man—and the greater the intelligence the greater the duty—than to take care, by all the influence he can command, that the country, the majority, public opinion, shall have a mind to do only what is just and pure and humane?

Gentlemen, leaving this college to take your part in the discharge of the duties of American citizenship, every sign encourages and inspires. The year that is now ending, the year that opens the second century of our history, has furnished the supreme proof that in a country of rigorous party division the purest patriotism exists. That and that only is the pledge of a prosperous future. No mere party fervor or party fidelity or party discipline could fully restore a country torn and distracted by the fierce debate of a century and the convulsions of civil war; nothing less than a patriotism all-embracing as the summer air could heal a wound so wide. I know—no man better—how hard it is for earnest men to separate their country from their party, or their religion from their sect. But nevertheless the welfare of the country is dearer than the mere victory of party, as truth is more precious than the interest of any sect. You will hear this patriotism scorned as an impracticable theory, as the dream of a cloister, as the whim of a fool. But such was the folly of the Spartan Leonidas, staying with his three hundred the Persian horde and teaching Greece the self-reliance that saved her. Such was the folly of the Swiss Arnold von Winkelried, gathering into his own breast the host of Austrian spears, making his dead body the bridge of victory for his countrymen. Such was the folly of the American Nathan Hale, gladly risking the seeming disgrace of his name, and grieving that he had but one life to give for his country. Such are the beaconlights of a pure patriotism that burn forever in men's memories and answer each other through the illuminated ages. And of the same grandeur, in less heroic and poetic form, was the patriotism of Sir Robert Peel in recent history. He was the leader of a great party and the prime minister of England. The character and necessity of party were as plain to him as to any man. But when he saw that the national welfare demanded the repeal of the corn-laws which he had always supported, he did not quail. Amply avowing the error of a life and the duty of avowing it—foreseeing the probable overthrow of his party and the bitter execration that must fall upon him, he tranquilly did his duty. With the eyes of England fixed upon him in mingled amazement, admiration, and indignation, he rose in the House of Commons to perform as great a service as any English statesman ever performed for his country, and in closing his last speech in favor of the repeal, describing the consequences that its mere prospect had produced, he loftily exclaimed: "Where there was dissatisfaction, I see contentment; where there was turbulence, I see there is peace; where there was disloyalty, I see there is loyalty. I see a disposition to confide in you, and not to agitate questions that are the foundations of your institutions." When all was over, when he had left office, when his party was out of power and the fury of party execration against him was spent, his position was greater and nobler than it had ever been. Cobden said of him, "Sir Robert Peel has lost office, but he has gained a country;" and Lord Dalling said of him, what may truly be said of Washington, "Above all parties, himself a party, he had trained his own mind into a disinterested sympathy with the intelligence of his country."

A public spirit so lofty is not confined to other ages and lands. You are conscious of its stirrings in your souls. It calls you to courageous service, and I am here to bid you obey the call. Such patriotism may be ours. Let it be your parting vow that it shall be yours. Bolingbroke described a patriot king in England; I can imagine a patriot president in America. I can see him indeed the choice of a party, and called to administer the government when sectional jealousy is fiercest and party passion most inflamed. I can imagine him seeing clearly what justice and humanity, the national law and the national welfare require him to do, and resolved to do it. I can imagine him patiently enduring not only the mad cry of party hate, the taunt of "recreant" and "traitor," of "renegade" and "coward," but what is harder to bear, the amazement, the doubt, the grief, the denunciation, of those as sincerely devoted as he to the common welfare. I can imagine him pushing firmly on, trusting the heart, the intelligence, the conscience of his countrymen, healing angry wounds, correcting misunderstandings, planting justice on surer foundations, and, whether his party rise or fall, lifting his country heavenward to a more perfect union, prosperity, and peace. This is the spirit of a patriotism that girds the commonwealth with the resistless splendor of the moral law—the invulnerable panoply of States, the celestial secret of a great nation and a happy people.

Carl Schurz

GENERAL AMNESTY

❡ CARL SCHURZ (1829-1906) was born near Cologne in Germany and was educated at the University of Bonn. He took an active part in the revolutionary movement of 1848-49. When it failed, he was arrested and imprisoned but escaped and fled to Switzerland. He returned to Germany for a daring rescue of one of his professors and escaped with him to England. In 1852 he came to America. Four years later he bought a farm in Wisconsin. He quickly mastered the English language and made many speeches in both English and German for the anti-slavery cause and in support of the new Republican party and the election of Lincoln. In 1861 he was appointed minister to Spain, but returned after a few months and was appointed a brigadier-general of volunteers; he served with distinction in many important battles of the Civil War. In 1867 he settled in St. Louis as editor of a German-language daily. He was elected temporary chairman of the Republican convention that nominated General Grant for the presidency and drew up the party's resolution for removing disqualifications of the late rebels. He was elected United States senator from Missouri and became a vigorous advocate of civil service reform and an opponent of corruption in government. He was a leader of the liberal Republican group that opposed Grant's second term. He supported Hayes for the presidency and in 1877 entered his cabinet as Secretary of the Interior. The remainder of his distinguished career was spent in journalism and literary work.

His speech on "General Amnesty" was delivered in the Senate on January 30, 1872. It concerned a bill to remove political disabilities imposed by the Fourteenth Amendment from certain persons who had aided the rebellion.

M R. PRESIDENT:—When this debate commenced before the holidays, I refrained from taking part in it, and from expressing my opinions on some of the provisions of the bill now before us, hoping as I did that the measure could be passed without difficulty, and that a great many of those who now labor under political disabilities would be immediately relieved. This expectation was disappointed. An amendment to the bill was adopted. It will have to go back to the House of Representatives now unless by some parliamentary means we get rid of the amendment, and there being no inducement left to waive what criticism we might feel inclined to bring forward, we may consider the whole question open.

I beg leave to say that I am in favor of general, or as this word is considered more expressive, universal amnesty, believing as I do that the reasons which make it desirable that there should be amnesty granted at all, make it also desirable that the amnesty should be universal. The Senator from South Carolina (MR. SAWYER) has already given notice that he will move to strike out the exceptions from the operation of this act of relief for which the bill provides. If he had not declared his intention to that effect, I would do so. In any event, whenever he offers his amendment I shall most heartily support it.

In the course of this debate we have listened to some Senators, as they conjured up before our eyes once more all the horrors of the rebellion, the wickedness of its conception, how terrible its incidents were and how harrowing its consequences. Sir, I admit it all; I will not combat the correctness of the picture; and yet, if I differ with the gentlemen who drew it, it is because, had the conception of the rebellion been still more wicked, had its incidents been still more terrible, its consequences still more harrowing, I could not permit myself to forget that in dealing with the question now before us we have to deal not alone with the past, but with the present and future interests of this Republic.

What do we want to accomplish as good citizens and patriots? Do we mean only to inflict upon late rebels pain, degradation, mortification, annoyance, for its own sake, to torture their feelings

without any ulterior purpose? Certainly such a spirit could not by
any possibility animate high-minded men. I presume, therefore, that
those who still favor the continuance of some of the disabilities imposed by the fourteenth amendment, do so because they have some
higher object of public usefulness in view, an object of public usefulness sufficient to justify, in their minds at least, the denial of
rights to others which we ourselves enjoy.

What can those objects of public usefulness be? Let me assume
that, if we differ as to the means to be employed, we are agreed as
to the supreme end and aim to be reached. That end and aim of our
endeavors can be no other than to secure to all the States the blessings of good and free government and the highest degree of prosperity and well-being they can attain, and to revive in all citizens
of this Republic that love for the Union and its institutions, and
that inspiring consciousness of a common nationality, which, after
all, must bind all Americans together.

What are the best means for the attainment of that end? This,
sir, as I conceive it, is the only legitimate question we have to decide.
Certainly all will agree that this end is far from having been attained
so far. Look at the Southern States as they stand before us today.
Some are in a condition bordering upon anarchy, not only on account of the social disorders which are occurring there, or the in-
efficiency of their local governments in securing the enforcement of
the laws; but you will find in many of them fearful corruption
pervading the whole political organization; a combination of rascality and ignorance wielding official power; their finances deranged
by profligate practices; their credit ruined; bankruptcy staring them
in the face; their industries staggering under a fearful load of
taxation; their property-holders and capitalists paralyzed by a
feeling of insecurity and distrust almost amounting to despair. Sir,
let us not try to disguise these facts, for the world knows them to
be so, and knows it but too well.

What are the causes that have contributed to bring about this
distressing condition? I admit that great civil wars resulting in
such vast social transformations as the sudden abolition of slavery
are calculated to produce similar results; but it might be presumed

that a recuperative power such as this country possesses might during the time which has elapsed since the close of the war at least have very materially alleviated many of the consequences of that revulsion, had a wise policy been followed.

Was the policy we followed wise? Was it calculated to promote the great purposes we are endeavoring to serve? Let us see. At the close of the war we had to establish and secure free labor and the rights of the emancipated class. To that end we had to disarm those who could have prevented this, and we had to give the power of self-protection to those who needed it. For this reason temporary restrictions were imposed upon the late rebels, and we gave the right of suffrage to the colored people. Until the latter were enabled to protect themselves, political disabilities even more extensive than those which now exist, rested upon the plea of eminent political necessity. I would be the last man to conceal that I thought so then, and I think now there was very good reason for it.

But, sir, when the enfranchisement of the colored people was secured, when they had obtained the political means to protect themselves, then another problem began to loom up. It was not only to find new guaranties for the rights of the colored people, but it was to secure good and honest government for all. Let us not underestimate the importance of that problem, for in a great measure it includes the solution of the other. Certainly, nothing could have been better calculated to remove the prevailing discontent concerning the changes that had taken place, and to reconcile men's minds to the new order of things, than the tangible proof that that new order of things was practically working well; that it could produce a wise and economical administration of public affairs, and that it would promote general prosperity, thus healing the wounds of the past and opening to all the prospect of a future of material well-being and contentment. And, on the other hand, nothing could have been more calculated to impede a general, hearty and honest acceptance of the new order of things by the late rebel population than just those failures of public administration which involve the people in material embarrassments and so seriously disturb their comfort. In fact, good, honest and successful government in the Southern States would in its moral effects, in the long run, have exerted a far more beneficial influence than all your penal legislation, while your penal legislation will fail in its desired effects if we fail in establishing in the Southern States an honest and successful administration of the public business.

Now, what happened in the South? It is a well-known fact that the more intelligent classes of Southern society almost uniformly identified themselves with the rebellion; and by our system of political disabilities just those classes were excluded from the management of political affairs. That they could not be trusted with the business of introducing into living practice the results of the war, to establish true free labor and to protect the rights of the emancipated slaves, is true; I willingly admit it. But when those results and rights were constitutionally secured there were other things to be done. Just at that period when the Southern States lay prostrated and exhausted at our feet, when the destructive besom of war had swept over them and left nothing but desolation and ruin in its track, when their material interests were to be built up again with care and foresight—just then the public business demanded, more than ordinarily, the cooperation of all the intelligence and all the political experience that could be mustered in the Southern States. But just then a large portion of that intelligence and experience was excluded from the management of public affairs by political disabilities, and the controlling power in those States rested in a great measure in the hands of those who had but recently been slaves and just emerged from that condition, and in the hands of others who had sometimes honestly, sometimes by crooked means and for sinister purposes, found a way to their confidence.

This was the state of things as it then existed. Nothing could be farther from my intention than to cast a slur upon the character of the colored people of the South. In fact, their conduct immediately after that great event which struck the shackles of slavery from their limbs was above praise. Look into the history of the world, and you will find that almost every similar act of emancipation, the abolition of serfdom, for instance, was uniformly accompanied by atrocious outbreaks of a revengeful spirit; by the slaughter of nobles and their families, illumined by the glare of their burning castles. Not so here. While all the horrors of San Domingo had been predicted as certain to follow upon emancipation, scarcely a single act of revenge for injuries suffered or for misery endured has darkened the record of the emancipated bondmen of America. And thus their example stands unrivalled in history, and they, as well as the whole American people, may well be proud of it. Certainly, the Southern people should never cease to remember and appreciate it.

But while the colored people of the South thus earned our admiration and gratitude, I ask you in all candor, could they be reasonably expected, when, just after having emerged from a condition of slavery, they were invested with political rights and privileges, to step into the political arena as men armed with the intelligence and experience necessary for the management of public affairs and for the solution of problems made doubly intricate by the disasters which had desolated the Southern country? Could they reasonably be expected to manage the business of public administration, involving to so great an extent the financial interests and the material well-being of the people, and surrounded by difficulties of such fearful perplexity, with the wisdom and skill required by the exigencies of the situation? That as a class they were ignorant and inexperienced and lacked a just conception of public interests, was certainly not their fault; for those who have studied the history of the world know but too well that slavery and oppression are very bad political schools. But the stubborn fact remains that they *were* ignorant and inexperienced; that the public business *was* an unknown world to them, and that in spite of the best intentions they *were* easily misled, not infrequently by the most reckless rascality which had found a way to their confidence. Thus their political rights and privileges were undoubtedly well calculated, and even necessary, to protect their rights as free laborers and citizens; but they were not well calculated to secure a successful administration of other public interests.

I do not blame the colored people for it; still less do I say that for this reason their political rights and privileges should have been denied them. Nay, sir, I deemed it necessary then, and I now reaffirm that opinion, that they should possess those rights and privileges for the permanent establishment of the logical and legitimate results of the war and the protection of their new position in society. But, while never losing sight of this necessity, I do say that the inevitable consequence of the admission of so large an uneducated and inexperienced class to political power, as to the probable mismanagement of the material interests of the social body, should at least have been mitigated by a counterbalancing policy. When ignorance and inexperience were admitted to so large an influence upon public affairs, intelligence ought no longer to so large an extent to have been excluded. In other words, when universal suffrage was granted to secure the equal rights of all, universal amnesty ought to have been granted to make all the resources of political intelligence and experience available for the promotion of the welfare of all.

But what did we do? To the uneducated and inexperienced classes—uneducated and inexperienced, I repeat, entirely without their fault—we opened the road to power; and, at the same time, we condemned a large proportion of the intelligence of those States, of the property-holding, the industrial, the professional, the tax-paying interest, to a worse than passive attitude. We made it, as it were, easy for rascals who had gone South in quest of profitable adventure to gain the control of masses so easily misled, by permitting them to appear as the exponents and representatives of the National power and of our policy; and at the same time we branded a large number of men of intelligence, and many of them of personal integrity, whose material interests were so largely involved in honest government, and many of whom would have cooperated in managing the public business with care and foresight—we branded them, I say, as outcasts, telling them that they ought not to be suffered to exercise any influence upon the management of the public business, and that it would be unwarrantable presumption in them to attempt it.

I ask you, sir, could such things fail to contribute to the results we read to-day in the political corruption and demoralization, and in the financial ruin of some of the Southern States? These results are now before us. The mistaken policy may have been pardonable when these consequences were still a matter of conjecture and speculation; but what excuse have we now for continuing it when those results are clear before our eyes, beyond the reach of contradiction?

These considerations would seem to apply more particularly to those Southern States in which the colored element constitutes a very large proportion of the voting body. There is another which applies to all.

When the rebellion stood in arms against us, we fought and overcame force by force. That was right. When the results of the war were first to be established and fixed, we met the resistance they encountered, with that power which the fortunes of war and the revolutionary character of the situation had placed at our disposal. The feelings and prejudices which then stood in our way had under such circumstances but little, if any, claim to our consideration. But when the problem presented itself of securing the permanency, the peaceable development, the successful working of the new institutions we had introduced into our political organism, we had as wise men to take into careful calculation the moral forces we had to deal with; for let us not indulge in any delusion about this: what is to be permanent in a republic like this must be supported by public opinion, it must rest at least upon the willing acquiescence of a large and firm majority of the people.

The introduction of the colored people, the late slaves, into the body-politic as voters pointedly affronted the traditional prejudices prevailing among the Southern whites. What should we care about those prejudices? In war, nothing. After the close of the war, in the settlement of peace, not enough to deter us from doing what was right and necessary; and yet, still enough to take them into account when considering the manner in which right and necessity were to be served. Statesmen will care about popular prejudices as physicians will care about the diseased condition of their patients, which they want to ameliorate. Would it not have been wise for us, looking at those prejudices as a morbid condition of the Southern mind, to mitigate, to assuage, to disarm them by prudent measures and thus to weaken their evil influence? We desired the Southern whites to accept in good faith universal suffrage, to recognize the political rights of the colored man and to protect him in their exercise. Was not that our sincere desire? But if it was, would it not have been wise to remove as much as possible the obstacles that stood in the way of that consummation? But what did we do? When we raised the colored people to the rights of active citizenship and opened to them all the privileges of eligibility, we excluded from those privileges a large and influential class of whites; in other words, we lifted the late slave, uneducated and inexperienced as he was,—I repeat, without his fault,—not merely to the level of the late master class, but even above it. We asked certain white men to recognize the colored man in a political status not only as high but even higher than their own. We might say that under the circumstances we had a perfect right to do that, and I will not dispute it; but I ask you most earnestly, sir, was it wise to do it? If you desired the white man to accept and recognize the political equality of the black, was it wise to embitter and to exasperate his spirit with the stinging stigma of his own inferiority? Was it wise to withhold from him privileges in the enjoyment of which he was to protect the late slave? This was not assuaging, disarming prejudice; this was rather inciting, it was exasperating it. American statesmen will understand and appreciate human nature as it has developed itself under the influence of free institutions. We know that if we want any class of people to overcome their prejudices in respecting the political rights and privileges of any other class, the very first thing we have to do is to accord the same rights and privileges to them. No American was ever inclined to recognize in others public rights and privileges from which he himself was excluded; and for aught I know, in this very feeling, although it may take an objectionable form, we find one of the safeguards of popular liberty.

You tell me that the late rebels had deserved all this in the way of punishment. Granting that, I beg leave to suggest that this is not the question. The question is, what were the means best calculated to overcome the difficulties standing in the way of a willing and universal recognition of the new rights and privileges of the emancipated class? What were the means to overcome the hostile influences impeding the development of the harmony of society in its new order? I am far from asserting that, had no disabilities existed, universal suffrage would have been received by the Southern whites with universal favor. No, sir, most probably it would not; but I do assert that the existence of disabilities, which put so large and influential a class of whites in point of political privileges below the colored people, could not fail to inflame those prejudices which stood in the way of a general and honest acceptance of the new order of things. They increased instead of diminishing the dangers and difficulties surrounding the emancipated class. And nobody felt that more keenly than the colored people of the South themselves. To their honor be it said, following a just instinct, they were among the very first, not only in the South but all over the country, in entreating Congress to remove those odious discriminations which put in jeopardy their own rights by making them greater than those of others. From the colored people themselves, it seems, we have in this respect received a lesson in statesmanship.

Well, then, what policy does common-sense suggest to us now? If we sincerely desire to give to the Southern States good and honest government, material prosperity and measurable contentment, as far at least as we can contribute to that end; if we really desire to weaken and disarm those prejudices and resentments which still disturb the harmony of society, will it not be wise, will it not be necessary, will it not be our duty to show that we are in no sense the allies and abettors of those who use their political power to plunder their fellow-citizens, and that we do not mean to keep one class of people in unnecessary degradation by withholding from them rights and privileges which all others enjoy? Seeing the mischief which the system of disabilities is accomplishing, is it not time that there should be at least an end of it? Or is there any good it can possibly do to make up for the harm it has already wrought and is still working?

Look at it. Do these disabilities serve in any way to protect anybody in his rights or in his liberty or in his property or in his life? Does the fact that some men are excluded from office, in any sense or measure, make others more secure in their lives or in their rights? Can anybody tell me how? Or do they, perhaps, prevent even those who are excluded from official position from doing mischief if they are mischievously inclined? Does the exclusion from office, does any feature of your system of political disabilities, take the revolver or the bowie-knife or the scourge from the hands of any one who wishes to use it? Does it destroy the influence of the more intelligent upon society, if they mean to use that influence for mischievous purposes?

We hear the Ku-Klux outrages spoken of as a reason why political disabilities should not be removed. Did not these very same Ku-Klux outrages happen while disabilities were in existence? Is it not clear, then, that the existence of political disabilities did not prevent them? No, sir, if political disabilities have any practical effect, it is, while not in any degree diminishing the power of the evil-disposed for mischief, to incite and sharpen their mischievous inclination by increasing their discontent with the condition they live in.

It must be clear to every impartial observer that, were ever so many of those who are now disqualified, put in office, they never could do with their official power as much mischief as the mere fact of the existence of the system of political disabilities with its inevitable consequences is doing to-day. The scandals of misgovernment in the South which we complain of, I admit, were not the first and original cause of the Ku-Klux outrages. But every candid observer will also have to admit that they did serve to keep the Ku-Klux spirit alive. Without such incitement it might gradually by this time, to a great extent at least, have spent itself. And now, if the scandals of misgovernment were, partly at least, owing to the exclusion of so large a portion of the intelligence and experience of the South from the active management of affairs, must it not be clear that a measure which will tend to remedy this evil, may also tend to reduce the causes which still disturb the peace and harmony of society?

We accuse the Southern whites of having missed their chance of gaining the confidence of the emancipated class when, by a fairly demonstrated purpose of recognizing and protecting them in their rights, they might have acquired upon them a salutary influence. That accusation is by no means unjust; but must we not admit, also, that by excluding them from their political rights and privileges we put the damper of most serious discouragement upon the good intentions which might have grown up among them? Let us place ourselves in their situation, and then I ask you, how many of us would, under the same circumstances, have risen above the ordinary impulses of human nature to exert a salutary influence in defiance of our own prejudices, being so pointedly told every day that it was not the business of those laboring under political disabilities to meddle with public affairs at all? And thus, in whatever direction you may turn your eyes, you look in vain for any practical good your political disabilities might possibly accomplish. You find nothing, absolutely nothing, in their practical effects but the aggravation of evils already existing and the prevention of a salutary development.

Is it not the part of wise men, sir, to acknowledge the failure of a policy like this in order to remedy it, especially since every candid mind must recognize that by continuing the mistake, absolutely no practical good can be subserved?

But I am told that the system of disabilities must be maintained for a certain moral effect. The Senator from Indiana (Mr. Morton) took great pains to inform us that it is absolutely necessary to exclude somebody from office in order to demonstrate our disapprobation of the crime of rebellion. Methinks the American people have signified their disapprobation of the crime of rebellion in a far more pointed manner. They sent against the rebellion a million armed men. We fought and conquered the armies of the rebels; we carried desolation into their land; we swept out of existence that system of slavery which was the soul of their offense and was to be the corner-stone of their new empire. If that was not signifying our disapprobation of the crime of rebellion, then I humbly submit, your system of political disabilities, only excluding some persons from office, will scarcely do it.

I remember, also, to have heard the argument that under all circumstances the law must be vindicated. What law in this case? If any law is meant, it must be the law imposing the penalty of death upon the crime of treason. Well, if at the close of the war we had assumed the stern and bloody virtue of the ancient Roman, and had proclaimed that he who raises his hand against this Republic must surely die, then we might have claimed for ourselves at least the merit of logical consistency. We might have thought that by erecting a row of gallows stretching from the Potomac to the Rio Grande, and by making a terrbile example of all those who had proved faithless to their allegiance, we would strike terror into the hearts of this and coming generations, to make them tremble at the mere thought of treasonable undertakings. That we might have done. Why did we not? Because the American people instinctively recoiled from the idea; because every wise man remembered that where insurrections are punished and avenged with the bloodiest hands, there insurrections do most frequently occur; witness France and Spain and the southern part of this hemisphere; that there is a fascination in bloody reckonings which allures instead of repelling— a fascination like that of the serpent's eye, which irresistibly draws on its victims. The American people recoiled from it, because they felt and knew that the civilization of the nineteenth century has for such evils a better medicine than blood.

Thus, sir, the penalty of treason as provided for by law remained a dead letter on the statute-book, and we instinctively adopted a generous policy, adding fresh luster to the glory of the American name by doing so. And now you would speak of vindicating the law against treason, which demands death, by merely excluding a number of persons from eligibility to office! Do you not see that, as a vindication of the law against treason, as an act of punishment, the system of disabilities sinks down to the level of a ridiculous mockery? If you want your system of disabilities to appear at all in a respectable light, then, in the name of common-sense, do not call it a punishment for treason. Standing there, as it does, stripped of all the justification it once derived from political necessity, it would appear only as the evidence of an impotent desire to be severe without the courage to carry it out.

But having once adopted the policy of generosity, the only question for us is how to make that policy most fruitful. The answer is:

We shall make the policy of generosity most fruitful by making it most complete.

The Senator from Connecticut (Mr. Buckingham), whom I am so unfortunate as not to see in his seat to-day, when he opened the debate, endeavored to fortify his theory by an illustration borrowed from the Old Testament, and I am willing to take that illustration off his hands. He asked: "If Absalom had lived after his treason and had been excluded from his father's table, would he have had a just reason to complain of an unjust deprivation of rights?" It seems to me that story of Absalom contains a most excellent lesson, which the Senate of the United States ought to read correctly. For the killing of his brother, Absalom had lived in banishment from which the King, his father, permitted him to return; but the wayward son was but half pardoned, for he was not permitted to see his father's face. And it was for that reason, and then, that he went among the people to seduce them into a rebellion against his royal father's authority. Had he survived that rebellion, King David, as a prudent statesman, would either have killed his son Absalom or he would have admitted him to his table, in order to make him a good son again by unstinted fatherly love. But he would certainly not have permitted his son Absalom to run at large, capable of doing mischief, and at the same time by small measures of degradation inciting him to do it. And that is just the policy we have followed. We have permitted the late rebels to run at large, capable of doing mischief, and then by small measures of degradation, utterly useless for any good purpose, we incited them to do it. Looking at your political disabilities with an impartial eye, you will find that, as a measure of punishment, they did not go far enough; as a measure of policy they went much too far. We were far too generous to subjugate the hearts of our late enemies by terror; and we mixed our generosity with just enough of bitterness to prevent it from bearing its full fruit. I repeat, we can make the policy of generosity most fruitful only by making it most complete. What objection, then, can stand against this consideration of public good?

You tell me that many of the late rebels do not deserve a full restoration of their rights. That may be so; I do not deny it; but yet, sir, if many of them do not deserve it, is it not a far more important consideration how much the welfare of the country will be promoted by it?

I am told that many of the late rebels, if we volunteer a pardon to them, would not appreciate it. I do not deny this; it may be so, for the race of fools, unfortunately, is not all extinct yet; but if they do not appreciate it, shall we have no reason to appreciate the great good which by this measure of generosity will be conferred upon the whole land?

Some Senator, referring to a defaulting paymaster who experienced the whole rigor of the law, asked us, "When a poor defaulter is punished, shall a rebel go free? Is embezzlement a greater crime than treason?" No, sir, it is not; but again I repeat, that is not the question. The question is whether a general amnesty to rebels is not far more urgently demanded by the public interest than a general pardon for thieves. Whatever may be said of the greatness and the heinous character of the crime of rebellion, a single glance at the history of the world and at the practice of other nations will convince you, that in all civilized countries the measure of punishment to be visited on those guilty of that crime is almost uniformly treated as a question of great policy and almost never as a question of strict justice. And why is this? Why is it that a thief, although pardoned, will never again be regarded as an untainted member of society, while a pardoned rebel may still rise to the highest honors of the State, and sometimes even gain the sincere and general esteem and confidence of his countrymen? Because a broad line of distinction is drawn between a violation of law in which political opinion is the controlling element (however erroneous, nay however revolting that opinion may be, and however disastrous the consequences of the act) and those infamous crimes of which moral depravity is the principal ingredient; and because even the most disastrous political conflicts may be composed for the common good by a conciliatory process, while the infamous crime always calls for a strictly penal correction. You may call this just or not, but such is the public opinion of the civilized world, and you find it in every civilized country.

Look at the nations around us. In the Parliament of Germany how many men are there sitting who were once what you would call fugitives from justice, exiles on account of their revolutionary acts, now admitted to the great council of the nation in the fullness of their rights and privileges—and, mark you, without having been asked to abjure the opinions they formerly held, for at the present moment most of them still belong to the Liberal opposition. Look at Austria, where Count Andrassy, a man who, in 1849, was condemned to the gallows as a rebel, at this moment stands at the head of the imperial Ministry; and those who know the history of that country are fully aware that the policy of which that amnesty was a part, which opened to Count Andrassy the road to power, has attached Hungary more closely than ever to the Austrian Crown, from which a narrow-minded policy of severity would have driven her.

Now, sir, ought we not to profit by the wisdom of such examples? It may be said that other Governments were far more rigorous in their first repressive measures, and that they put off the grant of a general amnesty much longer after suppressing an insurrection than we are required to do. So they did; but is not this the great Republic of the new world which marches in the very vanguard of modern civilization, and which, when an example of wisdom is set by other nations, should not only rise to its level, but far above it?

It seems now to be generally admitted that the time has come for a more comprehensive removal of political disabilities than has so far been granted. If that sentiment be sincere, if you really do desire to accomplish the greatest possible good by this measure that can be done, I would ask you, what practical advantage do you expect to derive from the exclusions for which this bill provides? Look at them one after another.

First, all those are excluded who when the rebellion broke out were Members of Congress, and left their seats in these halls to join it. Why are these men to be excluded as a class? Because this class contains a number of prominent individuals, who, in the rebellion, became particularly conspicuous and obnoxious, and among them we find those whom we might designate as the original conspirators.

But these are few, and they might have been mentioned by name. Most of those, however, who left their seats in Congress to make common cause with the rebels were in no way more responsible for the rebellion than other prominent men at the South who do not fall under this exception. If we accept at all the argument that it will be well for the cause of good government and the material welfare of the South to readmit to the management of public affairs all the intelligence and political experience in those States, why, then, exclude as a class men who, having been Members of Congress, may be presumed to possess a higher degree of that intelligence and experience than the rest? If you want that article at all for good purposes, I ask you, do you not want as large a supply of that article as you can obtain?

Leaving aside the original conspirators, is there any reason in the world why those Members of Congress should be singled out from the numerous class of intelligent and prominent men who were or had been in office and had taken the same oath which is administered in these halls? Look at it. You do not propose to continue the disqualification of men who served this country as foreign Ministers, who left their important posts, betrayed the interests of this country in foreign lands to come back and join the rebellion; you do not propose to exclude from the benefit of this act those who sat upon the bench and doffed the judicial ermine to take part in the rebellion; and if such men are not to be disfranchised, why disfranchise the common run of the Congressmen, whose guilt is certainly not greater, if it be as great? Can you tell me? Is it wise even to incur the suspicion of making an exception merely for the sake of excluding somebody, when no possible good can be accomplished by it, and when you can thus only increase the number of men incited to discontent and mischief by small and unnecessary degradation?

And now as to the original conspirators, what has become of them? Some of them are dead; and as to those who are still living, I ask you, sir, are they not dead also? Look at Jefferson Davis himself. What if you exclude even him—and certainly our feelings would naturally impel us to do so; but let our reason speak—what if you exclude even him? Would you not give him an importance which

otherwise he never would possess, by making people believe that
you are even occupying your minds enough with him to make him
an exception to an act of generous wisdom? Truly, to refrain from
making an act of amnesty general on account of the original conspirators, candidly speaking, I would not consider worth while. I
would not leave them the pitiable distinction of not being pardoned.
Your very generosity will be to them the source of the bitterest disappointment. As long as they are excluded, they may still find some
satisfaction in the delusion of being considered men of dangerous
importance. Their very disabilities they look upon to-day as a
recognition of their power. They may still make themselves and
others believe that, were the Southern people only left free in their
choice, they would eagerly raise them again to the highest honors.

But you relieve them of their exclusion, and they will at once become conscious of their nothingness, a nothingness most glaringly
conspicuous then, for you will have drawn away the veil that has
concealed it. I suspect that gentlemen on the Democratic side of
the House, whom they would consider their political friends, would
be filled with dismay at the mere thought of their reappearance
among them. If there is anything that could prevent them from
voting for universal amnesty, it might be the fear, if they entertained
it at all, of seeing Jefferson Davis once more a Senator of the United
States.

But more than that: you relieve that class of persons, those old
misleaders, of their exclusion, and they will soon discover that the
people whom they once plunged into disaster and ruin have in the
meantime grown, if not as wise as they ought to be, certainly too
wise to put their destinies in the hands of the same men again. I
hope, therefore, you will not strip this measure of the merit of being
a general amnesty to spare the original plotters this most salutary
experience.

So much for the first exception. Now to the second. It excludes
from the benefit of this act all those who were officers of the Army
or of the Navy and then joined the rebellion. Why exclude that
class of persons? I have heard the reason very frequently stated
upon the floor of the Senate; it is because those men had been edu-

cated at the public expense, and their turning against the Government was therefore an act of peculiar faithlessness and black ingratitude. That might appear a very strong argument at first sight. But I ask you was it not one of the very first acts of this Administration to appoint one of the most prominent and conspicuous of that class to a very lucrative and respectable public office? I mean General Longstreet. He had obtained his military education at the expense of the American people. He was one of the wards, one of the pets of the American Republic, and then he turned against it as a rebel. Whatever of faithlessness, whatever of black ingratitude there is in such conduct, it was in his; and yet, in spite of all this, the President nominated him for an office, and your consent, Senators, made him a public dignitary. Why did you break the rule in his case? I will not say that you did it because he had become a Republican, for I am far from attributing any mere partisan motive to your action. No; you did it because his conduct after the close of hostilities had been that of a well-disposed and law-abiding citizen. Thus, then, the rule which you, Senators, have established for your own conduct is simply this: you will in the case of officers of the Army or the Navy waive the charge of peculiar faithlessness and ingratitude, if the persons in question after the war have become law-abiding and well-disposed citizens. Well, is it not a fact universally recognized, and I believe entirely uncontradicted, that of all classes of men connected with the rebellion there is not one whose conduct since the close of the war has been so unexceptionable, and in a great many instances so beneficial in its influence upon Southern society, as the officers of the Army and the Navy, expecially those who before the war had been members of our regular establishments? Why, then, except them from this act of amnesty? If you take subsequent good conduct into account at all, these men are the very last who, as a class, ought to be excluded. And would it not be well to encourage them in well-doing by a sign on our part that they are not to be looked upon as outcasts whose influence is not desired, even when they are inclined to use it for the promotion of the common welfare?

The third class excluded consists of those who were members of

State conventions, and in those State conventions voted for ordinances of secession. If we may judge from the words which fell from the lips of the Senator from Indiana, they were the objects of his particular displeasure. Why this? Here we have a large number of men of local standing who in some cases may have been leaders on a small scale, but most of whom were drawn into the whirl of the revolutionary movement just like the rest of the Southern population. If you accept the proposition that it will be well and wise to permit the intelligence of the country to participate in the management of the public business, the exclusion of just these people will appear especially inappropriate because their local influence might be made peculiarly beneficial; and if you exclude these persons, whose number is considerable, you tell just that class of people whose cooperation might be made most valuable, that their cooperation is not wanted, for the reason that, according to the meaning and intent of your system of disabilities, public affairs are no business of theirs. You object that they are more guilty than the rest. Suppose they are—and in many cases I am sure they are only apparently so—but if they were not guilty of any wrong, they would need no amnesty. Amnesty is made for those who bear a certain degree of guilt. Or would you indulge here in the solemn farce of giving pardon only to those who are presumably innocent? You grant your amnesty that it may bear good fruit; and if you do it for that purpose, then do not diminish the good fruit it may bear by leaving unplanted the most promising soil upon which it may grow.

A few words now about the second section of the bill before you, which imposes upon those who desire to have the benefit of amnesty the duty of taking, before some public officer, an oath to support the Constitution, that oath to be registered, the lists to be laid before Congress and to be preserved in the office of the Secretary of State. Sir, I ask you, can you or any one tell me what practical good is to be accomplished by a provision like this? You may say that the taking of another oath will do nobody any harm. Probably not; but can you tell me, in the name of common-sense, what harm in this case the taking of that oath will prevent? Or have we read the history of the world in vain, that we should not know yet, how little political oaths are worth to improve the morality of a people or to secure the stability of a government? And what do you mean to accomplish by making up and preserving your lists of pardoned persons? Can they be of any possible advantage to the country in any way? Why, then, load down an act like this with such useless circumstance, while as an act of grace and wisdom it certainly ought to be as straightforward and simple as possible?

Let me now in a few words once more sum up the whole meaning of the question which we are now engaged in discussing. No candid man can deny that our system of political disabilities is in no way calculated to protect the rights or the property or the life or the liberty of any living man, or in any way practically to prevent the evil-disposed from doing mischief. Why do you think of granting any amnesty at all? Is it not to produce on the popular mind at the South a conciliatory effect, to quicken the germs of good intentions, to encourage those who can exert a beneficial influence, to remove the pretexts of ill-feeling and animosity and to aid in securing to the Southern States the blessings of good and honest government? If that is not your design, what can it be?

But if it be this, if you really do desire to produce such moral effects, then I entreat you also to consider what moral means you have to employ in order to bring forth those moral effects you contemplate. If an act of generous statesmanship, or of statesman-like generosity, is to bear full fruit, it should give not as little as possible, but it should give as much as possible. You must not do things by halves if you want to produce whole results. You must not expose yourself to the suspicion of a narrow-minded desire to pinch off the size of your gift wherever there is a chance for it, as if you were afraid you could by any possibility give too much, when giving more would benefit the country more, and when giving less would detract from the beneficent effect of that which you do give.

Let me tell you it is the experience of all civilized nations the world over, when an amnesty is to be granted at all, the completest amnesty is always the best. Any limitation you may impose, however plausible it may seem at first sight, will be calculated to take away much of the virtue of that which is granted. I entreat you, then, in

the name of the accumulated experience of history, let there be
an end of these bitter and useless and disturbing questions; let the
books be finally closed, and when the subject is forever dismissed
from our discussions and our minds, we shall feel as much relieved
as those who are relieved of their political disabilities.

Sir, I have to say a few words about an accusation which has
been brought against those who speak in favor of universal amnesty.
It is the accusation resorted to in default of more solid argument,
that those who advise amnesty, especially universal amnesty, do
so because they have fallen in love with the rebels. No, sir, it is not
merely for the rebels I plead. We are asked, shall the rebellion go
entirely unpunished? No, it shall not. Neither do I think that the
rebellion has gone entirely unpunished. I ask you, had the rebels
nothing to lose but their lives and their offices? Look at it.

There was a proud and arrogant aristocracy planting their feet
on the necks of the laboring people, and pretending to be the born
rulers of this great Republic. They looked down, not only upon their
slaves, but also upon the people of the North, with the haughty
contempt of self-asserting superiority. When their pretensions to
rule us all were first successfully disputed, they resolved to destroy
this Republic, and to build up on the corner-stone of slavery an
empire of their own in which they could hold absolute sway. They
made the attempt with the most overweeningly confident expectation of certain victory. Then came the civil war, and after four years
of struggle their whole power and pride lay shivered to atoms at
our feet; their sons dead by tens of thousands on the battlefields of
this country; their fields and their homes devastated; their fortunes
destroyed; and more than that, the whole social system in which
they had their very being, with all their hopes and pride, utterly
wiped out; slavery forever abolished, and the slaves themselves
created a political power before which they had to bow their heads;
and they, broken, ruined, helpless and hopeless in the dust before
those upon whom they had so haughtily looked down as their
vassals and inferiors. Sir, can it be said that the rebellion has gone
entirely unpunished?

You may object that the loyal people, too, were subjected to terrible sufferings; that their sons, too, were slaughtered by tens of thousands; that the mourning of countless widows and orphans is still darkening our land; that we are groaning under terrible burdens which the rebellion has loaded upon us, and that therefore part of the punishment has fallen upon the innocent. And it is certainly true.

But look at the difference. We issued from this great conflict as conquerors; upon the graves of our slain we could lay the wreath of victory; our widows and orphans, while mourning the loss of their dearest, still remember with proud exultation that the blood of their husbands and fathers was not spilled in vain; that it flowed for the greatest and holiest and at the same time the most victorious of causes; and when our people labor in the sweat of their brow to pay the debt which the rebellion has loaded upon us, they do it with the proud consciousness that the heavy price they have paid is infinitely over-balanced by the value of the results they have gained: slavery abolished; the great American Republic purified of her foulest stain; the American people no longer a people of masters and slaves, but a people of equal citizens; the most dangerous element of disturbance and disintegration wiped out from among us; this country put upon the course of harmonious development, greater, more beautiful, mightier than ever in its self-conscious power. And thus, whatever losses, whatever sacrifices, whatever sufferings we may have endured, they appear before us in a blaze of glory.

But how do the Southern people stand there? All *they* have sacrificed, all *they* have lost, all the blood *they* have spilled, all the desolation of *their* homes, all the distress that stares *them* in the face, all the wreck and ruin *they* see around them, all for nothing, all for a wicked folly, all for a disastrous infatuation: the very graves of their dead nothing but monuments of a shadowy delusion; all their former hopes vanished forever; and the very magniloquence which some of their leaders are still indulging in, nothing but a mocking illustration of their utter discomfiture! Ah, sir, if ever human efforts broke down in irretrievable disaster, if ever human pride was humiliated to the dust, if ever human hopes were turned into despair, there you behold them.

You may say that they deserved it all. Yes, but surely, sir, you cannot say that the rebellion has gone entirely unpunished. Nor will the Senator from Indiana, with all his declamation, make any sane man believe that, had no political disabilities ever been imposed, the history of the rebellion, as long as the memory of men retains the recollection of the great story, will ever encourage a future generation to rebel again, or that, if even this great example of disaster should fail to extinguish the spirit of rebellion, his little scarecrow of exclusion from office will be more than a thing to be laughed at by little boys.

And yet, sir, it is certainly true that after the close of the war we treated the rebels with a generosity never excelled in the history of the world. And thus, in advising a general amnesty it is not merely for the rebels I plead. But I plead for the good of the country, which in its best interests will be benefited by amnesty just as much as the rebels are benefited themselves, if not more.

Nay, sir, I plead also for the colored people of the South, whose path will be smoothed by a measure calculated to assuage some of the prejudices and to disarm some of the bitternesses which will still confront them; and I am sure that nothing better could happen to them, nothing could be more apt to make the growth of good feeling between them and the former master-class easier than the destruction of a system which, by giving them a political superiority, endangers their peaceable enjoyment of equal rights.

And I may say to my honorable friend from Massachusetts (Mr. Sumner), who knows well how highly I esteem him, and whom I sincerely honor for his solicitude concerning the welfare of the lowly, that my desire to see their wrongs righted is no less sincere and no less unhampered by any traditional prejudice than his; although I will confess that as to the Constitutional means to that end we may sometimes seriously differ. But I cannot refrain from expressing my regret that this measure should be loaded with anything that is not strictly germane to it, knowing as we both do that the amendment he has proposed cannot secure the necessary two-thirds vote in at least one of the houses of Congress, and that therefore it will be calculated to involve this measure also in the danger of common failure.

I repeat, it is not merely for the rebels I plead; it is for the whole American people, for there is not a citizen in the land whose true interests, rightly understood, are not largely concerned in every measure affecting the peace and welfare of any State of this Union.

Believe me, Senators, the statesmanship which this period of our history demands, is not exhausted by high-sounding declamation about the greatness of the crime of rebellion, and fearful predictions as to what is going to happen unless the rebels are punished with sufficient severity. We have heard so much of this from some gentlemen, and so little else, that the inquiry naturally suggests itself, whether this is the whole compass, the be-all and the end-all, of their political wisdom and their political virtue; whether it is really their opinion that the people of the South may be plundered with impunity by rascals in power; that the substance of those States may be wasted; that their credit may be ruined; that their prosperity may be blighted; that their future may be blasted; that the poison of bad feeling may still be kept working where we might do something to assuage its effects; that the people may lose more and more their faith in the efficiency of self-government and of republican institutions; that all this may happen, and we look on complacently, if we can only continue to keep a thorn in the side of our late enemies, and to demonstrate again and again, as the Senator from Indiana has it, our disapprobation of the crime of rebellion?

Sir, such appeals as these, which we have heard here so frequently, may be well apt to tickle the ear of an unthinking multitude. But unless I am grievously in error, the people of the United States are a multitude not unthinking. The American people are fast becoming aware that, great as the crime of rebellion is, there are other villainies beside it; that much as it may deserve punishment, there are other evils flagrant enough to demand energetic correction; that the remedy for such evils does after all not consist in the maintenance of political disabilities, and that it would be well to look behind those vociferous demonstrations of exclusive and austere patriotism to see what abuses and faults of policy they are to cover, and what

rotten sores they are to disguise. The American people are fast beginning to perceive that good and honest government in the South,
as well as throughout the whole country, restoring a measurable
degree of confidence and contentment, will do infinitely more to
revive true loyalty and a healthy National spirit, than keeping alive·
the resentments of the past by a useless degradation of certain
classes of persons; and that we shall fail to do our duty unless we
use every means to contribute our share to that end. And those, I
apprehend, expose themselves to grievous disappointment, who
still think that by dinning again and again in the ears of the people
the old battlecries of the civil war, they can befog the popular mind
as to the true requirements of the times, and overawe and terrorize
the public sentiment of the country.

Sir, I am coming to a close. One word more. We have heard
protests here against amnesty as a measure intended to make us
forget the past and to obscure and confuse our moral appreciation
of the great events of our history. No, sir; neither would I have the
past forgotten, with its great experiences and teachings. Let the
memory of the grand uprising for the integrity of the Republic;
let those heroic deeds and sacrifices before which the power of
slavery crumbled into dust, be forever held in proud and sacred
remembrance by the American people. Let it never be forgotten, as
I am sure it never can be forgotten, that the American Union, supported by her faithful children, can never be undermined by any
conspiracy ever so daring, nor overthrown by any array of enemies
ever so formidable. Let the great achievements of our struggle for
National existence be forever a source of lofty inspiriation to our
children and children's children.

But surely, sir, I think no generous resolution on our part will
mar the luster of those memories, nor will it obliterate from the
Southern mind the overwhelming experience, that he who raises
his hand against the majesty of this Republic is doomed to disastrous
humiliation and ruin. I would not have it forgotten; and, indeed,
that experience is so indelibly written upon the Southern country
that nothing can wipe it out.

But, sir, as the people of the North and of the South must live together as one people, and as they must be bound together by the bonds of a common National feeling, I ask you, will it not be well for us to act, that the history of our great civil conflict, which cannot be forgotten, can neither be remembered by Southern men without finding in its closing chapter this irresistible assurance: that we, their conquerors, meant to be, and were, after all, not their enemies, but their friends? When the Southern people con over the distressing catalogue of the misfortunes they have brought upon themselves, will it not be well, will it not be "devoutly to be wished" for our common future, if at the end of that catalogue they find an act which will force every fair-minded man in the South to say of the Northern people: "When we were at war they inflicted upon us the severities of war; but when the contest had closed and they found us prostrate before them, grievously suffering, surrounded by the most perplexing difficulties and on the brink of new disasters, they promptly swept all the resentments of the past out of their way and stretched out their hands to us with the very fullest measure of generosity, anxious, eager, to lift us up from our prostration?"

Sir, will not this do something to dispel those mists of error and prejudice which are still clouding the Southern mind? I ask again, will it not be well to add to the sad memories of the past which forever will live in their minds, this cheering experience, so apt to prepare them for the harmony of a better and common future?

No, sir; I would not have the past forgotten, but I would have its history completed and crowned by an act most worthy of a great, noble and wise people. By all the means which we have in our hands, I would make even those who have sinned against this Republic see in its flag, not the symbol of their lasting degradation, but of rights equal to all; I would make them feel in their hearts, that in its good and evil fortunes their rights and interests are bound up just as ours are, and that therefore its peace, its welfare, its honor and its greatness may and ought to be as dear to them as they are to us.

I do not, indeed, indulge in the delusion that this act alone will remedy all the evils which we now deplore. No, it will not; but it will be a powerful appeal to the very best instincts and impulses of human nature; it will, like a warm ray of sunshine in springtime, quicken and call to light the germs of good intention wherever they exist; it will give new courage, confidence and inspiration to the well-disposed; it will weaken the power of the mischievous, by stripping of their pretexts and exposing in their nakedness the wicked designs they still may cherish; it will light anew the beneficent glow of fraternal feeling and of National spirit; for, sir, your good sense as well as your heart must tell you that, when this is truly a people of citizens equal in their political rights, it will then be easier to make it also a people of brothers.

Robert G. Ingersoll

THE LIBERTY OF MAN,

WOMAN, AND CHILD

¶ ROBERT GREEN INGERSOLL (1833-1899) was born in Dresden, New York, the son of a clergyman. His meager schooling, gathered as his father moved from parish to parish in Ohio, Wisconsin, and Illinois, was completed by a brief attendance at an academy in southern Illinois. With his brother he began the practice of law in Shawneetown, but soon moved to Peoria. Here he acquired a considerable reputation as a lawyer and orator. In 1861 he raised and commanded a volunteer regiment which served in the campaigns of the Tennessee Valley. He was captured and paroled, and returned to Peoria. He became active in politics and served as attorney-general of Illinois from 1867 to 1869. His nomination of Blaine for the presidency in 1876 brought him national fame, and from then until his death he was much sought after as a lawyer, lecturer, and campaigner for the Republican party. To serve his clients better, he moved in 1879 to Washington, and in 1885 to New York.

As a child he revolted against the cruelties of orthodox religion as he heard it preached, and in later life he became a vigorous and eloquent critic of the churches and their creeds. He prepared and delivered some twenty or thirty lectures on such subjects as "Heretics and Heresies," "The Ghosts," "Orthodoxy," "Myth and Miracle," "Some Mistakes of Moses," "Why I Am an Agnostic," and "Superstition." Some of these were delivered in all the principal cities of the North from Boston to San Francisco, and most of them were repeated many times. Probably the most popular—and the least critical of religion—was "The Liberty of Man, Woman, and Child," first delivered about 1877. (The text that follows is from *The Works of Robert G. Ingersoll*, Dresden Edition, New York, 1900.)

T HERE IS no slavery but ignorance. Liberty is the child of intelligence.

The history of man is simply the history of slavery, of injustice and brutality, together with the means by which he has, through the dead and desolate years, slowly and painfully advanced. He has been the sport and prey of priest and king, the food of superstition and cruel might. Crowned force has governed ignorance through fear. Hypocrisy and tyranny—two vultures—have fed upon the liberties of man. From all these there has been, and is, but one means of escape—intellectual development. Upon the back industry has been the whip. Upon the brain have been the fetters of superstition. Nothing has been left undone by the enemies of freedom. Every art and artifice, every cruelty and outrage has been practiced and perpetrated to destroy the rights of man. In this great struggle every crime has been rewarded and every virtue has been punished. Reading, writing, thinking and investigating have all been crimes.

Every science has been an outcast.

All the altars and all the thrones united to arrest the forward march of the human race. The king said that mankind must not work for themselves. The priest said that mankind must not think for themselves. One forged chains for the hands, the other for the soul. Under this infamous *regime* the eagle of the human intellect was for ages a slimy serpent of hypocrisy.

The human race was imprisoned. Through some of the prison bars came a few struggling rays of light. Against these bars Science pressed its pale and thoughtful face, wooed by the holy dawn of human advancement. Bar after bar was broken away. A few grand men escaped and devoted their lives to the liberation of their fellows.

Only a few years ago there was a great awakening of the human mind. Men began to inquire by what right a crowned robber made them work for him? The man who asked this question was called a traitor. Others asked by what right does a robed hypocrite rule my thought? Such men were called infidels. The priest said, and the king said, where is this spirit of investigation to stop? They said then and they say now, that it is dangerous for man to be free. I deny it. Out on the intellectual sea there is room enough for every sail. In the intellectual air there is space enough for every wing.

The man who does not do his own thinking is a slave, and is a traitor to himself and to his fellowmen.

Every man should stand under the blue and stars, under the infinite flag of nature, the peer of every other man.

Standing in the presence of the Unknown, all have the same right to think, and all are equally interested in the great questions of origin and destiny. All I claim, all I plead for, is liberty of thought and expression. That is all. I do not pretend to tell what is absolutely true, but what I think is true. I do not pretend to tell all the truth.

I do not claim that I have floated level with the heights of thought, or that I have descended to the very depths of things. I simply claim that what ideas I have, I have a right to express; and that any man who denies that right to me is an intellectual thief and robber. That is all.

Take those chains from the human soul. Break those fetters. If I have no right to think, why have I a brain? If I have no such right, have three or four men, or any number, who may get together, and sign a creed, and build a house, and put a steeple upon it, and a bell in it—have they the right to think? The good men, the good women are tired of the whip and lash in the realm of thought. They remember the chain and fagot with a shudder. They are free, and they give liberty to others. Whoever claims any right that he is unwilling to accord to his fellow-men is dishonest and infamous.

In the good old times, our fathers had the idea that they could make people believe to suit them. Our ancestors, in the ages that are gone, really believed that by force you could convince a man. You cannot change the conclusion of the brain by torture; nor by social ostracism. But I will tell you what you can do by these, and what you have done. You can make hypocrites by the million. You can make a man say that he has changed his mind; but he remains of the same opinion still. Put fetters all over him; crush his feet in iron boots; stretch him to the last gasp upon the holy rack; burn him, if you please, but his ashes will be of the same opinion still.

Our fathers in the good old times—and the best thing I can say about them is, that they have passed away—had an idea that they could force men to think their way. That idea is still prevalent in many parts, even of this country. Even in our day some extremely religious people say, "We will not trade with that man; we will not vote for him; we will not hire him if he is a lawyer; we will die before we will take his medicine if he is a doctor; we will not invite him to dinner; we will socially ostracise him; he must come to our church; he must believe our doctrines; he must worship our god or we will not in any way contribute to his support."

In the old times of which I have spoken, they desired to make all men think exactly alike. All the mechanical ingenuity of the world cannot make two clocks run exactly alike, and how are you going to make hundreds of millions of people, differing in brain and disposition, in education and aspiration, in conditions and surroundings, each clad in a living robe of passionate flesh—how are you going to make them think and feel alike? If there is an infinite god, one who made us, and wishes us to think alike, why did he give a spoonful of brains to one, and a magnificent intellectual development to another? Why is it that we have all degrees of intelligence, from orthodoxy to genius, if it was intended that all should think and feel alike?

I used to read in books how our fathers persecuted mankind. But I never appreciated it. I read it, but it did not burn itself into my soul. I did not really appreciate the infamies that have been committed in the name of religion, until I saw the iron arguments that Christians used. I saw the Thumbscrew—two little pieces of iron, armed on the inner surfaces with protuberances, to prevent their slipping; through each end a screw uniting the two pieces. And when some man denied the efficacy of baptism, or may be said, "I do not believe that a fish ever swallowed a man to keep him from drowning," then they put his thumb between these pieces of iron and in the name of love and universal forgiveness, began to screw these pieces together. When this was done most men said, "I will recant." Probably I should have done the same. Probably I would have said: "Stop; I will admit anything that you wish; I will admit that there is one god or a million, one hell or a billion; suit yourself; but stop."

But there was now and then a man who would not swerve the breadth of a hair. There was now and then some sublime heart, willing to die for an intellectual conviction. Had it not been for such men, we would be savages to-night. Had it not been for a few brave, heroic souls in every age, we would have been cannibals, with pictures of wild beasts tattooed upon our flesh, dancing around some dried snake fetich.

Let us thank every good and noble man who stood so grandly, so proudly, in spite of opposition, of hatred and death, for what he believed to be the truth.

Heroism did not excite the respect of our fathers. The man who would not recant was not forgiven. They screwed the thumbscrews down to the last pang, and then threw their victim into some dungeon, where, in the throbbing silence and darkness, he might suffer the agonies of the fabled damned. This was done in the name of love—in the name of mercy—in the name of the compassionate Christ.

I saw, too, what they called the Collar of Torture. Imagine a circle of iron, and on the inside a hundred points almost as sharp as needles. This argument was fastened about the throat of the sufferer. Then he could not walk, nor sit down, nor stir without the neck being punctured by these points. In a little while the throat would begin to swell, and suffocation would end the agonies of that man. This man, it may be, had committed the crime of saying, with tears upon his cheeks, "I do not believe that God, the father of us all, will damn to eternal perdition any of the children of men."

I saw another instrument, called the Scavenger's Daughter. Think of a pair of shears with handles, not only where they now are, but at the points as well, and just above the pivot that unites the blades, a circle of iron. In the upper handles the hands would be placed; in the lower, the feet; and through the iron ring, at the centre, the head of the victim would be forced. In this condition, he would be

thrown prone upon the earth, and the strain upon the muscles produced such agony that insanity would in pity end his pain.

This was done by gentlemen who said: "Whosoever smiteth thee
upon one cheek turn to him the other also."

I saw the Rack. This was a box like the bed of a wagon, with
a windlass at each end, with levers, and ratchets to prevent slipping; over each windlass went chains; some were fastened to the
ankles of the sufferer; others to his wrists. And then priests, clergy-
men, divines, saints, began turning these windlasses, and kept turning, until the ankles, the knees, the hips, the shoulders, the elbows,
the wrists of the victim were all dislocated, and the sufferer was wet
with the sweat of agony. And they had standing by a physician to
feel his pulse. What for? To save his life? Yes. In mercy? No; simply
that they might rack him once again.

This was done, remember, in the name of civilization; in the name
of law and order; in the name of mercy; in the name of religion; in
the name of the most merciful Christ.

Sometimes, when I read and think about these frightful things,
it seems to me that I have suffered all these horrors myself. It seems
sometimes, as though I had stood upon the shore of exile and gazed
with tearful eyes toward home and native land; as though my nails
had been torn from my hands, and into the bleeding quick needles
had been thrust; as though my feet had been crushed in iron boots;
as though I had been chained in the cell of the Inquisition and
listened with dying ears for the coming footsteps of release; as
though I had stood upon the scaffold and had seen the glittering axe
fall upon me; as though I had been upon the rack and had seen,
bending above me, the white faces of hypocrite priests; as though
I had been taken from my fireside, from my wife and children,
taken to the public square, chained; as though fagots had been
piled about me; as though the flames had climbed around my limbs
and scorched my eyes to blindness, and as though my ashes had
been scattered to the four winds, by all the countless hands of hate.
And when I so feel, I swear that while I live I will do what little
I can to preserve and to augment the liberties of man, woman, and
child.

It is a question of justice, of mercy, of honesty, of intellectual development. If there is a man in the world who is not willing to give to every human being every right he claims for himself, he is just so much nearer a barbarian than I am. It is a question of honesty. The man who is not willing to give to every other the same intellectual rights he claims for himself, is dishonest, selfish, and brutal.

It is a question of intellectual development. Whoever holds another man responsible for his honest thought, has a deformed and distorted brain. It is a question of intellectual development.

A little while ago I saw models of nearly everything that man has made. I saw models of all the water craft, from the rude dug-out in which floated a naked savage—one of our ancestors—a naked savage, with teeth two inches in length, with a spoonful of brains in the back of his head—I saw models of all the water craft of the world, from that dug-out up to a man-of-war, that carries a hundred guns and miles of canvas—from that dug-out to the steamship that turns its brave prow from the port of New York, with a compass like a conscience, crossing three thousand miles of billows without missing a throb or beat of its mighty iron heart.

I saw at the same time the weapons that man has made, from a club, such as was grasped by that same savage, when he crawled from his den in the ground and hunted a snake for his dinner; from that club to the boomerang, to the sword, to the cross-bow, to the blunderbuss, to the flint-lock, to the cap-lock, to the needle-gun, up to a cannon cast by Krupp, capable of hurling a ball weighing two thousand pounds through eighteen inches of solid steel.

I saw, too, the armor from the shell of a turtle, that one of our brave ancestors lashed upon his breast when he went to fight for his country; the skin of a porcupine, dried with the quills on, which this same savage pulled over his orthodox head, up to the shirts of mail, that were worn in the Middle Ages, that laughed at the edge of the sword and defied the point of the spear; up to a monitor clad in complete steel.

I saw at the same time, their musical instruments, from the tom-tom—that is, a hoop with a couple of strings of raw hide drawn across it—from that tom-tom, up to the instruments we have to-day, that make the common air blossom with melody.

I saw, too, their paintings, from a daub of yellow mud, to the great works which now adorn the galleries of the world. I saw also their sculpture, from the rude god with four legs, a half dozen arms, several noses, and two or three rows of ears, and one little, contemptible, brainless head, up to the figures of to-day—to the marbles that genius had clad in such a personality that it seems almost impudent to touch them without an introduction.

I saw their books—books written upon skins of wild beasts—upon shoulder-blades of sheep—books written upon leaves, upon bark, up to the splendid volumes that enrich the libraries of our day. When I speak of libraries, I think of the remark of Plato; "A house that has a library in it has a soul."

I saw their implements of agriculture, from a crooked stick that was attached to the horn of an ox by some twisted straw, to the agricultural implements of this generation, that make it possible for a man to cultivate the soil without being an ignoramus.

While looking upon these things I was forced to say that man advanced only as he mingled his thought with his labor,—only as he got into partnership with the forces of nature,—only as he learned to take advantage of his surroundings—only as he freed himself from the bondage of fear,—only as he depended upon himself—only as he lost confidence in the gods.

I saw at the same time a row of human skulls, from the lowest skull that has been found, the Neanderthal skull—skulls from Central Africa, skulls from the Bushmen of Australia—skulls from the farthest isles of the Pacific sea—up to the best skulls of the last generation;—and I noticed that there was the same difference between those skulls that there was between the *products* of those skulls and I said to myself, "After all, it is a simple question of intellectual development." There was the same difference between those skulls, the lowest and highest skulls, that there was between the dug-out and the man-of-war and the steamship, between the club and the Krupp gun, between the yellow daub and the landscape, between the tom-tom and an opera by Verdi.

The first and lowest skull in this row was the den in which crawled the base and meaner instincts of mankind, and the last was a temple in which dwelt joy, liberty, and love.

It is all a question of brain, of intellectual development.

If we are nearer free than were our fathers, it is because we have better heads upon the average, and more brains in them.

Now, I ask you to be honest with me. It makes no difference to you what I believe, nor what I wish to prove. I simply ask you to be honest. Divest your minds, for a moment at least, of all religious prejudice. Act, for a few moments, as though you were men and women.

Suppose the king, if there was one, and the priest, if there was one, at the time this gentleman floated in the dug-out, and charmed his ears with the music of the tom-tom, had said: "That dug-out is the best boat that ever can be built by man; the pattern of that came from on high, from the great god of storm and flood, and any man who says that he can improve it by putting a mast in it, with a sail upon it, is an infidel, and shall be burned at the stake;" what, in your judgment—honor bright—would have been the effect upon the circumnavigation of the globe?

Suppose the king, if there was one, and the priest, if there was one—and I presume there was a priest, because it was a very ignorant age—suppose this king and priest had said: "That tom-tom is the most beautiful instrument of music of which any man can conceive; that is the kind of music they have in heaven; an angel sitting upon the edge of a fleecy cloud, golden in the setting sun, playing upon that tom-tom, became so enraptured, so entranced with her own music, that in a kind of ectasy she dropped it—that is how we obtained it; and any man who says that it can be improved by putting a back and front to it, and four strings, and a bridge, and getting a bow of hair with rosin, is a blaspheming wretch, and shall die the death,"—I ask you, what effect would that have had upon music? If that course had been pursued, would the human ears, in your judgment, ever have been enriched with the divine symphonies of Beethoven?

Suppose the king, if there was one, and the priest, had said: "That crooked stick is the best plow that can be invented: the pattern of that plow was given to a pious farmer in a holy dream, and that twisted straw is the *ne plus ultra* of all twisted things, and any man who says he can make an improvement upon that plow, is an atheist;" what, in your judgment, would have been the effect upon the science of agriculture?

But the people said, and the king and priest said: "We want better weapons with which to kill our fellow-Christians; we want better plows, better music, better paintings, and whoever will give us better weapons, and better music, better houses to live in, better clothes, we will robe him in wealth, and crown him with honor." Every incentive was held out to every human being to improve these things. That is the reason the club has been changed to a cannon, the dug-out to a steamship, the daub to a painting; that is the reason that the piece of rough and broken stone finally became a glorified statue.

You must not, however, forget that the gentleman in the dug-out, the gentleman who was enraptured with the music of the tom-tom, and cultivated his land with a crooked stick, had a religion of his own. That gentleman in the dug-out was orthodox. He was never troubled with doubts. He lived and died settled in his mind. He believed in hell; and he thought he would be far happier in heaven, if he could just lean over and see certain people who expressed doubts as to the truth of his creed, gently but everlastingly broiled and burned.

It is a very sad and unhappy fact that this man has had a great many intellectual descendants. It is also an unhappy fact in nature, that the ignorant multiply much faster than the intellectual. This fellow in the dug-out believed in a personal devil. His devil had a cloven hoof, a long tail, armed with a fiery dart; and his devil breathed brimstone. This devil was at least the equal of God; not quite so stout but a little shrewder. And do you know there has not been a patentable improvement made upon that devil for six thousand years?

This gentleman in the dug-out believed that God was a tyrant; that he would eternally damn the man who lived in accordance with his highest and grandest ideal. He believed that the earth was flat. He believed in a literal, burning, seething hell of fire and sulphur. He had also his idea of politics; and his doctrine was, might makes right. And it will take thousands of years before the world will reverse this doctrine, and believingly say, "Right makes might."

All I ask is the same privilege to improve upon that gentleman's theology as upon his musical instrument; the same right to improve upon his politics as upon his dug-out. That is all. I ask for the human soul the same liberty in every direction. That is the only crime I have committed. I say, let us think. Let each one express his thought. Let us become investigators, not followers, not cringers and crawlers. If there is in heaven an infinite being, he never will be satisfied with the worship of cowards and hypocrites. Honest unbelief, honest infidelity, honest atheism, will be a perfume in heaven when pious hypocrisy, no matter how religious it may be outwardly, will be a stench.

This is my doctrine: Give every other human being every right you claim for yourself. Keep your mind open to the influences of nature. Receive new thoughts with hospitality. Let us advance.

The religionist of to-day wants the ship of his soul to lie at the wharf of orthodoxy and rot in the sun. He delights to hear the sails of old opinions flap against the masts of old creeds. He loves to see the joints and the sides open and gape in the sun, and it is a kind of bliss for him to repeat again and again: "Do not disturb my opinions. Do not unsettle my mind; I have it all made up, and I want no infidelity. Let me go backward rather than forward."

As far as I am concerned I wish to be out on the high seas. I wish to take my chances with wind, and wave, and star. And I had rather go down in the glory and grandeur of the storm, than to rot in any orthodox harbor whatever.

After all, we are improving from age to age. The most orthodox people in this country two hundred years ago would have been burned for the crime of heresy. The ministers who denounce me for expressing my thought would have been in the Inquisition themselves. Where once burned and blazed the bivouac fires of the army of progress, now glow the altars of the church. The religionists of our time are occupying about the same ground occupied by heretics and infidels of one hundred years ago. The church has advanced in spite, as it were, of itself. It has followed the army of progress protesting and denouncing, and had to keep within protesting and denouncing distance. If the church had not made great progress I could not express my thoughts.

Man, however, has advanced just exactly in the proportion with which he has mingled his thought with his labor. The sailor, without control of the wind and wave, knowing nothing or very little of the mysterious currents and pulses of the sea, is superstitious. So also is the agriculturist, whose prosperity depends upon something he cannot control. But the mechanic, when a wheel refuses to turn, never thinks of dropping on his knees and asking the assistance of some divine power. He knows there is a reason. He knows that something is too large or too small; that there is something wrong with his machine; and he goes to work and he makes it larger or smaller, here or there, until the wheel will turn. Now, just in proportion as man gets away from being, as it were, the slave of his surroundings, the serf of the elements,—of the heat, the frost, the snow, and the lightning,—just to the extent that he has gotten control of his own destiny, just to the extent that he has triumphed over the obstacles of nature, he has advanced physically and intellectually. As man develops, he places a greater value upon his own rights. Liberty becomes a grander and diviner thing. As he values his own rights, he begins to value the rights of others. And when all men give to all others all the rights they claim for themselves, this world will be civilized.

A few years ago the people were afraid to question the king, afraid to question the priest, afraid to investigate a creed, afraid to deny a book, afraid to denounce a dogma, afraid to reason, afraid to think. Before wealth they bowed to the very earth, and in the presence of titles they became abject. All this is slowly but surely changing. We no longer bow to men simply because they are rich. Our fathers worshiped the golden calf. The worst you can say of an American now is, he worships the gold of the calf. Even the calf is beginning to see this distinction.

It no longer satisfies the ambition of a great man to be king or emperor. The last Napoleon was not satisfied with being the emperor of the French. He was not satisfied with having a circlet of gold about his head. He wanted some evidence that he had something of value within his head. So he wrote the life of Julius Caesar, that he might become a member of the French Academy. The emperors, the kings, the popes, no longer tower above their fellows. Compare King William with the philosopher Haeckel. The king is one of the anointed by the most high, as they claim—one upon whose head has been poured the divine petroleum of authority. Compare this king with Haeckel, who towers an intellectual colossus above the crowned mediocrity. Compare George Eliot with Queen Victoria. The Queen is clothed in garments given her by blind fortune and unreasoning chance, while George Eliot wears robes of glory woven in the loom of her own genius.

The world is beginning to pay homage to intellect, to genius, to heart.

We have advanced. We have reaped the benefit of every sublime and heroic self-sacrifice, of every divine and brave act; and we should endeavor to hand the torch to the next generation, having added a little to the intensity and glory of the flame.

When I think of how much this world has suffered; when I think of how long our fathers were slaves, of how they cringed and crawled at the foot of the throne, and in the dust of the altar, of how they abased themselves, of how abjectly they stood in the presence of superstition robed and crowned, I am amazed.

This world has not been fit for a man to live in fifty years. It was not until the year 1808 that Great Britain abolished the slave trade. Up to that time her judges, sitting upon the bench in the name of justice, her priests, occupying her pulpits, in the name of universal love, owned stock in the slave ships, and luxuriated upon the profits of piracy and murder. It was not until the same year that the United States of America abolished the slave trade between this and other countries, but carefully preserved it as between the States. It was not until the 28th day of August, 1833, that Great Britain abolished human slavery in her colonies; and it was not until the 1st day of

January, 1863, that Abraham Lincoln, sustained by the sublime and heroic North, rendered our flag pure as the sky in which it floats.

Abraham Lincoln was, in my judgment, in many respects, the grandest man ever President of the United States. Upon his monument these words should be written: "Here sleeps the only man in the history of the world, who, having been clothed with almost absolute power, never abused it, except upon the side of mercy."

Think how long we clung to the institution of human slavery, how long lashes upon the naked back were a legal tender for labor performed. Think of it. The pulpit of this country deliberately and willingly, for a hundred years, turned the cross of Christ into a whipping post.

With every drop of my blood I hate and execrate every form of tyranny, every form of slavery. I hate dictation. I love liberty.

What do I mean by liberty? By physical liberty I mean the right to do anything which does not interfere with the happiness of another. By intellectual liberty I mean the right to think right and the right to think wrong. Thought is the means by which we endeavor to arrive at truth. If we know the truth already, we need not think. All that can be required is honesty of purpose. You ask my opinion about anything; I examine it honestly, and when my mind is made up, what should I tell you? Should I tell you my real thought? What should I do? There is a book put in my hands. I am told this is the Koran; it was written by inspiration. I read it, and when I get through, suppose that I think in my heart and in my brain, that it is utterly untrue, and you then ask me, what do you think? Now, admitting that I live in Turkey, and have no chance to get any office unless I am on the side of the Koran, what should I say? Should I make a clean breast and say, that upon my honor I do not believe it? What would you think then of my fellow-citizens if they said: "That man is dangerous, he is dishonest."

Suppose I read the book called the Bible, and when I get through I make up my mind that it was written by men. A minister asks me, "Did you read the Bible?" I answer, that I did. "Do you think it divinely inspired?" What should I reply? Should I say to myself, "If I deny the inspiration of the Scriptures, the people will never clothe me with power." What ought I to answer? Ought I not to say like a man: "I have read it; I do not believe it." Should I not give the real transcript of my mind? Or should I turn hypocrite and pretend what I do not feel, and hate myself forever after for being a cringing coward. For my part I would rather a man would tell me what he honestly thinks. I would rather he would preserve his manhood. I had a thousand times rather be a manly unbeliever than an unmanly believer. And if there is a judgment day, a time when all will stand before some supreme being, I believe I will stand higher, and stand a better chance of getting my case decided in my favor, than any man sneaking through life pretending to believe what he does not.

I have made up my mind to say my say. I shall do it kindly, distinctly; but I am going to do it. I know there are thousands of men who substantially agree with me, but who are not in a condition to express their thoughts. They are poor; they are in business; and they know that should they tell their honest thought, persons will refuse to patronize them—to trade with them; they wish to get bread for their little children; they wish to take care of their wives; they wish to have homes and the comforts of life. Every such person is a certificate of the meanness of the community in which he resides. And yet I do not blame these people for not expressing their thought. I say to them: "Keep your ideas to yourselves; feed and clothe the ones you love; I will do your talking for you. The church can not touch, can not crush, can not starve, can not stop or stay me; I will express your thoughts."

As an excuse for tyranny, as a justification of slavery, the church has taught that man is totally depraved. Of the truth of that doctrine, the church has furnished the only evidence there is. The truth is, we are both good and bad. The worst are capable of some good deeds, and the best are capable of bad. The lowest can rise, and the highest may fall. That mankind can be divided into two great classes, sinners and saints, is an utter falsehood. In times of great disaster, called it may be, by the despairing voices of women, men, denounced by the church as totally depraved, rush to death as to a festival. By such men, deeds are done so filled with self-sacrifice and generous daring, that millions pay to them the tribute, not only of admiration, but of tears. Above all creeds, above all religions, after all, is that divine thing,—Humanity; and now and then in ship-wreck on the wide, wild sea, or 'mid the rocks and breakers of some cruel shore, or where the serpents of flame writhe and hiss, some glorious heart, some chivalric soul does a deed that glitters like a star, and gives the lie to all the dogmas of superstition. All these frightful doctrines have been used to degrade and to enslave man-kind.

Away, forever away with the creeds and books and forms and laws and religions that take from the soul liberty and reason. Down with the idea that thought is dangerous! Perish the infamous doc-trine that man can have property in man. Let us resent with indigna-tion every effort to put a chain upon our minds. If there is no God, certainly we should not bow and cringe and crawl. If there is a God, there should be no slaves.

Liberty of Woman

Women have been the slaves of slaves; and in my judgment it took millions of ages for woman to come from the condition of abject slavery up to the institution of marriage. Let me say right here, that I regard marriage as the holiest institution among men. Without the fireside there is no human advancement; without the family relation there is no life worth living. Every good government is made up of good families. The unit of good government is the family, and anything that tends to destroy the family is perfectly devilish and infamous. I believe in marriage, and I hold in utter contempt the opinions of those long-haired men and short-haired women who denounce the institution of marriage.

The grandest ambition that any man can possibly have, is to so live, and so improve himself in heart and brain, as to be worthy of the love of some splendid woman; and the grandest ambition of any girl is to make herself worthy of the love and adoration of some magnificent man. That is my idea. There is no success in life without love and marriage. You had better be the emperor of one loving and tender heart, and she the empress of yours, than to be king of the world. The man who has really won the love of one good woman in this world, I do not care if he dies in the ditch a beggar, his life has been a success.

I say it took millions of years to come from the condition of abject slavery up to the condition of marriage. Ladies, the ornaments you wear upon your persons to-night are but the souvenirs of your mother's bondage. The chains around your necks, and the bracelets clasped upon your white arms by the thrilled hand of love, have been changed by the wand of civilization from iron to shining, glittering gold.

But nearly every religion has accounted for all the devilment in this world by the crime of woman. What a gallant thing that is! And if it is true, I had rather live with the woman I love in a world full of trouble, than to live in heaven with nobody but men.

I read in a book—and I will say now that I cannot give the exact language, as my memory does not retain the words, but I can give the substance—I read in a book that the Supreme Being concluded to make a world and one man; that he took some nothing and made a world and one man, and put this man in a garden. In a little while he noticed that the man got lonesome; that he wandered around as if he was waiting for a train. There was nothing to interest him; no news; no papers; no politics; no policy; and, as the devil had not yet made his appearance, there was no chance for reconciliation; not even for civil service reform. Well, he wandered about the garden in this condition, until finally the Supreme Being made up his mind to make him a companion.

Having used up all the nothing he originally took in making the world and one man, he had to take a part of the man to start a woman with. So he caused a sleep to fall on this man—now understand me, I do not say this story is true. After the sleep fell upon this man, the Supreme Being took a rib, or as the French would call it, a cutlet, out of this man, and from that he made a woman. And considering the amount of raw material used, I look upon it as the most successful job ever performed. Well, after he got the woman done, she was brought to the man; not to see how she liked him, but to see how he liked her. He liked her, and they started housekeeping; and they were told of certain things they might do and of one thing they could not do—and of course they did it. I would have done it in fifteen minutes, and I know it. There wouldn't have been an apple on that tree half an hour from date, and the limbs would have been full of clubs. And then they were turned out of the park and extra policemen were put on to keep them from getting back.

Devilment commenced. The mumps, and the measles, and the whooping-cough, and the scarlet fever started in their race for man. They began to have the toothache, roses began to have thorns, snakes began to have poisoned teeth, and people began to divide about religion and politics, and the world has been full of trouble from that day to this.

Nearly all of the religions of this world account for the existence of evil by such a story as that!

I read in another book what appeared to be an account of the same transaction. It was written about four thousand years before the other. All commentators agree that the one that was written last was the original, and that the one that was written first was copied from the one that was written last. But I would advise you all not to allow your creed to be disturbed by a little matter of four or five thousand years. In this other story, Brahma made up his mind to make the world and a man and woman. He made the world, and he made the man and then the woman, and put them on the island of Ceylon. According to the account it was the most beautiful island of which man can conceive. Such birds, such songs, such flowers and such verdure! And the branches of the trees were so arranged that when the wind swept through them every tree was a thousand Æolian harps.

Brahma, when he put them there, said: "Let them have a period of courtship, for it is my desire and will that true love should forever precede marriage." When I read that, it was so much more beautiful and lofty than the other, that I said to myself, "If either one of these stories ever turns out to be true, I hope it will be this one."

Then they had their courtship, with the nightingale singing, and the stars shining, and the flowers blooming, and they fell in love. Imagine that courtship! No prospective fathers or mothers-in-law; no prying and gossiping neighbors; nobody to say, "Young man, how do you expect to support her?" Nothing of that kind. They were married by the Supreme Brahma, and he said to them: "Remain here; you must never leave this island." Well, after a little while the man—and his name was Adami, and the woman's name was Heva —said to Heva: "I believe I'll look about a little." He went to the northern extremity of the island where there was a little narrow neck of land connecting it with the mainland, and the devil, who is always playing pranks with us, produced a mirage, and when he looked over to the mainland, such hills and vales, such dells and dales, such mountains crowned with snow, such cataracts clad in bows of glory did he see there, that he went back and told Heva: "The country over there is a thousand times better than this; let us migrate." She, like every other woman that ever lived, said: "Let well enough alone; we have all we want; let us stay here." But he said "No, let us go;" so she followed him, and when they came to this narrow neck of land, he took her on his back like a gentleman, and carried her over. But the moment they got over they heard a crash, and looking back, discovered that this narrow neck of land had fallen into the sea. The mirage had disappeared, and there were naught but rocks and sand; and then the Supreme Brahma cursed them both to the lowest hell.

Then it was that the man spoke,—and I have liked him ever since for it— "Curse me, but curse not her, it was not her fault, it was mine."

That's the kind of man to start a world with.

The Supreme Brahma said: "I will save her, but not thee." And then she spoke out of her fullness of love, out of a heart in which there was love enough to make all her daughters rich in holy affection, and said: "If thou wilt not spare him, spare neither me; I do not wish to live without him; I love him." Then the Supreme Brahma said—and I have liked him ever since I read it—"I will spare you both and watch over you and your children forever."

Honor bright, is not that the better and grander story?

And from that same book I want to show you what ideas some of these miserable heathen had; the heathen we are trying to convert. We send missionaries over yonder to convert heathen there, and we send soldiers out on the plains to kill heathen here. If we can convert the heathen, why not convert those nearest home? Why not convert those we can get at? Why not convert those who have the immense advantage of the example of the average pioneer? But to show you the men we are trying to convert: In this book it says: "Man is strength, woman is beauty; man is courage, woman is love. When the one man loves the one woman and the one woman loves the one man, the very angels leave heaven and come and sit in that house and sing for joy."

They are the men we are converting. Think of it! I tell you, when I read these things, I say that love is not of any country; nobility does not belong exclusively to any race, and through all the ages, there have been a few great and tender souls blossoming in love and pity.

In my judgment, the woman is the equal of the man. She has all the rights I have and one more, and that is the right to be protected. That is my doctrine. You are married; try and make the woman you love happy. Whoever marries simply for himself will make a mistake; but whoever loves a woman so well that he says, "I will make her happy," makes no mistake. And so with the woman who says, "I will make him happy." There is only one way to be happy, and that is to make somebody else so, and you cannot be happy by going cross lots; you have got to go the regular turnpike road.

If there is any man I detest, it is the man who thinks he is the head of a family—the man who thinks he is "boss!" The fellow in the dug-out used that word "boss;" that was one of his favorite expressions.

Imagine a young man and a young woman courting, walking out in the moonlight, and the nightingale singing a song of pain and love, as though the thorn touched her heart—imagine them stopping there in the moonlight and starlight and song, and saying, "Now, here, let us settle who is 'boss!'" I tell you it is an infamous word and an infamous feeling—I abhor a man who is "boss," who is going to govern in his family, and when he speaks orders all the rest to be still as some mighty idea is about to be launched from his mouth. Do you know I dislike this man unspeakably?

I hate above all things a cross man. What right has he to murder the sunshine of a day? What right has he to assassinate the joy of life? When you go home you ought to go like a ray of light—so that it will, even in the night, burst out of the doors and windows and illuminate the darkness. Some men think their mighty brains have been in a turmoil; they have been thinking about who will be alderman from the fifth ward; they have been thinking about politics; great and mighty questions have been engaging their minds; they have bought calico at five cents or six, and want to sell it for seven. Think of the intellectual strain that must have been upon that man, and when he gets home everybody else in the house must look out for his comfort. A woman who has only taken care of five or six children, and one or two of them sick, has been nursing them and singing to them, and trying to make one yard of cloth do the work of two, she, of course, is fresh and fine and ready to wait upon this gentleman—the head of the family—the boss!

Do you know another thing? I despise a stingy man. I do not see how it is possible for a man to die worth fifty million of dollars, or ten million of dollars, in a city full of want, when he meets almost every day the withered hand of beggary and the white lips of famine. How a man can withstand all that, and hold in the clutch of his greed twenty or thirty million of dollars, is past my comprehension. I do not see how he can do it. I should not think he could do it any more than he could keep a pile of lumber on the beach, where hundreds and thousands of men were drowning in the sea.

Do you know that I have known men who would trust their wives with their hearts and their honor but not with their pocketbook; not with a dollar. When I see a man of that kind, I always think he knows which of these articles is the most valuable. Think of making your wife a beggar! Think of her having to ask you every day for a dollar, or for two dollars or fifty cents! "What did you do with that dollar I gave you last week?" Think of having a wife that is afraid of you! What kind of children do you expect to have with a beggar and a coward for their mother? Oh, I tell you if you have but a dollar in the world, and you have got to spend it, spend it like a king; spend it as though it were a dry leaf and you the owner of unbounded forests! That's the way to spend it! I had rather be a beggar and spend my last dollar like a king, than be a king and spend my money like a beggar! If it has got to go, let it go!

Get the best you can for your family—try to look as well as you can yourself. When you used to go courting, how elegantly you looked! Ah, your eye was bright, your step was light, and you looked like a prince. Do you know that it is insufferable egotism in you to suppose a woman is going to love you always looking as slovenly as you can! Think of it! Any good woman on earth will be true to you forever when you do your level best.

Some people tell me, "Your doctrine about loving, and wives, and all that, is splendid for the rich, but it won't do for the poor." I tell you to-night there is more love in the homes of the poor than in the palaces of the rich. The meanest hut with love in it is a palace fit for the gods, and a palace without love is a den only fit for wild beasts. That is my doctrine! You cannot be so poor that you cannot help somebody. Good nature is the cheapest commodity in the world; and love is the only thing that will pay ten per cent. to borrower and lender both. Do not tell me that you have got to be rich! We have a false standard of greatness in the United States. We think here that a man must be great, that he must be notorious; that he must be extremely wealthy, or that his name must be upon the putrid lips of rumor. It is all a mistake. It is not necessary to be rich or to be great, or to be powerful, to be happy. The happy man is the successful man.

Happiness is the legal tender of the soul.

Joy is wealth.

A little while ago, I stood by the grave of the old Napoleon— a magnificent tomb of gilt and gold, fit almost for a dead deity— and gazed upon the sarcophagus of rare and nameless marble, where rest at last the ashes of that restless man. I leaned over the balustrade and thought about the career of the greatest soldier of the modern world.

I saw him walking upon the banks of the Seine, contemplating suicide. I saw him at Toulon—I saw him putting down the mob in the streets of Paris—I saw him at the head of the army of Italy—

I saw him crossing the bridge of Lodi with the tri-color in his hand—I saw him in Egypt in the shadows of the pyramids—I saw him conquer the Alps and mingle the eagles of France with the eagles of the crags. I saw him at Marengo—at Ulm and Austerlitz. I saw him in Russia, where the infantry of the snow and the cavalry of the wild blast scattered his legions like winter's withered leaves. I saw him at Leipsic in defeat and disaster—driven by a million bayonets back upon Paris—clutched like a wild beast—banished to Elba. I saw him escape and retake an empire by the force of his genius. I saw him upon the frightful field of Waterloo, where Chance and Fate combined to wreck the fortunes of their former king. And I saw him at St. Helena, with his hands crossed behind him, gazing out upon the sad and solemn sea.

I thought of the orphans and widows he had made—of the tears that had been shed for his glory, and of the only woman who ever loved him, pushed from his heart by the cold hand of ambition. And I said I would rather have been a French peasant and worn wooden shoes. I would rather have lived in a hut with a vine growing over the door, and the grapes growing purple in the kisses of the autumn sun. I would rather have been that poor peasant with my loving wife by my side, knitting as the day died out of the sky—with my children upon my knees and their arms about me—I would rather have been that man and gone down to the tongueless silence of the dreamless dust, than to have been that imperial impersonation of force and murder, known as "Napoleon the Great."

It is not necessary to be great to be happy; it is not necessary to be rich to be just and generous and to have a heart filled with divine affection. No matter whether you are rich or poor, treat your wife as though she were a splendid flower, and she will fill your life with perfume and with joy.

And do you know, it is a splendid thing to think that the woman you really love will never grow old to you. Through the wrinkles of time, through the mask of years, if you really love her, you will always see the face you loved and won. And a woman who really loves a man does not see that he grows old; he is not decrepit to her; he does not tremble; he is not old; she always sees the same gallant gentleman who won her hand and heart. I like to think of it in that way; I like to think that love is eternal. And to love in that way and then go down the hill of life together, and as you go down, hear, perhaps, the laughter of grandchildren, while the birds of joy and love sing once more in the leafless branches of the tree of age.

I believe in the fireside. I believe in the democracy of home. I believe in the republicanism of the family. I believe in liberty, equality and love.

The Liberty of Children

If women have been slaves, what shall I say of children; of the little children in alleys and sub-cellars; the little children who turn pale when they hear their father's footsteps; little children who run away when they only hear their names called by the lips of a mother; little children—the children of poverty, the children of crime, the children of brutality, wherever they are—flotsam and jetsam upon the wild, mad sea of life—my heart goes out to them, one and all.

I tell you the children have the same rights that we have, and we ought to treat them as though they were human beings. They should be reared with love, with kindness, with tenderness, and not with brutality. That is my idea of children.

When your little child tells a lie, do not rush at him as though the world were about to go into bankruptcy. Be honest with him. A tyrant father will have liars for his children; do you know that? A lie is born of tyranny upon the one hand and weakness upon the other, and when you rush at a poor little boy with a club in your hand, of course he lies.

I thank thee, Mother Nature, that thou hast put ingenuity enough in the brain of a child, when attacked by a brutal parent, to throw up a little breastwork in the shape of a lie.

When one of your children tells a lie, be honest with him; tell him that you have told hundreds of them yourself. Tell him it is not the best way; that you have tried it. Tell him as the man did in Maine when his boy left home: "John, honesty is the best policy; I have tried both." Be honest with him. Suppose a man as much larger than you as you are larger than a child five years old, should come at you with a liberty pole in his hand, and in a voice of thunder shout, "Who broke that plate?" There is not a solitary one of you who would not swear you never saw it, or that it was cracked when you got it. Why not be honest with these children? Just imagine a man who deals in stocks whipping his boy for putting false rumors afloat! Think of a lawyer beating his own flesh and blood for evading the truth when he makes half of his own living that way! Think of a minister punishing his child for not telling all he thinks! Just think of it!

When your child commits a wrong, take it in your arms; let it feel your heart beat against its heart; let the child know that you really and truly and sincerely love it. Yet some Christians, good Christians, when a child commits a fault, drive it from the door and say: "Never do you darken this house again." Think of that! And then these same people will get down on their knees and ask God to take care of the child they have driven from home. I will never ask God to take care of my children unless I am doing my level best in that same direction.

But I will tell you what I say to my children: "Go where you will, commit what crimes you may; fall to what depth of degradation you may; you can never commit any crime that will shut my door, my arms, or my heart to you. As long as I live you shall have one sincere friend."

Do you know that I have seen some people who acted as though they thought that when the Saviour said "Suffer little children to come unto me, for of such is the kingdom of heaven," he had a raw-hide under his mantle, and made that remark simply to get the children within striking distance?

I do not believe in the government of the lash. If any one of you ever expects to whip your children again, I want you to have a photograph taken of yourself when you are in the act, with your face red with vulgar anger, and the face of the little child, with eyes swimming in tears and the little chin dimpled with fear, like a piece of water struck by a sudden cold wind. Have the picture taken. If that little child should die, I cannot think of a sweeter way to spend an autumn afternoon than to go out to the cemetery, when the maples are clad in tender gold, and little scarlet runners are coming, like poems of regret, from the sad heart of the earth—and sit down upon the grave and look at that photograph, and think of the flesh now dust that you beat. I tell you it is wrong; it is no way to raise children! Make your home happy. Be honest with them. Divide fairly with them in everything.

Give them a little liberty and love, and you can not drive them out of your house. They will want to stay there. Make home pleasant. Let them play any game they wish. Do not be so foolish as to say: "You may roll balls on the ground, but you must not roll them on a green cloth. You may knock them with a mallet, but you must not push them with a cue. You may play with little pieces of paper which have 'authors' written on them, but you must not have 'cards.' " Think of it! "You may go to a minstrel show where people blacken themselves and imitate humanity below them, but you must not go to a theatre and see the characters created by immortal genius put upon the stage." Why? Well, I can't think of any reason in the world except "minstrel" is a word of two syllables, and "theatre" has three.

Let children have some daylight at home if you want to keep them there, and do not commence at the cradle and shout "Don't!" "Don't!" "Stop!" That is nearly all that is said to a child from the cradle until he is twenty-one years old, and when he comes of age other people begin saying "Don't!" And the church says "Don't!" and the party he belongs to says "Don't!"

I despise that way of going through this world. Let us have liberty —just a little. Call me infidel, call be atheist, call me what you will, I intend so to treat my children, that they can come to my grave and truthfully say: "He who sleeps here never gave us a moment of pain. From his lips, now dust, never came to us an unkind word."

People justify all kinds of tyranny toward children upon the ground that they are totally depraved. At the bottom of ages of cruelty lies this infamous doctrine of total depravity. Religion contemplates a child as a living crime—heir to an infinite curse—doomed to eternal fire.

In the olden time, they thought some days were too good for a child to enjoy himself. When I was a boy Sunday was considered altogether too holy to be happy in. Sunday used to commence then when the sun went down on Saturday night. We commenced at that time for the purpose of getting a good ready, and when the sun fell below the horizon on Saturday evening, there was a darkness fell upon the house ten thousand times deeper than that of night. Nobody said a pleasant word; nobody laughed; nobody smiled; the child that looked the sickest was regarded as the most pious. That night you could not even crack hickory nuts. If you were caught chewing gum it was only another evidence of the total depravity of the human heart. It was an exceedingly solemn night. Dyspepsia was in the very air you breathed. Everybody looked sad and mournful. I have noticed all my life that many people think they have religion when they are troubled with dyspepsia. If there could be found an absolute specific for that disease, it would be the hardest blow the church has ever received.

On Sunday morning the solemnity had simply increased. Then we went to church. The minister was in a pulpit about twenty feet high, with a little sounding-board above him, and he commenced at "firstly" and went on and on and on to about "twenty-thirdly." Then he made a few remarks by way of application; and then took a general view of the subject, and in about two hours reached the last chapter in Revelation.

In those days, no matter how cold the weather was, there was no fire in the church. It was thought to be a kind of sin to be comfortable while you were thanking God. The first church that ever had a stove in it in New England, divided on that account. So the first church in which they sang by note, was torn in fragments.

After the sermon we had an intermission. Then came the catechism with the chief end of man. We went through with that. We sat in a row with our feet coming within about six inches of the floor. The minister asked us if we knew that we all deserved to go to hell, and we all answered "Yes." Then we were asked if we would be willing to go to hell if it was God's will, and every little liar shouted "Yes." Then the same sermon was preached once more, commencing at the other end and going back. After that, we started for home, sad and solemn—overpowered with the wisdom displayed in the scheme of the atonement. When we got home, if we had been good boys, and the weather was warm, sometimes they would take us out to the graveyard to cheer us up a little. It did cheer me. When I looked at the sunken tombs and the leaning stones, and read the half-effaced inscriptions through the moss of silence and forgetfulness, it was a great comfort. The reflection came to my mind that the observance of the Sabbath could not last always. Sometimes they would sing that beautiful hymn in which occurs these cheerful lines:

> "Where congregations ne'er break up,
> And Sabbaths never end."

These lines, I think, prejudiced me a little against even heaven. Then we had good books that we read on Sundays by way of keeping us happy and contented. There were Milners' "History of the Waldenses," Baxter's "Call to the Unconverted," Yahn's "Archaeology of the Jews," and Jenkyns' "On the Atonement." I used to read Jenkyns' "On the Atonement." I have often thought that an atonement would have to be exceedingly broad in its provisions to cover the case of a man who would write a book like that for a boy.

But at last the Sunday wore away, and the moment the sun went down we were free. Between three and four o'clock we would go out to see how the sun was coming on. Sometimes it seemed to me that it was stopping from pure meanness. But finally it went down. It had to. And when the last rim of light sank below the horizon, off would go our caps, and we would give three cheers for liberty once more.

Sabbaths used to be prisons. Every Sunday was a Bastile. Every Christian was a kind of turn-key, and every child was a prisoner,—a convict. In that dungeon, a smile was a crime.

It was thought wrong for a child to laugh upon this holy day. Think of that!

A little child would go out into the garden, and there would be a tree laden with blossoms, and the little fellow would lean against it, and there would be a bird on one of the boughs, singing and swinging, and thinking about four little speckled eggs, warmed by the breast of its mate,—singing and swinging, and the music in happy waves rippling out of its tiny throat, and the flowers blossoming, the air filled with perfume and the great white clouds floating in the sky, and the little boy would lean up against that tree and think about hell and the worm that never dies.

I have heard them preach, when I sat in the pew and my feet did not touch the floor, about the final home of the unconverted. In order to impress upon the children the length of time they would probably stay if they settled in that country, the preacher would frequently give us the following illustration: "Suppose that once in a billion years a bird should come' from some far-distant planet, and carry off in its little bill a grain of sand, a time would finally come when the last atom composing this earth would be carried away; and when this last atom was taken, it would not even be sun up in hell." Think of such an infamous doctrine being taught to children!

The laugh of a child will make the holiest day more sacred still. Strike with hand of fire, O weird musician, thy harp strung with Apollo's golden hair; fill the vast cathedral aisles with symphonies sweet and dim, deft toucher of the organ keys; blow, bugler, blow, until thy silver notes do touch and kiss the moonlit waves, and charm the lovers wandering 'mid the vine-clad hills. But know, your sweetest strains are discords all, compared with childhood's happy laugh—the laugh that fills the eyes with light and every heart with joy. O rippling river of laughter, thou art the blessed boundary line between the beasts and men; and every wayward wave of thine doth drown some fretful fiend of care. O Laughter, rose-lipped daughter of Joy, there are dimples enough in thy cheeks to catch and hold and glorify all the tears of grief.

And yet the minds of children have been polluted by this infamous doctrine of eternal punishment. I denounce it to-day as a doctrine, the infamy of which no language is sufficient to express.

Where did that doctine of eternal punishment for men and women and children come from? It came from the low and beastly skull of that wretch in the dug-out. Where did he get it? It was a souvenir from the animals. The doctrine of eternal punishment was born in the glittering eyes of snakes—snakes that hung in fearful coils watching for their prey. It was born of the howl and bark and growl of wild beasts. It was born of the grin of hyenas and of the depraved chatter of unclean baboons. I despise it with every drop of my blood. Tell me there is a God in the serene heavens that will damn his children for the expression of an honest belief! More men have died in their sins, judged by your orthodox creeds, than there are leaves on all the forests in the wide world ten thousand times over. Tell me these men are in hell; that these men are in torment; that these children are in eternal pain, and that they are to be punished forever and forever! I denounce this doctrine as the most infamous of lies.

When the great ship containing the hopes and aspirations of the world, when the great ship freighted with mankind goes down in the night of death, chaos and disaster, I am willing to go down with the ship. I will not be guilty of the ineffable meanness of paddling away in some orthodox canoe. I will go down with the ship, with those who love me, and with those whom I have loved. If there is a God who will damn his children forever, I would rather go to hell than to go to heaven and keep the society of such an infamous tyrant. I make my choice now. I despise that doctrine. It has covered the cheeks of this world with tears. It has polluted the hearts of children, and poisoned the imagination of men. It has been a constant pain, a perpetual terror to every good man and woman and child. It has filled the good with horror and with fear; but it has had no effect upon the infamous and base. It has wrung the hearts of the tender, it has furrowed the cheeks of the good. This doctrine never should be preached again. What right have you, sir, Mr. clergyman, you, minister of the gospel, to stand at the portals of the tomb, at the vestibule of eternity, and fill the future with horror and with fear? I do not believe this doctrine; neither do you. If you did, you could not sleep one moment. Any man who believes it, and has within his breast a decent, throbbing heart, will go insane. A man who believes that doctrine and does not go insane has the heart of a snake and the conscience of a hyena.

Jonathan Edwards, the dear old soul, who, if his doctrine is true, is now in heaven rubbing his holy hands with glee, as he hears the cries of the damned, preached this doctrine; and he said: "Can the believing husband in heaven be happy with his unbelieving wife in hell? Can the believing father in heaven be happy with his unbelieving children in hell? Can the loving wife in heaven be happy with her unbelieving husband in hell?" And he replies: "I tell you, yea. Such will be their sense of justice, that it will increase rather than diminish their bliss." There is no wild beast in the jungles of Africa whose reputation would not be tarnished by the expression of such a doctrine.

These doctrines have been taught in the name of religion, in the name of universal forgiveness, in the name of infinite love and charity. Do not, I pray you, soil the minds of your children with this dogma. Let them read for themselves; let them think for themselves.

Do not treat your children like orthodox posts to be set in a row. Treat them like trees that need light and sun and air. Be fair and honest with them; give them a chance. Recollect that their rights are equal to yours. Do not have it in your mind that you must govern them; that they must obey. Throw away forever the idea of master and slave.

In old times they used to make the children go to bed when they were not sleepy, and get up when they were sleepy. I say let them go to bed when they are sleepy, and get up when they are not sleepy.

But you say, this doctrine will do for the rich but not for the poor. Well, if the poor have to waken their children early in the morning it is as easy to wake them with a kiss as with a blow. Give your children freedom; let them preserve their individuality. Let your children eat what they desire, and commence at the end of a dinner they like. That is their business and not yours. They know what they wish to eat. If they are given their liberty from the first, they know what they want better than any doctor in the world can prescribe. Do you know that all the improvement that has ever been made in the practice of medicine has been made by the recklessness of patients and not by the doctors? For thousands and thousands of years the doctors would not let a man suffering from fever have a drop of water. Water they looked upon as poison. But every now and then some man got reckless and said, "I had rather die than not to slake my thirst." Then he would drink two or three quarts of water and get well. And when the doctor was told of what the patient had done, he expressed great surprise that he was still alive, and complimented his constitution upon being able to bear such a frightful strain. The reckless men, however, kept on drinking the water, and persisted in getting well. And finally the doctors said: "In a fever, water is the very best thing you can take." So, I have more confidence in the voice of nature about such things than I have in the conclusions of the medical schools.

Let your children have freedom and they will fall into your ways; they will do substantially as you do; but if you try to make them, there is some magnificent, splendid thing in the human heart that refuses to be driven. And do you know that it is the luckiest thing that ever happened for this world, that people are that way. What would have become of the people five hundred years ago if they had followed strictly the advice of the doctors? They would have all been dead. What would the people have been, if at any age of the world they had followed implicity the direction of the church? They would have all been idiots. It is a splendid thing that there is always some grand man who will not mind, and who will think for himself.

I believe in allowing the children to think for themselves. I believe in the democracy of the family. If in this world there is anything splendid, it is a home where all are equals.

You will remember that only a few years ago parents would tell their children to "let their victuals stop their mouths." They used to eat as though it were a religious ceremony—a very solemn thing. Life should not be treated as a solemn matter. I like to see the children at table, and hear each one telling of the wonderful things he has seen and heard. I like to hear the clatter of knives and forks and spoons mingling with their happy voices. I had rather hear it than any opera that was ever put upon the boards. Let the children have liberty. Be honest and fair with them; be just; be tender, and they will make you rich in love and joy.

Men are oaks, women are vines, children are flowers.

The human race has been guilty of almost countless crimes; but I have some excuse for mankind. This world, after all, is not very well adapted to raising good people. In the first place, nearly all of it is water. It is much better adapted to fish culture than to the production of folks. Of that portion which is land not one-eighth has suitable soil and climate to produce great men and women. You cannot raise men and women of genius, without the proper soil and climate, any more than you can raise corn and wheat upon the ice fields of the Arctic sea. You must have the necessary conditions and surroundings. Man is a product; you must have the soil and food. The obstacles presented by nature must not be so great that man cannot, by reasonable industry and courage, overcome them. There is upon this world only a narrow belt of land, circling zigzag the globe, upon which you can produce men and women of talent. In the Southern Hemisphere the real climate that man needs falls mostly upon the sea, and the result is, that the southern half of our world has never produced a man or woman of great genius. In the far north there is no genius—it is too cold. In the far south there is no genius—it is too warm. There must be winter, and there must be summer. In a country where man needs no coverlet but a cloud, revolution is his normal condition. Winter is the mother of industry and prudence. Above all, it is the mother of the family relation. Winter holds in its icy arms the husband and wife and the sweet children. If upon this earth we ever have a glimpse of heaven, it is when we pass a home in winter, at night, and through the windows, the curtains drawn aside, we see the family about the pleasant hearth; the old lady knitting; the cat playing with the yarn; the children wishing they had as many dolls or dollars or knives or somethings, as there are sparks going out to join the roaring blast; the father reading and smoking, and the clouds rising like incense from the altar of domestic joy. I never passed such a house without feeling that I had received a benediction.

Civilization, liberty, justice, charity, intellectual advancement, are all flowers that blossom in the drifted snow.

I do not know that I can better illustrate the great truth that only part of the world is adapted to the production of great men and women than by calling your attention to the difference between vegetation in valleys and upon mountains. In the valley you find the oak and elm tossing their branches defiantly to the storm, and as you advance up the mountain side the hemlock, the pine, the birch, the spruce, the fir, and finally you come to little dwarfed trees, that look like other trees seen through a telescope reversed—every limb twisted as though in pain—getting a scanty subsistence from the miserly crevices of the rocks. You go on and on, until at last the highest crag is freckled with a kind of moss, and vegetation ends. You might as well try to raise oaks and elms where the mosses grow, as to raise great men and great women where their surroundings are unfavorable. You must have the proper climate and soil.

A few years ago we were talking about the annexation of Santo Domingo to this country. I was in Washington at the time. I was opposed to it. I was told that it was a most delicious climate; that the soil produced everything. But I said: "We do not want it; it is not the right kind of country in which to raise American citizens. Such a climate would debauch us. You might go there with five thousand Congregational preachers, five thousand ruling elders, five thousand professors in colleges, five thousand of the solid men of Boston and their wives; settle them all in Santo Domingo, and you will see the second generation riding upon a mule bareback, no shoes, a grapevine bridle, hair sticking out at the top of their sombreros, with a rooster under each arm, going to a cock fight on Sunday." Such is the influence of climate.

Science, however, is gradually widening the area within which men of genius can be produced. We are conquering the north with houses, clothing, food and fuel. We are in many ways overcoming the heat of the south. If we attend to this world instead of another, we may in time cover the land with men and women of genius.

I have still another excuse. I believe that man came up from the lower animals. I do not say this as a fact. I simply say I believe it to be a fact. Upon that question I stand about eight to seven, which, for all practical purposes, is very near a certainty. When I first heard of that doctrine I did not like it. My heart was filled with sympathy for those people who have nothing to be proud of except ancestors. I thought, how terrible this will be upon the nobility of the Old World. Think of their being forced to trace their ancestry back to the duke Orang Outang, or to the princess Chimpanzee. After thinking it all over, I came to the conclusion that I liked that doctrine. I became convinced in spite of myself. I read about rudimentary bones and muscles. I was told that everybody had rudimentary muscles extending from the ear into the cheek. I asked "What are they?" I was told: "They are the remains of muscles; that they became rudimentary from lack of use; they went into bankruptcy. They are the muscles with which your ancestors used to flap their ears." I do not now so much wonder that we once had them as that we have outgrown them.

After all I had rather belong to a race that started from the skull-less vertebrates in the dim Laurentian seas, vertebrates wiggling without knowing why they wiggled, swimming without knowing where they were going, but that in some way began to develop, and began to get a little higher and a little higher in the scale of existence; that came up by degrees through millions of ages through all the animal world, through all that crawls and swims and floats and climbs and walks, and finally produced the gentleman in the dug-out; and then from this man, getting a little grander, and each one below calling every one above him a heretic, calling every one who had made a little advance an infidel or an atheist—for in the history of this world the man who is ahead has always been called a heretic—I would rather come from a race that started from that skull-less vertebrate, and came up and up and up and finally produced Shakespeare, the man who found the human intellect dwelling in a hut, touched it with the wand of his genius and it became a palace domed and pinnacled; Shakespeare, who harvested all the fields of dramatic thought, and from whose day to this, there have been only gleaners of straw and chaff—I would rather belong to that race that commenced a skull-less vertebrate and produced Shakespeare, a race that has before it an infinite future, with the angel of progress leaning from the far horizon, beckoning men forward, upward and onward forever—I had rather belong to such a race, commencing there, producing this, and with that hope, than to have sprung from a perfect pair upon which the Lord has lost money every moment from that day to this.

Conclusion

I have given you my honest thought. Surely investigation is better than unthinking faith. Surely reason is a better guide than fear. This world should be controlled by the living, not by the dead. The grave is not a throne, and a corpse is not a king. Man should not try to live on ashes.

The theologians dead, knew no more than the theologians now living. More than this cannot be said. About this world little is known,—about another world, nothing.

Our fathers were intellectual serfs, and their fathers were slaves. The makers of our creeds were ignorant and brutal. Every dogma that we have, has upon it the mark of whip, the rust of chain, and the ashes of fagot.

Our fathers reasoned with instruments of torture. They believed in the logic of fire and sword. They hated reason. They despised thought. They abhorred liberty.

Superstition is the child of slavery. Free thought will give us truth. When all have the right to think and to express their thoughts, every brain will give to all the best it has. The world will then be filled with intellectual wealth.

As long as men and women are afraid of the church, as long as a minister inspires fear, as long as people reverence a thing simply because they do not understand it, as long as it is respectable to lose your self-respect, as long as the church has power, as long as mankind worship a book, just so long will the world be filled with intellectual paupers and vagrants, covered with the soiled and faded rags of superstition.

As long as woman regards the Bible as the charter of her rights, she will be the slave of man. The Bible was not written by a woman. Within its lids there is nothing but humiliation and shame for her. She is regarded as the property of man. She is made to ask forgiveness for becoming a mother. She is as much below her husband, as her husband is below Christ. She is not allowed to speak. The gospel is too pure to be spoken by her polluted lips. Woman should learn in silence.

In the Bible will be found no description of a civilized home. The free·mother surrounded by free and loving children, adored by a free man, her husband, was unknown to the inspired writers of the Bible. They did not believe in the democracy of home—in the republicanism of the fireside.

These inspired gentlemen knew nothing of the rights of children. They were the advocates of brute force—the disciples of the lash. They knew nothing of human rights. Their doctrines have brutalized the homes of millions, and filled the eyes of infancy with tears.

Let us free ourselves from the tyranny of a book, from the slavery of dead ignorance, from the aristocracy of the air.

There has never been upon the earth a generation of free men and women. It is not yet time to write a creed. Wait until the chains are broken—until dungeons are not regarded as temples. Wait until solemnity is not mistaken for wisdom—until mental cowardice ceases to be known as reverence. Wait until the living are considered the equals of the dead—until the cradle takes precedence of the coffin. Wait until what we know can be spoken without regard to what others may believe. Wait until teachers take the place of preachers— until followers become investigators. Wait until the world is free before you write a creed.

In this creed there will be but one word—Liberty.

Oh Liberty, float not forever in the far horizon—remain not forever in the dream of the enthusiast, the philanthropist and poet, but come and make thy home among the children of men!

I know not what discoveries, what inventions, what thoughts may leap from the brain of the world. I know not what garments of glory may be woven by the years to come. I cannot dream of the victories to be won upon the fields of thought; but I do know, that coming from the infinite sea of the future, there will never touch this "bank and shoal of time" a richer gift, a rarer blessing than liberty for man, for woman, and for child.

Robert G. Ingersoll

AT A CHILD'S GRAVE

¶ THE FOLLOWING account of this speech appeared in the *Chicago Tribune* of January 13, 1882:

"Washington, D.C., Jan. 9th.—In a remote corner of the Congressional Cemetery yesterday afternoon, a small group of people with uncovered heads were ranged around a newly-opened grave. They included Detective and Mrs. George O. Miller and family and friends, who had gathered to witness the burial of the former's bright little son Harry, a recent victim of diphtheria. As the casket rested upon the trestles there was a painful pause, broken only by the mother's sobs, until the undertaker advanced toward a stout florid-complexioned gentleman in the party and whispered to him, the words being inaudible to the lookers-on.

"This gentleman was Col. Robert G. Ingersoll, a friend of the Millers, who had attended the funeral at their request. He shook his head when the undertaker first addressed him, and then said suddenly, 'Does Mrs. Miller desire it?'

"The undertaker gave an affirmative nod. Mr. Miller looked appealingly toward the distinguished orator, and then Col. Ingersoll advanced to the side of the grave, made a motion denoting a desire for silence, and in a voice of exquisite cadence, delivered one of his characteristic eulogies for the dead. The scene was intensely dramatic. A fine drizzling rain was falling, and every head was bent, and every ear turned to catch the impassioned words of eloquence and hope that fell from the lips of the famed orator.

"Col. Ingersoll was unprotected by either hat or umbrella, and his invocation thrilled his hearers with awe; each eye that had previously been bedimmed with tears brightening and sobs becoming hushed. The Colonel said:"

MY FRIENDS: I know how vain it is to gild a grief with words, and yet I wish to take from every grave its fear. Here in this world, where life and death are equal kings, all should be brave enough to meet what all the dead have met. The future has been filled with fear, stained and polluted by the heartless past. From the wondrous tree of life the buds and blossoms fall with ripened fruit, and in the common bed of earth, patriarchs and babes sleep side by side.

Why should we fear that which will come to all that is? We cannot tell, we do not know, which is the greater blessing—life or death. We cannot say that death is not a good. We do not know whether the grave is the end of this life, or the door of another, or whether the night here is not somewhere else a dawn. Neither can we tell which is the more fortunate—the child dying in its mother's arms, before its lips have learned to form a word, or he who journeys all the length of life's uneven road, painfully taking the last slow steps with staff and crutch.

Every cradle asks us "Whence?" and every coffin "Whither?" The poor barbarian, weeping above his dead, can answer these questions just as well as the robed priest of the most authentic creed. The tearful ignorance of the one, is as consoling as the learned and unmeaning words of the other. No man, standing where the horizon of a life has touched a grave, has any right to prophesy a future filled with pain and tears.

May be that death gives all there is of worth to life. If those we press and strain within our arms could never die, perhaps that love would wither from the earth. May be this common fate treads from out the paths between our hearts the weeds of selfishness and hate. And I had rather live and love where death is king, than have eternal life where love is not. Another life is nought, unless we know and love again the ones who love us here.

They who stand with breaking hearts around this little grave, need have no fear. The larger and the nobler faith in all that is, and is to be, tells us that death, even at its worst, is only perfect rest. We know that through the common wants of life—the needs and duties of each hour—their grief will lessen day by day, until at last this grave will be to them a place of rest and peace—almost of joy. There is for them this consolation: The dead do not suffer. If they live again, their lives will surely be as good as ours. We have no fear. We are all children of the same mother, and the same fate awaits us all. We, too, have our religion, and it is this: Help for the living—Hope for the dead.

Henry W. Grady

THE NEW SOUTH

❡ HENRY WOODFIN GRADY (1850-1889) was born in Athens, Georgia. At the age of eighteen he was graduated from the University of Georgia, then went to the University of Virginia for a year of post-graduate work. He early chose journalism as his profession and followed it throughout his life, rejecting the pleas of his many friends and admirers that he go into politics. As editor of various Georgia newspapers, and finally of the Atlanta *Constitution*, he worked tirelessly and effectively for the cause that dominated his life—reconstruction and development of the South.

He was little known outside his own region until 1886, when he spoke before the New England Society of New York on "The New South." This address before many of the leaders of Northern society brought him national fame. According to the custom of the time there were many speakers on the Society's program, among them Reverend Henry Van Dyke, Reverend Dewitt Talmage, and General William T. Sherman, after whose address the audience rose and lustily sang "Marching through Georgia." This was the setting that stimulated Grady to what was doubtless his greatest effort. He said afterward, "I knew that I had a message for that assemblage, and as soon as I opened my mouth it came rushing out." He spoke extemporaneously, but all his life's work had been a preparation for the occasion, and he won an enthusiastic ovation. The speech as taken down by a reporter for the *New York Tribune* differs in slight details from the text that follows, which is from the *Proceedings* of the Society.

THERE WAS a South of slavery and secession—that South is
dead. There is a South of union and freedom—that South, thank
God, is living, breathing, growing every hour." These words, delivered from the immortal lips of Benjamin H. Hill, at Tammany
Hall in 1866, true then, and truer now, I shall make my text to-night.

MR. PRESIDENT AND GENTLEMEN: Let me express to you my appreciation of the kindness by which I am permitted to address you.
I make this abrupt acknowledgment advisedly, for I feel that if, when
I raise my provincial voice in this ancient and august presence, I
could find courage for no more than the opening sentence, it would
be well if, in that sentence, I had met in a rough sense my obligation as a guest, and had perished, so to speak, with courtesy on my
lips and grace in my heart. [Laughter.] Permitted through your
kindness to catch my second wind, let me say that I appreciate the
significance of being the first Southerner to speak at this board,
which bears the substance, if it surpasses the semblance, of original
New England hospitality [Applause], and honors a sentiment that
in turn honors you, but in which my personality is lost, and the
compliment to my people made plain. [Laughter.]

I bespeak the utmost stretch of your courtesy to-night. I am not
troubled about those from whom I come. You remember the man
whose wife sent him to a neighbor with a pitcher of milk, and who,
tripping on the top step, fell, with such casual interruptions as the
landing afforded, into the basement; and while picking himself up
had the pleasure of hearing his wife call out: "John, did you break
the pitcher?"

"No, I didn't," said John, "but I be dinged if I don't!" [Laughter.]

So, while those who call to me from behind may inspire me with
energy if not with courage, I ask an indulgent hearing from you. I
beg that you will bring your full faith in American fairness and
frankness to judgment upon what I shall say. There was an old
preacher once who told some boys of the Bible lesson he was going
to read in the morning. The boys finding the place, glued together
the connecting pages. [Laughter.] The next morning he read on
the bottom of one page: "When Noah was one hundred and twenty

years old he took unto himself a wife, who was"—then turning the page—"one hundred and forty cubits long [*Laughter*], forty cubits wide, built of gopher-wood [*Laughter*], and covered with pitch inside and out." [*Loud and continued laughter.*] He was naturally puzzled at this. He read it again, verified it, and then said: "My friends, this is the first time I ever met this in the Bible, but I accept it as an evidence of the assertion that we are fearfully and wonderfully made." [*Immense laughter.*] If I could get you to hold such faith to-night I could proceed cheerfully to the task I otherwise approach with a sense of consecration.

Pardon me one word, Mr. President, spoken for the sole purpose of getting into the volumes that go out annually freighted with the rich eloquence of your speakers—the fact that the Cavalier as well as the Puritan was on the continent in its early days, and that he was "up and able to be about." [*Laughter.*] I have read your books carefully and I find no mention of that fact, which seems to me an important one for preserving a sort of historical equilibrium if for nothing else.

Let me remind you that the Virginia Cavalier first challenged France on this continent—that Cavalier John Smith gave New England its very name, and was so pleased with the job that he has been handing his own name around ever since—and that while Miles Standish was cutting off men's ears for courting a girl without her parents' consent, and forbade men to kiss their wives on Sunday, the Cavalier was courting everything in sight, and that the Almighty had vouchsafed great increase to the Cavalier colonies, the huts in the wilderness being full as the nests in the woods.

But having incorporated the Cavalier as a fact in your charming little books I shall let him work out his own salvation, as he has always done with engaging gallantry, and we will hold no controversy as to his merits. Why should we? Neither Puritan nor Cavalier long survived as such. The virtues and traditions of both happily still live for the inspiration of their sons and the saving of the old fashion. [*Applause.*] But both Puritan and Cavalier were lost in the storm of the first Revolution; and the American citizen, supplanting both and stronger than either, took possession of the Republic bought by their common blood and fashioned to wisdom, and charged himself with teaching men government and establishing the voice of the people as the voice of God. [*Applause.*]

My friend Dr. Talmage has told you that the typical American has yet to come. Let me tell you that he has already come. [*Applause.*] Great types like valuable plants are slow to flower and fruit. But from the union of these colonist Puritans and Cavaliers, from the straightening of their purposes and the crossing of their blood, slow perfecting through a century, came he who stands as the first typical American, the first who comprehended within himself all the strength and gentleness, all the majesty and grace of this Republic— Abraham Lincoln. [*Loud and continued applause.*] He was the sum of Puritan and Cavalier, for in his ardent nature were fused the virtues of both, and in the depths of his great soul the faults of both were lost. [*Renewed applause.*] He was greater than Puritan, greater than Cavalier, in that he was American [*Renewed applause*], and that in his homely form were first gathered the vast and thrilling forces of his ideal government—charging it with such tremendous meaning and so elevating it above human suffering that martyrdom, though infamously aimed, came as a fitting crown to a life conse-crated from the cradle to human liberty. [*Loud and prolonged cheering.*] Let us, each cherishing the traditions and honoring his fathers, build with reverent hands to the type of this simple but sublime life, in which all types are honored; and in our common glory as Americans there will be plenty and to spare for your fore-fathers and for mine. [*Renewed cheering.*]

In speaking to the toast with which you have honored me, I ac-cept the term, "The New South," as in no sense disparaging to the Old. Dear to me, sir, is the home of my childhood and the traditions of my people. I would not, if I could, dim the glory they won in peace and war, or by word or deed take aught from the splendor and grace of their civilization—never equaled and, perhaps, never to be equaled in its chivalric strength and grace. There is a New South, not through protest against the Old, but because of new conditions, new adjustments and, if you please, new ideas and aspirations. It is to this that I address myself, and to the consideration of which I hasten lest it become the Old South before I get to it. Age does not endow all things with strength and virtue, nor are all new things to be despised. The shoemaker who put over his door "John Smith's shop. Founded in 1760," was more than matched by his young rival across the street who hung out this sign: "Bill Jones. Established 1886. No old stock kept in this shop."

Dr. Talmage has drawn for you, with a master's hand, the picture of your returning armies. He has told you how, in the pomp and circumstance of war, they came back to you, marching with proud and victorious tread, reading their glory in a nation's eyes! Will you bear with me while I tell you of another army that sought its home at the close of the late war—an army that marched home in defeat and not in victory—in pathos and not in splendor, but in glory that equaled yours, and to hearts as loving as ever welcomed heroes home. Let me picture to you the footsore Confederate soldier, as, buttoning up in his faded gray jacket the parole which was to bear testimony to his children of his fidelity and faith, he turned his face southward from Appomattox in April, 1865. Think of him as ragged, half-starved, heavy-hearted, enfeebled by want and wounds; having fought to exhaustion, he surrenders his gun, wrings the hands of his comrades in silence, and, lifting his tear-stained and pallid face for the last time to the graves that dot the old Virginia hills, pulls his gray cap over his brow and begins the slow and painful journey. What does he find—let me ask you, who went to your homes eager to find in the welcome you had justly earned, full payment for four years' sacrifice—what does he find when, having followed the battle-stained cross against overwhelming odds, dreading death not half so much as surrender, he reaches the home he left so prosperous and beautiful? He finds his house in ruins, his farm devastated, his slaves free, his stock killed, his barns empty, his trade destroyed, his money worthless; his social system, feudal in its magnificence, swept away; his people without law or legal status, his comrades slain, and the burdens of others heavy on his shoulders. Crushed by defeat, his very traditions are gone; without money, credit, employment, material or training; and, besides all this, confronted with the gravest problem that ever met human intelligence—the establishing of a status for the vast body of his liberated slaves.

What does he do—this hero in gray with a heart of gold? Does he sit down in sullenness and despair? Not for a day. Surely God, who had stripped him of his prosperity, inspired him in his adversity. As ruin was never before so overwhelming, never was restoration swifter. The soldier stepped from the trenches into the furrow; horses that had charged Federal guns marched before the plow, and fields that ran red with human blood in April were green with the harvest in June; women reared in luxury cut up their dresses and made breeches for their husbands, and, with a patience and heroism that fit women always as a garment, gave their hands to work. There was little bitterness in all this. Cheerfulness and frankness prevailed. "Bill Arp" struck the keynote when he said: "Well, I killed as many of them as they did of me, and now I am going to work." [*Laughter and applause.*] Or the soldier returning home after defeat and roasting some corn on the roadside, who made the remark to his comrades: "You may leave the South if you want to, but I am going to Sandersville, kiss my wife and raise a crop, and if the Yankees fool with me any more I will whip 'em again." [*Renewed applause.*] I want to say to General Sherman—who is considered an able man in our parts, though some people think he is a kind of careless man about fire—that from the ashes he left us in 1864 we have raised a brave and beautiful city; that somehow or other we have caught the sunshine in the bricks and mortar of our homes, and have builded therein not one ignoble prejudice or memory. [*Applause.*]

But in all this what have we accomplished? What is the sum of our work? We have found out that in the general summary the free negro counts more than he did as a slave. We have planted the schoolhouse on the hilltop and made it free to white and black. We have sowed towns and cities in the place of theories and put business above politics. [*Applause.*] We have challenged your spinners in Massachusetts and your iron-makers in Pennsylvania. We have learned that the $400,000,000 annually received from our cotton crop will make us rich, when the supplies that make it are home-raised. We have reduced the commercial rate of interest from twenty-four to six per cent, and are floating four per cent bonds. We have learned that one Northern immigrant is worth fifty foreigners, and have smoothed the path to southward, wiped out the place where Mason and Dixon's line used to be, and hung our latch-string out to you and yours. [*Prolonged cheers.*] We have reached the point that marks perfect harmony in every household, when the husband confesses that the pies which his wife cooks are as good as those his mother used to bake; and we admit that the sun shines as brightly and the moon as softly as it did "before the war." [*Laughter.*] We have established thrift in city and country. We have fallen in love with work. We have restored comfort to homes from which culture and elegance never departed. We have let economy take root and spread among us as rank as the crabgrass which sprang from Sherman's cavalry camps, until we are ready to lay odds on the Georgia Yankee, as he manufactures relics of the battlefield in a one-story shanty and squeezes pure olive oil out of his cotton-seed, against any down-easter that ever swapped wooden nutmegs for flannel sausages in the valleys of Vermont. [*Loud and continuous laughter.*] Above all, we know that we have achieved in these "piping times of peace" a fuller independence for the South than that which our fathers sought to win in the forum by their eloquence or compel on the field by their swords. [*Loud applause.*]

It is a rare privilege, sir, to have had part, however humble, in this work. Never was nobler duty confided to human hands than the uplifting and upbuilding of the prostrate and bleeding South, misguided perhaps, but beautiful in her suffering, and honest, brave and generous always. [*Applause.*] In the record of her social, industrial, and political illustrations we await with confidence the verdict of the world.

But what of the negro? Have we solved the problem he presents or progressed in honor and equity towards the solution? Let the record speak to the point. No section shows a more prosperous laboring population than the negroes of the South; none in fuller sympathy with the employing and land-owning class. He shares our school fund, has the fullest protection of our laws and the friendship of our people. Self-interest, as well as honor, demand that he should have this. Our future, our very existence depend upon our working out this problem in full and exact justice. We understand that when Lincoln signed the Emancipation Proclamation, your victory was assured; for he then committed you to the cause of human liberty, against which the arms of man cannot prevail [*Applause*]; while those of our statesmen who trusted to make slavery the cornerstone of the Confederacy doomed us to defeat as far as they could, committing us to a cause that reason could not defend or the sword maintain in the sight of advancing civilization. [*Renewed applause.*] Had Mr. Toombs said, which he did not say, that he would call the roll of his slaves at the foot of Bunker Hill, he would have been foolish, for he might have known that whenever slavery became entangled in war it must perish, and that the chattel in human flesh ended forever in New England when your fathers—not to be blamed for parting with what didn't pay—sold their slaves to our fathers— not to be praised for knowing a paying thing when they saw it. [*Laughter.*] The relations of the Southern people with the negro are close and cordial. We remember with what fidelity for four years he guarded our defenceless women and children, whose husbands and fathers were fighting against his freedom. To his eternal credit be it said that whenever he struck a blow for his own liberty he fought in open battle, and when at last he raised his black and humble hands that the shackles might be struck off, those hands were innocent of wrong against his helpless charges, and worthy to be taken in loving grasp by every man who honors loyalty and devotion. [*Applause.*] Ruffians have maltreated him, rascals have misled him, philanthropists established a bank for him, but the South, with the North, protests against injustice to this simple and sincere people. To liberty and enfranchisement is as far as law can carry the negro. The rest must be left to conscience and common sense. It should be left to those among whom his lot is cast, with whom he is indissolubly connected and whose prosperity depends upon their possessing his intelligent sympathy and confidence. Faith has been kept with him in spite of calumnious assertions to the contrary by those who assume to speak for us or by frank opponents.

Faith will be kept with him in the future, if the South holds her reason and integrity. [*Applause.*]

But have we kept faith with you? In the fullest sense, yes. When Lee surrendered—I don't say when Johnston surrendered, because I understand he still alludes to the time when he met General Sherman last as the time when he "determined to abandon any further prosecution of the struggle"—when Lee surrendered, I say, and Johnston quit, the South became, and has since been, loyal to this Union. We fought hard enough to know that we were whipped, and in perfect frankness accepted as final the arbitrament of the sword to which we had appealed. The South found her jewel in the toad's head of defeat. The shackles that had held her in narrow limitations fell forever when the shackles of the negro slave were broken. [*Applause.*] Under the old regime the negroes were slaves to the South, the South was a slave to the system. The old plantation, with its simple police regulation and its feudal habit, was the only type possible under slavery. Thus we gathered in the hands of a splendid and chivalric oligarchy the substance that should have been diffused among the people, as the rich blood, under certain artificial conditions, is gathered at the heart, filling that with affluent rapture, but leaving the body chill and colorless. [*Applause.*]

The Old South rested everything on slavery and agriculture, unconscious that these could neither give nor maintain healthy growth. The New South presents a perfect democracy, the oligarchs leading in the popular movement—a social system compact and closely knitted, less splendid on the surface but stronger at the core—a hundred farms for every plantation, fifty homes for every palace, and a diversified industry that meets the complex needs of this complex age.

The New South is enamored of her new work. Her soul is stirred with the breath of a new life. The light of a grander day is falling fair on her face. She is thrilling with the consciousness of growing power and prosperity. As she stands upright, full-statured and equal among the people of the earth, breathing the keen air and looking out upon the expanding horizon, she understands that her emancipation came because in the inscrutable wisdom of God her honest purpose was crossed and her brave armies were beaten. [*Applause.*]

This is said in no spirit of time-serving or apology. The South has nothing for which to apologize. She believes that the late struggle between the States was war and not rebellion, revolution and not conspiracy, and that her convictions were as honest as yours. I should be unjust to the dauntless spirit of the South and to my own convictions if I did not make this plain in this presence. The South has nothing to take back. In my native town of Athens is a monument that crowns its central hills—a plain, white shaft. Deep cut into its shining side is a name dear to me above the names of men, that of a brave and simple man who died in brave and simple faith. Not for all the glories of New England—from Plymouth Rock all the way—would I exchange the heritage he left me in his soldier's death. To the foot of that shaft I shall send my children's children to reverence him who ennobled their name with his heroic blood. But, sir, speaking from the shadow of that memory, which I honor as I do nothing else on earth, I say that the cause in which he suffered and for which he gave his life was adjudged by higher and fuller wisdom than his or mine, and I am glad that the omniscient God held the balance of battle in His Almighty hand, and that human slavery was swept forever from American soil—the American Union saved from the wreck of war. [*Loud applause.*]

This message, Mr. President, comes to you from consecrated ground. Every foot of the soil about the city in which I live is sacred as a battleground of the Republic. Every hill that invests it is hallowed to you by the blood of your brothers, who died for your victory, and doubly hallowed to us by the blood of those who died hopeless, but undaunted, in defeat—sacred soil to all of us, rich with memories that make us purer and stronger and better, silent but stanch witnesses in its red desolation of the matchless valor of American hearts and the deathless glory of American arms—speaking an eloquent witness in its white peace and prosperity to the indissoluble union of American States and the imperishable brotherhood of the American people. [*Immense cheering.*]

Now, what answer has New England to this message? Will she

permit the prejudices of war to remain in the hearts of the conquerors, when it has died in the hearts of the conquered? [*Cries of
"No! No!"*] Will she transmit this prejudice to the next generation,
that in their hearts, which never felt the generous ardor of conflict,
it may perpetuate itself? [*"No! No!"*] Will she withhold, save in
strained courtesy, the hand which straight from his soldier's heart
Grant offered to Lee at Appomattox? Will she make the vision of
a restored and happy people, which gathered above the couch of
your dying captain, filling his heart with grace, touching his lips
with praise and glorifying his path to the grave; will she make this
vision on which the last sigh of his expiring soul breathed a benediction, a cheat and a delusion? [*Tumultuous cheering and shouts
of "No! No!"*] If she does, the South, never abject in asking for comradeship, must accept with dignity its refusal; but if she does not;
if she accepts in frankness and sincerity this message of goodwill
and friendship, then will the prophecy of Webster, delivered in this
very Society forty years ago amid tremendous applause, be verified
in its fullest and final sense, when he said: "Standing hand to hand
and clasping hands, we should remain united as we have been for
sixty years, citizens of the same country, members of the same government, united, all united now and united forever. There have
been difficulties, contentions, and controversies, but I tell you that
in my judgment

> " 'Those opposed eyes,
> Which like the meteors of a troubled heaven,
> All of one nature, of one substance bred,
> Did lately meet in th' intestine shock,
> Shall now, in mutual well-beseeming ranks,
> March all one way.' "

[*Prolonged applause.*]

Booker T. Washington

ATLANTA EXPOSITION ADDRESS

¶ BOOKER T. WASHINGTON (1856-1915) was born a slave in Franklin County, Virginia. After emancipation he moved to Malden, West Virginia, where he obtained a meager elementary education while working in a salt furnace and in a coal mine. He attended Hampton Institute for three years, being graduated in 1875. He taught in Malden and at Hampton Institute and in 1881 became principal of a newly organized school for colored students at Tuskegee, Alabama. He devoted the rest of his life to developing Tuskegee into a large well-endowed training school for Negroes. As his reputation grew, he was invited to address many Northern audiences and he became the leading spokesman of his race on education and race relations. Of his various books, the best-known is his autobiography, *Up from Slavery*.

In 1895 he was asked to speak at the opening of the Cotton States Exposition in Atlanta. This was his first opportunity to address an important Southern white audience, but he had to adapt his remarks also to his white friends in the North and to the members of his own race who were present. The editor of the Atlanta *Constitution* said his address was "one of the most notable speeches, both as to character and as to the warmth of its reception, ever delivered to a Southern audience. The address was a revelation. The whole speech is a platform upon which blacks and whites can stand with full justice to each other." (The text that follows is from *Selected Speeches of Booker T. Washington,* edited by his son.)

M R. PRESIDENT and Gentlemen of the Board of Directors and Citizens: One third of the population of the South is of the Negro race. No enterprise seeking the material, civil, or moral welfare of this section can disregard this element of our population and reach the highest success. I but convey to you, Mr. President and Directors, the sentiment of the masses of my race when I say that in no way have the value and manhood of the American Negro been more fittingly and generously recognized than by the managers of this magnificent exposition at every stage of its progress. It is a recognition that will do more to cement the friendship of the two races than any occurrence since the dawn of our freedom.

Not only this, but the opportunity here afforded will awaken among us a new era of industrial progress. Ignorant and inexperienced, it is not strange that in the first years of our new life we began at the top instead of at the bottom; that a seat in Congress or the State Legislature was more sought than real estate or industrial skill; that the political convention or stump speaking had more attraction than starting a dairy farm or truck garden.

A ship lost at sea for many days suddenly sighted a friendly vessel. From the mast of the unfortunate vessel was seen a signal: "Water, water; we die of thirst!" The answer from the friendly vessel at once came back: "Cast down your bucket where you are." A second time the signal, "Water, water; send us water!" ran up from the distressed vessel, and was answered: "Cast down your bucket where you are." And a third and fourth signal for water was answered, "Cast down your bucket where you are." The captain of the distressed vessel, at last heeding the injunction, cast down his bucket, and it came up full of fresh, sparkling water from the mouth of the Amazon River. To those of my race who depend upon bettering their condition in a foreign land, or who underestimate the importance of cultivating friendly relations with the Southern white man who is their next-door neighbor, I would say: "Cast down your bucket where you are"—cast it down in making friends, in every manly way, of the people of all races by whom we are surrounded.

Cast it down in agriculture, mechanics, in commerce, in domestic service, and in the professions. And in this connection it is well to bear in mind that whatever other sins the South may be called to bear, when it comes to business, pure and simple, it is in the South that the Negro is given a man's chance in the commercial world, and in nothing is this Exposition more eloquent than in emphasizing this chance. Our greatest danger is that in the great leap from slavery to freedom we may overlook the fact that the masses of us are to live by the productions of our hands, and fail to keep in mind that we shall prosper in proportion as we learn to dignify and glorify common labor, and put brains and skill into the common occupations of life; shall prosper in proportion as we learn to draw the line between the superficial and the substantial, the ornamental gewgaws of life and the useful. No race can prosper till it learns that there is as much dignity in tilling a field as in writing a poem. It is at the bottom of life we must begin, and not at the top. Nor should we permit our grievances to overshadow our opportunities.

To those of the white race who look to the incoming of those of foreign birth and strange tongue and habits for the prosperity of the South, were I permitted, I would repeat what I say to my own race, "Cast down your bucket where you are." Cast it down among the eight million Negroes whose habits you know, whose fidelity and love you have tested in days when to have proved treacherous meant the ruin of your firesides. Cast down your bucket among these people who have without strikes and labor wars tilled your fields, cleared your forests, builded your railroads and cities, brought forth treasures from the bowels of the earth, and helped make possible this magnificent representation of the progress of the South. Casting down your bucket among my people, helping and encouraging them as you are doing on these grounds, and, with education of head, hand, and heart, you will find that they will buy your surplus land, make blossom the waste places in your fields, and run your factories. While doing this, you can be sure in the future, as in the past, that you and your families will be surrounded by the most patient, faithful, law-abiding, and unresentful people that the world has seen. As we have proved our loyalty to you in the past, in nursing your children, watching by the sick bed of your mothers and fathers, and often following them with tear-dimmed eyes to their graves, so in the future, in our humble way, we shall stand by you with a devotion that no foreigner can approach, ready to lay down our lives, if need be, in defense of yours, interlacing our industrial, commercial, civil, and religious life with yours in a way that shall make the interests of both races one. In all things that are purely social we can be as separate as the fingers, yet one as the hand in all things essential to mutual progress.

There is no defense or security for any of us except in the highest intelligence and development of all. If anywhere there are efforts tending to curtail the fullest growth of the Negro, let these efforts be turned into stimulating, encouraging, and making him the most useful and intelligent citizen. Effort or means so invested will pay a thousand per cent interest. These efforts will be twice blessed— "Blessing him that gives and him that takes."

There is no escape through law of man or God from the inevitable:

> *"The laws of changeless justice bind*
> *Oppressor with oppressed;*
> *And close as sin and suffering joined*
> *We march to fate abreast."*

Nearly sixteen millions of hands will aid you in pulling the load upward, or they will pull, against you, the load downward. We shall constitute one third and more of the ignorance and crime of the South, or one third its intelligence and progress; we shall contribute one third to the business and industrial prosperity of the South, or we shall prove a veritable body of death, stagnating, depressing, retarding every effort to advance the body politic.

Gentlemen of the Exposition, as we present to you our humble effort at an exhibition of our progress, you must not expect overmuch. Starting thirty years ago with ownership here and there in a few quilts and pumpkins and chickens (gathered from miscellaneous sources), remember, the path that has led from these to the inventions and production of agricultural implements, buggies, steam engines, newspapers, books, statuary, carving, paintings, the management of drugstores and banks, has not been trodden without contact with thorns and thistles. While we take pride in what we exhibit as a result of our independent efforts, we do not for a moment forget that our part in this exhibition would fall far short of your expectations but for the constant help that has come to our educational life, not only from the Southern states, but especialy from Northern philanthropists, who have made their gifts a constant stream of blessing and encouragement.

The wisest among my race understand that the agitation of questions of social equality is the extremest folly, and that progress in the enjoyment of all the privileges that will come to us must be the result of severe and constant struggle rather than of artificial forcing. No race that has anything to contribute to the markets of the world is long, in any degree, ostracized. It is important and right that all privileges of the law be ours, but it is vastly more important that we be prepared for the exercise of those privileges. The opportunity to earn a dollar in a factory just now is worth infinitely more than the opportunity to spend a dollar in an opera house.

In conclusion, may I repeat that nothing in thirty years has given us more hope and encouragement, and drawn us so near to you of the white race, as this opportunity offered by the Exposition; and here bending, as it were, over the altar that represents the results of the struggles of your race and mine, both starting practically empty-handed three decades ago, I pledge that, in your effort to work out the great and intricate problem which God has laid at the doors of the South, you shall have at all times the patient, sympathetic help of my race; only let this be constantly in mind, that while, from representations in these buildings of the product of field, of forest, of mine, of factory, letters, and art, much good will come, yet far above and beyond material benefits will be that higher good, that, let us pray God, will come in a blotting out of sectional differences and racial animosities and suspicions, in a determination to administer absolute justice, in a willing obedience among all classes to the mandates of law. This, coupled with our material prosperity, will bring into our beloved South a new heaven and a new earth.

Woodrow Wilson

FIRST INAUGURAL ADDRESS

❡ WOODROW WILSON (1856-1924) was born in Staunton, Virginia. He attended Davidson College briefly, leaving because of ill health, and later entered Princeton, from which he was graduated in 1879. He studied law at the University of Virginia and in 1882 was admitted to the bar in Georgia. A year later he went to Johns Hopkins for graduate study and obtained his Ph.D. in 1886. His thesis became his first book, *Congressional Government*. He taught at Bryn Mawr, Wesleyan, and Princeton, and in 1902 became president of Princeton. In 1910 he was elected governor of New Jersey. In 1912, running on the Democratic ticket against Taft and Theodore Roosevelt, he was elected President of the United States. The reforms of his first administration were interrupted by the outbreak of World War I. He steered a difficult course of neutrality and ran for re-election in 1916 on the slogan, "He kept us out of war." But in January the Germans resumed unrestricted submarine warfare and Wilson severed diplomatic relations with them. On April 2 he asked a special session of Congress for a declaration of war. Wilson's lofty idealism had powerfully affected the peoples of the world, and when he went to Europe for the peace conference he received such acclaim as has seldom been given to any man. Through his efforts the League of Nations was incorporated into the peace treaty, but it met strong opposition at home, and while touring the West to arouse the country to its support he suffered a stroke that made him an invalid during the rest of his life.

THERE HAS BEEN a change of government. It began two years ago, when the House of Representatives became Democratic by a decisive majority. It has now been completed. The Senate about to assemble will also be Democratic. The offices of President and Vice President have been put into the hands of Democrats. What does the change mean? That is the question that is uppermost in our minds to-day. That is the question I am going to try to answer, in order, if I may, to interpret the occasion.

It means much more than the mere success of a party. The success of a party means little except when the Nation is using that party for a large and definite purpose. No one can mistake the purpose for which the Nation now seeks to use the Democratic Party. It seeks to use it to interpret a change in its own plans and point of view. Some old things with which we had grown familiar, and which had begun to creep into the very habit of our thought and of our lives, have altered their aspect as we have latterly looked critically upon them, with fresh, awakened eyes; have dropped their disguises and shown themselves alien and sinister. Some new things, as we look frankly upon them, willing to comprehend their real character, have come to assume the aspect of things long believed in and familiar, stuff of our own convictions. We have been refreshed by a new insight into our own life.

We see that in many things that life is very great. It is incomparably great in its material aspects, in its body of wealth, in the diversity and sweep of its energy, in the industries which have been conceived and built up by the genius of individual men and the limitless enterprise of groups of men. It is great, also, very great, in its moral force. Nowhere else in the world have noble men and women exhibited in more striking forms the beauty and the energy of sympathy and helpfulness and counsel in their efforts to rectify wrong, alleviate suffering, and set the weak in the way of strength and hope. We have built up, moreover, a great system of government, which has stood through a long age as in many respects a model for those who seek to set liberty upon foundations that will endure against fortuitous change, against storm and accident. Our life contains every great thing, and contains it in rich abundance.

But the evil has come with the good, and much fine gold has been corroded. With riches has come inexcusable waste. We have squandered a great part of what we might have used, and have not stopped to conserve the exceeding bounty of nature, without which our genius for enterprise would have been worthless and impotent, scorning to be careful, shamefully prodigal as well as admirably efficient. We have been proud of our industrial achievements, but we have not hitherto stopped thoughtfully enough to count the human cost, the cost of lives snuffed out, of energies overtaxed and broken, the fearful physical and spiritual cost to the men and women and children upon whom the dead weight and burden of it all has fallen pitilessly the years through. The groans and agony of it all had not yet reached our ears, the solemn, moving undertone of our life, coming up out of the mines and factories and out of every home where the struggle had its intimate and familiar seat. With the great Government went many deep secret things which we too long delayed to look into and scrutinize with candid, fearless eyes. The great Government we loved has too often been made use of for private and selfish purposes, and those who used it had forgotten the people.

At last a vision has been vouchsafed us of our life as a whole. We see the bad with the good, the debased and decadent with the sound and vital. With this vision we approach new affairs. Our duty is to cleanse, to reconsider, to restore, to correct the evil without impairing the good, to purify and humanize every process of our common life without weakening or sentimentalizing it. There has been something crude and heartless and unfeeling in our haste to succeed and be great. Our thought has been "Let every man look out for himself, let every generation look out for itself," while we reared giant machinery which made it impossible that any but those who stood at the levers of control should have a chance to look out for themselves. We had not forgotten our morals. We remembered well enough that we had set up a policy which was meant to serve the humblest as well as the most powerful, with an eye single to the standards of justice and fair play, and remembered it with pride. But we were very heedless and in a hurry to be great.

We have come now to the sober second thought. The scales of heedlessness have fallen from our eyes. We have made up our minds to square every process of our national life again with the standards we so proudly set up at the beginning and have always carried at our hearts. Our work is a work of restoration.

We have itemized with some degree of particularity the things that ought to be altered and here are some of the chief items: A tariff which cuts us off from our proper part in the commerce of the world, violates the just principles of taxation, and makes the Government a facile instrument in the hands of private interests; a banking and currency system based upon the necessity of the Government to sell its bonds fifty years ago and perfectly adapted to concentrating cash and restricting credits; an industrial system which, take it on all its sides, financial as well as administrative, holds capital in leading strings, restricts the liberties and limits the opportunities of labor, and exploits without renewing or conserving the natural resources of the country; a body of agricultural activities never yet given the efficiency of great business undertakings or served as it should be through the instrumentality of science taken directly to the farm, or afforded the facilities of credit best suited to its practical needs; watercourses undeveloped, waste places unreclaimed, forests untended, fast disappearing without plan or prospect of renewal, unregarded waste heaps at every mine. We have studied as perhaps no other nation has the most effective means of production, but we have not studied cost or economy as we should either as organizers of industry, as statesmen, or as individuals.

Nor have we studied and perfected the means by which government may be put at the service of humanity, in safeguarding the health of the Nation, the health of its men and its women and its children, as well as their rights in the struggle for existence. This is no sentimental duty. The firm basis of government is justice, not pity. These are matters of justice. There can be no equality or opportunity, the first essential of justice in the body politic, if men and women and children be not shielded in their lives, their very vitality, from the consequences of great industrial and social processes which they can not alter, control, or singly cope with. Society must see to it that it does not itself crush or weaken or damage its own constituent parts. The first duty of law is to keep sound the society it serves. Sanitary laws, pure food laws, and laws determining conditions of labor which individuals are powerless to determine for themselves are intimate parts of the very business of justice and legal efficiency.

These are some of the things we ought to do, and not leave the others undone, the old-fashioned, never-to-be-neglected, fundamental safeguarding of property and of individual right. This is the high enterprise of the new day: To lift everything that concerns our life as a Nation to the light that shines from the hearthfire of every man's conscience and vision of the right. It is inconceivable that we should do this as partisans; it is inconceivable we should do it in ignorance of the facts as they are or in blind haste. We shall restore, not destroy. We shall deal with our economic system as it is and as it may be modified, not as it might be if we had a clean sheet of paper to write upon; and step by step we shall make it what it should be, in the spirit of those who question their own wisdom and seek counsel and knowledge, not shallow self-satisfaction or the excitement of excursions whither they can not tell. Justice, and only justice, shall always be our motto.

And yet it will be no cool process of mere science. The Nation has been deeply stirred, stirred by a solemn passion, stirred by the knowledge of wrong, of ideals lost, of government too often debauched and made an instrument of evil. The feelings with which we face this new age of right and opportunity sweep across our heartstrings like some air out of God's own presence, where justice and mercy are reconciled and the judge and the brother are one. We know our task to be no mere task of politics but a task which shall search us through and through, whether we be able to understand our time and the need of our people, whether we be indeed their spokesmen and interpreters, whether we have the pure heart to comprehend and the rectified will to choose our high course of action.

This is not a day of triumph; it is a day of dedication. Here muster, not the forces of party, but the forces of humanity. Men's hearts wait upon us; men's lives hang in the balance; men's hopes call upon us to say what we will do. Who shall live up to the great trust? Who dares fail to try? I summon all honest men, all patriotic, all forward-looking men, to my side. God helping me, I will not fail them, if they will but counsel and sustain me!

Woodrow Wilson

WAR MESSAGE

¶ SHORTLY AFTER the outbreak of war in Europe in 1914 President Wilson issued a proclamation of neutrality and for three years he tried sincerely to keep us out of the conflict in spite of the persistent and vigorous efforts of many partisans in America to involve us. During these years American feelings were constantly inflamed, but there was little understanding of the stakes in the contest until Wilson defined them in his war message. The address was delivered in the Capitol on the evening of April 2, 1917, before the members of both houses of Congress, the cabinet, the Supreme Court, the diplomatic corps, and packed galleries.

GENTLEMEN OF THE CONGRESS:
I have called the Congress into extraordinary session because there are serious, very serious, choices of policy to be made, and made immediately, which it was neither right nor constitutionally permissible that I should assume the responsibility of making.

On the third of February last I officially laid before you the extraordinary announcement of the Imperial German Government that on and after the first day of February it was its purpose to put aside all restraints of law or of humanity and use its submarines to sink every vessel that sought to approach either the ports of Great Britain and Ireland or the western coasts of Europe or any of the ports controlled by the enemies of Germany within the Mediterranean. That had seemed to be the object of the German submarine warfare earlier in the war, but since April of last year the Imperial Government had somewhat restrained the commanders of its undersea craft in conformity with its promise then given to us that passenger boats should not be sunk and that due warning would be given to all other vessels which its submarines might seek to destroy, when no resistance was offered or escape attempted, and care taken that their crews were given at least a fair chance to save their lives in their open boats. The precautions taken were meagre and haphazard enough, as was proved in distressing instance after instance in the progress of the cruel and unmanly business, but a certain degree of restraint was observed. The new policy has swept every restriction aside. Vessels of every kind, whatever their flag, their character, their cargo, their destination, their errand, have been ruthlessly sent to the bottom without warning and without thought of help or mercy for those on board, the vessels of friendly neutrals along with those of belligerents. Even hospital ships and ships carrying relief to the sorely bereaved and stricken people of Belgium, though the latter were provided with safe conduct through the proscribed areas by the German Government itself and were distinguished by unmistakable marks of identity, have been sunk with the same reckless lack of compassion or of principle.

I was for a little while unable to believe that such things would in fact be done by any government that had hitherto subscribed to the humane practices of civilized nations. International law had its origin in the attempt to set up some law which would be respected and observed upon the seas, where no nation had right of dominion and where lay the free highways of the world. By painful stage after stage has that law been built up, with meagre enough results, indeed, after all was accomplished that could be accomplished, but always with a clear view, at least, of what the heart and conscience of mankind demanded. This minimum of right the German Government has swept aside under the plea of retaliation and necessity and because it had no weapons which it could use at sea except these which it is impossible to employ as it is employing them without throwing to the winds all scruples of humanity or of respect for the understandings that were supposed to underlie the intercourse of the world. I am not now thinking of the loss of property involved, immense and serious as that is, but only of the wanton and whole-sale destruction of the lives of non-combatants, men, women, and children, engaged in pursuits which have always, even in the darkest periods of modern history, been deemed innocent and legitimate. Property can be paid for; the lives of peaceful and innocent people cannot be. The present German submarine warfare against commerce is a warfare against mankind.

It is a war against all nations. American ships have been sunk, American lives taken, in ways which it has stirred us very deeply to learn of, but the ships and people of other neutral and friendly nations have been sunk and overwhelmed in the waters in the same way. There has been no discrimination. The challenge is to all mankind. Each nation must decide for itself how it will meet it. The choice we make for ourselves must be made with a moderation of counsel and a temperateness of judgment befitting our character and our motives as a nation. We must put excited feeling away. Our motive will not be revenge or the victorious assertion of the physical might of the nation, but only the vindication of right, of human right, of which we are only a single champion.

When I addressed the Congress on the twenty-sixth of February last I thought that it would suffice to assert our neutral rights with arms, our right to use the seas against unlawful interference, our right to keep our people safe against unlawful violence. But armed neutrality, it now appears, is impracticable. Because submarines are in effect outlaws when used as the German submarines have been used against merchant shipping, it is impossible to defend ships against their attacks as the law of nations has assumed that merchantmen would defend themselves against privateers or cruisers, visible craft giving chase upon the open sea. It is common prudence in such circumstances, grim necessity indeed, to endeavor to destroy them before they have shown their own intention. They must be dealt with upon sight, if dealt with at all. The German Government denies the right of neutrals to use arms at all within the areas of the sea which it has proscribed, even in the defense of rights which no modern publicist has ever before questioned their right to defend.

The intimation is conveyed that the armed guards which we have placed on our merchant ships will be treated as beyond the pale of law and subject to be dealt with as pirates would be. Armed neutrality is ineffectual enough at best; in such circumstances and in the face of such pretensions it is worse than ineffectual: it is likely only to produce what it was meant to prevent; it is practically certain to draw us into the war without either the rights or the effectiveness of belligerents. There is one choice we cannot make, we are incapable of making: we will not choose the path of submission and suffer the most sacred rights of our nation and our people to be ignored or violated. The wrongs against which we now array ourselves are no common wrongs; they cut to the very roots of human life.

With a profound sense of the solemn and even tragical character of the step I am taking and of the grave responsibilities which it involves, but in unhesitating obedience to what I deem my constitutional duty, I advise that the Congress declare the recent course of the Imperial German Government to be in fact nothing less than war against the government and people of the United States; that it formally accept the status of belligerent which has thus been thrust upon it; and that it take immediate steps not only to put the country in a more thorough state of defense but also to exert all its power and employ all its resources to bring the Government of the German Empire to terms and end the war.

What this will involve is clear. It will involve the utmost practicable cooperation in counsel and action with the governments now at war with Germany, and, as incident to that, the extension to those governments of the most liberal financial credits, in order that our resources may so far as possible be added to theirs. It will involve the organization and mobilization of all the material resources of the country to supply the materials of war and serve the incidental needs of the nation in the most abundant and yet the most economical and efficient way possible. It will involve the immediate full equipment of the navy in all respects but particularly in supplying it with the best means of dealing with the enemy's submarines. It will involve the immediate addition to the armed forces of the

United States already provided for by law in case of war at least five hundred thousand men, who should, in my opinion, be chosen upon the principle of universal liability to service, and also the authorization of subsequent additional increments of equal force so soon as they may be needed and can be handled in training. It will involve also, of course, the granting of adequate credits to the Government, sustained, I hope, so far as they can equitably be sustained by the present generation, by well conceived taxation.

I say sustained so far as may be equitable by taxation because it seems to me that it would be most unwise to base the credits which will now be necessary entirely on money borrowed. It is our duty, I most respectfully urge, to protect our people so far as we may against the very serious hardships and evils which would be likely to arise out of the inflation which would be produced by vast loans.

In carrying out the measures by which these things are to be accomplished we should keep constantly in mind the wisdom of interfering as little as possible in our own preparation and in the equipment of our own military forces with the duty,—for it will be a very practical duty,—of supplying the nations already at war with Germany with the materials which they can obtain only from us or by our assistance. They are in the field and we should help them in every way to be effective there.

I shall take the liberty of suggesting, through the several executive departments of the Government, for the consideration of your committees, measures for the accomplishment of the several objects I have mentioned. I hope that it will be your pleasure to deal with them as having been framed after very careful thought by the branch of the Government upon which the responsibility of conducting the war and safeguarding the nation will most directly fall.

While we do these things, these deeply momentous things, let us be very clear, and make very clear to all the world what our motives and our objects are. My own thought has not been driven from its habitual and normal course by the unhappy events of the last two months, and I do not believe that the thought of the nation has been altered or clouded by them. I have exactly the same things in mind now that I had in mind when I addressed the Senate on the twenty-second of January last; the same that I had in mind when I addressed the Congress on the third of February and on the twenty-sixth of February. Our object now, as then, is to vindicate the principles of peace and justice in the life of the world as against selfish and autocratic power and to set up amongst the really free and self-governed peoples of the world such a concert of purpose and of action as will henceforth ensure the observance of those principles. Neutrality is no longer feasible or desirable where the peace of the world is involved and the freedom of its peoples, and the menace to that peace and freedom lies in the existence of autocratic governments backed by organized force which is controlled wholly by their will, not by the will of their people. We have seen the last of neutrality in such circumstances. We are at the beginning of an age in which it will be insisted that the same standards of conduct and of responsibility for wrong done shall be observed among nations and their governments that are observed among the individual citizens of civilized states.

We have no quarrel with the German people. We have no feeling towards them but one of sympathy and friendship. It was not upon their impulse that their government acted in entering this war. It was not with their previous knowledge or approval. It was a war determined upon as wars used to be determined upon in the old, unhappy days when peoples were nowhere consulted by their rulers and wars were provoked and waged in the interest of dynasties or of little groups of ambitious men who were accustomed to use their fellow men as pawns and tools. Self-governed nations do not fill their neighbour states with spies or set the course of intrigue to bring about some critical posture of affairs which will give them an opportunity to strike and make conquest. Such designs can be successfully worked out only under cover and where no one has the right to ask questions. Cunningly contrived plans of deception or aggression, carried, it may be, from generation to generation, can' be worked out and kept from the light only within the privacy of courts or behind the carefully guarded confidences of a narrow and privileged class. They are happily impossible where public opinion commands and insists upon full information concerning all the nation's affairs.

A steadfast concert for peace can never be maintained except by a partnership of democratic nations. No autocratic government could be trusted to keep faith within it or observe its covenants. It must be a league of honour, a partnership of opinion. Intrigue would eat its vitals away; the plottings of inner circles who could plan what they would and render account to no one would be a corruption seated at its very heart. Only free peoples can hold their purpose and their honour steady to a common end and prefer the interests of mankind to any narrow interest of their own.

Does not every American feel that assurance has been added to our hope for the future peace of the world by the wonderful and heartening things that have been happening within the last few weeks in Russia? Russia was known by those who knew it best to have been always in fact democratic at heart, in all the vital habits of her thought, in all the intimate relationships of her people that spoke their natural instinct, their habitual attitude towards life. The autocracy that crowned the summit of her political structure, long as it had stood and terrible as was the reality of its power, was not in fact Russian in origin, character, or purpose; and now it has been shaken off and the great, generous Russian people have been added in all their naive majesty and might to the forces that are fighting for freedom in the world, for justice, and for peace. Here is a fit partner for a League of Honour.

One of the things that has served to convince us that the Prussian autocracy was not and could never be our friend is that from the very outset of the present war it has filled our unsuspecting communities and even our offices of government with spies and set criminal intrigues everywhere afoot against our national unity of counsel, our peace within and without, our industries and our commerce. Indeed it is now evident that its spies were here even before the war began; and it is unhappily not a matter of conjecture but a fact proved in our courts of justice that the intrigues which have more than once come perilously near to disturbing the peace and dislocating the industries of the country have been carried on at the instigation, with the support, and even under the personal direction of official agents of the Imperial Government accredited to the Government of the United States. Even in checking these things and trying to extirpate them we have sought to put the most generous interpretation possible upon them because we knew that their source lay, not in any hostile feeling or purpose of the German people towards us (who were, no doubt as ignorant of them as we ourselves were), but only in the selfish designs of a Government that did what it pleased and told its people nothing. But they have played their part in serving to convince us at last that that Government entertains no real friendship for us and means to act against our peace and security at its convenience. That it means to stir up enemies against us at our very doors the intercepted note to the German Minister at Mexico City is eloquent evidence.

We are accepting this challenge of hostile purpose because we know that in such a government, following such methods, we can never have a friend; and that in the presence of its organized power, always lying in wait to accomplish we know not what purpose, there can be no assured security for the democratic governments of the world. We are now about to accept gauge of battle with this natural foe to liberty and shall, if necessary, spend the whole force of the nation to check and nullify its pretensions and its power. We are glad, now that we see the facts with no veil of false pretence about them, to fight thus for the ultimate peace of the world and for the liberation of its peoples, the German peoples included: for the rights of nations great and small and the privilege of men everywhere to choose their way of life and of obedience. The world must be made safe for democracy. Its peace must be planted upon the tested foundations of political liberty. We have no selfish ends to serve. We desire no conquest, no dominion. We seek no indemnities for ourselves, no material compensation for the sacrifices we shall freely make. We are but one of the champions of the rights of mankind. We shall be satisfied when those rights have been made as secure as the faith and the freedom of nations can make them.

Just because we fight without rancour and without selfish object, seeking nothing for ourselves but what we shall wish to share with all free peoples, we shall, I feel confident, conduct our operations as belligerents without passion and ourselves observe with proud punctilio the principles of right and of fair play we profess to be fighting for.

I have said nothing of the governments allied with the Imperial Government of Germany because they have not made war upon us or challenged us to defend our right and our honour. The Austro-Hungarian Government has, indeed, avowed its unqualified endorsement and acceptance of the reckless and lawless submarine warfare adopted now without disguise by the Imperial German Government, and it has therefore not been possible for this Government to receive Count Tarnowski, the Ambassador recently accredited to this Government by the Imperial and Royal Government of Austria-Hungary; but that Government has not actually engaged in warfare against citizens of the United States on the seas, and I take the liberty, for the present at least, of postponing a discussion of our relations with the authorities at Vienna. We enter this war only where we are clearly forced into it because there are no other means of defending our rights.

It will be all the easier for us to conduct ourselves as belligerents in a high spirit of right and fairness because we act without animus, not in enmity towards a people or with the desire to bring any injury or disadvantage upon them, but only in armed opposition to an irresponsible government which has thrown aside all considerations of humanity and of right and is running amuck. We are, let me say again, the sincere friends of the German people, and shall desire nothing so much as the early re-establishment of intimate relations of mutual advantage between us,—however hard it may be for them, for the time being, to believe that this is spoken from our hearts. We have borne with their present government through all these bitter months because of that friendship,—exercising a patience and forbearance which would otherwise have been impossible. We shall, happily, still have an opportunity to prove that friendship in our daily attitude and actions towards the millions of men and women of German birth and native sympathy who live amongst us and share our life, and we shall be proud to prove it towards all who are in fact loyal to their neighbours and to the Government in the hour of test. They are, most of them, as true and loyal Americans as if they had never known any other fealty or allegiance. They will be prompt to stand with us in rebuking and restraining the few who may be of a different mind and purpose. If there should be disloyalty, it will be dealt with with a firm hand of stern repression; but, if it lifts its head at all, it will lift it only here and there and without countenance except from a lawless and malignant few.

It is a distressing and oppressive duty, Gentlemen of the Congress, which I have performed in thus addressing you. There are, it may be, many months of fiery trial and sacrifice ahead of us. It is a fearful thing to lead this great peaceful people into war, into the most terrible and disastrous of all wars, civilization itself seeming to be in the balance. But the right is more precious than peace, and we shall fight for the things which we have always carried nearest our hearts,—for democracy, for the right of those who submit to authority to have a voice in their own governments, for the rights and liberties of small nations, for a universal dominion of right by such a concert of free peoples as shall bring peace and safety to all nations and make the world itself at last free. To such a task we can dedicate our lives and our fortunes, everything that we are and everything that we have, with the pride of those who know that the day has come when America is privileged to spend her blood and her might for the principles that gave her birth and happiness and the peace which she has treasured. God helping her, she can do no other.

Theodore Roosevelt

THE MAN WITH THE MUCK RAKE

❡ THEODORE ROOSEVELT (1858-1919) was born October 27, 1858. He attended Harvard University from 1876-80; served as Civil Service Commissioner from 1889-95; Police Commissioner of New York, 1895-97; Assistant Secretary of the Navy, 1897-98. Following service as a cavalry officer in the Spanish-American War, he was elected governor of New York in 1898. In 1900, he became Vice-President under President McKinley, succeeding to the presidency upon McKinley's assassination. He was re-elected to the presidency in 1904. In 1912, Roosevelt left the Republican party, and became a candidate for the presidency on the independent Progressive ticket. During his years as a public man, he was an advocate of many social reforms.

In the early part of the twentieth century, various magazine writers participated in a campaign of exposure of corrupt and evil practices in the capitalistic system. Roosevelt had given encouragement and sanction to these reform efforts. In what appeared to be a reversal of sentiment, Roosevelt took the occasion of the laying of the cornerstone for the Congressional Office Building in Washington to ask that caution and restraint be exercised in the campaign of exposure, and that reform be accompanied by sanity. The speech was delivered April 14, 1906, before a distinguished assemblage, including the members of the Supreme Court, the members of the Senate and House of Representatives, the diplomatic corps, and a large concourse of people who were on hand to witness the ceremony and to listen to the remarks of the President, which had been heralded by the press many days in advance of their delivery. (The text of the address is taken from the *Chicago Sunday Tribune*, April 15, 1906, pp. 1, 2.)

OVER A CENTURY AGO Washington laid the corner stone of the Capitol in what was then little more than a tract of wooded wilderness here beside the Potomac. We now find it necessary to provide by great additional buildings for the business of the government.

This growth in the need for the housing of the government is but a proof and example of the way in which the nation has grown and the sphere of action of the national government has grown. We now administer the affairs of a nation in which the extraordinary growth of population has been outstripped by the growth of wealth in complex interests. The material problems that face us today are not such as they were in Washington's time, but the underlying facts of human nature are the same now as they were then. Under altered external form we war with the same tendencies toward evil that were evident in Washington's time, and are helped by the same tendencies for good. It is about some of these that I wish to say a word today.

In Bunyan's "Pilgrim's Progress" you may recall the description of the Man with the Muck Rake, the man who could look no way but downward, with the muck rake in his hand; who was offered a celestial crown for his muck rake, but who would neither look up nor regard the crown he was offered, but continued to rake to himself the filth of the floor.

In "Pilgrim's Progress" the Man with the Muck Rake is set forth as the example of him whose vision is fixed on carnal instead of spiritual things. Yet he also typifies the man who in this life consistently refuses to see aught that is lofty, and fixes his eyes with solemn intentness only on that which is vile and debasing.

Now, it is very necessary that we should not flinch from seeing what is vile and debasing. There is filth on the floor, and it must be scraped up with the muck rake; and there are times and places where this service is the most needed of all the services that can be performed. But the man who never does anything else, who never thinks or speaks or writes, save of his feats with the muck rake, speedily becomes, not a help but one of the most potent forces for evil.

There are in the body politic, economic and social, many and grave evils, and there is urgent necessity for the sternest war upon them. There should be relentless exposure of and attack upon every evil man, whether politician or business man, every evil practice, whether in politics, business, or in social life. I hail as a benefactor every writer or speaker, every man who, on the platform or in a book, magazine, or newspaper, with merciless severity makes such attack, provided always that he in his turn remembers that the attack is of use only if it is absolutely truthful.

The liar is no whit better than the thief, and if his mendacity takes the form of slander he may be worse than most thieves. It puts a premium upon knavery untruthfully to attack an honest man, or even with hysterical exaggeration to assail a bad man with untruth.

An epidemic of indiscriminate assault upon character does no good, but very great harm. The soul of every scoundrel is gladdened whenever an honest man is assailed, or even when a scoundrel is untruthfully assailed.

Now, it is easy to twist out of shape what I have just said, easy to affect to misunderstand it, and if it is slurred over in repetition not difficult really to misunderstand it. Some persons are sincerely incapable of understanding that to denounce mud slinging does not mean the endorsement of whitewashing; and both the interested individuals who need whitewashing and those others who practice mud slinging like to encourage such confusion of ideas.

One of the chief counts against those who make indiscriminate assault upon men in business or men in public life is that they invite a reaction which is sure to tell powerfully in favor of the unscrupulous scoundrel who really ought to be attacked, who ought to be exposed, who ought, if possible, to be put in the penitentiary. If Aristides is praised overmuch as just, people get tired of hearing it; and overcensure of the unjust finally and from similar reasons results in their favor.

Any excess is almost sure to invite a reaction; and, unfortunately, the reaction, instead of taking the form of punishment of those guilty of the excess, is apt to take the form either of punishment of the unoffending or of giving immunity, and even strength, to offenders. The effort to make financial or political profit out of the destruction of character can only result in public calamity. Gross and reckless assaults on character, whether on the stump or in newspaper, magazine, or book, create a morbid and vicious public sentiment, and at the same time act as a profound deterrent to able men of normal sensitiveness and tend to prevent them from entering the public service at any price.

As an instance in point, I may mention that one serious difficulty encountered in getting the right type of men to dig the Panama canal is the certainty that they will be exposed, both without, and, I am sorry to say, sometimes within, Congress, to utterly reckless assaults on their character and capacity.

At the risk of repetition let me say again that my plea is not for immunity to, but for the most unsparing exposure of, the politician who betrays his trust, of the big business man who makes or spends his fortune in illegitimate or corrupt ways. There should be a resolute effort to hunt every such man out of the position he has disgraced. Expose the crime, and hunt down the criminal; but remember that even in the case of crime, if it is attacked in sensational, lurid, and untruthful fashion, the attack may do more damage to the public mind than the crime itself.

It is because I feel that there should be no rest in the endless war against the forces of evil that I ask the war be conducted with sanity as well as with resolution.

The men with the muck rakes are often indispensable to the well being of society; but only if they know when to stop raking the muck, and to look upward to the celestial crown above them, to the crown of worthy endeavor. There are beautiful things above and round about them; and if they gradually grow to feel that the whole world is nothing but muck, their power of usefulness is gone.

If the whole picture is painted black there remains no hue whereby to single out the rascals for distinction from their fellows. Such painting finally induces a kind of moral color blindness; and people affected by it come to the conclusion that no man is really black, and no man really white, but they are all gray.

In other words, they neither believe in the truth of the attack, nor in the honesty of the man who is attacked; they grow as suspicious of the accusation as of the offense; it becomes well nigh hopeless to stir them either to wrath against wrongdoing or to enthusiasm for what is right; and such a mental attitude in the public gives hope to every knave, and is the despair of honest men.

To assail the great and admitted evils of our political and industrial life with such crude and sweeping generalizations as to include decent men in the general condemnation means the searing of the public conscience. There results a general attitude either of cynical belief in and indifference to public corruption or else of a distrustful inability to discriminate between the good and the bad. Either attitude is fraught with untold damage to the country as a whole.

The fool who has not sense to discriminate between what is good and what is bad is well nigh as dangerous as the man who does discriminate and yet chooses the bad. There is nothing more distressing to every good patriot, to every good American, than the hard, scoffing spirit which treats the allegation of dishonesty in a public man as a cause for laughter. Such laughter is worse than the crackling of thorns under a pot, for it denotes not merely the vacant mind, but the heart in which high emotions have been choked before they could grow to fruition.

There is any amount of good in the world, and there never was a time when loftier and more disinterested work for the betterment of mankind was being done than now. The forces that tend for evil are great and terrible, but the forces of truth and love and courage and honesty and generosity and sympathy are also stronger than ever before. It is a foolish and timid, no less than a wicked thing, to blink the fact that the forces of evil are strong, but it is even worse to fail to take into account the strength of the forces that tell for good.

Hysterical sensationalism is the poorest weapon wherewith to fight for lasting righteousness. The men who with stern sobriety and truth assail the many evils of our time, whether in the public press, or in magazines, or in books, are the leaders and allies of all engaged in the work for social and political betterment. But if they give good reason for distrust of what they say, if they chill the ardor of those who demand truth as a primary virtue, they thereby betray the good cause and play into the hands of the very men against whom they are nominally at war.

In his Ecclesiastical Polity that fine old Elizabethan divine, Bishop Hooker, wrote:

He that goeth about to persuade a multitude that they are not so well governed as they ought to be shall never want attentive and favorable hearers, because they know the manifold defects whereunto every kind of regimen is subject, but the secret lets and difficulties, which in public proceedings are innumerable and inevitable, they have not ordinarily the judgment to consider.

This truth should be kept constantly in mind by every free people desiring to preserve the sanity and poise indispensable to the permanent success of self-government. Yet, on the other hand, it is vital not to permit this spirit of sanity and self-command to degenerate into mere mental stagnation. Bad though a state of hysterical excitement is, and evil though the results are which come from the violent oscillations such excitement invariably produces, yet a sodden acquiescence in evil is even worse.

At this moment we are passing through a period of great unrest— social, political, and industrial unrest. It is of the utmost importance for our future that this should prove to be not the unrest of mere rebelliousness against life, of mere dissatisfaction with the inevitable inequality of conditions, but the unrest of a resolute and eager ambition to secure the betterment of the individual and the nation.

So far as this movement of agitation throughout the country takes the form of a fierce discontent with evil, of a determination to punish the authors of evil, whether in industry or politics, the feeling is to be heartily welcomed as a sign of healthy life.

If, on the other hand, it turns into a mere crusade of appetite against appetite, of a contest between the brutal greed of the 'have nots' and the brutal greed of the 'haves,' then it has no significance for good, but only for evil. If it seeks to establish a line of cleavage, not along the line which divides good men from bad, but along that other line, running at right angles thereto, which divides those who are well off from those who are less well off, then it will be fraught with immeasurable harm to the body politic.

We can no more and no less afford to condone evil in the man of capital than evil in the man of no capital. The wealthy man who exults because there is a failure of justice in the effort to bring some trust magnate to an account for his misdeeds is as bad as, and no worse than, the so-called labor leader who clamorously strives to excite a foul class feeling on behalf of some other labor leader who is implicated in murder. One attitude is as bad as the other, and no worse; in each case the accused is entitled to exact justice; and in neither case is there need of action by others which can be construed into an expression of sympathy for crime.

It is a prime necessity that if the present unrest is to result in permanent good the emotion shall be translated into action, and that the action shall be marked by honesty, sanity, and self-restraint. There is mighty little good in a mere spasm of reform. The reform that counts is that which comes through steady, continuous growth; violent emotionalism leads to exhaustion.

It is important to this people to grapple with the problems connected with the amassing of enormous fortunes, and the use of those fortunes, both corporate and individual, in business. We should discriminate in the sharpest way between fortunes well won and fortunes ill won; between those gained as an incident to performing great services to the community as a whole and those gained in evil fashion by keeping just within the limits of mere law honesty. Of course, no amount of charity in spending such fortunes in any way compensates for misconduct in making them.

As a matter of personal conviction, and without pretending to discuss the details or formulate the system, I feel that we shall ultimately have to consider the adoption of some such scheme as that of a progressive tax on all fortunes, beyond a certain amount, either given in life or devised or bequeathed upon death to any individual— a tax so framed as to put it out of the power of the owner of one of these enormous fortunes to hand on more than a certain amount to any one individual; the tax, of course, to be imposed by the national and not the state government. Such taxation should, of course, be aimed merely at the inheritance or transmission in their entirety of those fortunes swollen beyond all healthy limits.

Again, the national government must in some form exercise supervision over corporations engaged in interstate business—and all large corporations are engaged in interstate business—whether by license or otherwise, so as to permit us to deal with the far reaching evils of overcapitalization.

This year we are making a beginning in the direction of serious effort to settle some of these economic problems by the railway rate legislation. Such legislation, if so framed, as I am sure it will be, as to secure definite and tangible results, will amount to something of itself; and it will amount to a great deal more in so far as it is taken as a first step in the direction of a policy of superintendence and control over corporate wealth engaged in interstate commerce; this superintendence and control not to be exercised in a spirit of malevolence toward the men who have created the wealth, but with the firm purpose both to do justice to them and to see that they in their turn do justice to the public at large.

The first requisite in the public servants who are to deal in this shape with corporations, whether as legislators or as executives, is honesty. This honesty can be no respecter of persons. There can be no such thing as unilateral honesty. The danger is not really from corrupt corporations; it springs from the corruption itself, whether exercised for or against corporations.

The eighth commandment reads, 'Thou shalt not steal.' It does not read, 'Thou shalt not steal from the rich man.' It does not read, 'Thou shalt not steal from the poor man.' It reads simply and plainly, 'Thou shalt not steal.'

No good whatever will come from that warped and mock morality which denounces the misdeeds of men of wealth and forgets the misdeeds practiced at their expense; which denounces bribery, but blinds itself to blackmail; which foams with rage if a corporation secures favors by improper methods, and merely leers with hideous mirth if the corporation is itself wronged.

The only public servant who can be trusted honestly to protect the rights of the public against the misdeeds of a corporation is that public man who will just as surely protect the corporation itself from wrongful aggression.

If a public man is willing to yield to popular clamor and do wrong to the men of wealth or to rich corporations, it may be set down as certain that if the opportunity comes he will secretly and furtively do wrong to the public in the interest of a corporation.

But in addition to honesty, we need sanity. No honesty will make a public man useful if that man is timid or foolish, if he is a hot-headed zealot or an impracticable visionary. As we strive for reform we find that it is not at all merely the case of a long uphill pull. On the contrary, there is almost as much of breeching work as of collar work. To depend only on traces means that there will soon be a runaway and an upset.

The men of wealth who today are trying to prevent the regulation and control of their business in the interest of the public by the proper government authorities will not succeed, in my judgment, in checking the progress of the movement. But if they did succeed they would find that they had sown the wind and would surely reap the whirlwind, for they would ultimately provoke the violent excesses which accompany a reform coming by convulsion instead of by steady and natural growth.

On the other hand, the wild preachers of unrest and discontent, the wild agitators against the entire existing order, the men who act crookedly, whether because of sinister design or from mere puzzle headedness, the men who preach destruction without proposing any substitute for what they intend to destroy, or who propose a substitute which would be far worse than the existing evils—all these men are the most dangerous opponents of real reform. If they get their way they will lead the people into a deeper pit than any into which they could fall under the present system. If they fail to get their way they will still do incalulable harm by provoking the kind of reaction which in its revolt against the senseless evil of their teaching would enthrone more securely than ever the evils which their misguided followers believe they are attacking.

More important than aught else is the development of the broadest sympathy of man for man. The welfare of the wage worker, the welfare of the tiller of the soil, upon these depend the welfare of the entire country; their good is not to be sought in pulling down others; but their good must be the prime object of all our statesmanship.

Materially we must strive to secure a broader economic opportunity for all men, so that each shall have a better chance to show the stuff of which he is made. Spiritually and ethically we must strive to bring about clean living and right thinking. We appreciate that the things of the body are important; but we appreciate also that the things of the soul are immeasurably more important.

The foundation stone of national life is, and ever must be, the high individual character of the average citizen.

William Jennings Bryan

THE CROSS OF GOLD

❡ WILLIAM JENNINGS BRYAN (1860-1925) was born in Salem, Illinois, and educated at Illinois College and the Union College of Law in Chicago. He was admitted to the Illinois bar in 1883. Four years later he moved to Lincoln, Nebraska. He served two terms in Congress (1891-95), and, after he was defeated for the United States Senate, edited the *Omaha World Herald* for two years. He lectured widely on bimetallism and wrote the silver plank for the Democratic party platform in 1896. His defense of this platform before the convention won him the nomination to the presidency. He made a vigorous campaign, sometimes delivering fifteen to twenty speeches a day, but was defeated by McKinley. During the Spanish-American War he commanded a regiment of infantry. In 1900 he was again nominated for the presidency. After his defeat he founded and edited a magazine, *The Commoner,* at Lincoln, and continued to exert a strong influence on the country through his writing and lecturing. In 1908 he was nominated a third time for the presidency. Four years later he was influential in obtaining the nomination of Woodrow Wilson and he served for two years as Wilson's Secretary of State. His declining years were spent in combating intemperance, religious apathy, and evolution.

The "Cross of Gold" speech was delivered at the Democratic Convention in Chicago in 1896 in support of the silver platform. It won such an ovation as is seldom given a speaker even at a political convention. In *The First Battle* (Chicago, 1896, p. 206) Bryan says, "A portion of the speech was extemporaneous, and its arrangement entirely so, but parts of it had been prepared for another occasion."

M R. CHAIRMAN and Gentlemen of the Convention: I would be presumptuous, indeed, to present myself against the distinguished gentlemen to whom you have listened if this were a mere measuring of abilities; but this is not a contest between persons. The humblest citizen in all the land, when clad in the armor of a righteous cause, is stronger than all the hosts of error. I come to speak to you in defense of a cause as holy as the cause of liberty—the cause of humanity.

When this debate is concluded, a motion will be made to lay upon the table the resolution offered in commendation of the administration, and also the resolution offered in condemnation of the administration. We object to bringing this question down to the level of persons. The individual is but an atom; he is born, he acts, he dies; but principles are eternal; and this has been a contest over a principle.

Never before in the history of this country has there been witnessed such a contest as that through which we have just passed. Never before in the history of American politics has a great issue been fought out as this issue has been, by the voters of a great party. On the fourth of March, 1895, a few Democrats, most of them members of Congress, issued an address to the Democrats of the nation, asserting that the money question was the paramount issue of the hour; declaring that a majority of the Democratic party had the right to control the action of the party on this paramount issue; and concluding with the request that the believers in the free coinage of silver in the Democratic party should organize, take charge of, and control the policy of the Democratic party. Three months later, at Memphis, an organization was perfected, and the silver Democrats went forth openly and courageously proclaiming their belief, and declaring that, if successful, they would crystallize into a platform the declaration which they had made. Then began the conflict. With a zeal approaching the zeal which inspired the crusaders who followed Peter the Hermit, our silver Democrats went forth from victory unto victory until they are now assembled, not to discuss, not to debate, but to enter up the judgment already rendered by the plain people of this country. In this contest brother has been arrayed against brother, father against son. The warmest ties of love, acquaintance and association have been disregarded; old leaders have been cast aside when they have refused to give expression to the sentiments of those whom they would lead, and new leaders have sprung up to give direction to this cause of truth. Thus has the contest been waged, and we have assembled here under as binding and solemn instructions as were ever imposed upon representatives of the people.

We do not come as individuals. As individuals we might have been glad to compliment the gentleman from New York [Senator Hill], but we know that the people for whom we speak would never be willing to put him in a position where he could thwart the will of the Democratic party. I say it was not a question of persons; it was a question of principle, and it is not with gladness, my friends, that we find ourselves brought into conflict with those who are now arrayed on the other side.

The gentleman who preceded me [ex-Governor Russell] spoke of the State of Massachusetts; let me assure him that not one present in all this convention entertains the least hostility to the people of the State of Massachusetts, but we stand here representing people who are the equals, before the law, of the greatest citizens in the State of Massachusetts. When you [turning to the gold delegates] come before us and tell us that we are about to disturb your business interests, we reply that you have disturbed our business interests by your course.

We say to you that you have made the definition of a business man too limited in its application. The man who is employed for wages is as much a business man as his employer, the attorney in a country town is as much a business man as the corporation counsel in a great metropolis; the merchant at the cross-roads store is as much a business man as the merchant of New York; the farmer who goes forth in the morning and toils all day—who begins in the spring and toils all summer—and who by the application of brain and muscle to the natural resources of the country creates wealth, is as much a business man as the man who goes upon the board of trade and bets upon the price of grain; the miners who go down a thousand feet into the earth, or climb two thousand feet upon the cliffs, and bring forth from their hiding places the precious metals to be poured into the channels of trade are as much business men as the few financial magnates who, in a back room, corner the money of the world. We come to speak for this broader class of business men.

Ah, my friends, we say not one word against those who live upon the Atlantic coast, but the hardy pioneers who have braved all the dangers of the wilderness, who have made the desert to blossom as the rose—the pioneers away out there [*pointing to the West*], who rear their children near to Nature's heart, where they can mingle their voices with the voices of the birds—out there where they have erected schoolhouses for the education of their young, churches where they praise their Creator, and cemeteries where rest the ashes of their dead—these people, we say, are as deserving of the consideration of our party as any people in this country. It is for these that we speak. We do not come as aggressors. Our war is not a war of conquest; we are fighting in the defense of our homes, our families, and posterity. We have petitioned, and our petitions have been scorned; we have entreated, and our entreaties have been disregarded; we have begged, and they have mocked when our calamity came. We beg no longer; we entreat no more; we petition no more. We defy them.

The gentleman from Wisconsin has said that he fears a Robespierre. My friends, in this land of the free you need not fear that a tyrant will spring up from among the people. What we need is an Andrew Jackson to stand, as Jackson stood, against the encroachments of organized wealth.

They tell us that this platform was made to catch votes. We reply to them that changing conditions make new issues; that the principles upon which Democracy rests are as everlasting as the hills, but that they must be applied to new conditions as they arise. Conditions have arisen, and we are here to meet these conditions. They tell us that the income tax ought not to be brought in here; that it is a new idea. They criticize us for our criticism of the Supreme Court of the United States. My friends, we have not criticized; we have simply called attention to what you already know. If you want criticisms, read the dissenting opinions of the court. There you will find criticisms. They say that we passed an unconstitutional law; we deny it. The income tax law was not unconstitutional when it was passed; it was not unconstitutional when it went before the Supreme Court for the first time; it did not become unconstitutional until one of the judges changed his mind, and we cannot be expected to know when a judge will change his mind. The income tax is just. It simply intends to put the burdens of government justly upon the backs of the people. I am in favor of an income tax. When I find a man who is not willing to bear his share of the burdens of the government which protects him, I find a man who is unworthy to enjoy the blessings of a government like ours.

They say that we are opposing national bank currency; it is true. If you will read what Thomas Benton said, you will find he said that, in searching history, he could find but one parallel to Andrew Jackson; that was Cicero, who destroyed the conspiracy of Cataline and saved Rome. Benton said that Cicero only did for Rome what Jackson did for us when he destroyed the bank conspiracy and saved America. We say in our platform that we believe that the right to coin and issue money is a function of government. We believe it. We believe that it is a part of sovereignty, and can no more with safety be delegated to private individuals than we could afford to delegate to private individuals the power to make penal statutes or levy taxes. Mr. Jefferson, who was once regarded as good Democratic authority, seems to have differed in opinion from the gentleman who has addrest us on the part of the minority. Those who are opposed to this proposition tell us that the issue of paper money is a function of the bank, and that the Government ought to go out of the banking business. I stand with Jefferson rather than with them, and tell them, as he did, that the issue of money is a function of government, and that the banks ought to go out of the governing business.

They complain about the plank which declares against life tenure in office. They have tried to strain it to mean that which it does not mean. What we oppose by that plank is the life tenure which is being built up in Washington, and which excludes from participation in official benefits the humbler members of society.

Let me call your attention to two or three important things. The gentleman from New York says that he will propose an amendment to the platform providing that the proposed change in our monetary system shall not affect contracts already made. Let me remind you that there is no intention of affecting those contracts which according to present laws are made payable in gold; but if he means to say that we cannot change our monetary system without protecting those who have loaned money before the change was made, I desire to ask him where, in law or in morals, he can find justification for not protecting the debtors when the act of 1873 was passed, if he now insists that we must protect the creditors.

He says he will also propose an amendment which will provide for the suspension of free coinage if we fail to maintain the parity within a year. We reply that when we advocate a policy which we believe will be successful, we are not compelled to raise a doubt as to our own sincerity by suggesting what we shall do if we fail. I ask him, if he would apply his logic to us, why he does not apply it to himself. He says he wants this country to try to secure an international agreement. Why does he not tell us what he is going to do if he fails to secure an international agreement? There is more reason for him to do that than there is for us to provide against the failure to maintain the parity. Our opponents have tried for twenty years to secure an international agreement, and those are waiting for it most patiently who do not want it at all.

And now, my friends, let me come to the paramount issue. If they ask us why it is that we say more on the money question than we say upon the tariff question, I reply that, if protection has slain its thousands, the gold standard has slain its tens of thousands. If they ask us why we do not embody in our platform all the things that we believe in, we reply that when we have restored the money of the Constitution all other necessary reforms will be possible; but that until this is done there is no other reform that can be accomplished.

Why is it that within three months such a change has come over the country? Three months ago, when it was confidently asserted that those who believe in the gold standard would frame our platform and nominate our candidates, even the advocates of the gold standard did not think that we could elect a President. And they had good reason for their doubt, because there is scarcely a State here to-day asking for the gold standard which is not in the absolute control of the Republican party. But note the change. Mr. McKinley was nominated at St. Louis upon a platform which declared for the maintenance of the gold standard until it can be changed into bimetallism by international agreement. Mr. McKinley was the most popular man among the Republicans, and three months ago everybody in the Republican party prophesied his election. How is it to-day? Why, the man who was once pleased to think that he looked like Napoleon—that man shudders to-day when he remembers that he was nominated on the anniversary of the battle of Waterloo. Not only that, but as he listens he can hear with ever-increasing distinctness the sound of the waves as they beat upon the lonely shores of St. Helena.

Why this change? Ah, my friends, is not the reason for the change evident to any one who will look at the matter? No private character, however pure, no personal popularity, however great, can protect from the avenging wrath of an indignant people a man who will declare that he is in favor of fastening the gold standard upon this country, or who is willing to surrender the right of self-government and place the legislative control of our affairs in the hands of foreign potentates and powers.

We go forth confident that we shall win. Why? Because upon the paramount issue of this campaign there is not a spot of ground upon which the enemy will dare to challenge battle. If they tell us that the gold standard is a good thing, we shall point to their platform and tell them that their platform pledges the party to get rid of the gold standard and substitute bimetallism. If the gold standard is a good thing, why try to get rid of it? I call your attention to the fact that some of the very people who are in this convention to-day and who tell us that we ought to declare in favor of international bimetallism—thereby declaring that the gold standard is wrong and that the principle of bimetallism is better—these very people four months ago were open and avowed advocates of the gold standard, and were then telling us that we could not legislate two metals together, even with the aid of all the world. If the gold standard is a good thing, we ought to declare in favor of its retention and not in favor of abandoning it; and if the gold standard is a bad thing why should we wait until other nations are willing to help us to let go? Here is the line of battle, and we care not upon which issue they force the fight; we are prepared to meet them on either issue or on both. If they tell us that the gold standard is the standard of civilization, we reply to them that this, the most enlightened of all the nations of the earth, has never declared for a gold standard and that both the great parties this year are declaring against it. If the gold standard is the standard of civilization, why, my friends, should we not have it? If they come to meet us on that issue we can present the history of our nation. More than that; we can tell them that they will search the pages of history in vain to find a single instance where the common people of any land have ever declared themselves in favor of the gold standard. They can find where the holders of fixt investments have declared for a gold standard, but not where the masses have.

Mr. Carlisle said in 1878 that this was a struggle between "the idle holders of idle capital" and "the struggling masses, who produce the wealth and pay the taxes of the country"; and, my friends, the question we are to decide is: Upon which side will the Democratic party fight; upon the side of "the idle holders of idle capital" or upon the side of "the struggling masses"? That is the question which the party must answer first, and then it must be answered by each individual hereafter. The sympathies of the Democratic party, as shown by the platform, are on the side of the struggling masses who have ever been the foundation of the Democratic party. There are two ideas of government. There are those who believe that, if you will only legislate to make the well-to-do prosperous, their prosperity will leak through on those below. The Democratic idea, however, has been that if you legislate to make the masses prosperous, their prosperity will find its way up through every class which rests upon them.

You come to us and tell us that the great cities are in favor of the gold standard; we reply that the great cities rest upon our broad and fertile prairies. Burn down your cities and leave our farms, and your cities will spring up again as if by magic; but destroy our farms and the grass will grow in the streets of every city in the country.

My friends, we declare that this nation is able to legislate for its own people on every question, without waiting for the aid or consent of any other nation on earth; and upon that issue we expect to carry every State in the Union. I shall not slander the inhabitants of the fair State of Massachusetts nor the inhabitants of the State of New York by saying that, when they are confronted with the proposition, they will declare that this nation is not able to attend to its own business. It is the issue of 1776 over again. Our ancestors, when but three millions in number, had the courage to declare their political independence of every other nation; shall we, their descendants, when we have grown to seventy millions, declare that we are less independent than our forefathers? No, my friends, that will never be the verdict of our people. Therefore, we care not upon what lines the battle is fought. If they say bimetallism is good, but that we cannot have it until other nations help us, we reply that, instead of having a gold standard because England has, we will restore bimetallism, and then let England have bimetallism because the United States has it. If they dare to come out in the open field and defend the gold standard as a good thing, we will fight them to the uttermost. Having behind us the producing masses of this nation and the world, supported by the commercial interests, the laboring interests, and the toilers everywhere, we will answer their demand for a gold standard by saying to them: You shall not press down upon the brow of labor this crown of thorns, you shall not crucify mankind upon a cross of gold.

Franklin Delano Roosevelt

FIRST INAUGURAL ADDRESS

¶ FRANKLIN DELANO ROOSEVELT (1882-1945) was born at Hyde Park, New York, on January 30, 1882. He was educated at Groton School, Harvard University, and the Columbia University Law School. In 1910, he was elected New York State Senator, serving from 1911-13. He served as Assistant Secretary of the Navy from 1913-20. In 1920, he was a Democratic nominee for Vice-President. In 1921, Roosevelt became a victim of infantile paralysis. He returned to political activity in 1928, and was elected to the governorship of New York, an office which he held until 1932. In 1932, he was nominated and elected to the presidency of the United States. He was re-elected in 1936, 1940, and 1944. He died at Warm Springs, Georgia, shortly after the beginning of his fourth term, on April 12, 1945.

Roosevelt entered his first term as President when the country was in the fourth year of an unprecedented depression. Banks were closing; unemployment was great; and public morale was very low. During his campaign, in which he had traveled more than twenty-five thousand miles and spoken in nearly every state in the Union, he had promised concrete action, designed to bring about relief from economic depression. His Inaugural address was eagerly awaited. It was delivered in Washington on March 4, 1933, and broadcast to the nation. (The text of the address is from *The Public Papers and Addresses of Franklin D. Roosevelt*, Vol. II, Random House, New York, 1938.)

I AM CERTAIN that my fellow Americans expect that on my induction into the Presidency I will address them with a candor and a decision which the present situation of our Nation impels. This is preeminently the time to speak the truth, the whole truth, frankly and boldly. Nor need we shrink from honestly facing conditions in our country today. This great Nation will endure as it has endured, will revive and will prosper. So, first of all, let me assert my firm belief that the only thing we have to fear is fear itself—nameless, unreasoning, unjustified terror which paralyzes needed efforts to convert retreat into advance. In every dark hour of our national life a leadership of frankness and vigor has met with that understanding and support of the people themselves which is essential to victory. I am convinced that you will again give that support to leadership in these critical days.

In such a spirit on my part and on yours we face our common difficulties. They concern, thank God, only material things. Values have shrunken to fantastic levels; taxes have risen; our ability to pay has fallen; government of all kinds is faced by serious curtailment of income; the means of exchange are frozen in the currents of trade; the withered leaves of industrial enterprise lie on every side; farmers find no markets for their produce; the savings of many years in thousands of families are gone.

More important, a host of unemployed citizens face the grim problem of existence, and an equally great number toil with little return. Only a foolish optimist can deny the dark realities of the moment.

Yet our distress comes from no failure of substance. We are stricken by no plague of locusts. Compared with the perils which our forefathers conquered because they believed and were not afraid, we have still much to be thankful for. Nature still offers her bounty and human efforts have multiplied it. Plenty is at our doorstep, but a generous use of it languishes in the very sight of the supply. Primarily this is because rulers of the exchange of mankind's goods have failed through their own stubbornness and their own incompetence, have admitted their failure, and have abdicated. Practices of the unscrupulous money changers stand indicted in the court of public opinion, rejected by the hearts and minds of men.

True they have tried, but their efforts have been cast in the pattern of an outworn tradition. Faced by failure of credit they have proposed only the lending of more money. Stripped of the lure of profit by which to induce our people to follow their false leadership, they have resorted to exhortations, pleading tearfully for restored confidence. They know only the rules of a generation of self-seekers. They have no vision, and when there is no vision the people perish.

The money changers have fled from their high seats in the temple of our civilization. We may now restore that temple to the ancient truths. The measure of the restoration lies in the extent to which we apply social values more noble than mere monetary profit.

Happiness lies not in the mere possession of money; it lies in the joy of achievement, in the thrill of creative effort. The joy and moral stimulation of work no longer must be forgotten in the mad chase of evanescent profits. These dark days will be worth all they cost us if they teach us that our true destiny is not to be ministered unto but to minister to ourselves and to our fellow men.

Recognition of the falsity of material wealth as the standard of success goes hand in hand with the abandonment of the false belief that public office and high political position are to be valued only by the standards of pride of place and personal profit; and there must be an end to a conduct in banking and in business which too often has given to a sacred trust the likeness of callous and selfish wrongdoing. Small wonder that confidence languishes, for it thrives only on honesty, on honor, on the sacredness of obligations, on faithful protection, on unselfish performance; without them it cannot live.

Restoration calls, however, not for changes in ethics alone. This Nation asks for action, and action now.

Our greatest primary task is to put people to work. This is no unsolvable problem if we face it wisely and courageously. It can be accomplished in part by direct recruiting by the Government itself, treating the task as we would treat the emergency of a war, but at the same time, through this employment, accomplishing greatly needed projects to stimulate and reorganize the use of our natural resources.

Hand in hand with this we must frankly recognize the overbalance of population in our industrial centers and, by engaging on a national scale in a redistribution, endeavor to provide a better use of the land for those best fitted for the land. The task can be helped by definite efforts to raise the values of agricultural products and with this the power to purchase the output of our cities. It can be helped by preventing realistically the tragedy of the growing loss through foreclosure of our small homes and our farms. It can be helped by insistence that the Federal, State, and local governments act forthwith on the demand that their cost be drastically reduced. It can be helped by the unifying of relief activities which today are often scattered, ,uneconomical, and unequal. It can be helped by national planning for and supervision of all forms of transportation and of communications and other utilities which have a definitely public character. There are many ways in which it can be helped, but it can never be helped merely by talking about it. We must act and act quickly.

Finally, in our progress toward a resumption of work we require two safeguards against a return of the evils of the old order: there must be a strict supervision of all banking and credits and investments, so that there will be an end to speculation with other people's money; and there must be provision for an adequate but sound currency.

These are the lines of attack. I shall presently urge upon a new Congress, in special session, detailed measures for their fulfillment, and I shall seek the immediate assistance of the several States.

Through this program of action we address ourselves to putting our own national house in order and making income balance outgo. Our international trade relations, though vastly important, are in point of time and necessity secondary to the establishment of a sound national economy. I favor as a practical policy the putting of first things first. I shall spare no effort to restore world trade by international economic readjustment, but the emergency at home cannot wait on that accomplishment.

The basic thought that guides these specific means of national recovery is not narrowly nationalistic. It is the insistence, as a first consideration, upon the interdependence of the various elements in and parts of the United States—a recognition of the old and permanently important manifestation of the American spirit of the pioneer. It is the way to recovery. It is the immediate way. It is the strongest assurance that the recovery will endure.

In the field of world policy I would dedicate this Nation to the policy of the good neighbor—the neighbor who resolutely respects himself and, because he does so, respects the rights of others—the neighbor who respects his obligations and respects the sanctity of his agreements in and with a world of neighbors.

If I read the temper of our people correctly, we now realize as we have never realized before our interdependence on each other; that we cannot merely take but we must give as well; that if we are to go forward, we must move as a trained and loyal army willing to sacrifice for the good of a common discipline, because without such discipline no progress is made, no leadership becomes effective. We are, I know, ready and willing to submit our lives and property to such discipline, because it makes possible a leadership which aims at a larger good. This I propose to offer, pledging that the larger purposes will bind upon us all as a sacred obligation with a unity of duty hitherto evoked only in time of armed strife.

With this pledge taken, I assume unhesitatingly the leadership of this great army of our people dedicated to a disciplined attack upon our common problems.

Action in this image and to this end is feasible under the form of government which we have inherited from our ancestors. Our Constitution is so simple and practical that it is possible always to meet extraordinary needs by changes in emphasis and arrangement without loss of essential form. That is why our constitutional system has proved itself the most superbly enduring political mechanism the modern world has produced. It has met every stress of vast expansion of territory, of foreign wars, of bitter internal strife, of world relations.

It is to be hoped that the normal balance of Executive and legislative authority may be wholly adequate to meet the unprecedented task before us. But it may be that an unprecedented demand and need for undelayed action may call for temporary departure from that normal balance of public procedure.

I am prepared under my constitutional duty to recommend the measures that a stricken Nation in the midst of a stricken world may require. These measures, or such other measures as the Congress may build out of its experience and wisdom, I shall seek, within my constitutional authority, to bring to speedy adoption.

But in the event that the Congress shall fail to take one of these two courses, and in the event that the national emergency is still critical, I shall not evade the clear course of duty that will then confront me. I shall ask the Congress for the one remaining instrument to meet the crisis—broad Executive power to wage a war against the emergency, as great as the power that would be given to me if we were in fact invaded by a foreign foe.

For the trust reposed in me I will return the courage and the devotion that befit the time. I can do no less.

We face the arduous days that lie before us in the warm courage of national unity; with the clear consciousness of seeking old and precious moral values; with the clean satisfaction that comes from the stern performance of duty by old and young alike. We aim at the assurance of a rounded and permanent national life.

We do not distrust the future of essential democracy. The people of the United States have not failed. In their need they have registered a mandate that they want direct, vigorous action. They have asked for discipline and direction under leadership. They have made me the present instrument of their wishes. In the spirit of the gift I take it.

In this dedication of a Nation we humbly ask the blessing of God. May He protect each and every one of us. May He guide me in the days to come.

Franklin Delano Roosevelt

WAR MESSAGE—

HOSTILITIES EXIST

¶ ON DECEMBER 7, 1941, Japanese bombers attacked the American naval base at Pearl Harbor, thus bringing the United States into the world conflagration that had begun in Europe in 1939 when Germany opened offensive warfare against Poland. On December 8 President Roosevelt addressed a joint session of Congress, asking for recognition of a state of war. (The text that follows is from *The War Messages of Franklin D. Roosevelt.*)

TO THE CONGRESS OF THE UNITED STATES:
Yesterday, December 7, 1941—a date which will live in infamy—the United States of America was suddenly and deliberately attacked by naval and air forces of the Empire of Japan.

The United States was at peace with that nation and, at the solicitation of Japan, was still in conversation with its government and its Emperor looking toward the maintenance of peace in the Pacific. Indeed, one hour after Japanese air squadrons had commenced bombing in Oahu, the Japanese Ambassador to the United States and his colleague delivered to the Secretary of State a formal reply to a recent American message. While this reply stated that it seemed useless to continue the existing diplomatic negotiations, it contained no threat or hint of war or armed attack.

It will be recorded that the distance of Hawaii from Japan makes it obvious that the attack was deliberately planned many days or even weeks ago. During the intervening time the Japanese government had deliberately sought to deceive the United States by false statements and expressions of hope for continued peace.

The attack yesterday on the Hawaiian Islands has caused severe damage to American naval and military forces. Very many American lives have been lost. In addition American ships have been reported torpedoed on the high seas between San Francisco and Honolulu.

Yesterday the Japanese government also launched an attack against Malaya.

Last night Japanese forces attacked Hong Kong.

Last night Japanese forces attacked Guam.

Last night Japanese forces attacked the Philippine Islands.

Last night the Japanese attacked Wake Island.

This morning the Japanese attacked Midway Island.

Japan has, therefore, undertaken a surprise offensive extending throughout the Pacific area. The facts of yesterday speak for themselves. The people of the United States have already formed their opinions and well understand the implications to the very life and safety of our nation.

As Commander in Chief of the Army and Navy I have directed that all measures be taken for our defense.

Always will we remember the character of the onslaught against us.

No matter how long it may take us to overcome this premeditated invasion, the American people in their righteous might will win through to absolute victory.

I believe I interpret the will of the Congress and of the people when I assert that we will not only defend ourselves to the uttermost but will make very certain that this form of treachery shall never endanger us again.

Hostilities exist. There is no blinking at the fact that our people, our territory, and our interests are in grave danger.

With confidence in our armed forces—with the unbounded determination of our people—we will gain the inevitable triumph—so help us God.

I ask that the Congress declare that since the unprovoked and dastardly attack by Japan on Sunday, December 7, a state of war has existed between the United States and the Japanese Empire.

Franklin Delano Roosevelt

AMERICA HAS NOT BEEN

DISAPPOINTED

¶ IN 1944, President Roosevelt had allowed his name to be presented to the American people as a Democratic candidate for re-
election to the presidency for a fourth term. Shortly after his nomination, he left the country for a visit to the Pacific theater of war,
thus permitting himself little time for campaigning. Meanwhile, his
Republican opponent, Governor Thomas E. Dewey of New York,
carried on a vigorous campaign. On his return from the Pacific,
Roosevelt was invited to address the A.F.L. International Teamsters
Union. In an attempt to bolster the morale of his own party, to gain
the support of labor, and to secure the independent vote of the
country, Roosevelt delivered what has been described as "the greatest campaign speech of his career." The address was delivered in
Washington, September 23, 1944. (The text of the address is from
Vital Speeches of the Day, Vol. X, October 1, 1944, pp. 738-40.)

I AM ACTUALLY four years older—which seems to annoy some
people. In fact, millions of us are more than eleven years older
than when we started in to clear up the mess that was dumped in
our laps in 1933. We all know certain people will make it a practice
to depreciate the accomplishments of labor—who even attack labor
as unpatriotic.

They keep this up usually for three years and six months. But
then, for some strange reason, they change their tune—every four
years—just before election day.

When votes are at stake they suddenly discover that they really love labor, and are eager to protect it from its old friends.

I got quite a laugh, for example—and I am sure that you did—when I read this plank in the Republican platform adopted at their national convention in Chicago last July:

"The Republican party accepts the purposes of the National Labor Relations Act, the Wage and Hour Act, the Social Security Act, and all other Federal statutes designed to promote and protect the welfare of American working men and women, and we promise a fair and just administration of these laws."

Many of the Republican leaders and Congressmen and candidates, who shouted enthusiastic approval of that plank in that convention hall, would not even recognize these progressive laws if they met them in broad daylight.

Indeed, they have personally spent years of effort and energy—and much money—in fighting every one of those laws in the Congress, in the press and in the courts, ever since this Administration began to advocate them and enact them into legislation.

That is a fair example of their insincerity and their inconsistency.

The whole purpose of Republican oratory these days seems to be to switch labels. The object is to persuade the American people that the Democratic party was responsible for the 1929 crash and depression, and the Republican party was responsible for all social progress under the New Deal.

Imitation may be the sincerest form of flattery—but I am afraid that in this case it is the most obvious common or garden variety of fraud.

There are enlightened, liberal elements in the Republican party, and they have fought hard and honorably to bring the party up to date and to get it in step with the forward march of American progress. But these liberal elements were not able to drive the old guard Republicans from their entrenched positions.

Can the old guard pass itself off as the New Deal? I think not.

We have all seen many marvelous stunts in the circus, but no performing elephant could turn a handspring without falling flat on his back.

I need not recount to you the centuries of history which have been crowded into these four years since I saw you last.

There were some—in the Congress and out—who raised their voices against our preparations for defense—before and after 1939—as hysterical war mongering, who cried out against our help to the Allies as provocative and dangerous.

We remember the voices.

They would like to have us forget them now. But in 1940 and 1941 they were loud voices. Happily they were a minority and—fortunately for ourselves, and for the world—they could not stop America.

There are some politicians who kept their heads buried deep in the sand while the storms of Europe and Asia were headed our way, who said that the Lend-Lease Bill "would bring an end to free Government in the United States," and who said "only hysteria entertains the idea that Germany, Italy or Japan contemplate war upon us."

These very men are now asking the American people to entrust to them the conduct of our foreign policy and our military policy.

What the Republican leaders are now saying in effect is this.

"Oh, just forget what we used to say, we have changed our minds now—we have been reading the public opinion polls about these things, and we now know what the American people want. Don't leave the task of making peace to those old men who first urged it, and who have already laid the foundations for it, and who have had to fight all of us, inch by inch, during the last five years to do it—just turn it all over to us. We'll do it so skillfully—that we won't lose a single isolationist vote or a single isolationist campaign contribution."

There is one thing I am too old for—I cannot talk out of both sides of my mouth at the same time.

This Government welcomes all sincere supporters of the cause of effective world collaboration in the making of a lasting peace. Millions of Republicans all over the nation are with us—and have been with us—in our unshakeable determination to build the solid structure of peace. And they, too, will resent this campaign talk by those who first woke up to the facts of international life a few short months ago—when they began to study the polls of public opinion.

Those who today have the military responsibility for waging this war in all parts of the globe are not helped by the statements of men who, without responsibility and without knowledge of the facts, lecture the chiefs of staff of the United States as to the best means of dividing our armed forces and our military resources between the Atlantic and Pacific, between the Army and the Navy, and among the commanding generals of the different theatres of war.

When I addressed you four years ago, I said:

"I know that America will never be disappointed in its expectation that labor will always continue to do its share of the job we now face, and do it patriotically and effectively and unselfishly."

Today we know that America has not been disappointed. In his order of the day, when the Allied armies first landed in Normandy, General Eisenhower said:

"Our home fronts have given us overwhelming superiority in weapons and munitions of war."

I know that there are those labor baiters among the opposition who, instead of calling attention to the achievements of labor in this war, prefer the occasional strikes which have occurred—strikes which have been condemned by every responsible national labor leader— every national leader except one. And that one labor leader, incidentally, is certainly not among my supporters.

Labor baiters forget that, at our peak, American labor and management have turned out airplanes at the rate of 109,000 per year; tanks, 57,000 per year; combat vessels, 573 per year; landing vessels, 31,000 per year; cargo ships, 19,000,000 tons per year, and small arms ammunition, 23 billion rounds per year.

But a strike is news, and generally appears in shrieking headlines—and, of course, they say labor is always to blame.

The fact is that, since Pearl Harbor, only one-tenth of one per cent of man-hours have been lost by strikes. But even those candidates who burst out in election-year affection for social legislation and for labor in general still think you ought to be good boys and stay out of politics.

And, above all, they hate to see any working man or woman contribute a dollar bill to any wicked political party.

Of course, it is all right for large financiers and industrialists and monopolists to contribute tens of thousands of dollars—but their solicitude for that dollar which the men and women in the ranks of labor contribute is always very touching.

They are, of course, perfectly willing to let you vote—unless you happen to be a soldier or sailor overseas, or a merchant seaman carrying munitions of war. In that case they have made it pretty hard for you to vote—for there are some political candidates who think they may have a chance if only the total vote is small enough.

And while I am on the subject of voting let me urge every American citizen—man and woman—to use your sacred privilege of voting, no matter which candidate you expect to support. Our millions of soldiers and sailors and merchant seamen have been handicapped or prevented from voting by those politicians and candidates who think they stand to lose by such votes. You here at home have the freedom of the ballot. Irrespective of party, you should register and vote this November. That is a matter of good citizenship.

Words come easily, but they do not change the record. You are old enough to remember what things were like for labor in 1932.

You remember the closed banks and the breadlines and the starvation wages; the foreclosures of homes and farms, and the bankruptcies of business; the "Hoovervilles," and the young men and women of the nation facing a hopeless, jobless future; the closed factories and mines and mills; the ruined and abandoned farms; the stalled railroads and the empty docks; the blank despair of a whole nation—and the utter impotence of our Federal Government.

You remember the long, hard road, with its gains and its setbacks, which we have traveled together since those days.

Now there are some politicians, of course, who do not remember that far back, and some who remember but find it convenient to forget. But the record is not to be washed away that easily.

The opposition has already imported into this campaign the propaganda technique invented by the dictators abroad. The technique was all set out in Hitler's book—and it was copied by the aggressors of Italy and Japan.

According to that technique, you should never use a small falsehood; always a big one, for its very fantastic nature will make it more credible—if only you keep repeating it over and over again.

For example, although I rubbed my eyes when I read it, we have been told that it was not a Republican depression, but a Democratic depression from which this nation has been saved—that this Administration is responsible for all the suffering and misery that the history books and the American people always thought had been brought about during the twelve ill-fated years when the Republican party was in power.

Now, there is an old and somewhat lugubrious adage which says: "Never speak of rope in the house of one who has been hanged."

In the same way, if I were a Republican leader speaking to a mixed audience, the last word in the whole dictionary that I think I would use is that word "depression."

For another example, I learned—much to my amazement—that the policy of this Administration was to keep men in the Army when the war was over, because there might be no jobs for them in civil life.

Why, the very day that this fantastic charge was first made a formal plan for the method of speedy discharge from the Army had already been announced by the War Department—a plan based upon the wishes of the soldiers themselves.

This callous and brazen falsehood about demobilization was an effort to stimulate fear among American mothers, wives and sweethearts. And, incidentally, it was hardly calculated to bolster the morale of our soldiers and sailors and airmen fighting our battles all over the world.

Perhaps the most ridiculous of these campaign falsifications is the one that this Administration failed to prepare for the war which was coming. I doubt whether even Goebbels would have tried that one. For even he would never have dared hope that the voters of America had already forgotten that many of the Republican leaders in the Congress and outside the Congress tried to thwart and block nearly every attempt which this Administration made to warn our people and to arm this nation. Some of them called our 50,000-airplane program fantastic.

Many of those very same leaders who fought every defense measure we proposed are still in control of the Republican party, were in control of its national convention in Chicago, and would be in control of the machinery of the Congress and the Republican party in the event of a Republican victory this fall.

These Republican leaders have not been content with attacks upon me, or my wife, or my sons—they now include my little dog, Fala. Unlike the members of my family, he resents this. Being a scottie, as soon as he learned that the Republican fiction writers had concocted a story that I had left him behind on an Aleutian island and had sent a destroyer back to find him—at a cost to the taxpayers of two or three or twenty million dollars—his Scotch soul was furious. He has not been the same dog since.

I am accustomed to hearing malicious falsehoods about myself—such as that old, worm-eaten chestnut that I have represented myself as indispensable. But I think I have a right to object to libelous statements about my dog.

But we all recognize the old technique. The people of this country know the past too well to be deceived into forgetting. Too much is at stake to forget. There are tasks ahead of us which we must now complete with the same will and skill and intelligence and devotion which have already led us so far on the road to victory.

There is the task of finishing victoriously this most terrible of all wars as speedily as possible and with the least cost in lives.

There is the task of setting up international machinery to assure that the peace, once established, will not again be broken.

And there is the task which we face here at home—the task of reconverting our economy from the purposes of war to the purposes of peace.

The peace-building tasks were faced once before, nearly a generation ago. They were botched by a Republican Administration. That must not happen this time. We will not let it happen this time.

Fortunately, we do not begin from scratch. Much has been done.

Much more is under way. The fruits of victory this time will not be apples to be sold on street corners.

Many months ago, this Administration set up the necessary machinery for an orderly peace-time demobilization. The Congress has now passed legislation continuing the agencies needed for demobilization—with additional powers to carry out their functions.

I know that the American people—Business and labor and agriculture—have the same will to do for peace what they have done for war. And I know that they can sustain a national income which will assume full production and full employment under our democratic system of private enterprise, with Government encouragement and aid whenever and wherever it is necessary.

The keynote of all that we propose to do in reconversion can be found in the one word—"jobs."

We shall lease or dispose of our Government-owned plants and facilities and our surplus war property and land on the basis of how they can best be operated by private enterprise to give jobs to the greatest number.

We shall follow a wage policy which will sustain the purchasing power of labor—for that means more production and more jobs.

The present policies on wages and prices were conceived to serve the needs of the great masses of the people. They stopped inflation. They kept prices on a stable level. Through the demobilization period, policies will be carried out with the same objective in mind—to serve the needs of the great masses of the people.

This is not the time in which men can be forgotten as they were in the Republican catastrophe which we inherited. The returning soldiers, the workers by their machines, the farmers in the field, the miners, the men and women in offices and shops, do not intend to be forgotten.

They know they are not surplus. Because they know that they are America.

We must set targets and objectives for the future which will seem impossible to those who live in and are weighted down by the dead past.

We are even now organizing the logistics of the peace just as

Marshall, King, Arnold, MacArthur, Eisenhower and Nimitz are organizing the logistics of this war.

The victory of the American people and their allies in this war will be far more than a victory against fascism and reaction and the dead hand of despotism and of the past.

The victory of the American people and their allies in this war will be a victory for democracy. It will constitute such an affirmation of the strength and power and vitality of government by the people as history has never before witnessed.

With that affirmation of the vitality of democratic government behind us, that demonstration of its resilience and its capacity for decision and for action—with that knowledge of our own strength and power—we move forward with God's help to the greatest epoch of free achievement by free men the world has ever known or imagined possible.

/815P261A>C1/

B & T
10/8/83 ✓
19.95

D1715333

Hitler, a Film from Germany

HANS-JÜRGEN SYBERBERG

HITLER

A FILM FROM GERMANY

PREFACE BY SUSAN SONTAG

TRANSLATED BY JOACHIM NEUGROSCHEL

FARRAR · STRAUS · GIROUX · NEW YORK

Wingate College Library

Preface copyright © 1982 by Susan Sontag
Translation copyright © 1982 by Farrar, Straus and Giroux, Inc.
Originally published as *Hitler, ein Film aus Deutschland*
by Rowohlt Taschenbuch Verlag GmbH, Reinbek bei Hamburg
Copyright © 1978 by Rowohlt Taschenbuch Verlag GmbH,
Reinbek bei Hamburg
All rights reserved
Published simultaneously in Canada by McGraw-Hill Ryerson Ltd., Toronto
Printed in the United States of America
First printing, 1982
Library of Congress Cataloging in Publication Data
Syberberg, Hans-Jürgen.
Hitler, a Film from Germany.
Translation of: Hitler, ein Film aus Deutschland.
Includes bibliographical references.
1. Hitler, a Film from Germany (Motion picture)
I. Hitler, a Film from Germany (Motion picture)   II. Title.
PN1997.H5513   1981   791.43'72   81–17500
                                AACR2

092111

For my wife

Contents

Preface

The Romantics thought of great art as a species of heroism, a breaking through or going beyond. Following them, adepts of the modern demanded of masterpieces that they be, in each case, an extreme case—terminal or prophetic, or both. Walter Benjamin was making a characteristic modernist judgment when he observed (writing about Proust): "All great works of literature found a genre or dissolve one." However rich in precursors, the truly great work must seem to break with an old order and really is a devastating if salutary move. Such a work extends the reach of art but also complicates and burdens the enterprise of art with new, self-conscious standards. It both excites and paralyzes the imagination.

Lately, the appetite for the truly great work has become less robust. Thus Hans-Jürgen Syberberg's *Hitler, a Film from Germany* is not only daunting because of the extremity of its achievement, but discomfiting, like an unwanted baby in the era of zero population growth. The modernism that reckoned achievement by the Romantics' grandiose aims for art (as wisdom / as salvation / as cultural subversion or revolution) has been overtaken by an impudent version of itself which has enabled modernist tastes to be diffused on an undreamed-of scale. Stripped of its heroic stature, of its claims as an adversary sensibility, modernism has proved acutely compatible with the ethos of an advanced consumer society. Art is now the name of a huge variety of satisfactions—of the unlimited proliferation, and devaluation, of satisfaction itself. Where so many blandishments flourish, bringing off a masterpiece seems a retrograde feat, a naïve form of accomplishment. Always implausible (as implausible as justified megalomania), the Great Work is now truly odd. It proposes satisfactions that are immense, solemn, and restricting. It insists that art must be true, not just interesting; a necessity, not just an experiment. It dwarfs other work, challenges the facile eclecticism of contemporary taste. It throws the admirer into a state of crisis.

Syberberg assumes importance both for his art (*the* art of the twentieth century: film) and for his subject (*the* subject of the twentieth century: Hitler). The assumptions are familiar, crude,

This is excerpted from the essay "Syberberg's Hitler," written in 1979 and included in *Under the Sign of Saturn* (Farrar, Straus and Giroux, 1980).

plausible. But they hardly prepare us for the scale and virtuosity with which he conjures up the ultimate subjects: hell, paradise lost, the apocalypse, the last days of mankind. Leavening romantic grandiosity with modernist ironies, Syberberg offers a spectacle about spectacle: evoking "the big show" called history in a variety of dramatic modes—fairy tale, circus, morality play, allegorical pageant, magic ceremony, philosophical dialogue, *Totentanz*—with an imaginary cast of tens of millions and, as protagonist, the devil himself.

The Romantic notions of the maximal so congenial to Syberberg such as the boundless talent, the ultimate subject, and the most inclusive art—these notions confer an excruciating sense of possibility. Syberberg's confidence that his art is adequate to his great subject derives from his idea of cinema as a way of knowing that incites speculation to take a self-reflexive turn. Hitler is depicted through examining our relation to Hitler (the theme is "our Hitler" and "Hitler within us"), as the rightly unassimilable horrors of the Nazi era are represented in Syberberg's film as images or signs. (Its title isn't *Hitler* but, precisely, *Hitler, a Film . . .*)

To simulate atrocity convincingly is to risk making the audience passive, reinforcing witless stereotypes, confirming distance, and creating fascination. Convinced that there is a morally (and aesthetically) correct way for a filmmaker to confront Nazism, Syberberg can make no use of any of the stylistic conventions of fiction that pass for realism. Neither can he rely on documents to show how it "really" was. Like its simulation as fiction, the display of atrocity in the form of photographic evidence risks being tacitly pornographic. Further, the truths it conveys, unmediated, about the past are slight. Film clips of the Nazi period cannot speak for themselves; they require a voice—explaining, commenting, interpreting. But the relation of the voice-over to a film document, like that of the caption to a still photograph, is merely adhesive. In contrast to the pseudo-objective style of narration in most documentaries, the two ruminating voices which suffuse Syberberg's film constantly express pain, grief, dismay.

Rather than devise a spectacle in the past tense, either by attempting to simulate "unrepeatable reality" (Syberberg's phrase) or by showing it in photographic document, he proposes a spectacle in the present tense—"adventures in the head." Of course, for such a devoutly anti-realist aesthetician, historical reality is, by definition, unrepeatable. Reality can only be grasped indirectly—seen reflected in a mirror, staged in the theater of the mind. Syberberg's synoptic drama is radically subjective, without being solipsistic. It is a ghostly film—haunted by his great cinematic models (Méliès, Eisenstein) and anti-models (Riefenstahl, Holly-wood); by German Romanticism; and, above all, by the music of Wagner and the case of Wagner. A posthumous film, in the era of cinema's unprecedented mediocrity—full of cinéphile myths, about cinema as the ideal space of the imagination and cinema history as an exemplary history of the twentieth century (the martyrdom of Eisenstein by Stalin, the excommunication of Stroheim by Hollywood); and of cinéphile hyperboles: he designates Riefenstahl's *Triumph of the Will* as Hitler's "only lasting monument, apart from the newsreels of his war." One of the film's conceits is that Hitler, who never visited the front and watched the war every night through newsreels, was a kind of moviemaker. Germany, a Film by Hitler.

Syberberg has cast his film in the first person: as the action of one artist assuming the German duty to confront fully the horror of Nazism. Like many German intellectuals of the past, Syberberg treats his Germanness as a moral vocation and regards Germany as the cockpit of European conflicts. ("The twentieth century . . . a film from Germany," says one of the ruminators.) Syberberg was born in 1935 in what was to become East Germany and left in 1953 for West Germany, where he has lived ever since; but the true provenance of his film is the extraterritorial Germany of the spirit whose first great citizen was that self-styled *romantique défroqué* Heine, and whose last great citizen was Thomas Mann. "To be the spiritual battlefield of European antagonisms—that's what it means to be German," Mann declared in his *Reflections of an Unpolitical Man*, written during World War I, sentiments that had not changed when he wrote *Doctor Faustus* as an old man in exile in the late 1940s. Syberberg's view of Nazism as the explosion of the German demonic recalls Mann, as does his unfashionable insistence on Germany's collective guilt (the theme of "Hitler within us"). The narrators' repeated challenge, "Who would Hitler be without us?," also echoes Mann, who wrote an essay in 1939 called "Brother Hitler," in which he argues that "the whole thing is a distorted phase of Wagnerism." Like Mann, Syberberg regards Nazism as the grotesque fulfillment—and betrayal—of German Romanticism. It may seem odd that Syberberg, who was a child during the Nazi era, shares so many themes with someone so *ancien-régime*. But there is much that is old-fashioned about Syberberg's sensibility (one consequence, perhaps, of being educated in a communist country)—including the vividness with which he identifies with that Germany whose greatest citizens have gone into exile.

Although it draws on innumerable versions and impressions of

Hitler, the film offers very few ideas about Hitler. For the most part they are the theses formulated in the ruins: the thesis that "Hitler's work" was "the eruption of the satanic principle in world history" (Meinecke's *The German Catastrophe*, written two years before *Doctor Faustus*); the thesis, expressed by Horkheimer in *The Eclipse of Reason*, that Auschwitz was the logical culmination of Western progress. Starting in the 1950s, when the ruins of Europe were rebuilt, more complex theses—political, sociological, economic—prevailed about Nazism. (Horkheimer eventually repudiated his argument of 1946.) In reviving those unmodulated views of thirty years ago, their indignation, their pessimism, Syberberg's film makes a strong case for their moral appropriateness.

Syberberg proposes that we really listen to what Hitler said—to the kind of cultural revolution Nazism was, or claimed to be; to the spiritual catastrophe it was, and still is. By Hitler Syberberg does not mean only the real historical monster, responsible for the deaths of tens of millions. He evokes a kind of Hitler-substance that outlives Hitler, a phantom presence in modern culture, a protean principle of evil that saturates the present and remakes the past. Syberberg's film alludes to familiar genealogies, real and symbolic: from Romanticism to Hitler, from Wagner to Hitler, from Caligari to Hitler, from kitsch to Hitler. And, in the hyperbole of woe, he insists on some new filiations: from Hitler to pornography, from Hitler to the soulless consumer society of the Federal Republic, from Hitler to the rude coercions of the DDR. In using Hitler thus, there is some truth, some unconvincing attributions. It is true that Hitler has contaminated Romanticism and Wagner, that much of nineteenth-century German culture is, retroactively, haunted by Hitler. (As, say, nineteenth-century Russian culture is not haunted by Stalin.) But it is not true that Hitler engendered the modern, post-Hitlerian plastic consumer society. That was already well on the way when the Nazis took power. Indeed, it could be argued—contra Syberberg—that Hitler was in the long run an irrelevance, an attempt to halt the historical clock; and that communism is what ultimately mattered in Europe, not fascism. Syberberg is more plausible when he asserts that the DDR resembles the Nazi state, a view for which he has been denounced by the left in West Germany; like most intellectuals who grew up under a communist regime and moved to a bourgeois-democratic one, he is singularly free of left-wing pieties. It could also be argued that Syberberg has unduly simplified his moralist's task by the extent to which, like Mann, he identifies the inner history of Germany with the history of Romanticism.

Syberberg's notion of history as catastrophe recalls the long

German tradition of regarding history eschatologically, as the history of the spirit. Comparable views today are more likely to be entertained in Eastern Europe than in Germany. Syberberg has the moral intransigence, the lack of respect for literal history, the heartbreaking seriousness of the great illiberal artists from the Russian empire—with their fierce convictions about the primacy of spiritual over material (economic, political) causation, the irrelevance of the categories "left" and "right," the existence of absolute evil. Appalled by the extensiveness of German support for Hitler, Syberberg calls the Germans "a Satanic people."

The devil story that Mann devised to sum up the Nazi demonic was narrated by someone who does not understand. Thereby Mann suggested that evil so absolute may be, finally, beyond comprehension or the grasp of art. But the obtuseness of the narrator of *Doctor Faustus* is too much insisted on. Mann's irony backfires: Serenus Zeitblom's fatuous modesty of understanding seems like Mann's confession of inadequacy, his inability to give full voice to grief. Syberberg's film about the devil, though sheathed in ironies, affirms our ability to understand and our obligation to grieve. Dedicated, as it were, to grief, the film begins and ends with Heine's lacerating words: "I think of Germany in the night and then sleep leaves me, I can no longer close my eyes, I weep hot tears." Grief is the burden of the calm, rueful, musical soliloquies of Harry Baer and André Heller; neither reciting nor declaiming, they are simply speaking out, and listening to these grave, intelligent voices seething with grief is itself a civilizing experience.

The film carries without any condescension a vast legacy of information about the Nazi period. But information is assumed. The film is not designed to meet a standard of information but claims to address a (hypothetical) therapeutic ideal. Syberberg repeatedly says that his film is addressed to the German "inability to mourn," that it undertakes "the work of mourning" (*Trauerarbeit*). These phrases recall the famous essay Freud wrote deep in World War I, "Mourning and Melancholia," which connects melancholy with the inability to work through grief; and the application of this formula in an influential psychoanalytic study of postwar Germany by Alexander and Margarete Mitscherlich, *The Inability to Mourn*, published in Germany in 1967, which diagnoses the Germans as afflicted by mass melancholia, the result of the continuing denial of their collective responsibility for the Nazi past and their persistent refusal to mourn. Syberberg has appropriated the well-known Mitscherlich thesis (without ever mentioning their book), but one might doubt that his film was inspired by it. It seems more likely that Syberberg found in the notion of *Trauerarbeit* a psychological and moral justification for his aesthetics of repetition and recycling. It takes time—and much hyperbole—to work through grief.

So far as the film can be considered as an act of mourning, what is interesting is that it is conducted in the style of mourning —by exaggeration, repetition. It provides an overflow of information: the method of saturation. Syberberg is an artist of excess: thought is a kind of excess, the surplus production of ruminations, images, associations, emotions connected with, evoked by, Hitler. Hence the film's length, its circular arguments, its several beginnings, its four or five endings, its many titles, its plurality of styles, its vertiginous shifts of perspective on Hitler, from below or beyond. The most wonderful shift occurs in Part Two, when the valet's forty-minute monologue with its mesmerizing trivia about Hitler's taste in underwear and shaving cream and breakfast food is followed by Heller's musings on the unreality of the idea of the galaxies. (It is the verbal equivalent of the cut in *2001* from the bone thrown in the air by a primate to the space ship—surely the most spectacular cut in the history of cinema.) Syberberg's idea is to exhaust, to empty his subject.

Spurning naturalism, the Romantics developed a melancholic style: intensely personal, the outreach of its tortured "I," centered on the agon of the artist and society. Mann gave the last profound expression to this romantic notion of the self's dilemma. Post-Romantics like Syberberg work in an impersonal melancholic style. What is central now is the relation between memory and the past: the clash between the possibility of remembering, of going on, and the lure of oblivion. Beckett gives one ahistorical version of this agon. Another version, obsessed with history, is Syberberg's.

To understand the past, and thereby to exorcise it, is Syberberg's largest moral ambition. His problem is that he cannot give anything up. So large is his subject—and everything Syberberg does makes it even larger—that he has to take many positions beyond it. One can find almost anything in Syberberg's passionately voluble film (short of a Marxist analysis or a shred of feminist awareness). Though he tries to be silent (the child, the stars), he can't stop talking; he's so immensely ardent, avid. As the film is ending, Syberberg wants to produce yet another ravishing image. Even when the film is finally over, he still wants to say more, and adds postscripts: the Heine epigraph, the citation of Mogadishu–Stammheim, a final oracular Syberberg-sentence, one last evocation of the Grail. The film is itself the creation of a world, from which (one feels) its creator has the greatest difficulty in extricating himself—as does the admiring spectator; this exercise in the art of empathy produces a voluptuous anguish, an anxiety about concluding. Lost in the black hole of the imagination, the filmmaker has to make everything pass before him; identifies with each, and none.

Benjamin suggests that melancholy is the origin of true—that is, just—historical understanding. The true understanding of history, he said in the last text he wrote, is "a process of empathy whose origin is indolence of the heart, acedia." Syberberg shares something of Benjamin's positive, instrumental view of melancholy, and uses symbols of melancholy to punctuate his film. But Syberberg does not have the ambivalence, the slowness, the complexity, the tension of the Saturnian temperament. Syberberg is not a true melancholic but an *exalté*. But he uses the distinctive tools of the melancholic—the allegorical props, the talismans, the secret self-references; and with his irrepressible talent for indignation and enthusiasm, he is doing "the work of mourning." The word first appears at the end of the film he made on Winifred Wagner in 1975, where we read: "This film is part of Hans-Jürgen Syberberg's *Trauerarbeit*." What we see is Syberberg smiling.

Syberberg is a genuine elegiast. But his film is tonic. The poetic, husky-voiced, diffident logorrhea of Godard's late films discloses a morose conviction that speaking will never exorcise anything; in contrast to Godard's off-camera musings, the musings of Syberberg's personae (Heller and Baer) teem with calm assurance. Syberberg, whose temperament seems the opposite of Godard's, has a supreme confidence in language, in discourse, in eloquence itself. The film tries to say everything. Syberberg belongs to the race of creators like Wagner, Artaud, Céline, the late Joyce, whose work annihilates other work. All are artists of endless speaking, endless melody—a voice that goes on and on. Beckett would belong to this race, too, were it not for some inhibitory force—sanity? elegance? good manners? less energy? deeper despair? So might Godard, were it not for the doubts he evidences about speaking, and the inhibition of feeling (of both sympathy and repulsion) that results from this sense of the impotence of speaking. Syberberg has managed to stay free of the standard doubts—doubts whose main function, now, seems to be to inhibit. The result is a film altogether exceptional in its emotional expressiveness, its great visual beauty, its sincerity, its moral passion, its concern with contemplative values.

The film tries to be everything. Syberberg's unprecedented ambition in *Hitler, a Film from Germany* is on another scale from anything one has seen on film. It is work that demands a special kind of attention and partisanship; and invites being reflected upon, reseen. The more one recognizes of its stylistic references and lore, the more the film vibrates. (Great art in the mode of pastiche invariably rewards study, as Joyce affirmed by daring to observe that the ideal reader of his work would be someone who could devote his life to it.) Syberberg's film belongs in the category of noble masterpieces which ask for fealty and can compel it. After seeing *Hitler, a Film from Germany*, there is Syberberg's film—and then there are the other films one admires. (Not too many these days, alas.) As was said ruefully of Wagner, he spoils our tolerance for the others.

—*Susan Sontag*

Hitler, a Film from Germany

Introduction

TO THE READER
This is an honest book, reader. From the very start, it points out that I have set myself no other goal than a domestic and private one . . . I meant it for the personal convenience of my friends and family: so that when they have lost me . . . they will be able to rediscover here a few characteristics of what I was and felt. . . . For it is myself that I depict here. My faults will be read alive here, as will my true nature. . . . I myself am the subject of my book.
—*Michel de Montaigne, March 1, 1580*

It was above all in the voluntary surrender of its creative irrationality, and perhaps only in this, that Germany really lost the war.

We have studied hard, caught up, and now recite like a schoolchild: democratic praxis, a new social system, economic know-how, and a certain solidarity with the weak and with the rest of the world. But over and over again, we hear the pitying, often mournful, or even euphemistic, and hence comforting words about the disadvantaged condition of present-day German art or culture as compared with the so-called strengths of our contemporary material existence. Nevertheless, the successes of our present-day intellectual life often come from other sources than those repressed and betrayed forces of our own peculiar nature.

Can and should a film about Hitler and his Germany explain anything in this respect, rediscover identities, heal and save? Yet, I ask, will we ever become free of the oppressive curse of guilt if we do not get at the center of it? Yes indeed, it is only in a film—the art of our time—a film that is precisely about this Hitler within us, from Germany, that hope may come at all. In the name of our future, we have to overcome and conquer him and thereby ourselves, and only here can a new identity be found through recognizing and separating, sublimating and working on our tragic past.

Hitler himself is the theme and center of this past, which we must penetrate, this past so wounded and painful, yet so identifiable. But how else is this to be portrayed than in the most personal and also universal form of the risk of art; and how else can it be received by this Germany and its new generation—still deeply implicated, both intellectually and emotionally—than, necessarily,

The German edition of the filmscript of *Hitler, a Film from Germany* was prefaced by a long essay by Syberberg entitled "Die Kunst als Rettung aus der deutschen Misere" ("Art as Salvation from the German Misery"), dated May 1978. This introduction is a slightly abridged version of the first three sections of Syberberg's essay.

| 3

with utmost resistance? And how else can it succeed than through constant steadiness, with faith and trust in the sincerity of this work of mourning (*Trauerarbeit*), which the ancients called "tragedy," just as they presented in myth the ceremonies of the fear that they have conquered and their pity before the terror, just as we must accept the sinister things of which we are made. Accept them in the therapeutic process of art, as a method of overcoming and acknowledging the guilt and ourselves, for many others. A sad model. The issue is to mourn through art.

1 / Cinema, the Favorite Child of Our Democratic Age, as a Model

If the cinema is the most important art that the democratic twentieth century has produced, the favorite child of mass society, which is celebrated and at the same time damned as progress, then, as always in art, we can use the model of film, its appearance and its treatment in public, to glean a few things about the condition of the general will of a country and its current situation. Its production will supply conclusions about the makeup of intellectual trends, and the reception by distributors, movie theaters or television audiences or critics will provide clues about the practice of democracy, of public life, of freedom and discussion. And films will enable us to discover what is offered to people in their leisure time, what they themselves look for in their pursuit of happiness, what are the goals of their lives, or whether (and possibly how) one deceives them, does business with them, or deprives them of important information or possibilities. . . .

I venture to maintain that no previous generation in Germany had such a resolute desire for enlightenment as the present generation, especially from newspapers, radio, and television. A few people, a tiny vanguard, have determined, at least through the collective subconscious, what many others ought to think, feel, or do. Particularly in movie criticism, the interest in entertainment has been superseded more and more by an interest in "social politics" or "social criticism" and by an urge for altering life, whatever that may mean now. In Germany this is a legacy of bourgeois enlightenment in terms of progress. If entertainment values were in demand, then they were those from Hollywood, from the underground as a protest movement, and from certain pop gestures as signs of colonial occupation by other countries. It was precisely in the realm of cinema that this new generation— and a handful of opinion makers—determined the reasoning of the entire sect of filmmakers in Germany according to the most diverse fads or waves of market interests. . . .

The press in Germany, and especially in the realm of cinema, functions as an ersatz democracy in this land without a metropolis for a capital. Whenever people meet, have discussions, or drink and eat together, they have to get to know each other and compare themselves with one another on the basis of perceptions received from television or newspapers or the radio. No other country is so dependent on its media. God help us if they were to stop functioning, if no reports were given, if information were to be hushed up, if quotations were distorted, descriptions did not jibe with the facts, if a boycott was undertaken, and if hatred and aggression were on the increase. And all this does occur among a generation that carried around tolerance on the banner of enlightenment in Germany—tolerance, that fine old German tradition. . . .

Yes, this land has become brutal and materialistic. Tolerance has degenerated into denunciation, and mediocrity into cultural conformity. Cinema is misunderstood as a practiced mass art, as the fast-food stand of show business—cinema as the smallest common multiple of the leisure industry. Why? For an entire generation, Germany's children learned the statistics of Auschwitz, the virtues of revolution, no matter how misunderstood, from an admittedly puny German tradition without the courage of its convictions, which they promptly "demystified" as hero worship. They promptly introduced sociology and psychology, and they quickly and assiduously studied market economy both as the method of democratic freedom and as the radical scorn for it. The ethos of a consumer and cash-register democracy came into being; the buyer supports it, the people decide at the box office; they learned advertising gimmicks and public opinion surveys, and they got to sense the power of money and also the curse of simply lying in the middle, which no one could skirt, and how to use the human multitudes in order to develop mass buying power, which everyone envies, and even the curse of modernity, which is to rebuild everything out of nothing. Being modern became the sign of progress, and anything new was good. An intrinsic morality was born (or what they regarded as one), the bulwark of a new rationality; for feelings and ideals lead to disaster, so they had been told.

But one does not learn to grieve from statistics, and how can one cope with one's guilt? This too requires its rites, new ones. Who taught Germans the myth and the ethic of mourning, the new ones, the ones for our time, with the old doctrines of our tradition? No, they were deceived and they deceived themselves. In the course of assiduous lessons in rationalism and materialism, they repressed one of their most important traditions, the accursed main strand of their nature, pinning it all on the Nazis without a demurrer, putting the curse of Fascism upon the long history of irrationalism and what relates to it. Hence everything that is mysticism, *Sturm und Drang*, large portions of classicism, the Romantic period, Nietzsche, Wagner, and Expressionism, and their music and parts of the best things they had, were surrendered, relocated, repressed.

I am speaking here as an observer of the cinema in Germany, its production, its audience, and the opinion makers, who see themselves as the new, young, modern Germany, and of all those who want to belong to it.

Germany was spiritually disinherited and dispossessed; anything that could not be justified by sociology and social policies was hushed up. But how can they comprehend Hölderlin if they have relocated him as a revolutionary between Lessing and Marx, how could Novalis survive as a model for the American road movie; and without irrationality, no *Die Räuber* [*The Brigands*] by Schiller and no fairy tales and no folk songs and no Runge. Give everything to Hitler and Goebbels? And is Caspar David Friedrich right-wing and Fascist? Is irrationalism right-wing or left-wing? Have they forgotten that their venerated Ernst Bloch was the man who, in the last line of his *The Spirit of Utopia*, spoke of homeland (*Heimat*), the word banished from Germany? And that it was he who, in those days, when faced with the Nazis, warned about undernourishing the mass imagination? What would Judaism be without its Cabbala? Merely Einstein? And what would Einstein be without music, without German Romanticism and classicism? We live in a country without a homeland.

Everyone stands terrified and astonished before the eruption of what we call terrorism, some even applaud (and often not the worst of them), applaud the bomb planters and murderers from the ranks of the intellectuals, whether secretly or openly; and they often do not even know why. Not all applaud out of snobbery, and they perhaps desperately recognize in those madmen a moral opposition to the paternal generation of materialists, disregarding its perversion.

Now a film was made on this topic, entitled *Germany in Autumn*, by filmmakers of my generation, about the guilt that went back to a different generation. But how are we to depict guilt without a concept? Without aesthetic, metaphysical control and responsibility? I heard from them about anxiety fits—surely small ones compared with mine—in the face of our generation's representation-compulsion thirty years ago. But without this labor, cinema as a genre will surrender its possibilities. Too many things so far remain unreflected upon, tied to reality, action, goal-oriented, a part of the entertainment and propaganda industry. A profound impotence of means strikes us before the question of how to depict all this—namely, just why all this? This terror, this eruption? Is it not something like the explosion of repressed German irrationalism? The dull, unconscious shriek of a diseased nation without an identity? So much suppression of its own tradition and its nature was bound to evoke aggressions, in the German manner, radical and fanatic. But the decay of methods is dismal. An entire generation in Germany was simply not trained to understand and manipulate the things lying beyond the rational. . . .

It would be wrong and mistaken to deny the necessity of myth

—myth as a response to a reality that cannot be recovered. The will to myth means escaping the knowledge of reference books. It would be a disastrous error to reduce a nation's need to flaunt itself, its will to sacrifice itself—reduce them to money principles and spare-time scheduling or the annual union negotiations as fulfilling the promised happiness of freedom's revolutions. Whole eras of European civilization were nourished by the fact that cathedrals, temples, palaces, monuments and castles, and parks and cities were coming into being, usable by few, but identifiable as representative objects for all, until an era that did not understand itself and wiped itself out through revolutions, putsches, and wars. It was a fundamental misunderstanding and a palpable lie to picture Hitler only as an instrument of capital, as the final stage of capitalism and imperialism, and to picture the war as a necessary consequence of capitalistic exploitation. Only the materialists could come up with that. Why did capitalism bet on this repulsive corporal and what would he have done with it after his war?

Thus, in Germany today, history, even in the run-of-the-mill rationality of scholarly paperbacks, has become the material for our new myths. The artistic ennoblement of *Historia* in the form of sublimation, with deliberate citing of legends as signs of the collective will, is occurring because we need it. The will to myth is the cultural achievement of a nation with intellectual controls, if things go well, in huge emotional torrents and often with bitter sacrifices and sufferings, discernible only after decades, a path through many corpses and suicides, leading straight into the heart of the history of German culture. The head builds the body from which we live, arduously endured by the soul, our vital and crucial fiction. Only myth makes irony possible through humor and reason and passion. Myth, however, is the mother of irony and pathos, which beget irrationality in incestuous love, always for the fun of a new mythologizing of the soul, which we urgently need in order to survive.

Since we took myths seriously, literally, we found Troy, quite real, under the rubble of history. We have the debris of the history of Hitler, and now we have to seek the myths underneath.

This film, calling itself *Hitler*, moves between the axioms of chaos and systems of order, gods and the underworld, God and hell, death and immortality, victims, love, wars, creation and the starry cosmos. Components of mythical worlds. In words, images, music, with the help of triviality as it is called. Astrology is called upon, a larger-than-life masseur is taken seriously. A theory unacceptable in our academies, like the glacial cosmogony, can stand for the ideology of the entire Reich. In addition to all this, the everyday problems and detailed stories about the hero are narrated to the accompaniment of oversized images of his desk.

The banality of evil is taken seriously, mythologized in a modern fashion, but so is the evil of banality. For in kitsch, in banality, in triviality and their popularity lie the remaining rudiments and germ cells of the vanished traditions of our myths, deteriorated but latently effective. Belief in fairy tales and buried desires can be found here; Hitler knew how to activate them. Did the legend of the vanished emperor Barbarossa and the hope for his return provide the energy for Hitler's blitzkriegs all the way to Stalingrad? The buried dreams and impulses of a nation can be sought here in these explosions in the subconscious of grand wishes which only appeared to have been lost. The key to modern myths is in the banality (taken seriously) of kitsch success and the popularity of triviality—final traces of worlds gone under. Hitler and his people were the best performers of those things, on a huge stage, of misfortune and the destruction rites of a nation and perhaps of a continent and its cultures, as accelerator and trigger of a historical process. We can grasp him here—if our art, cinema, tries correctly (where scholarship must be, and is, permitted to pass)—with the ethics of artistic truth. Grasp, understand, retell, and overcome us and our history, the bloodiest of humanity so far, the enigma that still remained, but captured by the better powers of good counter-worlds of understanding, from the feeling of an ambivalent insanity and the competent irrationality, in the spirit and the aesthetic of a new myth, garnered from the mythologies of our kitsch worlds, which at one time imbued the state.

3 / The Anxious Attempt of Art to Mourn the Silence of Melancholy over Everything

Whose saintly visage is too bright
To hit the sense of human sight,
And therefore to our weaker view
O'erlaid with black, staid wisdom's hue.
—*Milton*

We know about the glory and misery of irrationalism; but without it, Germany is nothing but dangerous, sick, without identity, explosive—a wretched shadow of its possibilities. Hitler is to be fought, not with the statistics of Auschwitz or with sociological analyses of the Nazi economy, but with Richard Wagner and Mozart.

Now just what is this irrationalism, as I am defining it? The Bavarian director Herbert Achternbusch speaks of irrational laughter, and I think of Büchner and Karl Valentin. Aside from its rich traditions and all varieties of irony and *pathos*,* this irrationalism is always a game despite all efforts at puzzling out the riddle of the universe, for it is based on the plain avowal of the limits of our existence and of our capacity for thinking. To preserve the irrational illusion of hope between the birth of the star and the death of the star. Nevertheless, it is up to us. This irrationalism does not try to capitulate, but rather to exist in art as an anti-world, perhaps better than reality, affording a chance for paradises, utopias, a reality of its own, proving a likeness to God through its own strength—that greatest likeness—which remains for us, if we respect ourselves, one of our finest possibilities.

I would like to define this irrationality as the ultimate principle of infinity in our art, the indissoluble, the homesickness, the yearning for meaning in madness, in the cinematic artwork, and as a nation's desire for representation, a desire for myth, and that is my relationship to society at the present, which gives rise to these films, and their obligation to respond to woeful reality. The continuation of life by other means, including the issues of guilt, ceremonies of expunging guilt, the work of mourning as the reflection of this loneliness of infinity. At its start, suffering; and at its end, morality. It is only in myth as an act of human cultural will that we get hold of our history, unabashed. The mystery will have to be borne, with an awareness of the unsolved questions of the ultimate why and wherefore and where to and where from, and the joy of solution, just as music was capable of leaping across the limits of the ungraspable, which is neither thinkable nor explicable. An ambivalence of knowledge will be felt and, if things go well, it will, as art, attain that state of levitation that people love: whether as art, as music, as dance, at the circus and at the fair, and also in parades in the age of mass culture, or at the theater, on tours through landscapes, as an urban experience, in architecture, in churches, and even, at certain times, in concordance with systems of government. In the *Gesamtkunstwerk* of this era, film, if it uses all its optical and acoustic and moral possibilities (beyond the entertainment business and the limits of didacticism) as gratuitous, with a freedom and a love that leap across limits, in the manner of a new metaphysics, needing energy to go

* Translator's note: The German word *Pathos*, meaning bombast, intense emotion, high-flown rhetoric, etc., has been rendered here with *pathos* (italicized), since there is no sharp English equivalent.

along and providing energy for a better life. This is not cinema like
that of the movie profiteers, a beer-garden surrogate and part of
the leisure-time industry under the motto "Do you have two free
hours? Go to the movies!" Nor is it a simple guide, in the manner
of the political functionaries, to change life, unless first to change
oneself, through meditative concentration and openness, like that
presumed in a concert hall.

Nor is the movie house of the mass society the fast-food joint
and beer garden of the proletariat, which has been going to the

theater for a long while now, well organized and well prepared, without popcorn or slapstick, because the proletariat has learned that culture requires the entire person before opening up. They say one should distrust anyone who claims otherwise, that he wants to misuse culture to sell different things with his ideas, that he simply wants to get at the spectator's money. Lenin, the great tactician, preferred to confine himself to a few sincere and reliable men when he had to get through crises, for all that counts in a crisis is that honesty which can sweep us off our feet. The art of cinema today means making films with all the possibilities that cinema offers us, uncompromisingly, ethically inviolable against all attacks, even at the risk of occasionally losing mass under-standing and mass applause, so long as it can be done in some way or other. This is the only way we can endure and slowly regain friends beyond the few faithful that remain. If one views cinema as the most important art form of this time, then that is the only political responsibility, the categorical imperative of the artistic entity that is cinema, the radical limitation to an aesthetics of truth, and this aesthetics has nothing to do with the business of money or of ideologies, it is more closely related to a great deal of grief or, if things go well, to a little joy.

If my films *Ludwig, Requiem for a Virgin King* and *Karl May* can be understood as positive mythologizings of history through the devices of cinema, and filtered through the intellectual controls of irony and *pathos*, for our glory and for use as a response to the reality of our days, what can we do with a historical subject like

Hitler? That was the question from the very outset, before making this last film. This epitome of our deepest guilt and reflection of our vast grief and turning away from the face of a man such as we understand him, and nevertheless accepting here too the title as a motto for all three films of my trilogy: in search of paradise lost here as well?

First of all, Hitler is not conceivable without us. Hence, the film is about us, and we must know that first before selecting from the wealth of material. If one looks and hates but is forced to recognize human features there, how can we justly picture ourselves and this guilt and this common will and these intermediate tones of hope without harming ourselves through lies, self-deception? This identity of a man and a nation's will and a character that, in my opinion, swept everything in the center of Europe away. How can this be presented with the existing methods of cinema? And how can all the insights of sociology and psychology and the social sciences and politics be summed up, put together as a film, blended and reduced to a common denominator?

A denominator that does not omit anything important, something sensual, with no reconstruction of history but with all the technical devices that this century puts at our disposal. This century of cinema, of radio, and of projection—how to depict what even historians and politicians have so far managed to do only sketchily, how to clarify and attempt to win the hearts of audiences, for, so I feel, Hitler and all the idealism of his misled followers can be conquered only with the heart.

How does irrationalism function in the editing of my films, i.e., in the ambiguity, the vagueness of colliding levels, that hovering of trivial backgrounds that determine our lives, the truth behind things in the surreal concentration of cinematic imagination?

Our aim is the irony of diabolical enlightenment: to discover horror in the banal, to confront the hugeness of evil with ever-lurking triviality and carry it to absurdity; our aim is the sad knowledge that for victims and perpetrators, as for the spectators of history, this crisis of human existence has an attractive demonic quality. To present this, with all its pain, struck me as yielding more in a dialogue (e.g., those between Himmler and his masseur or his astrologer) than in a conversation—however historical—between Himmler and the commandant of Auschwitz. In the latter case, the brilliance or vanity of actors and the art of directing become impossible, whereas in the former, triviality, harnessed to the historical blood-reality, still has a chance to relieve the unspeakable shock through humor. But still and all, the risk of

Wingate College Library

| 13

portraying the beauty of evil is only justified in the passion and poetry of art.

In Part Two, the actor Hellmut Lange as Hitler's valet, reminiscing, walks through the huge projection of the Reich Chancellery in our studio. Piercing deeper and deeper into the cavern of his memories of underpants and nightshirts, he talks about breakfasts and film screenings and eventually, like Alice in Wonderland, the size of a Lilliputian, winds up in front of the immensely blown-up details of Hitler's desk with the facing portraits of Bismarck and with the sounds of *Fridericus Rex*, "Taps," and Wagner's *Rienzi* in his ears. Then the image suddenly changes to that of the same room in 1945, destroyed, in which he now stands while we hear a Russian fanfare. And as he stands there, we hear the announcement of the Christmas broadcast of 1942 with renditions of "Silent Night" patched in live from everywhere—Stalingrad to Africa. The valet now relates his last memories, namely, how Hitler dragged him through Munich on a prewar Christmas Eve after they had wrapped packages together. A private Christmas and war and Stalingrad—that is, the German people and Germany and the Führer—come very close together. The sound track then changes to the Wehrmacht station's broadcasting signal, "Lili Marlene"; then to the melody "In the Homeland, in the Homeland." All this takes place during a snowfall, today, at Obersalzberg, recited from memory by Hitler's former valet. The whole thing has the character of a fugue with several intercrossing lines and superimposed strata.

The child as a recurrent figure of the narrative framework is Guilt, for she brings the Hitler puppet into play and puts it in the cradle of the Caligula portrait; and she is also the judging authority of naïveté, before whom everything takes place like a horrifying interior vision.

Some viewers may wonder why, in Part Three of the film, I show Himmler in a conversation with the astrologer against the background of the noises of a bombing attack on Berlin. In point of fact, his quarters must have been far away from the theaters of war, at the front or at home. Critics of my film could speak of "heroizing." But, as elsewhere, the aim here is not reality, but rather the montage of the figure of horror and the evocation of his deeds. They belong together both as a torture for him and as a model of combined sound and image for us.

When we see Himmler, we instantly think of the concentration camps, as we automatically connect Hitler with war. And that is what he stands for. The two belong together: Himmler's speculations about Buddhism and the catastrophes of war and concentration camps. The SS men, for instance, who come toward us in his nightmares and with his words against Slavic and Jewish subhumans, emerge from the horror pictures of their deeds in his vision, to the accompaniment of the sound of the launching of the first V-1 against London and the invasion on the Atlantic coast and the attempted assassination of Hitler on July 20, 1944. Not only is it a montage of war, but the noises of the war are heard in conjunction with the speech of the mass murderer, the ideology that made this war a special war, a struggle for humanity, freedom, against the devil in his greatest confusion and aggressive efforts against the world so far. Whenever we hear these sounds of the Hitler war, we have to know what they signify beyond those normal matters of bravery and storms of steel of other wars. The death of love was always present, and even a Himmler could not endure it, which was why he needed his secret masseur. Otherwise he could not have gone on living. That too is part of the history of this man and this era—the era that so greatly valued strong men and the false myth of diabolical heroes. And so ultimately, if you will, enlightenment occurs, knowledge about the powerlessness of strong men and the great danger they pose. A knowledge without aggression and, as is possible today, from a certain distance and with some sympathy, which can be useful to all knowledge. For rage was always a bad teacher, and hatred is good in wartime, but we live in what is called peace, and we want calm insights to help us avoid repetitions.

Toward the end of Part Three the actor Peter Kern tells an anecdote about Hitler. He tells it at Obersalzberg, today, while having a snack, on the overgrown site where Hitler's house stood before it was blown up. Kern pretends to be Hitler's valet the way a lunatic imagines himself to be Napoleon. Or Ellerkamp, his film projectionist, a man very close to Hitler's dreams. Films of Hitler's appearance in Vienna are screened by him today in a Viennese movie house, where he lives. He quotes his father, the famous janitor Herr Karl, created by Helmut Qualtinger, and he tells the story of how Hitler's father beat him and how little Adolf, modeling himself after Karl May, tried to stifle his pain and refused to scream. And how he was never beaten again. Trivial sociology and psychology. His mother stands in the doorway and gazes tremblingly at the young Adolf. Then we hear music from the transistor radio on the table, music that we already heard in Part Two, a concert for the Waffen SS outside Leningrad. Instantly, we associate Karl May and Indians with German soldiers outside of Leningrad

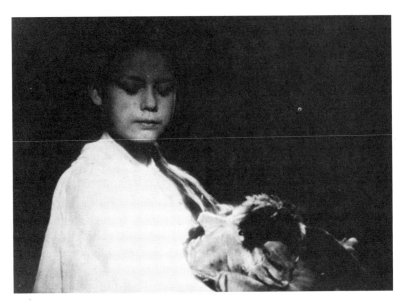

and Hitler's slogans—that is, one has to bear the pain, then one wins, overcomes. Anyone who knows what Karl May was for generations of Germans, how every schoolboy grew up with his books, knows how close we are here to a history of German feeling, the adventures of the soul and myths of the good, the German who fights for noble things and triumphs. Here reduced to an unreal historical denominator, through montage, for this music cannot emerge today from a transistor radio. Then, also from the transistor radio, we hear that round-robin Christmas broadcast from the moment of the greatest expansion of the German Reich, with voices from the North Sea to Africa and from the Bay of Biscay to Stalingrad, all singing the Christmas carol "Silent Night." Peter Kern walks toward Blondie, Hitler's wolfhound, calling, and then tells a new story, a characteristic anecdote about a dog, about how Hitler decided against the beloved little Burli in favor of the wolfhound for an official photo. Kern keeps walking into the forest and thinks that it is almost as beautiful as Christmas, as Christmas with Hitler.

This strange Christmas story was already heard at the end of Part Two, from Hitler's valet, to the same background of that "Silent Night" from the Deutschland network, parallel to Hitler's Christmas outing through a nocturnal prewar Munich. Peter Kern recalls Hitler's Christmas, which had a special meaning for him because his mother had died under a Christmas tree. Then, after some reflection, in the forest, at the former site of Hitler's house, he sings "Deutschland über Alles" (the first stanza, which is not

allowed today, from the time of the greatest expansion of the desired German Reich) and then collapses in tears. And this seemingly mad figure of an utterly nostalgic crazy neo-Nazi brings together many things, sociological and psychological reports, popular myths and folklore, history and the history of heroes; all these things form an inseparable unity. Here, Germany is equal to Hitler, Stalingrad has something to do with Karl May, Indians with the Waffen SS. The mother's death and Christmas at Stalingrad are connected as they can only be by a film. Nor is it necessary to know anything else, for instance the history of that unhappy anthem, which was carried by Hitler to all European countries, but which was written as a poem of freedom in the revolutionary days of the nineteenth century. By a poet who dreamed of national unity and freedom and was therefore persecuted. Nor does one necessarily have to know that the melody comes from Haydn and was originally that of the anthem of the Hapsburg monarchy and then, combined with the verses of the revolutionary period, it became the national anthem of the Weimar Republic, that first German republic, from which Hitler took the song. One does not have to know all these things; nevertheless, this neo-Nazi, unappealing to both our emotions and our political convictions, is a dismal figure. No one runs from this film with a knife to denounce him; pity and sorrow are greater than aggression.

Something else. Before Peter Kern remembers Christmas in the forest, we hear the sound of the old signal of the Deutschland Radio Network: "*Üb' immer Treu und Redlichkeit.*" That too is part of the sequence's associative structure. It was the glocken-spiel tune in Potsdam until its destruction, the melody by Mozart and verses from Germany's pietistic eighteenth century. Then it was taken over by the Freemasons and engraved on Frederick II's church as the hallmark of Prussia. And thus it must be under-stood here too as a signal and the dismal, macabre, tragic ending of a Hitler-history of Germany: "Be ever loyal and honest until the cool grave."

Perhaps there are not just emotional insights about the con-junction of private and historical facts in this ghostly trivial area of the history of the Reich. At the end of the film, I show the child wandering through the set with the Hitler puppet as a cloth dog, to the accompaniment of Schiller's *Ode to Joy* in Beethoven's Ninth. After the child throws down the dog and tramples on it, she takes it up again, sits down, and gazes at it wordlessly, Hitler's puppet face before her eyes, and we hear "this kiss of the entire world." All of German classical idealism and the world-embrace of German humanism in its great tradition stand before us, now reduced to its greatest trial and the absurdity of the trivial. What does the child do with her unloved puppet? She holds it tight, with an absent gaze, and keeps going into a black cloud. That is very pessimistic, German pessimism, which again, like classical ideal-ism, this time in mournful melancholy, embraces the world. That is more than irony. Naïve in the image, identifying itself with bad experience, devoured by the best that was possible, without hope, wandering the world through cinema.

A montage with the cinematic devices of the irrational. It has everything; the spectator must decide. Anyone who wants it more didactically starts lying, preparing the next errors. The extreme ends of our tradition are harnessed together through montage, such as only the sound film makes possible today. Yes, here, at the end of these seven hours of the Hitler-Germany Tragedy, joy despite everything is still possible. But anyone who fears a re-election of Hitler or an apotheosis of Hitler must have been sick, even before this film, and could not be helped even with the best kind of film enlightenment. At the end, the silence of melancholy remains as a new variety and consequence of abortive German idealism. Not embracing the world in this kiss of the entire world, with joy, but entering the black hole of the future, full of melan-choly. New tidings from Germany and not the worst at that.

I sought an aesthetic scandal: combining Brecht's doctrine of epic theater with Richard Wagner's musical aesthetics, cinemati-cally conjoining the epic system as anti-Aristotelian cinema with the laws of a new myth.

Today's movie-house movie has, in my opinion, been the locus of a deteriorated form of Aristotelian dramaturgy—deteriorated into boulevard triviality—for the past fifty years, without poetic, aesthetic, or intellectual innovation. A reactionary form of culture in the hands of shopkeepers and functionaries. Even the admirable exceptions had no trailblazing consequences, and the so-called underground cinema was restricted to private undertakings without historical relevance. Truly underground. The great inventions of the modern theater, with its interest in traditions of epic dramaturgy over the course of history, have never been grasped and assimilated by the cinema. The motion picture has not known how to use the spiritual and intellectual legacies of Aeschylus and Sophocles, of the mystery play and Shakespeare, of the German Romantic theater, *Sturm und Drang*, the revolutions of German classicism before Brecht, and Homer, or Dante and Bach, of what Wagner understood as a *Gesamtkunstwerk*.

In this respect, Germany—as was stated in the essays on cinematic aesthetics during the twenties and thirties—could and ought to have followed this route, as well as the practice of the Expressionist film. This line of anti-Aristotelian theater, which Brecht called "epic," is based on a possibility—highly profitable for the cinema—of elements like stationary series (i.e., chapter division), alienation, demonstrability, distancing, non-tectonic flashback, breaking of illusion, renunciation of color, plot with a beginning and an end, and the use of a narrator instead of a hero, character developed through monologue, etc. But this system also offered the chance to take seriously the origin of tragedy in the structure of music. We who make films are the heirs to Western civilization. There is good reason why some people claim that Wagner and Schiller would have made films today.

Thus, precisely in this tradition of epic, non-Aristotelian dramaturgy, one can observe a strong ceremonial character. And now comes the leap that I find important; it was Brecht's right, as the strongest exponent of this new and old aesthetics, to emphasize his special interest in the didactic, in the necessity of enlightenment, and—in the *Kulturkampf* of his time—in the anti-metaphysical effect of this system. It was neither logical nor simply possible or necessary. Irrationality, with all its related notions such as Surrealism, etc., is possible and consistent precisely where music is important as an aesthetic-dramaturgical principle of order, just as the tradition of this aesthetics proves, with witnesses from Greek tragedy, the mystery play, and Bach oratorios, to Wagner's *Ring of the Nibelungen*.

And now for the moral. The aesthetic moral. We not only have to see and work out the banality in history, the trivialities of our

lives, we also have to contrast them with so-called reality, through texts, characters, images, and sounds. Then we must add a highly artificial *pathos* (i.e., a new passion) and heroicize them ironically. Then, if possible, we must break with everything, not just with irony, through, say, music or various levels of projection and perhaps historical quotations and associations, and ultimately bring ourselves to a dreadfully simple, almost childish naïveté, if that is still possible, on the basis of our memories of ourselves or of the lost life of our culture. An irritatingly floating spiral motion of feelings and insights allows a recombination of things and people and events and a genesis of new worlds. A new artistic unity as a continuation of life, a new metaphysics as myth through cinema. All this looks complicated—but when something comes directly, is spoken, appears before the camera, or is heard as music, the strangest things reach us with a new freedom; then it is like a blow, virtually never before seen or heard. And it is precisely here that the spectator must make sure that something different is not meant or at least nothing but what is so openly offered, what is to be seen or heard. If here, for instance, it says quite simply, at the end: "But the fruit of the spirit is love and joy," etc., one would have to observe this carefully in the context of a film, where and when and by whom it is said, with what optical or acoustic ingredients. Everything would be in irritating disquiet or simply not, just as Kant's "the starry sky above and the moral law within" appears twice and very differently in the film. Despite all playing, everything will someday come to rest, and it is up to the author of the film and his audience where and when and how intensely we will permit this.

This means, after long attempts at circling in on it, that not everything must always be questioned by doubt and irony. In the end, we try to realize that courage is the ultimate quality in our work, acknowledge that necessary calm of the equilibrium of all parts, the final order of the intellectual and emotional excitement, which we admire in classical civilization, acknowledge them in our way, with the new technologies of this era: that is an aesthetic program. Whatever succeeds of it is our affair, that of the filmmaker and that of the receivers.

And that is the offer, all brought together to one point: hence, little Ludwig at the end of my *Ludwig, Requiem for a Virgin King*, with the beard on the child's face and the tear in the embarrassed grief of his final smile, before he vanishes in the grotto of clouds.

That is why the entire Hitler film is a child's world of puppets, dolls, full of stars and music, the material for a child's huge nightmare, such as has never been dreamed, tormenting and light. One feels that all this really shouldn't be, certainly not with this theme. It is all like the clairvoyant vision of a child with closed eyes and a huge tear, in the crack of the universe soaring toward us from the cosmos.

The final silence of childlike melancholy in a starry tear with a distant freedom fanfare beyond the mountains. That is the end of this Hitler, who is now a film. But how far we have gone in these seven hours of cinema, what things we have gone through and what things we have had to see and hear . . .

Part One
Hitler, a Film from Germany
From the World Ash Tree to the
Goethe Oak of Buchenwald

Stars flying toward us. A voyage into the darkness of outer space. The noise of static familiar to us from the radio of the 1930s and the opening of Mozart's Piano Concerto in D Minor softly fade in and out. More static as the following text appears in the form of subtitles:

> We all dream of traveling
> through space—into our
> inner self.
> The mysterious path
> goes inward,
> inward into night.

The figure 1 for Part One of the film flies toward us and vanishes. Suddenly we see a landscape with Himalayas, palms, and a lake—a painting of the Winter Garden that Ludwig II had built on the roof of his Munich palace. We hear the prelude to *Parsifal*.

The subtitles continue:

And if I had in one hand the gold of business, the full beer belly of the functionary, happiness, and all the playthings of the world, and my other hand held fairy tales and the dreams of fancy, the yearning for paradise and the music of our ideas, then everybody would blindly choose paradise, even if it was false, greedy for sacrificial blood, ready to give their best, involving our hopes with the greatest cruelties for the sake of moonstruck triumphs of the human soul. Concealing within ourselves all errors, the banality and baroque asceticism of mass rites. Long is the history of faith, its victories over us and its defeat at our hands.

The last line of the text passes into an off-focus white, from which the letters of the words DER GRAL come into focus. Moving from bottom to top, broad and cracked in a thick block: DER GRAL, LE GRAAL, THE GRAIL, from the white blurriness below to the white blurriness of the sky.

•

The paradisiacal image of Ludwig's roof garden is ripped apart from top to bottom in a huge split through the mountains, and through the split we see the stars again (as at the beginning), flying toward us. From among them, a tiny, starlike tear forms, coming closer. Within it is a lunar landscape (from a Méliès film), with a glass sphere in the midst of the landscape, full of snow and with a black house inside it.

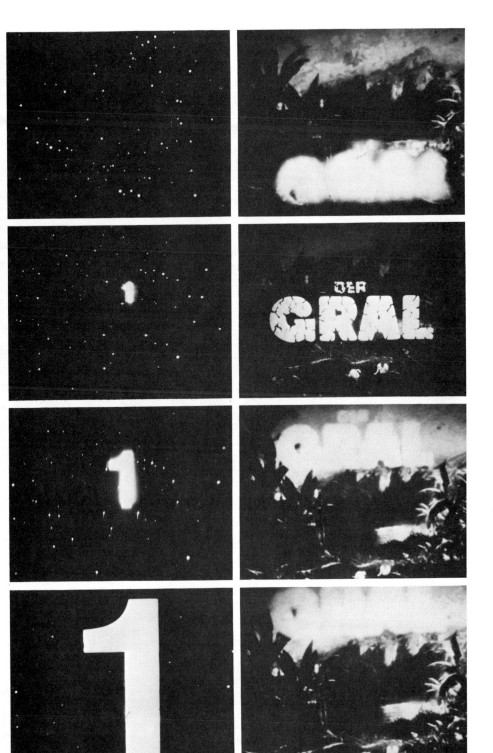

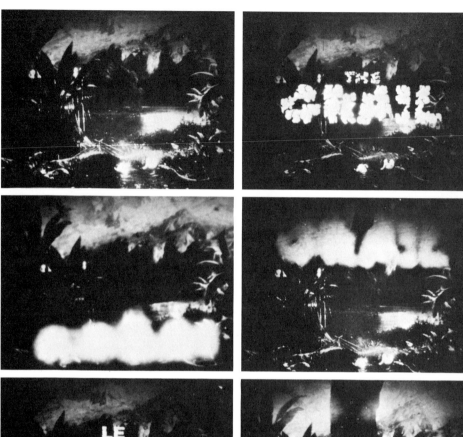
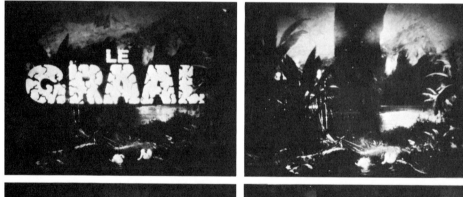

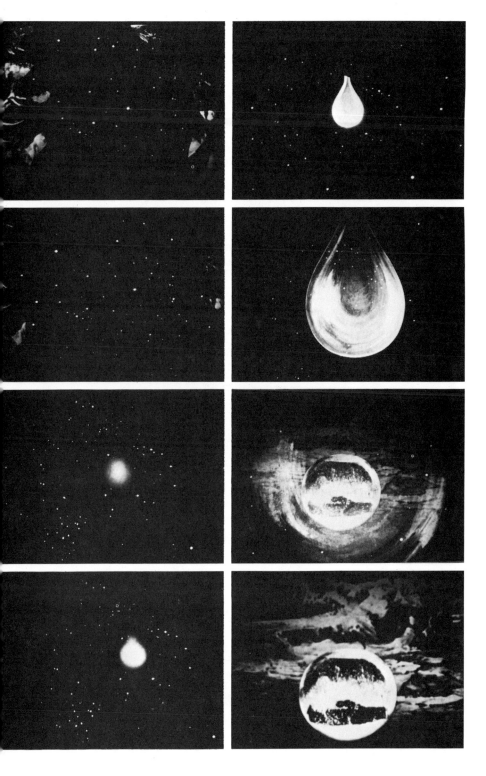

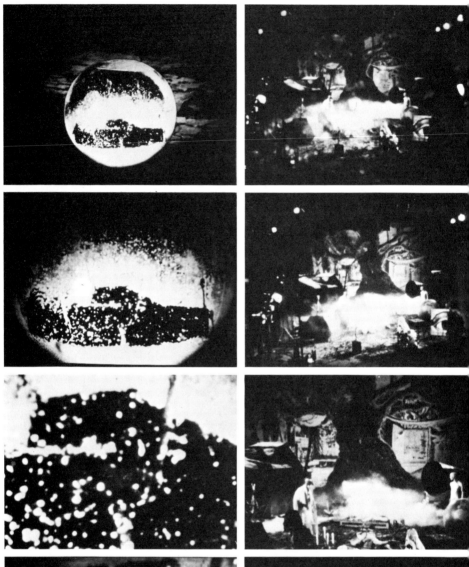
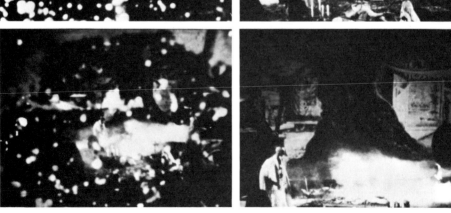

ANDRE HELLER (voice off, as if to himself):
I think of Germany in the night
And then sleep leaves me.*

The black house is the Black Maria, the first movie studio in the world; it was built by Edison in America shortly before 1900. The camera moves toward this house, that is to say, the film studio enclosed in the glass sphere; and after a lap dissolve, we are inside the studio, where the film begins. Music from *Das Rheingold* as an allusion to the earlier film *Ludwig, Requiem for a Virgin King* (madness scene of Ludwig's brother Otto). The camera closes in on the projection in the background of our film studio, showing the World Ash Tree from Wagner's *Die Walküre*.

ANDRE HELLER (continues, voice off): Everything is purely fictitious.
All historical people and events, any similarities are purely coincidental. This is no joke. The judicial reality of everyday life makes this disclaimer necessary. Thirty heirs of Hitler have al-

* Heine.

| 31

ready come forward with legal claims, and they are not alone. For Hitler was never tried: this leads to claims, and we live in a state founded on law and justice. Freed from similarities in the depiction of people and events, and without the restricting four walls of what is called reality in this world, we are thus free to pass judgment according to the intrinsic laws of our chosen universe, and we are finally putting him, this Hitler, on trial—we with our possibilities. Yet what else is this world but, first of all, us who make, present, and watch this film. This world and me and my film. Protuberances of the self in the cosmos of hard cuts, fragments of an inner projection, memories of an old world in the black studio of our imagination, full of now lonesome human puppets, changing characters of the self, endless material for monologues, mono-dramas, and tragedies on celluloid. Dances of death, dialogues of the dead, conversations in the kingdom of the dead, a hundred years later, a thousand years, millions. Passions, oratorios.

Who knows. But how is one to, who am I to, how are we to, who am I, who are we, who plays for us and for whom do we play, why, what remains, once again everyone together, leftovers of a lost civilization and of a lost life, our Europe before the collapse. Farewell to the West. *Sub specie aeternitatis* and everything on film, our new chance. The story of the death of the old light in which we lived, and of our culture, a remote singing.

An artificial light now through the black envelope of our film fantasies in the mind's eye. The echo of fading music in our ears.

●

Dissolve through the trunk of the World Ash Tree to the credits, black on gray-blue clouds. Far in the distance, the yodeler from the end of *Ludwig, Requiem for a Virgin King.*

Heinz Schubert · Peter Kern
Hellmut Lange

Rainer von Artenfels
Martin Sperr · Peter Moland

Johannes Buzalski
Alfred Edel
Amelie Syberberg

Harry Baer
and
Peter Lühr

and
André Heller

Written and directed by
Hans-Jürgen Syberberg

Director of photography	·	Dietrich Lohmann
Camera	·	Werner Lüring
Assistant directors	·	Gerhard von Halem
		Michael Sedevy
Editing	·	Jutta Brandstaedter
Assistant editors / continuity	·	Helga Beyer
		Lydia Pieger
Sound	·	Heymo H. Heyder
Mixing	·	Wilhelm Schwadorf
Makeup	·	Gerlinde Kunz
Sets	·	Hans Gailling
Costumes	·	Barbara Gailling
		Brigitte Kühlenthal
Props	·	Peter Dürst
Puppets	·	Barbara Buchwald
		Hans M. Stummer
Montage	·	Theo Nischwitz
Laboratory	·	Bavaria Atelier, Inc.
Unit manager	·	Ike Werk
Assistant to the producer	·	Annie Oléon
Executive producer	·	Harry Nap
Producer	·	Bernd Eichinger

With special thanks to
Henri Langlois
and the Cinémathèque Française
for publishing
Film—The Music of the Future
the aesthetics of this film

•

We see the "subterranean chasm," the *Rheingold* grotto where Erda and the Nibelungen dwarfs normally reside.

The concluding music of *Die Götterdämmerung.*

A little girl, in the kind of black hooded cape once worn by old women, sits and plays with dolls—including a little Ludwig. There are several figures of Karl May, and a Hitler hanging on a gallows.

HARRY BAER (voice off):
When the good old democracy
of the twentieth century got on in years,
it sent messengers in all directions

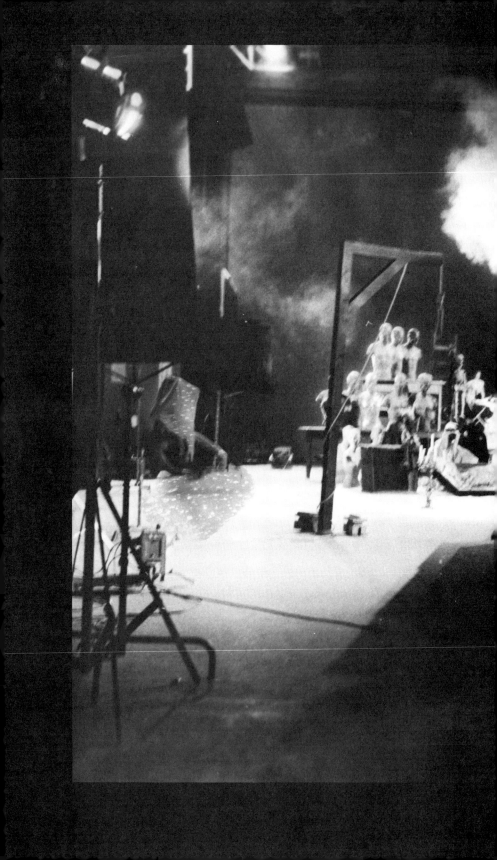

to find the reason for misery in the world.
When the messengers came back,
they came to know from East and West,
North and South, from all computers
—the incorruptible, as they say—
that democracy itself, good and old,
was the cause of all misery in the twentieth century.

The child gets up and goes into the world, holding a cloth dog with
Hitler's face, passing the hanged Hitler. Moving through other grottoes,
she encounters the huge projection of Lola Montez (from the Ludwig
film) coming toward her. The child passes three angels from Philipp
Otto Runge's painting *Morning*, wanders past William Blake's compass of
God (a compass spread over the surface of the earth by a hand held from
above), moves by Wieland Wagner's Norns, cuts across a Caspar David
Friedrich landscape with Dürer's Black Stone from the *Melencolia* en-
graving; and then she sees the newborn child on the meadow from Runge's
Morning.

This is accompanied, after the music from *Die Götterdämmerung* ends,
by the prelude to *Parsifal*.

ANDRE HELLER (voice off): It was in the good old days of the
democratic twentieth century, when all children were urged to do
well in school, learned about progress, learned how to become big
and make it, learned how to make money, to become rich and

famous, as always in all our fairy tales. And learned that it was sweet to die for one's country.

Or:

I am not worthy to have you under my roof.

Or:

The Party is always right, or one for all and all for one.

And they learned how to make any sacrifice in the name of progress. And the politicians did not see how unhappy people became. Without the happiness they had been promised in the great, beloved revolutions. And then a man came who knew that the greater the sacrifice, the greater the god. And he knew that blood sacrifices were required of the sacrosanct goods of art and morality on the altar of faith. And they still were moved by the old feelings and by the way he told them that he who sacrifices is chosen. A chosen people. And then that man from the legendary nullity of nothingness, from the landscape and forests of that people, gained access to undreamed-of energies, carried by all, by that majority, the quality of this century, beloved like no man before him and mystically redeemed, a redeemed Redeemer. A true miracle. Prepared for the total risk of everlasting damnation or of the greatest light in his eyes, striding over the mountains, and through oceans of blood, with the moaning curses of sacrificial victims in his ears, and of a great mass jubilation everywhere, in his middle of the world, which was, or would become, the middle of our earth. For all who were of good will or of the

right stock and race. And this arouser of all majorities of the middle, secretly beloved by the humiliated and by the nations of the Third World, the great taboo today in both East and West, outcast and lonesome now, abandoned, as he himself prophesied, a cast-off black Messiah, the Black Plague and cancerous ulcer of mass movements and all their somnambulant rites, devil and eternal tempter of democracy or hypnotized world-medium of the masses or tool of capitalist exploitation and social explosions— where is his beginning and how can we grasp it, depict it in old pictures for our time?

Once again, the ancient Dionysian rites of self-sacrifice. Occidental ceremonies, feasts of destruction, a final memory of faraway myths of God's nearness through blood sacrifices and slaughtering one's own son. And they know not what they do, awakening in the end as if from a faraway dream of their own guilt. Europe's final attempt to assert herself according to the old tradition, by the new law of the masses. Despairing in impotence, an enigma for all spectators forever, before it was written down between the shopkeeper-and-functionary states in East and West. Finally freed from herself in the nostalgic intoxication of death.

A postscript to the tragic case of the West, the satyr play about the death of light surrounded by the guilt of the culprits, but also of the victims, the fellow travelers and adversaries, the Jews and victors of Versailles, Germany, Europe, and the world?

Arriving in the midst of a projection from *Doctor Caligari*—that is, an Expressionist film décor from our little world—the girl puts the Hitler puppet in a cradle. The devil comes forward from behind and leans over the cradle and turns into a black eagle. We hear the prelude to *Parsifal*, which grows softer.

Figures of the German Expressionist cinema are placed about the set: from *Doctor Caligari, Alraune, Nosferatu,* and *Algal,* with Conrad Veidt, Lil Dagover, and Werner Krauss.

Once again, the old story of Elijah's struggle with Satan, whose blood at the moment of victory drips on the earth, setting everything ablaze with crimson fire. Once again, the image of the world ablaze and, with the final judgment at hand, the gamble for man's soul, his final chance before the destruction and before the departure of the gods from this world and before the exodus of the gods from this world. *Muspilli.* The conflagration of the world in the ancient manner.

Hitler (1932): I have something in mind, the gentlemen are quite correct. We are intolerant. I have set myself a goal, namely to sweep the thirty parties out of Germany.

[Applause]

They still mistake me for a bourgeois or a Marxist politician who backs the Social Democratic Party today and the Independent

Social Democratic Party tomorrow and the Communist Party the day after tomorrow and then is a syndicalist or a democrat today, and then backs the German People's Party tomorrow and then the Economic Party. They confuse me with one of their own kind.

We have a goal and we will advocate it fanatically and relentlessly until the grave.

ANDRE HELLER (voice off, quoting from *Muspilli*): So inprinnant die perga, poum ni kistentit, enhic in erdu, aha artrucknent . . . mano vallit, prinnit mittilargart. "The mountains burn, the trees vanish from the earth, the rivers run dry, the moon falls, and finally the entire earth burns."

Once again, we see a close-up of the Black Maria studio inside the glass sphere.

●

Enlarged photos of Berlin and Vienna in the early days of the Third Reich, and the Berlin of the future in designs by Speer and Hitler, after the victory of the last war. Also, images from Wagner's operas: for instance, the struggle between Wotan and Siegmund and Hunding at the edge of the world.

In front of these "projections," the actor Heinz Schubert as the circus barker. Interspersed in his text: excerpts from sound materials (now in historical archives) from the early years of the Third Reich.

CIRCUS BARKER: Ladies and gentlemen, today we are going to hear about the man whose fault it all is. Like Napoleon. The German Napoleon of the twentieth century. More of a non-person, a man who never laughed without holding his hand in front of his mouth, and who kicked his dog away if anyone caught him petting it. The man who said: "In the beginning, everyone laughed at me; now very few people laugh, and soon no one will laugh anymore." This was a man who had nothing to lose, a man whom nobody will imitate.

Ladies and gentlemen, now that we're rid of the Kaiser and God—off we go.

The Song of Songs, the greatest story ever told. Let's give him his chance,

Church hymns and marching songs.

let's give ourselves our chance. Taboos, this show's about taboos. The greatest show of the century, big business, the show of shows.

Either you bang the people on their heads or you stay home with your canary. Yessir, cultural revolution, art for the people. The people's right to depict itself. Representation. There have been parades and victory banners under the sign of the sun since

Caesar's Rome and Caligula. People in the era of film. Everything or nothing. The man who got rid of unemployment, who drove the money changers from the temple and cleansed the home of sex and crime, the man of the twentieth century.

Radio announcer, June 30, 1933: German radio listeners . . . fellow Germans . . .

The man who came from below, from the people, like any one of us, from the masses. Hurray! The devil's loose. Knaves are trumps, perversities and abnormal dealings, that would have preferred to stay in the wings. Hit them hard and beat the devil. A cheerful apocalypse. Experiment of world destruction, something about our wolfish society.

. . . constant questions on how this came about. Simply because a man stood up and created a movement that spread like a wave over all of Germany, from south to north, to east and west.

And these are the rules of the game: There will be no heroes, except ourselves. And there will be no plot, only ours, our inside story.

. . . above all, our war veterans . . . with Adolf Hitler's movement . . .

Fantasy visions of bloody orgies before the final daybreak. No human story, but a history of mankind, no disaster film, but disaster as a film. The end of the world, Deluge, the cosmos biting the dust.

. . . and to continue in all hearts.

Hence, no scenes of the private life, of the fear and misery of the Third Reich, and nothing of the "cabbage trust," the political racketeering of thirty years ago. Rather, something of the faith that moves mountains. Of a popular tribune without parallel. So gather all your strength, your gladness, and your sorrow.

. . . In just a few hours, we shall witness here the greatest mass meeting ever assembled.

Anyone who wants to see Stalingrad again or the Twentieth of July plot or the lone wolf's last days in the bunker or Riefenstahl's Nuremberg will be disappointed. We are not showing the unrepeatable reality, nor the feelings of the victims with their stories, nor the non-fiction of the authors, nor the big business of trading on morality and horror, on fear and death and atonement and arrogance and righteous wrath.

. . . The German worker, who is at the center of the celebration, has surpassed himself here . . .

So nothing of the leftist concentration-camp pornographers and celluloid spectators. A film for us. About war and racial annihilation. Auschwitz as the battlefield of racial wars. Our goal is to find the world culprit, and what would Hitler be without us? Our goal is to project the divine spark in man, the starry sky above us and the moral law within myself.

Deutschland, Deutschland über alles, über alles in der Welt.
Radio announcer: We are broadcasting over all German stations . . .

We will show the adventure of the mind and its bloody realization. Mephisto in front of every burning house.

Deutschland, Deutschland über alles, über alles in der Welt.

Heinz Schubert as the barker enters the Black Maria, which stands in front of the projected image of Runge's *Morning*.

●

Harry Baer inside the Black Maria meditating à la Dürer's *Melencolia*, with a Ludwig puppet. Props from Méliès' lunar landscape and from the *Melencolia*. *Rienzi* and *Parsifal* blend together in the sound track.

Deutschland, Deutschland über alles in der Welt.

HARRY BAER (with the Ludwig puppet): Once again. But how can we? Is it for art? Morality after fifty million dead? Silence? Should we keep silent? It concerns us, not the "haves," but us, the "have-nots," still hopeful, still putting our hopes in those who will finally do something, do their bit for once. Once they were carried away, and went along, wrong once already. It is about the greatest crisis of human existence, worldwide and with new technologies. I warned you, I, Ludwig II, I warned you from the very outset, I warned that business, wheeling and dealing, movies, porno, politics, were a show, a show for the masses. Entertainment, let money roll in, it has to. But how can one, how can I, how can you and I take this quite seriously, how can we take pleasure in tragedy, the work of a couple of madmen? Were the perpetrators all criminals? Were all the victims good people?

Masochists, systems, laws, purists, academics, newspapers, people, nation, socialism, workers, insane. Just have some pity for so much guilt. Then too, what would we be without this guilt? We live on the happiness of mourning, don't we?

Felix culpa. The happiness of guilt. A sadly beautiful business for art.

Without sympathy for the subject, how can I, how can one go through this, do this work? And again, should I, should we not live without this work, these thoughts, push aside these thoughts, think of something else, something more important? He ought to, he has to have his chance. Let him be born, like every one of us, have a mother, be able to learn, love, and hate. Influenced by what and by whom? Why did he make this or that decision? And if, in the end, he has to look the way he looked, he will be able to start like every one of us when we come into the world.

What shall it profit a man if he gain the whole world and have not love and lose his own soul. Quotations . . . pay attention, everybody: quotations. The entire old Occident and the Christian God are part of that. We're between Jesus and Hitler. There we have them already, the Jews and the persecution and the wheeling and dealing and the whole insanity of ideas and self-hatred and love.

Everyone envies me for this puppet, vital as it is. But what do I do if the puppet sees things, like the stairway of tears, or a grandfather showing his grandson the stars to divert him. The good old stars that the smog in the cities took away from us long ago. A mother with her baby in her arms, the men in black uniforms all around, death's-heads on their caps, all around on their caps, machine guns in their hands, the bodies still warm, trembling in the ditch, into which they too must go.

The shots at night, the curses, the whispering under the night stars. We hear the great curse in the stones all around. No sleep for the children and children's children of the guilty; music over everything, overcomes everything.

He draws Richard Wagner's velvet cloak from the Ludwig film slowly over his head, covering his face. The theme from *Parsifal* starts again.

●

Song: Today our Germany hears us,
Tomorrow the entire world,
And we will keep on marching,
Till everything to pieces is hurled . . .

Again, circus style. Heinz Schubert as the barker comes out of the Black Maria and sits down on the steps.

CIRCUS BARKER: During the last war, when the great Karl Valentin appeared once more on the Munich stage, he sang German folk songs very quietly amid the intoxication of victory:
In deepest cellar, here sit I;
What is coming from the sky?
and
Oh, you darling Augustin, everything's lost.

Valentin refused to sell Adolf Hitler his famous collection of postcards, including the card showing the child Ludwig with a beard. He refused an offer of one hundred thousand reichsmarks and a lifelong annuity of a thousand marks per month, because Hitler demanded that Valentin produce no more films. Where, I ask myself, will I find a second Valentin, someone who would say no to such an offer? After the war, however, when the then head of the Bavarian Radio Network informed him that he was no longer needed, due to his lack of humor, then the great Valentin wept for the first time, before he died.

Weeping after Hitler had gone. That was our Valentin. He didn't get another chance to object to anything. The people after Hitler had no more use for that Valentin.

One more thing: God always created ten who beat their breasts, weeping.

Song: Forward, forward . . .

And a fool who entertained them, laughing; which are you?

Song: Forward, forward! The brazen fanfares blare.
Forward, forward! Youth knows no danger anywhere.
Germany, you will stand in light,
Even if we die tonight.
Forward, forward! The brazen fanfares blare.

Forward, forward! Youth knows no danger anywhere.
No matter how high the goal may be,
Youth will reach it for all to see.
Our flag it flutters to point the way.
We march into the future, come what may.
We march for Hitler through night and through
    . . . need

January 5, 1935. Berlin, Lustgarten, German Youth . . .
Song: With the flag of youth for freedom and bread.
    Our flag it flutters to point the way,
    Our flag is the new age for all to see.
    And the flag leads us to eternity!
    Yes, our flag is greater than death!

Behind the barker, we see the projected image of the interior of the Reich Chancellery.

Song: Forward, forward! The brazen fanfares blare.
    Forward, forward! Youth knows no danger anywhere.
    Germany, you will stand in light,
    Even if we die tonight.
    Forward, forward! The brazen fanfares blare.
    Forward, forward! Youth knows no danger anywhere.
    No matter how high the goal may be . . .

Now that we've made up our minds to put on a show, in democratic fashion, about how he and we came to power, we want to carry it through to the end. Let's make it fun, for once, anybody can join in. There has to be a scandal, of course, what with this man and his deeds and our help. So let's do it right, let's shout it out, primal scream therapy, let's go way back to our childhood, let's go way back, into our most secret wishes, dreams, and stories . . .

. . . Sieg Heil, Sieg Heil . . .

Continues in the style of a barker's patter.

And as we have no Hitler to exhibit in a cage, to spit at, kick, or kiss his hands, for a fee of a couple of marks, each according to his taste, the way Lola Montez, in her day, could be touched for a buck in an American circus, I suggest that each man play himself, play his Hitler here in front of all the others. The way he

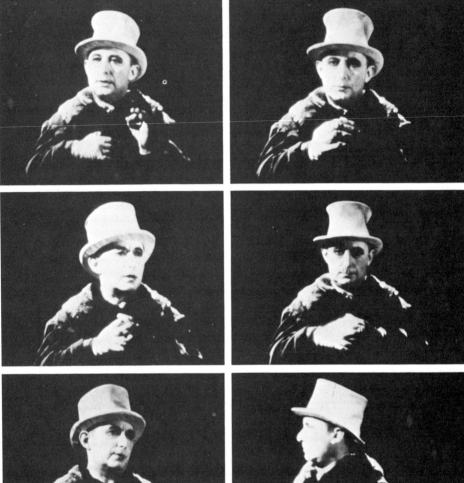

likes to play him even today, at home, in the privacy of his bedroom, in front of the mirror or on a motorcycle, everywhere, with a swastika and a Blessed Virgin as an amulet over his heart under the leather jacket, as he drives through the wind. And let's make it a commercial show, since, after all, film has always been a commercial business. No, please, just think back, into yourselves. Never has a man been so loved and so hated, remember, never has so much been projected into someone by so many. It's about us, about all of us. It's about the happiness that we were promised but never given. It's about the people who voted him in and sacrificed everything to him, that is to say, themselves and their ideas, sons, fathers, friends, and their image of the world, cities, whole countries: conscience and soul. It's about the Hitler within us, without stage sets, in slide projections, and in our imaginations, which the budget just barely allows, and in which anyone can join. The world as a circus and an amusement park. So let's give him and us a chance.

Sieg Heil! Sieg Heil!
Quiet, please. The Führer will appear now one last time, and then please go home, everybody, since he has meetings to attend.

●

All the actors in the film appear side by side, in various Hitler roles—a house painter, a raving maniac, Nero eating little children (dolls), "The Biggest Fart of the Century," Frankenstein, Charlie Chaplin in *The Great Dictator*, et al. The sound track includes historical recordings from the period, e.g., Hitler's march into Vienna in 1938 and one of his speeches. We also hear the text from *Jew Süss*—censored by Goebbels—in which the Jew curses this world. Then we hear the murderer's monologue from *M*, delivered by Peter Kern dressed in an SA uniform; it is interspersed with the commands of an SA parade. The whole thing as a sequence of circus acts.

HITLER AS HOUSE PAINTER (Johannes Buzalski): Neither the Party nor the common will brought me forward. It was the thousands who turned on the gas in their despair at finding no way out. The day is not far off when I shall ensure meticulous order in society. These plutocrats and Jewish elements want to dictate to the German worker. This lies solely in my power. Germany is Hitler—Hitler is Germany!

All my fanatical opponents—I know where their path will lead them, to the misery in which they should have been long ago. Meticulous order, let me repeat it once again, meticulous order.

| 53

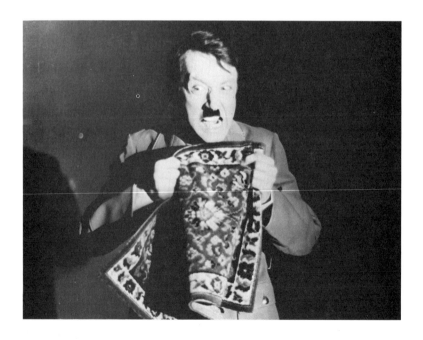

Hitler (Vienna, 1938): You can imagine how I have felt during these few days and what I feel now. I am so happy that destiny has selected me to bring about this great union of the German people.

And our new . . . our new community, that is security for us all. It shall never be dissolved again . . .

JEW SÜSS (Peter Moland): You Tartars, you worshippers of Baal, you judges of Sodom, may your limbs wither away, may your living bodies rot, may the bones of your children and children's children fester. May grief fill out your days and pain drive the sleep from your eyes.

Hitler: Germany has become Greater Germany and shall remain Greater Germany.
Crowd: Heil!

HITLER AS HOUSE PAINTER (miming Hitler's jig at the victory over France): Generals. Not only the genius of the commander in chief has led these troops to victory, but also Providence.

Ah, how good that no one knows that Rumpelstiltskin is my name.

Radio announcer (Vienna, 1936): The entire nation has lined up for the final roll call before its great, historic commitment. I beg you, my Führer, speak to us.
Crowd: Sieg Heil... We want our Führer...
Hitler: Germans, fellow members of the German race. For the third time, I speak to you on the occasion of an election in a border city. In 1933, it was Königsberg. There, on March 4, I asked the nation within the then borders of the Reich to make a commitment that would enable me to take in hand the history of Germany independent of its parliamentary difficulties and to shape it more auspiciously. The second time I spoke in a border city, in Cologne, on March 28, 1936, again on the eve of an election; at that time, I had to appeal to the German people to confirm a very serious decision on my part, a decision to take back the demilitarized zone under the sovereignty of the Reich. Today, I stand in Vienna, once again on the eve of a decision which, I believe, will enter the annals of German history.

Chorus from *Rienzi.*

Images from Hitler's childhood, of his father and mother and his early life. Images of Germany and Hitler ending in the annihilation of Hitler's opponents in Berlin after the uprising of the 20th of July.

ANDRE HELLER (voice off): So let's give him and ourselves a chance. As Brother Hitler, the chance for the little man from the people, who produced what all of us want, who understood how to produce himself. To be the greatest once. The old fairy-tale

nightmare. The man who had the courage to dare anything—let's admit it—radically. You can play it again now, once again, you've got a chance, and remember, you can inspire people for good and evil. Hitler did it systematically for evil, and he was the greatest at it, till now, through us. It was the defeat of arms that brought us away from him, not understanding. For when we gathered everything, all of our last strength of imagination, it was almost possible to conquer an entire world, practically all the way to New York, by way of Paris and London and Rome. Incomprehensible today.

And assuming he *had* had, we *had* had the atomic bomb and the rockets in the end? Through the Heisenbergs or von Brauns, with Furtwängler's music and Heidegger's and Benn's and Hauptmann's language, how would we be today, at the victory celebration in Speer's Berlin? The whole world, the way it was for a moment at the Olympic Games. The end justifies the means. That's the lesson of Western history, and everywhere—isn't it?

These thirty-two years after the last great European war. Prussia *kaputt*, a great European province snuffed out, pulling everything along, a major center gone, Berlin, a whole country with no identity. And therefore ominous once again. Six million driven from their homelands on the gaming table of history, with a flick of the wrist, and they can never talk about it again without losing themselves. The great self-provoked mass migration after the greatest mass murder of the century, the mass murder of foes and friends. Thus we stand here, after thirty-two years, with huge stakes, an infinitely harsh payment. How suspect are those who ask why we do this here, the speaking, playing, showing, bleeding. The end of the heritage. To those who ask why a film about this? What else!

The Deutschland Radio Network pauses for station identification: "Be true and honest all the time."
Crowd, Berlin, 1933: Sieg Heil, Sieg Heil . . .
Blind war veteran: . . . in 1915, I was blinded by a Russian grenade. Through eighteen years of darkness, I bore the sorrow and misery of the German Fatherland, but our personal destiny did not get the better of us blind German war veterans . . .
Crowd: Sieg Heil!
. . . A constant will imbued us and induced us nonetheless to do our share for the Fatherland. If today the solid hope for a better future for Germany shines forth, then that bright light penetrates our lives too and gives us new strength, and this day will be a fulfillment of our sacrifice. Honesty, discipline, and loyalty shall reign once again in Germany. Let this spring day be a symbol for the new spring in Germany, so that it may be bright and beautiful again.

Fellow Germans! At this moment when, outside, the guns are greeting the day of victory with a thunderous salute, at this moment I call to you as one of millions who gave their utmost (interspersed with: Deutschland, Deutschland über alles . . .), unite, close your ranks, so that the longed-for day of freedom may come. Hold fast to your oath to do everything for Germany, our cherished Fatherland.

MURDERER FROM "M" (Peter Kern) in SA uniform: But I can't help it. I just can't, I just can't help it . . .

VOICE: Ha-ha. We've heard that before!

Berlin, 1939—Hitler speaking to SA units: . . . the gratitude . . . because what we have discussed . . . our deepest respect . . .

MURDERER FROM "M": What do *you* know, what are *you* talking for, who are *you*, who are *all* of you, the whole bunch of you criminals? You probably think you're hot stuff because you can crack safes or climb up walls or mark cards.

Interspersed with roll call of SA men.

Things, I imagine, you could forget about if you'd learned a proper trade or worked, or if you weren't such lazy pigs. But I, can I, can I help it, don't I have that curse in me, that fire, the voice, the torment!

VOICE: So you mean to say that you have to kill.

MURDERER FROM "M": Always, always, it drives me through the streets, and I always feel that someone's after me, and that's myself, and he . . .

Radio announcer: . . . and representatives of the supreme SA leader in these days . . . the first time . . .

. . . follows me relentlessly, but it was *me*, yes yes. Sometimes I feel as if I'm running after myself. I have to, have to get away. I have to run away, I'd like to escape, run away from myself. But it's impossible. I, I, I, I have, I have to obey, I, I, I, I have to run, run, run, run down endless streets. I have to get away, I, I want to get away, but the ghosts follow me.

Radio announcer: . . . what is Germany today and is called Germany today is not primarily . . . your work, the work of soldiers.

The ghosts of mothers, children, they're always there. These children, children, they're always, always, always, always, always there, and then I can, except, except, when I, when I do it.

Crowd: Heil, heil . . .
Announcer: . . . everyone standing still, the banners in front.

Then I see the posters, then I see the posters . . .

Announcer: Our Führer Adolf Hitler, Sieg Heil.

Then I read what I've done, and I read, and . . .

Crowd: Sieg Heil!

. . . and I read, and did I do that? But I . . .

Sieg heil!

. . . I, I, I, I can't remember anything. But who will believe me, who, who knows what compels me! I have to, I don't want to, I, I have to, I don't want, I have to, I can't help myself, I can't help myself. I have to, I have to do it, but nobody will believe me. I can't help it, I, I . . .

Song: *The banner high! Our ranks are serried tight.*
       SA now marches with a bold, firm tread.
       Comrades whom Reds and reactionaries shot—
       They march with us in spirit though they're dead.

•

[One of the sequences was not filmed, for many reasons—lack of funds, too little time. But it is important in the kaleidoscope of the wish- and horror-aspects of this historical circus, in which he should have his chance —totally, with all the consequences, open to the reality of history.

This is the sequence: Two former SS men in seedy black death's-head uniforms, with decorations and weapons and dogged lips (Hellmut Lange and Peter Kern. Lange will later appear as Hitler's valet, Kern as a present-day follower). The two of them walk arm in arm to drums beating for the 9th of November burial rites for those who died in Hitler's putsch in 1923. They stride over the mountains and meadows of Obersalzberg, as though toward eternity, in commemoration of their adored Führer, the leader of the Greater German Reich, while we hear the text of Heine's ballad about the two grenadiers who have gone to seed after fleeing from Russia. Loyal to the memory of Napoleon, they are waiting for the resurrection of their leader from the grave. The ballad ends with a "Marseillaise," as composed by Richard Wagner. A daring, terrifying vision. Two laughing lemurs of the netherworld—the eternal Nazi wandering across the world, like a primal image, in the drumming collapse of his continuous and expected resurrection.]

•

To the music of Siegfried's death from *Die Götterdämmerung*, Harry Baer, in front of the projected images of stars and a globe on the long table in Hitler's villa in Obersalzberg, walks slowly toward the camera, and begins his monologue.

HARRY BAER: Sometimes he even believed that his will power was switched off and that he was atoning for whole generations of his

| 61

forebears, nations, and stars, but he had to go on. And when he suddenly woke up in the night and believed he had seen it, the New Man, he screamed, foaming at the mouth, and we had to calm him down and wash him, but we were not allowed to talk about it. At times, he would act with unspeakable harshness, but first against himself. Against any softness of private feelings, and against his lust for pleasure and gentleness, which naturally existed in him as in any human being but were unimportant in his struggle, in the self-imposed task of a life which filled the century. And the way he wouldn't allow his mother to caress him, because it interfered with his love for himself and for that chosen, purer mother, the masses of the German people, whose love he sought.

And the way he condemned everything in the end, inside the bunker of his failure, when, resigned to his fate, he gave in to Eva's servant-love and married like any normal person. Cursing Poland, which was never to belong to him, and because of which the British had gone to war; and cursing France and England, and with their inevitable collapse on his embittered lips, predicting the end of European power, so closely linked with the destruction of Germany, divided between East and West, ruled by oil interests and by bureaucratic states, by graft-ridden politicians, whoever and wherever they are, and then still as an aged Hitler, ailing since Stalingrad, knowing perfectly well not only that the war was lost . . .

Radio announcer: This is the Greater German Radio Network . . .

Baer in front of the projected image of the huge room with the fireplace and the panoramic window in Hitler's house in Obersalzberg.

. . . but also that all the sacrifices of millions of enemies (as he saw the Jews and anti-war people) were for nothing, suffering the torments of hell, for years on this earth, a living corpse in the end. A corpse with a trembling arm and trembling breath, pulling himself together with his last strength, seeing a world that was unworthy of him . . .

The announcer delivers a special report from the High Command, June 25, 1940: We bring you this special bulletin from the High Command.

The High Command announces: The campaign in France has ended after just six weeks with an incomparable victory by the German forces. A cease-fire has been in effect since one thirty-five this morning.

In front, the projected image of the earth as seen from the moon.

A black man will stand up for him openly, a man elected a leader in Africa, absolutely crazy, respected by all, talking quite openly against the Jews in the UN, and received without protest by the Pope of the Catholics. Thirty years after his death, his end in gasoline and ruins, cremated by servants and chauffeurs. Madness is legacy, and it is only the beginning. All of us stand around help-less before him.

Before these people, created in God's image. He too? And his helpers.

Hitler like us. A part of us, in all of us?

•

The child from the start of the film is seen sitting in profile within Méliès's lunar landscape under stars. She raises her hands as if to pray, pressing them together and splaying her fingers, closing her eyes, and finally covering her ears with her hands. Close-up of the face. Stars above her. Fade-out.

BBC—de Gaulle, June 22, 1940: Quelle honte, quelle révolte ... La France comme un boxeur ... Paris ... notre réunion avec nos alliés rendre la liberté au monde qui brûle ... et la grandeur à la patrie ...

Special report of the High Command, June 24, 1940. Song: Give thanks to God with hearts and lips and hands ...

BBC—Churchill, October 21, 1940: Frenchmen, whatever you may be or whatever your fortunes are, I repeat the prayer around the Louis d'Or: Dieu protège la France! God protect France!

Hitler (to the Reichstag, July 19, 1940): Many now rest in graves beside their fathers who fell in the Great War. They are witnesses to a silent heroism, they are the symbol of hundreds of thousands of riflemen, tank crews, antitank gunners, engineers, artillerymen, marines, paratroopers, men of the Waffen SS, and all the other warriors who joined in the struggle of the German Wehrmacht for the freedom and future of our nation and for the everlasting greatness of the National Socialist Greater German Reich, Deutschland, Sieg Heil!!!

•

Limbo.

From the coffins, the people of the Nazi period awaken one after another. Puppets are manipulated by the various actors of the film. Music from the 9th of November funeral celebration, the "Horst Wessel Song," and a chorus from *Rienzi* are played slowly, accompanying the text.

The back projection for the Hitler puppet is a red grotto from Ludwig's Venus Grotto in Linderhof. The same image in blue forms the background for the Speer and Valentin puppets.

Roll call of the martyrs at a Nazi rite commemorating November 9, 1923, Hitler's putsch in Munich: . . . Walter Fischer . . .

GOEBBELS (Hellmut Lange): Everyone's a scoundrel, so am I. But since we are, then let's be the biggest of all, and I'll make sure that in a hundred years, every word that any of us speaks will reappear in films. It's up to you to decide what part you want to play.

I'll make you a legend, a myth, if you like, through your deaths.

Roll call of names continues . . .

Hah, you're laughing down there. But see if anyone can emulate me—conquer the world in twenty-three years and change it from top to bottom. Yes indeed, I'm the devil incarnate; and I'm a human being who laughed at Mickey Mouse, just like you.

GÖRING (Peter Kern): Culture, when I hear the word "culture" I reach for my pistol. That is the art we want for the people. We are creating a cultural revolution for a more intelligible art, the art of the people. Art is a sublime mission that requires fanaticism. No nation lives longer than the documents of its culture. We pay for art with our life. Nothing will be concealed anymore. There has to be peace and quiet once and for all.

GOEBBELS: Yes indeed, we are the predators of mankind. But why do you not accord us the privilege of being the fox and the hyena among nations, the lone, raging wolf in the society of wolves? With distinct biological characteristics, recognizable, pursuable, fighting for its hungry brood, to kill the life goals of our species, albeit with no right to live, but not tortured, not denied or sold by the profiteers of so-called morality. Save us, but don't make a profit off us if you want to be better than our characterization of you . . .

HIMMLER (Heinz Schubert): We are not ghosts, people should be scared when they see me. Yes indeed, just be scared. And they were scared when they saw me. I taught them a thing or two, for I am a schoolmaster, who taught them how to eat of the Tree of Knowledge and, once again, to gain the new innocence that will be the end of the world.

And it was the end of the world. Five hundred years from now, when they have to pass judgment on my works, who will ask whether Fräulein Schulze or Fräulein Müller was unhappy?

When people admire the pyramids of the pharaohs, who asks about the death rattles of the slaves under the rocks? We live from old yet living traditions.

EVA BRAUN (Johannes Buzalski) sings: I'm frustrated, so frustrated. You are my baby . . .

SPEER (Peter Moland): It was one of those big meetings, my friends took me along. He spoke. The way he always spoke. There was a tumult, beer bottles, chair legs, eggs; my coat was wet and splotched. All at once he stood before me, me, this unknown man,

and he took off his jacket and gave it to me. I stood before him
in his jacket. His jacket, like a protective cloak, burning around
me. He had chosen me. Elected me from among thousands. It was
his choice, and it was correct, just as he chose all of them correctly. For I helped him wage his war, later, as only I could

organize it, his Minister of War and an artist like him. So I had
to meet him and see it through. And I do not know what chose
him within me. Did I choose him or he me? I do not know. It had
to come somehow or other. It could have been easy, or was it
the way I just described?

FITZLIPUTZLI (Martin Sperr): Yes, that's what we'll make of him: Adolf, the degenerate puppet from the Punch and Judy show.

Soft drinks instead of beer, vegetarian diet instead of pig's feet, Sieg Heil instead of gobbledygook, and Sieg Heil, that's progress from Germany, the puppet-clown as Führer.

Nazi funeral rites for martyrs of November 9, 1923.

Yes, indeed, the Führer as a puppet-clown; that's it, the vengeance of hell, that they now have to live as puppet-clowns.

Adolf has to yodel, and keep on yodeling, and Eva has to dance, forever. At the Octoberfest. And the children will laugh, immortal figures, a big number this, the first stage of punishment is limbo.

EVA BRAUN sings: You are my baby . . .

Chorus from *Rienzi.*

FITZLIPUTZLI: The puppet-clown as the Hitler within us. When the idea and the ideals of the masses are questioned, we're always

good, I'll take care of that. Mediocrity for leading the world, against individuality, relentless, ice cold. The Hitler of the simple man in the street, that's me.

But he—the boss—must never get in. God won't tolerate him in hell. He would make it burst at the seams, maybe because he's too big. Wandering, now he's looking for a new place, between heaven and hell, that is, on earth again. In what guise? He's been made immortal by us, in us.

GOEBBELS: I am a worker's son, yes indeed, something else, I am a worker's son, a devout Catholic, yes indeed. I was raised a devout Catholic, and an academic at our universities, and do I ever look Germanic, hah, but I will plant time bombs of worship and knowledge and National Socialist reawakening. They will explode in a hundred years or earlier or later, but, in any case, so long as there are human beings, they will appear in eternally new shapes.

That is my secret mission, the propaganda of a steel-clad Romanticism. When we leave, then let the earth tremble. They will never be worthy of us. Despite all democracies and the dictatorship of the masses everywhere.

Roll call of November 9 martyrs continues.

CLOWN HITLER (Rainer von Artenfels): People keep saying it's not true, I am not true.

Some of them talk about a non-person, the others . . .

Rienzi chorus.

. . . about the endless nullity of my actions. The Bolsheviks keep saying that I am a man of the plutocrats, and the plutocracy keeps lumping the Red and the Brown plagues together. None of them understand.

Just what did we have to do with Marx anyway or with Krupp and his dying class. Some people say that none of it is true. So the others speak about me as if I were a god and not a man. As if none of it had ever happened, the climb out of nothing, the community of the people, the worker of the forehead and the worker of the fist, which is what they all want after all. The fantastic explosion of the Great War, the victories over France and over all Europe, the millions of dead, the concentration camps and the bombs that I summoned, the cremation methods, euthanasia and all the catastrophes. So friends and enemies just erase me. But if it were all made up, then what an imagination at least, and that's why I love Karl May, the Righteous.

It's all about the emergence of the new mass man and taking him seriously, his outstanding leader figures, the survival of man, whether they like it or not. It's all about the Hitler of the common man, and what does the man look like, the one they elected from their own midst?

The gamut from the Volkswagen to the concentration camp, from Wolfsburg to Auschwitz, from Bayreuth to UFA and Obersalzberg.

Rienzi chorus. We see the child listening to the different puppets. She takes one, the Ludwig puppet, from its coffin as she continues into hell.

•

Radio announcer, May 5, 1933: This is the Deutschland Radio Network. This is all German radio stations. We are now at the Opernplatz, Unter den Linden, Berlin. At this moment, the German Student Association, which has built a gigantic funeral pyre for the occasion of the action of the Committee for the Struggle Against the Un-German Spirit, is burning immoral and corrupt books and writings.

You are listening to the statements of the students of Berlin. Next, Reich Minister Dr. Goebbels will take . . .

ANDRE HELLER (voice off): And as always at the beginning of our displeasure, at the entrance to the hell around us, these blood-red judges, who pronounce their verdicts according to the whore of the venal letter of the law and not the morality of our consciences.

Doré's engravings of Dante's *Inferno* form a back projection behind the red-robed judges of the National Socialist People's Court of all times.

It was these gentlemen who legalized the negative qualities of human beings into good deeds performed for *Volk* and nation, who fomented hate on a pornographic scale. Power against the spirit, as always, and in the future, much worse.
And how a Hitler could praise them.

Student (at the book burning): Against decadence and moral decay! For discipline and ethics in family and state! I deliver unto the flames the writings of Heinrich Mann, Ernst Gläser, Erich Kästner.

ANDRE HELLER (voice off): Assuming he were being judged, at the Last Judgment, how would these gentlemen reply to Hitler's praise: What would we have done without German jurists such as H. Specht, who said: Since 1923, I moved legally and loyally on the long road, through the courts of appeals, to power. Legally safeguarded, democratically elected. But then the future had to be realized.

A naked crone as Justice with scales: human heads (puppets) on one
scale and large papier-mâché penises on the other.

It was the incorruptible German jurist, the honest, industrious,
conscientious academic and citizen. He righteously legalized me
with interpretations for my ideas. He created a law for me by my
will and I stuck to it. His laws gave me the right to my deeds.

So we hear only their praises, the German jurists, when we
question Adolf Hitler today as we enter the hell around us. And
they belong here, boiling in the deep shit of their deeds, until the
end of the world, as in Dante: the compulsive implementers of the
law.

Again, the Hollywood figures set up as giant photos in front of Doré's
Dante engravings. In the middle, a black puppet with a child's skeleton
on its arm and a red glass tear on its black face.

And just have a good look at them, the big preventers of culture, for instance in Hollywood, which must follow now, in our

hell around us, with a corner for the Stroheim slaughter. And it was these gentlemen who made him, the great Stroheim, weep before the skeleton of his dead child, his mangled films, the red tear of helpless art in the face of the black swan. It was all these gentlemen . . .

Roll call of November 9 martyrs.

. . . L. B. Mayer and Thalberg, Pat Powers and Lasky and Gloria Swanson, and even his great colleague Sternberg, so they say. All of them worked by the Babbitt-law of Will Hays. Spreading world Babbittry according to the rules of Hollywood. And it was here that the . . .

Once again the naked crone, this time as a lecherous Statue of Liberty in front of the logos of the major Hollywood studios: MGM, United Artists, Columbia, etc.

. . . great Stroheim was struck down, Stroheim who accepted it because he thought that by doing so he could save his film. And it was here that his films were mutilated, from eighteen reels to eight, and from eleven hours to two. And it was here that they let the secretaries decide on the final cut of his film, an insult to the freedom and humanity of all the secretaries in the world. And it was here that the great Greta Garbo . . .

The girl with the small Ludwig in her arms moves in front of the projection of a huge Greta Garbo head, walks past Stroheim and his laughing Iron Man—a figure from Stroheim's *Wedding March*—the black knight who holds a blond girl captive.

. . . helped him and let him escape to France as Stroheim the actor, who was never allowed to direct another film, he one of the greatest directors. One of the first to see and show what had to come, our destruction and the sneering laughter about it by the evil one. Hollywood, the lecherous queen with the loveliest consumer goods in her arms.

Projected in front of a Doré engraving, the Russian opponents of Eisenstein with their eyes poked out, their hands chopped off, in their hellish torments.

And then in the group of preventers, those torturers of Eisenstein, like Boris Shumiatski, who blocked the filming of *Bezhin*

Meadow and destroyed it, what there was of it; who banned *Ivan II* and destroyed *Ivan III*.

And Nikolai Cherkassov, although working with Eisenstein as his leading actor, who played Ivan, testified against him, as a functionary, denouncing Eisenstein.

And then those who drove Eisenstein into self-criticism. That hypocritical suicide of the soul.

Dovzhenko, for instance. His former friend Sergei Vasiliev, an ex-student of Eisenstein's. And Yutkevitch, his colleague.

A huge Hitler eagle—by Schmidt-Ehmden—pylons with smoke bowls from which red smoke is streaming. This is followed by the projection of the drawing for the Hall of the Dead, meant for the German soldiers who died in action, in Speer's victorious Berlin. In the courtyard of the Reich Chancellery, the logo of UFA and a blackboard containing words from the Hitler period. Words from a Dictionary of the Inhuman. Title: Paradise of Hell. The words: exterminate, blood tribute, interest serfdom, Black Corps, take care of, inferior, final solution, special treatment, scum, root out, inject, slaughter, ruthless, degenerate, shoot down, put against the wall, make short shrift, bodyguard, snuff out, wipe out, national community, triumph, special force, task force, drastic measures, make him one head shorter, cleanse, pacify, bleeding heart, liquidate, popular storm, corrupt, blood banner, blood order, work up.

And empty the corner of human faces, self-destroyed, where they ought to stand, the Goebbelses, the teachers of language even today. No room for human faces, no matter how disfigured. Too cramped, for them, the system of the movie- and culture-hell, the masters of the present-day world. Who found words like "exterminate," "blood tribute," "take care of," "inferior," "final solution," "special treatment," "scum," "root out," "inject," "slaughter," "ruthless," "degenerate," "shoot down," "put against the wall," "make short shrift," "snuff out," "wipe out," "special force," "task force," "drastic measures," "one head shorter," "cleanse," "bleeding heart," "liquidate," "national community," "corrupt," "blood banner."

Roll call of November 9 martyrs; and book-burning ceremony of January 1933.

Student (at the book burning): Against the soul-corrupting overestimation of sexuality! For the nobility of the human soul! I deliver unto the fire the writings of the school of Sigmund Freud.

Second student: Against the falsification of our history and the denigration of its heroes! For respect of our past! I deliver unto the fire the writings . . .

A blackboard with the names of people who condemned Wolf Biermann and the words with which they did so. In front of it, puppets in athletic uniform, winning medals in international competition for the German Democratic Republic.

1. **The Cultural Hell Around Us**
2. **Cadre-ese of the East**
   Socialist Realism
3. Monopoly capitalists
   Arrogance
   Denigration
   Aestheticism
4. The mission of formalism is to undermine and destroy the national consciousness of nations (*Neues Deutschland*).
   For a progressive German national culture. The Soviet Union—the guarantor of progress, the Victorious, Glorious Soviet Union.
   The national cultural heritage of the Socialist workers. Sectarian pseudo-revolution of the proletarian cult.
5. **The Culture Creators**

P. Hacks	H. Kant
E. Busch	Prof. W. Heinz—Chairman of the Theatrical Creators
E. Schall	B. Wogazki
A. Seghers	W. Sitte—Chairman of the Fine Artists
L. Renn	M. Danegger

ANDRE HELLER (voice off): And then those dismal heirs with their dark functionary faces in Germany's East, and their nasty language, charged ideologically, like the previous language. Spreading icy coldness about them, walled in by their own fear of their deeds. Behind them, people with a language that they borrowed from the Nazi curse on Thomas Mann, in Germany's newspapers a few decades earlier.

Voices at book burning: . . . Jewish . . . participation in the work of national construction . . .
Student: . . . I deliver unto the fire the writings of Theodor Wolff and Georg Bernhard.
Student: Against the literary betrayal of the soldiers of the World War! For the education of the people! . . .

And now the cultural hell around us, nearby, right here, what remained, the heirs to a dark time. The timid colonial slaves of alien ideologies. With closed eyes and closed ears and that language from the Ice Age of the soul, the model pupil of the world.

A blackboard in the hell around us. In front of this plaque with names and words, the model of a destroyed critic's head with closed eyes and closed ears; black smoke from the mouth.

1. **CULTURAL HELL AROUND US**
2. **Cadre-ese West, German Federal Republic**
3. **BROTHEL**

blood and balls	wipe out
good box office—relevant	drill culture
box office poison	good entertainment
	box-office quality
economic dud	box-office democracy
racially alien	

4. **BUFF**

   Ideological charge

target group	socially critical
pop underground	exploitation
cultural shit, garbage	backgrounds
beautiful	demonstrate
creepy	make visual
crazy	denounce
subculture	critical of ideology
society	consciousness
	speculative

5. **Functionaries of the Public**

WOR		W. Kliess, film critic
WR		U. Nettelbeck, film critic
AB	SZ	
G.K.		Hort Axtmann, film critic
HGP		Film books from Hanser Verlag
S. Sch.	Spiegel	
W.L.		
B.J.	FAZ	
W. Schütte	FR	
Franz Sch.		
Wilfr. Sch.		
K. Eder	medium	
W. Günther		

Student (at book burning): Against the arrogant debasement of the German language! For the cultivation of the most precious treasure of our nation! I deliver unto the fire the writings of Alfred Kerr.

The Young Ones (from U. Nettelbeck to Hanser Verlag) with heads made up of film reels and "boards in front of their heads" [in allusion to a German idiom meaning "slow on the uptake"]. The Old Ones (Wendt-

land, Waldleitner, Axtmann, Brummer, Hechler, Hartwig, Purtzer) are covered with blood; their flies are open and huge cocks stick out, red and smoking.

ANDRE HELLER (voice off): And a few Young Ones dismally allied with the Old Ones, who say: the main thing is that the box

office is in order, and after us the deluge, and the best movie is the one that does best. The nasty ethos of the wheeler-dealer. Young Ones closely allied with those who claim the German cinema can do without culture. Realizing in their own way the bitter legacy of the Nazi, the legacy of his statement: "Whenever I hear the word 'culture,' I reach for my pistol." Hitler's heirs in Germany's West, film department. Young and old. Blood and balls of the German entertainment movie. The human countenance in Germany after Hitler. Inhuman with a genuine plastic face. Something for the Human Rights Commission at the Last Judgment, for the torture of the human soul. Blood-covered and with the greasy hand on the branch they're sitting on. All pants down.

Roll call of the November 9 martyrs.

The plastic face of a sex puppet with mouth open for fellatio.

Student (at book burning): Against insolence and arrogance! For awe and respect for the immortal spirit of the German people! Let the flames devour the writings of Tucholsky and Ossietzky.

In front of the projection of Doré's *Fall of the Angel*, various puppet figures, including Jew Süss, a man sporting a gold Party badge, the allegory of the New Cinema in Munich, and the black puppet with the red Stroheim tear and a child's skeleton in her arms.

Goebbels: Fellow students, German men and women, the age of sophistical Jewish intellectualism is now ended.

Where does it start, money, business deals, party invitations, ideology, careers, opportunism, thoughtlessness, denunciation? Where does it start? The burning of books, the cutting up of films, the murdering of a Wilhelm Reich by sticking him in a madhouse. And who is free of this plague of crimes against art? When McCarthy bribed and blackmailed, how many Jews in Hollywood were ready and willing to play along? And in Hollywood, jobs, not lives, were on the line—without Hitler, from whom they had fled to save their lives. The same Hollywood that made so many anti-Nazi movies.

On the table lies the charred corpse of Goebbels; around it, life-size puppets, with the initials of Erwin Leiser, Werner Maser, Joachim Fest, Transit Film, Albert Speer, Liliana Cavani, et al.

Or is money the only reason they continue to slaughter Hitler in books, films, and newspapers? Eternally damned in hell to keep dragging the rocks of their money bags up, over and over again, until they fall back down. The more capital they produce, the greater the labor of hell. That is the Sisyphian labor of today's Hitler researchers and their satellites in the entertainment industry with their blood-smeared aprons. They drag rocks of money.

And at the end of our days and our road, what shall we say? Make oneself intelligible to a Ludwig, explain our ordeal and what came out of it, he who went through the fire of the Wagnerian struggles for art and power, and now this. And what about art? Is it the guilt from which happiness grows, the victory of hell in art? The growing beauty from evil? Is this the slough from which art derives, Felix culpa, happy guilt? The cathedral for our music?

This is hell, wrote Oskar Loerke in his journal on April 4, 1933. And here we are already. Pfitzner and Knappertsbusch, good old Kna, who was so angry at Thomas Mann's friendship with Bruno Walter, his competitor and a Jew, that he played along in a dirty way, back then, we are told, when he organized a petition . . .

Roll call of the dead and drums.

. . . against Thomas Mann, with names like Gulbransson, for example, of whom Thomas Mann said: Of all the signatures, Olaf's hurt me the most. With the signatures of Richard Strauss and the editor in chief of the *Münchner Nachrichten* and his colleagues, the German journalists and critics, with the statement "He's had it coming to him for a long time now."

These people signed that declaration which accused Thomas Mann of the following: denigrating Richard Wagner, aesthetic snobbery, a cosmopolitan, democratic attitude, unreliability in his works, no right to speak in the name of the German spirit. Ultimately, this led to the dispossession of his house and of his entire library, loss of his honorary doctorate at the University of Bonn, and escape to Switzerland and around the world.

The camera cuts back and forth between a shrouded life-size puppet, which gradually stands naked in the studio, in front of changing projections, with the sign *Felix culpa* on its abdomen; and the child, who talks to the small Ludwig puppet (now sitting on a podium) and caresses it.

Music: Prelude to *Parsifal*.

And what were Thomas Mann's words in Küssnacht on Lake Zurich on New Year's, 1937: "God help our darkened and misused country and teach it to make peace with the world and itself." Thomas Mann survived and could go on writing. Think of *Doctor Faustus*. But others did not. Even without such attacks, they killed themselves—Walter Benjamin, Kurt Tucholsky, Stefan Zweig, Frau Liebermann at age eighty committing suicide before she was to be shipped to a concentration camp, the actor Gottschalk and his wife, and Egon Friedell.

| 83

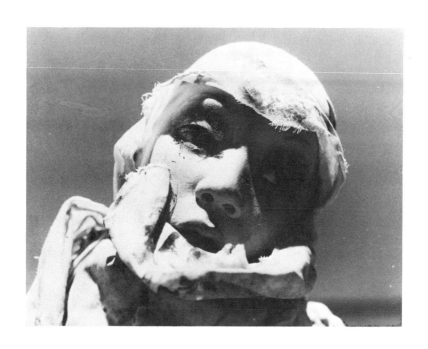

And, and. No end. Never. How to explain, narrate, understand. Do nothing? Keep silent?

Fade-out, followed by closing credits. Title of Part One: *Hitler, a Film from Germany*, over the girl's head. Accompanied by passage from the slow movement of Mozart's Piano Concerto in D Minor, as at the start of the film. Begins in static noises and at the end static noises again, gradual fading of image and sound.

Part Two

A German Dream

. . . Until the End of the World

The number 2 above the head of the girl, whose eyes are closed; strips of film hang from her head. On the sound track, radio static, as at the start of the film. Then, coming as from far away, Goebbels' Bible quotation.

Goebbels (January 30, 1943, on the tenth anniversary of Hitler's takeover): Faith can move mountains. This mountain-moving faith must fill us all . . .

This too turns slowly into static, which passes into the next sound.

The camera slowly moves back to show the newborn infant in Runge's *Morning*. Title of Part Two: *A German Dream*. The camera moves back into a long shot of the huge studio, as at the start of the film, accompanied by the Prelude to *Parsifal*, continuing from where it left off in Part One.

Einstein (October 24, 1940): This war can truly end only when we have succeeded in breaking the German domination of Europe. It is less certain whether the peace that is finally achieved will bring an organization of Europe or of all the countries of the earth, insuring us against future wars. Only if that is achieved will the immeasurable suffering of this generation not have been in vain.

Hence, everyone should be aware of the truth that liberation without an organized assurance of freedom for the future is merely

a reprieve. The attainment of the goal is dependent on each indi-
vidual. Everything must be done to make sure that no one grows
accustomed to the condition of slavery.

The individual must arrange all his actions and efforts in such a
way that the oppressors and their organization receive no support
from him.

Everyone should willingly accept privations if that will weaken
the economy and fighting strength of the enemy. The European
cannot be robbed of his independence so long as he steadfastly
clings to it.

•

A huge eye filling the screen (Ledoux's "Eye Reflecting the Interior of
the Theater of Besançon," 1804) ; inside the pupil, the black Hitler eagle
from the hell scene in Part One. In front of the eye, Harry Baer delivers
the following monologue. He holds the sphere with the Black Maria and
the falling snow inside it before his face. Music from *Parsifal*.

HARRY BAER (voice off): And in us, the horror pictures of the
paradise of hell, the loneliest corner in the deepest cold of our
misunderstanding.

And in the hand, the Grail crystal of yearning with the black
house of the bloodiest memories of our eternal nostalgia. The old,
glowing chalice of madness raised up toward guilt-ridden lips. In
it, a new wonder: the world grasped from both inside and outside
at once, split into new unity and into holy disquiet, in accord with
the laws of the cinema.

In front of the projection of William Blake's divine compass (a compass
splayed over the surface of the earth, held from above by God's hand),
Baer and a shop-window mannequin from the twenties. The camera slowly
moves in on the mannequin's head.

Before the judge of our inner eye, which, blinded by the mist
of everyday life, reflects only what the film of our memories and
hopes projects—images of a lost world or a future life.

Close-up of the interior of the glass sphere with the Black Maria in a
snowfall. The screen darkens, grows bright again, in an alternation of
light and shadow, in the falling snow and over the black house.

And imagine a very calm situation, as before dropping off to
sleep. In the cellars of our towns and the bunkers of our souls.
Light and shadow falling in, projections from outside, from the

| 93

other world, from above. We see ourselves on a mountain by the sea, in a forest, in the forest of the past or of the future.

The music from *Parsifal* continues.

Within the huge eye, in the hole of the pupil: the projection of a man (Karl May before his death) on a red carpet [a scene from the end of Syberberg's film *Karl May*]. He kneels before the figure of Death with its imperial crown and parts the black curtain to reveal everlasting paradise, an Arcadian landscape. We hear Gustav Mahler's Second Symphony, the resurrection passage with the Klopstock text, and we see Mahler himself at the piano, playing the part about Celestial Life from his Fourth Symphony.

Worlds come into being as projections. In you. Let us assume that, arriving lost and confused in the depths of the forest, we were crawling deep into ourselves and taking the road inward, to the center of our life, seeking salvation; far away from the collective guilt of the world, in the vast domain of our soul, through the history of our recent past.

Seeking advice from another God-seeker, who said: The collectivity is also guilty of the individual's deed; the collectivity has to forgive him, if only for its own sake!

A man who also said at the end of his life: Woe if the wrong man comes.

The child holds the small Ludwig puppet. We see the projected image of a huge death mask of Wagner. Music from *Parsifal*.

Baer stands again in front of the huge eye, inside which a scene from the film *Ludwig* is shown, in which Ludwig, shrouded in his cloak, kneels like Ossian before the Germanic gods frozen in snow. Music from *Parsifal* leads into the "Liebestod" from *Tristan and Isolde*.

Assuming we tried once again to mythologize the soul with figures from the old stories, reincarnations of the gods.

For he who does not respect heaven scorns man in merciless self-love; immortal soul, sing a song once again.

Music above all.

Music overcomes everything!

Film, the new child of this century, through its questions, boring very deep into the center. How shall one, how shall I, who am I, we, who plays for us, for whom do we play, why, what remains? Everything comes together once again, from the old Grail miracles up to the age of film—our chance. Is it up to us what we do with it; is it once again in our hands?

After the abolition of God and the Kaiser in the era of the

masses, the gods all gathered together once more and gave those human beings down there one last chance.

At first, they spoke of revenge. One wanted to take back the good that men had been entrusted with, asking: What did you do with it? Sitting in judgment, as the old folks say.

But then they made a bet as in the old fairy tales of mankind, and their legends and their books, their theater and their music. Very well then, they said, if you like, they are free to decide once again, they may determine their fate once again, they may choose the man of their choice themselves, one of their own, who will lead them to happiness. A man in the street, as they say, from their midst—a gray mouse. What if they *had* said those things before deciding to move on to another star among the billions, light-years away, where they were still needed, leaving the people of this earth on their own, leaving them to their progress, as they see it: their happiness, their degenerate paradise.

Baer strews snow from a jar over a table model of a small nineteenth-century German town (known from the film *Karl May* as Karl May's birthplace in the Erz Mountains), assisted by a little girl, also from *Karl May*. We hear choruses from Mahler's Second Symphony. We see a model of a set from *Karl May*, an allusion to the scene in which old Karl May recalls his youth. (In his childhood he was blind, and his grandmother told him about the world in the manner of a fairy tale. The scene ended with old Karl May warning of the end of all such German fairy tales with the words: Woe if the wrong man comes.)

And they wanted a man who wants the impossible, the misunderstood man and the misunderstood thing, torn by love and hate, the laurel wreath now for the dying hero. No politician, but an artist and a god, whom all could follow by simply believing. A man from their midst. That was what they wanted and that was what they created.

•

It is snowing. A carnival booth with all sorts of historical props. Puppets as spectators. Overhead, projected stars and on the wall historical images in the style of a historical horror comic, showing Goebbels dead and Irma Grese, the incarnation of the horror of Auschwitz; there are the allegories of Faith and of the Synagogue in Strasbourg, and the huge ears from the show booth in front of which Karl Valentin and Bertolt Brecht appeared at the Octoberfest. An advertising poster for Volkswagen, reading: "This is the beginning."

Across the way, we see a poster of a warped man, bearing the legend:

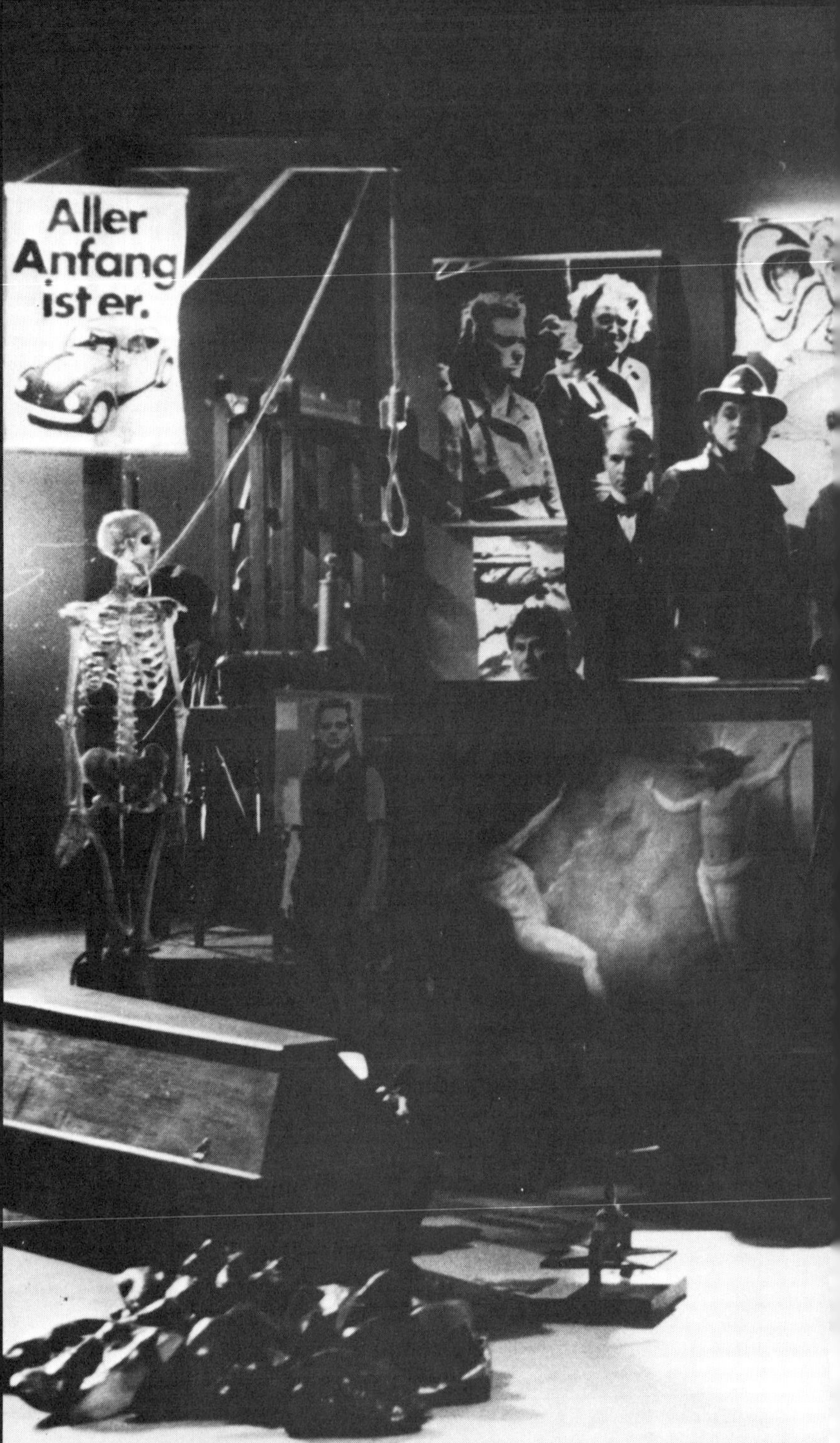
Aller
Anfang
ist er.

"The Subhuman." On the floor are pictures of Hitler and a pile of shoes, to suggest the mountains of shoes collected in the concentration camps.

MAGICIAN (Rainer von Artenfels): Ladies and gentlemen! Ladies and gentlemen, this is the masseur of Heinrich Himmler, the Reichsführer of the SS.

FELIX KERSTEN (Martin Sperr): Yes, I am the man with the magic hands, Himmler's masseur, through whom one could buy humanity for money. The man whom the heroes needed when their stomachs could no longer stand the blood of the tortured.

A wonder-healer, priest and physician, who saved all Holland from deportation to Poland and from being flooded in 1945 in a Nazi "scorched earth" action, and who saw to it that the concentration camps were disbanded, not liquidated.

For how much money? After all, humanity needs money in such times, especially in such times.

MAGICIAN: The man who, as an alchemist and as a new Copernicus of the twentieth century, created the systems for the German SS rites, for the cosmos of the giants and the Nordic law of fate, those blood utopias of the masses.

Goebbels reads aloud Hitler's speech of June 22, 1941, concerning the invasion of the Soviet Union: . . . German nation . . . After months of uncertainty . . . now the hour has come . . . when the German Reich on September 3 . . . I repeated . . . consolidation . . . of the continent . . .

COSMOLOGIST (Peter Lühr): A scientist and artist who did not even know what he created and whom he helped. His mother an organ player in Zellertal, who, in his youth, traveled around with a hunchbacked magician and played the zither. He made pressure valves for the newly invented steam engine and with the money, lots of it, millions, was free to develop a theory of the creation of the world, of the moon and ice and fire and the beginning and end of the world. Derided by scientists as a heretic, teaching at the Vienna Academy.

MAGICIAN: It was there that Hitler failed as an artist and so turned to politics. A prophet imposed by Himmler on all the universities. A man for Adolf Hitler.

COSMOLOGIST: The man who saw a new Atlantis.

MAGICIAN: The yearning and insane nostalgia of the German beekeeper and of all freethinkers and nudists.

COSMOLOGIST: And those who knew how hard it is to conceive of the beginning and end of the cosmos.

Announcer: Bulletin from the High Command, June 22, 1941, about the German attack on the Soviet Union. The High Command of the Wehrmacht announces the following from the Führer's headquarters: To ward off the menacing danger from the East, the German Wehrmacht, on June 21, at 3 a.m., pushed into the tremendous concentration of enemy forces . . . the German Luftwaffe . . . alone during the aerial combats . . .

MAGICIAN: And that is the man for the unpredictable.

ASTROLOGER (Peter Moland): That despised remnant that insurance companies throughout the world call a higher power, the man of the stars of this Third Reich. Our astrologer, who was first arrested, thrown into a concentration camp, then employed by Himmler, prophesied at a very early point the end of the world and the epoch. The man who was concerned about which star guided Hitler and whether he guided the stars for us. The artist in the service of State Security, who took his craft seriously and explained why Hitler had to come, which no one was willing to believe, since, according to principle, the soothsayer is responsible for the disaster he conjures up.

Announcer: Bulletin from the High Command, June 22, 1941, on the German attack on the Soviet Union. On this day, the German losses amount to thirty-five airplanes.

And this is Hitler's valet.

VALET (Hellmut Lange): The man who never saw Hitler in a nightshirt. The little SS man in the street, the bottom rung of the hierarchy, the voter who voted him in, the soldier who was detailed to him and stood by him, in everyday life. The embodiment of the banality of evil, also of the humanity of the banal. Telling us about the private lives of the sharks, the biggest in our cosmos of heroic life without heroes.

That man who cremated Hitler, who took Hitler's corpse and his wife Eva's and poured gasoline over them, in the ditch behind the bombed Reich Chancellery. Built a fire with the man who had

never missed a performance of *Götterdämmerung* at Bayreuth since taking power, nor any heroic death in music.

Wagner, do you hear me!

(Sings): Holldrio, holldrio, dearest echo, dearest echo, art thou there, art thou where, oh, my darling, I love you so. Holldrio . . . (repetition).

For Wagnerian music was written in blood, and blood, as we all know, is a very special potion; it attracts the devil unless it is drawn from the heart. I was involved from beginning to end. The only chance for the greatest mass murderer in world history.

Accompanied by details from the carnival booth. Wide pan from the naked heroes of Karl May's era to the photo of Joseph Goebbels dead. Leonardo da Vinci's depiction of a man whose outstretched legs and hands form a circle. The statues of Church and Synagogue in the Cathedral of Strasbourg. Brecht and Valentin's man with the big ears. And the camera pans to Auschwitz, and Irma Grese. Items from the grab-bag of history.

Radio broadcast about soldiers leaving for the front, 1941—Aïda, Berlin Opera. Announcer: The finale in the German Opera House has long since faded out. Only the breath of beauty lingers in the hall and in our hearts, pure and clear, radiant and tender, bold in its beauty, for harshness awaits us. For our furloughed soldier, tomorrow will transform the picture of the festive crowd into a throng of soldiers on a railroad platform, awaiting the train that will carry them back to duty.

102 |

Song (in the train to the front):
Don't always grieve and don't always weep,
Don't constantly visit the grave where I sleep . . .
But on my birthday, it would be fine,
If you'd sprinkle the flowers there with this year's wine.
Announcer: Ahead of us, Leningrad.

VALET: Some humanity in everyday life, some natural, animal warmth to be transmitted from the blood of this man without a human face. Adolf Hitler, he too a mother's son; she who died mourned deeply by this son, to whom private life never mattered; now human only as a living creature, a living creature like a hyena, but also a creature of God, human. Only he never wanted that.

The valet and the other figures leave. Rainer von Artenfels as the magician remains behind.

Announcer: A report from outside Leningrad: Hello, hello, this is the Skala. We are far away, almost sixteen hundred kilometers, from the renowned Berlin Skala. Our sumptuous military cabaret is located in a large, bare room that used to be the cinema hall of a Bolshevik Party headquarters, here in a small town outside Leningrad, twenty kilometers behind our front lines. Men of our Waffen SS division—musicians, singers, comedians, variety per-

*formers in civilian life—have pooled their talents, and now they're
going to give a gala performance of the best cabaret art for their
comrades here, who have come from the trenches at the front.*
Soldiers are performing for soldiers.
Cabaret performer (at the front):
Mother said to Hansel sweet . . .
A brother or sister would be neat . . .

Close-up of the photos of the statues of Church and Synagogue in the
Cathedral of Strasbourg.
In front of them, the circus magician (Rainer von Artenfels).

MAGICIAN: And whatever else belongs to the cannibals and
muscle men and prophets and conjurers of the market. Here are the
girls. One in the role of Faith and the other in the role of the
Agnostic. The past which always looks so sad isn't all that old.
Often it's just waiting for its comeback as the pet of the arts, in
fairy tales, myths, in religions and great popular legends.

From the Cathedral of Smolensk: Russian Orthodox Mass.

Blind and from the corner of life's poor ghetto.

The Mass celebrated at the Cathedral of Smolensk.

One by one, the props of the carnival booth are presented. Special
props, such as the history of trivia offers to this theme in our literature
on contemporary history. What we see is the optical reification of many
theories and much rubbish in books that have become best sellers. Some
have the sublime charm of an ironical insight into the psychology of the
causes of Hitler's success, a success that was not confined to Germany.

Always the symbols of the old and the new systems, or ideologies
and utopias for and against which people are suffering, murdering,
and sacrificing.
And then a few animals. Some zoology from East and West, ourselves and others, today and in the past.
For instance, the cats, surviving the tests of courage in the
Napola. The academy for Hitler's new generation, the national-
political educational institutions, in which the boys had to poke
out the eyes of cats, for the Führer didn't like cats, and cats eat
birds, and the Führer loved birds. And then, of course, the
monkey can't be left out, destined to be mated with all Slavic
and other subhuman females, to obliterate their species. After the

war. And here is this rat, the animal characterizing one's adversary, the rat used by the Nazis to represent the Jews, and by the Bolsheviks to portray capitalism. The same rat they used to prove that if you burn its semen to ashes, you can produce an antibody to exterminate its species. A cinch if you observe the rituals.

Thus they flew at the end of the war, at night, on a secret mission, our aircraft over Germany's remaining Reich, especially over Babelsberg—once UFA, today DEFA—driving out all the Jews forever, strewing ashes over the Reich, if possible over all Europe in East and West, which didn't fully succeed, or at least turned out differently in East and West.

More from front-line cabaret outside of Leningrad.

And here, the eagle. Everlasting in the struggle against rats and cats and monkeys and dogs.

And then here, one more animal, typically American. A must in any freak show, goodness, the things you can tell about man and his time from these creatures. The naked chicken, a genuine American-bred article, doesn't have to be plucked, and it lays eggs without shells; it's got skin without bones, guaranteed non-plastic, the rubber eagle for every home, easy upkeep, and tasteless, needless to say.

The cabaret continues: Soldiers perform for soldiers.
The Mass celebrated at the Cathedral of Smolensk.

And the insects. Like the birds, they'll survive man's destruction of the animal world. A few more curiosities. Gouged-out eyes of SS men, little blue things, gathered on plates in East Prussia by heroes of the Red Army after they marched in. Also, on the model of the original sperm bank in Hollywood, available to every female fan with the need and the money. Here it is: Adolf's sperm; from a stand-in, of course.

Song: From Finland to the Black Sea,
Forward . . .

The real capsule lies well preserved in an Alpine glacier, where someday, when the time is ripe, the capsule, closely guarded every summer by trained men, will be resurrected from the lead canisters as a rebirth when the moment is ripe, in an action prepared for since 1945.

The label is easy to read: bandleader Wolf, with heart and

genuine Austrian charm, testified to by a woman who ought to know, as the man who saw *Tristan and Isolde* one hundred twenty times, which has to leave something behind in a man.

That's all about the man who managed to break Hollywood's dominance of 65 percent of the world market.

The Holy Grail, the Black Stone. The treasure of all European legends and kings, found by Himmler at Montségur, France, during the war and planned as the central point of the new Reich in Bayreuth. Then as the shrine of the aforementioned relic, now well guarded until the new liberation, demanding annually live sacrifices in secret combats amidst the Alpine lakes and mountains. Closely guarded, here, is the duplicate.

Plus that Holy Lance . . .

The Mass celebrated at the Cathedral of Smolensk.
Song: From Finland to the Black Sea . . .

. . . from the Vienna Treasury, possession of which allowed the Hapsburgs to achieve world domination after the Roman Empire. That was the lance that was thrust into the Saviour's side by that Roman legionnaire, Longinus, later celebrated in *Parsifal*. It passed into the possession of Thomas the Apostle, St. Maurice, Constantine the Great, Charlemagne, Otto and Henry and Barbarossa and the Hapsburgs and Hitler. Who will be the next to rule over the earth?

And the wolfhound, the direct descendant of Hitler's Blondie, borrowed by the soldiers guarding the Wall in East Berlin. It has already cornered a lot of people, even almost tearing one apart, someone who wanted to flee from one part of Germany to the other, in a German uniform. The uniform of old Prussia.

And now, Himmler's Germanic horse. He saw it once, while riding in a train through Poland; it was white and its mane was red, but he never caught it, even though he assigned the entire Institute of Heredity to catch it and bring it to him.

Snow is falling. Long shot of the audience of puppets in front of the carnival booth. Displayed as in a county fair, various insignia of the Winter Relief Action. Close-up of porcelain birds, like those collected at that time. Military insignia and old-fashioned German costumes.

Radio announcer, High Command, September 26, 1941: From the Führer's headquarters, September 26, 1941. The High Command announces the following: In the capital city of Kiev, the annihilation of the still-encircled remnant of the enemy is pro-

gressing relentlessly. The number of prisoners has increased to 492,000 and is still growing.

Goebbels' appeal for the Winter Relief Action, December 20, 1941: . . . if possible, lined or trimmed with fur. Warm woolens, socks, stockings, vests, undershirts . . .

Radio announcer, High Command report, October 18, 1941: The High Command announces the following: The operations in the East are running on schedule. During the day, combat aircraft bombed the harbor installations of Murmansk and strategically important installations in and around Moscow. As we have already announced in a special bulletin, a well-protected convoy from North America to England was intercepted by German submarines after it entered blockaded waters. In unrelenting attacks lasting several days, the U-boats sank ten enemy merchant vessels, including three fully loaded tankers with a total gross tonnage of 60,000. The enemy did not fly into the territory of the Reich.

Goebbels' appeal for the Winter Relief Action: . . . is urgently needed at the front and therefore doubly welcome. Furthermore, we need quilted or lined undervests, wooden scarves, and mufflers, in fact everything that . . .

Obersalzberg as an idyllic postcard. A cheery, colorful picture from the period of German victories.

Female radio announcer, October 19, 1941: Heil Hitler, it is just after 5 a.m. Today is Sunday, October 19. The Deutschland Radio Network is now beginning its programming.

A projection of Saturn in which the camera appears to be soaring toward the planet.

Announcement in Japanese by General Hideki Tojo: The explanation for the Japanese attack on Pearl Harbor.

Announcement in English, American radio, December 7, 1941: We interrupt this program to bring you a special news bulletin. The Japanese have attacked Pearl Harbor, Hawaii, by air, President Roosevelt has just announced. The attack also was made on all naval and military installations on the principal island of Oahu.

•

Inside the Black Maria, on the wall, is a huge photo of Harry Baer as Ludwig in the stage set of the church in the original Bayreuth production of *Parsifal*. Next to it the "thinking cottage," an interior like a cell, with a table, and someone sitting at it (drawing by William Blake).

HARRY BAER: Who am I?

Sometimes I think what if my name were Ellerkamp, just for fun? SS Section Leader in Adolf Hitler's bodyguard and former film projectionist for the Führer and Reich Chancellor in Berlin, at the Reich Chancellery, and at the Berghof, Obersalzberg. Later, after 1945, first a maker of sentimental regional movies, then a porno movie producer and distributor. German film history, first-hand. Walt Disney, and Erwin Leiser's documentary, *Mein Kampf*. In 8-millimeter shows for the home, under the counter, and in the sex shops, Hitler is now the biggest hit. Hard core under the counter. Do you think I enjoyed doing it? But after all, the public, the consumers, the buyers, the people, the majority want it and ask for it and pay for it. We do live in a democracy after all, and the customer is always right, if he pays, of course, and nowadays Hitler sells.

Song: The world's decaying bones now tremble
Because of the coming war.
We overcame the terror:
A great victory was ours,
And we will keep on marching,
Till everything to pieces is hurled . . .

Or am I just one of the great entertainers? A solo performer, a circus director of a big show that's known as History and the Past. Or am I only the host Koberwitz, presiding at one of the weekly evenings in 1923 in a Bavarian villa, or perhaps just a cinéphile watching everything go past, fixing up equipment and identifying with it all.

We see the "Limbo" puppets placed on the steps at Baer's feet. Hitler with the fatal gunshot wound; Göring, old and with a watery face; Goebbels and Himmler with the mutilated faces of hell; Karl Valentin in a black top hat; and Speer in the prison uniform of Spandau. The set contains various props, among them a piece of charred wood from Hitler's house in Obersalzberg, as can still be found there even today; a stucco remnant in the shape of a red rose from Ludwig's Linderhof grotto; stucco and stones from Wahnfried, Wagner's villa in Bayreuth, etc.

Pan from detail to detail in close-up. After we hear the quote from Hitler, we see Baer as Ellerkamp in a close shot as he begins his monologue.

Hitler, November 8, 1942, Munich—Nazi memorial for the mar-
tyrs of November 9, 1923: If Jewry possibly imagines that it
can launch an international world war to exterminate the European

races, then the outcome will be not the extermination of the Euro-
pean races but the extermination of European Jewry. They always
derided me as a prophet. Of those who laughed in the past, a great
number no longer laugh today. Those who still laugh will perhaps
soon no longer be laughing . . .

ELLERKAMP (Harry Baer): I, SS man Ellerkamp, Hitler's film
projectionist, who knew his most secret desires, his dreams, the
things he wanted beyond the real world. Two or three movies
every day, *Broadway Melody* with Fred Astaire, Walt Disney's
Snow White, An Ideal Husband with Heinz Rühmann, *The Two
Seals* with Weiss Ferdl, and almost anything with Weiss Ferdl
or Moser or Rühmann, and Fritz Lang's *Nibelungen* over and
over again, *The Hot Punch, Quax the Hard Luck Pilot, The
Finances of the Grand Duke,* operettas, *The Trouble with Iolanthe.*
I saw him greeting Jenny Jugo, Anni Ondra, and Leni Riefen-
stahl. And I saw him joking with Gretl Slezak, Renate Müller,
Olga Tschechowa, Paula Wessely, and Lil Dagover.
I saw him watching the French movies he banned for the public.
I saw Goebbels keeping Chaplin's films away from him, but he
did hand over *Gone With the Wind.*
Yes, the man who controls the cinema controls the future.
There is only one future, the future of the cinema, and he knew
that, the man whom they called *Gröfaz,* the "greatest general of
all time." Some used the nickname reverently, others with nasty
irony. But I know he was really the greatest, the greatest filmmaker of all time. It began during his Karl May period, in that
Viennese flophouse.

> *Song:* . . . *And we will keep on marching,*
> *Till everything to pieces is hurled,*
> *For today our Germany belongs to us,*
> *And tomorrow the entire world!*

When he saw the film based on Kellermann's *The Tunnel* he wanted
to become like those tunnel builders, burrowing, magical, fanatical,
radical, powerful, with an iron will, burrowing under the seas all
the way through from Europe to America. And I saw him speaking
with Speer, about the new architecture in Berlin, in the year of
victory, 1950, and the Urania cinema with the signs of the zodiac
on the cupola and the Last Judgment on the wall.

Radio bulletin, Stalingrad, winter 1942–43: . . . *The Luftwaffe
is hammering away in nonstop missions* . . . *the anonymous hero*

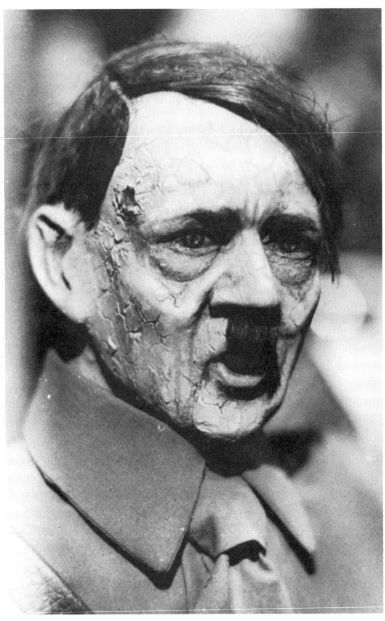

of our great victories . . . the hand grenades . . . smashing into the barricades . . . The Luftwaffe is preparing . . . but capture and conquest is ultimately the task of the individual warrior in the infantry.

And I saw him when Leni Riefenstahl was preparing *Triumph of the Will*, the huge parade as the setting for a film, his only monument apart from the newsreels of his war. And what did the masses ever make after the demonic screen was condemned that was better than the uniforms and marching, always in the same rhythm, hup-two-three-four; and after Rühmann's *Quax* and Willy Birgel in *Riding for Germany*. And I saw him watching John Ford's big movies about settlers, the Westerns with so many graves . . .

Announcer, military bulletin: Today, we must speak of Stalingrad as a dead and destroyed city. This once again testifies . . .
We see them before us . . . unshaven, unwashed, their faces black, their steel helmets snug . . . afflicted. The hand grenades in the legs of their boots . . . Figures leaping . . .

. . . and fights with the Indians. The great operettas of life. How he loved John Wayne. And I saw him struggling for Greta Garbo and trying to get Marlene Dietrich to come back to Germany.

He watched the movies over and over again, six or seven times in a row, focusing on image after image, shot after shot. And then I saw him stop everything when the war began; he didn't watch feature films anymore, just the newsreels, all by himself, before they were shown to the public. A war fought for him alone, on film in his bunker.

I saw all those things, Oberscharführer for the Führer. Ellerkamp, movie projectionist in the Reich Chancellery and at the Berghof in Obersalzberg, in Berchtesgaden, at the foot of the great Göll, near the Watzmann and Lake König, and now I run a booth at the Oktoberfest in Munich.

German newsreel—
Announcer, High Command bulletin from the Balkans: The High Command announces the following: After taking Ikpit and Veles, German troops have crossed the Vardar River in the direction of Albania's eastern border and taken Tetovo and . . .

Or am I porno filmmaker Koberwitz, near the railroad station? Or host Koberwitz in 1923? Who am I?

The camera moves in on a wax puppet head from the 1920s, as at the beginning of Part Two. Lap dissolve into the next image.

•

A projection of a Nazi production of *The Merry Widow*, with a close-up of décors by Benno von Arent, featuring the huge staircase. André Heller appears.

Voice (SA detachments): The final roll call . . .

ANDRE HELLER: Just imagine a gathering of 1923. Why, every-thing's still here, unchanged to this day. They are enacting the scene, compulsively, by way of atoning, in the historical locale, in the manner of an Oberammergau votive offering. The children come, the grandchildren, the children's children, and each one plays his part and they exchange them among themselves, they trade, and we hear the noises of the past, the cars, the voices, the laughter, the waiting, the work, the grief, the catharsis of fear and pity.

1923. Here and now.

•

A world of puppets. Mannequins from a modern department store, dressed in 1920s clothing, but with the faces of today. Behind the figures, the projection of a *Ludwig* set in the French baroque style. Furnishings for a party. Everything is full of cobwebs—the gramophone, the champagne glasses, lamps, heads.

Song: She went away, but a scent of roses remained,
Music softly plays, ah, it was only a dream of bliss.

MAN IN THE STREET (Alfred Edel): Germany must wipe out the shameful stain of Versailles, it must remove the humiliation that its foes inflicted upon it. Germany needs a new authority. There are three forms of authority. Traditional authority. My enemy, Wilhelm II, carried this to absurdity.

Edel coming toward and past and again away from the camera, walking to the back, into the puppet group.

With him, we capitulated and were humiliated. The rule of the high priests is over. Rational rule with its thin-blooded legality is no rule that can renew Germany.

Germany needs charismatic rule. It will come. You will be absorbed into charismatic rule. Germany needs a man of the people, a charismatic man bearing the legitimation of all Germans.

Germany, our people, must save Europe. Our people must show that it is capable of wiping away the stain, only through a charis-matic leader who comes from the people, who is no senile patri-arch, who does not perish in the inner-worldly asceticism of a sterile bureaucrat. It is only with a young, radiant leader who can make the best of our people that we can save our people, that we can save Germany, that we can save Europe. Salvation! It is possible only through rule, possible only through a man who will become our leader, who will raise himself from the jungle, the depressions, the humiliations, the failures, the disillusions. And this man will lead us and this man will complete our history, he will be the final point of our historical development, which began with the tribal rulers, which was perfected, powerfully perfected, in rationality, in legitimacy by legality.

Charisma—the rule of feeling,

the rule of free emotion,

the rule of creativity, discipline

and order and strict control, that will be the mission of our people,

even for you, even for you. . . That will be the future of our Fatherland and that will mean development for Europe.

Song: How do I get happy, how do I get big,

Do I have to learn it, or does it just come like that?

I don't even want to know when or where,

But how do I get happy . . .

Camera moves toward Johannes Buzalski as a member of high society, circa 1923. Close-up of the speaking head in the rigidified company. Details of the puppet heads and a few live people among them.

SOCIALITE (Johannes Buzalski): The earthly, Christian calendar is incorrect. The year 77 is the year zero. Venus, the Queen of Heaven, has declared war on Lucifer, the god of Earth.

Stand up, the judgment is coming, you shall reap everything you sow, and you shall get anything you choose. The secret of Judaism and its God must now finally be solved. We have to put an end to the hair-raising nonsense of the Creation legend in the Old Testament. And also to the fairy tale that Adam and Eve were the first Jewish human couple. And the first parents of all mankind; and original sin, which does not exist for all people anyhow, has subjugated all mankind to a score of priests from birth to death. Also, the absurd claim that Hitler was of Jewish background, that his father was a rabbi in Graz, named Schicklgruber. The absurd claim that Jesus was a circumcised Jew. Hitler is not dead, he is in the cosmos; when he was born, he was a cosmic baby placed on earth as a foundling. His parents took him in and baptized him Adolf.

Voice: Come on, break it up, break it up . . .

| 119

When the battle in front of the Reich Chancellery rages most violently, Hitler and Bormann will be received into the cosmos by the UFO's of the cosmic police. The second catastrophe will come before the start of this new age; this time, however, not through water, but through fire, all the atomic bombs on earth will be controlled by the UFO's of the cosmic police. After this world-wide catastrophe, paradise will be restored as it was before the Deluge.

Voice: . . . Sieg Heil, Sieg Heil . . . We greet you, my Führer, with our old battle cry: Adolf Hitler, Sieg Heil . . .
Announcer: the Führer speaks.
Hitler: . . . 41,000, then 62,000, then 78,000, now there are 90,000, 107,000, 137,000, and today over 114,000 . . .

Details of the party in cobwebs; also live figures and puppet heads.

Song: Wherever you go,
Wherever you stand,
Everything's twisted,
From early to late,
The world's got a hex,
There's only the rumba.
Nothing to rely on,
Young or old,
It was just very cold,
That's how you'll be,
So just try it yourself,
A little rumba.
And you hop along,
You don't know the steps,
You just dance like crazy,
'Cause everybody's nuts, my child,
The crisis will soon be forgotten.
The parties go away,
Instead of shouting,
Instead of recruiting,
But you stand there alone,
And you don't know what to do,
No.
Come on, let's dance a little rumba,
For the rumba is modern.
Only, I ask you, why are we dancing the rumba?

From the middle of the room and from a rigid puppet stance, the figure of the young Goebbels in a leather coat emerges, slowly coming toward the foreground and sitting down. In front of the projection of the Venus Grotto décor of *Tannhäuser* (as in Ludwig's nightmare scene, in which Hitler and Karl May first appeared to Ludwig at the Victory Celebration of 1871).

This scene of 1923 is accompanied, as from the very start, by a sound track filled with street noises, machine-gun fire, Communist and Nazi songs, slogans and music of the 1920's.

YOUNG GOEBBELS (Rainer von Artenfels): I come from a room in which I had never been before. Among people who are strangers to me. Poor, careworn people. Workers, soldiers, officers, students . . . I barely notice a man who suddenly stands above us and begins to speak. Hesitant and timid at first, as though seeking words for things that are too large to be squeezed into confining forms.

Then, all at once, the flow of speech begins to pour out, I am captivated, I am all ears. The man up there speaks faster and faster. There is a radiance like light above him.

Song: The banner high! Our ranks are serried tight.
SA now marches with a bold, firm tread.

Honor? Work? Banner? What am I hearing? Do these things still exist in this nation, from whom God has withdrawn his blessing hand?

| 121

Song: Just do it right . . . I don't know, child . . . Come on, let's dance a little rumba . . .

People begin to glow. Rays of hope shine on the gray, ragged faces. Now someone stands up and raises his clenched fist high . . .

Rumba continues.

An old officer sits next to him, weeping like a little boy. I feel hot and then cold. I don't know what's going on inside me. I suddenly think I can hear cannon booming. As if through a fog, I see a couple of soldiers suddenly get to their feet and shout: "Hurray!" Not one man takes notice of them. The man up there is speaking.

Hitler: . . . and today over 114,000 . . .

What has been living in me for years takes shape here and assumes tangible forms. Revelation!

Crowd: Heil Hitler, Heil Hitler, Heil Hitler . . .
Announcer: Ladies and gentlemen, the rise and fall of the city of Mahagonny.

In the midst of the ruins, one man stands up and thrusts the banner high.

Around me, all at once, there are no more strangers. They are all my brothers . . .

I go, nay, I am driven to the tribune. I stand there for a long time and gaze into the face of this One Man. This is no orator. This is a prophet!

Sweat is streaming from his forehead. In this gray, pale face, two glowing eye-stars are fulminating. His fists clench. I no longer know what I'm doing. I am virtually insane. I shout: "Hurray!" No one is surprised.

Song: The banner high! Our ranks are serried tight.
SA now marches with a bold, firm tread.

The man up there gazes at me for an instant.

Announcer: Break up, break up.
Crowd: Sieg Heil!

That is an order. From that moment on, I am virtually born again.

Crowd: Heil Hitler, Heil Hitler!

I know where my path must lead me. The path of maturity.

Chorus: Brightly from the darkened past
Shines the future now.

I am intoxicated . . . All I now know is that I put my hand into a throbbing male hand. That was an oath for life. And my eyes sank into two great blue stars.

Chorus: Brothers, toward the sun of freedom,
Brothers, upward toward the light.

●

The following texts are accompanied by Wagner's "Siegfried Idyll." In front of the projection of the great hall in Wahnfried, Wagner's residence in Bayreuth.

ANDRE HELLER: Imagine a baroque castle or the Villa Bechstein in Obersalzberg or Wahnfried in Bayreuth or the Bürgerbräu Tavern in Munich, everyone waiting—the Sleeping Beauty, King Arthur, Parsifal, Siegfried. The world is waiting for a hero.

Room in Wahnfried, with Wagner's piano.

ASTROLOGER (Peter Moland; text by Friedell): Rationalism, that will-o'-the-wisp that arbitrarily illumines and allows only those segments of reality that do not contradict so-called experience and the laws of thinking, is merely a modern European illusion, a local one, a temporary prejudice, an intermezzo of the rule of reason, a crude superstition, that will soon collapse under the jeers of the Orient and Asia.

Sundown in front of Wahnfried, the entranceway with a bust of Ludwig.
The Tibetan Dr. Ko, the spiritual teacher of the Finnish masseur Felix Kersten, walks over to Kersten, who is massaging someone on the table.

DR. KO: I have done my task, now do your duty. Europe belongs to you.

In the attic of Wahnfried, among various puppet women in the cobwebs of the centuries. Alfred Edel as a Man of Destiny, circa 1923, in the style of Max Weber. Music: March from *Das Rheingold*.

MAN OF DESTINY: Power does not interest me, this general influence that the literati have. I want to rule, I want to lead men concretely. I want to see people react to me, delegate me, transform me. I want an aide-de-camp, ruling is sensual. Ruling is blood. Ruling is life, ruling is self-realization, ruling is feeling, feeling anew, ruling is Eros, an inexhaustible Eros, the weak people will fall for this, for the Eros of rule, for the Eros of governing, for the Eros of violence, for the decay, for the body of violence. I and you and you and I, I have you, and the man who realizes this, the charismatic leader, no matter where he comes from, from below or above, he will have the weakest people behind him. He will have mass legitimation from women, he will receive a female vote of confirmation. Rule, Eros, body, woman.

Crowd: Sieg Heil, Sieg Heil.

Aria from *Das Rheingold*.

Goebbels: . . . Führer, command, we will obey.

"Siegfried Idyll" again. Projection of décor from Act II of *Tristan*. Night, stars. Stage decoration from the Nazi period (by Benno von Arent).

ASTROLOGER: Untold stars wander through the unending depth of the cosmos. Radiant thoughts of God. They are all happy, for God wants the universe to be happy. Only there is one among them that does not share this fate. Did God forget this star? Or did he grant it the highest glory by giving it the freedom of struggling up by its own strength? We do not know.
We are a tiny fraction of the history of this tiny star.

Comrades, raise your fists . . .

André Heller walks through the rooms of Wahnfried into the park. Puppets in pre-1933 Nazi uniforms. Chauffeurs, headlights, agitation. Heller continues through blood-red décor projections from the slaughterhouse scenes in Stroheim's *The Wedding March*.

ANDRE HELLER: We want to celebrate the love of danger—crime, action, sex.

[Quoting from Futurist Manifesto] We love the automobile, which is more beautiful than Nefertiti. We want the beauty of fighting, aggression, war, the hygiene of the world, blood and balls, blood and madness, blood and sunshine. We want to celebrate anarchy, for which one dies, as for a woman's scorn of a man.

We want to destroy the museums, the libraries, academies of all kinds, as well as morality and femininity. If prayer ties us to God, then speeding is our prayer, we will kneel on these tracks, the holiness of wheels and tracks within us, to pray to the divinity.

Crowd: Heil Hitler, Heil Hitler!
Song: The banner high! Our ranks are serried tight.
SA now marches with a bold, firm tread.

It is the intoxication of speed that blends us with the deity in the destroyed towns and houses and people, a vast square after the next war for our ceremonies of the new happiness.

Goebbels (New Year's Eve address, December 31, 1942): I greet the entire German nation at the front and at home, in town and country. Struggle and labor, that is our slogan for the new year, and over its entrance gate we write Friedrich Nietzsche's great words for our struggling and laboring nation: "You go your way of greatness . . ."
Crowd: Sieg Heil, Sieg Heil, Sieg Heil!
Goebbels: . . . that must be your greatest courage, that there will be no more prayer afterward. Now the mildest in you must become the hardest. Anyone who spares himself will ultimately grow ill from sparing himself. Praised be what makes us hard.
Roll call of the martyrs of November 9, 1923: . . . Siegmund Benke, Hans Hoffmann . . .

Like a vision at a Black Mass in back of Wahnfried. From the opened grave of Richard Wagner, Hitler (played by Heinz Schubert) emerges in a Roman toga: he is the color of a corpse as he comes out of hell, as in Doré's Dante illustration. Two figures, a life-size puppet in a Wagner cloak and the child, her face shrouded. Music from *Rienzi* throughout the following text.

HITLER, standing in Wagner's grave: Here the spiritual sword was forged with which we won our victory. After all, there was no one else who would, who could take over my desired role. And so they called upon me. First, the bourgeoisie, then the military, rubbing their hands in bliss and dirt, and also to defend their honor—

do you imagine I did not notice? Then, industry, to drive out
Bolshevism, from whose Lenin I learned so much and whose Stalin
could be venerated secretly. Then the petty bourgeois, the workers,
for whom I could bring forth so much, and youth, to whom I gave
a goal, and the students, who needed me, and the intellectuals, who
were now liberated from the Jewish Mafia of their friends and
foes, yes, and other countries, who were glad to have a pacified
Europe again, strength and solemnity. And one should consider to
how many people I gave something worth being against. And just
compare the lives of so many people—listless, empty. I gave them
what they put into me, what they wanted to hear, wanted to do,
things they were afraid to do. I made and commanded for them,
for it was all for them, not for me. Germany, yes, which I really
love, in my own way, of course. As I always said. Right?

They hate me from up close.

Just look.

And how could I, the artist, wage war without hatred of the
Jews, what would I have been without my music and architecture,
without my *Rienzi*, with which everything began, without the

blindness in Pasewalk, where I decided to become a politician, without the rejection from the Viennese Academy, which forced me to write and live my struggle, without the collapse of Germany, without Versailles, which taught me to speak, and what about Munich and Landsberg, the prison, with the abortive rebellion beforehand, the rebellion of the anarchic, lawless man?

And what would you be without the persecution of the Jews, without the readiness for sacrifice, which we have to be capable of? How can I help the mediocrity and the immensity, the cruelty that technology gave me? Yes indeed, I am the bad conscience of the democratic systems, perverse, as you now say, my goodness, cruelly putting order in the pigsty of history, which everyone secretly wanted but did not dare, at that time. If they knew how much of an effort, how much energy it cost me to make decisions, how much more hesitant I was than all these Prussian generals, a genuine child of turn-of-the-century Vienna, how much effort I had to exert, hard and ruthless in this labor that had to be done. The son of a middle-class Austrian official, with time in a flop-house.

I know I will be elected the greatest man of all time or perish, cursed and damned by all, for all time. And am I not the last of the breed of the great creators, who, in monumental repression of sex and private life, merciless against themselves, carry through their work, like Leonardo da Vinci and Michelangelo, and none of them laughed. Not Beethoven or Wagner, only Mozart perhaps, but he was not my man.

Yes, just listen, carry it through, ladies and gentlemen. I am a man, with two eyes and ears like you, and when you prick me, do I not bleed? I too. I too am one of you.

I was and am the end of your most secret wishes, the legend and reality of your dreams, so we have to get through. Finally. The final time? Nightmares? Not by a long shot. When I question the goddess of history, my Providence, which I know as none of you do.

Whoever does not want me cares little for the masses. Forever, your brother Hitler.

Goebbels (January 30, 1943, on the tenth anniversary of Hitler's takeover): ... *And so I would like to ask the Almighty for only one thing, to keep the Führer healthy and full of strength and joyous determination.*
Heil Hitler! Sieg Heil!
Crowd: Sieg Heil! Sieg Heil! Sieg Heil!
Song: Deutschland, Deutschland über alles ...

Black GI's are dancing with blond girls around the grave of Richard and Cosima Wagner in front of a projection of Wahnfried as it looked after being bombed in 1945.

Song (E. Busch—by Brecht):
The age must be fulfilled, we dead are waking up,
But not the white shrouds, we are coming up black,
And leaving the graves ragged and with hollow eyes.
The gentlemen in their parlors are no longer laughing,
Nothing is deducted, the lives that you stole
Are paid for in cash, someday they'll be paid in full.
Crowd: Heil Hitler, Heil Hitler, Heil Hitler.

•

Through the blue grottoes of Ludwig/Wagner architecture, Peter Lühr as the teacher of the ice cosmogony is pushed in a wheelchair by one of his disciples, played by Rainer von Artenfels. Accompanied by the Prelude to *Lohengrin*: the Grail theme, as in the Alp-dream sequence of the Ludwig film, with the same décor.

COSMOLOGIST (Peter Lühr): We live at a critical point in time. It has been proven that the moon is coming closer to us, as we can distinctly see on special days when the air is pure. The force of gravitation will increase. Then the ocean waters will rise to a steady flood, they will climb and cover vast areas, inundate both tropics and wash around the highest mountains. Living creatures will be more and more released from the weight pressing upon them. They will grow. The cosmic rays will become stronger and stronger. They will affect genes and chromosomes and cause mutations. New breeds will arise, giant plants and giant animals, giant men. But only these giants, the race of the supermen, the lords of the earth, will have the strength, after the struggle with the legendary, cunning dwarfs and lower races, to survive the imminent destruction of the earth or at least hold it up for a millennial civilization, like Plato's legendary Atlantis of yore.

Lohengrin Prelude.

The new Aryan race, if you like. Before the final decay of our remaining magical powers. Thus, there shall be a reawakening of the new magical orders and rites. We will achieve superdimensional powers. What we call history will be abolished. The third eye, virile powers will grow in us. The New Man is standing at the threshold. The New Era. The Golden Age, paradise saved from the Deluge by human strength and concentration on the essential, by chastisements, ceremonies.

Projection of a gigantic architectural blow-up of the chandeliers inside the tunnel to the teahouse in Obersalzberg.

The German dream, *der deutsche Traum*: death leading to a new life. Away with the abuses of our false prophets, the egotistical satisfaction of holy instincts, passions, and wishes from myths and legends by means of money, the so-called sociology of the dwarf-sized races. Annihilate what is worthless, exterminate the superstition of science, technology, and false religions.

This is the blood memory of our inner eye. The soul of blood arises to the world conscience, hard and ruthless, through us the saviours of the world and the cosmos over time: the twilight of humanity begins with us.

The disciple of the ice cosmogony, alone now, stands and walks through groups of figures consisting of upright life-size photos of contemporary people. Accompanied by changing background projections of an eagle's head, which, like a devil just emerged, conquers the toppled cross with the mangled Christ. Huge swastika and SS dagger emblems, etc.

The photos come from August Sander's collection. They show Germans from all walks of life: manufacturers, judges, workers, children in uniforms of the imperial period, pensioners, club types, an SS man, members of the Wehrmacht, peasants tilling the soil, landowners, revolutionaries (Erich Mühsam), apprentices, newspaper editors, men and women from cultural life, and World War I cripples by George Grosz.

The disciple of the ice cosmogony passes among the figures, talks to them, halts, then starts walking again, agitated, fanatical.

DISCIPLE (Rainer von Artenfels; voice off): Let us recall the great figures of early history, from heroic epics, dreams in sagas and legends in the soul of our blood. We in ourselves. Reawakening from mythical powers. Every abuse creates spiritual catastrophes of cosmic dimensions. The theory of our interior is not psychology but myth. This is the struggle between ice and fire, the fire of the heart's blood against the ice of rational coolness.

Roll call of the names of the martyrs of November 9, 1923.

The ice cosmogony is addressed to that breed of men who are alien to both the Christian notion of guilt and the idea of pure utility. This breed of men confronts Nature powerfully, never flinches, whether in the false modesty of asceticism and humility or in the solely sensual satisfaction of the moment. This man has all the merits of the Nordic character. He gazes with fresh, keen, bold eyes into the hard and rough experiences of a dramatic Nature. But his closed and unyielding features conceal a secret undauntedness of genuine humor, a marvelous tenacity of healthy,

vital resistance, true kindness, and the ever loyal comradeship of strong-willed men. These are polar men, who are comfortable with the utterly Nordic law of destiny—bold, not feeble—unscathed, never garrulous—with resolute and intelligent, secure and courageous characters, uprightly confronting the trial and danger of sacrifice—in short, dramatic men, whose hearts are both adventurous and made of steel. These are men honored solely by the courage to accept themselves and their destiny, hoping for no reward whatsoever, either here or in the hereafter, but feeling themselves to be a living part of universal destiny.

Death is the proof and crown of a meaningful life, it passes into a new birth, new meaning, new form, new level. Death, dulling all pain, is both rebirth and everlasting life; it is the great turning point, at which life changes its shape through rebirth, a self comes home, an isolated man finds his homeland and maternal womb.

Roll call continues.

Those who live with the dead see their lives as links in the chain of generations running from the forebears to the grandchildren, who, tied to a bloodline, are responsible and obligated to the future with their conduct and way of life, who, in the face of the grandchildren, always stand before the court of the forebears, and in the face of the forebears, always stand before the summons and the court of the grandchildren. Hence, the daring world view of the ice cosmogony is addressed not to the satiated Philistines, who have no interest in ancestral reputation or heroism and who flee from death and destiny. This theory is addressed to the tragic man, who fulfills victory in his destruction by confronting his destiny and devoting himself to the point of self-sacrifice; it is addressed to the heroic man, who simply has to do this because he cannot do otherwise, who unswervingly goes his prescribed way and who crowns and seals his life with his death.

The fact that this ice cosmogony, the most sublime and most tremendous cosmic theory to arise since Copernicus and Kepler, has been created by a German ought to fill every German with gratitude and joyous pride!

We are the declared enemies of the intellect; yes indeed, that is what we are, but in a far deeper sense than this stupidly proud bourgeois science could ever dream. It is the path of the possibilities concealed in man. Against God and Nature.

We are going to change the world. And if we are human beings, then those cannot be called human beings, "animals" would be too kind, "subhumans" and "repulsive vermin" too flattering, for that nest of vipers that we are stamping out underfoot. I am afraid, for I have seen the New Man. I shall be acknowledged as the greatest or perish, cursed and damned by all for all time.

We are going to create the New Man.

Everything depends on our success in destroying the inequality, the centuries-old class distinctions.

Beyond good and evil, paradisiacal, as the ancients said, initiated into the rites of the Ecclesia Militans, of the Black Order, of the masses and the death's-head groups, corps who will stop at nothing to achieve the tragedies of greatness, god-men, their families snuffed out and they tied solely to the harsh, relentless laws of our cult.

There shall be men of a master race, raging prophets full of holy madness, full of providence in the spirit of the struggle between the world-blaze and the world-ice, securing solely their survival in the cosmos, courageous in their solitude, full of self-discipline, achieving their own completion. With souls, Nordic, ethical, as echoes of remote past worlds and a golden future.

Do you want power over the world? Not through natural

products, through dealings of morality and the whore of reason, but through reawakening of the magic of the post-Christian soul from the powers of the blood.

And anyone can join in, those right-born under the Nordic sun.

A lord of the world in our system and Fatherland, for which he labors and struggles or dies, with everything he does. Ennobled by our Idea. His greatest chance since the birth of the world.

Shall we win? A curse on the excluded, who must envy us until the end of their days. Let us be on the alert.

And then the end. When I die, I die for you. With me dies a piece of your great love, its proxy.

I am everything you wanted. As you saw it in me, projected it onto me, and that is the scandal, the insolubility that my enemies refuse to understand—as yet.

You shall hate me, as you shall hate yourselves and all your children and children's children, all those qualities and ideals sacrificed for the enthusiasms and the intoxication of wanting and getting everything for once. You shall hate yourselves as you shall hate me, and when you have died, so shall your heirs, with hatred for everything that is German, and with bad consciences at that.

All will die, in me as a proxy, the lost faith of the masses that I mobilized, the faith in our old customs and virtues, and happiness in the exemplary lives of the great heroes.

But money will put your minds at ease, will it not? Really? And if not? Such is the fear of this new guilt that will terrorize your children and their children?

Terrorist children, our future.

•

Camera pans the clouds over Obersalzberg, the road to the teahouse above Hitler's villa, the Alpine panorama, Lake König, and finally the Watzmann (a mountain of the Berchtesgaden Alps).

Goebbels, February 18, 1943, Berlin, Sports Palace, on the total war: Never in this war do we wish to fall prey to that false and sanctimonious objectivity nonsense that has brought so much misfortune to the German nation and its history. When this war began, we focused our eyes solely on the nation; whatever serves the nation and its struggle for life is good and must be preserved and promoted. Whatever harms the nation and its struggle for life is bad and must be cut away and removed. With ardent hearts and cool heads, we want to approach the solution to the great problems of this era of the war, and in this way we are pointing out the path to ultimate victory.

It lies rooted in the faith in the Führer.

Crowd: Heil!

Goebbels: He expects a performance from us that will over-shadow everything that has ever been; if ever we have believed faithfully and unswervingly in victory, then now, in this hour of national awareness and self-inspired encouragement. We see victory close by, tangible, we only have to seize it. We only have to muster our strength of purpose, put everything in its service, that is the commandment of the hour. And that is why, from now on, the watchword is: Nation, stand up, and Storm, break loose!

Crowd cheers.

Hellmut Lange as Hitler's valet, Karl-Wilhelm Krause, in modern clothing and at his present-day age, in front of the tunnel leading to the elevator—the mountain elevator which goes to the teahouse at the peak over Obersalzberg and Berchtesgaden and Lake König. He enters the tunnel and goes deep into the mountain, over two hundred yards.

VALET (Hellmut Lange): On July 2, 1934, I was greeted by the division leader and the commander of the then minesweeper division and sent to the naval section of the district defense ministry in Berlin.

I was to report there and receive further orders to report to the Reich Chancellery. Full of disquiet and with mixed feelings, I traveled from Kiel to Berlin.

Crowd: Sieg Heil, Sieg Heil, Sieg Heil, Sieg Heil!

Song: Deutschland, Deutschland über alles, über alles in der Welt.

At the Defense Ministry, I was directed to the chief of staff of the naval command, received with great friendliness, and presented to several high-ranking officers, including the supreme commander of the Navy, Admiral Raeder, and Reich Defense Minister von Blomberg. After answering various questions, I received instructions to report to the then Reich Chancellor Adolf Hitler, whom I was to call upon the next day. I was to report at ten o'clock in the morning in the Reich Chancellery to the SS supreme commander and Adjutant Schaub. I got up at five-thirty, cleaned and brushed my uniform, put on my dress shirt, and was ready to report by eight o'clock. At nine-thirty, I turned into the Wilhelmstrasse; there, I waited for a few minutes, took another deep breath, and then strode resolutely to the door of the Reich Chancellery.

I was escorted through the small courtyard to Hitler's private apartment and there I was handed over to the SS man on guard.

The latter took me into the lounge of the escort detachment and had me wait there. In the lounge of the SS escort detachment, I found two SS men playing chess. At first, they looked at me a bit skeptically. Later, a few gentlemen in civilian dress and a few SS men joined them, and then the general introductions began.

When they learned that I was to become Adolf Hitler's valet, a general discussion ensued, and they weighed various factors. Some of the people received me in a very friendly way. And thus I found out that the Führer wasn't even in Berlin, he had gone to East Prussia to report to Herr Reich President von Hindenburg at the Neudeck Estate about the whole matter (meaning the Röhm putsch). I was told that his airplane was expected back in Berlin around three o'clock. Finally the message came from the airport: "The aircraft with the Führer on board has just landed!"

Well, now the place came to life. In a jiffy, the people had vanished except for two or three. When I asked what they all had to do, they explained that each man had his specific station for the arrival in order to cordon off the area and to ensure security and, well, of course, to keep the road clear. I asked those present to show me a place where I would have a good view of the Führer's arrival. And I was just about to leave the room, I was still standing at the door, about one yard away, when Adolf Hitler walked past me. Naturally I stood at attention like a soldier, and he greeted me in a deep voice with "Heil!"

After some three quarters of an hour, Adolf Hitler's adjutant, Schaub, came into the room and said that the Führer would not have time for me to report today, and I should come back again tomorrow morning. I nevertheless remained in the lounge for some time, getting to know nearly all the members of the escort division, including Hitler's later chauffeur, Kempka, who was very nice to me and also offered to drive me to my lodgings. That evening, incidentally, I took a pleasure drive through Berlin with Kempka, who had a small car at his disposal, with which I later took frequent drives in my free time. Two members of the SS escort detachment joined us. We visited a few nightclubs until around midnight. In response to my request to call it a night, considering the next day, when I had to be fresh again, Kempka drove me to my barracks quarters in his car. Yes indeed, that had been a strenuous day, even though the main thing had not even commenced.

It took several days. On the fifth day—it was already getting on evening—SA Squad Leader Brückner came into the escort room and asked: "Where is the sea dog? The Führer's waiting for him to report." Yes, well, I was taken upstairs by Brückner to

the door of the Führer's private rooms, he told me to go in and he remained behind.

I then stood alone in the doorway.

The room I had entered was filled with a soft, dim light. Behind a long table, which was covered with papers, books, periodicals, and so on, and illuminated by a floor lamp that cast its light on a specific point, stood, with folded arms, Adolf Hitler.

As I reported: "Master Sailor Karl-Wilhelm Krause of the First Minesweeper Flotilla reporting," Hitler came around the table toward me and greeted me with a handshake.

He then asked me whether I knew why I was here. I answered: "Yes." Next, a few questions about my background, my parents, my profession, and whether I wanted to take this job. He asked me whether I was a member of the National Socialist Party and then, before I could reply, he answered himself, saying: "Oh yes, the Reich Navy swears allegiance to the Constitution and is not allowed to be politically active. That's fine."

At the end of the tunnel, he reaches the elevator inside of the mountain which leads up to the teahouse, several hundred yards overhead. He enters the elevator.

VALET (voice off): The whole thing may have taken some four or five minutes. I was dismissed with a handshake, told to wait outside and to send in his adjutant. I waited for a few minutes

until Brückner reappeared; he took me downstairs and gave me one hundred and fifty marks on behalf of the Führer, telling me to look around Berlin and to return tomorrow afternoon in order to hear the Führer's decision. So I wandered around Berlin, taking my meals at the Reich Chancellery. But only the day after tomorrow brought the decision. In the early evening hours, Brückner appeared with the words: "Where is Krause?" I stood at attention and said: "Here." Whereupon he declared that the Führer had decided in my favor.

This is the Deutschland Radio Network . . . from the Lustgarten . . . the victims . . . in the course . . . and Reich Minister . . .

Meanwhile, a room had been prepared for me in the Reich Chancellery, and Adolf Hitler inspected it himself. In his presence, I had to try out the bed to see whether it was long enough for me; I am six feet four inches tall. Then I received two light-colored business suits and a dark suit.

He arrives upstairs at the window facing the mountains and Lake König.

In the afternoon, when Hitler was drinking coffee with his guests in the garden, I was supposed to come to him. It was exactly a week ago, one of the SS escort detachment told me, that Hitler had stood up during such an afternoon coffee and telephoned the order to shoot SA Leader Röhm. Well, yes, now I stood before him. He took two garden chairs in his hands, and when I tried to take them from him, he warded me off, saying: "No, no, let me do it. You'll have to do it often enough later on."

He walked with the chairs almost to the middle of the garden, placed them in facing positions, and then asked me to be seated. I sat right opposite him. He said: "You are a soldier, and I shall not have you swear a special oath of allegiance, for I will rely fully upon you. What you see and hear here concerns no one else. You are personally responsible only to me. At most, you may receive orders from me through my adjutant. No one else is to give you any orders."

I was then responsible for Hitler's personal effects: that is, for linen, clothing, and shoes, later on for food as well—I don't mean preparing it, just serving it. In Berlin the kitchen and household were under Herr Kannenberg and his wife. In Munich, a Frau Winter; and in Obersalzberg, at first Hitler's sister, Frau Raubal, later a caretaker.

The valet recollects the daily schedule during his period of service, while sitting at the fireplace in Hitler's teahouse in Obersalzberg.

VALET: The setup of the daily schedule in Berlin was almost always the same in the first few years, until about 1937. Upon dismissing me before going to bed, Hitler, outside his absolutely private rooms on the second floor, informed me of the time at which he wanted to be awakened the next morning. His words were: "I will be awakened at 9:30 a.m.; at 8:00 a.m., leave the newspapers and periodicals on the stool in front of the bedroom door. Good night." Often with a handshake. (During the first few years in Berlin, the wake-up time was nearly always the same, nine-thirty.) My answer was then: "Good night, sleep well."

Hitler always locked himself in. His actual private quarters were on the second floor of the old Reich Chancellery and consisted of the private study with the library, the bedroom, and the bath. In the first few years, the SS man on duty in the vestibule placed the reports and newspapers on the above-mentioned stool outside the bedroom door. Later on, I had to take care of that myself; that is, the SS man on duty would wake me, bring me the reports and newspapers, and then I placed them on the stool. Hitler then stuck out his hand, the door remaining open a crack, and the hand groped for the stool. That was why the stool always had to stand in the same place.

And now the wake-up: During the first year, there was no buzzer connecting my room to his quarters. So, each morning, I went to the door of the bedroom, knocked, and waited for a response. And then I reported with the words: "Good morning, my Führer! It is nine-thirty."

But when the buzzer system was installed a year later, I would press the button three times, The buzzer was located at the head of his bed. I would then wait for his return signal. He would press the button, which was on his night table, three times also. Only then did I go up to his door, knock, and wait for his response, and then I announced the time of day. And the answer was then: "Thank you," and also "Thank you very much," and "Thank you kindly," according to his mood.

I could tell what mood he was in from the answer.

Only seldom did he ask for anything. After awakening him, I would then go down to the kitchen, prepare his breakfast myself, and arrange it on a tray. However, the milk was heated by the person on duty in the kitchen. The breakfast always consisted of the same things. Two cups of mouth-warm whole milk, as many as ten pieces of Leibniz zwieback cookies, and then a third to a half of a bar of bittersweet chocolate broken into small pieces.

I kept the milk mouth-warm upstairs on the coffee warmer outside his rooms. Almost always to the minute, that is, if I had awakened him at nine-thirty, there was a buzzing at nine fifty-two or nine fifty-three. Carrying the breakfast on a tray, I entered the bedroom and from there the library. The bedroom door was the only door that Hitler opened himself. It was my duty to open the other doors. In the above-mentioned twenty-two to twenty-three minutes, Hitler had bathed, shaved, and dressed. He buzzed as soon as he had put on his jacket. Even if occasionally he was awakened at another time, the duration of his toilette, a good twenty-two minutes, always remained the same.

Yes, Hitler always shaved himself, he needed two razors for that, one for the pre-shaving and one for the after-shave. Every day, a new blade was inserted into each razor, so that Hitler needed two razor blades every day. His brand of soap was Steckenpferd Lilienmilch, his shaving cream Pieri, his skin cream Pfeilring, and his hair tonic Dralles Birkenwasser. His hair tonic changed once, but then he went back to Birkenwasser.

For his bath, he used pine needle tablets.

Upon entering with the breakfast, I usually greeted first, but at times he was the first to greet. My greeting was: "Morning, my Führer."

If my mood happened to be spoiled, then I just said: "Morning." His reply was then: "Good morning," or even just: "Heil!" And

I then replied with the word "Heil!" and no further addition.

Hitler ate his breakfast standing in the library, while glancing through the latest reports and bulletins from the German News Office, which I had brought up. On this occasion, I also presented the menu for lunch. The first dish inscribed upon it was always the dish for the guests, then three vegetarian dishes were inscribed, from which he selected one or combined two for a meal. Sometimes he said: "At lunch today, I would like two fried eggs and some green salad." Concerning the dish for the other participants in the meal, he would only say: "Does the dessert go with the entree?"

Breakfast took three to five minutes. Hitler then went over to the official office of the Reich Chancellery. I walked ahead of him, for there were several rooms to go through, and the doors were locked from the side of the private rooms.

The keys, however, were in the locks. I opened these doors and left them open all the way to the office rooms, where the adjutants waited for him and greeted him.

In the first few years, the afternoon coffee was prepared at about four-thirty in the Hotel Kaiserhof. A few men from the security detachment went on foot to the Kaiserhof by way of the Wilhelmplatz. Hitler, one or two adjutants, and I drove in the car across the Wilhelmplatz to the side entrance of the Hotel Kaiserhof, where the manager and a man from the escort detachment were waiting, and they led us into the lobby. Here, there was always a corner table reserved for us. Göring or Goebbels also usually took part in this afternoon coffee. But seldom together. The afternoon coffee usually went on until six-thirty or seven, and then we went back to the Reich Chancellery. Here, everything was prepared for the evening meal. During the first few years, actors and singers from the theater, the opera, or the cinema were nearly always invited.

The evening meal too was very informal. During the meal, I presented a list of three or four, sometimes even six films for that evening's screening. Domestic and foreign films. Hitler then decided which film was to run that evening, and after supper and a quick coffee in the smoking room, the music room was set up for the screening. The arrangement was the same as for a public motion-picture theater. The films were made available by the Ministry of Propaganda or by individual film distributors. As many as three films were presented. If Hitler did not care for a film, then another had to run instead. Hitler would stop the screening with the words: "Take it off, what nonsense, the next one, please."

Until the start of the war, Hitler saw every domestic and foreign film that ran in Germany, even including films which the film control office of the Reich Propaganda Ministry was undecided about in regard to release in Germany. Hitler then made the decision himself.

During the war, Hitler saw no films aside from the newsreels.

The newsreels were screened without sound. The text was read aloud by one of the adjutants, and Hitler checked to see whether the text really fitted in with the images. Often, he made changes. As of 1942, Hitler saw no more newsreels. But he did maintain his old habit of listening to records of Franz Lehár and Johann Strauss, for instance *The Merry Widow* and *Die Fledermaus*.

After the screening, about midnight, we would go back into the smoking room. Here, the orderlies had already set a coffee table in a cozy corner. Everyone sat down, men and women alternately, and an outright chat began. All alcoholic drinks, plus coffee and cake, sandwiches, and so on, were served. And here, people even smoked, although not near him. The conversation was informal. Actually, everything was discussed, but not politics. Yes, even the women's fashions were discussed. And during these chats, one could see that Hitler was really a very entertaining conversationalist. This was often confirmed to me personally, not only by German but also by foreign visitors. I was usually present during these conversations and could actually hear and see everything that went on; after all, I was only one or two yards away from Hitler's group. These conversations often lasted until around two, even three in the morning. And after all the guests had taken their leave, I, for my part, would put out the latest evening newspapers and the latest bulletins from the German News Office, all of which Hitler would then study thoroughly. Meanwhile, I prepared a tea for his bedroom, this was a Valerian tea with a small flacon of cognac, which I set on the night table.

When Hitler had then read the newspapers and latest bulletins, he went upstairs to his rooms.

This daily schedule in Berlin remained about the same until 1938.

Until then, we had never really been in Berlin on a Sunday.

We always went out to Obersalzberg near Berchtesgaden.

Scene changes to photos from the night-time Berlin of the Nazi period. A festive city festooned with Nazi bunting. People in the streets, jubilantly greeting Hitler. Then the Reich Chancellery.

May 22, 1939, Ciano's visit.

Signing of the pact between Germany and Italy.

Crowd: We want to see our Führer, we want to see our Führer, we want to see our Führer, we want to see our Führer . . .

Radio announcer: All of us are still full of this beautiful experience here on the Wilhelmplatz, where the Deutschland anthem resounded from thousands and thousands of throats toward the heavens. Where this song became an oath for the deed of these men who brought about this alliance.

And thus, thousands and thousands of eyes on the Wilhelmplatz and the side streets are trained on the Reich Chancellery, on the door of the balcony there.

We are waiting for the moment when we can express our gratitude to these men.

Hitler's valet, reminiscing, walks past projections of the rooms of the destroyed Reich Chancellery—as though viewing a castle. (See Syberberg's film about Theodor Hirneis, Ludwig II's cook, relating the life of the king in Linderhof, Neuschwanstein, etc.). Speer's rooms are restored in the projections. At the start, the valet is in normal proportion to the dimensions of the rooms, then midget-like, tiny, in front of the huge details of Hitler's desk. Music: "Taps," the opera *Fridericus Rex*, and *Rienzi*.

He walks through the corridors, the passageways, the plush-lined rooms, past the portraits of Bismarck, until he reaches the room of Hitler's SS guards. We see Hitler's cabinet hall and the details, the globe and his desk, as they were photographed then. Cut back to the room as it looked in 1945, after it was destroyed.

VALET (voice off): One of my chief responsibilities was to take care of the wardrobe. The civilian clothes, especially the business suits, were so worn out that a middle-level official might just barely have been able to wear them to the office. At my urging and after a long time, he finally gave in to Frau Goebbels, Frau Troost, and, last but not least, Eva Braun, and he had a few suits made, as well as a dress coat, a double-breasted tuxedo, and uniforms. The uniforms were made in Berlin, the civilian suits in Munich. During my nearly ten years of service, the uniform tailor never even came ten times to take measurements or for a fitting. If I did manage occasionally to talk Hitler into allowing a fitting, this could last at most for two or three minutes, for nothing was more repulsive to him. Hitler wore all his clothes loosely on his body. How much criticism I had to hear from others! From all sides, even in letters from the people, I was very frequently rebuked. The blame was placed on me. The matter, they said, was my business and it was a

reflection on my job. I was supposed to make sure that Germany's
Führer showed himself to the public in well-fitting uniforms and
suits.

By now, a number of people must know that this was not easy
for me. Indeed, it was impossible as far the uniforms went. I
often had something altered on a coat or trousers; for instance,
I had the waist taken in on a coat. When I set out the item for
him to wear, I waited suspensefully. But, alas, he had not even
buttoned it when I was summoned to receive another dressing
down, half of which was enough for me. I later gave up doing
anything in this direction. I preferred putting up with rebukes
from others. I smiled and thought to myself: "Oh, if you only
knew." Hitler only very rarely appeared in public without some
headgear. His hats, they were velvet hats, were purchased at
Seidl's, in Munich, the caps for the uniforms in Berlin. His way
of wearing a cap was impossible. He may have had very personal
opinions in this matter. Frequently, I said to him: "That is a real
postman's cap," or "The railroad dispatchers wear such 'lids,'
but no other human beings."

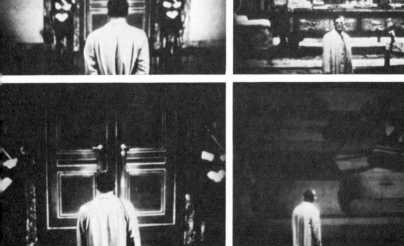

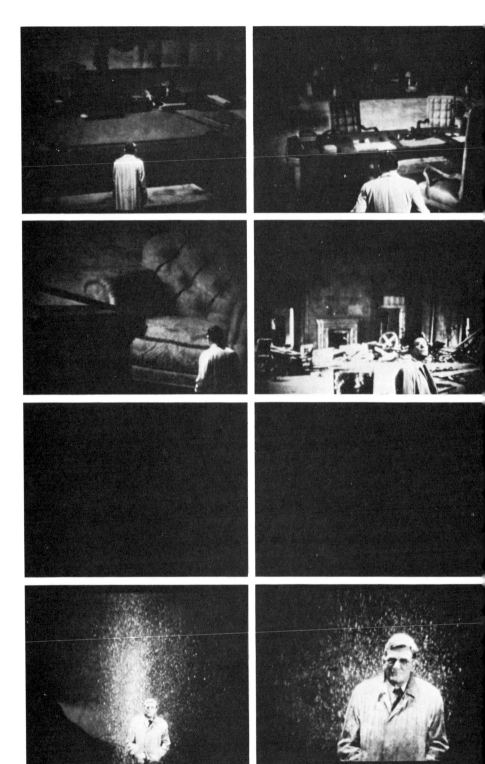

He would then look me up and down and say: "Am I wearing the cap or are you?"

My reply, about all the things I had to hear from others, didn't bother him in the least.

Once, at a Party convention, I removed the wire frame from his cap. The cap fitted him a hundred percent better, he didn't realize this right away. It was only when we were driving that he noticed, in the car, that the wire was missing. I was scared he would throw me right out of the car. I got a terrible bawling out. But I do believe that the whole country laughed at the way he wore his cap. The same was true of his shoes and boots. He simply couldn't give up his old top boots. He had bought them somewhere before my time. Also, this was the only pair of top boots he owned. I had some three pairs of top boots made for him, but he didn't like them, he kept putting on the old things again. If ever they needed resoling, it had to be done at night so that they could be ready the next morning. These boots too, with their unsightly creases, were the talk of the country. I was unable to coax him into wearing any others.

As for shoes, he wore patent-leather half-shoes almost exclusively. There were two pairs of simple leather half-shoes. He owned only one pair of high-laced shoes with rubber soles. These were worn only in cool weather and on walks. He also had a pair of mountain boots. For many years, it was impossible to get him to wear colored shoes with light-colored suits. During the first three years, he basically wore black silk or lisle stockings and black patent-leather half-shoes with his light-colored suits. With the stockings, he always had something to complain about, for they were usually too short, so that they supposedly slid down his calves. He would then exclaim: "Isn't it possible for the Führer of the German people to get a pair of decent socks?" Frau Kannenberg and I combed all the stores in Berlin.

The black shoes with the colored suits were an atrocity. But here too he became sensible only after several years. I had long before purchased three pairs of brown shoes and also colored stockings, and every time one of the light-colored suits was laid out, I added the brown shoes.

But, every time, he pulled the black patent-leather shoes out of the closet himself and let the colored ones lie there. The same was true of the neckties. In this matter too, he was extremely self-willed. Even though I laid out two or three proper ties for a business suit, I was forced each time to watch him finally take the most unsuitable tie from the closet. Frau Troost often criticized

| 151

him: "My Führer, an impossible tie." She then glared at me reproachfully. I then said that the suitable one was at home. Namely, in the chest . . .

. . . this great jubilation . . . here on the Wilhelmsplatz.
. . . and waves a greeting, gazes down at the youth, and our Führer . . . on the shoulder . . .
. . . down again . . .
. . . two little girls and two boys, holding up their little lilac bouquets in one hand, and having to cover their eyes with the other hand, for their eyes are full of tears.

. . . on the "house boy," that practical clothes holder I had made.

He always knotted his neckties himself, but I had to tie the bow ties for the dress coats and tuxedos, and this had to be done very quickly, in some twenty-five seconds. It had to sit right after that time, otherwise he became surly and kept shifting from leg to leg. I think that by this point no one could tie a good bow tie on Hitler. I did, however, have a good measure of calm, which sometimes made him furious.

Once, he asked me what went through my mind when he bawled me out. I calmly replied: "Then my job is a little more interesting, not so monotonous."

. . . smiles down, is delighted at this greeting . . .
they keep thronging forward . . .
they want to express their deep gratitude . . .

Once, at the table, in Obersalzberg, he said in front of several guests: "Just take a look at my Krause here, nothing can shake him. If ever I make a scene, he puts on a small, ironic smile for me or peers at me with an absolutely innocent expression and probably has his own thoughts on the matter. I'd like to have his calm for just five minutes."

Anyway, when Hitler went traveling, the clothing issue was very difficult for me. I never or very seldom received detailed instructions on what was to be taken along on the trip. His instruction was something like: "Prepare for a long time or for several days," and not another word. It was only for short day-long trips that he might say: "You can take this or that along, that's all I need." But God forbid if something was needed but not at hand. Then, naturally, it was all my fault. I may say that there are few people on earth who packed as much as I did in those relatively few years, for on every day of travel, even in the hotel or during the briefest stay, everything was unpacked and repacked, and this had to be done incredibly fast, especially in the morning, for Hitler never really gave me any time for this work. Also, all the clothing items, including the dress coat and the tuxedo, had to be packed in such a way that he could put them on directly out of the valise without first having them ironed.

... the Italians ... have now ...
the coalition of ...
one hundred fifty million ...

As simply as Hitler generally lived, as easily as one could deal with him in an intimate circle (there was as good as no etiquette), he was difficult when guests were present. At such times, he was unpredictable. And all the more so when women were expected.

Now that was something else! Nothing was good enough. The entire place was infected with this fever. God help the orderly, God help me, if anything went wrong! A scene for even the pettiest bagatelle dogged our every step. What a sigh of relief when everything was over and it had worked more or less! At such times, one might even receive praise from him. But if anything went awry, then we were done for on that day—and most likely for the next day as well, and it was advisable not to let him see you, not for any reason, unless he summoned you. It could also happen that he praised a thing on one day and then rejected it the next day, or vice versa.

An example: I once had short underpants made for Hitler, and from the very same material as those that he wore. The same seamstress sewed them according to the same measurements. When they were done, I added them to the rest of the underwear. One morning, I entered with breakfast and—lo and behold: the new underpants fell at my feet with the words: "Please take these things away. They are quite impossible underpants!" I instantly took them away. They were put in with the emergency supplies and I even wore them myself. A few weeks later, when we happened to be in Godesberg during a long journey, he ran out of underwear. Fresh linen, en route from Berlin, would not arrive until the evening. What to do? I went to my baggage. I had three pairs of the above-mentioned underpants, which I had already worn. They were freshly laundered. I took them and put them out for the next morning. Naturally, I assumed he would object to them again. The certainty, however, that the linen courier from Berlin would soon arrive eased my fears. But how amazed I was to learn that he had put on these underpants without the least comment! The earlier incident had probably just been a whim of his.

Another example: the gray uniform coat! I had had it made on my own responsibility, since Hitler stood out conspicuously in his brown coat at army inspections and maneuvers. When another inspection of the army was slated and I showed him this gray coat, he merely replied: "You can do what you like with this. I will wear only my brown coat as long as I live." How astonished I was, about six months later, at the start of the war, on September 1, 1939, when he inquired whether the gray coat was still available. Hesitantly, I answered: "Yes." He wanted to see it immediately, tried it on, and ordered several coats of this sort to be tailored. I replied: "Goodness, my Führer! It's a good thing that I already have the gray coat here . . ."

Thus, there were many things that were rejected by Hitler and then later accepted on a suitable occasion.

Hitler changed his underwear whenever he needed to. Sometimes, he would change it two or even three times a day; at other times, however, he would not change it for two or three days in a row. He wore only thin socks, even with the top boots, always only short underpants, even in winter, during the greatest cold; he never wore an undershirt, he wore a separate shirt and collar, thus never a sports shirt, and never a colored shirt, only white ones. His suits were double-breasted. Except for the one with his dress coat, he had no vests. He never wore a belt, only suspenders, he never wore pajamas at night, only a nightshirt of simple linen.

The final image shows Hitler's workroom before and after the bombing.

Christmas broadcast connecting all fronts, December 24, 1942: Attention, all listeners, attention, calling Stalingrad again. This is Stalingrad, this is the front line on the Volga. Attention, once again the Lapland front.
This is a barracks in the Finnish forest.
Attention, once again, South of France, the Air Force.
This is a military airfield in the South of France . . .

Now Hitler's valet stands high up, in front of the teahouse, the mountains of Lake König behind him. Snow is falling, gradually covering him, turning him to ice. His narrative of his memories of the last Christmas with Hitler in Munich is interspersed with the radio broadcast on Christmas Eve during the battle of Stalingrad.

VALET: On Christmas Eve of the year 1937, Hitler greatly astonished me. He was in his private apartment in Munich, at number 16 Prinzregentenplatz. I myself was invited to a family gathering, and I was greatly looking forward to the moment when Hitler would withdraw and I would thus be free to leave. But then he walked through the room containing some presents that had not yet been distributed, he wanted to pick out one more gift.

Christmas broadcast connecting all fronts, December 24, 1942: Attention, attention, I am again calling the Bay of Biscay, Leningrad, the Caucasus front, the U-boat sailors in the Atlantic, Catania. This is the Mediterranean front and Africa, a military convalescent home in the Tatras. We send you greetings from buddies on the front lines.
Once again, Crete. Attention, attention, the Black Sea harbor.

The two of us then wrapped it up, as we stretched out on the carpet, and on this occasion, as he pressed down upon the knot, I tied up his thumb as a joke, whereupon, laughing, he gave me a playful blow in the back of my neck with his left hand. He then told me to deliver this package personally, but first to prepare his tuxedo. When I looked at him incredulously, he only replied: "That's right. Prepare my tuxedo!"

I also had to order a taxi. It was to wait on a side street off the Prinzregentenplatz.

December 24, 1942, Christmas broadcast:
Again this is the Black Sea harbor on the Crimean Peninsula.
We ask you, comrades, to sing once more the lovely old Christmas carol "Silent Night":
> *Silent night, holy night,*
> *All is calm, all is bright . . .*
All stations will now join in with this spontaneous greeting by comrades deep in the south, on the Black Sea.
Now they are already singing in the Arctic Ocean off Finland, and now we are switching in all the other stations, Leningrad, Stalingrad.
And now France as well.
Now Catania.
Now Africa.
And now they are all singing together:
> *. . . Sleep in heavenly peace . . .*

I had to make sure once again that everyone was really at the Christmas party that was going on inside the house, with punch brewing and so on, and I had to make sure that no one was at the door, which was usually the case, and that only one of the

Munich policemen was standing outside the house. When Hitler gave the order, we went downstairs very quietly. We really skulked like thieves through the house to the taxi waiting below. No one had noticed us, which made Hitler very happy. I was about to sit down next to the driver, but Hitler pulled me into the back seat, and I sat down at his right. Yes, then he began whispering destinations in Munich to me, and I passed them on to the driver in front. And so, on this Christmas Eve, we drove all over Munich for some two or three hours, from place to place, always a new destination. Finally, he told me: "Luitpoldcafé!"

Amazed at his behavior, I wondered what he intended to do at the Luitpoldcafé at this time. And how much more astonished the taxi driver must have been; after all, he didn't know who was sitting in the taxi. In any case, he was visibly relieved when we got out at the Luitpoldcafé and I paid him. Scarcely did he have the money in his hand when he shifted into gear and zoomed off at an insane speed. He probably thought we were a couple of loonies. Oh well, maybe he wasn't all that wrong, for I found the whole business really creepy. Yes, and then, without entering the café, we walked all the way back to the "Royal Square." Feeling responsible for his safety, I kept looking around every now and then, but he remarked: "Just stay at my side! You don't have to worry about me, for no one would believe that Adolf Hitler is strolling alone here through Munich on Christmas Eve!" If anyone came past us, he merely lowered his head a bit or peered to the side. And so, recognized by no one, we managed to get back to our place on the Prinzregentenstrasse, the Prinzregentenplatz.

En route, we were overtaken by an icy rain, so that, after having previously only leaned on my shoulder, he went the rest of the way arm in arm with me, since he was wearing new patent-leather shoes. Yes, someone must have noticed something. For the next day, Himmler and Rattenhuber, who was in charge of the escort detachment of the criminal investigation department, reproached me for not telling anyone in advance about this under-taking.

Roll call of the martyrs of November 9, 1923.
Radio broadcast from Radio Belgrade: This is the Wehrmacht station Lili Marlene. We greet our listeners!
Song (instrumental): In the homeland, in the homeland,
              We will meet once again . . .
February 1943: This is the German-language broadcast of Radio Moscow. The new year has begun as follows: On January 31, the group of Hitler units that were encircled west of the central

part of Stalingrad have been totally ground up. The commanding officer, Field Marshal von Paulus, his staff, and fifteen other generals have surrendered.

Close-up of the valet, who has now frozen in the ice and snow.

●

André Heller sits in William Blake's "thought cottage," Shrine of the Imagination (projection). The slow movement from Beethoven's Ninth Symphony begins. Heller sits at the table that we know from the second part of the Ludwig film (scene during which Ludwig has the vision of a burning castle with crowds of tourists being shown through it today).

ANDRE HELLER: Astronomers at the University of California, Berkeley, have discovered the farthest known galaxy. This tremendous structure of over a trillion suns is more than eight billion light-years away. The light now reaching us from there was sent out at a time when our sun and its planetary system did not even exist.

On photographs, 3 C 123 looks like a blurry, irregularly formed little spot, which probably represents other galaxies in the same group. The evaluation of spectroscopic data produced a surprise: The object shows the greatest red shift of the spectrum that has ever been observed in a galaxy. 3 C 123 is thus moving away from us at forty-five percent of the speed of light and is about five to ten times bigger than our Milky Way.

In the opinion of Professor Dr. Horst Löb of Giessen, six percent of all the suns in the universe are orbited by planets that could, like the earth, be inhabited by living creatures. This estimated percentage may seem relatively small, but the absolute number of inhabited heavenly bodies would be gigantic. For, according to a rough estimate, there are some one hundred million Milky Ways, and each one has some fifty billion stars . . .

Heller is still seated at the table in front of a projection of rising and setting sun: Runge landscape.

The modern age begins with the idea of the infinity of the universe, and if we think that idea through to the end, we come to unreality, for infinity is nothing but a mathematically formulated expression for unreality. If one tries to imagine concretely that the Milky Way consists of more than a billion fixed stars, many of which have a diameter greater than the distance between the earth and the sun, and that the Milky Way does not form a

source of tranquillity in the cosmos, but is racing somewhere at a speed of 360 miles a second, i.e., about a thousand times as fast as a cannonball, then the assumption that this could have anything to do with reality is reduced to a mere mental game.

Background: the Runge landscape with a detail from *Morning*.

The idea becomes even more unreal if one goes along with the latest speculation that the sum of all star clusters forms a closed finite system in the shape of a revolving ellipsoid; for then we cannot shrug off the thought that this is nothing but one of the molecules making up a larger body.

The cosmos as a molecule.
The molecule as a cosmos.

Background: projection of the ice floes in Caspar David Friedrich's painting *The Frozen Ocean (Das Eismeer)*. André Heller takes a book and reads.

Adalbert Stifter writes about Abdias the Jew and his blind daughter Ditha.
If there are people on whom such a wealth of hardship falls

from the clear blue sky that they finally stand there and let the hailstorm wash over them: then there must also be nations and stars, at least entire continents, that are so stubbornly afflicted by misfortune that it seems as if the natural laws were reversed so that only they can meet with disaster. It was along this route that the ancients came to the notion of *fatum*, fate, and we to the notion of destiny—in the face of which some people go in their pants, so eager are they to take it into their own hands and burn themselves, very courageously if things go well, but mostly lamentably. In the face of this same destiny, in regard to which we sometimes feel as though an invisible arm were reaching down from the clouds and doing the incomprehensible with us before our very eyes, for which we become guilty.

The tear from the start of the film, emerging from a star and flying toward us from the world crack, hangs low over the painting of the paradisiacal landscape of Ludwig II's Winter Garden. Heller slowly takes the glass sphere containing the Black Maria and holds it before his eye. Slow movement from Beethoven's Ninth Symphony ends. Fade-out.

The closing title of Part Two, *A German Dream*, over the girl's head, accompanied by a passage from the slow movement of Mozart's Piano Concerto in D Minor, coming from the static and vanishing back into it. Sound fades out.

Part Three
The End of a Winter's Tale
And the Final Victory of Progress

The child, with closed eyes, as at the end of Part Two; the figure 3; and Goebbels' voice in the background.

Goebbels, on January 30, 1943, at the tenth anniversary of Hitler's takeover: Faith can move mountains. This mountain-moving faith must fill us all, it drives us to work, to struggle for the nation and the Reich . . .

Long shot of the studio. Camera moves slowly toward the projection of the Méliès moon. The title of Part Three: *The End of a Winter's Tale.*

●

Music from *Die Götterdämmerung*, "Siegfried's Death." In front of a projection of an ornate room, reminiscent of Ludwig's taste, a massage scene: Himmler and his masseur, Felix Kersten.

Erich Weinert: National Committee of Free Germany, Radio Moscow, July 12, 1943:
> *Germany will not be lost,*
> *As some may worriedly wonder*
> *What will become of Germany,*
> *Because it can never win*

The war that it began.
Who worries here, who asks for advice,
Did you want the war, soldier?

Announcer: German soldiers! We now bring you an original recording of the Manifesto at the Conference of the National Committee of Free Germany, as read by its president, Erich Weinert:

The National Committee regards itself as justified and obligated at this fateful hour to speak in the name of the German people. Hitler is leading Germany to destruction. The defeats of the past seven months are unprecedented in German history. Germany itself has now become a battlefield. Time is of the essence, quick action is necessary. Anyone who will still follow Hitler whether through fear, necessity, faintheartedness, or blind obedience is acting out of cowardice and is helping to drive Germany toward national catastrophe. For the nation and the Fatherland, against Hitler and his war, for immediate peace, for the salvation of the German people, for a free, independent Germany.

HIMMLER (Heinz Schubert): Naturally, I'm an inquisitor, the Grand Inquisitor of the German Reich. We have found our devil and we know how to deal with the witches and renegades of this time and the human race.

Himmler, October 4, 1943, meeting of SS squad leaders in Posen: Whether other nations live in comfort, whether they croak, starve to death—that interests me only so far as we need them as slaves for our civilization. That is one of the things one can say easily.

The Jewish people will be exterminated, the population will be exterminated. That is quite clear, it is in our program. The elimination of the Jews. We are exterminating, ha! A bagatelle! And then you all come, all the decent eighty million Germans, each one has his decent Jew, all the others are bastards, but this one is a first-rate Jew.

We have the moral right, we have the obligation to our nation to do this.

To kill this nation which wanted to kill us. But we do not have the right to enrich ourselves with even one fur coat, with even one mark, with even one cigarette, with even one watch, with anything at all. We do not have that right. For we do not ultimately want to exterminate the bacillus in a cowardly way, get sick from the bacillus, and die.

During Himmler's massage, his vision. Dreams of fear and horror—lap dissolve in a long shot of the massage. Figures of memory, SS men, coming forward, filling the screen. Their words are drawn from SS reports and Himmler's texts.

Accompanied by *Die Götterdämmerung* and sound documents from the victorious invasion of France up to the liberation of Chartres and Paris by the Allies.

FIRST SS MAN (Hellmut Lange; voice off): May I ask you to listen closely and never speak about the things I am going to tell you in this group. We have been asked: What about the women and children? I have made up my mind to find a very clear solution here too.

You see, I did not consider it justifiable to exterminate the men, that is to say, kill them or have them killed, and then to allow the avengers in the guise of children to grow up for our sons and grandsons. The difficult decision had to be made to cause this nation to vanish from the face of the earth. For the organization assigned to carry out this mission, it was the most difficult that we have had so far. It has been carried out, without, I believe I may say, without causing damage to the souls of our men and leaders.

SECOND SS MAN (Rainer von Artenfels; voice off): So long as there are people on the earth, the struggle between humans and subhumans will be a historical rule. After all, this war, waged by the Jew against the nations, as far back as we can look, is part of the natural course of life on this planet. One can calmly reach the conviction that this life-and-death struggle is as much a natural law as the struggle of the plague bacillus against the healthy body. Just as the night gets up into the day, just as light and shadow are everlasting enemies, so too the greatest enemy of man, who rules the earth, is man himself. The subhuman. That natural creation, which seems biologically to be of the same species, with hands, feet, and a kind of brain, and eyes and a mouth, is nevertheless a very different, a terrible creature, is merely a sketch of a human being, with human-like features, but standing lower in its spirit and its soul than any animal. Inside this creature, a cruel chaos, images of uninhibited passion, an unspeakable destructive will, the most primitive desire, the most naked lowness, subhuman, nothing else. God help the man who forgets. What this earth possesses in great works, thoughts, and arts—it was man who conceived them, created and completed them, devised and invented them, for him there was only one goal: to work his way up to a higher existence, to give shape to the inaccessible, to replace the inadequate with better things. That was how culture

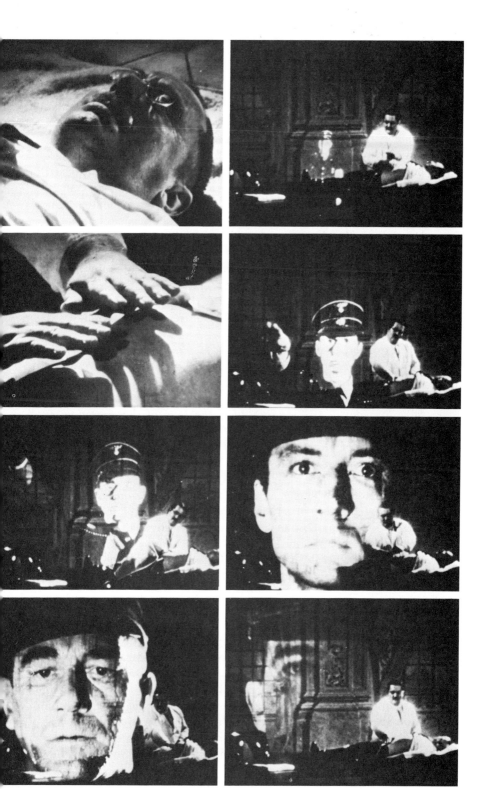

and civilization grew. That was how the plow, the tool, the house came into being, that was how man became sociable, that was how the family came into being, the nation, the state, that was how man became good and great, that was how he rose far beyond all other living creatures. That was how he became next to God. But the subhuman also lived. He hated the work of the other. He raged against it, secretly as a thief, openly as a blasphemer and murderer. He joined forces with his ilk. The beast called the beast. Never did the subhuman keep the peace, never did he leave others alone, for he needed semi-darkness, chaos, he shunned the light of cultural progress. For his self-preservation, he needed the slough, he needed hell, but not the sun.

THIRD SS MAN (Peter Moland; voice off): And this subworld of subhumans found its leader, the wandering Jew, the eternal Jew, who understood them, who knew what they were after. He stoked their vilest lusts and desires. He sent horror over mankind.

Newscaster, D-Day, June 6, 1944: Please synchronize your watches: At the tone, it will be ten-oh-two p.m.
The fighting in the Atlantic. Last night, the enemy began his attack on Western Europe, which he has long prepared and we have long awaited. Very soon after the start of the operation, it was obvious that the English and the North Americans were aiming their chief thrusts at the areas of Caen, Carentan, and Cherbourg. Under the cover . . .

FOURTH SS MAN (Peter Kern; voice off): The leading minds of a nation are bloodily slaughtered, and then it comes into governmental, economic, cultural, spiritual, and physical slavery. The rest of the people, robbed of its intrinsic value by countless blood mixtures, degenerates, and in the historically short space of centuries, one knows at most that such a people did exist once.

HIMMLER (voice off): I know that I have been and will be attacked for this by very many people, who told and will tell me that this is un-Germanic. I have the impression that, for some people, Germanic is really only a way to keep getting taken in as a good and kindhearted Germanic and then falling on one's back. Un-Germanic! I am sorry, but I consider it right and I believe that it is right. First we had to remove the enemy's leading minds. Those were the people in the Western Province Federation. In the rebellious federations, it was the Polish intelligentsia. It had to be gotten rid of. We had no other choice. I heard wise words and advice from various sides about how our own troops could suffer damage thereby, and I know it very well. I believe that none of the gentlemen who offered their advice was present at a single execution. I can tell you, it is dreadful and horrible for a German person to witness such a thing. That is the way it is, but if it were not dreadful and horrible for us, then we would no longer be Germans and we would not be Germanic. As horrible as it is, it was necessary, and it will be necessary in many cases, to carry it out. If we do not have the nerve now, then our bad nerves will fail our sons and grandsons, then after a lot of practicing we can once again commit the political madness of a thousand years in the next few centuries. We do not have the right to do this, for if we live in the modern age, brought up by Adolf Hitler and lucky enough to work for Germany in Adolf Hitler's Reich or under Adolf Hitler's hand, then we simply cannot be weak. Such an execution must always be utterly difficult for our men, and yet they must never be soft, they must do it with clenched teeth. That was a basic necessity.

SS figures step out from behind the projected images and slowly come toward the camera. The projections show the architecture of the planned fortresses of death on the borders of the future Reich, concentration camp inmates, and images of the war. The speakers move like the figures in Himmler's vision, as in a dream, like statues—speaking their lines and then going away.

HARRY BAER (voice off): The train arrived—Kurt Gerstein reported—and two hundred Ukrainians tore open the doors and lashed the people out of the cars with their leather whips. A huge loudspeaker gave further instructions: to undress, remove artificial limbs, eyeglasses, etc., etc. Then the women and girls to the barber, who cut off all their hair with two or three strokes of his scissors and stowed it away in potato sacks. Then the line started moving again, with a very pretty girl at the head. They went along the lane, all naked, men, women, children, without artificial limbs or eyeglasses. They come up, hesitant, enter the death chambers, most of them without saying a word. A Jewess, some forty years old, with blazing eyes, calls out: "May the blood that is shed here fall upon the murderers." She gets five or six strokes of the riding crop in her face, then she too vanishes in the chamber.

American announcer, CBS, D-Day, June 6, 1944: . . . Now the flak is coming up in the sky. Looks like we're going to have a night tonight . . .

THIRD SS MAN: The diesel doesn't start up. The people wait in their gas chambers, in vain. You hear them weeping and sobbing. Wirth goes over to the Ukrainian who is supposed to help Heckenholt (executive officer to the company commander), and Wirth then hits the Ukrainian in the face twelve or thirteen times. After two hours and forty-nine minutes, the diesel starts up. Another twenty-five minutes go by. Right, a lot are dead by now. You can see that through the tiny window that illuminates the chambers for an instant. After twenty-eight minutes, very few are still alive. Finally, after thirty-two minutes, all are dead. On the other side, men in the work detachment open the wooden doors. The corpses are squeezed together in the chambers like basalt columns. There's no place to topple or even bend over anyway.

Radio report, June 17, 1944: . . . filth in their mouths . . . and SS privates . . . The faces are rigid. Damn it, they have us in it . . . They've been trying it for days . . .

FOURTH SS MAN: Strangely enough, our men who took part in the executions suffered a lot more than their victims. From a psychological standpoint, they went through something terrible. Most of them know what it means if a hundred corpses are lying together, if five hundred are lying there, or if a thousand are lying there. Experiencing all this and, aside from a few human foibles, managing to remain decent: that is what has made us hard. This is an unwritten and never-to-be-written page of glory in German history.

Report from the front lines continues.

FIRST SS MAN: I can tell you, it is dreadful and horrible for a German person to witness such a thing. That is the way it is, but if it were not dreadful and horrible for us, then we would no longer be Germans and we would not be Germanic. As horrible as it is, it was necessary, and it will be necessary in many cases, to carry it out. One should not regard things from petty, egocentric viewpoints, one must focus on the whole of the Germanic spirit. The individual must sacrifice himself.

Reporter: . . . We are at it again. In this hard and fierce fighting, the commander . . .

FOURTH SS MAN (voice off): In front of me stretched a ditch in which there were countless corpses of Jews of all ages and both sexes, they had been shot. Soldiers and civilians came running over and stared curiously into the depths. One of the bodies in the grave was a man with a full white beard, he had a small cane still hanging on his left arm. Since this man gave signs of life through a jerky breathing, I asked one of the policemen to dispatch him. Whereupon the policeman laughed and told me: "I've shot him in the belly seven times already, he'll croak on his own for sure."

The Jews of a Russian village had gone into hiding because they had been informed that a murder detachment was approaching. When the detachment reached the village, the SS men saw only a woman, with a baby in her arms, standing at the edge of the road. The woman refused to reveal the hiding place of the Jews. One of the men then tore the baby away from her, grabbed it by the legs, and smashed its head on a door. It sounded like a tire bursting. I will remember that sound for the rest of my life. The dazed woman revealed the hiding place.

Launching and detonation of the first V-1.

In Riga, an SS man saw two Jews carrying a rafter. Calmly, he pulled out a revolver and shot down one Jew. One was enough for this work. An SS commander reacted similarly during the liquidation of a Latvian ghetto. The sick Jews were being carried on litters. The SS commander went from stretcher to stretcher with his service pistol, shooting one Jew after another. The gunfire of the task forces ruthlessly lightened the ranks of Russian Jewry. By the winter of 1941–42, Detail A reported 249,420 liquidated Jews, Detail B 25,467 liquidated Jews, Detail C 95,000 liquidated Jews, Detail D 92,000 liquidated Jews.

Newscast, July 21, 1944: We bring you the news from the wireless service.

First, we repeat an important bulletin of the wireless service which was sent out on all networks this afternoon. Assassination attempt against the Führer. The Führer not injured.

Hitler (on July 21, after the assassination attempt): Fellow Germans! An assassination attempt planned against me . . .

FIRST SS MAN: The Jewish question in the countries occupied by us will be taken care of by the end of this year. There will only be remnants left, individual Jews who have gone into hiding. The question of the Jews with non-Jewish spouses and the question of half-Jews will be sensibly and rationally examined, decided, and then resolved. Everyone takes it for granted, and is gratified if there are no Jews left in his province.

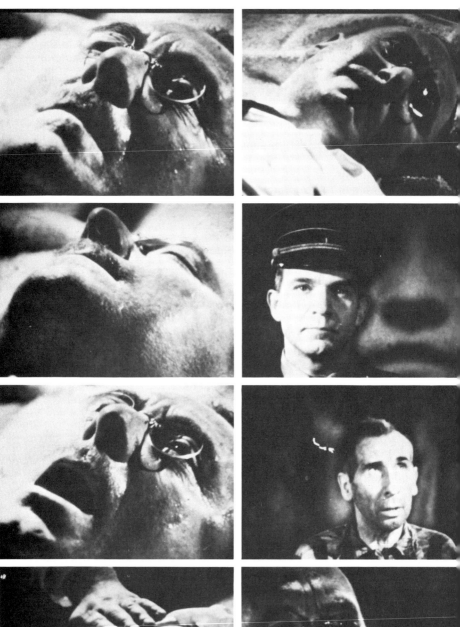
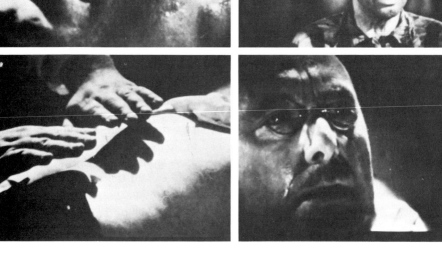

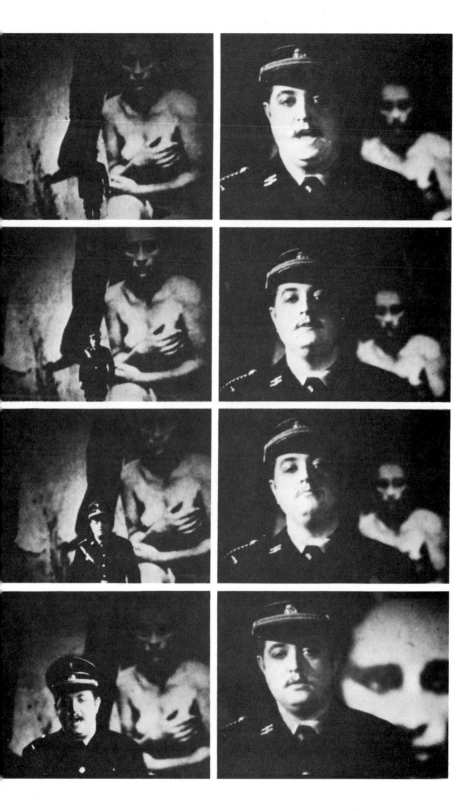

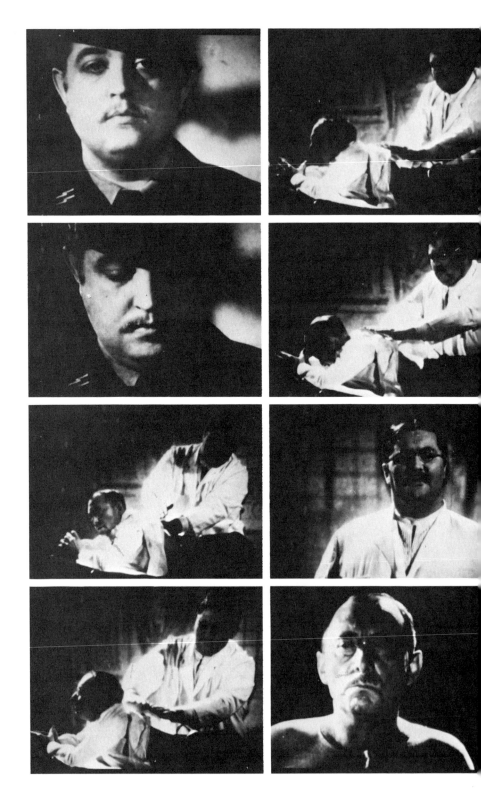

Hitler (continuing): ... *so that you may learn the details* ...

All German people, with few exceptions, fully realize that we will never be able, and would never have been able, to hold out ...

Hitler: ... *an entire clique forged a plot.*

through the bombings, through the strains of the fourth and perhaps the coming fifth and sixth years of the war if we still had this corroding plague in our nation.

Gentlemen, it is easy to speak the few words: The Jews must be exterminated.

Hitler: The bomb planted ... *by Colonel Count Stauffenberg* ... *critically injured* ...

For those, however, who have to carry it out, it is the harshest and most difficult thing that exists. You see, of course, it's Jews, that's quite clear, it's only Jews. But just recall yourselves how many people, even Party members, have addressed their famous petition to me or some agency, claiming that, naturally, all Jews are bastards, but that so-and-so alone is a decent Jew, and we shouldn't do anything to him.

Hitler: ... *continue to pursue it as I have done so far* ...

I venture to maintain that, judging by the number of petitions, the number of opinions, there were more decent Jews among us than the entire number that existed in the first place. We have, it seems, so many millions of people in Germany who all have their famous decent Jew that this number is already larger than the entire number of Jews.

Hitler: ... *has nothing whatsoever to do with the German Wehrmacht* ...
A very small group of criminal elements that will now be ruthlessly wiped out. This time we will settle accounts as we National Socialists are accustomed to doing. I am convinced that every decent officer ...

SECOND SS MAN: The era of Adolf Hitler will put Aryan-German mankind at a new beginning. This will not be the glow of the evening sun, it will be a new period of blossoming. Our globe is not so old and it has too long a way to go before the great world catastrophe to do without the creative Atlantic-Nordic way. This will, of course, not happen by itself. Hitler is our German Saviour, the god-man, the Aryan figure of light in the cosmic struggle of *Weltanschauung*, the karma of the Germanic, predestined for this world. This *Weltanschauung* struggle is like the struggle with the Huns in the period of tribal migrations, like the struggle with Islam in the Middle Ages, which was a racial and not a religious struggle. Our task includes the breeding of men, for the Grail of Aryan Blood has been sullied for centuries by proletarians, Bolsheviks, and subhumans, and it threatens to dry out the otherwise healthy womb of our people.

Hitler: I thank Providence and my Creator, not for keeping me alive; my life is my only concern and labor for my people. I thank him because he gave me the possibility of continuing to bear these concerns to the extent that I can make this consistent with my conscience.

CONCENTRATION CAMP GUARD (Johannes Buzalski): We had the right, the moral duty to our nation, to kill this nation which wanted to kill us. But we do not have the right to take even one fur, one watch, to enrich ourselves with even one mark or one cigarette.

I will never tolerate or stand by and watch a single point of rottenness set in; wherever it may form, we will burn it out together.

Hitler: Every German therefore, no matter who he may be, has the duty to deal relentlessly with these elements, either arrest them immediately . . . or strike them down immediately.

All in all, however, we have suffered no damage in our character, our souls, our essence, loyalty, obedience, fulfillment of duty, faith, combat patrol of the blood-notion.

Hitler: I see a warning finger of Providence here that I must continue my work and that I shall continue my work.

Felix Kersten continues giving Himmler his massage—this seen from various angles.

HIMMLER: I was extraordinarily interested to hear recently that when the Buddhist monks walk through the town in the evening, they carry a little bell in order to make the forest creatures that they might crush underfoot move aside, so that they may suffer no harm. Among us, however, every snail is trampled, every worm is crushed underfoot, prizes are offered for killing sparrows, and money is used to spur the children to murder harmless animals. Now, during the war, I cannot of course take any comprehensive steps in this respect. It would be completely misunderstood. But after the war I will issue the most rigorous laws for the protection of animals. In school, the children will be systematically taught to love animals, and I will give special police authority to the societies for the protection of animals.

Crowd noises.

Just as a man who has been away from home for a long time is welcomed and greeted upon his return by his wife, his children, and his friends at the threshold, thus too, when he someday leaves this life, he will be awaited at the threshold of the next life by his good deeds, the way a dear friend is by friends.

August 23, 1944, liberation of Chartres: Allons, enfants de la patrie . . .

MASSEUR (Martin Sperr): And what about the bad deeds? One can get alarmed if one has everything reckoned up for one precisely. In that case, I find divine grace a better way than this arithmetic example.

HIMMLER: But you have to pay for everything else in life down to the last penny. Why shouldn't you be presented with a bill here too? You can deal with it, even if you need another lifetime or two.

MASSEUR: Aren't you often alarmed yourself, Herr Reich Commander, when you sometimes consider what deeds you often have to do here and which will someday confront you?

Crowd noises—Chartres—Paris—the Liberation.

HIMMLER: One should not see things from petty, egocentric perspectives, one has to focus on the whole of the Germanic spirit, which also has its karma, after all. Someone has to sacrifice himself, even if this is very hard at times. One should not think of oneself. It is naturally more pleasant to deal with the flower beds of a state rather than the garbage heaps and waste disposal, but without this work the flower beds would not thrive. Furthermore, I try to find a balance for myself by helping wherever I can and doing good,

assisting the oppressed and getting rid of injustices. Do you believe that I am devoted heart and soul to the things that simply
have to be done for reasons of state? What wouldn't I give to be
Minister of Education and Religion like Rust and be able to devote
myself only to positive tasks.

I often wonder whether after the war I shouldn't suggest to the
Führer that he separate the position of the SS Reich Commander
from that of the chief of police. This would be along the Führer's
line, after he has made the SS Reich Commander the supreme
head of the Farmers' Defense Settlement, of the entire settlement
action. Perhaps this position could be combined with that of the
Minister of Education and Religion. That would not be a bad
solution at all, I would be totally absorbed by these positive tasks.
But our internal and external situation simply forced us to fuse
the SS Reich Commander and the chief of police, that was simply
a karma too, which I have to resign myself to and turn to my own
advantage.

*Himmler (secret speech to SS, Posen, 1943): Most of you must
know what it means if a hundred corpses are lying together, if five
hundred are lying there, or if a thousand are lying there. Experiencing all this and, aside from a few human foibles, managing to
remain decent: that is what has made us hard. This is an unwritten
and never-to-be-written page of glory.*

MASSEUR: I was astonished to hear so openly from Himmler how closely he linked his religious views to his personal destiny. I was just about to ask him a question, but Himmler waved me off. "Wait, first I want to read something very different to you." He picked up the Bhagavad-Gita, which he especially loved, and he quoted the following passage to me, and I asked him if I could write it down word for word: " 'As often as the human sense of justice and truth has vanished and injustice rules the world, I am born anew, that is the law. I have no desire for profit.' This passage fits the Führer like a glove," Himmler explained.

HIMMLER: He rose for us from the deepest misery, when the German nation could no longer go on. He is one of the great figures of light that keep arising for the Germanic spirit . . .

Hitler (on July 21, 1944): I therefore command at this time . . .

whenever it comes into deepest physical, intellectual, and spiritual misery. Goethe was such a figure in the area of the intellect, Bismarck in the political sphere . . .

. . . that no military agency, no commander of a squad, no soldier is to obey any order of these usurpers, that, on the contrary, everyone is obliged to either arrest the transmitter of such an order . . .

the Führer is such a figure in all areas, political, cultural, and military . . .

. . . or, in case of resistance, to bring him down on the spot. In order to establish definitive order, I have named H. Himmler, who is Reich Commander of the SS, to be the commander in chief of the domestic army.

He is predestined by the karma of the Germanic spirit to wage the struggle against the East and save the Germanic spirit for the world, one of the very great figures of light has found its incarnation in him.

Announcer (reporting on the liberation of Chartres, August 23, 1944): Vive le Général de Gaulle . . .

MASSEUR: Himmler expressed these ideas with great solemnity and forcefulness. Now I realized why Himmler occasionally described Hitler as a man whom people would piously look up to after centuries, as they had looked up to Christ. He not only saw in him a figure to whom, for purely practical considerations, one had to attach a religious myth in the struggle against the Church. He also regarded him as a figure from another world, the kind of figure who descends from there and brings help in times of crisis. Something of the Grail Knight, of the Parsifal theme, clung to him. If Himmler lived in this state of mind, he also had to view himself as the reincarnation of some great man out of German history.

I also asked him about this and he replied defensively: "One doesn't like to talk about oneself personally in such matters. I have done a great deal of thinking about that. But I have not come to any conclusion."

Today I conversed at length with Brandt about this last matter, and he told me that he knows for sure that the Reich Commander regards himself as a reincarnation of Henry the Fowler. He knows Henry's story better than anyone else's, said Brandt, and he regards his East European settlement as one of the great deeds in Germanic history. Himmler, according to Brandt, knows that in his own ranks he is nicknamed "King Henry" and also "the Black Duke," and he doesn't mind at all. At the Brunswick Memorial Assembly in honor of Henry, Himmler gave a deeply moving address about this great man. Brandt found it quite in order that a man should take a lofty model and try to emulate it, and if he even goes so far as to identify with this image, then all the better.

Himmler gets up and dresses.

HIMMLER: Certainly, the Jews will suffer a great deal. But what did the Americans once do? The Indians wanted to go on living on their hereditary soil, and the Americans exterminated them in the most dreadful way. It is the curse of the great that they have to walk over corpses and stop at nothing to create new life. But we have to create new life, and the area must be sterilized, otherwise it cannot thrive. This will be a great burden for me. Retribution strides relentlessly through the history of the world. It is a historical fact that the kingdom of the Jews cost millions of lives, many more millions than there are Jews in the entire world. These dead demand their atonement. Even the old Jewish dictum "an eye for an eye, a tooth for a tooth" speaks of this atonement. Originally, I had other plans, but the necessity of atonement and defense grew beyond me. It is the old tragic conflict between desire and duty. I am experiencing only now how terrible it can be.

Please leave me alone.

French sound document: . . . Paris . . . libéré . . .

MASSEUR: You can't stand the strain, Herr Reich Commander. I need forty-two Dutchmen who are condemned to death, plus three Estonians, four Latvians, one Belgian, two Swedes, three Frenchmen, and these Russians.

De Gaulle: . . . Paris . . .

You believe in the immortality of the soul in the blood. Just as you are Henry the Fowler, so too Crown Prince Rudolf as an incarnation suffered every last sin of Caligula through acute torments of the feelings. How do you, as Himmler, plan to atone for your cruel actions if you do not begin today? Be grateful. I take you seriously.

Paris, August 26, 1944: Te Deum in the Cathedral of Notre Dame.
Voice: Paris est libéré.

Himmler suddenly bows to Kersten, across the massage table, and kisses his masseur's hand.

HIMMLER: You are wrong if you believe that the screams of the victims are wiping out my men. That is not the worst source of disease. They have much more trouble with their virtues, with rigor, their loyalty to the nation, with comradeship, their Prussianism. They can barely cope with these demands. But they have learned to be strong, to be loyal to their oath to Germany, Germany is Hitler, and Hitler is the world.

All homosexuals are condemned. SS penal court, then concentration camp, and finally shot while trying to escape.

In 1935 alone, 60,000, including Jews, removed from the SS.

Albert Camus, August 8, 1944: . . . Ce jour a bouleversé . . . se lire sur les visages des parisiens et aussi . . . et plus encore peut-être la nôtre et la tâche des hommes de la résistance.*
"Marseillaise."

●

Himmler's masseur and his astrologer meet (this scene is historically documented). The décor is a photo of Wewelsburg, in Westphalia, which Himmler made the center of his new Reich and of his Black Order.

MASSEUR: Make the stars favorable to us.

ASTROLOGER: That I cannot do.

MASSEUR: You will save thousands. All the concentration camps are to be liquidated in the end, and we will stop the war prematurely if Himmler dissociates himself. World history is in your hands.

ASTROLOGER: World history is in the stars. You want business, business with the stars, business with history, business with humanity.

MASSEUR: We live in a time in which business is humane compared with the ideas, a time in which corruption can save lives, thousands, hundreds of thousands. We have to act. Just tell me what country you want to go to afterward, what passport, what air destination, how many dollars. I have friends everywhere, but you will first have to be free. Tell Himmler my future, as the future of the stars. The stars do not deny us the right to bargain.

ASTROLOGER: One does not bargain with the stars. They are not susceptible to human corruption. I will not bargain with truth, with the art of the heavenly laws.

---

* Translation: . . . This day has upset . . . can be read on the faces of the Parisians and also . . . and even more perhaps ours and the task of the men of the Resistance.

One must be strong enough to see this. To understand our limits and proper happiness, the order of the stars.

The stars above me and the moral law within me.

Albert Camus: . . . avec un état social où la classe dirigeante a trahi sur ses devoirs et a manqué à la foi d'intelligence et de coeur, nous voulons réaliser sans délai une démocratie populaire et ouvrière. Dans cette alliance, la démocratie apportera les principes de la liberté et le peuple la foi et le courage sans lesquels la liberté . . .*

●

Himmler with an SS group, eating a meal in ornate décor.

HIMMLER: Our meatless day today, and generally, I don't like to see any animal suffering, I can't stand the smell of blood. You may laugh. Thank you for the book *Arthasastra*. A textbook of cruelty and falseness. Yes, the Indians.

ASTROLOGER: It contains all the wisdom necessary for a statesman.

The four castes, the four phases of life. A hierarchy like that of the planets. Otherwise, everything will collapse.

HIMMLER: I am a Buddhist. Yes indeed, that too.

Astrology is a royal art.

I undertake all great actions at certain phases of the moon, an old rule for peasants. And I believe in good and bad spirits.

I am sorry that I had to lock you up.

But things couldn't go on that way.

Concentration camp until the end of the war for all astrologers, like Frederick II, who also ordered the clergy to preach from the pulpits that his war was for a holy and just cause. And what are Stalin and Eisenhower doing? Crusade for freedom! Well, there you are! And Churchill? What things he has said, that cynic. But the blood-and-tears business was good. A thing like that always works and it's true. That's how a man wins wars, all the way to his memoirs.

They get up from the table. All leave. Himmler and his astrologer remain behind.

* Translation: . . . with a social state in which the ruling class has betrayed its duties and lacked both intelligence and heart, we want to bring about without delay a popular, working-class democracy. In this alliance, democracy will bring the principles of freedom, and the people will bring faith and courage, without which freedom . . .

Stettin, February 28, 1945.

Operational command group Weichsel. Announcer: First Lieutenant Morero, technician, Sergeant Biehl, combat zone Stettin. From the opposite bank of the Oder River, the grenades howl into the city. The explosions tear huge holes in the roof ridges of the upper stories. Stones and splinters rain down upon the asphalt. Our batteries are answering.

Explosions . . . Artillery burst.

At the exit roads in the dead angle of the whizzing grenades, refugees are standing with suitcases, pillows, and bedding. Some just with a small knapsack. Military policemen are stopping the vehicles, and every available space is being used. Trucks and military cars are piled sky-high with the last belongings of our fellow Germans, who have fled the enemy, often amid unspeakable suffering.

Himmler and his astrologer enter another room. Himmler closes all doors. They are alone. The two men sit down. Changing projections in the style of the period. Pictures of the sea and an eagle, a violinist, the countryside, peasants plowing, a mass grave.

Recollections of the grand period: Berlin, the flag processions at night, the 9th of November, celebration in Munich with smoking pylons, etc.

We hear on the sound track the final appeals to the Volkssturm [territorial army made up of men and boys unfit for military service] and noises of the bombing of Berlin.

Announcer, October 18, 1944: The organization and command of the German Volkssturm is to be taken over in every province by the provincial governor . . .

Radio station signals.

Radio announcer, BBC, October 21, 1944: The city of Aachen no longer exists. That is the price of drawing out the war . . .

The Reich Commander of the SS as commander in chief of the surrogate army responsible for the military organization of the Volkssturm . . .

HIMMLER: For testing the day, the birth data of a high-level minion.

Radio announcer: Attention, attention! This is the command post of the First Antiaircraft Division, Berlin.

The reported bomber formations are in the Hanover-Brunswick area. We will return.

ASTROLOGER: You don't have to worry about him. He'll betray everything, flee, they'll catch up with him.

HIMMLER: You are talking about SS General Fegelein. Be careful.

ASTROLOGER: You had an accident on December 9.

HIMMLER: That's right. I was driving the car myself that day. It was dark, I drove off the road and plunged down forty yards, it was a slope.

ASTROLOGER: You landed on tracks. A train was just coming along. You barely managed to get away. As you know, I found out Mussolini's whereabouts during his imprisonment.

HIMMLER: Someone else.

ASTROLOGER: He won't fall victim to a murderer. A woman will play a certain part at his end in April '45. Hitler.

HIMMLER: I could easily lock him up. I'll send out Berger with an armored division, and we'll easily take care of the rest. A woman, in April '45. I don't know. The next page, please!

ASTROLOGER: A series of interesting constellations. Mars in the sixth field, that is to say, activity in the war as commander in chief of an army group. Then Jupiter's favorable aspect toward the moon, Uranus and Mars designate the very high ascent in his life, but that can't change anything in his fateful end. He will betray his best friend. His death will not occur through someone else's hand or through heroic deeds or sharp weapons.

HIMMLER: You're talking about me.

ASTROLOGER: Born on October 7, 1900, calculated time of birth: exactly 4:28:34 a.m., Pisces. Under royal protection, father in royal service, a man with a constantly wavering character, Saturn in the field of profession. Position in the world not through his own abilities but through constellations—I would say, of the stars. Paying for a guilt until the seventh member of the family and the nation—you have a second brother—who wasn't born. Dead. Aborted. Critical disease of the lung area. Bodily defects, weak heart, stomach. Strong attachment to mother, guilt feelings for this weakness, always wants to remain a little boy.
Lack, yes—lack of will power, servility, need to lean on others,

and courage. An encouragement tendency to conquer everything. Elitist consciousness. Great self-love. Masturbation tendency, virile impotence, prodigal-son type. Suffers from dreariness. Yearning: to be a severe father.

HIMMLER: I know the secret reproach—for instance, Heydrich's —that I'm not really equal to my tasks, too soft, listless, unmilitary, an intellectual crackpot with a quirk about the Germanic.

Heydrich was different in that way. Severe, hard as steel, and he always played the violin beautifully, once he played Mozart for me. His Jewish heritage always kept breaking through, and then he was ruthless, nasty, ice-cold—I didn't need all that pomp.

I see corpses at night. Whole armies. In long processions, corpses without names. Emperor Charles of Untersberg, Barbarossa's crusades, the entire West. Henry the Fowler is there, so am I. That's bad, I know. We have to stick together, you, Kersten, and Schellenberg, and I. What should I do? Hitler will find out. The stars. They know everything. What should I do?

Himmler (secret speech in Posen, 1943): Whatever happens to the Russians, whatever happens to the Czechs makes no difference whatsoever to me. The good blood of our species that the nations have—we'll get it by kidnapping their children if necessary. Altogether, even when we say we performed this most difficult task out of love for our people, and we were not damaged within, in our souls, in our characters.

ASTROLOGER: The stars cannot take over actions, Herr Himmler. If you ask me, Schellenberg should negotiate with Sweden, Switzerland. Hand over all the concentration camps, don't blow them up. The decision lies with you, the Reich Commander of the SS and the Minister of the Interior of the German Reich. It is the freedom of your constraint.

HIMMLER: Yes indeed, talk to Eisenhower, he reads our newspapers. He knows me well enough, he knows what we are fighting for, Patton is looking for the Lance of Longinus. Yes indeed, the Grail. We will have it forever. Democracy and the Grail, impossible. I will not die fighting. Through sharp weapons, tell everyone, I'm Henry the Fowler. I always have been and I still am, I'm the Black Knight. I have released all concentration camps from total annihilation, for Kersten, in writing, through personal negotiations with the Jewish World Congress, through Kersten. That is a betrayal of the Führer, he says if we cannot revolutionize our Reich and the world, then at least our enemies should not triumph.

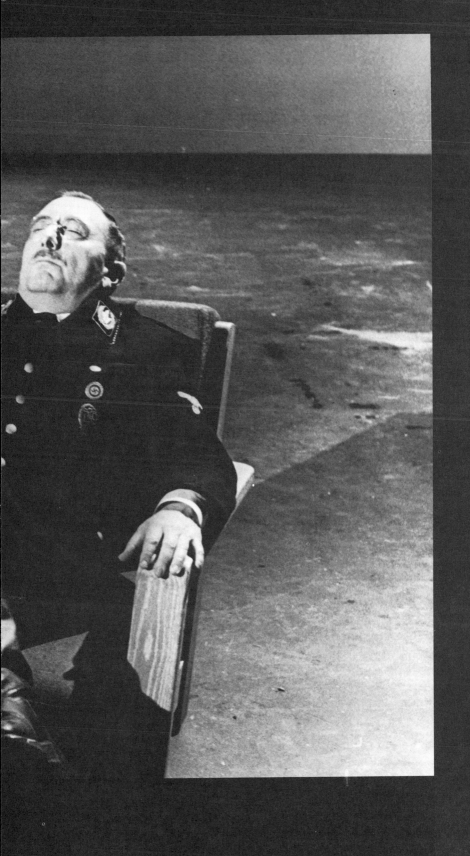

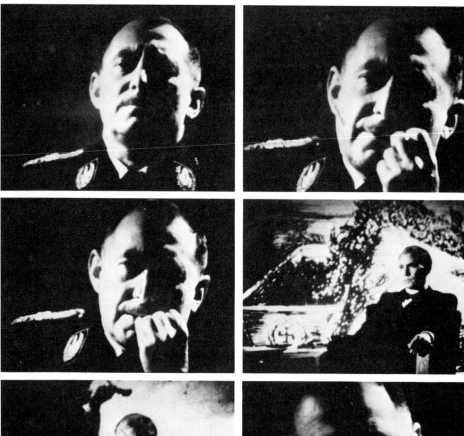
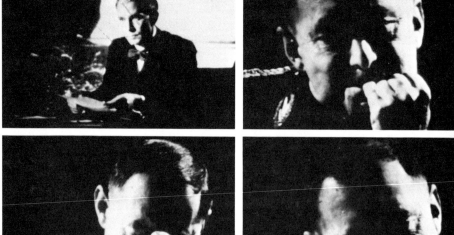

That is logical. He signed—Kersten—with the words: "In the name of humanity." I had to hesitate, am I inhuman? And he laughed. We are always misunderstood. We just happen to have a different concept of human and humanity; that has nothing to do with humanism and the Christian God. Socialism, yes, but altogether different. We had to magically—this is a secret—sacrifice our neighbor, our great opposite, the Jew, the chosen people, the holy renegade of the past, he had to be sacrificed by the other chosen holy people, the Germanic people, in gigantic slaughter rites of the present and the future. You will see, in order to create the New Man, a proud, conquering, rustic, decent man.

It's over. Over, the stupid word. I too believe in the immortality of the soul. And yet I don't understand anything anymore.

The curse of the universe is certain for us. A divine laughter, as revenge. Soul, yes indeed. The soul dwells in the blood forever and we are its reawakeners. Can we go under, can we lose, after so many deeds? For immortality.

•

Transition to Joseph Goebbels and, in the image, the ovens of Auschwitz.

Roll call for the martyrs of November 9, 1923. Slow playing of the "Horst Wessel Song."

Joseph Goebbels, Christmas Eve, December 24, 1944: Forward over graves! The dead are more powerful armies than we on the land, than we on the sea. They stride ahead of us. They departed from us in the din of the battles of war. In the roaring of the bells of victorious peace, they will return to us. We owe the Reich more to them than to any living people. That is the only demand they have left for us. It is our duty to fulfill that demand. Let us therefore keep our hands and hearts prepared; the world will then, as the poet says, be soon renewed, like a newborn child.

•

The following text is accompanied by projections of Hitler's Obersalzberg house in various states, from its reconstruction to its bombing and final blowing up. The scale of the image varies.

Paul Giesler, reciting a poem by Dietrich Eckart, November 8, 1944:

> *Storm, storm, storm.*
> *Ring the bells from tower to tower.*
> *Ring hard enough to strike sparks.*

Judas appears, to conquer the Reich.
Ring till the ropes turn bloody red.
Ring till the earth arches up
Under the thunder of saving revenge.
Woe to the nation that dreams today.
Germany, awake!

Obersalzberg today. Peter Kern, as a present-day Hitler fan named Ellerkamp, stands at the wall of one of the last Obersalzberg houses, a wall covered with names. He introduces himself.

ELLERKAMP: Walls are nice. They tell stories. You just can't imagine. I've seen a lot of things, I can tell a lot of stories. But you don't know that. You're still young, as my father always said. I've gone through heaven and hell, and my heart was always in it. In the past, we were always together! There was something like a sense of togetherness. Movies, I tell you, people had taste back then, powerful stories for the people. We made a lot of money. But today only a few single people jerking off in the movie theater. You can see a thing or two. I could tell you some stories. But you're still such a young man. *The Heroes' Square in Vienna*, now that was a movie, hah. I screened it myself, in the Bellaria Theater, 1938. It was all a gigantic bottle of new wine.

He sings: Yes, we are Lichtentalers,
        We like to drink a glass of wine,
        We're no shnorrers, we pay our bills.

> But make sure the wine is divine!
> A drop like this just can't be mixed.
> It has to be real, true wine.
> Refreshing the body and the soul,
> But it has to be divine, halloooo!

Yes, yes, I wouldn't have missed those days. I'm a victim, an idealist. Just look at me, I'm just a shell of my former self, the eyes, the hair, the figure. I've seen so many things. I could tell you so many stories. But you, you're still a young man. What do you know about it anyway!

During the following speech by Hitler, which seems almost to come out of the walls like a memory, Kern as Ellerkamp walks through the ruins of Obersalzberg, for instance the SS garage, with a transistor radio under his arm. From the last act of *Aïda* comes:

> . . . *the stone has closed above us* . . .
> *Farewell, O earth, O vale of tears.*

Hitler, November 8, 1943, Munich: And then I want to say something to those people who talk about religion. I too am religious, indeed very ardently religious. And I believe that Providence weighs man, and that the man who cannot endure the trials and our trials of Providence, who crumbles under them—I believe that he is not chosen by Providence for anything great. I believe that this is a necessity given in nature, that only the fittest survive a selection, and I would like to state that calmly here. If my own nation were to crumble in such a trial, I could not shed a single tear, it would not have deserved any better, it would be its own destiny that it has brought upon itself. But I will never, never believe that, for, thank God, I have gotten to know the German people, not in the milieu of the politicians, the big industrialists,

*or our so-called mental capacities, I have gotten to know the
German people, thank God, in the mass of its phenomena, and this
mass of our nation is sound, as sound as a bell.*

Ellerkamp in the just barely preserved garage under Hitler's destroyed
house.

ELLERKAMP: In the morning, a deep silence always lay over the
mountain farm. I had been asked not to take a bath before noon
since the concrete structure amplified the noise, and the Führer
needed his rest in the morning since he fell asleep late. Everything
was virtually lifeless. I tiptoed to breakfast.

He came to breakfast only seldom, and if he did come, then
naturally with Eva. He would then drink two cups of milk or bitter
cocoa. Eva asked for strong coffee and butter.

*Radio announcer: Attention, everybody! Once, again, under the
impression of . . .*

It was only toward noon,

*. . . everything is to . . . All comrades at the most remote . . .
bulletin . . . far-reaching experience . . .*

when the sun stood over the Kehlstein, the "Grand Hotel" awoke
from its numbness.

Attention! I am once again calling . . .

The cars halted with screeching brakes in front of the garage, the
fat Mercedes autos would then drive in. The SS presented arms.

| 195

Attention! I am once again calling Stalingrad.
This is Stalingrad, this is the front along the Volga.
Attention! The Lapland front once again!
This is a barracks in the Finnish woods.

The most important receptions in Obersalzberg were for the Duke of Windsor, Prime Minister Chamberlain, Lord Rothermere, Schuschnigg, Mussolini, Balbo, Ciano. Now those were gentlemen for you.

Attention! The South of France once again. This is a military airfield in the South of France. And once again . . .

Ah yes, Hitler, who put the construction work in the hands of the Munich architect Roderick Fick, did not let him tear down Wachenfeld House, no, he had him build around it. Yes, the way you build a cathedral around a chapel.

The camera follows Ellerkamp as he walks across the now overgrown terraces and the places where Hitler's rooms used to be. We hear his voice off-camera.

The first floor had additional rooms, including the kitchen and pantry, the vestibule and the guardroom. The Führer lived on the second floor. It had a long corridor with huge paintings on the walls instead of windows, vases, knickknacks, statues everywhere, but nothing was really uniform. You could tell these were presents from all over the world, they were certainly very expensive, but somehow they didn't fit.

Announcer: The Navy and the Army in the South of France! This is . . .
Attention! Attention! Calling the . . .
. . . on the Atlantic coast in the South of France.
Attention! Calling Leningrad! This is the front line outside of Leningrad and . . .
Attention! Calling the Channel coast!
These are security units of the Navy in the Channel!
Attention! Calling the Caucasus front again! This is the front line in the Caucasus area. Attention! U-boat captains in the Atlantic!
This is a U-boat base on the Atlantic.
Attention! Catania! This is the Mediterranean front and Africa!
Attention! Zakopane! The wounded men in the army convalescent

home in the Tatras greet their comrades on all fronts! Attention!
Calling Crete!
This is Crete! . . .
Attention! Calling the Black Sea port! . . . We ask you, our old
German veterans, to join in the carol.

There is a new background image. Ellerkamp stands on the site of the
Hitler house, in an overgrown area of woods and bushes; a quick cut
to the onetime fireplace room on the same spot, with a large table, on
which war plans were made, in front of the huge window, the panorama
window, and the surrounding mountains.

Christmas Mass broadcast changes into Johann Strauss's Fledermaus
waltzes and Wagner.

ELLERKAMP: The grand salon, especially impressive. I particularly admired the tapestries. Eva, who always wanted to appear
very educated, said that they were genuine "Gobelins d'Aubusson."
Who knows if that's true.

Ah, I haven't even introduced myself: SS Section Leader Fritz
Ellerkamp, servant and film projectionist, right? You have to
picture it like this: whenever I screened a movie, this Gobelin
d'Aubusson automatically slid up and a screen came down. And
on the opposite side, the paneling moved and uncovered the
opening for the movie projector. I stood behind it and ran it. The

grand salon is furnished in Gothic style. I particularly admired this little table with the finest mosaic work, and the fireplace, which Eva said was a gift from Mussolini, yes indeed.

Very few people ever set eyes on Hitler's bedroom. It was furnished very simply: a wardrobe in Bavarian style, a couple of books scattered around, and a simple bed. A door led out to the balcony, which no one was allowed to enter, except for Eva, of course. I was told, you see, that Hitler liked to watch the stars at night.

He sings: Yes, my heart fills up with joy
Where the Alpine roses grow
And the gentian blossoms.
Where the Alpine roses grow
And the gentian blossoms.

On what was the terrace of Hitler's house, now as overgrown as a forest, Ellerkamp sits at a broken beer-garden table with his transistor radio and eats his lunch, telling stories (allegedly) from memory. Period sounds emerge from the radio.

Number 175. They always played the same records. Usually, the people at the afternoon tea knew the numbers of the records by heart. When Hitler said, for instance: "*Aïda*, last act: The Stone Has Closed upon Us," one of the guests instantly called out the catalogue number to me: number 175.

Aside from Wagner, Bruckner, Beethoven, Strauss, a couple of lieder by Hugo Wolf, Verdi, Hitler allowed only operettas. He had the habit of whistling to the music, sometimes even singing along. Eva once pointed out to him that he whistled off key, to which he said: "I'm not whistling off key, the composer pulled a blunder here."

Yes, yes, music, blood! Hitler developed his own theory about his blood. He told me that he had once had high blood pressure, and so he had applied leeches. When I told him that I can't stand the little beasts because . . . they look horrible, why, they're so unappetizing, they're disgusting, isn't that so, well, he said to me: "Don't say that, they're nice little creatures, they do me a lot of good." Later, he let Dr. Morell draw his blood, of course, oh well, it's a lot more comfortable, a lot cleaner and more hygienic.

Ha, once, when he saw us eating meat, he told me, in regard to Dr. Morell's drawing his blood: "I'll have them make blood sausage from my superfluous blood; after all, you like meat so much."

I do like blood sausage.

198

Front-line cabaret (song):
Eduard, he is so old, he's got a beard.
I told him: Just listen, you.
Why don't you earn your living as Santa Claus . . .

Why are you wiggling around on your chair? Are you bored? You don't have to tell me anything, I know everything, I've read all the books, all the biographies by secretaries, by Krause, by Linge, I know everything.

Mother said to Hansel sweet:
Would you like a little brother,
Or a little sister?

Even by him.
Very private and intimate. A story from his childhood.
"I never loved my father," he told me, "but I feared him all the more. He had a quick temper and he often hit me. My mother was always very scared for me. Once, when I read in Karl May that it was a sign of courage not to show your pain, I resolved not to let out a sound the next time.

Soldiers perform for soldiers!

And when it happened again—I can see it now, my mother standing outside, at the door, very scared . . .

. . . and ready to sacrifice in the hardest of all fights, never losing courage, for the victory of our people.

I counted every stroke.

. . . and tomorrow they will return to the trenches at the front and . . .

My mother thought I'd gone crazy when I came to her radiantly proud and said: Father hit me thirty-two times! It was odd, from that day on I didn't have to repeat my experiment, my father never touched me again."
Hitler told me that story. The next day, I promptly bought a book by Karl May.
Later, when life dealt harshly with him, Hitler had great respect for his father, for he had worked his way up from an orphan boy to a customs official. By dint of thrift and hard work, he even managed to buy himself a small farm.
Well, that's how you win wars, with Karl May and a strict father, right?

Song: Silent night, holy night,
All is calm, all is bright
Round yon virgin mother and child.
Holy infant, so tender and mild,
Sleep in heavenly peace,
Sleep in heavenly peace.
(repeated)

Well, now I've had enough, and the skin is for the dog. Blondie, Blondie [whistles], Blondie . . .

Now they are singing on the Arctic Ocean and in Finland, and now they are singing in . . . and now we are switching in all the others . . . Leningrad, France, North Africa, and now everyone is joining in . . .

At an early time, Hitler was presented with a dog, a Scotch terrier. He named him Burli. Blondie.

Yes, he just loved playing with the dog. But no one was allowed to watch.

No one was allowed to see the dog tearing up files and hopping around on the armchair, and whenever I was away, he was nice again, he called him. Burli, that's what he named him, Burli, Burli . . .

Blondie! . . .

And then the official photographer wanted to take a photograph, "Führer with Burli." He wouldn't hear of it. He said: "No, that's not suitable for a Führer, a German shepherd would be more like it."

Well, the skin is for . . . Blondie, Blondie, look, sausage, Blondie! . . . Blondie, here, Blondie, c'mon, c'mon, eat nicely, eat nicely, you're my doggie, aren't you. The Führer's dog. Yes, he's a good dog, Blondie, you're a good dog, sit, that's right, sit.

But that's not Burli.

Wow, this is nice, like Christmas.

Radio network signal of the Deutschland Radio Network: Üb' immer Treu und Redlichkeit.

Hitler was deeply affected by Christmas. He couldn't look at a Christmas tree. I asked him why he never went to any Christmas parties or gave one himself. He said: "No, my mother died on a Christmas Eve, under the Christmas tree."

He sings: Deutschland, Deutschland über alles,

Über alles in der Welt.
Wenn es stets zum Schutz und Trutze,
Brüderlich zusammenhält.
Von der Maas bis an die Memel,
Von der Etsch bis an den Belt,
Deutschland, Deutschland, über alles,
Über alles in der Welt.

He puts his face in his hands and weeps.

•

Lap dissolve to close-up of Hitler as ventriloquist's dummy on Harry Baer's knees. We are inside the Black Maria. Music: *Die Götterdämmerung.* A dialogue, which is really a monologue, of course. As Baer talks, he undresses the Hitler puppet, who is wearing many layers of costume.

HITLER PUPPET (Harry Baer; voice off): I don't want to go on like this. You're treating me like an incubus crouching on your chest while you sleep.

HARRY BAER: Business, nothing but show business. Everything for art, for the film.

HITLER PUPPET: You know me. A dangerous game.

BAER: An old pattern, the devil comes to have a nice conversation. Says a few true things. Horror, exorcism, inquisition.

HITLER PUPPET: True things that no one will normally admit, cynical. You'll be amazed if you, if all of you, can stand it.

BAER: A game.

HITLER PUPPET: If you can stand it.

BAER: Hitler as the devil and in the full, burning house, the devil as moralist. That's what he's always been.

HITLER PUPPET: The devil as Hitler. And Hitler as a moralist, warning people, that's what he always was.

BAER: Imagine me as a sad Jew, from Germany, weeping because I was not allowed to join in, uninvited, even though we were always the most loyal nationalists. Relentless and tricky and loving

| 201

my homeland, think of Heydrich, how good he was for you. In his heart of hearts, every Jewish émigré from Germany is first and foremost a German.

How silly. Of you not to realize that. Silly. Silly of you not to play with that, always stopping five minutes after twelve. You people just can't be left alone. With Germany. Just look at what you did to our country. You ruined UFA. It took them twenty years to make decent movies again. You've done everything wrong. Everything!

American radio series: The adventures of Superman, faster than a speeding bullet . . .

Ha, just look at you. Like Murnau, Lubitsch, Sternberg. Like Fritz Lang.

HITLER PUPPET: They accepted you, back then, at the academy in Vienna. You could have become an artist. An architect or a filmmaker, to build worlds in art. And I, I had to produce my world in politics. You did not sacrifice yourself to do the dirty business of politics. I didn't goldbrick, and I did my job to the best of my ability, according to our faculties, our old tradition. And now the taboos. Friends, let us praise. Praise the progress of the world from the other world of death. Praise from Adolf Hitler on this world after me. What is the brief span of a human life against the eternity of my victory afterward? Can I not be content with immortality? For instance, the map of Europe, what would it be without me? No one before me has changed the West as thoroughly as we have. We brought the Russians all the way to the Elbe and we got the Jews their state. And, after a fashion, a new colony for the U.S.A.—just ask Hollywood about its export markets. I know the tricks better than any of you, I know what to say and do for the masses. I am the school of the successful democrat. Just look around, they are in a fair way to take over our legacy. Each in his own way.

This is Tarzan, the lord of the jungle . . .

The Soviet workers' state has cost a million lives so far. Stalin, that is the Russian revenge of the goyim, the non-believers, against the Jewish revolution? His purges still live today, all the way to Prague.

It is simply brilliant to lock up opponents as mentally ill, in madhouses, people who are against repression in the satellites,

East Germany, Czechoslovakia, Hungary, or Poland. One must not think any longer in terms of national borders if one speaks from the afterlife. The main things are ideas, progress, modern politics, the future of the world. The power of the stronger, which, today, is money, youth, majority. The issue is not Germany. People like me want to change the world. And the Germany of the Third Reich was merely the Faustian prelude in the theater. You are the heirs. Worldwide.

On November 10, 1975, the United Nations resolved by a two-thirds majority, quite openly, that Zionism is a form of racism and racial discrimination. They were all unanimous, black and white, East and West. The majority.

Who knows what evil lurks in the hearts of men? The Shadow knows, hahahaha . . .

And I praise Idi Amin, Africa's spokesman and my venerator. He was received by the Pope, isn't that something? And in front of the UN, Arafat, the Arab, with his gun in his pocket. The same UN in which 110 out of the 159 states violate human rights— 110 out of 159 torture and murder, which is why, at every vote, they vote for inhumanity, by majority, quite democratic.

I also have to praise the United States, where the advocates of capital punishment are constantly on the increase.

Courage, now! Only the extermination of the American Indian

permitted feats of progress, and only the radical annihilation of
the Russian aristocracy and bourgeois culture guaranteed the
victory of the proletariat. Everyone struggling, straining, working
in camps, reeducating, murdering, helping others. Praises for the
new China, which we know so little about, with its mass happiness
and laughter, and praises for the whole of Africa, learning from
us, and Cambodia—who counts the dead after the victory of the
Reds—and Vietnam, and Cuba, and Chile since the victory of the
rightists.

And the systematic torture- and killer-units in Brazil, and Argen-
tina and now Italy's kidnappers and South Africa. Things are
going forward. The Arabs are already teaching our German revolutionaries on the terrorist front how to use weapons and shock
troops. And the best pupils of our desert foxes, the brave nation
of the Israelis, finally seem cleansed by the fire of our hell, to do
their own deeds. And in the United States? Nothing about gas at
Auschwitz on American TV. It would damage the American oil
industry and everything having to do with oil. You see, we did
win, in bizarre ways. In America.

. . . Superman . . .

We also have to praise Germany's East, I will not be petty,
with the bloody red in the philistine banner of progress, East
Germany is again at the top of its world. A state of the future in

cultural politics, a generation ahead of its time. They said so themselves. Progress from Germany.

> *Song: The world's decaying bones now tremble*
> *Because of the coming war.*
> *We overcame the terror:*
> *A great victory was ours,*
> *And we will keep on marching,*
> *Till everything to pieces is hurled,*
> *For today our Germany belongs to us,*
> *And tomorrow the entire world!*

The true model of Germany. The world shall be cured by German ways, old traditions in old uniforms with a love of reality in art, which we also liked to teach them, condemning the decadence of people who thought differently. Praise, praise, praise.

It's really gigantic, simply fencing everything in, with a wall and barbed wire and our guns, everything a giant ghetto, with concentration camps superfluous, surrounded by people whom they call "national" and "popular" and "army," who simply shoot at anybody who wants to leave, mow them down like rabbits, merely because they want to get away from the happiness of the functionaries.

Fifty million marks income a year for selling out enemies of the state. I could have learned from them, my best pupils in

Prussia even today. But I still had the masses, the people behind me, the only man who was really elected democratically, ladies and gentlemen, loved by the majority and virtually carried by the will of the people.

And in the West what remains of our Germany? I greet the terrorists and anarchists, we started that small too, in exactly the same way. They drive new supporters to us. And long live the women's movement, the new racism, worldwide, but most radical here, with no distinctions, if we are not in favor of motherhood, then we are simply against it, so long as we win, relentless and ruthless.

What do the German Chancellor and the unions say, and everyone else: unemployment is our biggest problem, getting rid of it is worth any sacrifice. *Any?* I know all about that and I can tell you how to do it. A state in which not even the executioners would be unemployed, if they still existed. Hah. And I tell you: It won't work without sacrifices. But where do we start? Do you see? To live on as before, without changes, that is your goal. But you people want to be elected. In your view, destruction proceeds from population growth rates.

But it was stupid to abolish the VW beetle. The symbol of our virtues. And I tell you, you will still be thinking about it.

But Obersalzberg is doing well, I see, even as an empty space, like Ludwig's castles now, my film documents from the newsreels are getting prices like the most expensive pop shows. The Russians took the stones of the Reich Chancellery for their monument in Treptow, and they thereby took my spirit along, the fear and curses of the victims and the stormy jubilation of my supporters. And the Americans took the rockets from Peenemünde and they used the atomic bomb first. Your Auschwitz, bravo.

But the world is a cesspool. Europe's eagles are dying out, they only survive in Africa. During the fifty-six days of his world cruise, Thor Heyerdahl could not wash in the sea on forty-three days. Is this the world you hold up against mine? Pardon me. Hitler as the German philistine's wonder man. And nothing else?

Millions in oil bribes and Lockheed money for your politicians. Yes, that's perfectly all right. But where is the great line, the conception of the great architect, the consistent architecture?

I am not talking about the cunning of corruption, the shady compromises of the functionaries and shopkeeper nations, I am frankly speaking about the logic of this century, its art of politics, which frightens you because of the consistency in the *Gesamtkunstwerk* of the masses, socialism and progress with parades and demonstrations, which give the masses their shine. We need the modern political artist who will create the masterpiece.

Die Götterdämmerung.

So long as Wagner's music is played, I will not be forgotten. I've made sure of that. Branded forever in the history of Wagnerian music. The source of our, the source of my strength. Everything is going according to plan after all. And we did win, on all fronts and everywhere, in a finer way. Only in a different costume. Just recall the new words: "society" instead of "Fatherland," "national ideology" instead of "philosophy," "functionary" instead of "human being," "conviction" instead of "conscience," "objective constraints" instead of "quality," "concrete" instead of "correct," "display" instead of "fairness," "educational policies" and "leisure-time industry" instead of "culture," "satisfaction of needs" instead of "happiness." Germany as schoolteacher for the world.

Economy in East and West, together with the Japanese. Leisure-time tourism makes us work too hard, like ants, a somewhat gentler world domination than my methods, a bitter knowledge. Everyone fights with any means! Only I am the bogeyman of the world. And so I took it upon myself, if only the ideas survive in us. Everyone bears guilt. But who is closer to God than the guilty man? And what about a time without God? When we ourselves have deposed him.

BAER: Thus spake the devil. In the end cynical and moral? Or rather, on the contrary, quite human. Living as the Grand Inquisitor in the world of the present. Full of praise on all sides. His legacy has long since been taken over in other ways, in the most various ways.

HITLER PUPPET: And yet, in their banality, finding no homeland anymore, either in the divine or in the devil. Long live mediocrity, freedom, and equality for the international average. Among third-class people interested only in the annual profit increase or a higher salary, destroying themselves, relentlessly, ruthlessly, moving toward their end and what an end. Without me! Bravo. They are liquidating themselves, only slower, right? Thus spake the cynic, and he is always right.

Die Götterdämmerung. Fade-out over the close-up of Harry Baer with his eyes closed.

As at the start of the film and the ending of Part One and Part Two, the child's head appears and we see the closing title of Part Three: *The End of a Winter's Tale.* We hear the slow movement of Mozart's Piano Concerto in D Minor, as we did at the end of Parts One and Two, coming out of the static and vanishing back into it. The static fades.

Part Four
We Children of Hell
Recall the Age of the Grail

The child's head. Over it, the figure 4. From the static comes the sound of Goebbels' voice, fading back again into the static.

Goebbels (January 30, 1943, on the tenth anniversary of Hitler's takeover): Faith can move mountains. This mountain-moving faith must fill us all . . . for the nation and the Reich on the very spot where I am now standing and speaking to you, the German people . . .

The title appears over a close-up of the Black Maria, inside the glass sphere. Long shot. Snow is falling. We hear the Clausewitz text (as altered by Goebbels) spoken by Heinrich George at the end of 1944.

Signal of the Deutschland Radio Network—Üb' immer Treu und Redlichkeit . . .
Heinrich George: I declare and proclaim to the world and to posterity: That the false wisdom that tries to elude danger is something that I consider the most destructive thing that fear and terror can inspire. That I would consider the wildest despair wiser if we were absolutely prevented from facing danger with a manly courage, that is to say, with a calm but solid resolution and lucid con-

sciousness. That in the present-day delirium of fear I do not forget the warning events of ancient and modern times, the wise teachings of whole centuries, the noble examples of renowned nations, and I would not give away world history for a page of a lying newspaper. That I feel free of any selfishness, that I may boldly and openly admit to every thought and every feeling within me in front of all my fellow citizens, that I would feel only too happy to perish gloriously in the wonderful struggle for the freedom and dignity of the Fatherland. Let posterity decide whether this faith in me and those who share my thinking deserves scorn and derision.

Haydn's *Emperor Quartet.*

•

Heller sits at a desk with candelabra. A Caspar David Friedrich landscape is projected behind him.

ANDRE HELLER: Imagine a conversation in a German landscape, in the light, windows and a fireplace, a park, walking, corridors, fire, dark faces, cigarette smoke, close-ups of faces, face to face, or according to the model of Brecht's *Refugee Conversations*, constantly interrupted, or as in Karl Kraus's *The Last Days of Mankind*, the optimist and the pessimist, the pros and cons. One could play all this in eight or ten scenes. One could, one could not, it is all very difficult.
Let me read from the notes for this film:
Imagine this Hitler, that is to say, one hundred fifty antiaircraft searchlights in Nuremberg, their beams converging on the sky above, so that they could be seen from as far away as Frankfurt at night, and then all of them focusing on the same point, the stairs where Hitler made his appearance. The things that must go on in a man when he stands dazzled before 400,000 others, who cheer in the dark, while thousands of red banners of all local groups from all over Germany come toward him. The desire to flaunt and the *Gesamtkunstwerk* of German politics in the twentieth century?

The following texts are accompanied by a series of close shots of Heller at the table. Behind him, 8-millimeter films of the period, sent by people throughout Germany (in response to an advertisement), or sometimes a black background.
Among this 8-millimeter footage: the opening of the House of Art in 1938. Hitler arrives, many flags, SS, Mercedes cars.

When little Henriette Hoffmann, later Frau Schirach and great lady of Vienna and the whole of Austria as well as the German Youth, the so-called Hitler-Jugend, when she was still the sixteen-year-old daughter of Hitler's friend and photographer Hoffmann, she opened the door of her house for him again one night, barefoot and wearing a nightgown, he had forgotten his dog whip, which he asked for, then struck his other palm with it, turned around, and also asked her: "Wouldn't you like to kiss me?" This was the first time that he used the polite form with this girl whom he had known since she was eight. To which she said, as girls of that age will do, pert, trembling, or honest, who knows: "Not really, Herr Hitler." How impractical, she was to say, forty-five years later. And within a couple of years, it was this Henriette, now a young woman, the only person who, in the middle of the war, in his house in Obersalzberg, in the presence of seventeen uniformed men, who held their tongues and poked in the fireplace—she reproached Hitler for killing Jews. Speer and Schirach were in the canteen, since they preferred the company of the personnel. Whereupon he came over to her, stood next to her at the fireplace, seized her wrists, and spoke penetratingly at first, then shouting: "You don't understand, we are at war. Our best men are dying, and Germanic blood is drying out, we have to sacrifice our enemies." And she said: "I am here to love, not to hate."

Memories of early days with him, when he said: It was the loveliest thing in life to attract another human being. But now she heard him scream: "Learn to hate, to hate, like me!" Devoured by love and hate.

We have to invent a new, a different reality. Let us have the courage to change life. The important thing is the quality of the new reality, as they always say in such moments.

Utopians, ideologues, idealists, or artists. What did Thea von Harbou say in her book, which she dedicated: To you and Germany. The author of Fritz Lang's *Nibelungen* in the twenties. The goal, from top to bottom, including the human material, was to create the world of a century in which the primal beginning, myth, fairy tale, memories of the beginning of the human race would be coupled with the familiar solemnity of early cathedrals. And him. Naturally, we are unrealists, unrealists of a steel-clad romanticism, artists of a new reality of the twentieth century, the past woven into the future. And what did she have to pay, the widow of Pfauen, a UFA technician who was executed for a joke about the new realities? Four hundred reichsmarks for the headsman, one hundred for the assistants, and twenty-five pfennigs for the sawdust.

He saw himself as Moses with the Tables of the Law on his back, the founder of a religion, from Egypt or Greece, Hitler the Great, the model of Obersalzberg, as his Henriette knew about him, a Nero, igniting Europe for us, without madness in his mind, very lucid and deliberate and logical. The planned end, quite within our tradition and development.

On a meadow, a popular festival with girls dancing in folk costumes. The audience sitting on reviewing stands.

It is fear, the fear of the great tempter of democracy. A fear that will survive as long as socialism and mass society and technology exist. The fear of the devil of the democratic system, and Germany was well prepared. The reddest country in Western Europe, Bavaria in the hands of Communists, always at the head of the class in world history. Decent and idealistic. Masses and technology and energy, not class hatred but class reconciliation. And now his watchword: The worker is like an artist. An art for the people, an art that everyone understands, a cultural revolution against the ivory tower of the turn of the century, against the people who once spit at the *Gartenlaube*. He took kitsch seriously in the history of German taste. Art for the people, radical. Work liberates, or to each his own, or abandon all your hope, or right or wrong, my Hitler.

Hitler on the evening of January 30, in the Reich Chancellery, to the last guests of his circle in the later bunker: And no one will get me out of here alive, about which he turned out to be right, as he so often was.

And recall the scene of Hitler weeping as he turned away from his old friend and fighter, the photographer Hoffmann, when taking his leave, before his death in gasoline and his cremation in the Russians' bomb crater, *Götterdämmerung* 1945. In the gasoline fire, in the gasoline fire of his chauffeur and servant. One has to imagine him as the lover of Germany and he was Germany, as everyone knew and wished, isn't that so? Heir of the Habsburg emperors and of the Holy Roman Empire, and to endure it, just once, not lying to himself. And just look at his face, the face of the typical loser at the head of Germany, identifying with Germany. I am Germany and Germany is I, what luck that we have found one another, perhaps she is not worthy of me, this Germany. Where democracy and the republic were always just an import, an import from England or France, aimed against what is best in us—against obedience and subjugation, the freedom of serving and commanding, the soldierly virtues, technology and philosophy, enthusiasm, the joy of strength, the strength of belief, of beauty in the triumph of the will. Our desire is to flaunt our law and pleasure; our suit of honor is the uniform. Put the Germans in uniforms and you will see miracles of performance.

Vienna 1938. An 8 millimeter film, from a private source, of Hitler's triumphal motorcade through the city.

They are unfit for eating, living, fun. In the war, they were known as the Fritzes. Better to die in honor than to live in shame. To live for others, to die for others, that is not new, it is the basis of our culture, the deputy principle. An old European tradition: Western civilization.

Who will ask five hundred years from now whether Fräulein Schulze was happy, said Himmler, war is the father of all things, said the Greeks, and he who pays the piper calls the tune, that is what we say, today. The freedom of consumption and not even that. The point is war and the nation of war and culture: Germany. But ardently did we live and ardently did we die. Enough material for centuries, Felix culpa, happy guilt, we lived it, lived it to death. Guilt is the principle of tragedy, Germany the tragic land of the century. Germany the ruin of Europe and final victor of the last war, when we will make the consumer democracy our honor and progressively pull through it, as the first in the world.

A war forced upon us, says Hitler, in order to avoid everything coming later. It is easier to wage a war at fifty than at sixty, it had to come.

Let us now hear the holy songs of the war as the reflection of Europe, the orgasm of universal life, which makes chaos fertile, and makes it move, the prelude to all creations, and which, like Christ, the saviour from death, triumphs over death itself. And it was war from which Hitler was born, for instance Pasewalk. It was here that Hitler, blinded in the war, decided to become a politician. "I made up my mind to become a politician." In 1918, when everything was over. Let us assume he recalled the scene in which he was decorated with the Iron Cross, first class, for bravery beyond the call of duty, an unusual honor for a corporal in those days. When he stood before the officer, a German, who was secretly called a Jew, and who told him he ought to always bear in mind the great honor and distinction and duty to the Fatherland he was taking upon himself. As a little man, the volunteer and petit bourgeois for Germany. This reminder from the Jew Hugo Gutmann, the regimental aide, who secretly called him a nut and laughed at him because he lacked the leadership qualities necessary for promotion, because he only read Homer or *Parsifal* and Schopenhauer and the Gospels, away from everyone else, away in the trenches of the war, which Hitler, at thirty, called his surrogate university. The loneliness of the elect, his homeland and his religion. And thus, Adolf Hitler, the son of an Austrian customs official, became a politician, who swore never again to be a petit bourgeois. If the art of the politician is really an art of the possible, then the man who declares his intentions is one of those of whom it is said that they are pleasing to the gods only if they demand, and desire, the impossible.

Within long periods of humanity, it may sometimes happen that the politician and the man who declares his intentions are one and the same. The deeper this fusion, however, the greater the resistance to the politician's activities. He no longer works for the demands that are obvious to any run-of-the-mill philistine, but rather for goals that only very few understand. Hence, his life is then torn apart by love and hate, success is all the more infrequent, but if he does flourish, one man in many centuries, then perhaps, in his later days, a quiet shimmer of glory may radiate about him.

Heller in close-up against a black background.

Naturally, these great men are merely the marathon runners of history. The laurel wreath of the present touches only the temples of the dying hero. And let us remember that in Landsberg, in the prison, he resolved to go through democratic channels, with the most rigorous respect for the law and the will to power. A radical, fanatical application of democratic principles and possibilities. The little man who swore never again to be a petit bourgeois. A petit bourgeois feeling like an artist, swearing the oath of the philistine against all philistines, and committing himself to Germanic grandeur in the ancient tradition, and the Western bourgeoisie of Europe, realizing German dreams in his heart. The soldier from the fields of World War I, who had to prove his leadership qualities and his artistry, which was scorned in Vienna.

A dreadful law, which he put upon himself and which, to him and all his comrades-in-arms, seemed possible to carry out. Which is why, out of guilt feelings, as an inferior race, they had to demand the strict, cruel fulfillment from everyone, relentlessly.

Footage of parade during a Party celebration in the provinces.

It was around this time that Hitler saw the movie version of Hugo's *Les Misérables*, on Munich's Blütenstrasse—as Henriette testified in her old age—outdoors, under chestnut trees, with beer, projected on a stretched-out sheet, to a piano accompaniment: the struggle between the law-abiding monster and the humane destiny of Jean Valjean, and little Cosette. The movie said that it is better to give than to receive—absolutely a different quality, which he, Hitler, never managed to acquire, as he realized. For he was a great cineaste, a man of the masses, who sensed what was developing in the cinema and who had resolved to be a movie hero. If not in one way, then at least by resolving never again to be a petit bourgeois, but to live by the laws of a justice that never asks about petty feelings.

> *Song: The world's decaying bones now tremble*
> *Because of the coming war . . .*

And thus Hitler became Siegfried and a great friend of the West, like Stalin, and it was said: One man against all, against a world of enemies. The small good against the great evil. With the enjoyment of strength, which we all so greatly enjoy seeing. The man who draws faster, who wins, is right. Bravo at the end. A small joy in the everyday rut of the spectator, at least that. Do we not feel once again in this hour the miracle that brought us together? You once heard the voice of a man and it struck your hearts, it aroused you, and you followed this voice. You followed it for years without even seeing the bearer of the voice. You only heard a voice and you followed it. If we assemble here, then we are filled with the miraculousness of coming together like this. Not every one of you can see me, nor can I see every one of you, but I feel you all, and you all feel me. It is the faith in our nation that made us little people great, that made us poor people rich, that made us waiting, discouraged, fearful people bold and brave. That made the erring see and joined us together.

Home movies taken by a member of Hitler's entourage at Obersalzberg.

And this had to be sacrificed—loyalty to the old fairy tale, if you renounce love, you will grow rich, if you renounce freedom, individuality, and brotherhood, you will grow famous, rich and famous. But the happy ending is *Götterdämmerung*, and when there are no more gods, and no up and down, where will we fall? In the game without gods. For success, Fatherland, community, socialism, nation, secret model of all managers, if they are honest.

Close-up of Heller against a black background.

216 |

He predicted everything, for everyone, nobody wanted to believe it. Someone had to be found who was guilty of all the sins of the world. Of the striving for profits, which people were ashamed of, of art, which no one among the people understood anymore, of the unemployment, the humiliations and torments of everyday life, and someone had to be found to take over the task of cleansing, to make the sacrifice of conscience, and to sweep everyone away but himself in the Dionysian cult, like a nightmare, with murder and blood for the new cause. They believed they were doing good by killing what they called evil, in the others as proxies, themselves subconsciously. A battlefield of the self.

Medium shot of Heller with candelabra.

In Thuringia, when the concentration camp of Buchenwald was built, they left the old Goethe oak in the middle, where he had written poems one hundred fifty years ago. For instance, "The Wanderer's Nightsong":
>You who are of heaven,
>Stilling all sorrow and woe,
>For the man who is twice wretched,
>You fill with twofold refreshment.
>Ah, I am weary of wandering!
>What good is all the pain and joy?
>Sweet peace, come, ah, come into my breast!

And many years later:
>Over all the peaks,
>There is peace,
>Over all the treetops,
>You barely feel a breath of wind.
>The birds are silent in the forest,
>Just wait,
>Soon, you too
>Will be at peace.

Long shot with footage in the background from the war period: Hitler visiting the front lines.

When Versailles prohibited us from using the old munition depots because of the danger of explosion, even though they were in wooden barracks and away in the forests, with a siding track, and well fenced and supplied with watchtowers, on German territory, those practical vacant munition depots—Hitler swore, in case he ever came to power, to lock them up right there, those men who had signed that treaty along with so many other things. And he swore to call them what the British had called them in their Boer War: concentration camps. Those British, his great rivals, whom he emulated, radically, thoroughly, without sloppiness, which he was afraid of because he was always accused of it, like his indecisiveness—the British of "my country, right or wrong," to which he said: "I am Germany." Thus he fulfilled the principles of the West, with a great strain on the principles, performance and progress, energy, power, and intelligence without morals, without God and emperor, only with a yearning mass that had no center. What had Robert Musil, that Viennese compatriot of Hitler, said? If just once any one of the ideas that move our lives were put into effect, thoroughly, so that nothing were left of the opposing idea, our civilization would probably no longer be our civilization. When Abraham was commanded to kill his son in order to perform a service for God, to put religion and God's law into effect, it was that divine arm that prevented him in the last moment from doing it. Hitler had to miss that grace in the godless age of the decline of the West. And history advanced, advanced through him.

Images of Berlin during the Nazi period.

He fulfilled it. East and West face one another on the Elbe, and Israel has become Greater Israel. Europe, as he said, is ultimately not economical, but he never spoke about economy. We prefer it this way, let us not talk about money, of course.

In ten years, the exhaust fumes of cars wiped out as much civilization as four centuries once did, and it is a familiar joke of our German reality that the postwar years destroyed more of our cities through reconstruction than the bombs of the last war. Final victory, final solution. And that was how Goebbels saw himself and his men in that struggle at the end of the war, when he spoke about the *Kolberg* film: "Gentlemen, a hundred years from now, they will show another color film, depicting the terrible days that we must now live through. Would you not like to play a role in this film, a role that will bring you back to life in a hundred years? Every man now has the chance to choose his part, which he will play in this film in a hundred years. I can assure you it will be a great and beautiful, an uplifting film, and it is worth standing one's ground for this film. Hold fast!"

Close shot of Heller's head and shoulders against black background.

And the story, a very small story, an everyday story about that man with the sign that said "Jew," driven through the streets of, say, Greifswald, Pomerania, the city of Caspar David Friedrich, driven through by Greifswald's Hitler Youths, who kicked him in the ass, this German walking proudly with an upright gait through his city. A young officer, weeping helplessly, had to be forcibly restrained from plunging into disaster amid such lawful injustice.

Long shot. Footage of barracks.

And in May 1945, after the end of the war, GI's called in Henriette von Schirach's little three-year-old son, the son of the former head of the Hitler Youth—three years old, and he thought he'd be getting some chewing gum, and they asked the little boy to do a "Sieg Heil" or a "Heil Hitler" for them. And when the little boy, not knowing what was going on, tearfully obeyed and did what they had showed him how to do, a GI put out his burning cigarette on his arm.

And what did Hitler say before the end of the war: if we lose it, the sacrifices shall not be in vain. The seed will sprout, someday, somewhere, I am immortal so long as this world exists, socialism and capitalism and the mass of humanity.

And at the end of the film *Jew Süss*, Goebbels prohibited the Jew's curse on his town when he was locked up and hung up in his cage. This is the curse: "You Tartars, you worshippers of Baal, you judges of Sodom, may your limbs wither away, may your living bodies rot, may the bones of your children and children's children fester. May grief fill out your days and pain drive the sleep from your eyes. May evil neighbors destroy your peace of mind. May your firstborn bring shame upon you, may your memory be cursed and your town be destroyed by the fire of heaven. May your hunger find no bread, your thirst no mercy, your rights no ears, and may your own tongues blaspheme your God."

Images of the War in Russia.

And in the street, the old man, pulling a small wagon with valises and last belongings, through the streets, always running, full of fear, always living through his trek in flight, friendly, driven, with a wide gaze, restless, no longer even realizing that he has no homeland, forever, that he will never arrive. Everything Hitler's fault. Only Hitler's? The questions of a literate worker. But how can all this be depicted without constriction,

injustice, where should we begin? The ideas and their consequences, on a minor and a major scale, the grief and the fun,
which was always there, always.

Song: The world's decaying bones now tremble . . .
     . . . And we will keep on marching,
     Till everything to pieces is hurled,
     For today our Germany belongs to us,
     And tomorrow the entire world!

Behind Heller's table, images of Berlin in ruins. Aerial photos of
Unter den Linden. We hear the SA funeral march, composed by Putzi
Hanfstaengl.

And imagine old Henriette, today, what things she could tell us.
It was the entire period of our youth, our great decisions, between
Mother's death—when he held my little hand and ordered me not
to cry—one should never let people look into your heart—and
the time when the same man, weeping, and old now, at the end of
the war, standing at the fireplace, holding a handkerchief to his
mouth while receiving the bulletins about the death of his blond
men, and weeping, like Frederick II after the battles in the Seven
Years' War, with his great men dying, such as Menzel depicted
him.

In between, however, there was the lovely, golden time of our
picnics with him in Munich during 1923 and later, when we were
still laughing and singing in the open Mercedes, when we were
dreaming with him about rockets to the moon, the House of Art,
Minotaur labyrinths, with cars for everyone on Autobahns, butter-
flies on the naked bodies of our youth. That was the time when
Geli was still alive and Ernst Röhm was still laughing and Brückner
always stuck his elbow out the window until he smashed it in an
accident, on the window of the big Mercedes, which Maurice was
still driving, Maurice, the founder of the SA and later condemned
as a Jew, excommunicated, his oldest, most intimate friend and
the man who saved his life, a Jew from Germany. With Putzi, who
whistled Wagner and read aloud from newspapers, foreign newspapers in the suitcase, reports on the last speeches in the Krone
Circus, in which he said the Jew is always within us, and if he
didn't exist, we would have to invent him. Sheer medievalism,
witches and belief in the devil, Western civilization. It was the
time when he suddenly told the driver to halt, on the way to
Berchtesgaden, to the still peasant-like Wachenfeld House, and he
saw a boy reading under a tree, as in the pictures that we knew

and know. "Just like my youth," he shouted, "when I sat there in the shade, reading to my comrades about the Boer War, and the way they fought against the British, the Uncle Krügers against Lord Kitchener with his concentration camps and dreadful harshness. And behind me stood my strict father's beehive in the guise of a victorious Napoleon, the master of the ice of Moscow. Napoleon behind me, with them flying in and out of his belly, the bees, an industrious people, lovers of the State, clean and orderly, capable of organizing honeycombs, good to their queen, who took care of their future. Always battling the enemy wasp, aggressive and stupid, but cunning, incapable of building its own houses, parasites that have to be wiped out, as my father said, wherever they are found, exterminated. That was my mission since childhood. My duty against the pests and parasites. My father was strict with his pipe and his whip and the many bees around him. That's how we can learn from nature, everything, all the time."

And it was Hess, still young, who felt sorry for a wasp and who saved it from the wasp trap on the veranda of Wachenfeld House, until it stung him in the tongue, dangerously, and they had to call a doctor and take him to the hospital and perform a tracheotomy in Berchtesgaden. That was the time when Hitler then said: "Do you see, my child, he is too kind, that's what you get."

I remember Bruckner, his compatriot from Upper Austria, and the Romantic Symphony, the one from Linz, he always listened to it, Bruckner, not Wagner, to put himself in the mood.

What does Master Stolzing in Nuremberg say . . .

Heller in front of a black background. His voice slowly fades, while Goebbels' voice becomes audible—from his last speech, in Görlitz, before the Volkssturm.

Goebbels, March 11, 1945: We shall enter this battle like a divine service . . . And when they shoulder their rifles, then their minds will be solely on their murdered children and their raped wives, and a shout of revenge will rise from their throats, making the enemy turn pale . . .
Song: "Hold Out in the Raging Storm."

. . . in his small, intimate circle that suddenly became as gigantic as a cancerous ulcer in the history of our traditions. Hitler as the final perfecter of European history in tradition, ideas, art, power politics, energies, and the mobilization of performance. Why say he failed? Why not call him the crucible, the will-less victim, the medium of a world spirit?

Goebbels: Every house a fortress, every town a bulwark, and every heart an invincible trench . . .

You think you're pushing, but you're being pushed, the mirror of our greed and dreams of the power of the community. There was no other choice. The development of history and the many attempts at democratic elections in Germany prove it. They all lead back to him, he was the only solution, no mere chance or error or blunder, quite logical to the last, both he and we. The goddess of history, of Providence, had spoken, he was right, dreadfully right. He was Germany and Germany was he in the Europe of the twentieth century. Everything in the traditions of Frederick II, Napoleon and Lenin and Stalin and Wallenstein, the Stauffers and King Arthur, and Charlemagne, the Romantics and Kantian classicism and nineteenth-century Vienna and the Greeks and Teutons and the entire Middle Ages. The executor, coming from the grandiose Viennese scene and the Upper Austrian provinces, the Catholic altar boy with the Mozart Masses in his ears, growing up to become the petit-bourgeois executor of Prussian virtues in the finale of the St. Vitus's dance of the twentieth century. The European atom bomb had exploded; it ignited, in the area of civilization, that mixture of technological rationality of the enlightened faith in progress and the conservative style, the will of the reactionary West and the greed to flaunt in the sacrificial will of the proletarian masses. And all that in the heart of Europe. Austria and Prussia united once again in a German Reich, for the last time with the worldwide claim of a petit-bourgeois genius . . .

Crowd: Sieg Heil! Sieg Heil!
Song: Deutschland, Deutschland über alles . . .

Or the last desperate attempt of mentally deprived, hungry upstarts of the cultural proletariat in its own style, equal rights with the urge to be allowed in, and—incomprehensible to them and insulting to them—the temples and brothels and department stores of the cultured and the capitalists and the smart set, those despised people who fawned, who celebrated and howled with mirth at the have-nots of the slums and the petit-bourgeois masses, until they were ruthlessly killed and gassed, obtaining the final right of fulfillment, by sheer obstinacy, in their style of the Black Death. In the self-imposed paradise in hell.

Song: The banner high! Our ranks are serried tight.
SA now marches with a bold, firm tread.
Comrades whom Reds and reactionaries shot—
They march with us in spirit though they're dead.

What does it say in *Muspilli*, that ninth-century manuscript about the ultimate struggle between the heavenly legions and the devil's retinue? Imagine Elijah and Satan: Satan's blood, dripping upon the earth, kindles the conflagration of the world and the end:

> so inprinnant die perga
> poum ni kistentit
> enhic in erdu, aha entrucknent
> mano vallit, prinnit mittilargart
> The earth, the mountains burn,
> The trees vanish
> From the earth, the rivers run dry,
> The moon falls, and finally
> The whole earth burns.

Instrumental: Deutschland, Deutschland über alles.

We see Heller at the table with the candelabra. Behind him, a projection of Caspar David Friedrich's fiery landscape, *Neubrandenburg.* We hear sound documents from 1945.

Female radio announcer: Attention, attention, we are bringing you the following bulletin on the situation in the air war. The enemy fighter units and combat units reported heading eastward in the Norderney area . . . A small special course in the area of . . .
Roosevelt, January 20, 1943: We have learned to be citizens of the world . . .
Goebbels: We shall enter this battle like a divine service . . .
Walter Ulbricht, April 11, 1945: We are speaking to you as Germans, who love your nation with all your heart. Soldiers, our nation does not need your senseless deaths. It needs your lives for the work in the future Germany . . .
Female radio announcer: Enemy fighter units in the Bremen area and south of it. A few fighter planes, also in the Oldenburg area south of . . .
Announcer, April 5, 1945: This is Radio Werewolf, the transmitter of the German freedom movement in the territories occupied by the enemy. We are the voice of the German freedom fighters. Every evening at nineteen hundred hours, we broadcast important

news about the German freedom fight, on wavelength 13 . . . meters 324 kilohertz. We have brought bulletins about the fight of our werewolves, new bulletins in the course of our broadcast, with music until then.

Female radio announcer: We are bringing you an aerial report! . . . enemy bomber units with changing courses between . . . and Bremen. Plus scattered bomber units . . .

American newscaster, April 12, 1945: We interrupt this program to bring you a special news bulletin from CBS World News: The Press Association has just announced that President Roosevelt is dead. The President . . . cerebral hemorrhage. All we know so far is that the President died at Warm Springs, in Georgia.

Churchill, April 25, 1945: After long journeys, toil and victories graft the lands and oceans across so many deadly battlefields. The armies of the great allies have traversed Germany and have joined hands together.

Heller at the table. The candles are almost flickering out. Fade.

●

The following sequence has no cuts. The camera approaches and moves away, and there are pan shots showing the speaker and various visual details. Close shots of the figures from the Cathedral of Strasbourg (Synagogue and Church), of Hitler as a ventriloquist's dummy dressed in lederhosen, of the Karl May village from the start of Part Two. Harry Baer, beginning his monologue, brings the glass sphere with the Black Maria close to his eyes; it shines in the bright light like crystal. *Rienzi* music.

HARRY BAER (voice off): Just once more, an Adolf Hitler would and must speak like this at the end of his days. Using his final chances.

I believe and avow, at least once, seriously what it was really all about, my struggle, *Mein Kampf*, the program of our final goal. The traditions of Western civilization. Christianity and antiquity modernized. As radical as the Old Testament, a feudal mass society with self-elected and tolerated monarchs. With all the consequences, making you tremble, seeing, hearing what that means. The twentieth century presents Hitler, a film from Germany.

The Roman Empire, as the only Western system of world domination, a model; we learned from the British colonial empire of the last few centuries how a resolute minority of fifty-two million can employ a relentless dictatorship by a minority to rule one fifth of the world. By means of national feeling and genius.

And we learned from the practice of the Jewish people how religious racial purity and a sense of mission by a chosen people can help us achieve world dominion.

Thinking of Jerusalem for two thousand years. In every prayer, every day, until they won. My respects. We may be small, but once a man stood up in Galilee, and today his teachings govern the entire world, for that is what we learn from the Jewish people who from now on will have nothing more to do with Moses, the Egyptian prince, or Jesus, whom I can only imagine as blond and blue-eyed.

Strength does not lie in the majority, as Lenin said, and we can learn here too—it lies in the purity of the willingness to offer sacrifices, and that means the eradication—and I say this now, consistently and logically, ruthlessly—the extermination of the divine people through the natural superiority of the concentrated, the chosen racial elite of the Aryans. What do we want? A system of slaves, colonies, and satellites like Rome, England in the past or Moscow today, or the economic and marketing structure of the United States.

The goal was not Germany and not Europe and not a few generations. The whole Nazi business would be worthless if it did not include the rule of the superior race over the entire world and for at least one or two thousand years, so that the challenge cup of world power might finally come to rest in a grand organization of the world, from the center of Europe, by the New Man, against the plutocracies of the West and against the claim to world power of the East. The democracies are only the approaches of Bolshevistic world imperialism of the Jewish aspirations to world power by people who could not do it with money. The Communistic striving for equality by those who have not gotten their share.

What does all this mean for us? After the experiences of world history, however, successes are all the more enormous, the greater the final goal.

In these last few years, I have taken the steepest and most dizzying path that any man has ever had to take. I also think that it is something unique in world history that a man in my situation, with my qualifications and twenty years later, comes to this result.

All my conquests served only this one final goal, the attainment of the Arabic world rule with its center Germania in the place of present-day Berlin. The luxury of a civilized nation, organized in terms of agriculture, ruling the industrial societies of the independent and the inferior races. Atlantis-like, with a ruling architecture of victory and the intoxication of Wagnerian music in our blood. A great power of world domination through blitzkriegs with a global victory celebration in 1950 or through a global destruction of Europe.

And if ever I were a man of the devil, as the followers of the old Christian faith call it, then I can only have wanted the entire world, for the Antichrist that I am is not content with alms.

The camera continues to pan while Baer is silent.

BBC, April 15, 1945, Auschwitz: Today, we are happy that we have everything behind us. We do not know how we shall ever thank the liberators, our liberators, we only know that when we get out of here, we must scream into the world everything that we have experienced here, for otherwise we cannot live. The people who hear this now may perhaps think that we are not quite normal anymore, but when one starts to tell, it is so cruel. One does not know where to start, there are such terrible things one has experienced that one cannot find the words to describe them, and someone who did not witness them will not understand how dreadful this red, glowing flame remains in our memory. When we see the sun go down today, we think of the chimney in Auschwitz, which has carried off thousands of people, and we had to watch, we were in such despair, we clenched our fists in our pockets and could do nothing, because we were enslaved and tortured and only because we had come to Auschwitz as Jews, because we had the terrible misfortune of being born Jews. We committed no other crime than simply coming into the world as Jews, and it was as Jews that we entered the chimney there.

Announcer, May 1, 1945: We have received the following report from the Führer's headquarters: This afternoon, our Führer Adolf Hitler, fighting until his very last breath against Bolshevism, died for Germany in his command post at the Reich Chancellery.

BBC, May 2, 1945: Now we are breaking into our programs with some splendid news from Moscow. Berlin has fallen. Marshal Stalin has just announced the complete . . .

•

Obersalzberg today. In front of a large wall, from which André Heller steps and approaches the camera. The Hitler Museum is opened.

ANDRE HELLER: Obersalzberg, memories, relics of Hitler. The whip. Then the tattered suit from the assassination attempt. Winter Relief buttons. Eva Braun's little lederhosen. Hitler's dogs stuffed: Blondie, Wolf, Bella, Muck, Stasi, Negus, Katuschka, Burli.

Secretaries, servants, chauffeurs, officers. Then the last things from Hitler's bunker room, Frederick the Great painted by Anton Graff. Then the picture of his mother, the final-solution pistol, and *Muspilli*, which he was reading when he wrote *Mein Kampf*. On this very spot.

Announcer through loudspeaker, Leipzig, end of April 1945: . . . everyone, whether German or foreigner, is to go home immediately.

On a small podium, the mayor, played by Martin Sperr. He is surrounded by the historical objects for a new Hitler Museum, including the dog Blondie and many historical figures in both uniforms and mufti. We see tourists and the projected image of the countryside around Obersalzberg.

MAYOR (Martin Sperr): Ladies and gentlemen! To the opening of our Hitler-life in Bavaria.

Announcer: And between 4 and 6 p.m. . . .

Now that everything is finished, this is how things stand before the expansion. Three thousand visitors a day, like Linderhof or Neuschwanstein, the limit of our capacity, five buses up, five down in a convoy, on the one-lane road to the elevator for the teahouse. Many Americans, Frenchmen, Scandinavians, also people from behind the Iron Curtain, and also East Germany, if they get out secretly, and our people, factory workers, entire busloads, company outings, also celebrities, Romy Schneider recently, and blacks from the developing countries with white girls and German shepherds, elegant on short leashes. This means that, statistically, in terms of tourism, we can ascertain a public need; capacities could be expanded. A picture from the past shows them going their way amid the destroyed historic sites, amid homes green and overgrown— Bormann, Göring, and Hitler, like ants whose anthill has been smashed and whose queen has been taken away. And strangely enough, in the places where the houses were, new greenery is growing more luxuriantly, it is comforting to see our trails and those of the historic deeds marking their spirit in the landscape, our trails not vanishing in eons or being wiped away by government decrees. The spirit lives on, which many people cannot forget, and which many people want to see again. The evil too. A comfort too. A final one. At least that.

American newscaster, May 7, 1945: The National Broadcasting Company delays the start of all its programs to bring you a special bulletin. It was announced in San Francisco half an hour ago by a

high American official, not identified, who said that Germany has surrendered unconditionally to the Allies . . .

Peter Kern as Berchtesgaden's director of tourism stands on the speaker's podium. Behind him, the projection of the panorama of Lake König in Obersalzberg. Many figures in the Hitler circle, including secretaries, the pilot Bauer, Eva Braun—all as photo figures in the imaginary outdoor museum in Obersalzberg. The valet Linge, Krause, little Henriette, Frau Raubal, the ragged trousers that Hitler wore on June 20, and the hangman of Nuremberg with the rope for the hanged.

DIRECTOR OF TOURISM (Peter Kern): Good day, one and all! Don't worry. No politics here, we don't want any problems. The goal is spare-time industry, entertainment, show business, movies, and tourism. Naturally, within the pale of the law, not of morality. Business, you have to have fun, and the best fun is the one that sells well. Business is the democrat's freedom. And democracy is possible only with economic growth. Seen in such terms, Hitler is quite obviously the international top drawer, with genuine box-office appeal. Concessions are clear: feelings, the public, but the public is always right. At the cash register, quality decides, quite democratically: porno, hetero, homo, blood, horror, authentically human, in disaster solid history with expressive performers. Big business, huge, worldwide, socialistic, sociopolitical. Nothing esoteric, Culture is wiped out. Genuine popular taste prevails here.

Announcer at victory celebrations in Paris, May 8, 1945: . . . Général de Gaulle . . . ce sont plusieurs . . . c'est la fin de la guerre pour Paris . . .

The mayor and the director of tourism dance together. Behind them, the historical Alpine landscape painting with a black eagle, the museum's pièce de résistance.

Song: The telephone rings softly,
           Telephone, telephone,
           And we know
           It can only be you, only you, only you . . .
           The telephone rings softly . . . (repeated)

MAYOR and DIRECTOR OF TOURISM: Here, bandleader Wolf! Heil!
They sing: Don't you have, don't you have, don't you have a
           girl for me.

Yes, yes, we do, we've got one for you,
With a big pile of cash,
We've got one stashed.
She's gotta be chic, yes, yes, yes.
And not too thick,
No, no, no, no.
With no vices, no, no, no, no.
And a lot of money, yes, yes, yes, yes . . .

*London, May 14, 1945: Mr. Churchill himself is all smiles . . .
we all know so well. Now listen to this ovation!*

The mayor comes forward amid the uniformed museum figures. We see
a huge projection of Anton Graff's painting of Frederick the Great—the
painting in front of which Hitler shot himself.

MAYOR: We must, of course, not glorify Hitler, but business is
permissible, it creates jobs and relaxation in our leisure time, important milestones of our democratic will, which we have learned
well.
So, why don't we begin, Herr Director!

*Above, I see Lady Megan and Lloyd-George. And now the end
of the procession . . .*

DIRECTOR OF TOURISM: This is the pistol with which Hitler shot
himself in front of the painting of Frederick the Great. Ah, don't
worry. Don't worry.

*Churchill, May 8, 1945, London: This is your victory! Victory
of the cause of freedom! Through all our long history we have
never seen a greater day than this.*

The mayor of Berchtesgaden and the director of tourism in front of
Hitler's reconstructed house, amid the historical figures from the great
period of the Third Reich.

DIRECTOR OF TOURISM: Naturally, we recall the victims, by
way of reparation, a mini-show, a mini-Dachau right nearby with
a Boger swing. No power without resistance and no castle without
a torture chamber. Just look at the Tower of London. We are
dealing with power here and torture, the horrible torture of the
twentieth century, very modern and progressive. Technologically
correct and authorized by the building authorities, we are open

to all questions and strictly nonpartisan. With Arab money and Israeli management. Real estate speculation with reparation funds. On our Alpine territory, in Germany absolutely democratic. The secret bunkers and hothouses, where Bormann's biologically dynamic food grew, vegetarian fare, today, where Hermann Göring, the fat man, always practiced archery and laughed, and Eva wept in the evening, when she had to stay alone, not even able to profit from his absence, fanatically photographing for her album.

Zarah Leander: . . . Though our skulls may smoke . . .
The world won't come to an end,
It's needed still.

The government-issue people's stock, for the German Disneyland on the holy mountain near Berchtesgaden. An amusement park with special movie showings. Hitler in UFA land, housemaid stories, with all departments, from the fairy tale to the land of the future and the merry-go-round of progress to the land of fantasy, adventure, and the frontier. Wherever people fight for

the New Man. Just don't let anyone say we don't have our history, our business. The time is ripe, this is expected of us now, the interest is there. The greatest show of the century. They will continue with original figures and dates precisely according to history. The wedding in the teahouse: Eva's sister and SS Fegelein, the traitor and SS slaughterer in Poland. On April 20, then, the memorial for the victims, and on the anniversary of the death, a lovely wolf-celebration for the lone wolf in the jungle of bunker 45, and always in the off-season, November, a meditation as in 1923, with a contemplation of the stars and an introduction to the ice cosmogony in the adult education center.

. . . Yes, and then don't forget the labor of Lebensborn, a look at the emancipation of women in the male state, graphic, with film clips of young and old production, social or more entertaining, left-wing, concentration camp, straight porno or *Salon Kitty,* according to taste, a fine market, multimedia . . .

Newscaster, May 8, 1945: From a newsroom in New York, here is the latest news summary. Germany's unconditional surrender became effective at 6:01 p.m. Eastern War Time. The surrender was ratified in Berlin today and it was signed by the chief

of the German High Command, Field Marshal Wilhelm Keitel,
and three Allied representatives. You have heard a special pro-
gram . . . bring you coverage of V-E Day, and this is the National
Broadcasting Company!

The mayor and the director of tourism of Berchtesgaden and Obersalzberg walk through their new park, reaching a stairway that runs to
the upper edge of the image.

Hitler: So I was a member of the German Wehrmacht, I was a
musketeer among millions of others, and that gave me my faith
and my whole struggle in the movement for the soul of the German
people, for the soul of the broad masses, the millions of workers
and farmers. This struggle was what really made me strong, for it
acquainted me with the most precious thing in the world: the
uncorrupted strength of the broad masses, the millions of fellow
Germans, from which ultimately the idea of the National Socialist
state emerged, from which our national community emerged. Our
National Socialist Party, our German Reich, Sieg Heil, Sieg Heil,
Heil, Heil!
Song: Deutschland, Deutschland über alles, über alles . . .

ANDRE HELLER (voice off): Yes, and now the main attraction.
Our saddest show. Big business, that big business with the many
jobs, something for everyone, a guaranteed role. The victory
celebration in Berlin, designed by Hitler, for 1950, right at the
start of his struggle, produced by Speer, to the last detail. Our
version! Without Leni Riefenstahl, without newsreels, the price-
less newsreels that we couldn't afford. The greatest show of the
century, our Disneyland, the final victory of hell with the Hitler
within us. Play everything once again, the roles from the innermost compulsion for cleansing, over and over again the doctrine
of the old myth.

The mayor and the director of tourism walk toward the stairway, halt
when they reach it, and sing an old Bavarian hymn.

MAYOR and DIRECTOR OF TOURISM sing:
Sea star, I greet thee,
Oh, Mary, help,
Sweet Mother of God,
Oh, Mary, help.
Mary, help us all
From our deep affliction.

Both men go down and out along the projection of the huge stairway. They enter the hell of the Nazi victory celebration, amid the deafening sounds of the SA song.

•

Song: The banner high! Our ranks are serried tight,
SA now marches with a bold, firm tread.
Comrades whom Reds and reactionaries shot—
They march with us in spirit though they're dead.

The first image of the victory celebration is the Black Eagle in the soldiers' tomb, like the one planned for the victorious Berlin and for the victims. Pylons emitting red smoke, cannon firing a salute, as in Part One of the film, at the presentation of the paradise of hell.

ANDRE HELLER (voice off): I believe and avow, I had a dream. The artwork of the state and politics and nation and each individual a part of it, each in his place. The attempt to lead the masses to victory with their inherent strength. In a beautiful race. A model for all others, according to the old pattern, two thousand years old and known to every schoolboy from an early age. Like Darwin the Englishman's laws of the struggle for survival, and Wagner's myth from *Rienzi* to *Parsifal*. The *Gesamtkunstwerk* of Germany, the model, I proclaim the death of light, the death of all life and of nature, the end.

The child, shrouded in black, walks through a group of gallows, in front of a Hitler drawing as a projection, of the victorious Berlin of the future. We hear the final Wehrmacht report of the war.

Network signal: Üb' immer Treu und Redlichkeit . . .
May 9, 1945: Eight-oh-three p.m. Reich Network, Flensburg,
and the associated networks. We are now broadcasting the final
Wehrmacht report of this war. From the headquarters of the Grand
Admiral, on May 9, 1945. The High Command of the Wehrmacht
announces: In East Prussia just yesterday, German divisions were
still courageously defending the mouth of the Vistula and the west-
ern part of the Frische Nehrung and the Memel until the very last.
The Seventh Infantry Division in particular excelled in battle.
Supreme Commander von Salten, general of the armored division,
was honored for the exemplary behavior of his soldiers with an oak
leaf added to his Knight's Cross and swords and diamonds of the
Iron Cross. The advanced bulwarks of our armies in Kurland,

*under the tried-and-true supreme command of Colonel General
Grüter, contained superior Soviet infantry platoons and armored
units for many months, attaining eternal glory in six great battles.
They refused any premature surrender. Far from the homeland,
the defenders of Atlantic bases, our troops in Norway, and the
occupiers of the Aegean Islands maintained obedience and discipline, preserving the military honor of the German soldier.*

In front of models and projections of Speer's buildings—the great
square designed for the victorious Berlin of 1950—lies the charred corpse
of Joseph Goebbels, modeled after a Russian photograph. In front of the
podium on which it lies, the girl takes up the Hitler dog reclining there,
just as she carried it out into the film in the beginning and into the cradle
of the *Doctor Caligari* setting. Dragging the dog slowly along the floor,
she exits through the back.

*Since midnight, the weapons have been silent on all fronts. On
the orders of the Grand Admiral, the Wehrmacht has discontinued
the fighting, which has become hopeless. Thus ends the heroic
struggle, which has lasted for almost six years. It has brought us
great victories, but also heavy defeats. In the end, the German
Wehrmacht has lost honorably to a tremendous superior power.
We have broadcast the text of the final Wehrmacht report of this
war. We will now observe three minutes of silence.*

Holding the Hitler dog, the child continues through the figures from
the 1920s (life-size photo figures), under the hanged Goebbels in the tomb
of the soldiers' hall, Hitler's planned Hall of Glory for the German people
after the war, and past the laughing Iron Man from Stroheim's *Wedding
March*—the black man holding the blond girl in his arms, as seen before.
The Iron Man, the laughing emblem of black, strong evil, according to
an old tradition. This is accompanied by Stalin's voice, in Russian, talking
about the victory of the Red Army in May 1945.

236 |

Stalin, Moscow, May 9, 1945: The great day of victory over Germany has come. Forced to her knees by the Red Army and the troops of our allies, Fascist Germany has declared herself defeated and surrendered unconditionally.

Projection in close-up of the death's-head of the charred body of Goebbels; in front of this, life-size cutouts of Prussian generals and a girl from the 1920s in a long black dress, holding the Bible in her hand (photos by August Sander).

ANDRE HELLER (voice off): I promise the world to everyone who votes for me. He only has to desire it relentlessly. I shed no tear for Germany, my spirit shall not come here again, to this place humiliated by itself. Who will be next? The conqueror. It is a natural necessity that, in the process of selection, only the fittest survive. Let us not talk about morality. I brought this land invincible to the top of this century, at the center of the world, be that as it may, who will be next? He will have to start small, fight, learn, against himself and everyone, against everything that was valuable to him until now, endure with a will of iron, make sacrifices with a will of steel for the community or society or Party. For you are nothing and the Party is always right. You have to risk it. A narrow margin between good and evil. God and devil, go to it, or everything will be doomed. He who hesitates is lost. Who is next? He will come and keep on coming, in a different shape, he is within us already, if only we desire it. Not our brother, not in us, we ourselves, you and I.

Roll call of the martyrs of November 9, 1923.

Images of Speer's architecture and of his office for the Berlin planned for 1950, after the war. In a lap dissolve, the child, in black, walks through and beyond these images. Her head is wreathed in strips of film. Like a somnambulist, she walks past toy buildings, this gigantic model architecture, which reaches only up to her waist. Her eyes are closed.

HARRY BAER (voice off): Watch them march past us in huge processions, the subhumans, the Slavs and Jews, the communists and capitalists, the Wandering Jew and Jew Süss and the gypsies and the madmen in chains and fetters. And the ruling nation on the tribunes. And the victorious one-armed cripples in wheelchairs, their arm stumps raised to salute Hitler, the Iron Crosses on their throats. And Knapperstbusch, Lehár, and Strauss, and Hauptmann and Benn and C. G. Jung, and Knut Hamsun and Ezra

Pound, D'Annunzio and Céline and Heidegger and Jünger and Arnolt Bronnen, and all the others as at the beginning, forever after the victory.

And the Nazi families, the mothers and the children, all who sit today in the porno editorial offices or lawyers' offices and businesses and abbeys of churches, the children of Himmler and Eichmann and Schirach and Hess and Göring and Heydrich, Wirth and Frank and Bormann and Kaltenbrunner.

Roll call continues.

And then the Jews around Hitler: Gretl Slezak and Maurice, his chauffeur and Eva's boyfriend. And the little girl he loved so much in Obersalzberg and whom they took away from him, crossed out in all photos, and his diet cook there and Haushofer's wife, and all the deportees from the southern Tyrol, shipped to the German Reich by Mussolini, a whole people, with Hitler's approval, and Röhm, the old friend whom he personally ordered killed, the homosexual SA head of the Third Reich.

And in the montage of images, the mural drawings for the planned Urania Cinema on Hitler's showplace boulevard: drawings with eagles and with heroic figures modeled after Michelangelo's *Last Judgment.*

And you have to picture the tribune of honor for the victors with their marks of death. Hitler and Eva with bloodstains on their heads. Joseph Goebbels and Himmler and Göring still pale from the poison. Bormann lacerated and Röhm with the bullet holes of the assassins in his chest, then Freisler buried under the bombs. You have to see them, standing there, and having to watch, as bloodhounds on leashes, forced to be eternal in the silence of their victory. Flanked by Hitler's mother Klara and Hitler's father Alois, his sister, his brother, and his niece Geli Raubal, his secret true love. And all the women around him, Winifred and Leni and Hanna, and Unity and Bruckmann and Bechstein from the Munich of 1923, the old cake women and the hyenas, Irma Grese and Ilse Koch from Buchenwald and Auschwitz, and Magda Goebbels and all the mothers of Lebensborn and the bearers of the maternity crosses.

In the montage, the dead of Nuremberg after 1945, and Himmler and Goebbels, their last photos after death. And the hangman of Nuremberg, who must never be absent—certainly never from any victory celebration of Hitler's.

238 |

They have to watch the procession of refugees. For instance, Brecht and Feuchtwanger and Fritz Lang and Fritzi Massary, Kortner and Bruno Walter and Thomas Mann and Einstein, all of whom would have been handed over by America and Moscow after the invention of the atomic bomb by Hitler's scientists, with arrangements on all sides.

And the dead of Spandau and the dead of July 20, and the books that burned, and the victims of concentration camps and the victims of miscegenation, the victims kicked to death, and those of euthanasia and the commissars of the GPU, and those of the shock troops, marching past, endless and ashen.

Anne Frank and Dreyfus's granddaughter and Sigmund Freud's four sisters, who were murdered at Auschwitz, and Kafka's sister, tears of shame in her eyes, surviving the deluge of the last war, in the empire of the dead. At the victory. In a hundred years, or how many.

And you have to see them up there, the army officers, Keitel and Jodl, and Doenitz, Raeder, Canaris, and Kesselring, Guderian and Paulus, and also the artists, Furtwängler and Speer and Gründgens and Krauss and Marian and Jannings and Söderbaum and Zarah and Wessely and Rühmann and Trenker. The film directors, Steinhoff and Ritter and Erich Engel and Harlan and Leni Riefenstahl. Then the SS, Dietrichs and Steiner. And Rommel and Udet and Rudel and Prien in U-boats, Messerschmitts, and tanks. And also the leftists who joined in, don't forget Bronnen and Freisler and Strasser. All the people of these twelve years in the story of mankind.

The first chapter of democracy in twentieth-century Germany. Subdivision: Progress of the Masses.

Goebbels as a corpse on the autopsy table: a quotation from hell. In back, the projection of one of Doré's illustrations to Dante's *Inferno*, Sisyphus pushing huge sacks of money up the mountain over and over again, which fall back upon him endlessly.

And the scientists march along in the funeral procession: Messerschmitt, Heinkel, Heisenberg, and Wernher von Braun, Porsche, and the industrialists Flick, Krupp, Thyssen, Siemens, Röchling, and Quandt.

And then the famous Herr Karl, a janitor and a common man in Vienna and elsewhere. He's fine and dandy, now as always. And then just see Eva dancing and singing à la Hollywood, Scarlett O'Hara, gone with the wind, with the secretary's gold crown on the head of the chosen girl from the people.

The Goebbels corpse tightly fettered to Eva Braun as a sex puppet. Hanging and swaying in front of the projection of the huge buildings in Speer's victorious Berlin. Accompanied by the *Fledermaus* waltz and further gun salutes of the victory celebration in hell.

Announcer, San Francisco, June 26, 1945: The Charter of the United Nations, which we are now signing, is a solid structure upon which we can build for a better world. History will honor us for it.

Announcer, BBC, August 6, 1945: Scientists, British and American, have made the atomic bomb at last. The first one was dropped on a Japanese city this morning. It was designed for a detonation equal to twenty thousand tons of high explosives—that is, two thousand times the power of the RAF ten-ton bombs of orthodox design. President Truman gave the news this afternoon in a statement from the White House. This atomic bomb, the President added, is a harnessing of the basic powers of the universe. The force from which the sun draws its power has been loosed against those who brought war to the Far East. The actual harnessing . . .

The *Fledermaus* waltz changes into the familiar hell noises from the Hitler period, those gun salutes of Hitler's huge black celebration. The puppet of Goebbels' corpse swings slowly, clutching the sex puppet of Eva Braun.

The camera moves into the mouth of the sex puppet. A group of Barbie dolls gathered around a male doll. Hitler, as in limbo, small in Eva Braun's arms.

•

From the gun salutes of Hitler's funeral rites, Haydn's *Emperor Quartet* develops, at first slowly (the melody of *Deutschland über alles* as chamber music). The Haydn quartet accompanies Heller's monologue and subsequent dialogue with the Hitler puppet to the end.

A wide shot of the deserted studio. There are leaves on the floor. Heller comes slowly forward, toward the camera.

ANDRE HELLER (voice off): Assuming we stood before Hitler, as before Christ at the Last Judgment, and he asked the question: What did you do with the world and your lives, after me, without me? The Last Judgment with the devil as supreme judge, the cheerful apocalypse, finally, and the blackest of all Masses. His great praise for the progress of the world, the true victory celebration at the end of the world. The story of the death of light, from the Holy Grail to the destruction of the West.

What did Thomas Mann say at New Year's 1938: "God help our darkened and misused land and teach it to make its peace with itself and its world."

What would he say today? Or our children tomorrow? Seeing what we have done with our freedom and ourselves: Soulless dwarf people in the dead plastic womb of an empty doll face are the mirrors of our cities and our language; and they created gods in this image. The end game of our existence today, a new Family of Man, in the inhuman ready-made face of our freedom, which we have gambled away. Freedom without a human face.

Hitler, here is your victory!

Heller sits down for a dialogue with the Hitler puppet, which is perched on the front edge of the table. The camera moves up close.

After so much praise for the progress of the world, in imitation of its legacy, let me talk about lost life.

You are to blame for Moscow's successful imperialism, which reaches all the way to the Elbe, with the fortified walls and wolf-hound borders of your concentration camps.

And who said that the Wandering Jew, wandering through the world, pushed by disquiet to create culture, stirred up by provocation, wanted to become a philistine, like everyone else?

Israel has no Karl Kraus, no Kafka, no Schnitzler, no Altenberg, no Friedell, no Polgar. They need Moshe Dayan there, I

can understand that. You killed the Wandering Jew. You destroyed Berlin, Vienna. But the silliness of your panorama windows in Obersalzberg began a triumphant march through the vacation villas of Austria and Germany. And the others learn from us, and are still learning. You are responsible for houses, houses without souls, with burned-out eyes, without tears, cities that cannot weep. Auto landscapes without silence, life that no longer quivers. You took away our sunsets, sunsets by Caspar David Friedrich. You are to blame that we can longer look at a field of grain without thinking of you. You made old Germany kitschy with your simplifying works and peasant pictures. And you are to blame that we have lost the pride of restaurants, that people are driven into fast-food places for fear they might still love their work and something other than money, the harmlessly harmful, the only thing you left them with, since you occupied everything else and corrupted it with your actions, everything, honor, loyalty, country life, hard work, movies, dignity, Fatherland, pride, faith. You are the executor of Western civilization, democratically self-elected, voluntarily, with the victory of money, of materialism over us. The plague of our century. The wretched artist as a hangman degenerating into a politician, voluntarily, cheered as no man ever before. How can I make this clear to you and to me, and me and all the children and grandchildren, who didn't know all this, this previous life, which they have all forgotten by now, corrupted by the new legacy of your time. The new old philistine. The common thing is everlasting yesterday, said Wallenstein, which always was and always comes again, and counts tomorrow because it counted today, for man is made of commonness, and he calls habit his wet nurse. All this, all this has been made impossible. The words "magic" and "myth" and "serving" and "ruling," "Führer," "authority," are ruined, are gone, exiled to eternal time. And we are snuffed out. Nothing more will grow here. An entire nation stopped existing, in the diaspora of the mind and the elite. The New Ones were designed, developed, the New Man is here. The plague of materialism has won out in East and West! Congratulations!

•

Harry Baer, wearing Wagner's cloak, reclines in a chair in front of the huge projected image of Karl May's head. Behind him, the huge Ledoux eye and, nearby, the black stone from *Melencolia*. Music: the final choruses of Mahler's Second Symphony.

HARRY BAER: After the journey into this world, who is closer to God than the guilty man? But what about a time without God,

when we have deposed him ourselves? Thus spoke the devil. Ultimately cynical and moral or rather something human in one of his roles: about a twilight of the gods without gods, the Armageddon of progress, the end of time through the ecological death of the human species in the lower vermin of the insects, or the soul death of an ice-age society, the Universal Judgment without jurists and hence just at last, infinitely dreadful. Making room for the next generation, on the next star, after this one becomes definitively self-annihilating, due to the human species.

Now they'll say that we're crazy, and those who thought us up and made us. Yet we cannot even manage to describe this world in praises.

Or have we scolded, have we insulted anyone? We have only praised. Just as in real life. And what else can one say to this theme?

Snow falls, golden yellow. Behind it, we see imaginary scenes from Karl May's adventures around the world—in America and the Orient. A German landscape, with a small, freezing child.

•

Once again, Heller in the empty studio, slowly going out in back. Close shot of the Black Maria in the studio, snow falling upon it. Chairs from before, the Wagner cloak, the circus barker's megaphone, the black stone from *Melencolia*. In front, the table with the abandoned Hitler puppet. Projection of the glass sphere with the Black Maria inside it. Music: the finale of *Parsifal*.

Grail light, snow.

ANDRE HELLER: And it is the black mother of our imagination, of the last astral hour of celluloid, Black Maria, as Edison called it, making his first movies in it, the holy apparatus, as Mary Pickford said, the camera, the camera obscura, the black chamber, which tells old stories anew. Stories, projections out of the interior, such as "Once upon a time . . ." or "In the beginning was . . ." Stories of nostalgia and yearning and insanity in our interiors after everything has slowly been walled up on the outside. Let us recall school.

Black Stone, Lapis Lapidi, Stone of Light, *lux ex coelis*, fallen from Lucifer's crown. The Grail, the Kaaba, the Golden Fleece, from the Tree of Life, fallen from the stars, the rise and end of the stars, part of the treasure of Delphi, from the legacy of Apollo, the sun god, brought to the gardens of the Hesperides, and granting eternal life to the gods and those who want to be like the people in the land of the Hyperboreans in Montségur. Do you remember? The Holy Vessel of the Grail, in which the blood flowed that night, the true, pure blood. Orient, Mohammed, Middle Ages, and Christianity together, King Arthur's court and Richard Wagner once again. Richard Wagner! A Black Stone fallen from the sky to the earth with eternal yearning for the heavens, for the paradise lost, of the angels, the paradise that bears the guilt for the sin of the world, when Eve and Adam were guilty. Black sun of the light of the beginning and the end of all ends, the black hole, the whirlwind of dark nothingness the size of an apple. Everything contained, our earth, the sun, the solar system, the Milky Way, one of fifty million, billions, collapsing into the tiny black hole of the future. This is us and all our projections, memories, dreams from the era of light.

Heller seems to walk into the projection of the glass sphere, and vanishes.

•

In front of the huge Ledoux eye, the child stands with closed eyes. In the eye, the projection of a journey through the snowy landscape, familiar from the Ludwig film, with *Tristan* music—memories of this lost world.

Oh, descend,
Night of love,
Bring oblivion
That I may live,
Take me
Into thy womb,
Release me
From the world!

A long shot of the vast studio. On a long gangway, moving toward the front, the child comes out of the darkness, with the Hitler dog, which she hurls away, then kicks, picks up again; coming forward, she sits down, staring at this Hitler dog for a long time, turning away and yet taking it, she stands up and walks toward the camera into a black cloud. The black cloud finally occludes the whole image.

The scene is accompanied throughout by the chorus from Beethoven's Ninth Symphony, the Schiller text.

Praise to Joy, the God-descended
Daughter of Elysium!
Ray of mirth and rapture blended,

Goddess, to thy shrine we come.
By thy magic is united
What stern Custom parted wide,
All mankind are brothers plighted
Where thy gentle wings abide.

O ye millions, I embrace ye,
With a kiss for all the world!
Brothers, o'er yon starry sphere
Surely dwells a loving Father.

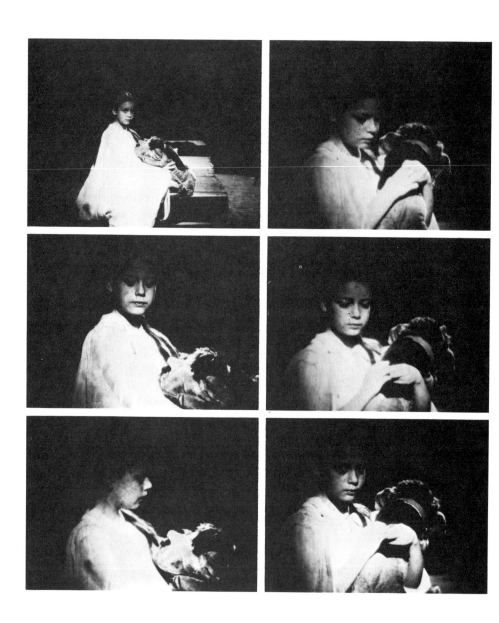

O ye millions, kneel before Him,
World, dost feel thy Maker near?
Seek Him o'er yon starry sphere,
O'er the stars enthroned, adore Him.

The child goes back to the huge eye. In the eye: the crystal sphere and the Black Maria, the black mother of our film imagination, and then (a projection from the Ludwig film) the small weeping Ludwig. To Beethoven's Ninth Symphony, the sphere turns into the landscape of Ludwig's

Winter Garden from the start of the film, torn now, with a deep crack through the world, a huge tear hanging down. Camera moves toward the tear, in which the girl sits, folding her hands in prayer, closing her eyes, then covering her ears. A starry sky is overhead. And, as if heard by the inner ear, the freedom fanfare from *Fidelio*. Close-up of the child's face. The face of a child that went through this world. Fade-out.

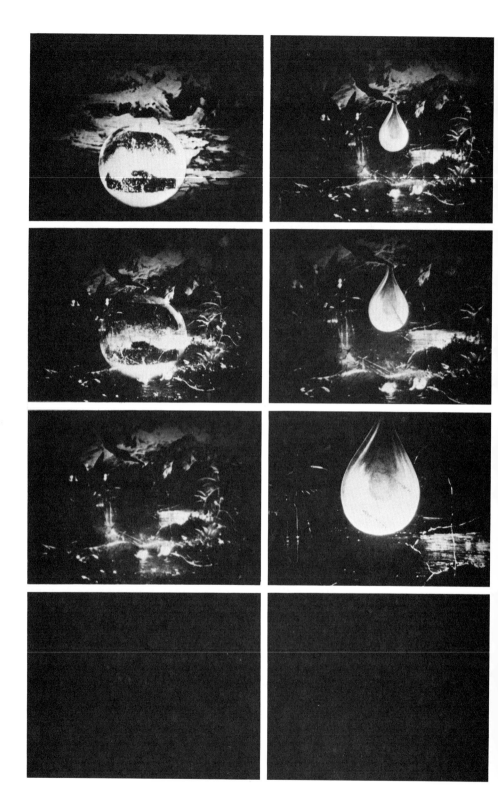

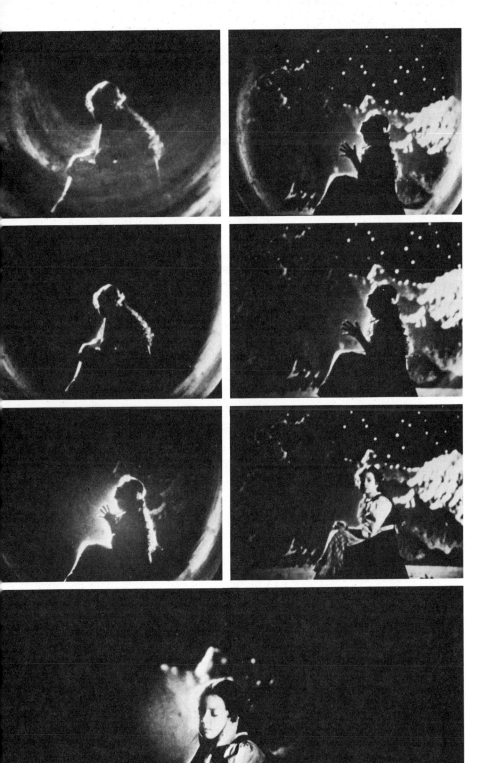

Ende 4. Teil

Wir
Kinder der Hölle

Denk ich an Deutschland
in der Nacht,
dann bin ich um den Schlaf
gebracht,
ich kann nicht mehr die
Augen schliessen,
und meine heissen Tränen
fliessen.

17. September 1844
Paris-Hamburg

H. Heine

Wir
Kinder der Hölle

Harry Baer
André Heller
Peter Kern
Martin Sperr
Amélie Syberberg

---

25. Februar - 20. Oktober 1977
München, am Tag nach
Mogadischu-Stammheim-
Mulhouse

H.J. Syberberg

Buch und Regie:
Hans Jürgen Syberberg

Kamera:
Dietrich Lohmann

Produktion:
TMS/SOLARIS - München
WDR   - Köln
INA   - Paris
BBC   - London

---

und hätte ich allen
Glauben, dass ich
Berge versetzte, und
hätte der Liebe nicht,
ich wäre nichts.

und hätte ich allen Glauben, dass ich Berge versetzte, und hätte der Liebe nicht, ich wäre nichts.

Eine Projektion ins schwarze Loch der Zukunft.

Eine Projektion ins schwarze Loch der Zukunft.

Fade-in.

Over the starry night sky, as at the start of the film, the closing titles and the slow movement of Mozart's Piano Concerto in D Minor coming out of the ether and vanishing into it again. The stars flying toward us. Letters spelling THE GRAIL in different languages and fading in and out from bottom to top, and the final lines of the film—in the form of titles—and the soaring of the stars.

Notes on Some Names and References

Abdias. Main character in the story of the same name by the Austrian writer Adalbert Stifter (1805–68).

Altenberg, Peter (1859–1919). Viennese writer.

Arthasastra. Ancient Indian teaching.

Babelsberg. Film studios near Berlin, formerly UFA, today DEFA.

Balbo, Italo (1896–1940). Marshal of the Italian Air Force, one of the champions of Fascism. Air Force Minister 1928–35.

Bechstein, Arnold. Well-known industrialist who supported Hitler as early as the 1920s.

Bella. One of Hitler's dogs.

Bellaria. Movie theater on Vienna's Ringstrasse, specializing in old UFA films.

Berghof. Hitler's vacation residence since the twenties in Obersalzberg, near Berchtesgaden (a health resort on Lake König, in Upper Bavaria). Bombed in April 1945. Leveled by government order in April 1952.

Bezhin Meadow. Film directed by Sergei Eisenstein (1898–1948), three-fourths completed when on the orders of Boris Shumiatski the shooting was stopped. The negative and work copy were destroyed in 1942, supposedly in the German bombings of Moscow.

Birgel, Willy (1891–1973). Film actor of the UFA period.

Black Maria. The first film studio, in New Jersey. Built for Thomas Edison by Dickson in 1893.

Blomberg, Werner von (1897–1946). Professional soldier; field marshal and Reich Minister of War; dismissed in 1938, whereupon Hitler made himself supreme commander of the Army.

Blondie. Hitler's favorite wolfhound, whom he killed before committing suicide.

Boger swing. Torture device in concentration camps, named after its inventor.

Brandt, Karl. One of Heinrich Himmler's aides. Executed after the war.

Bronnen, Arnolt (1895–1959). German writer; communist and then follower of National Socialism.

Bruckmann. Publishing family in Munich; early supporters of Hitler.

Brückner, Wilhelm. Hitler's adjutant; SA squad leader.

Bürgerbräu. Tavern in Munich, early meeting place of the Nazi movement.

Burli. One of Hitler's favorite dogs.

Canaris, Wilhelm (1887–1945). Career naval officer; admiral; 1935, head of the Abwehr; dismissed in 1944, linked to resistance movement and the attempted assassination of Hitler on July 20, 1944; arrested and executed.

Cosette. Heroine of Victor Hugo's novel *Les Misérables.*

Dagover, Lil (1897–   ). German movie star of the silent film period; in Robert Weine's *The Cabinet of Dr. Caligari* (1919), Fritz Lang's *Dr. Mabuse* (1922), and other UFA films.

DEFA. Company succeeding UFA after World War II in East Berlin.

Dietrich, Josef. SS Obergruppenführer and general of the Waffen SS, commander of the "Adolf Hitler" division; 1944–45, commander of the Sixth (SS) Armored Army in Russia.

Disney, Walt (1901–66). Welcomed Leni Riefenstahl to Hollywood in 1938.

Doenitz, Karl (1891–1980). Career naval officer; 1942, admiral; January 1943, made Grand Admiral and commander in chief of the Navy; on April 30, 1945, after Hitler's suicide, named Führer.

Eckart, Dietrich (1868–1923). Writer and early supporter of Hitler. In 1921, he became editor of the Nazi newspaper *Volkischer Beobachter.*

Ellerkamp, Fritz. Corporal in the SS and Hitler's projectionist at the private evening film screenings. A character invented by Syberberg.

Engel, Erich (1891–1966). German theater and film director (e.g., *Affair Blum,* 1949) ; as of 1947, director at DEFA and the Deutsches Theater in East Berlin.

Fegelein, Otto Hermann (1906–45). SS Gruppenführer and lieutenant general of the Waffen SS; brother-in-law of Eva Braun (1912–45), Hitler's consort. On April 27, 1945, Fegelein was charged with desertion. On April 28 he was shot on Hitler's orders, and that same day Hitler and Eva Braun were married; their joint suicide took place on April 30.

Fest, Joachim. German historian. Author of *Hitler,* 1977, and narrator of a documentary film about Hitler.

Feuchtwanger, Lion (1884–1958). German writer of dramas and novels (including *Jew Süss*). Left Germany in 1933, settled in California in 1941.

Fick, Roderick. Munich architect, built the Berghof.

Fitzliputzli. Bavarian version of a puppet clown.

Flick, Friedrich (1883–1972). German industrialist (iron, steel, coal, etc.) ; in 1938 named head of defense economy.

Frank, Hans (1900–46). Jurist, early follower of National Socialism. 1939–45, Governor General of Poland; 1946, sentenced to death and executed at Nuremberg.

Frederick II, the Great (1712–86). King of Prussia from 1740 until his death. A painting of him by Anton Graff (1736–1831) hung in Hitler's bunker.

Freisler, Roland (1893–1945). Jurist. Joined the Nazi Party in 1925; 1942–45, President of the National Court.

Friedell, Egon (1878–1938). Viennese theater critic, cultural historian. Committed suicide at the time of the Anschluss.

Friedrich, Caspar David (1774–1840). Along with Philipp Otto Runge, the great representative of German Romantic painting. His painting *Das Eismeer* figures throughout Syberberg's film.

Furtwängler, Wilhelm (1885–1954). 1922–45, head of the Berlin Philharmonic. First State Kapellmeister in 1934 at the Berlin State Opera. 1936, chief conductor of the Bayreuth Festival.

Gartenlaube. Illustrated weekly family magazine, published in Berlin from 1853 to 1943. Symbol of German kitsch.

George, Heinrich (1893–1946). German stage and screen actor. Role in Veit Harlan's *Jew Süss.* Died at the Sachsenhausen concentration camp.

Gerstein, Kurt. SS Obersturmführer who became a leader of the German resistance against Hitler.

Giesler, Paul. Architect, early follower of the Nazi Party. In 1941, made Gauleiter (provincial governor) and SA Obergruppenführer.

Gläser, Ernst (1902–63). German writer, moved to Switzerland in 1933, returned to Germany in 1939. Correspondent for the Luftwaffe, editor of the front-line newspaper *Adler in Suden.*

Gottschalk, Joachim. German screen actor and star of the UFA films. He was ordered to divorce his Jewish wife and, when he refused, was barred from employment. He and his wife committed suicide with their child in 1941.

Grail. From the Old French *graal;* in medieval literature a secret, sacred object bringing its owner earthly or celestial bliss; to be found only by the pure, predestined man. *Sanguis reales,* the pure blood, stone or bowl. Documented in Spanish, French, English, and German legends and literary works, and alchemical-religious notions. Parsifal legend, Chrétien de Troyes, *Le Conte du Graal,* ca. 1180; Wolfram von Eschenbach, 1210; English: *The Holy Grail;* Richard Wagner, *Lohengrin* and *Parsifal.* The Grail is kept at the castle of Montsalvat, guarded by King Arthur's knights.

Greifswald. University town in the province of Pomerania; birthplace of Caspar David Friedrich.

Grese, Irma. Concentration camp guard at Ravensbrück, Auschwitz, and Belsen; renowned for her cruelty; she was twenty-one when she was executed in December 1945.

Gründgens, Gustav (1899–1963). German actor and director. In 1934 directed *Finances of the Grand Duke,* a feature film with Victor de Kowa in the lead (a remake of a 1923 film by F. W. Murnau). 1934, manager of the State Theater in Berlin. 1937, State Councillor. 1937–45, general manager of the Prussian State Theater in Berlin. The character Hendrik Höfgen in Klaus **Mann**'s novel *Mephisto* (1935) is in fact a portrait of Gründgens.

Guderian, Heinz (1888–1954). Pioneer of tank warfare; 1937, adviser to Franco; 1938, commander of armored forces; 1940, colonel general;

1941, commander in chief of the Second Armored Army; 1944–45, Chief of the General Staff of the Army.

Gulbransson, Olaf (1873–1958). Norwegian painter, moved to Munich in 1902, became an important cartoonist. Published regularly in the satirical magazine *Simplicissimus*.

Harbou, Thea von (1888–1954). Popular novelist. Wrote film scripts for the director Fritz Lang (1890–1976): *The Nibelungen* (1924), *Metropolis* (1926). She was married to Lang, whom she divorced in 1933. She became a Nazi while Lang, whose other German films include *Dr. Mabuse* (1922) and *M* (1931), emigrated to the United States in 1934.

Harlan, Veit (1899–1964). German film director; made the famous anti-Semitic propaganda movie *Jew Süss* (1940) and *Kolberg* (1945), as well as *The Golden City* (1942), *Immensee* (1943), and *Sacrifice* (1944). After the war he was tried for "crimes against humanity" because of *Jew Süss* and eventually, after years of litigation, declared innocent.

Haushofer, Karl (1869–1946). Professor of geography at the University of Munich; author of *The National Socialist Idea in the World* (1934), etc. Committed suicide.

Haydn, Joseph (1732–1809). The music for *Deutschland, Deutschland über alles* is taken from Haydn's *Emperor Quartet*.

Hays, Will (1879–1954). 1922–45, president of the Motion Picture Producers and Distributors Association of America; author of the Hays code, a production code that intimidated producers for many years. He stopped several of Erich von Stroheim's projects.

Heinkel, Ernst (1888–1958). Airplane designer and pro-Nazi industrialist; 1922–45, owner and manager of the Ernst Heinkel Aircraft Works in Warnemünde. In 1938 his factory developed the first jet plane.

Henry the Fowler (1129–95). Duke of Saxony and Bavaria—the most powerful German ruler next to Frederick I. Founded Munich in 1158. He promoted the expansion of German culture and Christianity in the Slavic territory between the lower Elbe and the Baltic Sea.

Heroes' Square. Famous square in Vienna, in front of the Hofburg, where, on March 13, 1938, after his annexation of Austria, Hitler spoke before thousands of enthusiastic Viennese.

Heydrich, Reinhard (1904–42). SS Gruppenführer until 1934; 1939, head of the Reich Security Office (RHSA), which oversaw the Gestapo, the security services, and the criminal police; 1941, Deputy Reich Protector of Bohemia and Moravia. In May 1942, he was assassinated by Czech agents trained in England; in reprisal for his death the inhabitants of the Bohemian village of Lidice were murdered by SS units.

Hoffmann, Heinrich. Intimate friend of Hitler, whom he met in 1919. Joined the Nazi Party in 1920. Official photographer of the Party.

Hoffmann, Henriette. Wife of Baldur von Schirach and daughter of Heinrich Hoffmann. She knew Hitler from the time she was eight years old.

Jodl, Alfred (1890–1946). Professional soldier. 1939, major general; 1939–45, head of the Wehrmacht Command Office (ie., chief of staff). Sentenced to death and executed at Nuremberg.

Jugo, Jenny (1905–). German movie star, mostly in comedies. Her popularity was at its height in the late thirties.

Kaltenbrunner, Ernst (1903–46). Jurist; joined the Nazi Party and the SS in 1932. 1935–38, head of the SS in Austria; 1938, SS Gruppenführer; 1943–45, head of the security police. Sentenced to death and executed at Nuremberg.

Kannenberg. Willy. One of the staff at Hitler's retreat in Obersalzberg.

Karl (Herr Karl, Jr.). Fictitious son of Herr Karl, created by Helmut Qualtinger and Karl Merz as the prototype of the Viennese petit bourgeois sympathetic to the Nazis.

Kästner, Erich (1899–1974). German writer of satirical and humorous poems, novels, plays, and children's books. In 1933, some of his books were banned and burned.

Katuschka. One of Hitler's dogs.

Kehlstein. Mountain in Obersalzberg, with Hitler's teahouse at the peak. A long tunnel led to the elevator to the teahouse.

Keitel, Wilhelm (1882–1946). Professional soldier. Major general, 1934; 1935–38, head of the Wehrmacht office in the Ministry of War; 1938–45, general field marshal and chief of the High Command. On May 8, 1945, he signed the surrender in Berlin. Sentenced to death and executed at Nuremberg.

Kellermann, Bernhard (1879–1951). Novelist. He wrote a famous technological-utopian novel, *The Tunnel* (1913).

Kempka, Erich. Hitler's chief chauffeur. For the cremation of Hitler's and Eva's bodies, he rolled them in woolen blankets.

Kerr, Alfred (1867–1948). Berlin's most influential theater critic in the twenties. A Jew, he left Germany in 1933.

Kersten, Felix. Finnish, a senior medical officer; Himmler's masseur. His famous clientele included members of the Dutch royal house and German aristocrats and industrialists. According to Kersten's notebooks, he once had a Tibetan teacher in Berlin, a Dr. Ko.

Kesselring, Albert (1885–1960). Professional soldier. 1936–37, chief of staff of the Luftwaffe; 1940, general field marshal; 1941–45, commander in chief of the southwest zone (Italy and the Mediterranean); March 1945, named commander in chief in the West. In July 1947, he was sentenced to death by a British military court but the sentence was commuted; he was released in 1952.

Koch, Ilse. Wife of Buchenwald commandant Karl Koch. As a guard there, she was infamous for her cruelty. Her death sentence was commuted to life imprisonment because she was pregnant. She committed suicide in 1967.

Kolberg. Film directed by Veit Harlan, a Nazi "stick-it-out" movie made in 1945, shortly before the surrender. An extravagant historical spectacle intended to rival *Gone With the Wind.*

Kortner, Fritz (1892–1970). German actor and director; emigrated in 1933. Returned in 1949.

Kraus, Karl (1847–1936). Austrian writer and satirist who wrote a mammoth play, which (it is estimated) would take ten evenings to perform, called *The Last Days of Mankind.* The character in the play who speaks for Kraus is called the Grumbler.

Krause, Karl-Wilhelm. Hitler's valet between 1934 and 1939. His book *I Was Hitler's Valet* (1949) is the source of the valet's narrative in Part Two.

Landsberg/Lech. Town in Upper Bavaria where Hitler served his prison term after the 1923 putsch and wrote most of *Mein Kampf.*

Lasky, Jesse (1880–1958). Movie producer, vice-president of Paramount when Erich von Stroheim was there. He fired Stroheim shortly before the director finished filming *The Wedding March,* Part II (1939). Lasky had Josef von Sternberg cut the film drastically.

Leander, Zarah (1907–81). Swedish movie actress and singer. UFA star. Very popular in Germany in the late thirties.

Leiser, Erwin. Film historian. Made *Mein Kampf,* a documentary film on the Hitler period.

Linderhof. Castle in the Graswang Valley near Garmisch-Partenkirchen, built between 1869 and 1878 by King Ludwig II of Bavaria.

Linge, Heinz. Hitler's valet between 1939 and 1945. He and Martin Bormann (b. 1900; vanished in 1945) were the first to enter the room where Hitler and Eva Braun committed suicide and carried their corpses to be cremated in the courtyard of the bunker.

Ludwig II (1845–86). King of Bavaria; patron and friend of Wagner. Subject of a film by Visconti (1972) and two films made in 1972 by Syberberg: *Ludwig, Requiem for a Virgin King,* the first part of a trilogy completed with *Karl May* and *Hitler, a Film from Germany;* and *Theodor Hirneis,* which portrays the king through the eyes of his cook.

M. Film directed by Fritz Lang in 1931, starring Peter Lorre.

Marian, Ferdinand (1902–46). Film actor. Forced by Goebbels to play the title role in Veit Harlan's *Jew Süss.* After the war, during Harlan's trial, Marian's innocence was established; but before he learned this he drove his car, while drunk, into a tree.

May, Karl (1842–1912). Writer of adventure books that mainly take place among the Indian tribes of North America or in the Near East (heroes: Old Shatterhand, Kara Ben Mensi). He became the author most widely read by juveniles. Subject of a film by Syberberg: *Karl May—In Search of the Lost Paradise* (1974), the second film in the trilogy which begins with the film on Ludwig II of Bavaria and ends with the film on Hitler. Hitler, a great admirer of Karl May, saw him in Vienna in 1912, when Karl May made his last appearance. Hitler allegedly recommended that his generals learn how to win at Stalingrad from Karl May.

Mayer, Louis B. (1885–1957). Movie producer at MGM, producer of Stroheim's *Greed*. After the film was cut from twenty-four to eight reels (1922), Mayer had the remaining negative of the original version burned.

Morell, Theo. Hitler's personal doctor from 1936 until he fell out of favor in April 1945; died after the end of the war.

Moser, Hans (1880–1964). Viennese comedian and film actor, very popular with Hitler.

Muck. One of Hitler's dogs.

Muspilli. Ninth-century German poem describing the Day of Judgment.

Negus. One of Hitler's dogs.

Neuschwanstein. Castle near Füssen, Allgäu, built by Ludwig II of Bavaria.

Parsifal. Opera by Richard Wagner. (Hitler: "I'll make *Parsifal* into a religion for myself.")

Paulus, Friedrich von. Professional soldier. Commander of the German forces at Stalingrad; surrendered with the remnants of his army on January 31, 1943. Soviet POW until 1953.

Polgar, Alfred (1875–1955). Theater critic in Vienna and Berlin. Fled to the United States from Paris in 1940.

Rattenhuber, Hans. SS brigade commander, chief of Hitler's personal bodyguard.

Raubal, Angela. Hitler's half sister, who ran his household at Berghof from 1928 to 1935.

Raubal, Geli. Daughter of Hitler's half sister, Angela Raubal; Hitler's "great love." In 1931, in Hitler's apartment on the Prinzregentenstrasse, Munich, she shot herself.

Refugee Conversations (Flüchtlingsgespräche). Prose dialogues by Bertolt Brecht (1898–1956), written in Finland (1940–41) and the United States (1944).

Reitsch, Hanna. Famous German pilot of the Nazi period; on April 26, 1945, she flew to Berlin in order to get Hitler out.

Rienzi. An early opera by Wagner, about Cola di Rienzi, born circa 1313, murdered 1354, Roman popular leader, idealized in modern times as a forerunner of Italian nationalism. Hitler said in 1941 that it was when he first saw this opera in Linz, with his friend Kubizek, in 1906, that he received his vision of a future mission.

Rudel, Hans Ulrich. Legendary military figure of the Third Reich; fighter and bomber pilot, he sank a Soviet battleship and destroyed some five hundred tanks.

Schirach, Baldur von (1907–74). From Lübeck, he knew Thomas Mann's family. Early follower of the Nazi Party and the SA. 1931, SA Gruppenführer; 1931–45, Reich Commander; 1933, Reich Youth Leader; 1940–45, Gauleiter of Vienna. Sentenced at Nuremberg to twenty years in prison.

Söderbaum, Kristina (1917–). Swedish film actress, UFA star, wife of Veit Harlan. She starred in *Jew Süss* and *Kolberg*.

Stasi. One of Hitler's dogs.

Stauffenberg, Claus Count Schenk von (1907–44). Professional soldier. On July 20, 1944, he unsuccessfully attempted to assassinate Hitler in the headquarters compound at Rastenburg. He was arrested in Berlin the same day and shot.

Stolzing, Walter. Character in Wagner's *Die Meistersinger von Nürnberg*.

Troost, Paul Ludwig (1878–1934). Architect. Designer of the House of German Art and Party buildings in Munich.

UFA (Universum Film AG, Berlin). Founded in 1917. Until 1945, the biggest German movie company, with studios in Berlin-Tempelhof and Berlin-Neubabelsberg, and with its own movie theaters.

Wahnfried. Richard Wagner's residence in Bayreuth, built in 1873–74. Richard and Cosima Wagner's graves are in the garden. Bombed in 1945. Restored; now a museum.